£1-50.

FLYING THE FLAG

BRITISH VICTORIES OVER
OUR EUROPEAN PARTNERS

FLYING THE FLAG

BRITISH VICTORIES OVER
OUR EUROPEAN PARTNERS

To Graham

John C Taylor

John

January 2008.

First published in Great Britain 2007 by WritersPrintShop

ISBN 1904623530

Designed by e-BookServices.com

Drawings by Rachael Holifield

Dedication

This book is dedicated to all those in the past from Clifton in Bedfordshire who served their country and in particular those who have sacrificed their lives for their country.

Clifton Roll of Honour

The First World War 1914 - 1918

Frank Armour
Fred Arnold
Horace William Arnold
Arthur Baldock
Herbert Bland
Charley Bland
William Burnage
William Cooper
Jim Cooper
William Copperwaite
Daniel Dilley
George Dilley
William Dodd
Frank Earl
Joesph Goss

Ernest Gray
Ernest Kiteley
George Legate
Albert Legate
Fred Meeks
Frank Pateman
Arthur Sharp
Wilfred Slater
William John Stevens
Alex Taylor
William Walker
Bertie Watts
Percy West
Richard Woodring
Frederick Wright

The Second World War 1939-1945

Vernon Cockroft
Robert Cockroft
James Dunbabin
Stanley Gosby
Stanley Napier
George Napier
Stanley Page
Ted Rainbow

Other Conflicts

Jonathan Kitulagoda

Acknowledgements

This book is written out of the resources of a private library. The augmentation of that library, since the book does not pretend to have involved research on original documents and is informative in intent and not academic, has been aided substantially by the help of John Leeson of Eric.T.Moore's Bookshop in Hitchin who has unendingly lived up to the designation made by Country Life of Eric. T.Moore's Bookshop as one of the best eight in Britain and I am very grateful to him for all which he has done.

Being a long-timer hater of typewriters the text was written in my own hand. I am therefore deeply in debt to Mrs Clare McGill for having typed the text for me. Her powers to discern and reproduce the text have filled me with awe and appreciation. There were many times in my long years in Court when in full flow I was unable to read my own written notes. She mastered that problem and I am grateful to her.

Finally, the patience of my wife must be properly acknowledged as for endless hours and days I disappeared in the house to work on the book avoiding all social discourse. I am grateful to her too for without that forbearance this book would not have been finished.

The Flag

The Union Jack was introduced in 1606 after the personal union of the Crowns of England and Scotland by James I of England and VIth of Scotland. The 'Jack' was the expression used to describe the bowsprit-end flag on boats and the term Union Jack came into use in the sixteen – seventies. The original flag comprised the red cross of England with its white ground superimposed on the Saltire of St Andrew's Cross which formed the blue ground. It was not until 1801 that the red Saltire of St Patrick was added at the time of the union of Britain and Ireland. Thereafter the Union Flag was always to be flown with the 'thick' white band in the Saltire above the red cross line of St Patrick nearest to the flagpole.

The use of the flag was closely connected with the Royal Navy. King Charles I in 1634 limited its use to ships of the navy. It was in the mid-seventeenth century that the 'Union' flag first began to be carried on a staff on the poop deck, although during the Commonwealth the Union Jack was replaced excluding the Saltire of Scotland after the death of King Charles I. The Union Jack was to be re-used with the Restoration. In 1674 merchant ships were first permitted to use an ensign containing the Union Flag in the first quarter on a red ground and in the early eighteenth century the current naval ensign emerged of a union flag in the first quarter on a white ground with the red cross of St George superimposed. On seagoing vessels the colours for the ground in each case were derived from the command flags of the fleet which were devised for the purpose of action in battle in three squadrons, white for the van, red for the centre and blue for the rear. Blue ensigns with the union flag in the first quarter are still flown today on boats owned by members of certain yacht clubs under royal warrant such as the Royal Ocean Racing Club.

The national flag reflects the basis of the moral order of the country in that it is the only national flag to contain the flags of three saints of the Christian church.

The Town and Country Planning (Control of Advertisements) (England) Regulations 2007 permits the erection of a flagpole and the flying of national flags without the need for any planning consent. The flagpole may be vertical or affixed to a roof or wall. It is not permitted to use the flagpole in any way save for the flying of the flag itself. There are a number of conditions which apply to the deemed consent, namely, that the flag can only be flown on the site with the owner's consent, that it should not be sited to affect safety on the highway or of other transport installations or obscure or hinder the operation of traffic and transport signs or signals. The flagpole and flag has to be properly maintained so that visual amenity is not impaired or the public endangered and, if the flagpole is removed, the site must be properly restored. In Areas of Special Control defined under the Regulations consent for the flagpole will be required from the local authority. The detailed provisions are in the Regulations.

Historical Chronology

The Hundred Years War with France

1340	The Battle of Sluys	(24 June)
1346	The Battle of Crecy	(26 August)
1356	The Battle of Poitiers	(19 September)
1367	The Battle of Navarette	(3 April)
1415	The Surrender of Harfleur	(22 September)
1415	The Battle of Agincourt	(25 October)
1424	The Battle of Verneuil	(17 August)
1426	The Battle of St James	(6 March)
1429	The Battle of the Herrings	(12 February)

The War against Philip II of Spain

| 1587 | The Singeing of the King of Spain's Beard | (19 April) |
| 1588 | The Defeat of the Spanish Armada | (29 July) |

The Dutch Wars of the Seventeenth Century

1652	The Battle of the Kentish Knock	(28 September)
1653	The Battle of Portland	(20 February)
1653	The Battle of the Gabbard Bank	(3 June)
1653	The Battle of Texel	(31 July)
1665	The Battle of Lowestoft	(3 June)
1666	The Battle of the North Foreland	(25 July)

The War of the League of Augsburg

| 1692 | The Battle of Barfleur-La-Hogue | (19 May) |

The War of the Spanish Succession

1702	The Battle of Vigo Bay	(12 October)
1704	The Storming of the Schellenberg	(2 July)
1704	The Taking of Gibralter	(24 July)
1704	The Battle of Blenheim	(13 August)
1704	The Battle of Malaga	(14 August)

1705	The Battle of Marbella	(10 March)
1705	The Capture of Barcelona	(3 October)
1706	The Battle of Ramillies	(23 May)
1708	The Battle of Oudenarde	(11 July)
1709	The Battle of Malplaquet	(11 September)

The War against Spain

| 1718 | The Battle of Passaro | (11 August) |

The War of Jenkins's Ear and the Austrian Succession

1743	The Battle of Dettingen	(28 June)
1749	The First Battle of Finisterre	(3 May)
1749	The Second Battle of Finisterre	(14 October)

The Seven Years War

1759	The Battle of Minden	(1 August)
1759	The Battle of Lagos	(18 August)
1759	The Surrender of Quebec	(18 September)
1759	The Battle of Quiberon Bay	(20 November)
1762	The Capture of Havana	(11 August)
1762	The Capture of Manila	(6 October)

The War with France and Spain and the Rebellion of the Colonies

| 1780 | The Moonlight Battle | (16 January) |
| 1782 | The Battle of the Saints | (12 April) |

The War with Revolutionary France

1794	The Glorious First of June	(1 June)
1795	Cornwallis's Retreat	(17 June)
1797	The Battle of St Vincent	(14 February)
1797	The Battle of Camperdown	(11 October)
1798	The Battle of the Nile	(1 August)
1799	The Siege of Acre	(20 May)
1801	The Battle of Aboukir	(21 March)
1801	The Battle of Copenhagen	(2 April)

The Napoleonic War

1805	The Battle of Trafalgar	(21 October)
1806	The Battle of Maida	(4 July)
1807	The Taking of Copenhagen	(7 September)
1808	The Battle of Rolica	(17 August)
1808	The Battle of Vimiero	(21 August)
1809	The Battle of Coruna and Evacuation of the Army	(17 January)
1809	The Naval Action in the Aix Roads	(11 April)
1809	The Battle of Talavera	(28 July)
1810	The Battle of Borrosa	(5 March)
1811	The Battle of Sabugal	(3 April)
1811	The Battle of Fuentes de Onoro	(5 May)
1811	The Battle of Albuera	(16 May)
1811	The Battle of Arroyo dos Molinos	(28 October)
1812	The Battle of Cuidad Rodrigo	(19 January)
1812	The Taking of Badajoz	(6 April)
1812	The Battle of Salamanca	(22 July)
1812	The Battle of Garcia Hernandez	(23 July)
1813	The Battle of Vitoria	(21 June)
1813	The Battle of Sorauren	(28 July)
1813	The Taking of Saint Sebastian	(8 September)
1813	The Crossing of the Bidassoa	(7 October)
1813	The Battle of Nivelle	(10 November)
1814	The Battle of Orthez	(27 February)
1814	The Investment of Toulouse	(10 April)
1815	The Battle of Waterloo	(18 June)

The First World War 1914-1918

The battles on the Western Front on land are described in the entry for Armistice Day, 11th November 1918. Naval battles listed are –

1914	The Battle of the Falkland Isles	(8 December)
1915	The Battle of the Dogger Bank	(23 January)
1916	The Battle of Jutland	(31 May)

The Second World War 1939 – 1945

1939	The Sinking of the Admiral Graf.Spee	(17 December)
1940	The Deliverance at Dunkirk	(2 June)

1940	The Seizure and Destruction of the French Fleet	(3 July)
1940	The Battle of Britain	(15 September)
1940	The Destruction of the Italian Fleet at Taranto	(11 November)
1940	The Battle of Sidi Barrani	(15 December)
1941	The Victory at Beda Fomm	(7 February)
1941	The Battle of Matapan	(28 March)
1941	The Conquest of Italian East Africa	(18 May)
1941	The Sinking of the Bismarck	(28 May)
1941	The Surrender of Lebanon and Syria	(14 July)
1941	The Relief of Tobruk	(10 December)
1942	The Battle of El Alamein	(4 November)
1943	The Turning of the Mareth Line	(27 March)
1943	The Breakthrough at the Medjerda Valley	(6 May)
1943	The Conquest of Sicily	(14 August)
1944	The Battle of Monte Cassino	(17 May)
1944	The Battle of Normandy	(20 August)
1945	The Crossing of the Rhine	(24 March)
1945	V.E. Day	(8 May)
1945	V.J. Day	(15 August)

Other Entries

24th April	St George's Day
24th May	Empire Day
29th May	Oakapple Day

Of Patriotism

Flying the flag is conceived not as an academic history but as a book just for reading, having a serious purpose. Its evolution was twofold. The house flagpole had been broken by storm and needed replacement. The successor in place, the question became, asked idly, like most questions put to themselves by the retired with empty moments to hand, on which days should the flag be raised. The concept that the Union Flag or the Flag of St. George should be used to mark the commemoration of British Victories seemed obvious, but, search for a list in being shewed that none was to be found. Creation of a list was to involve judgement as to the action to be included as a 'victory' and how far the scope of the list should go. There then came the two-hundredth anniversary of the Battle of Trafalgar in 2005 and, planning for a party and fireworks, I asked the gardener, a young man of twenty-eight, what did he know about Nelson. The reply shocked me, "Nothing", he said. I asked what he had studied in history at school and after a pause was told, "Oh, about Celtic pots, slavery and rubbish of that sort." Further inquiring among those under thirty elucidated a not dissimilar position. The ignorance of British history for the state educated of the country seemed to me to be manifest. A generation was being brought into being whose sense of nation and of recollected history had been emulsified into a hotpotch of politically correct recollection, most of it irrelevant to the remembrance of the memory of being British. The Holocaust seemed to figure large as an area of study. No one can doubt the benefit of reminding people of the horror into which men can be led by blind nationalism of race and the cruelty of the century of the common man, although it would be perhaps more balanced to recall as well the slaughter and starvation in the nineteen thirties of millions of Russians in the interest of Marxist Socialism, about which the so called 'liberal' intelligentsia maintains almost total silence and which seems not to be taught in schools. The point is that neither of these happenings was the responsibility of the British and it is not their history. In an age when to many the visual transmission of information is so dominant with state funded literacy achieved often by education so low, given the national curriculum, it is perhaps inevitable that possibly out of idleness and certainly out of political correctness so much of history teaching should centre on the topic of the Holocaust and Adolf Hitler, but the failure to educate the young in the deeds of their forefathers is a betrayal. It betrays the idea of nation and it betrays those who gave their lifeblood for that idea down the centuries. In that context this book seeks to shine a light into the deeds of the past where the British forged and showed those characteristics of duty, courage, endurance and sacrifice that has so marked our history. It does so for the short attention span, eschewing the need to swim through the dense chronology of events, and its focus is the British people.

Duty, courage, endurance and sacrifice as qualities for mankind are not compelling morally by themselves, because they can be abused as in Nazi Germany where in a context of evil their transforming characteristics were turned to an objectionable end. They need to exist within an overall patriotic ideal which is founded soundly on a civilised cultural base.

Patriotism has long had a bad press among "intellectuals". Dr. Johnson early defined it as the last resort of the scoundrel and that allegation has persisted into our age reinforced by the political correctness of the London left-Liberal elite and the media, which reflect their views. Patriotism however, needs to be kept distinct from crude nationalism, which the French "invented" and which under Napoleon Buonaparte was spread across Europe to undermine the political and cultural unity of the continent in the early nineteenth century and to bare its worst fruit in the twentieth. Read in one sense for the people of Britain the words of Nurse Edith Cavell, when she was shot in Bruxelles by the Germans on the 12th October 1915 that she realised "patriotism is not enough. I must have no hatred or bitterness towards anyone," contained a false analysis of the historic nature of British patriotism predicating a formulation of patriotism to which "hatred and bitterness" must be inclusive. Read in another way the words can be seen as an essential requisite of British patriotism of which she is reminding herself. In the former sense the statement ignores the peculiar characteristic of the medieval idea of the Christian king, the influence of which has flowed down a continuous and unbroken history of these islands gaining force by its unity with the essential belief in freedom and representative government which formed the institutions for the people living in them. The role-call of the victories through the centuries echoes this patriotism rooted in the peculiar chosen myth of Britain, that of King Arthur and his Knights of the Round Table. From Edward III with the founding of the order of the Garter, his adoption of the emblem of St.George, to Churchill's aphorism "In war victory: in peace magnanimity" the idea of a crude nationalism without chivalry and moral respect for the people, with whom the fighting is done and the war engaged, has not been part of the way and the idea for which our wars with scant exception have been fought. The idea of British patriotism is in fact the total antithesis to the expressed idea of Clemenceau, the French Prime Minister in 1918 that the time of revenge had arrived and that he would bust the new German Republic. With its destructive consequences, Lloyd George sadly, despite his expressed view on 12th November 1918 (see 11 November 1918: Peace) about the Armistice, became party to the degraded approach of vindictiveness embodied in the Treaty of Versailles, which were the fruits sought and won by France and the price for which Europe was to pay .

The main ideas of the Christian king and representative government which join together can be seen as early as the fourteenth and fifteenth century in the campaigns of Crecy (27 August 1346) and Agincourt (25 October 1415). Edward

III and King Henry V could only make war with the consent of their Parliaments which provided the resources to do so. They had in their distinctive campaigns to carry the people with them and give the sense to their armies of a shared identity. Henry V and the Battle of Agincourt (25th October 1415) is the exemplar, although the example like much of human activity is flawed. The King in France forbids his army to destroy and loot; he hangs the soldier thief who takes a pyx from a church; he falls before battle into prayer and fights dismounted, he and his great nobles, on foot among the yeoman, the ordinary bearers of arms and the Welsh bowmen. He is at one with his people making the idea of monarchy a part of their minds and hearts. His victory is marred by the wanton killing of the fallen French knights and men at arms, but, that flaw interestingly the chroniclers feel they need to explain away. It is seen as inconsistent, an angry lapse after the French had massacred the young squires and boys left to shelter with the baggage and is a matter proper for apology. The chivalrous Christian king before his God must love his neighbour and even in the exigency of war offer aid, mercy and compassion. The Black Prince made explicit the notion of chivalric duty flowing from this idea after his victory at Poitiers (19 September 1356) by serving at table on his prisoners, King John II of France and his great nobles on the very night of his victory. The Kings of England too, their nobles and knights did not ride down their own men like the nobles and knights of France at Crecy, as the latter advanced trampling through and on the poor defeated crossbowmen retreating towards them. Henry V at Agincourt is pivotal because his conduct in and among his people created the image of country and unity between monarch and people which is the very essence of being British and suffuses the expression of patriotism to come. As the Civil War period in the seventeenth century shows in its outcome the British people felt rootless without their King. Charles II was welcomed back with enthusiasm in 1660 and the day of his return celebrated for two hundred years on 29th May as Oakapple Day.

The thread runs down the years. Henry VI was noted for his piety and as the founder of Eton College and King's College, Cambridge, cared for the education and moral life of his people. Henry VII completed, despite his well-known parsimony, the last five bays of King's College Chapel, which had been for half a century unfinished. His successor was to forge the foundations of that quintessential quality of Englishness, the Church of England which with slow fuse was to burn itself into every corner of English life and define the qualities of patriotism down the ages.

In the popular mind Henry VIII is seen only as a rumbustious King with six wives given to violent action and tyranny. His claim however to lie in the mould of the Christian king is formidable. Out of his action there emerges as well the wholly sovereign English state, which lasts over four hundred years and the strengthening of representative government which defines its institutions. The monarch as

Defender of the Faith is the heir directly of Henry VIII's own cast of mind and expressed view. He was well educated and percipient. As the Reformation erupted in Europe from Germany his concern led him to write a book replying to Martin Luther in defence of Roman Catholicism and its traditional medieval doctrines. Its publication won for him the title of 'Fidei Defensor' from Pope Leo X. His move to the creation of the Church of England stemmed both from his conscience as he saw it and his determination to have a male heir. He had married in Katherine of Aragon his dead brother's wife following a dispensation from Cannon Law given by the Pope. Henry regarded Katherine's failure after many miscarriages as a judgement of God for a breach of the biblical law of Leviticus XX, verse 21, which defines such a marriage as impurity. He sought from the Pope a decree of nullity of the marriage as against cannon law based on an invalid dispensation and the Pope would have been disposed to grant such a declaration had the Holy Roman Emperor Charles V, who was Catherine of Aragon's nephew not acted to prevent it by the threat of force. This political interference from Europe in English matters determined Henry VIII to free himself from constraints on his Sovereign rights to exercise power in England. He was determined to marry Queen Anne Boleyn and resorted to Parliament for their support. The religious and monarchical revolution brought the role of popular consent in the legislature for executive act to a higher point. The notion of the Christian King and representative Government became fully embraced. Parliament embarked for the King on a stream of legislation to remove the power of the Pope from the English Church and to establish a reformed English church.

The Act in Restraint of Appeals 1533 gave exclusive control of the church in England to the King and made illegal resort to the Pope's jurisdiction. Two Acts of Annates in 1534 prevented the Pope from appointing bishops and the payment of money to Rome. In the same year the Act of Supremacy made Henry VIII Supreme Head on earth of the Church of England. Failure to accept the King's authority became punishable as treason and in 1535 and 1536 the Crown seized the property of the Church and suppressed the monasteries. Those, who would not accept his marriage to Ann Boleyn and his headship of the Church were put to death for treason like the Carthusian priors of London in May 1533 and Sir Thomas More, Henry VIII's one time Lord Chancellor. Henry saw state and church as one and men were expected to be loyal to both.

Although Henry VIII desired no doctrinal change he appointed in 1532 as his Archbishop of Canterbury, Thomas Cranmer a sympathiser with the Protestant reformers. He was the architect of the English Bible, its reading in Church and of the beginnings of the Liturgy. His was the hand that preserved in the vital words of the Eucharist the medieval doctrine of the spiritual presence of Christ with his people as opposed to the notion of a physical presence at the consecration of bread and wine. The middle period of the sixteenth century under Edward

VI and Queen Mary, eldest daughter of Henry VIII was an era when extreme Protestant and Roman Catholics struggled over the soul of England. Married to a Spanish King, Philip II, under Mary the methods of the continent were imported and Protestants were burnt and martyred including the Archbishop Thomas Cranmer. The record of the persecution produced a book which for generations would be widely read on Sundays, Foxe's Book of Martyrs, speaking a protest at government interference with men's religion and conscience and implicitly warning of the danger of continental institutions such as the jurisdiction of the Pope and the structure of the Catholic church being returned to England.

The reign of Queen Elizabeth I was to draw together these threads. Her intelligence, character and beliefs were to mould England. Her people and their descendents were to transmit ideas which were born while she was Queen to the world at large. Some of those ideas were yet to grow to assume the form recognisable today, but, the essence of their meaning for the English was in place. First as befitted "the Christian King" she turned her attention to religion. She was firm in restoring the doctrine and practice of the church of Henry VIII as a Catholic and Apostolic Church but she did so with moderation and tolerance. Henry had made himself Supreme Head of the Church with the aid of Parliament: Elizabeth however in the Act of Supremacy only declared herself "the only Supreme Governor of this realm, as well in all spiritual and ecclesiastical things or causes as temporal". The monarch today remains that Supreme Governor and the establishment of the Church of England as a spiritual expression of the state continues in the public expression of the spiritual in Government. Elizabeth did not build the church as a sect, which with disestablishment it would become, but as a gift to all the English people. She found a nation divided with a substantial catholic minority and zealot puritans. Her method was one of moderation and a messy "English" compromise of unexpressed toleration. None of the Roman Catholic Bishops appointed by Mary were put to death although they were deprived. There was no massacre like that in France by King Charles IX and his mother Queen Catherine de Medici of the Huguenots on St. Bartholomew's Day 1572. Neither were there the persecution of the Protestants, forcible conversions, forced bullying and dragonards that accompanied the revocation of the Edict of Nantes by Louis XIV in 1685, when toleration previously granted was nullified. Conformity to the notion of the identity of church and nation rested on the idea of government by consent, on persuasion and only force in the clearest necessity. She did not desire a 'window into men souls' but loyalty to the Government. An oath of Supremacy was required of office holders and people could be fined for non attendance at Church, but the latter restraint was lightly enforced. An Act of Uniformity restored the Prayer Book of 1552 with minor changes. If they took the Oath parish clergy could remain, otherwise they were deprived, and most did remain.

As John Foxe who died in 1585 said of these evictions in his Book of Martyrs, "A reformation being soon resolved upon, the Queen desired that changes might be so managed as to occasion as little division as possible among her subjects." It was so managed.

For the first twelve years of the reign with a quiescent Catholic minority no Roman Catholic was executed. In 1572 however Pope Pius V influenced by Philip II of Spain, issued the 'decretal Regnans in Excelsis' in which Elizabeth was declared a heretic and excommunicated; Roman Catholics were freed to assassinate her and for the next thirty odd years she and King James I were under threat to their lives. The speech at Tilbury in 1588 (see the Defeat of the Armada, 29 July 1588) is only explicable in this context and re-affirms the unity of Crown and people in a common nationhood. The assassins were but a small fundamentalist minority, but, they were Englishmen, many minor country gentry of education. Politically correct commentators without history are astonished or concerned, that Muslim suicide bombers of today are similarly British bred but with an adhesion to an alien spiritual ideal: Elizabeth and her Government faced the same religious zealots grown from the large minority of Catholics of the time. The threat was broken by the use of informers, torture, and special courts, the Courts of Star Chamber and of High Commission. But even at the end of Elizabeth's reign only eight Roman Catholics were executed each year out of an estimated recusant population of 120,000. In terms of civil liberties the decree was a disaster and led to the tightening of state control over the Roman Catholic population. An act of 1581 declared members of the Church of Rome to be traitors and increased the fines for absence from Church. In 1588 Catholics were required to return to their homes and confined to a five mile radius of movement from there.

The attempt by Philip II to restore Roman Catholicism and the hegemony of the Pope to England was broken in the epic of the Defeat of the Armada and the self-confidence of England as a nation was hardened, touched by a suspicion of foreigners beyond the Channel. The reign of Elizabeth ended with a people conscious of a defined nationhood around the crown and a spirituality suffusing society, which embodied recognition of individual human difference of ideas, and accepted a kind of toleration in a society founded on compromise. Elizabeth governed by consent and accepted that Sovereignty rested with the Queen in Parliament in legislative matters but she stood firm on her prerogative and chided Parliament for their attempts to bring her to and to discuss her marriage. Christian and representative government were maintaining their inter-twined journey to the future and evolving into the sense of patriotism distinctive to Britain which continental nationalisms were not to share.

The other problem for the Queen was the growing challenge of the Puritans who, absorbing the doctrines of the Lutherans and the more extreme views of Zwingli and the Calvinists, wished to tear down the Anglican compromise, eliminate the bishops and purge the liturgy of the church of papistical practices. These too she put down with a firm hand. It was for the new king from Scotland, James I to meet this challenge in a conference at Hampton Court, out of which emerged in 1611 the Authorised Version of the Bible with its beauty of language and poetry of expression, a book which was be at the very heart of the heritage of England. Many of those who were unable to achieve their aims with the King left for the United States carrying with them a dogmatic Calvinist Protestantism, which was to colour the early "theocracy" of Massachusetts, and a wistful regret for their native land which was to cause them to name New England places with names such as Boston, Bedford, New London, Suffolk County, Dorchester, Cambridge and even the Thames River. They took too the notion of representative Government by consent which was to well up in the Rebellion of the Colonies at the end of the eighteenth century led by the landed gentry of Virginia and the rich heirs of the Boston protestants.

The difference between the assault made on the position of Elizabeth I and King James as between the Roman Catholics and the Puritans was to influence the course of events for two hundred years. The former were suspected of seeking to replace the Church of England with a continental hegemony and re-introducing the power of foreign kings and bishops into England, while the latter were less suspect in that their end was solely the replacement under the Crown of Anglican practice in the Church with Puritan doctrine and liturgy. The Gunpowder plot of 1605 was to stamp the threat of Roman Catholicism and its corollary of interference by a foreign power indelibly on the mind of Englishmen. Once more the laws on recusancy were tightened. Charles I was to uphold the Henrician approach of identifying the Church and state as one, making loyalty to Crown and Church intrinsic to the civic functions of English subjects. He was determined to protect the traditional Anglican settlement and its liturgy as, to quote the king, in the "purest times of Queen Elizabeth's days" between "the pomp of superstitious tyranny and the meanness of fantastic anarchy." Archbishop Laud was thus empowered by the king to defend the Anglican settlement from the Puritans and exercised a strong pro-active intervention to secure traditional practices of ritual and liturgy in the churches but, when the Parliamentarians and Puritans united against Charles I in the Civil War, was to be executed. Under Oliver Cromwell with the monarchy and church destroyed there was in the sixteen-fifties a need to restore within the state a religious order, the need for which was undoubted. A church was established, but, it was not Episcopalian but Presbyterian in character, each independent congregation having a freedom from among people vouched to be "godly" to choose their pastor, whether Presbyterian, independent or Baptist. Atheists, Anglicans and Roman Catholics were excluded but there was no great persecution of Episcopalians meeting quietly or of Roman Catholics acting privately. It set the first foundation of real toleration of religious opinion since outside the state structure there was liberty of dissenters, apart from Quakers, to form congregations of their own.

With the restoration of King Charles II the nature of England as a Christian monarchy formed by the Crown in Parliament was restored, but, the next fifty years were to be marked by a tension between the notion of state and church as one and the principle of toleration by the state of Christians without the Church. Charles II was to express the more modern view in the Declaration of Breda promising "a liberty to tender consciences, and that no man shall be disquieted or called in question for differences of opinion in matters of religion, which do not disturb the peace of the kingdom." The Royalist Parliament however in 1662 passed an Act of Uniformity in support of the restored Anglican Church, which was to lay the foundation of the distinction between conformity and non-conformity until 1828. The Book of Common Prayer and the liturgy were to be restored in every church, chapel or place of public worship and people preaching required licences from the church authorities. In 1664 the same Parliament sought to constrain the rise of non-conformist congregations by requiring persons preaching in any unlawful assembly, conventicle or meeting under the colour or pretence of any exercise of religion to take an oath to the King and not to work for any alteration to the state or church. They could be fined if within five miles of any town or place where they had preached without making the oath to five or more people under the Seditious Conventicles Act of 1670. In 1672 Charles II dissatisfied with the policy issued under his prerogative suspending power a Declaration of Indulgence suspending the execution of "all penal laws ... in matters ecclesiastical against whatsoever sort of non-conformists, or recusants "i.e. Roman Catholics. Opposition came from Parliament challenging the right of the Crown to suspend Acts of Parliament and the controversy went to the heart of the conflict between the Crown and Parliament that shook England in the seventeenth century. Charles II backed down and the Declaration was cancelled. The Parliament, absorbed by the idea of the danger posed by Puritanism as experienced under Cromwell and by Roman Catholicism from the continent driven by King Louis XIV of France, then set about strengthening the laws to establish the unity of the Crown and Church of England as one. The Test Acts of 1673 and 1678 were purported to be aimed at Roman Catholics but in fact also encompassed non-conformists since it required all persons who wished to be eligible for any office, civil or military, to repudiate publicly Roman Catholicism and produce certificates that they were partakers of the sacrament in the Church of England. The 1678 Act applied the provisions to Parliament and in the House of Lords Roman Catholic peers were forced to relinquish their seats. It was not until 1828 that the Tests Acts and the other Acts effecting the disability to hold office of any non-conformist were replaced and 1829 before the disability on Roman Catholics was to be lifted. For one hundred and fifty years society was to be formed by the notion that service to the Crown in Parliament was dependent on a loyalty given to the monarch and the Anglican Church together and the patriotic ideal of the English was built in that context.

The legal joinder of Crown and Church left a legacy down to the later 20th century in which no public function or institution was without a statement of Christian belief or order in the conduct of its activities – such as Parliamentary prayers, local civic services, Ascension day as a red-letter day for judges, church parades, compulsory school chapel and prayers and people were able freely in the workplace to exhibit statements of their belief. It is only with the present obsession with multi-culturalism founded on an extreme secular notion of toleration that the British have come to face the deracination of the open civic practice of their Christian beliefs.

King James II was to re-ignite the dispute over the Prerogative Power by dispensing in favour of individuals with the operation of the Test Acts and was suspected as a Roman Catholic sympathiser. His attempt at toleration by use of the suspending power in the Declaration of Indulgence in 1687 and 1688 was an act of Government outside Parliament and was to loose him his throne creating an alliance of Tories, Whigs and Dissenters ready to welcome William III and Mary as joint King and Queen. William reflecting his political instinct for compromise made his acceptance of the Crown conditional on toleration of dissent. He declared that he wished to see freedom of conscience for Roman Catholics, freedom of public worship for dissenters and a revision of the Penal Laws, but, would not abrogate the Test Acts and other laws which precluded members of the Church of Rome from office. It was therefore on the footing of the toleration of Protestantism in England outside the Anglican church and an end to the persecution of Roman Catholics that the Parliamentary monarchy of 1688 rested. In 1689 the Toleration Act was passed opening the door to public worship for all protestant sects, save the Unitarians. The Penal laws against Roman Catholics were laxly enforced allowing mass to be said in private houses. Up to 1720 attempts were made to restore complete Anglican primacy and toughen the application of the penal laws, but, the efforts were not long lasting. Britain had moved into an age, when toleration among Christians became an attribute of the Crown in Parliament. The settlement of the Glorious Revolution did not extend toleration of religious practice to those who served the Crown in England but there was no break with the notion that the Crown stood for the protection of the ideal of Christian action as the impulse upon which the state acted. In Scotland the established Presbyterian church was similarly in the history of the seventeenth century protected and saved by William III. The Act of Settlement of 1707 guarded that establishment and the monarch was henceforth to become an Anglican in England and a Presbyterian in Scotland.

The Seventeenth century in its struggle over religion and the Church had its reflection in the battle between the notion of a Crown able to tax and make laws outside the consent of the people assembled in Parliament and of a Crown under law acting by consent and subject to oversight of independent judges. The latter was not a novel idea but had started its life in the thirteenth century expressed in Magna Carta in the concept of the feudal king in "contract" with his Barons. It was in counterpoint to the notion of the theocratic king answerable not to law but only to God, a model which was to flourish in the monarchies of Europe. Its operation has been seen under Henry VIII and Queen Elizabeth, but, its scope was to be defined in the Civil War and the political conflicts of the Restoration. The Parliamentary Monarchy of William III and Queen Mary was to see the struggle resolved in the settlement enacted in the Declaration of Rights 1689, the Triennial Act of 1694 and the Act of Settlement of 1701. The Crown henceforth was under the rule of law, and lawmaking was dependent on representative government embodied in the Houses of Lords and Commons so that the engine of sovereignty, of the Crown in Parliament, was the consent of the people. The Crown came in 1688 thereafter to stand for freedom under the law, government by consent and a moral order suffused by the precepts of Anglicanism, and thus of Christian order, and the notion of toleration of conscience within that order. To be a free, law abiding nation of Christian morals under its King formed the minds of the people and shaped their action. Life became saturated with the feeling embodied in these concepts and they were put to work in every sphere.

It would be inappropriate to follow further the working of this idea of nation in Britain and its consequences. The toleration of non-confromity after 1688 and the removal of all civil disabilities on dissenters and Roman Catholics in the early nineteenth century gave room for the enlargement of Christian action within society and within all classes of the people. The contribution of Methodism, the Baptists, the Quakers, the Evangelists, the Anglo-Catholics, revived Roman Catholicism and the 'Salvation Army' all were to stamp in large cities, the valleys of Wales and emerging industrial Communities, the moral order of life with Christian values and was to impel the touching of British life with the impulse of charity, concern for others, tolerance of difference and human treatment of each man's neighbour. The abolition of slavery, the redress of unendurable practices of treatment at work, the drive for acceptable housing and the attack on poverty all were the fruits of the climate of thought, which the national order created.

In the army and navy and in warmaking the Christian Crown in Parliament was to be exemplified in the life of the men involved and in their attitudes. The roll call of the battles won is marked by Admirals and Generals formed out of the distinctive way of life that Anglicanism fostered. The sons of the clergy are the seed-bed of many of the officers in the Navy in particular, but, the army too has its examples from that background. Nelson, if anyone the archetype of British heroes, was the son of the village parson at Burnham Thorpe in Norfolk. Before he went to command in the Mediterranean the influence of this past led him to seek

874 Bibles and prayer books for his men from the Society for the Promotion of Christian Knowledge. Susceptible to human weakness, his personal morals had a latitude which breached the notion of Christian marriage, but, yet before Trafalgar he fell in his cabin to his knees to compose his moving prayer for victory not just for King and Country but for the benefit of Europe. His sense of duty and patriotism were more than a narrow nationalism. That worldly-wise courtier, the Duke of Marlborough, spent much of the night before the Battle of Blenheim with his Chaplain, Dr.Francis Hare and took Communion on 13th August 1704. The late eighteenth century men-at-war had their Chaplains, although the kindly Earl St Vincent, considerate of his men, could not resist the humour of calling them in rough seas by gig and cutter to the flagship. Even in the twentieth century in North Africa in 1942, among the first concerns of Fieldmarshal Montgomery, the son too of a Clergyman, was to improve and re-organise the supply of Chaplains to his men. In a "secret" visit to Cairo he insisted on reading the lesson at a service in the Cathedral. This continuous tradition of the union of church and state in the role and function of the armed forces and the interaction of naval and military practise with religious teaching and the ministry of the clergy has in its turn formed vital attitudes to the practice of war for the British. The role of Chaplains in succouring the wounded on the battlefield of the Second World Wars evidenced the nexus in action. The Reverend Ted Brabyn conducting his service under air attack in Belgium in 1940 is an image to be remembered and valued.

The identity of Crown and Church also suffused the responsibility felt by military and naval leadership towards their men. The rule of action for the Cavalry Officer on return to barracks or to camp was to attend upon the horses, his men and then only on himself. The principle therefore of responsibility to the men as primary before oneself as an officer might be argued as an emanation from the Christian ideal of Christ as both leader and servant and as shepherd. Whatever its source and it may stem also from a sense of reciprocal feudal bonds between the lord and the men of his manor, taken to war, the need to care for the well-being of the men embodies as an idea the notion of providing for their comfort and so their safety consonant with the nature of war. Marlborough in his great two hundred mile march from Holland to Bavaria in 1705 meticulously planned the logistics and created supply dumps of food and shoes on the way. Hawke fought the corrupt and inefficient victuallers for provisions for his men in 1759. Lord Howe distributed his own wine and comforts to the wounded men. Nelson mortally wounded on his way to the orlop deck ordered that care be taken of the wounded Midshipman Rivers, whose leg had been injured by a cannonball. Undoubtedly to the modern eye conditions of service were often cruel and hard and comforts few. Amelioration was also left to individuals and applied without uniformity. The ideal was however there and could be deeply felt. Wellington cried publicly for the 3000 dead in the breach at the siege of

Badajoz when he visited the scene afterwards. At Ciudad Rodrigo he rode thirty miles to inspect the condition of the wounded left in open bivouac, ordered their removal to officer's barracks and cashiered the officers who subsequently evicted them. General Alexander commanding the rearguard at Dunkirk waited to the final moment of evacuation to insure his men were safely gone. Much of the success of Fieldmarshal Montgomery stemmed from the direct relationship which he achieved with his fighting soldiers, first in the lines of El Alamein in 1942, and in the sense which he radiated of his care for their comfort and safety. He had served in the First World War, and having experienced the casualties of that war was to seek to return to the care for the safety of the men in battle in the tradition of Wellington, who liked to choose positions for his battles where his infantry might lie down and shelter from bombardment on the reverse slopes of hills until the moment came for them to rise and deliver their fusillade of shot to decisive purpose. The unease which the record of the First World War strongly arouses is that the Generals seem to have forgotten their duty to care for the safety of the men and were wanton in their approach to the things which the men were asked to undertake. Yet Earl Haig seems to have been well thought of by his men and had to fight at the historic point when military technique and technology imposed effective limits on the capacity of action to forward the outcome of the conflict. The enormity of that war was to colour strongly the approach to battle in the Second World War as the example of Montgomery shows and was to return the conduct of the army to the long tradition of the past. Quite apart from issues of military tactic, which underpinned the reservations of General Von Rundstedt and other German Generals to orders often given by Hitler, the idea of defending to the death without sensible military necessity positions such as that at Stalingrad at the end of 1942 and in the Falaise Gap in 1944 are not to be found in the record of British military action because the army was seen not as a mere instrument, but, as people to whom a proper moral conduct for their care and safety was owed by their leaders founded on the medieval image of the Christian King among his men. It would have been inconceivable for a British Commander to speak of his army as Adolf Hitler spoke to Feldmarschall Rommel in 1943 saying that the army and the men in Africa did not matter.

The flexibility of the ideal of British patriotism for which men fought is to be found in its distinctiveness as a result of the history of this country. It depends on only one crucial element loyalty to the Crown. Because the Crown is a composite reference to the ideas of freedom, Government under law and Government by consent founded on a Christian moral order no statement of values, ideals or guarantees is needed. The person of the monarch is the living embodiment of the principles for which the British have stood as their history witnesses. There is no need for a constitution, a document to express the disposition of what it means to be British. The essence of the matter is to be found in the heart. The simplicity of the principle enabled the peoples of India to fight in the armies of the Crown, loyal to their King-Emperor. The Government of India may not have been a Government elected on a franchise, but, the small numbers needed to maintain the law and give order in a mighty population was a token of consent in exchange for the civic peace, which the King Emperor brought. Loyalty in the Crown also carried with it as a value for which it stood, the idea of self-government, and the dissolution of Empire was inherent in its very existence. The example of the Muslims, Sikhs and Ghurkhas and their heroism – the Victoria Cross, for example, of Khudadad Khan in 1914 and Kamel Ram in 1944 – are testimony that in loyalty to the Crown in Parliament immigrant communities can be British and at the same time, Muslim, Sikh and Hindu.

In the last forty years the public clarity of loyalty to the Crown as the basis of British patriotism and moral order has suffered endless assault and few among the Governments and metropolitan establishments of that period have not set their hands to the destruction of the Britain that in mid-twentieth century was evoked in the Coronation of Queen Elizabeth II where thanks to the benefit of film and television the dedication of the monarch to the institutions and moral order, for which the Crown stands, could be shared by the people as a whole. That Britain was innate in its history and Christian practice and the attack on and marginalisation of both has led to a situation in which politicians and the media, the principal architects of the destruction, talk of the need to discover Britishness and to set out the values for which it stands, as if they were continental Jacobins in some new found republic. The destruction of history and religious education in the schools under the impact of political correctness and multi-culturalism destroy the growth and habit of mind that is crucial to the existence of the British patriotic ideal. Even the ending of symbols such for example, as the cancellation of the Royal Yacht, the constant merging of historic regiments, the ejection of hereditary peers from the House of Lords, who by their names were living witnesses to the past, are phenomena stemming from the uprooting of history. As a result of membership of the European Union, the symbolic unity for individuals of the Crown in the Commonwealth has also been fractured by the ending at airports and ports of the dedicated Immigration Controls that recognised the special position of Commonwealth citizens, some of whom remain subjects of the Crown such as Canadians, Australians and New Zealanders, and who now are banished to joining foreigners outside the Union, while the British, for whom they fought, are themselves submerged in an undifferentiated mass of Europeans. For those from the Dominions, who acknowledge the Crown, and who recall the past, this situation is hurtful, apart from the corrosiveness which it causes to the link with the Crown which eats away at the idea of a worldwide union based on common history. In terms of the moral order the modern secularism of some of the bishops undermines the idea of a Christian order. Toleration can be pressed too far as can adherence to the sexual rules of biblical authority and the formulations of St Paul in reaction to the licentiousness of Rome. The sphere of private conscience and action needs constantly to be distinguished from the public. Equal treatment under the law for homosexuals, for example can be justified on the basis of a moral order in which toleration is a principal element. A requirement that Catholic Adoption Societies should accept homosexuals in civil partnerships as prospective parents strikes however at the Christian moral order fundamental to Britain and the freedom which is innate to it. Perhaps the most basic real attack, however, on the moral order inherent in Britishness has been found in the change in religious education which is made compulsory under the Education Act 1944. Until fifty years ago children were exposed in school to the basic tenets of Christian religion. They knew the Ten Commandments, of the life and preaching of Christ, the Lords Prayer, Psalm 23 and some of the great hymns, such as God Our Help in Ages Past, sung on so many public occasions. Even if subsequently non-church going, they were touched by the Christian order. The marginalisation of the general act of common worship required by law in many schools abets the destruction of this tradition. Relativism in religious education in which children study all religions with the unspoken premise that all are of equal validity destroys belief in a Christian moral order and leaves many rootless without moral sense and the instinct to faith destroyed. The result has been seen in the continuing withdrawal of people from the churches, declining moral imperatives in conduct and materialism pursued seven days a week. There is probably no way of completely restoring an inherent Christian order to British society and the modern populist politician edges away from the idea, but the knowledge of it could be restored as a datum in schools, to be taught save where the religion of pupils is predominantly different. Diversity should not require the destruction for the majority population of the historic bases of their state founded on Anglicanism. Education alone cannot of course restore the Christian social moral order of the past: that needs the return of the people of this country and their families to their churches and their chapels and their essential ethic.

In the end the patriotic ideal of loyalty to the Crown in Parliament is a valid benchmark of this nation as in the past. It needs to be kept alive and celebrated. Those, who have come to these shores to live, should have it made plain that on that benchmark rests the civil order and freedom that they wish to share and is more vital to their lives than the commandments of zealots or customs founded on long held religious traditions. They must remember with all of us that they are subjects of the Queen not citizens of some vacuous secular state. The idea of the Christian king requires however that the monarch too remains Defender of the Faith and not Defender of Faiths.

Of the Battles

Any selection of battles won in the continuous history of a society long established and with a defined cultural identity involves the problems of selection. As in all decision making the subjective choice needs to be diminished in impact, although as in all human affairs it cannot be eliminated. The goal is to achieve selection on the basis of an objective test. In searching for the criteria of success in battle there still after almost one hundred and eighty years is no better source than Lieutenant-General Karl Von Clausewitz's Dem Kriege. Only Book One of this work was published at his death but his wife was able from his notes to create the last few books of the work. Von Clausewitz analyses extensively the nature of war and discusses carefully the character of battles. The issue for this book is by which criteria should one select the battles, which are chosen as Victories. A battle is defined by Von Clausewitz as a conflict waged with all the forces to hand for the attainment of a decisive victory. Since the existence and effectiveness of an army depends on maintaining the artificial formation which constitutes an army and the cohesion which sustains it, the breaking up of this formation is the event which constitutes the victory. The ability to wage war for both opponents rests heavily on the existence of the morale of each of the forces involved, so that success in battle can be measured by its effectiveness on the morale of the vanquished. Where the object of the battle is not primarily the destruction of the opponent's military or naval formation, but the taking of land, such might constitute a victorious decision, the efficacy of which is to be tested in the context of the impact on the defeated army or navy or the defeated nation. The taking of land needs to be judged also by the question of whether the objective, for which the land is to be taken, is realised. Quite apart from existence of morale in the troops or nation being at the heart of the matter, it has to be remembered that the war of a community – of whole nations and particularly of civilised nations – always starts from a political condition and is therefore a political act. It is against these criteria that in relation to each battle in the period 1340 to 1945, three tests have been applied, first, if the objective was the destruction of the enemy's fighting force or a part of it, was that achieved? Second, if the objective was the taking of land, were the objectives of that taking realised? And third, to what extent was any political object achieved in whole or in part by victory in the battle? Few single battles ever decide by themselves a war, although such instances as the Battle of Waterloo are capable of doing so. Most form part of continuous campaigns designed to secure the political objective for which the war was fought. It follows therefore that there are greater or lesser degrees of outcome evident in history. Thus, not all carry the same importance – the Battle of Trafalgar might be contrasted with the Battle of Garcia Hernandez (23rd June 1812) which gains its place solely as the most audacious cavalry charge of the Peninsular War by the King's German Legion. Objection might be made on the other hand that none of the extensive western front battles of the First World War are separately listed but are all subsumed under Armistice Day 1918 while at the time politicians and media claimed these ultimately fruitless struggles as victories. Set against the realistic acid of the theories of General Von Clausewitz, none meet the three tests which have been used. The Battle of the Somme in 1916 exemplifies the costly failure of the first World War battles until the German collapse in 1918. The Somme battle was forced on the British by the French (see Campaign of 1916, the 11th November 1918) and after he was reluctantly forced into the strategy, Haig set four objectives for the outcome, first, a break through of the first line of defence, second the taking of the main ridge where the German second line was located, third a wheel left from the Bapaume ridge to Arras to 'roll up' the Germans, and fourth, an advance generally to Cambrai and Douai. At the end of the battle only the first two objectives had been gained in part at the cost of 419,564 casualties: the land taken was a salient twenty five miles long and seven-miles in depth, still penned in by a third line of defence. While the 465,000 German casualties might be arguably a destruction of part of the enemy's fighting force, the specified major objective of the break-through was not achieved. While the continuous frontal assault on the German lines in the west, taken with the naval blockade and Russian sacrifices in the East were to wear the German forces and nation down over four years, the effect of the Battle of the Somme cannot be separately isolated to cloak an event which to the modern mind, namely the taking of a waste of mud where the objectives were not met at such great cost, with the habiliments of victory. The western front in the First World War has to be seen as a long siege and in a siege the commander is not entitled to claim success when a breach is made in the wall which is immediately blocked.

Those of sceptical bent may well ask, when the First War Battles have been excluded, why there should be found in the text, Cornwallis' Retreat (the 17th June 1795), the Battle of Coruna (17th January 1809) and the Deliverance at Dunkirk (2nd June 1940). It is admitted that there was soul-searching as to their inclusion, but, it was decided that all three sufficiently answered the three essential questions on the nature of a victory to justify inclusion. Admiral Cornwallis retired before a French fleet four times as powerful, fighting all day, and by deception persuaded the French fleet that the Channel fleet was near, causing their retirement to port and helping to save a convoy from attack. At Coruna Sir John Moore, by his deft retreat from Spain and the check given to Marshal Soult before the town, enabled the evacuation of the army by the Royal Navy. It had been the objective of the Emperor Napoleon to destroy that army and drive Britain from the Iberian Peninsula. Moore prevented the realisation of that objective and the army saved and re-equipped was to return to Lisbon to be commanded by Sir Arthur Wellesley. Morale was not broken, the army was not destroyed and the political objective not achieved. The event is two faced, because for the British, it can be said, that morale of the army was enhanced at Coruna, the army survived and returned to Lisbon ultimately to succeed against the French in Portugal and Spain. The Deliverance at Dunkirk has similarly a duality. The pause of the German Panzers short of Dunkirk, whatever its cause, enabled the army to be saved. The fighting retreat was carried out with skill and the army retained a substantial degree of cohesion. The Royal Navy in Operation Dynamo organised the evacuation effectively and instead of the 45,000 troops, which the Cabinet had been told might be rescued, 224,320 British troops were brought home. The sea operation was a brilliant success and the army was kept in being to re-enter the war. 113,906 non-British troops were also embarked. The saving of the army strengthened national morale, thwarted the German objective of destroying the army and demonstrated the versatility and efficiency of the navy and air force. In Von Clausewitz's terms the Germans had no victory: the British had been rescued to the support of national morale and resolution to see the war through to the end. The object of saving the army, the purpose of the naval operation was achieved. As in any categorisation of human events then these battles are touched by ambiguity and the outcome of classification is subjective, but they are not out of place.

Because the book is not intended to be an indigestible academic work of modern style but a book suitable for reading in a country house the greater part of the sources relied on are derivative. The text is built on works, which include the primary facts and inferential facts based on them. Sources for the description of the same battle are sometimes not clear, the inferential description of events the subject of greater or lesser conflict with one another and in evolving the text analysis has sought to describe the battles drawing together a view of the facts without ambiguity, with clarity, and absence of conflict of the facts one with another. In not every battle did the need for constructive interpretation arise but the scale of divergence at its worst is to be seen in relation to the Battle of Matapan (28th March 1944) where Winston Churchill in his Second World War refers to the aircraft carrier involved as the Illustrious, but, Admiral Cunningham the naval commander in the Mediterranean at the time states that the carrier was the Formidable. The latter statement of fact has been preferred because other sources suggest that Illustrious was undergoing repair in March 1941 in Alexandria. The battles do fall in the shadowy world which is truth in human events and the outcome carries a degree of the subjective.

In describing the battles the attempt has been made to put them briefly in their setting so that the question can be answered why were these battles fought? Those prior to the sixteenth century can be seen as wars by the Crown for land and dynastic objectives, but, from the Armada onwards the battles are conducted with modern objectives in view. Henry VIII by his repudiation of the continental jurisdiction of Rome in the affairs of England gave the country a sovereign shared identity, a sense of being a nation, fostered the more by Queen Elizabeth I. In that context the foundation of action flows from the principle enumerated by General von Clausewitz, namely that "the war of a community – of whole nations and particularly of civilised nations – always starts from a political condition. It is therefore a political act." With the possible exception of the three Dutch Wars of the mid-seventeenth century, the principal purpose of the wars fought with the European powers was the preservation of the distinctive character of the English state, its idea of freedom and sovereignty being embodied in the Crown set in the context of a peaceful order in Europe. Acquisition of land as a political aim was not primary, although its protection and the preservation of the British economic outreach in commerce and through the seas formed an important but secondary leit-motif. Who controlled the Low Countries was a constant factor in the wars, but, as an adjunct to resistance to the political hegemonies and systems, with which the essence of the struggled rested. The early period represents a period of opposition to the re-imposition of Catholic jurisdiction in England coupled with the political objective of renewing an authoritarian monarchy deriving from the doctrine of divine right. The objectives of King Philip II of Spain to replace the protestant Anglican settlement with Catholicism was a clear-cut challenge to English freedom. Louis XIV after 1685 was driven by his recovered Catholic zeal, his desire to plant the borders of France on the Rhine and his support for the restoration of the Stuart Dynasty, embodied in the deposed King James II, whose attempts at toleration had resulted in his downfall as a Catholic sympathiser. The extension of Bourbon power with its threat of a hegemony of France and Spain over Europe in the War of the Spanish succession drove on British resistance. That merged into a period of resistance to the attempt by France to extend its influence in Europe and elsewhere. The Revolutionary War marks the second phase of resistance to the imposition of a uniform political structure throughout Europe based on the programme of liberty, equality and fraternity carried by marching columns of troops and backed by a controlling central structure of civil administration. The anarchy of the revolutionary attempt to disturb the order of Europe and its effects in France were of course to lead to the autocracy of the Emperor Napoleon, who disguised his drive to the creation of a total French power in Europe and the creation of effective bureaucratic Government with the trumpet call of the revolutionaries. Not only was his idea of government a threat to Britain, but, in his continental system of trade banning trade with Britain, he sought to expel British commerce from Europe. The third and final phase is the resistance to aggressive military Prussianism and an amoral nationalism, whose populist roots are found in the destructive effects of the French Revolution and the reaction to the aggression of Napoleon Buonaparte stirring a populist nationalist idea throughout Europe. Common to all these systems, to which the

British were opposed, is the existence of authoritarian government carrying the marginalisation of the idea of the state resting on the consent of the people. The acts done by the aggressors tearing the peaceful order of the states affected also made the war arising just, but it is the securing of the safety of the style of government by a sovereign Crown in Parliament with its guarantee of freedom, moral government and the primacy of law binding even the Crown, which constitutes the "political act" leading to resistance to Spain, France and Germany in turn and the fount of public morale sustaining that resistance and puts Britain in direct counterpoint from those countries.

The primary armed force by which the safety of Britain was secured throughout the greater part of these wars was the Royal Navy. The army after the Glorious Revolution of 1688 was regarded with suspicion necessitating an annual act in Parliament to authorise its existence and was to retain save in times of dire emergency a limited size. The necessities of action by land against France, Spain and Germany, meant that with small armies victories were dependent on the existence of alliances. While in the War of the English Succession and its continuation in the War of the Spanish Succession, the British Navy was in alliance at sea with the Dutch, the greater number of British naval victories were solely national in character, reflective of the arm of war in which the principal power resided. Many of the victories on land in contrast were the outcome of alliance, where Allies have contributed to success to a larger or lesser extent under a British Commander. The Duke of Marlborough at Blenheim commanded with Prince Eugene Imperial troops from Austria, Hessians, Danes, Prussians and other Germans from Wurtemburg and Hannover. The Duke of Wellington in the Peninsula fielded the King's German Legion, the rebuilt Portuguese army and a Spanish army. At Waterloo his force contained Dutch contingents and he jointly campaigned with Prince Blucher and the Prussians. Lord Nelson in his prayer before Trafalgar asked for a great and glorious victory for his country and for the benefit of Europe and in so doing acknowledged the alliance, which William Pitt had formed with the Austrian Empire and the wish to remove from the Continent the danger of French hegemony. It is that danger, which from the time of King Louis XIV in the mid-seventeenth century to the downfall of the Emperor Napoleon in 1815, was to be the mainspring of British policy. The national allies, whom we had, were the German powers, who felt as much, if not more threatened. Despite the defeat at Waterloo the French political class did not in the nineteenth century abandon their pretensions to control others in the interests of France, turning their attention to North Africa and under the Emperor Napoleon III to Italy and inter-meddling so far as they could in the southern German states. Britain stood apart save for an uneasy alliance with France to campaign against the Russians in the Crimea. Lord Raglan, who had been aide-de-camp to the Duke of Wellington in Spain and commanded the

British army there, preserved his sound instinct about the French in, it is said and it may be apocryphal, always referring to his French allies as "the enemy." It was only the aggressive economic expansion of the German commercial classes taken up unwisely by Kaiser Wilhelm II and forwarded under the impulse of the anti-British Admiral Turpitz by the building of a potent navy that impelled Britain to abandon its natural allies in Europe for the questionable twentieth century alliance with the French. Allies for war on land remained essential to Britain but the record of the First and Second World Wars speaks of the damage done to Britain and its armies by France in the implementation of the latter's military strategies, as in the Somme and in 1940, and by acquiescence of the British political class of the time in the vengeful Treaty of Versailles engineered and promoted by the French Prime Minister, Clemenceau. Marshal Petain is the embodiment of the French alliance of the two World Wars apparently standing beside us but with dislike, and in the Second World War holding a dagger to wound, as he agreed with Hitler that the defeat of the British was in the interests of France in the Autumn of 1940. The commitment of the French as a people to the alliance with Britain in 1940 and 1941 its moreover exemplified in the small numbers of the French navy and army, given the opportunity of adhering to the Free French forces of De Gaulle (see the Seizure and Destruction of the French Fleet 3rd July 1940 and the Surrender of Lebanon and Syria 14th July 1941), who in fact did so. The rescuers of Britain as Allies were the United States and Russia bringing about the successful outcome of the war, and the debt to both should be acknowledged. That with the United States reflects the permanent interest of Britain in the age of American power giving protection to the diffused still existing sinews of the economic and political interest of Britain, which remain across the oceans and distinguish this nation from those on the continent. The relationship to Russia is of less weight but still a permanent interest and signs of the recognition of the wartime alliance have a moving quality. On a bright October day to find at the Seelow Saure, where the towering memorial of a Russian soldier stands as testimony to the fallen, who had stormed in March 1945 the River Oder visible below, a faded wreath of poppies from the 52nd Engineers Regiment has the power to prompt memory of what is owed.

Memorial of the dead is at the heart of this sequence of victories. The purpose is not the glorification of war whose inhumanity and horror is demonstrated by the events narrated but the record of the men who took part in the wars, which have preserved Britain and its special identity since 1340. It is a record of duty, courage, honour, heroism and endurance and the object is to celebrate those virtues and the patriotic idea, which brought them into play. They are virtues which the modern world may find old-fashioned and disdain, but, their exercise has helped to conserve a world, which seeks to rest on moral order and government by consent. Until the First World War the history is of men, who were the inhabitants of these islands – England, Welsh, Scots and Irish – and their deeds resound through the regiments of the army which carried their separate identities and were embodied in the traditions of lines of naval ships' names, echoed in descent one to another. The creation of the Victorian Empire brought in the British overseas – Canadian, Australian, New Zealanders, Rhodesian and South African – but, because of the nature of its political outreach making men the subjects of the Crown and the test of belonging loyalty to the monarchy, it brought within the roll of honour and sacrifice French Canadians, Boers, Indians, men from the Caribbean, India, Nepal and Africa, whoever took the "King's Shilling." It is their record and their history as well, and they made their stand in the same cause. Whether they marched or sailed home or fell in battle these men were the beating heart of Britain and its Empire and ignorance of their deeds and action is a betrayal of them. A state education, which pencils out in the interest of political correctness these deeds of the people in the past, fails the cause of nation. Betrayal by ignorance pales however into the insubstantial beside the political betrayal which has eviscerated the object for which the battles were fought. A sovereign nation ruled by the Crown in Parliament resting on law-making by consent was the source of the belief and sense of duty, which imbued the seamen and the soldiers to do their duty. Riotous, anarchic they may have been, but, the Crown in Parliament was at once the guarantor of identity and freedom. Paradoxically the seamen of Lord Nelson's time, who had no vote for the House of Commons, had more freedom than do their successors, who have the benefit of universal suffrage: the effect of moving to populist democracy has laid upon the people more chains and not removed them. The Sovereign Government of Britain is no more. The accession treaties to the European Union have progressively sucked out the ability for Britain to regulate national affairs in whole areas of action – agriculture and fishing are obvious examples – and reforged the ability for the interference of others in our affairs, which Henry VIII and Elizabeth broke and which for three centuries was so courageously resisted. The betrayal has been cloaked in deceit by the Government politicians of the time of both Conservative and Labour parties and the destruction done without recourse to gaining the consent of the people. Edward Heath, a leading figure in the betrayal of the past, who was conscious that the 'sovereignty' of Britain had been given away (see the 8th Corbishley Memorial Lecture 1984) thought to castigate it as outdated and irrelevant and invented in order to explain the European Union the notion of a system of "pooled Sovereignty". As any reader of John Austin's Province of Jurisprudence Determined however must know, sovereignty as such is indivisible, although there can be argument as to its precise location. "Pooled sovereignty" is judicially an absurd concept. In all the areas where by treaty the European Union has been given competence or seized it by the use of the political judiciary of the European Court of Justice, sovereignty no longer rests with the Crown in Parliament and thus the people of Britain have lost their ability, which their predecessors possessed, of governing themselves in relation to the competences given away. As the competences are extended the loss is ever greater. More unforgivable than loss of sovereignty is the elimination of representative government in a real sense guaranteeing freedom for people to live their lives under historic modes of lawmaking, whose application rested on the essential fundamental of individual freedom and consent. The century of the common man has arguably ravaged and destroyed the careful polity, made first by the lawmakers of the Glorious Revolution, replacing, particularly since 1945, representative government by rule by a London based inward-looking group of the politically elite, who in the terms of John Locke operate an alternating 'tyranny' of "the people" embodied in themselves. The fact that they are subject to the needs of open lawmaking, the vagaries of Parliamentary procedure and the ability in a General Election for the holders of power to be replaced means that the shadow of representative government remains, even if its substance is weakened. The institutional structure of the European Union gives no such safeguard and is the antithesis of the mode of Government for which the people whose lives are recorded in this book fought. The present is not the place to develop this point, but, the lawmaking function alone demonstrates the grave defect of the mechanism. The Council of Ministers as the chief lawmaking and policy body evolving the basic treaties meets in secret session, no minutes are published, its decisions are announced as unanimous and no one knows how much those who are supposed to speak for Britain have given away or conceded and for what purpose. As an exercise of the law making power it affronts the very concept of lawmaking by consent done openly which first began to evolve effectively under King Edward III. The Commission which has its own legislative power as the executive arm of the union is unelected. This structure is not answerable to the European Parliament, in the way that the Crown and its Ministers have always been answerable to the British Parliament even in its modern attenuated and weakened form. The authoritarian nature of the European structure is readily understandable if it is realised to which constitution it is a close analogy. When Germany was unified in 1870 and Prince von Bismarck wished to insure the primacy of Prussia, its Crown and his role as Chancellor, Imperial Germany was given a constitution which insured that primacy. Executive powers were vested in the Emperor and the Chancellor, policy powers and lawmaking in the Bundesrat, an assembly representative of the states with some decisions made by majority vote of the members among which Prussia dominated and some by qualified majority voting, the latter having the main purpose of reducing the influence of Bavaria and the Southern States. The Reichstag was largely consultative with limited lawmaking, financial and budgetary powers. Bismarck's goal was not representative government, but, the supremacy of a controlling Prussian Crown, guided by himself. In both Germany and France the tradition of effective bureaucratic administration over the widest area of action which grew out of Prussianism and Bonapartism infect the climate of Bruxelles, where early on the French style of administrative action formed the structure of implementation. These habits of lawmaking and regulation reverse the old presumption of English government that action to intervene with the individual, his property, trade and social customs should be taken only out of the strongest necessity so that freedom is preserved. The deliberate de-construction of the bases of the British state by politicians, who have preferred so-called, but never precisely calculated or assessed, Cobdenite advantages of an economic market, poses the issue how did we allow ourselves to be party to the betrayal of those whose story is told in these battles. Co-operation of Britain with the continental powers of Europe is a long tradition in our history as the alliances show, even with quondam enemies: legal subservience of British interests and of the British to a combination of states in which Britain has but a minority voice is a violent breach of our history, which has never had directly the consent of the people.

Of the Wars

In the City of God written in the fifth century A.D. St Augustine remarks that anyone, who pays regard to human affairs and man's common nature, knows that there is no one who avoids joy or shrinks from peace. He concedes however that those who want war, want nothing but to conquer in that they wish to arrive by waging war at an honourable peace. As an ideal the peace of the city of God, the heavenly city, is orderly and harmonious in fellowship in the enjoyment of God and of each other in God. As war by violence and destruction breaks that serenity of order and yet exists as a real event in human life, St Augustine evolved the notion of the just war. "A wise man", he said, "will only wage just wars .... If he remembered he was a man, he would grieve all the more at the necessity of waging just wars. If they were not just, he would not have to wage them and then for the wise man, there would be no more war". He further adds in this context that those who are willing that an existing peace should be disturbed, do not hate peace but may desire to have something they judge better.

The notion of the just war as an instrument for achieving the serenity of order innate in peace, or a more peaceful order than existing, and the criterion that the wise man's resort to arms must be on the basis of evident 'necessity', has played a potent part in British history since the sixteenth century as a reflection of the concept of the state governed by a Christian king. St Augustine's formulation as a rule for action has influenced the attitude of politicians to war and the action taken. What may be the needs of the preservation of peace, what may be 'just' or 'necessary' can be inevitably a matter of argument in the context of the circumstances in which the idea is applied, but it does have a normative objectivity, if applied reasonably.

Sir Robert Walpole, the first Prime Minister, in relation to the outbreak of the War of Jenkins' Ear in 1735, was an early exponent of the principle. The dispute over Spanish ships seizing British ships and cargoes in the Caribbean had been the subject of negotiation and the British Ambassador in Madrid had entered into the Convention of Pardo for Spain to pay compensation. There was a public clamour for war, particularly in Parliament, and Walpole was opposed to it. "A war with Spain", he asserted, "after the concessions she has made by this very Convention would on our part be unjust, and if it is unjust, it must be impolitic and dishonourable". Walpole was forced to give way in resisting the war, but his attitude has influenced policy more often than not since this time. Its roots can be found earlier. Queen Elizabeth I, despite the strength of opinion of some around her, advised by Cecil and Burghley, was reluctant to wage war officially with Spain, even on the brink of the Armada (see the Singeing of the King of

Spain's Beard, 19th April 1587) and was only driven into war after 1572, by the attack of Philip II of Spain, the threat of dethronement and the return of Roman Catholicism. Oliver Cromwell was himself opposed to the War against the Dutch in 1652, which was forced on him by Parliament under the influence of the City of London and was a competitive war for commercial dominance over the seas. The seventeenth century wars with Holland (see the Battle of the Kentish Knock, 28th September, the Battle of Portland, 20th February 1653, the Battle of the Gabbard Bank, 3rd June 1653, the Battle of Texel, 31st July 1653, the Battle of Lowestoft, 2nd June 1665 and the Battle of the North Foreland, 25th July 1666) do not therefore fit within the pattern.

Under William III the commitment of England to the War of the League of Augsburg was a direct response to the threat to the peace of Europe made by the vaulting ambition after 1678 of Louis XIV of France to be predominant in west Europe. It was France which attacked the Spanish Netherlands and sought to push its boundaries to the Rhine. It was France also that threatened the Parliamentary monarchy established in 1689 by William III by the consistent support given to James II the deposed Stuart King and his son, the Old Pretender. The war was therefore 'just' in the sense that its object was to preserve the peaceful order of the low countries and the order existing in England created with the consent of the people. The War of the Spanish Succession follows the same pattern. The prospective ending of the Hapsburg dynasty in Spain had resulted in a series of Partition Treaties between the powers including France by which Spain and the Spanish Netherlands, the control of which was crucial to England and Holland, would be inherited ultimately by the Archduke Charles, son of the Emperor Leopold I of Austria. By the Treaty of Rhyswick of 1697 Louis XIV had also agreed to recognise William III as King and abandon his support for James II and his son. In 1700 Charles II of Spain died leaving Spain to the Duke of Anjou the grandson of Louis XIV and Queen Maria Theresa of France. Louis XIV decided to break the Partition Treaty in order to unite Spain and France under the Bourbon dynasty and recognised the Old Pretender, son of James II as King of England. William III died in March 1702, but, Queen Anne continued his policy of joining into a grand alliance of Britain, Holland, Austria and other powers to oppose France and war was declared in May 1702. Once more disturbance of the peaceful order of Europe and breach of clear treaty obligations, reviving the threat of the Jacobite line to the Parliamentary monarchy of 1688 made for a war which was "just".

This thesis could be pursued down the eighteenth century to 1815 as France, first under Louis XIV, then under Louis XV, and Napoleon pursued an aggressive policy to establish French control in western Europe. Even under the pacific Louis XVI the French absence of peaceful intent was to be seen for in 1777 Louis's Minister, Vergennes, deliberately provoked a war with Britain by aiding the American colonies as revenge for the Peace of Paris (1763) under which Canada was ceded away. The skein of events is not always straightforward, but, every British war had its origin in the breach of international treaty designed to establish a peaceful order or specific threat to British interests. The wars have thus been essentially defensive and directed to the support of peaceful order. Even the war of Jenkin's Ear as it merged into the War of the Austrian Succession came to have a justifiable basis in the preservation of the peaceful order of Germany – as it affected George II's Electorate of Hannover, and the attack by France on the Austrian Netherlands in 1743 (Belgium). The Battle of Dettingen, 28th June 1743, was in fact fought before the French, having joined a new family compact with Spain, declared war on Britain in 1744. Pre-emptive fighting or warfare thus occurred. The Battle of Passaro, 11th August 1718, was fought against Spain before any declaration of war, although Admiral Byng was instructed to negotiate first with the Spanish. That war was directed to preserve the terms of the Treaty of Utrecht. Although hostilities in the Seven Years War commenced in North America with the French, when George Washington clashed with a French force near Fort Duquesne in May 1754, the Duke of Newcastle did not declare war on France, until the French invasion of Minorca in May 1756, having devoted his energies to finding allies for Britain. (See the Taking of Quebec, 18th September 1759).

With the French Revolution the clarity of the issue whether British wars with other European powers have been "just" does not need to be argued. Revolutionary France, Napoleon Buonaparte as First Consul and Emperor, tried determinedly to subvert the peaceful order of Europe and to establish in its place a hegemony of one power achieved by a new means of destructive warfare. It is interesting to see William Pitt, the Younger, between 1790 and 1792, despite the open threats to peace and order, having the patience to deal with the Revolutionaries (see the Glorious First of June, 1 June 1794). There was no hurry to war by Pitt; he stood aside from the attempts of Austria and Prussia to restore the King in France, but, he was not content to allow Revolutionary France to seize the Netherlands and pledged the support of Britain, if France invaded, in November 1792. As the French moved into the Austrian Netherlands and took Antwerp he warned the French that action against Holland would mean war. Preparations were put in hand and on 30th January 1793 the French announced the intention to take the Austrian Netherlands and declared war. The example is evocative of the future, if set beside the reason for Britain to enter the Great War in 1914 and the guarantee given to Poland as a small country in April 1939 as stated by the Foreign Secretary, Lord Halifax in the House of Lords (see Battle of Britain, 15th September 1940) and Pitt's action exemplifies the need for a "just" war to be a necessity.

The test of "necessity" predicates a substantial criterion to be met. It implies that what is done "cannot be otherwise", "that which is unavoidable", "essential" or "imperative". This application in the context of the wars the subject of the victories recounted in not without significance. At the end of January 1801 for instance William Pitt the Younger, the Prime Minister, resigned over the issue of Catholic Emancipation and a new ministry took office under Addington. This Government was inclined to make peace with France and a Preliminary Treaty was signed on 1st October 1801 against the background of the Treaty of Luneville made between France and Austria in February 1801. In the latter the independence of the Cisalpine and Ligurian Republic was guaranteed, of the Helvetic Republic (Switzerland) and the Batavian Republic (Holland). In the Preliminary Treaty with Britain free entry of British trade to the Continent was to be permitted, conquered colonies were to be returned, and Malta was to have the Knights of St John of Jerusalem restored as independent rulers of the island and their future secured by France, Spain and Italy from whom subsidies were to come. Even before the terms of the Preliminary Treaty were embodied in the Treaty of Amiens signed in March 1802, the French acted in breach of the terms and disregarded them and continued to do so. British trade was not re-admitted to France; French agents were sent throughout Italy to undermine the independence of the states. The terms relating to Malta were not acted upon. Buonaparte kept his troops in Holland, took over the Cisalpine Republic, seized Switzerland, to whose people even Addington promised arms and money, occupied the Grand Duchy of Parma on the death of its Duke and tried to intrigue with Russia to undermine the Ottoman Empire. Addington's Government, although backed by British public opinion, was outraged by this behaviour, but negotiated with Buonaparte to maintain the peace from November 1802 until May 1803 particularly over the crucial issue of the independence of Malta on the Mediterranean sea route to Italy and the East. On the 18th May the British at last declared war. War had become a "necessity" to uphold the Treaties of Lunéville and of Amiens; although the British were not parties to the former, the need had become to preserve the "serenity of order ", which they guaranteed and the implementation of their terms. In 1914 (see Armistice Day, 11th November 1914) the reluctance of the British to go to war, embodied in the divided views of the Liberal Government, was turned to a 'necessity' for war when Germany invaded Belgium in breach of the guarantees to her integrity made under the Treaties of London. The peaceful order was subverted and the refusal of the Kaiser's Government to desist created the clear "necessity." The policy pursued by Neville Chamberlain and his Government from 1937 and 1939 of the much derided appeasement of Nazi Germany (see The Deliverance at Dunkirk 2nd June 1940 and the Battle of Britain 15th September 1940) was wholly within the tradition of British Governments of the past to make war only once alternative action was exhausted. The appeasement policy also has significance in that the attempts made by Chamberlain for peace were founded on a desire for something judged better than the existing peace, to quote St Augustine, namely to undo the settlement of Versailles, based on French desire for revenge and hegemony in Europe and to give to Germany a more just order.

Both the invasion of Czechoslovakia and the attack on Poland were however, a destruction of the integrity of an existing 'just' order, which involved the guarantee of the independence of small states. There can be disagreement when the point of "necessity" is reached, as in Chamberlain's appeasement policy before the Second World War, but he was, as Churchill said, a devoted man of peace and in St Augustine's terms 'a wise man'.

The working out of the Christian doctrine of the just war in the political action of consistent Governments stems from the determinative of the Crown in Parliament as the guardian of a Christian order. Its importance is not just in the realm of diplomacy and state action, but, it is significant in the fighting morale of the armed forces. To act in loyalty to the Crown has now for centuries implied that no soldier, sailor or airman will be required to face the heat and sacrifice of war, if the cause is unjust and there is no clear necessity for war. It is important that those who fight know that. The long line of courage, endurance and sacrifice that the ages record by the people of Britain rests on that premise. Their deeds in century after century done by men, whom the London metropolitan elite of today would describe in contrast to themselves as "ordinary people", made them extraordinary. The motive power of love of country, which had transmuted them, would not survive, if loyalty to the Crown failed to embody the principles, for which the image of the Christian king stands as evolved in our society. The principle of just war is fundamental.

The British approach in this matter can be contrasted with the attitude of the European powers, with whom the wars have been fought, principal of whom since 1688 are the French and Germans. The French pro-active desire for control in western Europe, first under Louis XIV, predicated action which of its very nature aimed at destruction of the existing peaceful order, at the taking of the land of others and the imposition upon defeated 'enemies' of French control. As Walpole might have noted from the outset the impetus was "dishonourable" yet the ambition for a French hegemony in Europe has been consistently pursued. The Emperor Napoleon not only had French supremacy in all Europe as his objective, but, added to the process an escalation of violence in war and a shift to war of armies on the whole people, which was to leave its legacy to the twentieth century. Karl von Clausewitz in Dem Kriege is the witness to this change; his career as an army officer covered the period of the Napoleonic Wars and during the Waterloo campaign he was Chief of Staff to the Third Prussian Corps commanded by Lieutenant General von Thielmann. Under Napoleon, he commented that war had suddenly become an affair of the people once more and that of a people numbering thirty millions, everyone of whom regarded himself as a citizen of the state. The means available for war no longer had limits, so that by the extent of the means and the wide field of possible results, as well as by the powerful excitement of feeling which prevailed, the energy with which war was pursued was vastly increased. The energy of war thus broke loose with all its natural force. There was therefore a tendency for violence to escalate and war as an act of violence is pushed to its ultimate extreme. The model of the French armies and the campaigns of Napoleon were to influence military thinking through the theories of von Clausewitz down to the First World War. The French did not abandon their urge to control western Europe and the policy was revived by the Buonapartist Emperor Napoleon III until his defeat by the Germans at Sedan in 1870. The pre-eminence of the needs of French State policy and strength over-riding other considerations remained in Clemenceau and De Gaulle to be applied even in the Framework of peace and lives yet in the European Union resting on the mutual alliance with Germany of the two powers.

If Napoleon and the French increased the violence of war, King Frederick II of Prussia models the example of war as an act of aggression without moral justification. Such was his attack in 1740 on the Austria of the Empress Maria Theresa with a view to acquiring Silesia and also his invasion of Saxony and Bohemia subsequently. There was no restraint such as that imposed on the Christian King and for Hohenzollern Kings of Prussia making war was an instrument solely of the needs of state policy without moral dimension. In the mid-nineteenth century based on the Theory of War set out by Von Clausewitz the German General Staff developed from a selective reading of his works the notion of the need for great battles, for massive armies striking bloodily at decisive points and the legitimacy of the escalation of violence. The success of Prussia in 1866 against Austria and of the Germans in 1870-1871 against France led to an admiration of the General Staff and the dissemination of these theories of violence through the armies of Europe. Marshal Foch was indeed to remark perhaps not surprisingly given the Buonapartist tradition that "blood is the price of victory. You must resort to it or give up waging war." Overlooked particularly was von Clausewitz's observation that the defensive was the strongest form of strategy, an omission which was to be reflected in the bloody slaughter of the trenches in the First World War. In Germany in that war the theory that war was a legitimate element without constraint in the policy of a state combined with another idea, taken from a false reading of Dem Kriege, and expressed by Feldmarschall Helmut von Moltke, the victor of the Franco-German War of 1870 that the politicians should fall silent the moment that mobilisation begins. The result was first the slide into war and second, the inability of the Kaiser's Government to end the war by negotiation against the opposition of Hindenburg and Ludendorff, who commanded on the western front (see 11th November 1914 Armistice Day). It does not need to be said that the theory of war unfettered by moral constraint was carried on by Adolf Hitler and adopted by Benito Mussolini in his attacks on Ethiopia, Albania, Greece, Britain and France. It cannot be said, finally, that the British army commanders were not infected by the theories emanating out of the approach of the German

General Staff to the Conduct of war. The result in the First World War was the shedding of blood without victory. Given that the technology of mobility based on the cavalry arm was incapable of overwhelming the static infantry defence of machine guns and mortars, the constant problem of attack and the expectation of it called for by the politicians over-seeing the armies gives one ground for taking the view that the Generals of the First World War were not stupid and uncaring, but, found themselves in an unsolvable dilemma which it was their misfortune to have to handle.

The escalation in violence of the Second World War with the total bombing of cities and towns, the use of the atomic bombs in Japan and the extensive impact of war on civil populations has presented new challenges to the application of the Augustinian idea of a just war with all its innate clarity. The extent of potential harm from the violence of war can be a factor which it might be argued effects its 'justice', but such a concept is not in the world of the real without difficulty. The major effect however of the Second World War was the attempt to create the United Nations as a universal body to preserve the "serenity of order" and protect it. Unfortunately and probably inevitably its structure is flawed, because the sovereignty and interest of the most powerful states through the process of veto in the Security Council, who are charged under the Charter with the authorisation of the use of force, can distort the objectivity of decision. The resolution authorising military action in Korea, for example, only passed because the Soviet Union had absented itself, although the invasion of south Korea was a clear instance of naked aggression. There is thus still a need to resort to the moral idea of the just war in deciding action, whatever the implications in relation to treaties and international law may be. The assessment of whether a war is just ethically must legitimately pay regard to the proceedings of the United Nations, but, because of the flawed nature of this world body cannot be exclusive of other moral considerations. Politicians involved in military action are of course driven into interpretation of the interstices of resolutions of the Security Council to justify their arguments for war but in the last analysis legitimacy depends on the moral clarity of the doctrine of just war, which is unspoken as the basis of Articles 2(3) and 2 (4) of the Charter. Article 51 also reflects the just war idea of the "the necessity" for action in that it recognises the inherent right of individual or collective self-defence, if an armed attack occurs on any member. In the final analysis the United Nations process is a procedure only for determining on the basis of consent whether a war is just but it cannot give the comprehensive and only answer to whether such is so morally, because of the institutional flaw which stems from the world of political reality in which the interests of the 'veto' powers are not identical.

The Church of England in the new context has endeavoured to reformulate the elements which need to exist for a war to be just. They are five, first, the war must be a defensive response to unjust aggression; second, there must be a realistic chance of success; third, there must be some proportion between the costs and the post-war settlement; four, only military targets can be chosen, and five, the use of force must never be an end in itself. The present is not the place to discuss the problems, which arise from these principles in a modern situation, where the "aggression" may not be perpetrated by a state, but, by an extensive association of zealots seeking to impose their own order of society on others and the "action" does not involve a war properly so called. There are however elements introduced to affect the clarity of the Augustinian principle, which may be debateable. They are to be found in the second, third and fourth points set out, which go to the conduct of war rather than to the principle whether the war is just.

It is quite plain that as the objective of war as a political act as its leading principle the destruction of the enemy's military force, a military judgement that there is no reasonable chance of success is unlikely to result in war. War is however, as von Clausewitz pointed out, the province of chance and three quarters of those things upon which action in war must be based are more or less hidden in clouds of great uncertainty. Desirable as it may be therefore to act as if the chance of success can be successfully judged, there is no clarity in this criterion, which in any event may not deal with the need to make war to preserve the peace, where objective opinion might suggest that there is little chance of success but there is a "necessity". Item (iii) raises an innate conflict between the proper manner of conducting a war and the end results of its conduct. When von Clauswitz wrote, the contemporary armoury of rockets, atomic and hydrogen bombs, guided missiles, heavy bombs and guns was non-existent and it was easy for him to write, "let us not hear of Generals who conquer without bloodshed. If a bloody slaughter is a horrible sight, then that is a ground for paying more respect to war but not for making the sword we wear blunter by degrees of humanity until someone steps in with one that is sharp and cuts of the arm from the body." The proportionality of the use of weapons, as opposed to a policy of total annihilation of the enemy's force, an objective believed in by Lord Nelson, by whatever force, is now arguably a legitimate element in deciding in practice whether a war is 'just', but, the military principle of aiming at destruction of the opposed forces is still applicable and the issue turns on the extent to which it is necessary to secure the peace. Thus, using an atomic bomb on a non-nuclear opponent could not be justifiable, but, using explosive rockets on troops not so armed would be. Von Clausewitz's point is still therefore correct in that the prospective bloodshed is a ground for paying more respect to whether a war is just if the prospect is the mutual destruction by rockets armed with atomic and hydrogen bombs by the combatants of each other, a respect which was visible in the Cold War where mutual deterrent kept and held the peace. The criterion of attack only being justifiable on military targets (Point (iv)) is supported by the theory of war in that the prime objective must be the destruction of the opposed forces. Thus attack on non-military targets should not be relevant, but, unclear issues arise as to the nature of a military target, the problem of the interweaving of military and civilian activities in contemporary societies, for example, weapon and aircraft production in towns. To fulfil this object may be a desirable mode of conducting war as an aim of conduct but to be determinative of the character of a war as an unjust war may be problematical. One has only to ask the question-did the bombing of German cities and towns make the Second World War unjust? – to realise the inadequacy of a test dependent on confinement of operations to military targets. The bombing campaign in retrospect can however perhaps now be regarded as beyond a proper conduct of a war, a disproportionate infliction of damage for the advantages achievable in pursuit of the principal aim and which proved ineffectual in breaking morale. Modern directional weapons, however, make the need for such general bombing less compelling. But the position is not however clear-cut, since the destruction caused by the atomic bombs on Japan forced submission of that country to the allies and in so doing inevitably saved thousands of American and British lives. There is no doubt that participants should so conduct themselves that the horrors of war are mitigated. Hospital ships should not be bombed, for example, but the objective is to win. A principle that goes to conduct only as a test of "the just" confuses ends and means, although not wholly to be disregarded. It is none the less a subordinate consideration.

None of this discussion of the concept of "just war" in context after 1945 has purported to consider the international law implications inherent in the points made and the moral considerations only in the briefest way. The point made is the continued essential relevance to the conduct of war by Britain of St Augustine's concept of the just war.

In an age where the threat to the "serenity of order " may stem from international associations of religious fundamentalists urged on by Governments, whose policy like that of France in the past, has an overwhelming ambition to spread its religious order and control over vanished empires, the issue of whether a war is 'just' may be difficult to apply. Action may be needed which is pre-emptive, but, that of itself is not prohibited: action must however be politic and honourable, to cite Sir Robert Walpole, and certainly above else "a necessity."

January

The Moonlight Battle

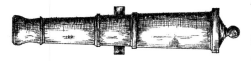

The American colonies rebelled against the British in 1776 and in October 1777 defeated a British army at Saratoga. France, filled with a desire for revenge for defeat in the Seven Years War, and pursuing her traditional policy of enmity to Britain, made an alliance with the Rebels on 6th February 1778. She then set upon the task of persuading King Charles III of Spain to adhere to the alliance. The latter was reluctant but succumbed to the temptation offered by the hope of regaining Gibraltar. In April 1779 he made a secret treaty with France, and declared war on Britain in June. A combined fleet of sixty-seven men-of-war supported by frigates sailed to attempt an invasion of England. The British for their part could muster but thirty-five ships of the line. The summer and autumn were spent by the French and Spanish manoeuvring in the entrance to the Channel, but the combination of lack of co-operation between them, poor seamanship and sickness led to the dispersal of the fleet. The one disaster for the British was the capture by the Spanish of the joint East and West Indies convoy of merchantmen as they went south, a prize valued at £1.5million. At Brest, in October, 7,000 sick seamen were landed from the enemy fleet.

In October 1779 Admiral Rodney was appointed to take a squadron of five men-of-war to the station on the Leeward Isles in the Caribbean. On his arrival in Portsmouth Roads he found a fleet whose discipline was broken down and which had neither been completely refitted or provisioned. He energetically set himself to put matters right and much was done, but not finished, by December. The First Sea Lord. Lord Sandwich, was urging him in the interest of the Government to sail. Although ready, apart from the frigates, on 11th December, strong westerly and south-westerly winds prevented his departure from Spithead. That weather persisted until 23rd December when the sea fell calm, presaging a change of wind. On the 24th he was finally able to sail on an easterly. His mission had in the waiting period been enlarged. He was to escort both the West and East Indies convoys south and proceed to the relief of Gibraltar and Minorca. Gibraltar had been invested in July 1779 and was to remain besieged until the peace in January 1783. He left therefore accompanied by twenty-one men-of-war, nine frigates and an extensive convoy of merchant ships. On 4th January the West Indies convoy went off and on the 5th he rounded Finisterre. As he sailed south on the 8th he saw twenty-two ships to his north-east. They were a convoy of twenty-two Spanish store and provision ships on route from San Sebastian to Cadiz, escorted by a 64 gun man-of-war, the Guispuscoano. Taken by surprise, the convoy was captured together with its escort, two frigates and two corvettes. The store ships were ordered away as prizes to England, but the Guispuscoano was renamed and put into commission as the Prince William in honour of the Duke of Clarence, who served as a Midshipman on the flagship and became King William IV (1830-37).

On his way down the coast of Portugal, some frigate captains learnt that a Spanish fleet was patrolling off the coast from Cape St Vincent to Cadiz and the Straits of Gibraltar. Rodney prepared the fleet for battle and rounded Cape St Vincent on the morning of 16th January. The winds were westerly and making as the Poniente, which blew through the Straits, gathered force. At one o'clock the Bedford (74 guns) signalled a fleet to the north east. It had come upon the expected Spanish force comprising eleven ships of the line supported by two frigates under the command of Don Juan de Langara in his flagship the Fenix (80 guns). They were of course closer to the shore and the Spanish ports than the British and were assisted by the westerly wind. Nonetheless, Rodney, who was prostrate in his cabin with severe and painful gout, ordered his captain, Captain Young to order the fleet into line abreast. Langara was completely surprised by the appearance of the British as he had sent out no frigates to patrol. He signalled his dispersed fleet to form line and proceed towards the coastal ports and safety. The Spanish, with poorer seamanship and slower ships, were gradually overhauled. Rodney altered his orders, having discovered that the eleven-ship squadron was alone, to that of general chase, but directed that the attack should come from leeward between the Spanish ships and the shore. As the westerly wind mounted in force, the position on the lee shore, full of shallow shoals, would become full of danger, apart from the risk of leaving the convoy undefended. Rodney took that risk, trusting his seamen and their skill.

At four o'clock in the fading winter afternoon the leading British ships, the Defiance (74 guns), Resolution (74 guns and 7th of the name) and Edgar (74 guns) all of which had been made copper-bottomed, came up to the Spanish line and a running fight was to begin. Firing heavy broadsides as they went into the Spanish the leading ships sailed up to the van. Dusk was falling and Rodney signalled to the fleet to engage the enemy closely. For himself in the flagship, Sandwich (90 guns and 2nd of the name) he told the Master to lay him alongside the largest ship. Darkness came on, but the sea was lit by a hovering full moon. Bienfaisant (64 guns) engaged the San Domingo (70 guns) which suddenly blew up. By six o'clock the first Spaniard had struck. In the moonlight, strong wind and high seas the fleet fled on, the Spaniards striving to gain the coast, its ports and safety. By two o'clock in the early morning, five ships had struck their colours, including the flagship, the Fenix. The Sandwich attacked the Monarcha with crashing broadsides and it struck at about two in the morning. In the high seas the San Augustin managed to slip away and the British were being driven ever closer on to the Lee shore. Securing the prizes in the crashing seas and wind was hugely difficult, and they too were driven towards the shore by the wind. Two prizes, the San Julian and the San Eugenio, drifted leeward. One went aground and the other was reseized by its Spanish crew. By 6 a.m. in the moonlight battle Rodney had taken or destroyed six of the eight Spanish men-of-war, but the fleet was coming dangerously near the shoals of San Lucar de Borromeda at the estuary of the River Guadalquiver The Royal George, Sandwich, Prince George and others were being driven towards these shallow waters, and the fleet had to claw itself to windward. The foul weather continued the next day but Rodney and his ships were able to join the convoy and proceed to the relief of Gibraltar. Provisions and ammunition were landed to sustain the garrison's fierce resistance. Rodney moved on to Minorca and then departed in the flagship supported only by Ajax (74 guns and 1st of the name) Montagu (74 guns) and Terrible (74 guns). The rest of the fleet returned to England.

Although Rodney had been confined to his cabin during the action, his bold and decisive orders had ensured the victory, but his captains, including his own Captain Young, continued to disparage him to the Admiralty. No doubt exasperated by all this, he wrote to the First Sea Lord, Lord Sandwich, that discipline in a very great measure was lost and officers presumed to find fault and think, when their duty was implicit obedience, a maxim which would have sorely inhibited naval heroes of the future if observed strictly. The victory in London was however appreciated and there were salutes of guns, illuminations and votes of thanks by both Houses of Parliament.

On 12th April 1781 Gibraltar was again re-supplied and in October 1782 Lord Howe arrived once more to succour the garrison with thirty-four ships of the line. The Spanish had 30,000 troops on shore and a fleet of forty-nine ships of the line in Algeciras bay. The latter avoided all attempts to join battle with Howe, despite their superiority of numbers. Gibraltar was provisioned and was still holding out at the peace in 1783.

17th January 1809
The Battle of Corunna and the Evacuation of the Army

The attack on Portugal in 1807 by the Emperor Napoleon and the gradual seizure of Spain culminating in April 1808 in the forced abdication of King Charles IV of Spain and his son Ferdinand VII (see the Battle of Rolica, 17th August 1808) brought about the intervention of the British in Spain and Portugal. An army commanded by Sir Arthur Wellesley won a victory at Vimiero (see the Battle of Vimiero 21st August 1808) which forced the French in Lisbon into an armistice. The two Commanders of the Army, Sir Hew Dalrympole and Sir Harry Burrard, agreed to the proposal that Marshal Junot and his army should be free to go with all their property back to France. The convention of Cintra (as the agreement was called) so disturbed public opinion that Dalrympole, Burrard and Wellesley, who had been compelled to sign against his inclinations, were recalled to London. The army within the Peninsula was then entrusted to Major-General Sir John Moore, who had previously been appointed as third in command.

Sir John Moore was the son of a Glasgow doctor and had entered the army in 1776. In 1784 he became a Member of Parliament, backed by the Duke of Hamilton. His qualities as a soldier were appreciated by William Pitt, the younger, the Prime Minister and the Duke of York, the Commander in Chief of the army. At the battle of Aboukir (21st March 1801), he had distinguished himself and was wounded five times. In 1803 he was appointed to command at Shorncliffe camp, and there he spent three years creating the Light Infantry. The Duke of York had already experimented with a Rifle Corps at Horsham but Moore was to set out to create one with the 95th Regiment, soon joined by the 52nd and 43rd. The object was to create troops similar in character to the French *tirailleurs*, which preceded their dense columns and demoralised the traditional slow-moving infantry formations. The object was to create men who were active, disciplined, mobile and self-thinking. Fitness was regarded by Moore as essential and a humane discipline which encouraged men to exercise their judgement, skills and observation, to use the terrain for their benefit and fire accurately their new Baker riffles, which had a range of 300 to 500 yards depending on the skill of the user. Officers were to learn to know their men individually, to exercise care on their behalf and share their training. The men were taught to cook and sow and to bivouac in the open. At the end of their training it was noted of the 52nd Regiment that their discipline and enthusiasm was in a high state and there was no recourse to the cat o' nine tails.

The Emperor Napoleon's attempt to place his brother King Joseph on the throne of Spain, and the occupation of Spain by the French, appeared initially to be peacefully achieved, although in different areas of the country *Juntas* were being formed with armies of support to maintain Spanish independence. In August 1808 General Castanos defeated a French army under General Dupont at Baylen and all Spain rose to expel the invader. On the 23rd he re-occupied Madrid and King Joseph fled north to Vitoria. Only two areas of Spain were retained by the French after the uprising. While there was a central Junta, the individual regional Juntas were fiercely parochial. They each maintained their own armies and were loath to co-operate. An appeal was made to Britain for money and arms and for military support. Sir John Moore was therefore in early October instructed that he should act in co-operation with the Spanish armies in an attempt to encircle the French. His task would be to move north-east to support the Spanish on the Ebro River. His forces were divided between those in Portugal and the force under General Sir David Baird being sent to Corunna of 12,000 infantry, cavalry and artillery. He therefore needed to march towards Salamanca, with a view to joining Baird's army at Burgos or Valladolid. The operation involved a three hundred-mile march over mountains rising to 4,000 feet in winter; the state of the road was thought to be such that it was not easily passable by artillery and transport. He decided to split his force, sending the artillery, but for twelve light 6-pounders, with 4,000 cavalry via Elvas, Badajoz and then north near Madrid to Salamanca under the command of General Sir John Hope. The main body was to proceed across the mountain tracks. These were effectively dirt tracks winding round the mountains with steep precipices to their sides. There were few villages and those were squalid and poverty-stricken.

Sir John Moore remained with the army in Portugal at Queluz until 11th October. At that stage the French on the Ebro faced the Army of Galicia under Blake in the west, the Army of Castile under General Castanos in the centre and the Army raised by General Palafox based on Saragossa. Count Belvedere was in Madrid and Somosierra south of Burgos. There were therefore in northern Spain four Spanish armies in existence. Following the battle of Baylen, the Spaniards became supremely confident that they could oust the French from Spain despite the disorganised and largely untrained character of their armies. The troops were poorly led by their officers, badly armed in the main, wretchedly fed and cared for and with few guns. The Junta in Seville spent its time arguing about a new constitution and were unable because of their jealously one for another to appoint a Commander in Chief. It was with these armies that Moore had been ordered to co-operate by a government in London which listened only to optimistic reports about the Spanish army. As Moore set out for the Ebro, however, tumultuous events were in process. The Emperor

Napoleon, incensed by the reverses in Spain, which he thought might encourage insurrection elsewhere in Europe, had decided himself to come to Spain to reduce the Peninsula. An army of 130,000 had been raised with regiments withdrawn from Germany. On 3rd November Napoleon reached Bayonne to command a force of 120,000 on the Ebro. There immediately followed as Moore marched north, having reached Almeida on 8th November and entered Salamanca on the 13th, a series of crushing defeats of the Spanish armies. On 11th November Blake and the Army of Galicia were over-whelmed at Espinosa, on 10th November Count Belvedere at Gamonal and on 23rd November Castanos at Tudela.

The march to Salamanca had tried the morale and endurance of the troops. A large number of women and children had managed to accompany the army to Portugal and Moore tried to encourage them to stay in Portugal and go home. Very few left, the majority accompanying the army on its long and bitter trek. Across the coastal area of farmland and pinewoods the weather remained mild, but after about a week of marching it began to rain and icy winds to blow as the column marched higher into the mountains with their pervasive mists, causing even the Portuguese guides at times to lose their way. The tracks in the persistent rain became middens of mud and the horses and mules of the transport struggled ever more desperately to mount the slopes. The troops were soaked, their shoes deteriorating and food and supplies scarce, since the staff of the Quartermaster-General was inexperienced. The villages became more squalid, the peasants more sullen and shelter in the bitter night non-existent. Brigadier Anstruther with the advance guard reached Almeida in the first week of November and Moore arrived on the 8th.

General Sir David Baird had arrived in Corunna on 13th October with one hundred transports carrying his 12,000 strong force. The Junta of Galicia made every objection possible to his landing at Corunna and it was not until the 26th that the Spaniards (who had sought British help) permitted the army to land. It was 15th November before he could leave on the march to join up with Sir John Moore. The two hundred miles to Astorga was very slow, the troops being beset by conditions not dissimilar from those which Moore and his army had experienced. His problem was compounded by an absence of supplies and the failure of the Horse Guards to provide him with adequate funds to purchase any. Forage was scarce, but in twelve days Baird urged his army on over one hundred and eighty miles.

Sir John Moore, on his arrival in Salamanca, had learnt of the reverse suffered by Blake at Espinosa and that the French were at Burgos and Valladolid, the meeting point planned for the British Army. These reports caused him to worry about the risks inherent in continuing to advance, since his army was divided into three parts, the infantry at Salamanca, Hope one hundred miles south with the cavalry and artillery and Baird at that time one hundred miles north at Lugo. He considered that junction of the armies was not without risk and that the British army could face overwhelming French forces in the north east with little help from the Spanish. Lord William Bentinck arrived to warn him of the condition of the Army of Castile and the want of confidence of the generals in their men and the men in their generals. Moore gradually formed the view that once Hope arrived he should withdraw from Salamanca. He then learned of the defeat of the armies of Castanos and Palafox, which left him with a force of 17,000 to confront a possible 80,000 French force in the North. Meanwhile, Sir David Baird had on arrival at Astorga heard of the defeats of Blake at Espinosa and Belvedere at Gomunal and decided that he ought to consider returning to Corunna, and sent a message to Sir John Moore requesting his approval of such a course.

While Moore and Baird were considering retreat, the Emperor Napoleon was advancing on Madrid with 70,000 men of his army. The Spanish spoke of resistance and Howard Frere, the Foreign Office Representative in Madrid, sent a letter and messenger calling upon Moore to come to the city's relief. 12,000 Spaniards were set to guard the Somosierra pass over the Guadarrama mountains north of Madrid, but they were swept aside in the morning mist by Napoleon's Polish Lancers of the Imperial Guards and the supporting artillery. On 1st December the French vanguard was in the outskirts of Madrid. The Spanish still spoke of resistance but on 4th December Napoleon entered the capital. The French drive south had meant that the pressure was taken off the British army and Valladolid was evacuated by the French. Napoleon was of the view that the British were retreating back to Portugal.

In the new circumstances Moore again faced the dilemma whether to retire in order to save the army or whether to press north to bring help to the Marques de La Romana, who had taken command of the remnants of Blake's Army of Galicia on the Asturian border. The advantage of moving forward was that the continuing presence of a British army in Spain would draw the French north from Madrid and give time for new armies to be raised and organised in southern Spain. Moore decided, his duty being to support the Spanish, that he should not retire, but go north to join with Baird. On 11th December the advance towards Valladolid began. The weather was so cold that the pigtails of the 71st Highlanders froze to the ground in the night. At Alaejos Moore was handed papers from a murdered French courier which showed that Napoleon had 300,000 troops in Spain, that the French were going to march on Badajoz and Lisbon and that Marshal Soult in the north with 18,000 men was across the River Carrion and could threaten the retreat route to Corunna. A united British army could, however, strike at Soult's force on the Carrion. Baird was ordered to go east to meet Moore at Mayorga. On 15th December the army crossed the River Douro at Toro and Zamorra with a cavalry screen to the east. It was now snowing and there were violent gale force winds. There was still a shortage of all supplies and fuel was unobtainable. On 20th December the British forces were united at Mayorga and moved forward to Sahagun. Lord Paget's cavalry had a skirmish with French dragoons involving 500 men of the 15th Hussars and chased them off. On the approach of the British Marshal Soult drew back across the Carrion River.

On 19th December the Emperor Napoleon, as he was setting off to pursue the British army towards Badajoz, learnt that their army was in the north posing a threat to communications with France. He immediately halted the westward march and ordered a concentration north on the plains of Castile. Marshal Ney was ordered from Aragon to support Soult, whose task was to decoy the British towards Burgos. He pushed on himself through the snowbound high Guadarrama pass, marching at the head of his men with arms linked to the foot guards on either side of him. On 23rd December he reached Villacastin, sixty miles south of Valladolid, where he thought Sir John Moore was. Moore was in fact fifty miles further north and on the 22nd he had ordered an attack. On the 23rd the vanguard moved forward in the snowy night cheering loudly. They had not gone far before a messenger was sent ordering them to retire. News had reached Moore that Napoleon was crossing north and was over the Guadarramas. This new information changed the military position in northern Spain. To avoid the probable destruction of the British army, Moore had to retreat at once westwards. The Grande Armée was moving up south of Moore's flank; Junot with the army returned from Portugal was advancing to support Marshal Soult. Lefebvre was marching towards the Galician passes to the rear. Moore had to get across the Esla River and make the mountain defiles beyond Astorga before he was cut off. On Christmas Eve Hope's and Fraser's divisions left; on Christmas Day Baird's and Edward Paget's Reserve Division. The route lay through Benavente, to the Esla River some fifty miles away, and then one hundred and fifty more miles to Corunna and a similar distance to Vigo. On the 25th Napoleon rested his army at Tordesillas, some twenty miles from Benavente. With all the skill of a twenty-first century government to lie and spin, he ordered that reports be circulated to Paris and the Empire that he was to the rear of the British at Benevente, that they had abandoned the Spanish in a cowardly retreat and were surrounded.

Despite his statement as to his position, on 27th December Napoleon resumed his northern march to Sahagun. The halt had allowed Moore to escape with the army: by the end of day on the 27th all but the rearguard were across the bridge over the Esla. The army had been forced along at a hard pace and retreat was not to the liking of many of the men. The retreat began in a thaw – the roads were slush by day and frozen by night. Discipline and order began to crack and the Duchess of Ossuna's palace at Benavente was vandalised and sacked. Napoleon came up to Valderas and began to probe beyond the river with his cavalry. The Chasseurs of the Imperial Guard under General Lefebvre-Desnouettes crossed the river and encountered the 10th Hussars, the 3rd King's German Hussars and the Rifles, and were severely mauled, losing two hundred men, while General Lefebrve was captured. The rearguard hurried on to Astorga: the sooner the

British army reached the mountains the safer they were, since Napoleon wished to force a battle, while Moore wished to avoid it. The greatest worry which afflicted Sir John Moore was that the French would outflank the army.

On 29th December the threat was made real when Marshal Soult defeated the Marques de La Romana at Mansilla, south-east of Leon, leaving bridges undamaged over the Esla and giving access to Leon and Villafranca on the line of the march. At Astorga there were only two days' rations and there had been no transport to bring supplies from Villafranca. The shortage of food undermined discipline and the wilder and more criminal elements of the battalions took to drink and plunder. Hundreds of men roamed the streets, wild with drink and mutinous. The Marques de La Romana's remnant army had fallen back and fell on the local Spanish to loot with avidity. Moore thought the behaviour of the army disgraceful and was horrified by the failure of officers to control it effectively. At Astorga the army divided, the Light Brigades commanded by Major General Robert Crawford and Baron Alten of the Kings German Legion being sent to Orense and Vigo. The justification for this split was Moore's worry that he might be outflanked through Orense and that he needed a shield in the valley of the River Minho.

The absence of supplies meant that the army needed to reach Villafranca, a supply depot, with all speed, but after Astorga the route lay over soaring mountains. The road was knee-deep in snow; there was no shelter or fuel and the severe winds whipped the snow around the soldiers and the women and children struggling up the passes. The ice made standing and walking difficult and horses fell and died. The top of the pass before Beimbre was a white bleak waste. In the sound-deadening snow the air was full with the groans and cries of the fallen and dying. Men and women could not struggle on and lay beside the road, the quiet being pierced by the shooting of the horses and their distressed whinnying. At Beimbre the cellars of the town were broken open, the casks of wine smashed until wine ran in the streets. Soldiers with their families and children lay in drunken heaps in the street. On 1st January as the rearguard passed through, they tried to raise the fallen men and women and urge them on. Behind them came in the French cavalry slashing at all left behind, cutting at ears, hands, heads and limbs. Some of those so attacked regained the column and were exhibited in Villafranca as a caution to keep up. Once Moore had entered the mountains, however, and Napoleon could see no prospect of a battle, he removed the Imperial Guard to Madrid and from there returned to Paris. Marshal Soult was left to pursue the British.

At Villafranca the army behaved no better. The troops refused to wait for an orderly distribution of the fourteen-day supply of biscuit, salt beef and rum, and they plundered the supplies, trampling some underfoot. The scavenging hordes were uncontrollable and the officers were unable to stop the pillage. On 2nd December Moore arrived however, and immediately locked up the stragglers; survivors of Beimbre were paraded as a lesson and plunderers of a magazine shot. He rebuked the men and told the 28th Regiment of Foot that they were not as they had been. Major-General Paget had his reserve form hollow squares and flogged plunderers and the undisciplined within the square, only finishing one punishment as the French vanguard started to appear. After a sharp exchange with the French, the rearguard marched eighteen miles that night without losing a straggler.

The next fifty miles to Lugo, over the Cantabrian Mountains, were an even greater calvary for the army. The journey was to take five days. There was torrential rain, snow at the highest passes over the mountains, and a steep climb up the slope of Monte Del Cabiero. There was a trail of dying women and children and, in the defile beyond Villafranca, as the route wound round the bends of the River Valcaso between precipitate cliffs, the members of the trudging column were constantly falling out and at times going over the lip into the precipice. On the snow-covered heights men lay at night clasped in each others arms. The plight of women and children became even more pitiful as they sank in the snow. There was neither bread nor shelter, only the loud moaning of the wind. Nonetheless, whenever attacked by the French vanguard, who at times tried to outflank the marching column, the men stood to arms to resist attack. The Light Brigade on the route to Vigo had experiences of the same kind as "Black Bob" - as the men called General Crawford - urged them on. He marched with them, offering them at times as he moved up and down the columns cups of rum from his own canteen. He made his officers suffer with the men; on one occasion a soldier carrying an officer on his shoulders across an icy stream was ordered to put him down in the water and the officer was told to go back and wade the stream as others did. On the 6th January the army reached Lugo. Moore prepared to give battle and discipline improved despite the foul weather. Soult did not however appear, and in a dark night of sleet and hail the march began again. The army had become a mob almost without order, muddled up and incoherent, protected only by the discipline and firmness of the rearguard. At last on 10th January at Betanzos the columns came into the coastal plain, where a light sun warmed the air and the orange trees were breaking into flower. The next day with intense pleasure the army saw the sea and the ships at anchor in Corunna harbour. The army was re-organised and entered into Corunna on 11th January in reasonable order. Two battalions of the Foot Guards marched in with drums beating, led by the drum major twirling his baton. The ships in the harbour were only hospital and store ships, with few men-of-war. The transports had gone to Vigo, where the Light Brigade was to arrive on the 12th January.

Sir John Moore faced a problem; there could be no rescue until the transport fleet arrived, and so he had to provide a defence for Corunna until the ships came. The army was unfortunate in that, while in January the pre-dominant winds are south and south-west on the north-west coast of Spain, the fleet was faced at Vigo by a wind which required beating into the Atlantic to round Cape Finisterre. To keep Soult at bay for an indefinite time was crucial. The French would need to cross the River Mero at Burgo about four miles from the city, so it was essential to hold the bridge for as long as possible, and then blow it up. The next question for Moore was where to site his lines. Nearest to the town was a ridge rising to four hundred feet from the Heights of Santa Margarita in the west, continuing east as the Monte Mero, stretching as far the river. Further to the south was a higher range dominating these shallow hills, stretching from the Heights of San Cristobel on to the Heights of Penasquedo and Palavea near the river. The road from Burgo followed the river through the small villages of Palavea Abaxo and Piedralonga. A shallow valley ran between the hills in which stood the village of Elvina, turning then north between the Monte Mero and Santa Margarita. The southern ridge was too long for Moore successfully to defend it and so he was forced to place the army along the Monte Mero, despite the ability of the French to overlook those heights with their guns. The configuration of the land was such that Moore realised that there could only be one section of the front where a decisive attack could be made, and that was through the village of Elvina with an attempt to outflank him on the right. The left on the heights near the sea was less vulnerable.

Until the transports arrived there remained a serious shortage of food. Moore however began to embark his wounded and sick. At the same time, with the enthusiastic help of the townspeople, fortifications were thrown up at the entrance to the isthmus on which Corunna town lay. Given the absence of the transports and the uncertainty of their arrival, a number of his subordinate commanders suggested to Moore that he should seek an armistice from Marshal Soult, allowing the army to depart, similar to that given to Marshal Junot at Cintra. With great scorn and indignation Sir John Moore rejected that. Soult had come up to the bridge at Burgo on the 12th. The rearguard covered the bridge from the advancing French patrols while the engineers struggled to place their charges to explode it. They had on a number of occasions failed to blow bridges on the retreat, but with a huge charge late on the 12th the bridge was wrecked, the bang of the explosion being heard in Corunna four miles away. Soult had sent out his cavalry to seek for another crossing and found one at Celo, some seven miles upstream, which the Spanish had failed to destroy. On the 13th Corunna was rocked in the morning by two explosions which Moore had ordered to destroy barrels of powder stored for delivery to the Spanish on San Christobal. The amount destroyed was over four thousand barrels, in two stores which ignited one after another, high black clouds rising in the air and lingering while in the town windows were broken, the ships in the harbour rocked and the more timid of the townspeople fell on their knees in the streets to pray.

The destruction of surplus horses began, to be continued the next day with greater intensity. Only 1,000 of the best horses were to be taken. The remainder were brought to the cliffs, shot and thrown over to the beach. Some had their throats cut and where the work was ill-done, wounded horses dashed up and down on the beach whinnying and neighing. Some were to be seen roaming the streets of the town. About noon on the 14th the transports entered harbour escorted by twelve men-of-war - Ville de Paris, Victory (7th of the name), Barfleur, Zealous, Implacable, Elizabeth, Norge, Plantagenet, Resolution (7th of the name) Audacious, Endymion and Mediator. On their arrival the last of the sick were embarked and the embarkation of the cavalry began, since in a defensive battle before the port, their use would be without advantage. All the guns were embarked but for nine. Most of the supplies had by the 14th been destroyed.

Moore spent the 14th inspecting the disposition of the troops. Given his belief that Marshal Soult would attack the British centre and right in an attempt to outflank Monte Mero through the low-lying land past Elvina and leading down to the road to the port between the Heights of Monte Mero and San Cristobal, he placed one-third of his army on the right. Sir David Baird's division (comprising Warde's, Bentinck's and Manningham's Brigades) was placed on the western part of the ridge above Elvina. Lord William Bentinck's brigade was on the right comprising the 4th (the King Own Regiment) the 42nd (Royal Highland) and the 50th (West Kent) Regiments of Foot. Warde's Foot Guards were in reserve behind Bentinck's Brigade and Manningham's 1st (Royal Scot's), 26th (the Cameronians) and 81st Regiments on the left forming the centre. Between them and the River Mero was stationed Hope's Division, made up of Leith's, Hill's and Crawford's Brigades. Behind Baird, straddling the valley towards the town, was Sir Edward Paget's Division in reserve, made up of Anstruther's Brigade, comprising the 20th (East Devonshire Regiment of Foot, the 52nd (Oxfordshire Regiment of Foot) and the 95th (Rifles) and of Disney's Brigade, the 28th (West Gloucestershire) Regiment of Foot and the 91st (Argyllshire Highlanders) Regiment of Foot. Fraser's Division, with Fane's and Beresford's Brigades, were based on the Heights of Santa Margarita to the rear on the Vigo road, guarding the far right flank and entrance to the port.

Sir John Moore in the course of the day moved through the lines talking to the officers and men, not finishing his inspection until after night fell. Of the nine guns, six were placed on the right and Paget was provided with three. On 15th January Marshal Soult's force came up, pushing back the outposts and occupying the outer heights of San Cristobal and Penesquedo and the slope above the village of Palavea Abaxo on the British left rear the Mero River. The day was spent in deploying the French army and twelve guns were pulled up the Height of San Cristobal overlooking Elvina and the western end of ridge. Skirmishing and intermittent cannonades occurred. On the far right Soult placed Francheski's cavalry with Lehoussaye on the slopes above San Christobal village. Mermet's division was placed to oppose Baird on the western end of the ridge above Elvina, Merle's Division to his right and Delaborde's in the vicinity of Palavea Abaxo to oppose Hope's Division.

On the morning of 16th January Sir John Moore was up at six o'clock. A sea mist lay over the harbour and stretched in the low valleys inland. He went to visit Monte Mero, where the skies were clear and the French opposite on the English right were beating to arms. The troops on Monte Mero remained undisturbed throughout the morning however. About 10 a.m. Moore issued a general order authorising the embarkation. He had promised Paget's reserve the right to embark first for their fine performance throughout the retreat. They were given an early dinner and about noon began to march down to the docks. About one o'clock the French, however, began to move and an aide-de-camp was hastily sent to recall Paget. Under the cover of the bombardment by their guns of the British on the western end of the Monte Mero ridge, the French of Mermet's Division began to move forward downhill in three columns, from the Penasquedo Heights. They were led by a force of tirailleurs commanded by General Jordan, a hard-swearing revolutionary, who was not thought to change his linen over much. At the same time the French Cavalry were to be seem moving on the right, commencing their encirclement action towards the low valley leading to Corunna. They were hampered by the country, where the low stone walls and small fields made the cavalry charge impossible and constantly slowed progress. Jordan pushed the British skirmishers and the light company of the 59th (2nd Nottinghamshire Regiment of Foot) out of Elvina and began to approach the Monte Mero heights. The British on the ridge were subjected to continuous fire from the batteries, while the French columns came on under the cover of the intense fire. Lord William Bentinck rode nonchalantly through his Brigade on a mule, smoking and carrying on soft conversations with the troops. When Sir John Moore came up to inspect the brigade on the ridge, a round shot frightened his horse, which almost threw him. A soldier of the 42nd Regiment nearby, whose leg had been shattered, lay screaming, affecting the morale of those around him. Moore turned to the man and said, "This is nothing, my lads, Take that man away. My good fellow, don't make such a noise. We must bear these things better."

After Elvina was taken and Mermet's Columns began to move up the slope of Monte Mero, the French 31st Regiment split and the right-hand column halted to deploy. Moore ordered the 42nd to go into the attack. Led by Colonel Sterling the Highlanders charged down on the French firing a volley and crashing on with bayonets fixed. There was a ferocious struggle but the French gave ground and it was not until the 42nd was almost down the slope that they were held among the low stone walls weaving across the lower slopes. At this point the 50th came to their support, closing up on Elvina and clambering over the walls. The commander of the 50th, Major Charles Napier was in the lead with Major Charles Stanhope. Down they ran under heavy fire; two ensigns carrying the colours fell but the colours were seized and held high again by two sergeants. Fearlessly the two majors led the men into the village advancing up a lane at the end of which the French were reforming. Napier's impetuosity had outrun his men, only three officers and thirty other ranks remaining with him as he took cover behind a wall. Stanhope stood on the top of a wall to urge his men into the murderous fire and then went on only to be shot in the heart. The French had been driven out of Elvina and only started to re-enter the village cautiously.

The cavalry activity on the British right and the movement of the infantry to the western flank of Mont Mero resulted in the 4th Regiment being commanded to bend their line in part to face the flank, and orders to General Edward Paget to come up as quickly as possible. The latter sent on the 95th in an extended line after Moore's first order. Later they were joined by the 52nd, the 28th regiment and two battalions, the 20th and 91st, coming up the shallow river valley to where the French cavalry was struggling forward through the walled fields. General Lahoussaye's cavalry could not charge and had to dismount and act virtually as individuals or groups of skirmishers as Paget advanced upon them, while the 52nd and the 20th battalion faced the French Infantry, already under fire from the 4th Regiment on their flank on Monte Mero. Inexorably the French were held and pushed back towards the Heights of Penesquedo.

On the left the French Divisions of General Delaborde were to take Palavea Abaxo and the village of Piedralonga, but their task to mount the ridge was harder than on the right since the slope was steeper and Hope's men robustly held them. Ultimately, with the French repulsed, Hill's Brigade fought their way forward and the 14th (Bedfordshire) Regiment of Foot retook Palavea Abaxo. On the far right, Fraser's Division was holding General Francheski's cavalry on the Heights of Santa Margarita. Sir John Moore, seeing the French cavalry of Lahoussaye and Mermet's Infantry being pushed back, decided to endeavour to take the batteries which were doing so much damage among the British infantry on the ridge. He therefore ordered up Warde's Brigade of Foot guards. Their first objective was a large house on the outskirts of Elvina from which a fierce fire was maintained on the 42nd, who being short of ammunition started to slip back. Moore hurried to prevent that: "My brave 42nd, if you've fired your ammunition", he shouted to them, "you've still your bayonets. Remember Egypt! Think on Scotland! Come on my gallant countrymen" The reference to Egypt is to the Battle of Aboukir (21st March 1801). The Highlanders heard him and at once returned to the fight.

Sir John Moore was standing with some of his aides-de-camp at a crossroads just northwest of the village of Elvina and a French battery had observed the place as a frequent rendezvous for officers. Henry Hardinge had just come up to him to report the arrival of the Foot Guards and Colonel Thames Graham was beside him. Moore raised his hat and turned to view the Guards coming up when he was hit by round shot and fell from his saddle at the feet of Graham's horse. He had not cried out and Hardinge ran to his aid, squeezing his hand. The round shot which had hit him had torn off his arm and smashed his collarbone and ribs, exposing his lungs and slashing into strips the muscles of his chest. Hardinge tried to staunch the blood with his sash; Surgeon McGill examined him and he saw that Moore could not be helped, only removing a lapel and two buttons from the wound. Moore asked whether the 42nd were advancing. Gently he was helped on to a blanket on poles by soldiers of the 42nd and the Foot Guards, who carried him back to his lodgings. On the way two surgeons came up, but he ordered them away to help the wounded for whom something could be done. Colonel Anderson remained with him and Moore told him that he had always wished to die this way.

General Sir David Baird having been injured, the command devolved to General Hope. The short winter day was ending and the French had been fought to a standstill. Firing went on until six o'clock when it ceased. Hope had no reserves to exploit the situation and knew that Marshal Soult still had further forces which he could call up. He decided that the army should take its opportunity to evacuate Corunna.

Sir John Moore was laid on the floor of his lodgings. Colonel Anderson supported him in his arms and Moore asked whether the French were beaten, hoping that the people of England will be satisfied. "I hope" - he softly said – "my country will do me justice." For long periods there was silence, while a chaplain helped Anderson support him. From time to time he roused himself to speak, concerned over the safety of his aides-de-camp, his will, the provision for his servants, and his promise to Major Colborne to give him a colonelcy, whom he asked again whether the French were beat, to which came the reply "In every point, Sir." In reply he expressed his satisfaction and again hoped that his country would do him justice. Colonel Graham and James Stanhope came to join him, but Moore was sinking. Seeing Stanhope he whispered "Remember me to your sister". Those were his last words. He clutched Colonel Anderson's hand more tightly and just after the eight o'clock gun sounded from the Admiral's ship in the harbour, died. At twelve o'clock, Sir John Moore's body was removed to Colonel Graham's quarters in the citadel.

In the dark, the bivouac fires were lit on Monte Mero along the line and left burning, while in proper order the troops, filthy and hollow-eyed, marched down to the ships. In the mist in the harbour it was impossible for the cutters and small craft to find the allotted transports and the men were taken to the nearest ships until full and then gradually through the fleet. By morning half the army was aboard. The rest were to board on the 17th, apart from a rearguard of 1500. The Spanish townspeople rallied and manned the ramparts south of the town to delay the French. A party of the 9th (East Norfolk) Regiment of Foot bore the body of Sir John Moore to the landward ramparts in the early morning to a grave next to that of Brigadier Anstruther. The watch fires still flickered on the hills. As the French guns started the Reverend Henry Symons, Chaplain to the Brigade of Guards, began the moving, sonorous recitation of the Funeral Service from the Book of Common Prayer. The body of Sir John was clad in his full regimentals, wrapped with a blanket and a cloak. At the internment, Colonel Anderson, Major Colborne, Captains James Stanhope and Henry Percy lowered the body into the grave with their long red officer's sashes.

About noon the French opened fire on the harbour from the guns brought up to the heights above Santa Lucia on the city outskirts. Some of masters cut their cables precipitously and four vessels ran on shore: the Royal Navy's cutters however rescued the soldiers and took them aboard other ships. The rearguard of Beresford's Brigade was safely embarked early on 18th January from behind the citadel. As they were evacuated, the French opened fire on the fleet from the heights of San Diego immediately above the harbour, but little damage was done. It was time for the great convoy to leave and it sailed through gales in the Bay of Biscay to the safety of home.

A ragged, typhus-ridden army arrived home in the ports from Falmouth to Dover and the press and sections of public opinion rushed to condemn Sir John Moore for his failure and near destruction of the army. The Times was critical of his failure to make a stand in the passes of Galicia. The Duke of York, in a General Order, praised Moore as an example of a gallant officer to be admired and followed. Colborne was given his colonelcy and Thomas Graham made a Major-General. On 24th February however Mr Ponsonby, a critic of Moore, introduced a motion in the House of Commons for an inquiry into the events in Spain. In the middle of the debate Sheridan announced that the Drury Lane Theatre was on fire and there was debate as to whether the house should be adjourned. At last Canning, the Foreign Secretary spoke, ending his speech with the words "If we have been obliged to quit Spain, we have left it with fresh laurels blooming on our brows." "Whatever", he added, "may be the fruits of Bonaparte's victories in other respects, the spirit of the Spanish nation is yet unsubdued". The motion was lost by a majority of 94.

Sir John Moore's last words referred to James Stanhope's sister, Lady Hester Stanhope, whom he had met while she lived at 10, Downing Street with her Uncle, William Pitt the Younger, the Prime Minister. She formed an attachment for Moore, who was strikingly handsome, and told her brother Charles, killed at Corunna, that she thought he had the most perfect body. His reply was that she should see him unclothed, when he looked like a God. She was desolated by Moore's death and began vigorously to campaign to achieve proper recognition for his achievement. Finally in 1810 she left London to travel and settled to live in the high mountains of Lebanon with the Druses, virtually as a local chieftain. In 1835 Alexander Kinglake visited her in the half-ruined convent which she inhabited, guarded by Albanians, and thought that she had the character of a prophetess, discussing with him for hours sacred and profane mysteries. She died in 1839.

The Reverend Charles Wolfe was the author of a poem, first published in 1817 and his only poem of note, entitled *the Burial of Sir John Moore after Corunna*, and it was constantly learned by children down to the mid-twentieth century, although factually inaccurate.

Gradually Moore's achievement was recognised, first, in creating the Light Infantry regiments of the army, and second, in the skill with which he used his small army to obstruct the attempt by Napoleon to gain control of all Portugal and Spain. His campaign of 1808 – 1809 diverted the French north. The south was left unconquered and was free to organise new armies and new resistance.

The failure of the French to destroy Britain's army as a result of the well-conceived retreat and stand at Corunna preserved the army in being and kept the foundation for its return to Portugal under Sir Arthur Wellesley. Marshal Soult made his own tribute to Moore by ordering a monument to be placed on his grave. In 1816, after a vote in Parliament, a monument was placed in St Paul's Cathedral.

Sir John Hope subsequently became the Earl of Hopetown, a title now held by the eldest son of the Marquess of Linlithgow. Henry Hardinge became a Fieldmarshal and a Viscount.

The 4th Marquess of Linlithgow and the 6th Viscount Hardinge were ejected from the House of Lords in 1999.

> Not a drum was heard, not a funeral note,
>> As his course to the rampart we hurried;
> Not a soldier discharged his farewell shot
>> O'er the grave where our hero we buried.
>
> We buried him darkly at dead of night,
>> The sods with our bayonets turning,
> By the struggling moonbeam's misty light
>> And the lantern dimly burning.
>
> No useless coffin enclosed his breast,
>> Not in sheet or in shroud we wound him'
> But he lay like a warrior taking his rest
>> With his martial cloak around him.
>
> Few and short were the prayers we said;
>> And we spoke not a word of sorrow;
> But we steadfastly gazed on the face that was dead,
>> And we bitterly thought of the morrow.
>
> We thought, as we hollow'd his narrow bed
>> And smooth'd down his lonely pillow,
> That the foe and the stranger would tread o'er his head,
>> And we far away on the billow!

Lightly they'll talk of the spirit that's gone,
  And o'er his cold ashes upbraid him-
But little he'll reck, if they let him sleep on
  In the grave where a Briton has laid him.

But half of our heavy task was done
  When the clock struck the hour for retiring;
And we heard the distant and random gun
  That the foe was sullenly firing.

Slowly and sadly we laid him down,
  From the field of his fame fresh and gory;
We carved not a line, and we raised not a stone,
  But we left him alone with his glory.

The Taking of Ciudad Rodrigo

During 1811 the Duke of Wellington made attempts on Cuidad Rodrigo and Badajoz, the cities guarding the entrance to Spain from Portugal. Both were unsuccessful and as the year came to an end he drew back to winter quarters on the border, while Marshal Marmont, with the Army of Portugal, withdrew to his base at Almaraz. The front was quiet; the British army was weakened by sickness. The Emperor Napoleon, misled by the inactivity, withdrew troops from the Army of Portugal to assist Suchet to take Valencia. The French army in Spain was also being weakened by withdrawal of troops for the campaign to invade Russia in 1812. Wellington had been strongly reinforced, particularly with cavalry, enabling him to raise that force from three to six brigades. By December the weather had turned bitterly cold, but nonetheless he resolved that the moment had come to strike at Ciudad Rodrigo. An effective siege train had arrived from England and the army could field thirty twenty-four pounders and eighteen pounders. Long forage and straw for the cavalry however, was short and for eight or nine days there was no corn. The horses had only the sustenance of grass so short that they often swallowed stones as they cropped the ground. The men were quartered in villages between Guarda and the River Agueda. In all, Wellington's combined Anglo-Portuguese force amounted to 45,000 effective troops, of which 33,000 were seasoned regulars. The Army of Portugal, on the other hand, had been reduced to only 30,000 centred on Marshal Marmont's base at Salamanca.

The city and fortress of Ciudad Rodrigo stood on the west bank of the River Agueda on a small rise, surrounded by a wall about thirty-two feet high. The ground fell away on the south and south-eastern side to the river. To the south lay the convent of Santa Cruz, which had been fortified, and to the north-west the convent of San Francisco near a village of that name, which had also been turned into a fortress. The walls of the city were not in a good state and the defences not improved since 1810, apart from the creation of an outlying redoubt on a hill above the San Francisco convent. The force garrisoning the town amounted to 2,000 of which 1,500 were effective, comprising a weak French regiment, a German and an Italian regiment. The Governor, Baron Barrié, General of Brigade, commanded however a force of 100 guns in the hands of two companies of artillerymen. The Diarist William Gratton recorded that to be safe the city would need a garrison of 5,000 to 6,000 so that, unless relieved, it could not hold out for long. The city was made subject to a loose blockade by Spanish Guerillas and the Connaught Rangers who on one occasion made off with 200 store cattle from the glacis near the city and captured the previous Governor, General Renaud, when a sortie was made to rescue the cattle.

While the men waited in the rain and cold, the troops entertained themselves with point to points across country between church towers, fox hunting and boxing. Orders finally came to march on 4th January. After sleet, rain and snow the roads were mired in mud through which the marching columns struggled. The men waded through the River Agueda in water up to their shoulders – five dying of cold, while the engineers worked in the water to throw a bridge across for the guns and baggage. Ciudad Rodrigo was reached on the 7th. Wellington wasted no time. He was determined to take the city before Marshal Marmont could come to its relief. On the night of the 8th a force of three hundred from the Light Division led by Colonel Colborne of the 52nd were sent to take the redoubt built by the French on the hill overlooking the San Francisco convent. There was no preliminary bombardment and the troops were pressed forward. They had been provided with ladders made from Spanish rails but many of them gave way and the mass had to mount the earthworks, using their bayonets, stuck in the wall as steps. The surprise of the attack was such that the redoubt was soon taken, two officers and fifty men surrendering. Because the redoubt was open to the town, as a position it was untenable, but its taking enabled the first parallel to be started on the 9th.

The siege works were to last for ten days. The troops of the Light, First, Third and Fourth Divisions were used in relays to dig out the approach trenches and the parallels. In the bitter cold and snow it was bruising work, but at least the men bivouacked in the open were kept warm. The French guns played over the works and substantial casualties were incurred from the grapeshot, mortars and howitzers fired at the working parties. Occasional veins of rock gave rise to visible sparks, attracting the fire. Nonetheless the works advanced. On the 13th the Kings German Legion took the convent of Santa Cruz and a night assault was made by the 40th on that of San Francisco. A second parallel was started nearer the city on the 13th. On the morning of the 14th, however, Barrié and the French, taking advantage of the change-over of the divisions' working parties, made a sortie, retaking Santa Cruz and wrecking the works on the second parallel. The convent was retaken and the French retired. The same day twenty-four of the large guns were placed at five hundred and fifty yards to bombard the walls. A five-day cannonade was to begin. Approaches were created beyond the first parallel, while the second was completed on the 17th. On the 18th seven heavy guns were placed on the left, in advance of the second parallel. The works were nearing the walls, but there still remained two ditches to cross, created by the French, the tops of whose glacis were battered by the guns. The constant bombardment had created two practicable breaches in the walls – one to the right of the Salamanca gate in the northerly wall, the greater breach, and one to the left, the lesser.

Although the siege works were not complete, Wellington decided that an assault should be made on the 19th, before Marshal Marmont could arrive to succour the garrison. The Light Division was assigned the lower breach and the 3rd Division the greater.

From early afternoon the troops who were to take part began to muster in the area behind the parallels, now full of troops relaxing, sutlers, women accompanying the troops and their families and their bivouacs. Late in the afternoon the band of the 43rd Regiment marched past and the column was inspected. The Light Division was formed up, their band playing "Over the hills and far away". General Picton inspected the 88th (the Connaught Rangers) and told them that it was not his intention to expend any powder that evening. "We'll do this business with cold bayonet" -he said. Darkness began to fall at five o'clock and the night was piercingly cold. The men engaged in the assault left their knapsacks in rows guarded by sentries to preserve them from Spanish and Portuguese scroungers around the camp. The start time was set for seven o'clock. As they waited, the clouds cleared the moon, and in the moonlight the bayonets of the French could be seen glittering on the ramparts. Lieutenant Mackie, the Senior Lieutenant of the Connaught Rangers, volunteered and was appointed to lead into the main breach the 'forlorn hope' of twenty men from the Rangers, backed by three hundred men of the 74th (Highland Regiment of Foot) under Major Russell Manners.

Three simultaneous attacks were planned, that on the main breach, the lesser breach and a feint on the southern walls by Portuguese brigades and the light company of the 83rd Regiment of Foot led by Colonel O'Toole and Brigadier General Pack. At seven o'clock, on the signal, the columns moved forward. Generals Picton and Crauford dismounted to join their troops on foot. At the main breach the 3rd Division emerged from the covered way at the parallel and had to cross three hundred yards of open land to the breach. The French from the ramparts delivered a withering fire of grapeshot. The charge rushed on and the ditch was reached. The division pressed on; the 45th (Nottinghamshire) Regiment of Foot, the 88th (Connaught Rangers) and the 74th (Highland Regiment of Foot) met up to cheers with the 5th (Northumberland) Regiment of Foot and the 94th (Scots Brigade) of Foot; who joined them at the ditch. The latter had picked off the French on the ramparts and resolved to go with the storming party. The breach was stormed, despite the *chevaux de frise* and logs which had been used to block it, and despite the twenty-five foot high rubble which had to be scaled, and the French abandoned their position, leaving a drop of eleven feet still to be negotiated. Once the British had taken the top, the French began with two twenty-four pounder guns to left and right of the breach to enfilade the troops on the lip. The first lines there were swept away and the French returned to seize back the breach.

Picton set about rallying his men and once more they stormed through the ditches and up to take the breach. Led by General Mackinnon the troops pressed forward, when a gun magazine near one of the enfilading guns blew up. Mackinnon was blown up and killed together with three hundred British and French. The diarist William Gratton noted that the hole left was like a small quarry. It was still necessary to try to silence the remaining gun on the left and the only surviving officer in the breach, Major Thompson of the 74th, called on the men to take it, but it was difficult to approach up to where it stood. Three soldiers from the 88th were to disable the gun and the five gunners who stood effectively firing it. Sergeant Patrick Brazil of the Grenadier Company and Privates Swan and Kelly unscrewed their bayonets and came up to the gunners to engage them in hand-to-hand fighting. Private Swan killed the first gunner of the five on the left of the gun only to have his left arm severed from his body by a sabre blow of the second gunner. Kelly, as Swan lay bleeding to death, scrambled under the gun and bayoneted two more. Sergeant Brazil took the fourth and a soldier of the 5th shot the last. The gun was silenced.

At the lesser breach the Light Division, comprising the 95th Regiment of Foot, whose toast was, "The first in the field and the last out of it, the bloody, fighting ninety-fifth", the 43rd (Monmouthshire Light Infantry and the 52nd (Oxfordshire) Light Infantry had more success. Prior to action General Crauford addressed the storming party in the lee of a convent. That party comprised Lieutenant Gurwood with twenty-five men making up the forlorn hope and three hundred men of the 42nd (Royal Highland Regiment of Foot) commanded by Captain Napier. Crauford led the way and was the first to fall in the breach from the canister shot. George Napier was to lose an arm as the men two-thirds up the breach prepared to attack with their bayonets. The French defence was however weaker than at the great breach and the men were soon over, although Gratton observed that the dead appeared more numerous than at the great breach. Led by Captain Ferguson, the troops of the Light Division moved along the ramparts in both directions, taking the defenders of the great breach on the flank.

The Portuguese and the light company of the 83rd Regiment of Foot led by O'Toole and Pack met only slight resistance in their assault and were soon in the city. The defenders of the great breach retired when taken in the flank and retreated into the streets, skirmishing as they went towards the Citadel and still resisting. Shooting was to be heard throughout the city and resistance only stopped when the fighting debouched into the Plaza Mayor. The Governor, General Baron Baril surrendered his sword to Lieutenant Gurwood, who had been slightly wounded in the head while leading the 'forlorn hope' Ciudad Rodrigo had been taken at a cost of 160 officers killed and wounded and 1,032 men, of which the losses during the period of the siege works were 101 officers and 529 men. Lieutenant General Crauford, who had been hit in the spine, died on 24th January. It had taken twelve days to seize the city; 1700 prisoners were taken and one hundred and fifty heavy guns. The French losses were of the order of 500.

Once the firing stopped, the troops set themselves to loot the city, becoming drunk on wine and spirits seized from the bodegas and stores. Large candles taken from a chandlers lit the scene. Valuables and clothes were plundered and taken from houses and churches. Pillage and orgies engulfed the streets going on through the night. Officers were powerless to control the men and even had on occasion to draw their swords on them. At daybreak the sack of the city stopped and the troops moved out festooned in the loot taken; silk gowns, priests' vestments and fine clothes, and carrying the valuable items taken, – silver and gold, crosses and plate. It took three days to re-organise the army. Thirteen deserters were found in the city, five from the 60th and 88th. Of these four were shot and one of good character pardoned. Wellington himself gave particular attention to alleviating the suffering of the wounded of all ranks. On hearing that soldiers who were wounded had been left in the open, he rode thirty miles by night to their bivouac and ordered them taken to officers' quarters. On hearing that the officers had had the sick men thrown out he had them taken back and the officers were cashiered.

News had only reached Marshal Marmont on 12th January that Ciudad Rodrigo was invested, much to his surprise and anger, since he had taken the view that the fierce cold weather would deter Wellington from any action. There was no time for him to reach the city before it fell. Both he and General Dorsenne were horrified, but he took no action until Emperor Napoleon ordered him to recover the place, Meanwhile Wellington set the 5th Division to repairing the defences of the city and prepared the army to march on to besiege Badajoz in the South. (See the taking of Badajoz 6th April 1812). The army left on 8th March, leaving a garrison of three thousand Spaniards. In accordance with Napoleon's orders, Marmont arrived near Ciudad Rodrigo on 30th March. He had no siege guns, since Wellington had captured those in the city and moved off towards Almeida. After a few days, the efforts of insurgents in his rear, together with the absence of supply trains and a barren countryside led him to retreat back to his base, having lost 1,500 horses.

On news of the victory, Wellington was advanced to an Earldom and given a pension of £4,000.

23rd January 1915
The Battle of the Dogger Bank

Information reached the Admiralty in the middle of January 1915 that there was considerable naval activity at Kiel and Wilhelmshaven. Both the battle-cruiser Seidlitz, Admiral Hipper's flagship, and the battle-cruiser Derflinger, had gone seaward from the Jade. Commodore Tyrwhitt carried out a reconnaissance in the vicinity of Heligoland but found nothing and returned to Harwich. In fact, Admiral Ingersohl planned a foray to the Dogger Bank with a view to interfering with the British fishing fleets. On 22nd January Admiral Hipper in Seidlitz, with the battle-cruisers Derflinger and Moleke, accompanied by the armed cruiser Blucher, the light cruisers Kolberg, Stralsund, Rostock and Graudenz and a torpedo flotilla went out on this mission. Knowledge of this departure led the Admiralty to warn the battle-cruiser squadron commanded by Admiral Sir David Beatty and the light cruiser and destroyer flotilla at Harwich commanded by Commodore Tyrwhitt to search out the German Squadron. A rendezvous was fixed to the north-east of Dogger Bank. Tyrwhitt had difficulty in getting to sea in the dense harbour fog and the last elements of the Harwich flotilla was not at sea until 7 a.m. The flotilla was thus strung out, but in the early morning the Arethusa (6th of the name, a light cruiser) with seven destroyers was near the rendezvous. Admiral Beatty, who was a keen rider to foxhounds, and a strong polo player, and who was thought to have a Nelsonian dash, on his flagship Lion (8th of the name, a Battle-cruiser) had reached the area with his squadron of battle-cruisers, Tiger, Princes Royal, New Zealand and Indomitable.

In the course of their progress Arethusa and the destroyers accompanying it had crossed the line taken by the Germans north. The Aurora (7th of the Line, a light cruiser) and twenty-eight other ships of Commodore Tyrwhitt's, force were some twelve miles behind. The Aurora was the first to see the Germans, becoming engaged with the Kolberg four and half miles away. The Kolberg turned east and warned Hipper of the presence of the British. Hipper ordered the fleet to turn south-east and proceed at full speed back to their bases. By 7.30 a.m. the Southampton (4th of the name, light cruiser) which was probing ahead of the line forward of the battle-cruisers came in touch with the line of fleeing Germans. Southampton signalled Lion and Beatty ordered his squadron to speed up. By that time the light was pretty good, skies clear and the sea calm. General Quarters were ordered. The German squadron was on the port side and to the windward and became visible to the British squadron about 7.30 a.m. The two fleets moved south east: by 8.15 a.m. the battle-cruisers had made speed up to twenty-five knots and were soon to reach twenty-nine knots, closing the gap. Indomitable began to fall behind, and New Zealand. The smoke of destroyers and Light Cruisers and of the German squadron obscured from time to time the German Squadron. At 9 a.m. Lion fired its first salvo from the 13.5" guns in the fore turrets at the rear ship, the Blucher, at a distance of 20,000 yards.

There were problems getting the range. The Germans began to reply, straddling the on-coming battle-cruisers in the van. Lion passed on, firing at Moltke, the next ahead, and Tiger took up the attack on Blucher. Three of the Germans began to concentrate their fire on Lion and it was hit for the first time on the waterline at 9.28 a.m. The 13.5" shells of the battle-cruisers devastated Blucher and it began to slow. One German account averred that the first shot from Tiger to hit went down the funnel. First Princess Royal and then New Zealand began to fire on Blucher, while Tiger moved on the German flagship, the Seidlitz, and Princes Royal took its place attacking Moltke. Beatty ordered the squadron to turn from ahead to quarter line. Lion and Derflinger kept up their mutual engagement. At 9.40 a.m. Tiger struck Seidlitz in the stern. The 13.5" shell pierced the armour of the rear turret, which exploded causing damage in the rear chambers and ammunition ducts, with the result that the other rear turret exploded. The fore turrets of Seidlitz fell out of action. Fire was concentrated on Lion for almost one and a half hours. It lost its wireless masts: fire raged in the forward turret; its armour was pierced; waterline hits put out of action the port engine and parts of the ship up to main deck forward. Signals could only be run up by flags or conveyed by semaphore. The harm done to the boilers lowered the speed, as Lion listed, to fifteen knots. In the heat of the battle, Beatty's signals became unclear and misinterpreted. Beatty first signalled a 90° degree turn to port to avoid possible torpedo hazards and then to turn north-east. He followed it up with Nelson's signal at Trafalgar "Engage the enemy more closely."

The British battle-cruisers had been closing up on the German squadron, although in the clouds of smoke masking the German ships the shooting had become poor in accuracy. Rear Admiral Sir Archibald Moore, faced by the two signals, turned New Zealand away towards the Blucher, where Indomitable had come up to the attack. Tiger meanwhile had put Derflinger on fire and herself received a hit which shook the conning tower, although no one was hurt and Midshipman Ouvry recorded "everyone kept cool and no one was hurt." The shell had pierced the armour and exploded in the intelligence office and battery. After Lion had slowed and drawn back, the Germans had concentrated on Tiger and she was hit in a storm of shells eight times. Meanwhile, the Blucher had stopped, although she continued to fire solitary shells. Almost without warning she turned on her side and sank, the crew clambering out over the hull. British destroyers tried to carry out a rescue but were only able to save 237 members of her crew. Both Tiger and Princess Royal had moved on Blucher. The turn away from the pursuit of the German squadron insured their escape. Beatty, who had had to move his flag to the destroyer Attack, was enraged by their escape, but there had been a victory, although far less than complete. Blucher had been sunk, Seidlitz significantly damaged, Derflinger damaged by fire and only Moltke returned undamaged. The Lion was towed back to port. Despite the damage done to the British ships, only 15 sailors were killed. Seidlitz had lost 192 men and of the crew of Blucher 782 were lost.

February

7th	Victory at Beda Fomm	1941
12th	The Battle of the Herrings	1429
14th	The Battle of St.Vincent	1797
20th	The Battle of Portland	1653
27th	The Battle of Orthez	1814

7th February 1941
Victory of Beda Fomm

After the fall of Sidi Barrani (see the Battle of Sidi Barrani 15th December 1940), the Western Desert force came to a standstill on the frontier. Before them on the coastal road of Cyrenaica stood the fortified seaports of Bardia and Tobruk. Bardia had a seventeen-mile perimeter defended by mine-fields, an anti-tank ditch, wire and concrete bunkers; within, there was a second defensive line. Tobruk sat within a twenty-seven mile perimeter similarly defended, but with an anti-tank ditch which in places was shallow. After reorganisation and the bringing up of supplies, Bardia was attacked on 3rd January 1941.

The 7th Armoured Division moved to block the north and north-west exit on the coast road to Tobruk. The Royal Navy bombarded Bardia from the sea. The main assault however came from the west where, under cover of heavy gunfire by the artillery made up of one field and one medium Regiment of Corps Artillery, the mines were cleared and one Australian battalion of the 6th Australian Division broke through the perimeter. Behind them the engineers filled the anti-tank ditch. Two Australian brigades took the attack to the east and south-east of the enclosed area so that by the afternoon of the 4th the tanks of the 7th Battalion Royal Tank Regiment, supported by the 16th British Infantry Brigade and the Australians, were able to take the seaport itself. On 5th January the whole area of Bardia was in British hands. 45,000 prisoners of war were taken, with 462 guns and 12 tanks.

The 7th Armoured Division pressed on and by 6th January Tobruk had been isolated. The absence of food and water in the desert wastes of rock and sand meant that no forward moves could be made without a build-up of supplies. For that the Royal Navy was crucial, and each day during this campaign from December 7th to its end 2,500 tons of supplies per day were brought up for the advancing desert force. It was not until 21st January that the assault on the Tobruk perimeter could be made. Within that area was one complete Italian Division, the remnants of others and their Corps Headquarters.

Once more the 6th Australian Division was to spearhead the attack. Their leading brigade has reached Tobruk on the 7th to back up the armoured blockade on the city. Using similar methods to those at Bardia, the Australians broke through on the southern perimeter, fanning out east and west through the fortified area. By dusk about a third of the area had been taken and on the morning of 22nd January the whole garrison had surrendered. 30,000 prisoners of war were taken, 236 guns and 87 tanks.

Winston Churchill was anxious to take Bengazi in western Cyrenaica and urged Sir Archibald Wavell to go on. He and Major-General Richard O'Connor devised a plan for that advance. There were still substantial Italian forces in this part of Libya – the 60th Division between Tobruk and Derna on the coast road and fifty miles south at Mekili one brigade of the 60th and 160 tanks. On the night of 26 to 27th January the latter retired to Barce, north-east of Benghazi on the coastal route. The plan devised involved splitting the Western Desert force. The 7th Armoured Division, now comprising only 50 cruiser tanks and 95 light tanks, were to speed through the desert and cut the coastal road in two places south of Benghazi. The remainder of the force was to pursue the Italians along the coast road, forcing them west. The navy was still in place to maintain the bombardment of that route and the Royal Air Force by constant attack and bombing had progressively destroyed the Regia Aeronautica and gained control of the skies.

The discovery that Mekili had been abandoned and that the Italians were moving back on Barce led O'Connor to begin his strike by the 7th Armoured Division to the coast south of Benghazi on 30th January, without waiting for fuel supplies to be in place. On 5th February the 7th occupied Msus, and General Crearer sent two detachments forward. A few hours later in the day the coastal road was cut south of Benghazi at Beda Fomm. Colonel John Combe with a force of about 2,000 reached the road two hours before the vanguard of the Italians retreating from Benghazi arrived at his position. He had the 11th Hussars, the 2nd Rifle Brigade and three artillery batteries. The retreating Italians amounted to at least 20,000 with tanks and guns. The odds were ten to one in manpower. The van of the Italian army, amounting to some 5,000 men, came up and attacked against the crashing frontal fire of the Rifle Brigade, E Squadron of the 11th Hussars and the Royal Horse Artillery. As his front was narrow, Colonel Combe almost at once extended it by sending E squadron to the right to prevent the Italians outflanking the position. The Italians persisted with frontal attacks on the Rifles, which failed. At about three hours into the fight the first tanks of the 4th Armoured Brigade, the 7th Hussars arrived to the left and rear of the Italian command. An attack with guns blazing was immediate, spreading destruction and confusion among the retreating troops and refugees. Their trucks were put on fire and in the panic many tried to be taken prisoner. These, for so small a force as the British, posed a problem.

The next day the main column of the Italians came up the road with numerous tanks and guns, being pursued to the rear by the 6th Australian Division, who had taken Benghazi on the 5th. The 6th February for the embattled cordon of troops across the line of retreat was to be a testing day. Under constant attack they managed to destroy 100 tanks and hold on. In the night the Italians persisted in their attempt to break out, attacking nine times and being on each occasion repulsed by the Rifle Brigade. Their last assault came at dawn on 7th February with their remaining 30 tanks. Their forces were squeezed on a twenty-mile stretch of road at risk of naval bombardment and bombing. With the failure of the dawn attack General Berganzoli surrendered. The Italian army in Cyrenaica had been destroyed. In the course of the campaign from 7th December to 7th of February the Western Desert Force had advanced five hundred miles, taken 130,000 prisoners, 400 tanks and 1290 guns. General Wavell wanted to go on west to Tripoli but German aid to the Italians, who had attacked Greece, caused Churchill to direct Wavell to put as his priority assistance to Greece and concentrate the British forces at the Delta in Egypt. Benghazi was to be held, but the 7th Armoured and 6th Australian Divisions were withdrawn to rest and be reformed. They were replaced by a brigade from the 2nd Armoured Division and part of its Support Group and the 9th Armoured Division. Neither were fully trained and had been stripped of tanks and transport to build up the army for Greece. One brigade of the 9th was held at Tobruk with a brigade of motorised Indian Cavalry which was reforming. The gains of the campaign were therefore left to be protected by weakened, relatively inexperienced troops.

12th February 1429

The Battle of the Herrings

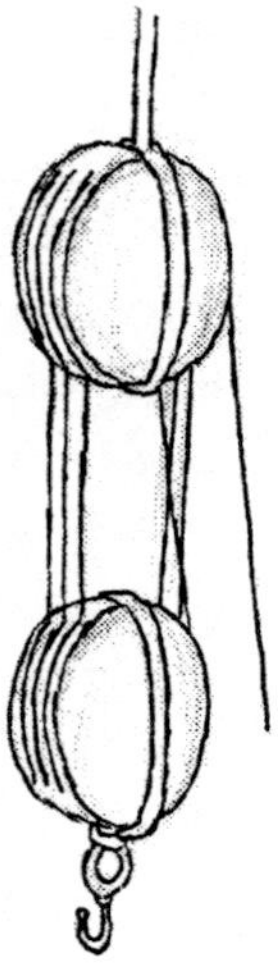

After the battle of Agincourt (25th October 1415) Henry V pursued a campaign to reduce the north of France to his control. In this he was successful, and he was married in Paris to the daughter of the King of France in 1420. His son, Henry VI, became King of England on his father's sudden death in 1422. Up to 1428, there were only limited attempts to enlarge and sustain the areas held by English power, but in 1428 new efforts were made to subdue Northern France, and the English under the Earl of Salisbury advanced to besiege Orleans. He died in October 1428 and was succeeded by the Earl of Suffolk. The English had inadequate forces with which to enclose the whole city of Orleans and carried on the siege through a system of redoubts and fortifications around the city. A problem was supply. In February 1429 Sir John Fastolf, whose name was probably used by Shakespeare for his character Falstaff, was conveying a supplies column south to Orleans from the North of France. A principal part of the merchandise was a load of herrings required for the lenten fast, hence the name of the battle.

The column composed some 300 wagons escorted by a mounted contingent of militia men from Paris and 1,000 archers. On 12th February near Rouvray, a French army under Count Clermont appeared and was making to attack. Sir John Fastolf circled his wagons, leaving two entries filled with archers. The French, unlike the English, had a number of low power cannons and began a bombardment, but the Scots contingent of the French army under Sir John Stuart could not contain itself. His men dismounted and ran in a mass to attack. The English archers fired on them once they were in range and they were forced to withdraw. The French Cavalry then attacked but were halted by the stakes driven to guard the entries and by the deadly archery. Sir John ordered a counter-attack and the archers mounted and fell upon the disorganised French army, which was scattered.

The provisions were delivered and the army before Orleans succoured, the siege being sustained until May. On hearing of this battle, the besieged in Orleans began to negotiate surrender. Before these negotiations were ended, another French army appeared with Joan of Arc at its head, and the siege of Orleans was raised.

Salisbury, 'the great Commander', was killed in the siege and Suffolk was forced by the new French army to retire. The French moved north and the Dauphin was crowned as Charles VII of France. Joan of Arc was captured subsequently and burnt as an incorrigible heretic and apostate. The consequences of the battle were therefore limited, but England retained its extensive power in Northern France until 1444 – 1456 when the English were ejected during the War of the Roses, the civil war in England between the Lancastrians and Yorkists.

The Battle of St. Vincent

In 1796, a strange alliance came into being between revolutionary France and Bourbon Spain. The instigator in Spain was Godoy, "the Prince of Peace", the Chief Minister, who believed that the time had come to settle old scores with England, such as the taking of Gibraltar and attacks in the West Indies.

Godoy thought that, with seventy-six ships of the line and revolutionary France triumphant on land at Castiglione at the end of July 1796, the advantage was in an alliance with France. On 5th October Spain declared war on Britain. The loss of the Spanish ports and the previous success of Buonaparte in May led to the evacuation by the Navy of the Mediterranean. Sir John Jervis returned to Gibraltar. He visited Lisbon, escorted a Brazil-bound convoy into the Atlantic and returned to his station of Cape St. Vincent in order to intercept attempts by the Spanish to take a fleet to join the French in Brest. On 31st January a fleet of twenty-three battle ships and twelve large frigates left Cartagena for Brest.

The Spanish fleet passed the straits on 5th February sailing on to battle the Atlantic gales. On the night of 13th February the British and Spanish fleets drew near to one another. Sea mist gathered, and the Spanish fleet became strung out over a long distance. They were unaware of the presence of the British fleet, whose frigates had shadowed the Spanish vessels, which were sailing in two divisions about three miles apart.

Sir John Jervis, the Commander of the British fleet, was the child of poor parents whose successful career included piloting General Wolfe (see Taking of Quebec September 28th 1759) on his last journey to the heights of Abraham. He had tempered himself to become a man of steel, without fear, having a strong sense of duty and sound judgement. Called by his sailors "Old Jack", he could be humorous (it is said that in rough weather he always took the opportunity to summon the ships' chaplains to the flagship for a conference) and had an eye for pretty women. He commanded in addition to the frigates, only 15 ships of the line – Victory and Britannia (100 guns) Barfleur, Prince George, Namur and Blenheim (98 guns), Diadem (64 guns) and eight two-deckers of 74 guns – Egmont, Culloden, Goliath, Captain, Colossus, Excellent, Irresistible and Orion. He was therefore materially inferior to the Spanish in firepower. His strength lay in the sense of duty, courage and training of his sailors: their "strong nerves and truly manly sense" as he told the Admiralty.

Horatio Nelson, as Commodore, carried his flag on "Captain", with Captain Miller, an American.

On sighting the Spanish fleet, as it emerged from the mist at 5'o clock on 14th February the flag lieutenant on Victory called the odds – "There are twenty sails of the line, Sir John." "There are twenty-three sails of the line, Sir John." "There are twenty-seven sails of the line, Sir John." At last Jervis quietly replied, "even if there are fifty sails of the line I will go through them." Sir John, gradually merging his two columns into a line of battle so close that sterns and bows of the ships almost touched, then took the fleet between the dispersed Spaniards into the gap between their two divisions. The object was to take the line to a point where the fleet could tack into the wind in turn and meet the Spanish ships on a parallel course. The Principe de Asturias (112 guns) tried to break through the line to give succour to the Spanish ships to the leeward. It encountered Victory, whose broadsides rendered its topmasts wrecked and sails rent. It drifted away. Culloden tacked first to pass the Spanish in line and as each ship came up with a Spanish opponent the guns fired, battering the vessels as they passed. At one o'clock the end of the British line was nearing the head of the Spanish fleet. The Spanish fleet could now turn to leeward to join their isolated leeward division before Jervis could catch up, thus realising their whole strength.

Nelson, in Captain, saw the need to prevent that union and without orders attacked. He was supported by Collingwood in the Excellent. The change of direction brought the Captain (the smallest two-decker) straight into the course of the Santissima Trinidad (a four-decker), in which Don Josef de Cordoba carried his flag, and of four more ships. The Captain lost her topmast and had her wheel carried away. She, however, survived and the Spanish line broke in confusion, allowing Jervis to beat back into the battle with the rest of the fleet. Nelson now ordered Captain Miller to drive into the stern of an 80 gun two-decker, the San Nicholas.

That in its turn was entangled with the 112-gun San Josef, which had drifted into it. Gathering a boarding party, Nelson, with a shout of "Victory or Westminster Abbey" ran across the bowsprit into the stern gallery of the San Nicholas, the second on board. The St. Nicholas was taken but as Nelson and his party emerged on the quarter-deck they were fired on from the San Josef. The party then turned their attention to boarding and taking the San Josef. The Spaniards soon surrendered, Nelson receiving the swords of the officers on the quarterdeck. The Victory, as it passed, gave three cheers, as did every ship in the fleet. Throughout the fleet the taking of the San Nicholas, as a step to the taking of the San Josef, was commonly referred to as "Nelson's patent bridge for boarding first rates."

Others that day achieved heroic results: in the course of the action Orion, Excellent and Blenheim engaged the 74-gun Sans Isidro and Salvador, causing their surrender. Four battleships remained in the victors' hands and the Spanish fleet withdrew in the night to Cadiz. The great four-decker the Santissima Trinidad was almost taken but was saved by the Spanish and towed away. The junction of the Spanish and French fleet had been prevented and the Spanish threat proved insubstantial. Nelson was knighted and Sir John Jervis became Earl St. Vincent.

The 6th Earl St. Vincent was ejected from the House of Lords in 2001.

20th Febraury 1653

The Battle of Portland

The first Dutch War broke out between England and Holland as a result of a conflict of commercial interest. Philosophically the Long Parliament, in 1652 reduced to a Rump, and the Dutch Republic were natural allies, but the City of London, whose influence in Parliament was great, looked longingly at Dutch world trade. Some seven-eighths of the Dutch population was dependant on commerce. Fleets of merchantmen, often up to 200 in number, traded through the Baltic, to the East and to the Caribbean. On the return to Holland, passage had to be made up the English Channel and round Britain, or through the North Sea from the Baltic. To protect these fleets, the Dutch States General authorised the increase of the navy, making 226 ships in all. Dutch naval vessels however were smaller than the English, seldom exceeding 40 guns, being mainly converted merchantmen. Van Tromp, the Dutch Admiral, thought that at least 50 English ships were more powerful than his own.

The English Navy had its foundations laid in the ships built by Charles I with Ship Money, and a significant building programme by Parliament between 1649 and 1652.

In 1651 Parliament passed the Navigation Act, restricting trade between Britain and its overseas colonies to British ships. That, together with a demand that foreign warships dip their ensigns to English naval vessels in the British seas (the whole Channel and part of the North Sea) led to the outbreak of fighting in July 1652. In February 1653 the Dutch Admiral Van Tromp appointed a rendezvous with a merchant fleet at the Isle de Ré. Clarendon (in his History of the Rebellion) states the numbers at 100 men-of-war and 150 merchantmen. Others say there were only 75 men-of-war.

Admiral Blake (the Commander of the fleet and leading the White Squadron in the Triumph) awaited the Dutch in the Channel, spread from Portland to the Cotentin peninsula. Admiral Penn commanded the Blue Squadron. Blake, says Clarendon, was inferior in numbers but intercepted the Dutch near Portland. A very sharp battle, said Clarendon, took place from midday until night, the battle proceeding up the Channel. The Triumph took much battering in the fight. Blake was wounded in the thigh and had his Flag Captain and secretary killed. The ships "Vanguard" and "Lion" fought strongly but "Samson" was lost. The English fleet pursued the Dutch up the Channel, pinning them down with Cap Gris

Nez to the leeward. However, in the night the Dutch with great skill extricated their remaining fleet and fled on towards the shelter of their home ports. The English followed up at dawn. In all Van Tromp lost 17 men-of-war and over 50 merchant vessels. Clarendon states that on that morning the Dutch were engaged "so unprosperously that, after the loss of two thousand men, who were thrown overboard, besides a multitude lost, they were glad to leave 50 merchantmen to the English, that they might make their flight more securely." The English lost only 10 ships of their fleet.

Admiral Blake was in fact by origin a soldier, a member of the Long Parliament who won renown by his defence of Taunton. Later, in 1657, he destroyed the Spanish fleet at Santa Cruz, but died of fever while returning to England.

27th February 1814

The Battle of Orthez

In mid-December of 1813 the campaign came to a standstill as the British crossed the River Nive and approached Bayonne (see the Battle of Nivelle 10 November 1813). The intensely wet weather made roads and country impassable almost continuously and Marshal Soult drew off to establish positions on a series of rivers, which Wellington and the British Army needed to cross before penetrating deeply into south-west France. Operations were delayed for two months, and there was some restlessness in London that Wellington was not pressing on. Marshal Soult had been deprived by the Emperor Napoleon of part of his force – three cavalry brigades, two infantry divisions and five batteries of guns – in order to rebuild his army after the defeat at Leipzig by the combined armies of Austria, Prussia and Russia in October. Many of the troops left were inexperienced new recruits. Soult therefore inclined to a defensive strategy to meet the larger combined force of the British, Portuguese and Spanish armies. Wellington however had also lost part of his manpower, as he ordered the Spanish army back to Spain after an orgy of looting and plundering in a captured French town.

Marshal Soult first established a position behind the Gave de Oleran, which flowed from the Pyrenees north-west to join the River Adour. The strategy adopted by the Duke of Wellington was to move north-east with the object of turning his position. Picton's 3rd Division was sent on to attack the French forward positions at Sauveterre and Navarreux, while Hill moved to the east to cross the river. Picton met strong opposition at Sauveterre and was repulsed. However, a bridge of boats was constructed across the river by Hill further east without opposition, and by the night of 24th February the army, 20,000 strong, was across the river on the French left flank. Soult immediately moved to withdraw to the next river line, the Gave de Pau at Orthez.

The position taken up by the French was a strong one. Behind the town of Orthez, which stood on the river, there ran from east to west a ridge through which the line of retreat for Soult ran to the north-east. In the section of the ridge from the Dax road north the ridge threw out a number of spurs. Marshal Soult, conscious of the weakness of his army, decided to station the army on the ridge back from the river save around Orthez. The allied army would thus have to attack strong points up hill. The right wing under General Reille, comprising the Divisions of Rouget and Taupin, guarded the approach up the western end

41

of the ridge to the village of St Boes on the Dax Road. The centre, commanded by Count d'Erlon and consisting of Foy and Darmagnac's Divisions, lay on the ridge and filled the gap between the ridge and the town of Orthez. The town itself was guarded by Harispe's Division, and the east end of the ridge near the road to Sault de Bavailles was held by Villatte's Division, which Soult hoarded as a guard for any retreat. The French army comprised 33,000 infantry, 3,000 cavalry and 48 cannons. The Duke of Wellington's force was larger, amounting to 40,000 infantry, 3,000 cavalry and 54 cannons.

On the 26th Wellington set down his directions for the battle, sitting in the rain under an umbrella provided by a passing officer. The plan was to attack the French strongly on both flanks and having defeated the flank divisions, roll up the army from each end. Marshal Beresford the same day crossed the Gave de Pau west of the town of Orthez virtually unopposed save by patrolling cavalry. The troops moved forward to engage at 8.30a.m. on 27th February, mounting the spurs of the ridge where the French were embedded on the British left wing, while Sir Rowland Hill began the attack on Orthez on the British right. Both wings were weighted in accordance with the tactics, while Sir Thomas Picton's Third Division held the centre. General Cole's 4th Division, which was to spearhead the attack on the left up the spur to St Boes village, comprised the largest number of units which had seen action since 1812 (the 27th (Inniskillen) Regiment of Foot, the 40th (2nd Somerset) Regiment of Foot, the 11th (North Devonshire) Regiment of Foot, the 7th (Royal Fusiliers) Regiment of Foot, the 23rd (Royal Welsh Fusiliers) Regiment of Foot and the 48th (Northamptonshire) Regiment of Foot. Sir Rowland Hill's 2nd Division had four long-serving regiments back to 1812; (the 50th (West Kent) Regiment of Foot, the 71st (Highland Light Infantry) Regiment of Foot, the 34th (Cumberland) Regiment of Foot and the 39th (Dorsetshire) Regiment of Foot. General Walker's 7th Division contained three; the 52nd (Oxford Light Infantry) Regiment of Foot the 51st (Second Yorkshire West Riding) Regiment of Foot and the 95th (Rifle Corps) Regiment of Foot. The 6th Division contained only the 36th (Herefordshire) Regiment of Foot. The remainder of the force was made up of regiments brought to the Peninsula later than 1812 and of course the Portuguese Division, including the seasoned 1st Cacadores. Qualitatatively therefore the most experienced soldiers were on the wings.

The 4th Division attacked, mounted the hill and moved up the spur to St Boes in a fusillade of fire and initially succeeded in pushing Taupin's French out of the village. The latter rallied and repulsed the British, driving them from the village, only in their turn to be driven back. The French guns meanwhile pounded the artillery on the left wing and much of the artillery was put out of action. In the centre Picton's 3rd Division could not move forward until St Boes was secure and had to wait under decimating fire. A second attack by the French led to Cole retiring from most of the village; Brigadier Ross and two-thirds of his men had become casualties. The 1st Cacadores went to assist the Light Division. Cole called for reinforcements. Picton committed the 3rd Division in the centre to attack along a spur towards Darmagnac and Foy. The former started to push back the 3rd Division along the spur. Meanwhile in the east

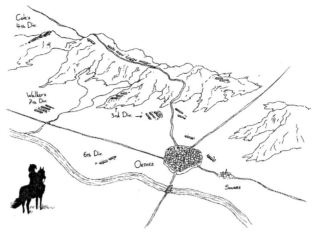

Hill pressed Harispe hard at Orthez. Foy continued to be pressed by the infantry, and so effective a bombardment that his force began to crumble. He commenced gradually to retire, drawing Darmagnac, who was being pushed by the 3rd Division, with him on his right and Harispe on the left. The 7th and part of the Light Division were then sent in by Wellington to reinforce the 4th and savage fighting again occurred around St Boes. Harispe's retirement cleared the way for Hill to get two divisions of his forces across the river east of the town on the French left flank. The withdrawal of Darmagnac affected Rouget, and a gap opened between the retiring French army and Taupin at St.Boes. The 52nd Regiment forced their way up and into the gap and Taupin's force left the spur in disorder. Harispe's retreat enabled him, with Villatte's waiting reserve, to screen the retreat which, after twelve o'clock was in flood towards Sault de Navailles. Towards the end of the engagement Wellington, who was riding with the Portuguese commander General Alava, was hit by a round shot ball which struck the scabbard of his sword, leading only to severe bruising and inability to gallop about for some days, as was his wont.

The disorganised French streamed north-east towards Aire on the upper Adour, falling into ever-mounting disorder as the conscripted young soldiers deserted. Initially the Allied pursuit was languid but on 2nd March Sir Rowland Hill forced Harispe out of the town. Meanwhile Marshal Beresford advanced on Bordeaux, from which the French army withdrew. It was entered on 12th March and the Bourbon Lilies of France flew again over the town.

The Battle of Orthez was not an easy engagement, and Wellington's tactics had not carried the day until the French left centre began to dissolve. On the British left the resistance had been particularly strong. Allied casualties amounted to 2,200, although the French lost 4,000 with 1,350 prisoners. In the later nineteenth century twenty-seven Regiments carried "Orthez" as an Honour on their colours.

March

5th	The Battle of Borrosa	1811
6th	The Battle of St.James	1426
10th	The Battle of Marbella	1705
21st	The Battle of Aboukir	1801
24th	The Crossing of the Rhine	1945
27th	The Turning of the Mareth Line	1943
28th	The Battle of Matapan	1941

5th March 1811

The Battle of Borrosa

At the end of 1809 the only European nations still resisting the Emperor Napoleon were Britain and Portugal. Elsewhere, apart from Spain, all resistance had ended and the nations had accepted the overall hegemony of France. In Spain, the people had risen up against their French occupiers and Napoleon's brother, King Joseph. Spanish armies remained in the field but they were of poor quality, often ineptly led. Marquis Wellesley, Wellington's brother, had reflected this state of affairs in a remark to a Spanish deputy, while in Seville, that he would not trust the safety of a favourite dog to the whole Spanish army. The Spanish were however effective in *guerilla* warfare in the countryside, where informal bands, sometimes as large as regiments, constantly harassed the French, necessitating the protection of messengers by troops of cavalry and the spreading of garrisons throughout the countryside. Priests, peasants, deserters from the armies all participated in the insurgency against the French, and cruelty and savagery were used as a weapon by both sides. Sanchez, a typical leader of one of these bands provided, for example, to Wellington a constant supply of decapitated couriers and their dispatches. Another boiled a general alive and sawed another in half. The French army therefore, amounting to 350,000, had its power dissipated by the need to deal with these partisans throughout the country. By early 1810 the French had succeeded in bringing under control the centre and north of the country. King Joseph and Marshal Soult therefore decided to set out to conquer the south and Andalusia. The Spanish were driven back and the Regency Council was forced to return to Cadiz, the Spanish naval base, which was besieged by Marshal Victor. It was vital to Britain to keep Spain in the field and so in early 1810 the Prime Minister, Lord Liverpool, decided to send a force under Sir Thomas Graham to help to defend the city.

James Graham, later Lord Lynedoch (see the Taking of San Sebastian 8th September 1813) was born in 1748 at Balgowan, and became the heir to extensive estates. In 1774 he married Mary Cathcart, whose uncle was Sir William Hamilton, husband of Lord Nelson's mistress and a beauty whose captivating portrait was painted by Gainsborough (it is still in the Scottish National Gallery). Always strong, vigorous and a man of courage, just before Christmas of that year, when the carriage, in which were his wife and her sister, was held up by three footpads in Park Lane in Mayfair on the way to a party at Hay Hill, he flung himself on the leader of the three, who had opened the carriage door, pistol in hand, and wrestled him to the ground, the other two thieves running off. After marriage he retired to Balgowan, where the Perthshire Hounds kennels were next to the stable yard and he indulged his passion for hunting, salmon fishing and shooting. Mary was of poor health and they began to travel to the Mediterranean for the sun, on one occasion in 1780, after a chase of fourteen hours having their ship taken by the American privateer, the Cicero, whose Captain Hill treated them with great civility, took none of their possessions and put them ashore at Vigo in Spain. When his wife died, Thomas Graham was desolate and became a volunteer aide-de-camp to Captain Elphinstone at Toulon in 1793. On his return to Britain he was given a commission to raise a regiment of ten companies. He acted with expedition and the 90th Regiment (Perthshire volunteers) came into being, later becoming the 2nd Battalion of the Cameronians. At the age of forty-five his military career had begun. He was a friend of Sir John Moore, whom he had met in Gibraltar, and beside him at Corunna in January 1809 when Moore was struck by a round shot ball and fell at the feet of Graham's horse.

The city of Cadiz was in an almost impregnable position from the point of view of defence. It lay at the northern end of a five mile isthmus running between the sea and the inner harbour on the west and stretching out from the Isla de Leon, which was separated from the mainland by the Rio Santi Petri, a waterway varying in width from three-quarters of a mile to one mile and guarded by salt marshes on the mainland and on the south-east of the island. The French investment line ran from Rota to the north of the Bay of Cadiz, south to Chiclana and west to the Bermeja Ridge, south of the half-mile wide mouth of the Rio Santi Petri to the Atlantic Ocean. South of the Bermeja Ridge, separated by pine woods, lay the Barrosa Ridge east of the coast road south to Conil.

Graham arrived at Cadiz at the end of March 1810 and on the 25th inspected the defences. His mission was both political and military - to bolster Spanish morale and effectiveness - and was complicated by the responsibility he held towards three masters; the Prime Minister, Lord Liverpool, Sir David Dundas, the Commander in Chief and Wellington as Commander in the Peninsula. In the end he was made second-in-command to Wellington but left on independent commission in Cadiz. His inspection of the defences showed him that they were virtually non-existent and ineffective and with characteristic determination he set about remedying the position. The absence of available tools delayed the work and made it difficult. Fortunately the French, who were pre-occupied with organising a fleet of small boats, were quiescent during 1810, taking only Fort Metagorda opposite the isthmus on the east of the inner harbour. General Blake, the Spanish Commander, and Graham agreed to organise an attack to raise the siege against the French. Graham and Wellington were opposed to the scheme but acquiesced in the interest of the alliance. In fact the campaign never took place and Blake was superseded by General La Pena. The latter lacked judgement and was weak, ineffective and indecisive; he was known even to his own troops as the Lady Manuela. Graham was given a specific direction not to join in unnecessary or inexpedient operations. By the end of the year Victor had been reinforced by shipbuilders and marines; however in January 1811 a large part of his force had to be detached to assist in the protection of Badajoz. Victor was left with an army of 19,000 opposed to 25,000 Spanish, British and Portuguese in Cadiz. The disparity in forces led Graham to consider, with the Spanish, the notion of a dual assault upon the French. The final plan involved an attack by 4,000 from the south of the Isle de Pena across a bridge of boats and one by 14,000 (9000 Spanish and 5000 British) from Chiclana, to be co-ordinated and taking place on 3rd March. Because the greater part of the latter force was Spanish, Graham, with reluctance and some distrust, accepted for diplomatic reasons that La Pena should be in command.

On 21st February Sir Thomas Graham and the British and Portuguese contingent left Cadiz for Tarifa. Heavy weather at sea forced the expedition to divert to Algeciras to land, where they bivouacked in the open. A two-day march was necessary to reach Tarifa, fifteen miles away across the southern ridges of the Sierra del Ronda where they debouched to the sea. The roads were poor, rock strewn and almost impassable for wheel transport. As so often in Spain, rations were unobtainable. The marching troops arrived at their destination in ice and heavy torrents of rain. It was not until 27th February that La Pena and the Spanish arrived. At last the march along the coast fifty miles back to Cadiz began, the Spanish making up the van and the British the rear.

The line of march was affected by La Pena's irresolution and incompetence. After the first twenty miles north the road diverged, the right fork continuing via Casas Viejas to Medina Sidonia, the left to Vejer and Conil and going along the coast north towards Chiclana. Le Pena chose the inland route north to Medina Sidonia and took the force over impassable hilly country, wading through streams as far as Casas Viejas. There he heard that Marshal Victor had sent 3,000 troops to Medina Sidonia to oppose him and so he decided to retreat back to the Vejer road, as he could not take Victor by surprise. The troops had struggled an unnecessary ten miles. At eight o'clock on 3rd March the marching column started again but was soon in trouble. A lagoon lay alongside the route to Vejar, the Embalse de Celemin, and with the rains the road causeway had become covered by three feet of water. The Spanish vanguard had piled up in front of the waters and blocked the way in a confused mass. Sir Thomas Graham came up to the edge, had the depth tested and stationed men along the causeway. He then dismounted and stood in the water to cheer the troops on as they crossed.

The delay caused by the impotence of General La Pena had not been communicated to General Zayas in Cadiz. On 2nd March, in accordance with the plan, he prepared his bridge of boats across the southern entrance of the Rio

Santi Petri and on the 3rd mounted a frontal attack on the French lines. He was however, being unsupported from the south, thrown back and repulsed.

Having passed Vejer, La Pena decided on the morning of the 4th that he would not set out until the day's end for yet another night march to Conil and Chiclana. There had been a number of such marches and they had exhausted the troops. In the event the column started at six o'clock on a march which was to last fourteen hours. As it approached the French lines, Sir Thomas Graham had seen the importance of the Barrosa ridge to the east of the road and urged La Pena to occupy it. Two Spanish brigades and two battalions of Light Infantry were sent and took the summit.

Marshal Victor had anticipated the coming of La Pena's force and prepared a trap for the marching column. General Villatte's division was placed on and at the Bermeja ridge near the sea and his other two divisions, commanded by General Ruffin and General Leval, were sent south to wait on the flank of the marching column in the Chiclana Forest. The Spanish vanguard and General Lardizabal's column marched on and attacked La Villatte, who was also taken from the rear by General Zayas's force, which had issued across a restored bridge, and he retreated east across the Almanga Creek. La Pena ordered Graham to move his divisions through the woods as a reserve support for the Spanish. Meanwhile the Spanish troops abandoned the Barrosa Ridge, leaving the two battalions of British Light Infantry. As Graham moved through the woods, an officer warned him that two French divisions were marching on Barrosa in column to his flank and rear. He immediately reversed the line of march. General Dilke was deputed to look to Ruffin to the rear on the right and General Wheatley to deal with Leval on the left. Colonel Browne's five hundred light infantry were descending the ridge, when Graham met them on horseback, and Ruffin was deploying with his division on the abandoned ridge. Quickly he ordered the three companies of the 9th (East Norfolk Regiment of Foot), the 38th (North Gloucestershire Regiment of Foot) and the 82nd (Prince of Wales' Volunteers Regiment of Foot) to close up to prevent them being seen as a string of skirmishers, and led them back to retake the hill. They were to be backed by Dilke and their task was to delay the column until his division could come up.

Led by Colonel Browne, who told the men that General Graham had given them the honour of being the first to attack, and singing Hearts of Oak are Our Men, they advanced uphill. Ruffin with his whole division had his guns unlimbered and met them on the open slope with a hail of shot. 200 out of 470 fell at the first cannonade; the men closed ranks and marched on, despite further losses, to within one hundred yards from the French, where shielded by boulders they kept up constant fire on the French column. Dilke pressed on to back up the attack; his hurrying regiments in the move forward fell into some disorder, but they mounted the hill steadfastly and speedily. Breathless, the 1st and

3rd Guards Regiments and the 67th (South Hampshire Regiment of Foot), toiled up the slope spraying the French column with their deadly discharges of fire. The French Division broke and Dilke's men drove 3,000 retreating soldiers before them over the ridge.

Graham had also to deal with General Leval's Division on his flank on the east edge of the Chiclana pinewood forest. A similar tactic was employed; 700 light infantry under Colonel Bushe and Colonel Barnard were to move speedily to check the French column, allowing General Wheatley to back them up. 400 men of the 95th (Rifles) and 200 Portuguese Cacadores were deputed for the task and emerged to hold the column. Barnard was wounded and Bushe killed in the attack before they began to fall back, but by that time Wheatley with his regiments, the Coldstream Guards, the 28th (North Gloucestershire Regiment of Foot) and the 82nd (Prince of Wales' Volunteers Regiment of Foot) had come up with ten guns and after they had destroyed the French 8th Regiment of Foot, Leval with his Division retreated. An Eagle was taken by Sergeant Masterton of the 87th Foot and four guns. General Ruffin, who had been captured, told Graham of his surprise by so rash an attack made upon his Division. The allied casualties were 1,740, about one third of the force, and the French 2,400 out of 7,000. The battered French force under Marshal Victor drew off towards Chiclana.

During the two-hour struggle General La Pena and his Spaniards had remained inactive by the sea near the Bermeja Ridge, and no attempt was made to send help to the outnumbered British. Graham with his sore losses and no reserve was unable effectively to pursue the French. His men, after a fourteen-hour night march and the battle, were exhausted, without provisions and rest. General La Pena made no move to pursue Victor and so Graham decided to return to Cadiz. He was soon followed there by the Spanish. Victor to his surprise was therefore left unpursued and was almost immediately able to re-establish his siege of the city. The victory had been thrown away by Britain's Spanish allies.

Sir Thomas Graham was properly reticent about his views concerning the conduct of General La Pena, but the latter soon claimed the victory as his own and criticised Graham and his troops. The Regency Council established an inquiry, but Graham's anger was ignited by an account of the campaign written by General Lascy, La Pena's chief of staff. Sir Thomas immediately sent Colonel Frederick Ponsonby to ask for an apology and stating his willingness, if none were forthcoming, to face him in a duel. Lascy at once apologised, unwilling to measure arms with Graham. A similar challenge was sent to General La Pena, asking for a public disapproval of Lascy's comments. He too was unwilling to face Graham, apologised and promised to require Lascy to withdraw his comments. In late June Graham was recalled from Cadiz to join Wellington as his second-in-command of the British Army in the north of the Peninsula.

6th March 1426
The Battle of St.James de Beuvron

This battle was an incident in the struggle after the death of Henry V in 1422 to defend the conquests which followed the battle of Agincourt (25th October 1415) and the right of King Henry VI, the son of the victor of Agincourt, to be King of France, under the terms of the Treaty of Troyes (1420) made by Charles VI. The Duke of Brittany, John V, decided in 1424 to abandon his support for England and adhere to the Dauphin, the son of Charles VI who claimed the throne and was based at Bourges. An English army of small numbers invaded Brittany and established a base at the town of St.James. The Constable of France, Arthur de Richemont with an army, it is said, of 16,000 moved to assist his brother the Duke of Brittany and besieged St.James, which was held by Sir Thomas Rampston with a garrison of 600. On 6th March a strenuous assault lasting all day was made by the French. Night fell and the defenders resolved to respond by attacking the enemy. The bulk of the garrison quietly slipped out by a sally port and with cries of "Salisbury (a Commander of the English army in France with an outstanding record of success in battle) and St.George" attacked the French besiegers in the rear. The surprised French did not withstand the attack and fell back, some being forced into a lake and drowned, and some fleeing back to their base. Here panic set in; tents were burned and the camp abandoned, the army retreating away. Arthur de Richemont retreated to Anjou. After the victory an English army arrived two days later and the forces were united.

The importance of this battle, although not long lasting, was strategic. England had only sustained its position in Northern France and elsewhere by reason of its alliance with the Duke of Burgundy, a signatory of the Treaty of Troyes, and up to 1424 the support of the Duke of Brittany. After the battle of St.James the latter returned in 1427 to the English alliance.

10th March 1705

The Battle of Marbella

In 1700 Charles II, King of Spain, died childless, leaving no direct heir. The nearest claimants were respectively in the families of the King of France and of the Holy Roman Emperor of Austria. After diplomatic attempts to resolve the succession, the vast lands of Spain were given to the French king's grandson who, backed by Louis XIV, became Philip V of Spain. The Emperor of Austria claimed the throne for his second son, the Archduke Charles. Louis XIV proceeded to occupy the Spanish Netherlands (Flanders and Belgium,) seized the barrier forts designed to protect Holland, and sought to exploit the Spanish overseas empire for the benefit of France. These actions led to war and a coalition with which to fight it, including Britain, Austria, Holland, Prussia and other states. Campaigning was to take place in Hannover, Germany and in the Mediterranean. The Duke of Marlborough and his political supporters saw the virtue of striking at France and Spain from the Mediterranean, and naval forces and troops were committed there. In 1704 Gibraltar was taken. Various attempts were made to besiege the fortress and recover it. After the success at the Battle of Malaga, the larger part of the British fleet sailed home leaving a small squadron under Admiral Leake at Lisbon.

Throughout the winter of 1704 – 1705 vigorous attempts were made by Marshal Tessé with 12,000 men to assault Gibraltar as part of an eight-month siege. Sir John Leake's force was deployed to protect the garrison and command the Bay of Algeciras. In February 1705, the French Admiral Pointis was sent with 12 ships of the line and seven frigates to assist the assault of Marshal Tessé. Before the storming of Gibralter could begin, however, a westerly gale familiar in the Straits, the *Poniente*, began to blow powerfully, sending most of the French fleet to leeward, but leaving Admiral Pointis with only five ships. The unusual weather of the Straits then probably played its part. As the Poniente blew itself out, mist formed in the eastern straits where the cool Atlantic water met the *Levante*, (the east wind) which can often build, following a pause, after the westerly gale. Sir John Leake coming out of this mist at daybreak fell upon the French. Three out of five three-deckers were taken and the others were driven ashore and burnt. The ships previously driven by the gale along the Straits, at the sound of battle made sail in order to escape to Toulon. As a result Marshall Tessé was forced to raise the siege and Gibraltar and the Straits were held. As a naval base Gibraltar was immediately of little use, being without the facilities and stores to fit out the fleet, but its retention by virtue of the Treaty of Utrecht of 1715 was of long-term significance.

The date of this battle is given sometimes as 28 February. It was the custom of the sailors of Queens Anne's navy to use as log dates the old-style dating, some eleven days behind the new style calendar. The log date has been adopted here.

21st March 1801

The Battle of Aboukir

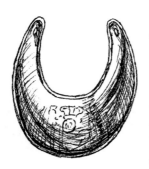

After his victories in Italy General Buonaparte returned a hero to the public in France. The governing Directorate were uneasy at the potential threat his popular support posed to their position and accordingly in 1798, in order to be rid of him, acceded to his strategy of striking at Britain by seizing Egypt and gaining control of the Ottoman Empire, which at the time stretched from Belgrade to Basra. Buonaparte was appointed General of the army to carry out the task and in May 1798 with the navy under command of Admiral Brueys and four hundred transports, he left Toulon. He managed to elude Nelson, took the surrender of Malta from the Knights of St John and arrived at Aboukir Bay and landed on 2nd July. While Egypt was nominally ruled by Murad Bey, as viceroy for the Supreme Porte in Constantinople, effective power rested with the Mamelukes. Within twenty days Buonaparte and his army, comprising largely veterans of his Italian campaign, defeated the Mamelukes and had seized the whole of lower Egypt, making his capital in Cairo. On 1st August Lord Nelson attacked and destroyed the French fleet at Aboukir Bay (see the Battle of the Nile, 1st August 1798). The French were thus marooned in Egypt without the means of returning to France. The only recourse for Buonaparte and the French was to seek to move on the Turks and their armies in Syria and to hope to return by land through the Ottoman Empire. At the time Syria was the name given to present day Syria, Lebanon, Palestine, Israel and Jordan. The march north would be through parched deserts, and wastes with nothing but brackish waters and few sources of food. On 11th March 1799 the march began with 12,000 men, of whom half were to be lost in the campaign. The push north was to come to an end after the French failed to take Acre and retreated on 20th May, reaching Cairo on 14th June.

In July 1799 the Ottoman Government sent a force of 15,000 troops under Mustapha Bey to attack Alexandria. The troops were landed at Aboukir Bay on the isthmus and soon overcame Aboukir town and castle at the east end, slaughtering the French garrison of 300. He then formed up his army, leaving a flank lying on open sands. Five days after the seizure of Aboukir, Sir Sidney Smith arrived with a squadron of the British fleet. The news of the landing was brought to Buonaparte in Cairo and he moved with alacrity. On 23rd July he arrived at Alexandria and decided to attack immediately. The Turks were easily routed and fled towards the sea, only a very small proportion of them being saved by the British fleet. Sir Sidney Smith, having courteously entertained a French officer sent on a truce mission, provided him with newspapers describing disasters in Italy suffered by the French for the perusal of Buonaparte. According to de Bourienne, Buonaparte's private secretary, the latter read the papers and remarked. "Ah! The fools have lost Italy. All the fruits of our victories have disappeared: I must leave Egypt". On 23rd August Buonaparte deserted his army, sailing with five hundred men on the frigates La Murion and La Carriére. On 8th October 1799 he arrived at Frejus, having escaped the surveillance of the Royal Navy. General Kleber was left in command. At the end of the year Buonaparte became 1st Consul and effective ruler of France.

In the spring of 1800 the British Government nerved itself to send troop reinforcements to the Mediterranean, with the expectation that they might be based on Minorca to assist the Austrians in Italy. Sir Ralph Abercrombie finally left on 15th May 1800 with Major-Generals Moore and Hutchinson to collect together armies already at sea. The troops were to spend most of the year being transported around the Mediterranean. In the autumn of 1800 Henry Dundas, later 1st Viscount Melville, against the opposition of William Pitt the younger, persuaded the Government to destroy the French in Egypt. Orders for the expedition were given on 6th October and on 24th November Abercrombie and Moore reached Malta. The army of 16,000 collected, and escorted by the Mediterranean fleet, the expedition sailed and anchored in Marmoris Bay in January. Six weeks were to be spent by the army and navy under the tutelage of Major-General Moore, practising amphibian landings from the sea onto the beach. The force was to co-operate with the Turks and obtain supplies for the invasion of Egypt. In fact, not much help was to be gained from the Turks. Moore visited their army in January at Jaffa and found it to be a "wild, ungovernable mob" with a corrupt and incompetent leadership. Abercrombie himself was pessimistic, thinking his troops ill-equipped and concerned at the absence of cavalry.

The French position in Egypt was not without strength. There were 24,000 troops including cavalry. Supplies of ordinance and stores had arrived in Alexandria on frigates from Toulon and a squadron under Admiral Gantaume was at sea with the object of succouring the garrison. Any British landing would be against an experienced force and would be an operation not without risk. On 2nd March, escorted by the fleet under Lord Keith, two hundred transports anchored in Aboukir Bay.

Aboukir Bay (otherwise called Lake Maadieh) was enclosed on the west by an isthmus upon which stood Aboukir town and castle. The isthmus stretched west, bounded by the Mediterranean on the north and on the south by Aboukir Lake and Lake Mareotis. The latter at the time of arrival by the British was a dry lake. At the west end of the isthmus lay the town of Alexandria. The isthmus contained a ridge of varying height and its surface comprised rock, sand and scrub. A few groups of palm trees sprinkled the desert isthmus and nearer to Alexandria there were extensive ruins of Graeco-Roman buildings breaking the surface. The army was to land at the west beach of Aboukir Bay, commanded on the north by the castle of Aboukir and on the south by the Block House.

Five days of strong winds and heavy swell precluded landing and the French garrisoning Alexandria had the opportunity to station a force at the east end of the isthmus. On the 7th orders were given to land the next day. At 2 a.m. a rocket went up from the Foudroyant to give the signal for the landing force to begin to embark in the craft assembled for the landing. On the night General Moore was in overall command of the landing itself, but was directly to command the 23rd (Royal Welsh Fusiliers) Regiment of Foot, the 28th (North Gloucestershire) Regiment of Foot, and the 40th (2nd Somersetshire) Regiment of Foot on the right and General Oates the 42nd (Royal Highland) Regiment of Foot, the 58th (Rutlandshire) Regiment of Foot, and the Corsican Rangers. The Guards Regiments (Cold stream and Scots Guards) were to land to support the 42nd and 58th. The sector of the beach to the front of Moore's troops comprised a desert hill rising steeply to about two hundred feet. The sector on the left was a plain between the hill and the lakeshore.

The men clambered down into the flat-bottomed landing boats fifty men to a boat. Having embarked, the boats were mustered in three lines, the first comprising some fifty-eight at fifty-foot intervals. The men sat upright in the boats, each equipped with three days of rations and sixty rounds of shot. The second line of eighty-seven cutters preceded a third line pulling launches bearing fourteen field guns. This line was commanded by Sir Sidney Smith, the hero of the siege of Gaza. The distance to the landing beach was some five miles and the seamen of the fleet had to row the longboats lustily, drawing the beach boats over that distance. Keeping proper lines in order, the flotilla began to pull into the beach around 8 a.m. with the sun risen high above: the lines of boats were enfiladed by guns from Aboukir Castle to the North and the Block House to the south. General Friant with 2,000 men waited on the beach and in the dunes in order to repulse the landing. Where the plain met the beach, French infantry peppered the boats with volleys of musquetry: men toppled and two boats carrying the Coldstream Guards were hit by gunfire and sunk. Naval vessels bombarded the beach as the troops went in, rowing through the rushing surf which overwhelmed some of the boats. The first of the flat-bottomed boats to reach the shore carried Captain Cochrane, who leapt onto the beach, and the first rank of the boats grounding almost in line, the troops waded in and formed up in lines and companies under their colours. Encouraged by General Moore they rushed through the scrub and rock up the hill, not firing until the summit was reached. Firing a massive volley they fixed bayonets and rushed down on the 61st demi-brigade, which was pushed back and broken.

The artillery beached and the guns dragged up by 300 seamen began to enfilade the French. On the left the 42nd and 58th and the Corsican Rangers were heavily attacked by the enemy, supported by dragoons. The Guards behind them, assaulted by the cavalry, moved to their support in some confusion. Order re-established, they stormed down on the French on their flank, advancing and pushing them back into the plain. In the afternoon, the beach secure, the rest of the army landed. The Navy had lost 100 casualties and the army 625, of whom 135 were killed and missing. Sir Ralph Abercrombie, lacking cavalry, did not immediately push forward and the army rested during the cold desert night. It is said that soldiers of the 92nd (Highland) Regiment of Foot spent much of the night discussing how the Bible statement that there was no rain in Egypt was justified in the light of the showers which had been experienced. To find water the troops, on the advice of Sir Sidney Smith, dug down to the roots of the palm trees. The next morning the army pushed on, only lightly resisted by cavalry patrols and skirmishers, for some four miles through deep loose sand in order to establish a new position nearer Alexandria. A force was left to besiege Aboukir and the castle surrendered on 12th March.

The French for their part withdrew to take up a new line among the archaeological ruins between the sea and the extreme west end of Lake Aboukir. The army was brought up and at 6 a.m. on 13th March again attacked the entrenched French. The Reserve on the right, separated from the Guards by a small valley, went forward. As the line moved on, two regiments of Scots pushed ahead of the general mass. The French thought that the 90th (Perthshire Light Infantry) were dismounted cavalry and the French cuirassiers came on towards them. As they deployed, the young Colonel Hill (later General Sir Rowland Hill, victor of Arroyo de Molinos (see the battle of Arroyo de Molinos, 28th October 1811) avoided death when musquetry shot hit the peak of his cap. The 90th moved into line six to eight deep to receive the shock. At fifty yards the volleys crashed into the French horsemen, savaging their ranks. As they whirled round, the 92nd in its turn ravaged their ranks. Both regiments, although hard pressed, held the line and gradually the army pushed the French out of position into a plain before the heights of Nicropolis. Being unable to hold the plain, the British army withdrew to the line along the ruins taken from the French. They were now eight miles from Alexandria.

The bulk of the French forces in Egypt were in Cairo, and on hearing of the landing, General Menou, who had succeeded General Kleber, decided to move to meet the threat. Kleber had been stabbed to death by a Muslim fanatic on 14th June 1800. Menou and his reinforcements reached Alexandria on 20th March. He decided to attack at once. The French force amounted to 12,000 men and the British about 13,000, the army having been reduced by casualties and sickness. The time between 13th March and the 20th had been spent fortifying the line under Moore's supervision. On the left, covering the plain, two batteries were embedded, and a redoubt was thrown up on the lower slope of a towering roofless ruin on the right, close to the Mediterranean. The weakest point in the line was on the left where Moore discovered that the dry lake, Lake Mareotis, could bear cavalry.

An Arab spy had warned the British of the approach of Menou and the French army. The 21st was the day upon which General Moore was the field officer in command. He remained until 4.00 a.m. with the piquets on the left, but hearing the commotion on the right of the French assembly and approach, moved to the right where the 'Reserve' Division was stationed. The approach of the French, drums beating, with shouts of 'Vive La République' and 'Vive La France' could be heard in the darkness as the main columns marched to attack the roman ruin and half-built redoubt. French troops meanwhile under General Reynier attacked on the left near to Lake Mareotis. The 28th (North Gloucestershire) Regiment of Foot were the first to encounter the marching French columns of General Lanusse and discerned their cap badges glinting in the moving flashes of the battle in the darkness. They stood ready until the French were within fifty yards, before unleashing their battering volleys. The 58th (Rutlandshire) Regiment of Foot, immediately to their right between them and the 'redoubt' and sea were engaged next, struggling with the experienced French marching columns. Meanwhile a contingent of French cavalry had broken through behind the 42nd (Royal Highland) Regiment and had begun to attack them in the rear. The 42nd, holding off the infantry in front, faced about to fight the dragoons at the rear.

Meanwhile Moore had called up the 23rd (Royal Welsh Fusiliers) Regiment and four flank companies of the 40th (2nd Somersetshire) Regiment of Foot to the support of the 58th and embattled 28th Regiments. The 42nd forced back the French cavalry towards the 23rd and 40th and they were pushed on to the ruin to be taken by the 58th. Led by General Moore, who had been slightly wounded, the 42nd then moved to their flank toward the redoubt, only to have to meet a new French attacking column and cavalry. Sir Ralph Abercrombie had come up to the front accompanied by only one or two officers and was to be seen encouraging the 42nd near its rear, "My brave Highlanders! Remember your country! Remember your forefathers!" The 42nd were to charge the new column vigorously and went too far, meeting the French cavalry and having to fight them individually on foot. The cavalry had broken past to the rear of the 28th, who still faced the on-coming infantry. Their Colonel ordered the rear rank to face about and firm fire as if from a single shot hit the French dragoons, to be followed by further volleys. The reserves brought up by Moore were still near, helping to resist the strong infantry attack on the 58th in the ruins and half-built redoubt. As the French cavalry moved back and forth between the steady British troops, Sir Ralph Abercrombie was attacked by a small knot of dragoons, defended himself with his sabre and would have been cut down had the dragoon attacking him not been shot. His aide-de-camp offered his horse, but as he moved to dismount had his head shot off. Abercrombie was wounded in the thigh by round shot, but stayed on encouraging the embattled troops. The 40th then marched to the help of the 42nd firing on the dragoons who had broken them.

The dragoons were driven off, but not without casualties among the 42nd. By 9.30 a.m. shortages of shot were developing and the French began to pull back to reform away from the line, although firing still persisted on both sides. About ten o'clock Sir Ralph Abercrombie allowed himself to be carried to the Foudroyant. An officer covered him with a soldier's blanket apologising that there was no other covering. Abercrombie turned to him, "Only a soldier's blanket! A soldier's blanket is of great consequence: you must send me the name of the soldier to whom it belongs." The French started to withdraw to Alexandria, but no pursuit could be made because of the shortage of cavalry. The French had lost 3,000 and the British 1,500. The 42nd lost over half its strength and Moore said of his army that he had never seen men more determined to do their duty.

The victors of Lodi and Arcola, who under Buonaparte had blown away the Austrians and Italians, had been defeated. Slowly the army moved up to besiege Alexandria, but in the absence of a siege-train it could only be taken by starving the garrison. A Turkish army arrived on 25th March which besieged Rosetta, the town falling on 19th April. By 26th May the French had been expelled from the Delta. To help blockade Alexandria the British on 13th April opened the derelict canal between Lakes Aboukir and Mareotis, flooding a number of villages, but breaking potential communications to the south. Only Alexandria and Cairo remained in French hands. In mid July, the army now being commanded by General Hely-Hutchinson, Cairo was surrendered to him on terms, including the return of the French to France, and on 16th August Alexandria was taken. General Menou and his troops were to return to France under a capitulation of 2nd September 1801. The French adventure in Egypt was over.

On the Foudroyant Sir Ralph Abercrombie lay seriously injured. It was impossible to remove the bullet lodged near the groin and on 26th March gangrene set in, with his death following on 28th March. The Duke of York, in a General Order of the day, commended his ever watchful attention to the health and wants of his troops, the splendour of his actions in the field and the heroism of his death, which he declared was "worthy of the imitation of all, who deserve, like him, a life of honour and a death of glory." Sir John Moore was to recover from his wound and have a military career of distinction, culminating in the Spanish campaign of 1808.

The poet Thomas Campbell (1777 – 1844) wrote a poem to celebrate the battle entitled *Lines written at the request of the Highland Society in London, when met to commemorate the 21st of March, the day of Victory in Egypt.*

> Pledge to the much-loved land that gave us birth!
> Invincible romantic Scotia's share!
> Pledge to the memory of her parched worth!
> And first, amidst the brave, remember Moore!

And be it deemed not wrong that name to give,
In festive hours, which prompts the patriots sigh!
Who would not envy such as Moore to live?
And died he not as heroes wish to die?

Yes, though too soon attaining glory's goal,
To us his bright career too short was given,
Yet, in a mighty cause his phoenix soul
Rose on the flame of victory to Heaven!

How oft (if beats in subjected Spain
One patriot heart) in secret shall it mourn
For him – How oft on far Corunna's plain
Shall British exile weep upon his own!

Peace to the mighty dead – our bosom lands
In sprightlier strain the living may inspire!
Joy to the chiefs that lead Old Scotia's ranks,
Of Roman garb and more than Roman fire!

Triumphant be the thistle still unfurled,
Dear symbol wild! On freedom's hill it grows,
Where Fingal stemmed the tyrants of the world
And Roman eagles found unconquered foes

Joy to the band * this day on Egypt's coast,
Whole valour tamed proud France's tricolour,
And wrenched the banner from her bravest host
Baptised Invincible in Austria's gore!
Joy for the day on red Vimiero's strand
When, bayonet to bayonet opposed,
First of Britannia's host her highland brand,
Gave but the death shot once, and foremost closed?

Is there a son of generous England here
Or fervid Erin? – he with us shall join,
To pray that in eternal union dear,
The rose, the shamrock and the thistle twine!

---

* The 42nd (Royal Highland) Regiment. The asterisk appears in the text of the poem. (See also the
   Battle of Vimiero, 21st August 1808). It is to be noted that Campbell was educated at Glasgow
   University and was heavily engaged in the foundation of the University of London (University
   College) in the 1820s.

Types of a race who shall th'invader scorn
As rock resist the billows round their shore;
Type of a race who shall to time unborn
Their country leave unconquered as of yore!

For the death of General Sir John Moore see the Battle of Corunna 16th January 1809.

24th March 1945

The Crossing of the Rhine

The disintegration of the German army in the west after the Battle of Normandy and the rapid sweep of the Allied armies across France and into Belgium had not been anticipated and, as the rush across France developed, the British and Americans in the SHAEF command had to decide on the strategy to be adopted for the battle to be carried into Germany in order to secure its defeat. In the United States the President, the Commander-in-Chief, General Marshall, and public opinion had become insistent that the ground forces should be commanded by an American for the future campaign. That attitude was not unreasonable in that by the end of August the great balance of forces were American. Prompted by General Marshall, General Eisenhower told Montgomery on 19th August that he was to take over from him as commander of the ground forces, General Montgomery remaining in command of the 21st Army Group. Given his personality, the latter did not accept the decision easily. He liked Eisenhower, but had a low opinion of him as a military strategist. There was moreover a division of view as to the way forward between the British and Americans.

The British believed that the Allied armies should strike north across the Rhine, take the Ruhr and thrust across the north German plain to take Berlin. Both Fieldmarshal Brooke, the Chief of the Imperial General Staff and Winston Churchill supported Montgomery's view about this. Eisenhower on the other hand, pressed by Generals Patton and Omar Bradley, commanding the US 3rd and 12th armies, thought that there should be pressure put on the Germans on more than one front. He conceived of an attack through to the Saar and then north towards the Ruhr. The objective of ultimately taking Berlin was still however in September 1944, to quote Eisenhower, the "main prize." The pull of these two alternative theories was to cloud allied co-operation, because of the problem of supplies that the quick pace of the advance across France had called into existence. The armies remained dependent on supplies coming through the Mulberry harbour on the Normandy beaches north of Bayeux: any assault on Germany itself needed access to the deepwater port of Antwerp, which had surprisingly been taken by the British 21st Army group on 4th September with the installations intact. On 23rd August General Montgomery and General Eisenhower met and discussed the 'two thrust' strategy and Eisenhower conceded that Montgomery's northern arm should have priority, to the subsequent annoyance of Bradley and Patton, to whom only restricted supplies of fuel were given. Bradley was arguing for a thrust forward by the American 1st and 3rd Armies through the Frankfurt gap, but Eisenhower rejected this. With the supply journey at three hundred and seventy miles it was plainly sensible to go north in the hope of clearing a port which could be used, as an objective apart from that of crossing the Rhine, which the Allies saw as the most formidable obstacle to German defeat. In furtherance of the northern thrust the British and Fieldmarshal Montgomery began to prepare a plan for a speedy advance to take five bridges over canals and rivers to open access to Germany, the last being that at Arnhem.

By early September however the disorganised retreat of the Germans was coming to an end and Feldmarschall Von Rundstedt, who had returned on 5th September, had begun with system and skill to rebuild German military formations along the Siegfried Line and across southern Holland. The hardening of resistance was illustrated by the fact that it took until 8th September for 30th Corps to cross the Albert and Meuse-Escaut canals. On 2nd September Eisenhower gave way to Bradley and Patton, conceding them a greater share of the fuel supplies to enable them to push up to the German frontier and the Siegfried Line. On 10th September Eisenhower and Montgomery met and the latter pressed again for a single thrust into Germany from the North. Eisenhower refused to scale down the operation towards the Saar and told Montgomery that he did not have "absolute priority" for fuel supplies. He did however approve of the proposals for the operation to cross the rivers, called operation Market Garden, the plans for which had been finalised in the first week of September. Before that took place however, President Roosevelt and Winston Churchill met from 13th to 16th September in Quebec and confirmed two matters which had an influence on the course of future events. First, it was agreed that the part of Germany not occupied by the Russians and preliminarily assigned to them for occupation should be divided between the British and American.

The future of Germany had already been touched on at the Teheran Conference in November 1943 between Churchill, Stalin and Roosevelt, who there produced a plan for its division into five. Second, Churchill was persuaded to endorse a plan promoted by the U.S. Secretary to the Treasury, Morgenthau, to restrict German industry after the war and limit the country to a pastoral economy. The first point as finally hammered out was ultimately to influence strategy at the end of the war, and the second fortified German resistance, coupled with the principle of unconditional surrender, giving to the Nazi propaganda minister Dr. Goebbels effective arguments for the Germans people to remain firm and fight on. These were backed by the Nazis with relentless punishments introduced against defeatism and desertion by the troops, which was redefined to cover mere separation of individuals from their units.

At the time of its conception Operation Market Garden was not an unreasonable strategy, although subject to risk. The British Army and the Canadians had in a matter of three weeks swept across northern France and Belgium up to Antwerp, having started at Caen in Normandy. They had not faced coherent strong resistance. The remnants of the 15th Army were being pressed back to the mouth of the Scheldt. In Holland, the German forces under the command of General Student, the 1st Parachute Army, was comprised of 18,000 reservists and young men stretched from Antwerp to Maastricht, with a few infantry divisions elsewhere in the country. It could be conceived against this background that a "Rapid and violent threat", as Fieldmarshal Montgomery described it, could take the bridges and open the German plain. With his obsession about the need for a dominant northern thrust into Germany north of the Ruhr, the 'gamble' was worthwhile particularly before he lost total influence over ground operation to Eisenhower and the Americans. Execution of the operation had difficulties, which were only resolvable if the attack was blessed with good luck. Market Garden necessitated an armoured drive some 60 miles along a single road to Arnhem. That road ran through open, flat country with polders on either side. The bridges needed to be taken and held before they could be blown and then defended from counter-attack until the relieving troops could reach them. The operation depended on a mass airborne attack and the existence of fair weather to facilitate that attack, and the dropping of supplies and the provision of air cover. The hitherto cautious Montgomery was to abandon that caution and take a gamble.

The planning of the operation called for airborne landings to take the bridges over the Maas, Waal, and lower Rhine. The U.S. 101st Division was to be dropped at Eindhoven, the U.S. 82nd Division at Nijmegen and the British 1st Airborne and 1st Polish Paratroops Brigade at Arnhem. The latter was expected to hold out for two days, the time predicted for the Armoured corps to travel to the Bridge. 20,000 vehicles were amassed to bring the British 2nd Army up the road. There were 5,000 aircraft and gliders to enable the drop to take place simultaneously, but because of the inadequacy of that number the drop had to be planned as incremental over one to three days. The Guards Armoured Division and the 50th were to spearhead the road attack. All these plans predicated the continuance of a weak German position through Belgium into Holland.

Events were however to be changed by the posting from the Eastern front to the vicinity of Arnhem of two SS Panzer Divisions (9th and 10th SS Divisions) to reform and recuperate immediately prior to the attack. The resistance sent messages as to their presence and the troop movement and position of this armoured corps was picked up on ULTRA. Aerial reconnaissance found the tanks hidden in the woods. General Sir Frederick Browning in command of 1st Airborne took scant interest and thought it no reason for postponing the operation. General Bedell Smith at SHAEF raised the matter with Montgomery, but he brushed it aside.

Unlike the situation at the bridges over the Orne on D Day (see the Battle of Normandy 20th August 1944) the drop zones were not planned immediately next to the bridge at Arnhem. The combination of the presence of the Panzer Divisions and the absence of drop zones at the bridge was to prove a fatal weakness. There was some unease by the men of 1st Airborne about this, but it resulted from representations made by the air force about the danger of anti-aircraft fire close in to the bridge.

On the morning of Sunday 17th September on a bright and clear day the massed aircraft carrying the airborne troops, British and American, met over Bruxelles and between 1 and 2 p.m. simultaneous drops were made to secure the bridges. At the south end of the road a bombardment opened up on the defending Germans from 17 Artillery regiments and at 2.30 p.m. the push forward commenced. The British 1st Airborne troops, amounting to 5,700 men, dropped north and south of the river to the west of Arnhem. Feldmarschall Model had his headquarters at Oosterbeck north-west of the town and immediately mobilised the two SS Panzer divisions, some of which were based near the drop zones. Fierce fighting broke out on the north of the river as the British moved towards and through the town to the bridge. The 1st and 3rd Battalions of the Parachute Regiment tried to force their way towards the bridge but were brought to a stop just over half a mile from it. The 2nd Battalion under Colonel John Frost however, coming from the south, met no resistance and reached the bridge which they stormed, establishing themselves in a bridgehead in the houses on the northern side. As the day wore on, the weather deteriorated and it began to rain heavily. Fighting in and around the town went on; tanks with rocket-firing mortars on the one side and bren-guns and rifles on the other. Elsewhere the vanguard of XXX Corps (the Irish Guards) moved down the road towards Eindhoven, where the U.S. 101st Airborne division had taken a twenty mile-long sector. By nightfall the tanks of the Irish guards were ten miles south of the town.

The second wave of 1st Airborne was due to be dropped on 18th September. Fierce fighting was moving in a scattered way through the streets of Arnhem. The 2nd Battalion of the Parachute Regiment continued to hold under devastating fire at the bridge. The radios carried could not be made to work properly, and Major General Urquehart, in command of the Airborne troops, set out on a reconnaissance to investigate the position. He became entangled in the street fighting and had to hide in an attic in a friendly Dutch house. Finally he went back to Oosterbeck where he established a headquarters in the Hartenstein Hotel. Bad weather delayed the dropping of the second wave of 1st Airborne, which did not arrive until 4 p.m. to meet heavy German fire from Tiger and Panther tanks. The troops, armed only with Bren-guns and rifles, moved through the suburbs and streets of the town, and the South Staffordshires and Paratroops tried again to break through to the bridge against the fire of the panzers, but by the evening of the 19th they were being driven back to an area on the west and north-west of the town around the headquarters which was subjected to constant artillery fire from the 85mm guns.

At Eindhoven the U.S. 101st Airborne Division managed to take the town on the 18th, but the armoured advance was held up on the Wilhelmina Canal, which had to be crossed by Bailey bridge. The next morning the Guards began to push north and by 9 a.m. had joined up with 82nd U.S.Airborne at Grave on the Maas, where the latter had taken the bridge. At Nijmegen, eleven miles south of Arnhem, the advance was again halted by heavy German resistance. The strike north was falling well behind its time schedule of two days to the Arnhem Bridge. On the 18th and 19th the 2nd Battalion of the 1st Parachute Regiment continued to hold out under increasingly heavy fire and with numerous casualties. Bad weather meanwhile delayed the third wave of the airborne troops to Arnhem and the 1st Polish Parachute Brigade was not dropped as planned on the 19th.

On the 20th the Guards and the U.S. 82nd Airborne cleared Nijmegan, the Guards rushing the road bridge, which was unblown. In the afternoon, using canvas boats, the Americans crossed the Waal River to take the northern bank. At the end of the day, instead of pushing on, the Guards were held back for the night and it was to be the 21st before they went on. The paratroops under Colonel Frost at the bridge were on the 20th having to lurk in destroyed houses and had suffered numerous dead and wounded. By evening they were short of ammunition and forced to surrender. The 1st Airborne was still holding out in a zone that was being compressed and they too were short of supplies, the supplies dropped commonly being outside the area occupied. Out of 390 loads of supply only 31 were received. By the 21st they occupied an area only 1300 yards by 820 yards north of the river. That day the Polish Parachute Brigade was dropped south of the river, arriving to a murderous crossfire. Only 200 men succeeded in crossing the river. That same day, with the surrender of Colonel Frost and his paratroopers, General Bittrich was able to cross the bridge with Panzers to confront the oncoming British. The Airborne area continued under a savage attack and the Poles dug in south of the river at Driel, where on the 22nd armoured cars made contact with them, to be followed on the evening of the 23rd by 43rd Wessex Division. These troops were now in contact with the 1st Airborne north of the river. The battle was sustained on the 24th but on the morning of the 25th at 6 a.m. 1st Airborne were told to break out and withdraw south of the river. On the 25th and 26th that attempt was made, but only some 2,183 men returned. 1,400 had been killed and 6,000 were prisoners.

The battle at Arnhem was over. Had it been a success north Germany would have been open, with Munster outflanking the Ruhr eighty-seven miles away and Osnabruck one hundred and twenty. Bad weather and the presence of the two Panzer Divisions had defeated the plan. While the strike north initially created a narrow salient, the campaign had value: it founded a base for the Allies to attack towards the Lower Rhine from Eindhoven and Nijmegen, and it increased the isolation of General von Zangen's 15th Army in South Beveland and Walcheren, complicating his supply problem. Fieldmarshal Montgomery had lost his gamble. In a comment on the Duke of Wellington he denied him recognition as a great general because he was averse to risk, but Wellington, unlike Montgomery, never lost a battle. The campaign had another result, in striking at the notion of one primary great thrust across the plains to Berlin. Had Arnhem been held, the case against such a strategy would have become almost unarguable. The failure also left the problem of clearing the access to Antwerp along the River Scheldt directly. General Eisenhower now ordered Montgomery on 9th October to make that his priority.

The West Scheldt, which gives access to Antwerp, stretches over fifty miles from the sea. The southern bank is part of Belgium and the Netherlands mainland, but the north consists of an island, Walcheren, won largely from the sea, and a long isthmus, South Beveland, which separates the West from the East Scheldt. The entrance had been heavily fortified and was dominated by batteries commanding the estuary. At the western entrance there stands on the south side the town of Breskens and on the north Flushing. General Gustav von Zangen's 15th Army had been forced north along the coast and had ended at the mouth of the Scheldt. There he was able to become entrenched south of the West Scheldt in an area defined by the Leopold Canal from Zeebrugge to a limb of the river west of Terneuzen. The island of Walcheren could only be approached on land along a causeway across the Sloe Channel separating the island from the isthmus of South Beveland.

When Antwerp fell with its docks undamaged to 21st Army Group on 4th September, it would have been feasible to press north and west to prevent the 15th Army crossing from Breskens to Flushing (this was achieved in a skilled operation organised by General Schweble) and to isolate South Beveland. Concentration on Operation Market Garden and want of resources precluded such operations although two Canadian Divisions of General Crerar's army did endeavour to reach Breskens but were not in time. A Polish Infantry Brigade reached Terneuzen on 20th September. On the 17th the air attack on Walcheren had begun with the bombing of the defences and the batteries. It was not until after the Arnhem failure that the assault on the German "Scheldt Fortress South" and on the South Beveland isthmus was to begin. On 3rd October, 247 bombers attacked the dykes protecting Walcheren using bombs similar to those invented by Dr Barnes Wallis which had destroyed the Mohne Dam, flooding the Ruhr valley. One hundred yards of the dykes were smashed, allowing the sea to flood into the interior of the island. On 6th October the attack by the 2nd Canadian Army, supported by 49th Division and 52nd Lowland Divisions, on the German salient around Breskens and north in order to cut off South Beveland, began.

Thrusts across the Leopold Canal began to penetrate the area and on 9th October an attack was launched from Terneuzen. The Germans put up a strong resistance and supplies limited progress, but by the 16th Woemsdrecht at the east of the South Beveland isthmus had been taken. On the 21st Breskens fell to the 3rd Canadian Division and the surviving defenders were forced back to the west of the salient. The 2nd Canadian Division and the 52nd Lowland Division began to move along the South Beveland isthmus on the 23rd. By 31st October the Sloe Channel had been reached and the Canadians stood at the east end of the 1200-yard causeway to Walcheren. By 2nd November the salient south of the river had been eliminated and Zeebrugge was open. Three times the Canadians tried to take the causeway to Walcheren but were driven back. On 31st October however, the 52nd Lowland Division managed to cross the Sloe Channel and began to move on Middleburg. An invasion of Walcheren was also about to be launched involving British Commandos, the use of an amphibian brigade and of U.S. Amphibians and Weasels to go in through the broken dykes. A strong naval bombardment of the island batteries announced the assault on 1st November but bad weather precluded effective air support. Specially designed landing craft to carry guns to bombard the beaches were used but only 7 out of 20 were relatively undamaged. The Westkapelle attack by the British Commando Brigade with tank support and against the most formidable defence moved north-east, taking Domburg, and south-east towards Flushing. In the town it required two days street fighting to clear it and on 5th November the German Commander at Middelburg surrendered. The batteries threatening the estuary by that date had all been taken. The whole experience cost the 1stCanadian Army 12,873 dead, wounded and missing. The river was then swept for mines and on 28th November the first supply convoy arrived at Antwerp. The new base of supply for the invasion of Germany, with reasonable access to the front, had been established. Antwerp was however not free of the war, since the Germans used Holland to bombard the city with VI and V2 rockets.

The debate about the strategy for that invasion had continued throughout these events and on into December. The division of strategy between the British and Americans had already emerged in August, before Operation Market Garden. General Eisenhower had to deal on the one hand with Fieldmarshal Montgomery, whom he thought the most difficult person whom he had ever met, and on the other with Generals Omar Bradley and Patton, who refused to serve under Montgomery again, and argued for a southern thrust through the Frankfurt gap by the Americans with less emphasis on a northern push into Germany. Eisenhower had temporised over Operation Market Garden and for the time rejected a southern thrust as a main route of invasion. He, in line with traditional American military thinking, adapted to a nation with endless men and resources, favoured pressure along the whole line, giving the enemy no opportunity to move armies to oppose attack wherever it came. While however the strategic objective remained Berlin, Eisenhower accepted the need for a strong northern attack into the German plains. He rejected criticism from Generals Bradley and

Patton of Montgomery for the Arnhem debacle and took the blame himself. In early October however, he stressed to Montgomery that unless the approaches to Antwerp were taken by mid-October, the move into Germany would grind to a standstill. Fieldmarshal Montgomery did not abandon his attempt to persuade Eisenhower of the paramount nature of the northern approach, arguing even on 7th December that fifty divisions should be committed to it to take the Ruhr. General Omar Bradley was still backing his south Germany strategy. Throughout Montgomery was backed by Fieldmarshal Brooke, the CIGS, and the Prime Minister, Winston Churchill, who had begun to worry about the Soviet threat to a free Poland, for which Britain and the Empire had gone to war, and the risk of Soviet penetration into Western Europe. He saw a need to take as much of north Germany as possible to give the Allies a negotiating position with Stalin. On 15th December however, the strategy to be adopted became a less urgent issue, as the Germans struck through the Ardennes at the American 1st Army.

Meanwhile throughout Autumn a policy had been pursued of edging up as near as possible to the Rhine and of securing the front west of the Siegfried Line. The Siegfried Line stretched some three hundred and fifty miles from the Swiss Frontier to Mönchen Gladbach; from there north to Cleve, it consisted only of isolated bunkers and trenches. It varied in density and strength, the strongest fortifications being in the sector covering Saarbrucken. Feldmarschall von Rundstedt worked on reforming the broken divisions of the army, and troops for the defence of the line were gathered from every source available. The Germans had lost vast numbers of men; in September alone 345,000 and probably all told since D Day one million. Naval and Luftwaffe personal were taken and placed in the line. The young, the old and the sick were mobilised, the weaker divisions being used to man the fortifications south of the line and the most experienced the north, where the line was at its most tenuous. In the north the 1st Canadian Army and 2nd British Army moved up to the Maas by 4th December and were east of Nijmegen. The 1st and 9th U.S. Armies came up against the Siegfried Line at Aachen in mid-September, where it comprised two thin lines, and tried to penetrate it south of city. It was not until 21st October that Aachen surrendered after bitter fighting in the city. The progress up to the Roer Valley, a tributary of the Maas, again engaged those forces in a costly offensive from 15th November to 3rd December, carried out in bad weather through the Hürtgen Forest. General Patton's 3rd Army was involved around the Metz forts, which were only taken on 22nd November. Unlike the dashing races from Normandy, against firm and stubborn resistance Patton's forces from September to December only advanced twenty-five miles. The 7th U.S. Army in the south had however reached the Rhine on 20th November and turned south towards the Colmar pocket.

The Fuehrer Adolf Hitler began to conceive the idea of a major armoured thrust from the Ardennes to Antwerp in mid-September 1944. It represented a bold strategic conception, which if successful could cut off the British 21st Army Group from the Americans, continue to prevent the use of Antwerp for supplies, and win for Germany a useful delay in invasion from the west. It echoed the triumph of 1940 in the push from the Ardennes which drove the British army from Europe and brought France to its knees. The difference however was that Germany now no longer had command of the air and the resources of men and weapons. For two and half months, throughout the Autumn, Feldmarschall von Rundstedt had worked at and rebuilt the strength of the army so far as possible. Quite apart from stabilising the west wall he had achieved a re-organisation which could furnish for the great offensive over twenty divisions, to which some seven reserve divisions could be added. The Supreme Command (OKW) worked on the plans in secret and by November was ready to produce them to the commanders involved. Characteristically, von Rundstedt was to regard it as a nonsensical operation, but carried out its execution as a Fuehrer command.

Feldmarschall Model tried to persuade OKW and Hitler to modify the plan to a less ambitious alternative towards Maastricht, which could take the British in the rear. At a conference on 2nd December in Berlin the Fuehrer indicated that he had refused to look at that. The plan conceived provided for an attack west from the front between Monschau and Echternach. The right wing comprised the 6th SS Panzer Army, with four panzer divisions and five infantry under Colonel-General Sepp Dietrich, with the 5th Panzer Army of four panzer divisions and three infantry under General Hasso von Manteuffel on the left wing. Their flank on the south was to be protected by the 7th Army of one panzer and six infantry divisions under General Brandenberger. The object was to be a quick thrust to the bridges over the Meuse between Liege and Namur and then on to Antwerp. The logistic problems for the armies were however formidable. There was a shortage of fuel for the tanks and motor transport, and reliance would need to be placed on captured American supplies. The danger from bombing to the German rail network meant that movement of trains was slowed and constrained, some tunnels being blocked by stationary trains and people. Supplies by train had therefore to be unloaded well behind the lines. The roads in the Ardennes were narrow, became icy on the hills and resulted in slowing all traffic down.

The armies for the drive were brought up at night and many troops were held to the east of Aachen to create the deception that they were reserves for the battle there. By mid-December the armies were in place. Along the ninety-mile front the Americans had only four divisions deployed: the 41st and 28th had been posted on this front, where no action was expected, in order to rest and recuperate, and the 106th and 9th Armoured Division were untested troops. Action "Herbstnegel" (Autumn fog) was launched on the dark and crisp night of 15th December. It began with small groups of infantry penetrating the front and pushing on past strong points, a tactic used in the First World War. To increase disorganisation among the American infantry, German troops, trained by Obersturmbannfuehrer Otto Skorzeny, who had rescued Mussolini from imprisonment, were sent in to direct traffic movement and mislead American columns by doing so. The Fuehrer, whose idea it was, was well pleased with this concept, but as General von Manteuffel records, it had little effect and most were captured and shot. There were two towns which were important road junctions, which needed to be taken, St Vith in the north and Bastogne in the south. On the first day and on the 17th the 6th SS Panzer army faced strong opposition in the north, failed to take Monschall and made only limited progress. The 7th Army on the flank in the south also were held up.

Only the 5th Panzer Corps was able to push through, crossing the River Oure and taking Clerf, thrusting aside the 28th and 106th US Divisions. The bad weather, which had prevented the use by the Allies of their aircraft to target the moving columns, began to worsen, and four feet of snow fell. The roads became passages of snow, ice and mud slowing the columns down. On the 17th St Vith was reached and the Americans put up a stout defence, until they were forced to evacuate the town on the night of the 22nd. On the 19th, units of the 5th Panzer Army reached the outskirts of Bastogne. That day there also arrived in the town itself the hardened 101st Airborne Division, driven from Rheims and snatched from their rest period to fortify the defence.

For the 5th Panzer Army a difficult question now arose; whether all the effort should be applied to taking Bastogne and securing the rear of operations, or whether, in accordance with the overall strategy, the town should be by-passed and the drive forward to the Meuse pressed. The decision was to send 2nd Panzer Division west, while 47th Panzer Corps was to detach the Panzer Demonstration Division to support the 26th Volks-Grenadier Division in its attack. 2nd Panzer drove on, taking Ortenville.

The response of the American command to the attack on the 16th had been somewhat laggardly. General Omar Bradley dismissed it at first as a local attack and did not arrive at his headquarters until thirty-six hours after the attack began. The 1st U.S. Army had been divided by the bulge created by the Germans, and it was difficult for Bradley from his headquarters in the south to co-ordinate the 1st Army response in the north. On the 20th General Eisenhower, in order to remedy the problem, gave Fieldmarshal Montgomery command over the 1st U.S. Army. The latter drove to the U.S. Army headquarters in his staff car flying the largest Union Flag he could find. He immediately brought up British troops as a reserve, consolidated a front line, pulling back from hopeless positions, and organised a striking force under General "Lighting Joe" Collins to counter-attack. Meanwhile, the 101st Airborne were "digging in" around Bastogne. The icy earth and snow made foxholes difficult to make; supplies were limited, winter clothing scarce; there were few tanks and only 130 pieces of artillery. For six days the defenders were to withstand the German push to take the town: the rounds available to the artillery units fell to ten a day, but they held on. General von Manteuffel said that at one time nine divisions were tied down by the resistance made. On the 22nd two German officers came with white flags to offer General McAuliffe a truce in order to avoid annihilation. His reply was "Nuts."

Although 2nd Panzer Division were going forward on the 20th, General von Manteuffel told Feldmarschall von Rundstedt that it would be impossible to reach the Meuse bridges. The latter sought the consent of the Fuehrer to withdraw but it was refused. On the 22nd the 2nd Panzer Division was nearing the Meuse. That day the bad weather ended, the skies cleared and the Allies were able to mount air force attacks on the German armies. On the 24th nonetheless the advance Panzers were three miles from Dinant. The bombing hit supplies to the German forces seriously and fuel began to be even more scarce for the advancing columns. The 23rd and 24th December brought a maelstrom of fighting at Bastogne following an order for 5th Panzer Command to take the town, with parachute troops trying to penetrate in two places. The advance of Panzer Lehr west was held up by the aircraft attack and the offensive finally came to a standstill.

On the south of the salient created, General Patton's 3rd Army was pressing north and on 25th December entered Bastogne to relieve the 101st Airborne and the garrison. Once more the 101st Airborne Division had shown the endurance and courage which so characterised them. The crisis was over and a slow squeeze from north and south compressed the bulge. On 3rd January Montgomery launched his northern counter-attack and finally on 8th January the Fuehrer agreed to withdrawal. By the 16th the American troops from north and south met at Houffalize near the original starting point. During the retreat the icy weather which had returned, and shortage of fuel, meant that many tanks and other vehicles had to be abandoned. By that time the Russians had opened their offensive on the eastern front and the 6th SS Panzer Army, with its four SS Panzer Divisions, Fuehrer Escort and Grenadier Brigades, departed from the front. The failure of the Ardennes offensive had been inevitable from the outset, because it combined large objectives with inadequate resources with which to achieve those objectives, but it had shaken the complacency of the Allies and marginally delayed - by six weeks - their attack on Germany. The allies took 50,000 prisoners and the Germans had casualties amounting to 120,000. They lost 600 tanks and assault guns and 1,600 aircraft. The Allies had some 50,000 total casualties.

The issue of future strategy came to a climax in December. Fieldmarshal Montgomery was still pressing for a dominant northern attack towards Berlin, with combined British and American armies, which he would command, and had a meeting with General Eisenhower on 27th December, where he once more pressed his views. The latter had again been told by General Marshall, the United States Chief of Staff in Washington, that such an arrangement was not acceptable. Generals Omar Bradley and Patton were threatening to resign if Eisenhower gave into Montgomery. Eisenhower once more temporised but given that Berlin remained the invasion objective, adopted a compromise strategy. The northern thrust was to remain paramount, Montgomery being allowed to retain command of the 9th U.S. Army to the annoyance of General Omar Bradley. There was however to be a second thrust virtually as strong further south. The broad front policy adopted predicated a thrust in the north by the British 21st Army Group and the 9th U.S. Army crossing the lower Rhine north of the Ruhr area, a thrust by the 12th U.S. Army through to the river from Düsseldorf south to Mainz and a third attack by the 6th U.S. Army Group to clear the area up to the Rhine in the south, eliminating the Colmar pocket. The object of Berlin was not abandoned. Neither Winston Churchill or Fieldmarshal Brooke, the CIGS, were entirely happy about the broad front strategy, because they had become more conscious of the need to block entry by the Soviet armies too far into Europe, and of the need of the Western Allies to take land in east Germany as a negotiating position to secure concessions from Stalin. To them Berlin, was an essential political and strategic objective.

In mid-January the first steps towards the crossing of the Rhine were taken in the clearance of the Roermond triangle. The main campaign in the north however began on 8th February 1945. The troops involved comprised the 30th Army Corps, the 15th, 31st, 43rd and 53rd Divisions, the 2nd and 3rd Canadian Divisions, and the 4th Canadian Armoured Division, to which were added the 49th Infantry Division, the Guards Armoured Divisions and 11th Armoured. The assault was announced by a bombardment of 1,050 guns. The direction of attack was south-east towards the bank of the Rhine, but necessitated the penetration of and taking of the Reichswald Forest covering an area of eight by three miles. The snow had thawed, the roads were full of holes and the ground waterlogged; at times the troops had to wade almost waist-deep in water. The weather remained bad, the forest roads were inadequate and narrow and the German resistance determined. General Alfred Schlemm, Commander of the 1st Parachute army, had prepared positions to meet attack facing north-west. They were manned by personnel taken from the Luftwaffe in part, most under twenty-five and convinced Nazis. As the campaign proceeded the defenders were consistently reinforced. Progress until these defence lines were reached was reasonable. On 13th February Cleve was taken and the Rhine reached east of Nijmegen. By that date the Reichswald Forest had also been cleared. On the 19th Goch was taken but by the 22nd Schlemm had stabilised his front, now having some nine divisions; three infantry, three parachute and three armoured. Strung out on a front of twenty miles, the fighting was fierce and ruthless and German discipline iron, as evidenced by the corpses, alleged deserters, found hanging from the trees by the men of 21st Army group as they advanced.

It had been planned that the 9th U.S. Army and elements of the 1st U.S. Army should begin an offensive north-west to the Rhine at the same time as the British and Canadian assault took place in the Reichswald Forest area, but on 10th February the Germans opened the Schmidt Dams on the River Roer and the water rose some four feet. The 9th and 1st U.S. Armies were supposed to strike across the Roer from Julich and Düren towards the Rhine from Duisburg to Köln. The rise of the river waters delayed the attack until 23rd February. Julich was taken and on the 24th Düren. As the Americans drove north they moved towards the rear of General Schlemm's army. He was forced to retreat towards Wesel as the armour came up from the south. By 2nd March the Allies had taken Mönchen Gladbach and Venlo and had reached the Rhine at Neuss. That day the 7th Corps of the 1st U.S. Army reached Köln on the east bank of the river. On 3rd March the 30th British Corps and the 16th Corps of the 9th U.S. Army joined up at Geldern. General Schlemm had moved north and east and occupied a pocket on the west bank of the river opposite Wesel. There were within it nine bridges across the Rhine, all of which Adolf Hitler ordered blown. By 8th March the pocket was only 15 miles by 15 and subject to constant bombing and artillery fire. It contained the remains of nine divisions, three Corps headquarters and the army headquarters. A colonel from OKW in Berlin visited the pocket and on 10th March Schlemm was ordered to withdraw and the bridge to Wesel was blown. Of the 70,000 troops lost in three battles, 50,000 became prisoners. The German army was disintegrating.

Southwards the 3rd Corps of the U.S. 1st Army had reached the "Lüdendorf" railway bridge at Remagen on 7th March. As the armoured column approached the bridge the Germans attempted to detonate it. However, due to inadequate fuses, the bridge was merely shaken, rising a few feet and falling back into place. The bridge was taken by the infantry, the engineers cutting the fuse wires as they crossed, and the U.S. troops moved over the bridge, putting four to five divisions on the poorly defended east bank, thus establishing a salient 25 miles by 10 miles deep almost immediately. While a valuable crossing, the country to the east was wooded and hilly and not ideal for a breakout. On 17th March the bridge collapsed. By that time the remnants of ten divisions, including three panzer divisions, were thrown against the salient but the build-up of the Americans was not prevented. The attempt to contain it however weakened the Rhine defences elsewhere. Further south still General Patton and the 3rd Army crashed through the weak defences of the Eifel and reached the Rhine on 9th March. Thus by 11th March the whole west bank of the Rhine was cleared north of the Moselle and south to Manheim. In this stage of the battle the German army in the west had lost half a million men, of whom 350,000 surrendered. Two million had been lost from the armies since D Day.

Consonant with his broad front strategy, General Eisenhower planned the crossing of the Rhine and the break out into Germany for 24th March 1945. North of the Ruhr the task was committed to Fieldmarshal Montgomery's 21st Army Group. The self-obsessed General Patton was determined to be the first to have his troops across the river and so on the night of 22nd/23rd March he deceived the Germans south of Mainz by a feint and opportunistically pushed a division across at Oppenheim against a weak Panzer-Grenadier Division. Montgomery in contrast planned the lower Rhine crossing, defended by General Schlemm commanding the 1st Parachute Army with his five divisions, with meticulous care and deliberation, relying on massive fire power and a co-ordinated planned assault. The railway approaches around and to the north of the Ruhr were prior to the assault subjected to heavy bombing by the 8th and 9th U.S. Airforces in order to impede supplies to the defending armies. Prior to the river crossing, at 9.a.m. on the 24th, some 3,500 guns bombarded the defences east of the river on the sector to be attacked from Rheinberg to Rees. The British 2nd Army was to deploy on the left and the 9th U.S. Army on the right. Assembled for the river crossing (Operation Plunder) were Buffaloes (amphibian vehicles) and landing craft.

The first wave of British troops to cross comprised the 1st Commando Brigade near Wesel, the 15th Division north of Zantern and the 51st (Highland) Division at Rees. The town of Wesel was bombed and a thousand fighter-bombers were ready to give air-cover. The 9th U.S. Army attacked south of Wesel in the area of the Lippe Canal. Within two hours the troops were established on the east bank, much of the opposition being light. During these events, some 1,696 transport planes and 1,348 gliders had met up over Bruxelles carrying 22,000 men for airborne assaults inland from the area of ground attack. Some 20 minutes after the British troops went in, the British parachute troops were dropped behind the German front line, the 3rd Parachute Brigade north of Bergen, the 5th near the village of Hammiklen and the 6th south of it. The British gliders arrived some fifty-five minutes after the parachute drop and the Americans forty-three minutes later. The American parachute drop was more dispersed and fierce fighting took place in and around the village of Diersfordt. The day was spent by these ground and airborne forces establishing their position and clearing the area to build a unified salient. Hammiklen was only taken by a joint attack by the 6th Paratroops Brigade, 13th Devonshire Regiment and the 513th U.S. Division, which landed north of their allotted zone. At Rees by the late afternoon the German 1st Paratroop Army hung on only to a small area where they were pressed by the Gordon Highlanders and the Black Watch. By dark the landing areas were united and the movement to enlarge and exploit it could begin. By the 28th the river was secured from east of Emmerich to north of Duisburg and the advance had reached Haltern, north of the Ruhr, inland some twenty-five miles east of Wesel. On the 25th the 1st U.S. Army had broken through at Remagen and gone on by the 28th to Marburg, while Patton's 3rd U.S. Army had crossed the Main at Aschaffenberg and Hanau and reached Lauterbach, 80 miles across the river, by the 28th.

The successful crossing of the Rhine was followed by a sharp break in the joint strategy of the British and Americans. Berlin had always been publicly held out as the prime objective. On 27th March, the bridgehead having been established, Montgomery signalled Eisenhower that he had issued orders to the 2nd British Army and 9th U.S. Army for their armour to move forward to get to the Elbe with the utmost speed. On the 28th Eisenhower replied that he was co-ordinating his future strategy with 'Stalin', that Montgomery should unite with the 12th U.S. Army east of the Ruhr, at which point the 9th U.S. Army was to revert to the command of General Omar Bradley, and that henceforth the advance to the east was to be on the southern axis from Frankfurt and Leipzig to the Elbe, the 21st army Group acting only in support. Eisenhower had discussed no word of this change at his meeting on the 25th with Montgomery, Fieldmarshal Brooke and Winston Churchill, who had been present to see the Rhine crossing. Later Eisenhower was to tell his generals in conference that Berlin had "no tactical or strategic value", the implication being that the changed strategy was purely military with no political content. General Patton, who was present at the meeting, was non-plussed and thought it an error in the long term not to go on quickly to Berlin and then the River Oder. There had been no consultation with the British about this decision, which had significant political implications, and its genesis is clouded. Stalin of course greeted Eisenhower's new approach with enthusiasm, agreeing that Berlin had no importance and endorsing his proposed thrust east in the south.

The origin of this change is likely to have stemmed from a shift in the policy of President Roosevelt and his advisors as the war ended, arising from the desire of the United States to establish the United Nations, in which they wanted Stalinist Russia as a member, and the belief that there should be trust shown towards Stalin in the hope that such an approach would draw him into a peaceful settlement over Germany and Europe. One of the core issues was the treatment of Germany after unconditional surrender. The matter was raised at Teheran but had become urgent at the Yalta Conference from 4th February to 11th February 1945. At the Quebec Conference in September 1944 a plan had been ratified to divide Germany into three zones of occupation, with its eastern border on the River Oder. At Yalta the issue arose of whether France should have an occupation zone. Stalin objected to that on the sound basis that France had played no substantial part in the war, but in the end the point was conceded, if their zone came out of the Anglo-American allocation. It was also agreed that the future policy towards Germany involved its dismemberment, the occupation zones establishing some basis for that as a preliminary approach. The conference did however fend off huge reparation claims by Russia, achieve Russia's endorsement of the United Nations and tie Stalin to pledges of free democracies in Poland and Eastern Europe. It is arguable that Roosevelt may have seen these results of the conference as helping in shifting the American public out of isolationism and in preparing them to resist breaches of these principles. As a corollary, the good faith of Stalin needed to be tested.

On that logic, to take East Germany, as a bargaining counter in the way urged by Churchill, would be inconsistent with the 'trust Russia' approach.

There was therefore a political basis for Eisenhower's change of policy, to which might be added the practical point that it would be wasteful of men to fight for land which by agreement was designated to the Russians. It is almost inconceivable that these political issues did not result in some direction given to General Eisenhower over the campaign to take Berlin. To pretend as he did that it was his mere "strategic" decision, free from political context, seems ingenuous and certainly, if true, naïve. Churchill did lobby Roosevelt and Truman to alter their approach, pressing the need to have an effective bargaining position with Russia over Poland and East European countries, but without success.

In the end the British armies were to go north-east towards Hamburg and the Baltic in order to protect Denmark from Russia invasion. The forces locked in the Ruhr were surrounded. The 5th Panzer Army, 1st Parachute Army and the remnant of 15th Army were caught in the trap. By 18th April 317,000 troops had surrendered, including twenty-five generals and one admiral. Feldmarschall Model shot himself to avoid capture.

27th March 1943
The Turning of the Mareth Line

During 1942, after the United States had entered the war, President Roosevelt and the people of America lent all their great energies, enthusiasm and dynamism to the task of creating huge armies, torrents of ammunition, tanks, guns aircraft and ships to meet their enemies. In the European theatre of operations the first objective agreed between the President and Winston Churchill was the taking of North Africa. It had been hoped that the invasion of Algeria and Morocco, both French territories, could take place in early Autumn, before the attack at El Alamein (see the Battle of El Alamein 4th November 1942) in order to create two fronts upon which the Axis armies had to fight, but delay in assembling landing craft meant that the necessary forces being gathered were not ready. The yet untried and newly-trained American Divisions were brought to Europe. From the Clyde on the 25th October a great fleet was to set out to attack. In addition, General Patton with his army was to come from the United States. Six hundred and fifty fighting ships and transports were to be involved in the operation, Operation Torch. The landings in North Africa were conceived as a three-pronged invasion at Casablanca, Oran and Algiers, made simultaneously. There was to be no landing east of Algiers since the Allies still did not hold air supremacy in the central Mediterranean around Sicily and southern Italy, and the Royal Navy could not provide adequate protection, since there were not enough aircraft carriers. Gibraltar was to be used as the base. Since the beginning of the war, extensive tunnelling had been carried out inside the rock in order to convert it into a well protected and supplied fortress. The spoil had been used to create a more effective airfield and fourteen squadrons of Spitfires were to be based there to give air cover. The plan was for American forces to take Casablanca and Oran, and for a mixed American and British force to take Algiers. The latter was under the command of Major General Anderson, and the British element comprised two commando units, 11th and 36th Brigade Group, a mixed British and United States force, 1st Guards Brigade and the 78th Division of infantry.

A crucial problem for the whole operation was the likely reaction of the French to the invasion. It was uncertain whether or not they would resist and their forces in North Africa exceeded in number the 65,000 troops of the Anglo-American force. In addition there was the worry that Adolf Hitler might order an invasion of Spain in order to attack Gibraltar, the Allies' base. The latter danger was not to emerge as events in Russia meant that the Fuehrer did not have the resources to implement such a plan. The former problems were only resolved on landing. President Roosevelt's attitude to General De Gaulle and the Free

French was such that the Americans put out feelers to the army Commanders in French North Africa to test their attitude to the invasion and sponsored General Giraud, who had been rescued from the Riviera with his two sons by submarine after his escape from German imprisonment, as a possible future commander of French forces and Governor. He was brought to Gibraltar to meet General Eisenhower who, since Operation Torch was principally an American project, had been made commander-in-chief of the forces in North Africa. He did not prove very tractable.

In fact, events were to take a wholly unexpected course. President Roosevelt and Winston Churchill did however agree that General De Gaulle should not be told of the proposed operation beforehand, since the French were considered not sufficiently reliable, and the plans could leak out as they did in relation to the unsuccessful attack on Dakar in 1940. The Germans did become aware that operations were in hand, but were uncertain of their objective and came to the view that a new attempt was to be made at Dakar. Over forty U-boats were as a consequence sent to wait south and east of the Azores. On the night of 5th to 6th November the great convoy began to enter the Mediterranean and was observed by German spies at La Linea, who informed the High Command in Berlin. On the evening of 7th November an American representative went ashore to speak to General Juin, the French Army Commander, to warn him of the assaults at dawn on the 8th and invite him to order non-resistance. He was however outranked by the chance presence in Algiers of Admiral Darlan, who had come to see his sick son. Darlan had become a Minister in the French Government of Marshal Petain. Juin said he had to be told and at 2 a.m. Darlan was woken. At 7.40 a.m. he telegraphed to Petain. By that time the landings had begun. Marshal Petain met his cabinet that morning and ordered Darlan to resist. Prime Minister Pierre Laval invited a German guarantee of metropolitan France and its Empire.

At 1 a.m. the landing east and west of Algiers commenced. The French opposed the landing and fighting went on all day in and around the city, but at 7 p.m. Admiral Darlan ordered a ceasefire. At Oran the American landing was also opposed by the French from Syria and the French navy. On 18th November, as resistance continued, the port was shelled by the navy including HMS Rodney (4th of the name, launched 1925). At Casablanca resistance was also met and the French navy had to be put out of action: the battleship Jean Bart, stationary in the harbour was severely damaged and seven naval ships sunk. It was only on 11th November that Admiral Nogues surrendered. After Darlan had informed the French Government of the Algiers city ceasefire, he discussed an armistice for all Algeria and Tunisia with the Americans, if Marshal Petain's Government were recognised as the French controllers of the country. Petain was informed. The French Prime Minister Laval hurried to see Hitler in Bavaria. The Fuehrer was becoming increasingly suspicious of the French, who were not hurrying to give him access to, and use of, their airfield facilities in North Africa. As Laval arrived in Munich, the Fuehrer ordered the occupation of Vichy France and the German troops began to move in on 11th November. Darlan had continued to receive messages to resist from Petain, but after the German invasion, he entered into an armistice and telegraphed to the fleet to sail from Toulon. He then made terms with the Allies, who thought him the person best able to command the French forces not to fight on. He was to remain in control until 24th December, when he was assassinated. The Germans did not enter the port of Toulon immediately and only moved to do so on 27th November, when the Commander at Toulon, Admiral de La Borde, who was fiercely anti-British, nonetheless scuttled all the ships.

After resistance ceased, although his logistic support had not all landed, being designated to the second wave, General Eisenhower acted with alacrity to send his forces east into Tunisia. On 10th November 36th Brigade Commando took Bougie and on the 12th, 6th Commando landed by sea at Bone, while paratroops in their first drop took the airfield. The Navy in inshore vessels facilitated the movement west of the army from Algiers. The airfields further south at Souk el Arba and Tebessa were also taken. The 78th Infantry Division moved inland and east, finally meeting the Germans forty miles west of Tunis near Medjez El Bab. The 2nd US Corps in the north reached Sedjenane by 30th November. In the south, the Free French and Americans had gone through the Kasserine pass and were into Tunisia. By the end of the month the Germans and Italians, using air transport, carrying as many as a thousand men a day, had built up 15,000 troops in Tunisia with 100 tanks, 60 field guns and 30 anti-tank guns.

Meanwhile, General Montgomery and the 8th Army were forcing Feldmarschall Rommel and his army back west across the Libyan desert and a series of fighting retreats were fought. It was not until 23rd January 1943 that Tripoli was taken and Rommel retreated to the Mareth Line, which formed the southern boundary of Tunisia. The twenty-mile line had been built by the French as a protection against the Italians. The eastern end lay on the sea coast and the fortifications were protected by the Wadi Zigzaou, which in places was fifty feet deep and eighty yards wide and constituted an impassable obstruction to tank movement. Beyond the Wadi the line comprised pill boxes, ditches, minefields and wire as far as the Matmata Hills, which were a further barrier to vehicular movement forward. The French were therefore of the view that the line was impregnable. The 8th Army did not go up to the Mareth Line immediately and Rommel had time to put it into order. The 7th Armoured Division, 51st British Infantry Division and 2nd New Zealand Division moved up to Medenine, but there were no minefields to protect them. However, 500 guns were deployed with this force.

Rommel was not initially reinforced, but Germans troops and weapons were continually brought in during the rainy winter season, when operations all but ceased. In November Rommel visited Hitler and was treated for the first time to a violent Hitler scene, when he suggested withdrawal of the Afrika Korps from North Africa. He was denounced for defeatism, berated as a coward, told to stand fast at Tripoli and, after pleading to save his troops to fight in Italy, was told they did not matter. Rommel's disillusion with the Fuehrer began at that point: In mid-December, the 10th Panzer Division, 334th Infantry Division and a Grenadier Regiment arrived in Tunisia. The 501st Tank Battalion, with new mark II tanks, was added and the Herman Goering Panzer Division was on its way. Two armies were now formed in the country. In the north stood that of Feldmarschall von Arnim, composed of the new forces sent and in the south under the Italian General Messe, the 20th and 21st Italian Corps and the Afrika Corps, named as the First Italian Army. On 22nd February Army Group Afrika was formed, consisting of these forces, and Rommel became its commander as well as commander of the German-Italian tank forces. The view of the German High Command was that holding Tunisia for as long as possible would pin down the Anglo-American forces in the Mediterranean and delay any invasion in southern Europe.

On 14th February 1943 the campaign in Tunisia was to burst again into activity. The British and Americans had spent the winter building up their forces in North Africa, the merchant ships returning with cargos of dried dates and figs which were to become - in suet puddings - a staple of school dinners. Rommel was under threat in the rear from the US 2nd Corps in the north-east around Sbeitla and Gafsa and he had collected together a striking force of the Herman Goering Division, paratroops, 10th Panzer and 21st Panzer supported by Italian Young Fascists. Under cover of Stuka bombers, Focker-Wolfs and Heinkels, his armoured forces, with new mark VI Tiger tanks, fell on the 1st and 34th United States Division and thrust through, going on to the Kasserine pass, through which he went on 20th February. His success potentially imperilled the rear of the 1st US Army to the north and General Alexander was appointed on 19th February as commander of all ground forces to co-ordinate steps to avert the crisis which had arisen. He invited Montgomery in the south to create a diversion. Despite the underlying weakness of his position, Rommel decided to strike out north-west towards Tebessa and north towards Thala. The British 6th Armoured and the Guards Division met the Afrika Corps near Thala on 23rd February and after a scorching encounter Rommel, quickly appreciating that his raid had failed, decided to retreat, withdrawing to Gafsa. Alexander was then to embark on bringing an ordered structure to the 1st Army, where the Americans, British and Free French acted without coherence.

On 6th March Rommel and his Afrika Corps were to attack again. The likely offensive had been disclosed to the 8th Army by means of the use of ULTRA (see Battle of El Alamein 4th November 1942) and Montgomery placed at Medenine General Freyberg VC and his 2nd New Zealand Division, the 201st Guards Brigade joining the 7th Armoured Division and 51st (Highland) Division. The troops were equipped with the new seventeen-pounder anti-tank guns. Committing the tank formations available, the Germans of the 15th and 21st Panzer crossed the open flat land to Medenine. As they approached, they saw the front-line gunners leave their bunkers and emplacements and bolt back to the main line. When the panzers were close, the artillery opened with the new guns, a crushing fire. Four times the Germans attacked without success and finally had to withdraw. The Germans lost fifty-two tanks, all to the anti-tank guns. No British tanks were involved and the British killed and wounded amounted to 130. It was the last attack in North Africa that Rommel was to make. On the 12th March he flew back to Germany and Hitler refused to give him consent to return. Rommel was ill and was to spend six weeks in hospital at Semmering.

Alexander and Montgomery still had the problem of passing the Mareth line to push the Germans north. Ever since the Autumn of 1941, where it was first used by parachute unsuccessfully in the November campaign, there had been in existence a striking force formed into small patrols of experienced soldiers who went behind the enemies' line to reconnoitre and to strike unexpectedly at enemy supply dumps, installations, aircraft and airfields. This informal force emerged as the Long Range Desert Group, under Colonel Stirling, and was the precursor of the present Special Air Service. By January 1943 it had an establishment of 400 officers and men in four squadrons. A route was known to exist round the Matmata hills to the west of the Mareth line through Tetalowie to the north from where a pass led to the plain south of El Hamma and west of Gabes on the coast. The route was however one hundred and fifty miles long. The Long Range Desert Group were given the task of surveying the route and returned to pronounce that it was not impossible for an army to use it. The strategy was therefore developed of a double attack: one directly on the Mareth Line to the front and the other an outflanking attack round the Matmata hills to the 'Plum Pass', and then into the plain to the rear of the Mareth Line. The outflanking movement was to be committed to 2nd New Zealand Division and 8th Armoured Brigade. They were to join with General Le Clerc's Free French, who had crossed the Sahara from Chad.

The 8th Army moved up to the Mareth Line after the battle of Medenine and with the Western Desert Air force a closer integrated strategy, the "Blitz" strategy perfected by the Germans, was evolved in support of the ground troops. In the winter of 1942-3 the German air force in North Africa and the Mediterranean had been reinforced and at one time twenty-five percent of its strength was in this sector of operations. Air cover for army attack was therefore critical. Stationed in the Mareth Line the Germans had 6 divisions – alternate Italian and German – on the coast; the 15th Panzer Division, then the Italian Trieste Division, the German 90th Light Division, the Italian and Spezia Pistoia Divisions and finally the 164th Division beside the Matmata hills. On 19th March the outflanking column under General Freyberg VC left for 'Plum Pass'. On the 20th the British 50th Division after an artillery bombardment went across the Wadi Zigzaou against fierce opposition and they succeeded in establishing a bridgehead on the German side, but were without tanks or anti-tank guns. They were to hold on desperately against bombardment and counter-attack on the 22nd by the 15th Panzer Division supported by infantry. By the 20th the New Zealanders had reached 'Plum Pass' after their desert march and were ready to attack. Before both attacks the German airfields had been bombed and the assault on the pass was preceded by 'a blitz' sustained by forty light bombers, five Spitfire squadrons as cover and sixteen squadrons of Kittyhawk bombers, of which two squadrons at a time spent flights of two and half hours at a time over the battlefield. The six thousand yard wide 'Plum Pass' could not be forced by the New Zealand Division and so on 21st March General Montgomery detached to aid them the Headquarter force of XIth Corps and 1st Armoured Division. The 50th was withdrawn on the 23rd from across the Wadi and the 7th Armoured Division sent to the Mareth Line front, where the attack continued, including a push by 4th Indian Division along the Matmata hills.

From the 21st massive air bombardment continued on the defenders at Plum Pass, reaching a crescendo before a new attack on the evening of the 28th. The air assault was halted at dusk, but after the moon rose the armoured forces pushed beyond the pass to near El Hamma, where they were met by anti-tanks guns. The threat to their rear made the Mareth Line untenable and the Germans and Italians on the night of 27th March withdrew north to Wadi Akarit, ten miles north of Gabes. The position was thus threatened from the west by the American 2nd Corps at Gafsa, who were on the Gabes road, being opposed by 10th and 21st Panzer Divisions. Gabes had fallen to General Patton's first Infantry division on 17th March but they were to come up with the Germans dug in fifteen miles west at El Guettar, where on 23rd March the 10th Panzer Division, with one hundred tanks, tried to drive back the Americans. The German effort expired in a hail of anti-tank fire and 40 tanks were destroyed. Other pushes were held at Fondouk and Macaassy as General Alexander attempted to squeeze the Axis along the coast. The Americans were to keep up the pressure of these attacks: indeed they tried to break through at El Guettar on 31st March. In April, Montgomery launched an attack on Wadi Akarit using bombardment by massed artillery of 450 guns and sending forward the 50th, 51st and 4th Indian Divisions. They were subject to counter-attack and by nightfall the line had not been taken. Having regrouped, the attack was renewed in the darkness and the front was overwhelmed, letting the British columns through. On 7th April the United States 2nd Corps and the 4th Indian Division met to the north of Gabes. General Messe and the Axis army, under air attack, rapidly fell back.

28th March 1941

The Battle of Matapan

After Italy declared war in June 1940 and the Government of France deserted Britain without the sought guarantees regarding her navy, Britain faced the problem that the union of the battle fleets of these countries under Nazi control could undermine Britain's access to the Mediterranean and jeopardise its interests in the near East. The battle of Cape Matapan was the last of three actions designed to restore the predominance of naval power in Britain's favour.

Intelligence was obtained that the Italians were moving a fleet to the Aegean. A modern battleship, the Vittorio Veneto, was accompanied by five cruisers, three with 8-inch guns, and seventeen destroyers. The naval force stationed at Alexandria was alerted and Admiral Cunningham sailed in Warspite (built 1913 and 8th of the name) with Valiant (built 1914 and 8th of the name) and Barham (built 1915 and 4th of the name). The modern aircraft carrier, Formidable, and destroyers supported the battleships, together with light forces from Crete, comprising 4 cruisers, the flagship Orion (launched 1932 and 5th of the name) and 4 destroyers. Searching aircraft located part of the Italian fleet at dawn and by 7.45 a.m. the Orion and cruiser fleet was able to engage the Italians. The initial fighting was without outcome but the Italians retired towards their main fleet. By 9.45 a.m. Orion and the cruisers were within 16 miles of the Vittorio Veneto, which opened fire. Orion and the British carriers retired towards the battle fleet some seventy miles away. Aircraft from Formidable were launched against the battleship Vittorio Veneto, which withdrew, damaged by a torpedo after the second attack, its speed limited to 15 knots. The enemy battleships were protected by a force of five cruisers and five destroyers and the aircraft were the subject of an anti-aircraft barrage. Nevertheless the heavy cruiser Pola was hit and stopped. After dark Admiral Cunningham set out to find the cruisers and stricken battleship. At 10.10 p.m. Pola was picked up on the radar and two cruisers that had gone to its assistance, the Fiume and the Zara. At 10.20 p.m., when the Valiant, upon which the Duke of Edinburgh was serving, was 4.5 miles distant, it opened fire and was joined by Warspite. The Fiume was struck by fifteen broadsides from Warspite and Valiant and the Zara was reduced by Valiant to a wreck under concentrated fire - 62 shells from the 15-inch guns. The Zara sank and the destroyer Jervis completed the destruction of the Pola by torpedoing it. The whole action had taken twenty-one minutes without naval loss. As Churchill noted in his speech to the House of Commons, the battle disposed of the challenge to British naval supremacy in the Mediterranean for the rest of the year. Between June 1940 and March 1941 the naval actions undertaken meant that out of six Italian battleships one had been sunk and three damaged.

The Admiral commanding the fleet in the Mediterranean at the time of this operation was created in 1946 Viscount Cunningham of Hindhope.

April

<h1 style="text-align:center">2nd April 1801</h1>

The Battle of Copenhagen

In 1793 France declared war on Britain and Holland and resolved to seize Belgium. The principal means by which Britain itself was to fight the French Revolutionary War was by the use of its naval strength, and an effective means of using that power was by way of blockade of French ports. One facet of the blockade was the need to stop, search and, if necessary, seize neutral merchant ships and any contraband goods within them. This power of search and seizure, evolved by Britain as being based on international law and practice, was not unchallenged but due to Britain's naval success was a practice which could be put into effect. Buonaparte, as First Consul of France, decided to use the dislike of the practice to foment unrest among the Baltic states – Denmark, Sweden and Russia – in relation to the effect on their shipping.

In the summer of 1800 a British squadron stopped a Danish convoy in the North Sea, forced its protective frigate, the Freja, to strike its colours and then took the convoy into the Downs anchorage. The ships were let go but an Embassy was sent to Copenhagen to re-assert the right to search and sequester contraband goods. The matter appeared to be settled when the Danish dropped their claim to be free of search, but in November 1800 Tsar Paul I of Russia embargoed English shipping, putting some crews in chains and marching them into the interior, and burning ships. He revived the League of Armed Neutrality with Denmark and Sweden in December 1800. The threat to Britain from naval challenge in the Baltic and the Russian embargo was heightened by the importance of the Baltic trade in grain, naval stores and timber.

The cabinet decided to act by sending a fleet to the Baltic to deal with the challenge presented. The fleet was to be commanded by Sir Hyde Parker (known to his contemporaries as 'Old Vinegar'), who had served in the West Indies and who had just married a young wife of 24. His appointment embodied typical bureaucratic caution (which persists to this day), having the objective of containing the firebrand Lord Nelson, who was thought, while heroic, to be unreliable. The fleet assembled at Yarmouth and Sir Hyde Parker lingered there, putting off sailing to the Baltic until after a ball to be given by his new wife. Nelson arrived and, knowing the need to reach Russian waters before the ice closing Kronstadt had thawed, complained secretly to the Admiralty; Earl St. Vincent ordered the fleet to sail. There were fifteen ships of the line at Yarmouth including the 98-gun London, in which Sir Hyde Parker had his flag, the St. George (Nelson's flagship),

Ramillies and Defiance. In addition the fleet had two 50-gunners, frigates and brigs, and carried one thousand troops. Three more ships of the line were ordered to the fleet but one, the Invincible, ran aground in Norfolk and was pounded to pieces on the beach. All her complement was lost.

The fleet arrived in the Kattegat, near the entrance to the Oresund, on 19th March. A continuation of an attempt at diplomacy, irresolution on the route to be taken to the Baltic by Sir Hyde Parker, and an unfavourable wind delayed further action until 30th March. This delay permitted the Danes to make further preparations to resist the British fleet. The Oresund at its narrowest is three miles wide and the Danish coast was lined with batteries of guns. Their fleet was drawn up at Copenhagen, a part within the inner harbour channel, but the main force, mostly dismantled, along the shore line in the King's Channel with the flagship, Dannebrog, in the middle of the line. The northern end of their line was protected by Trekroner castle.

Nelson wished to sail on to attack Reval, but Sir Hyde Parker was reluctant to proceed to Russia while the Danish fleet remained behind him. Finally he agreed to an attack on Copenhagen and the fleet. At daybreak on 30th March a northwesterly wind blew and the whole fleet set sail in line through the Oresund. The guns on the Danish coast fired on the fleet, but no guns spoke from the Swedish shore so that the bombardment fell short of the ships as they stood to that shore. Once through the Oresund, the plan conceived by Nelson was put into operation.

Two channels served Copenhagen, separated by a shoal known as the Middle Ground. The Danish fleet lined the western side of the inner and less deep channel. Nelson's plan was to take the lighter vessels – 10 ships of the line and 27 others with lesser draughts up the inner channel and to direct the attack individually boat to boat on the line as it lay. Success was therefore dependent on the initiative and boldness of individual ship's captains. Nelson transferred his flag to the Elephant and spent the nights of 30th and 31st March sounding the shoals of the inner channel, laying buoys and formulating his plan. The heavier ships under Sir Hyde Parker were to sail north of the middle ground from their anchorage in the Oresund to meet with Nelson's squadron near the entrance channel of Copenhagen north of the Trekroner fort. On 1st April Nelson and his squadron sailed through the outer channel and anchored to the south of the Middle Ground. During the night the wind veered to south – south-east and at 9.30 am anchor was weighed and buoyed by the following wind the squadron moved towards the line of Danish ships. Bellona and Russell went aground on the Middle Ground shoal, but led by Edgar, each ship went to its allocated station, anchoring by the stern, so that broadsides could be fired at each Danish ship. The distance between vessels was about half a cable, with the Elephant a cable's length from the Dannebrog, the Danish flagship. By 11.30 action was general, and it lasted for four hours. Resistance was stiff; the battle was a series of duels conducted in the encompassing gun smoke at close range. So fierce was it that

Nelson wrote in despatches: 'I have been in one hundred and five engagements but that of today is the most terrible of all'.

Sir Hyde Parker, due to tide and wind, had not been able to come near to assist Nelson, but observing the battle from a four-mile distance, decided to order Nelson to disengage. There was certainly a problem, since Nelson had only frigates to attack the Trekroner batteries, having lost the benefit of the Bellona and Russell. Parker made his signal in the early afternoon and Lieutenant Langford on the Elephant told Nelson of the signal. Nelson ordered the Lieutenant to look out for the Danish Commodore's signal of surrender and keep his eye fixed on that. He told him to acknowledge the signal but kept his signal for close action flying. He then turned to Captain Foley and said 'You know Foley I have only one eye – I have a right to be blind sometimes'. Putting the glass to his blind eye, he then said, 'I really do not see the signal'.

The battle went on for another hour or so until the wrecked Danish fleet began to fall silent. The flagships were drifting in the wind, burning, and then blew up. Some Danish ships surrendered, but shore batteries continued to fire on the boats sent with prize crews. Nelson, incensed, penned out a message to Crown Prince Frederick threatening to set the Danish ships on fire with their crews on board unsaved, and to bombard Copenhagen. Negotiations resulted in a twenty-four hour truce.

About the time at which the message was sent, two of Sir Hyde Parker's division of ships of the line arrived at the action and all the Danes ahead of Elephant struck their colours. Nelson took the opportunity of the truce to secure the passage of his most damaged vessels past the Trekroner batteries. The Danish prizes, apart from one, were burned and sent to the bottom. Nelson and Sir Hyde Parker were re-united and they stationed themselves at a point from where Copenhagen could be bombarded. The British loss amounted to over one thousand men and the Danes more. With the approval of Sir Hyde Parker the truce was renewed daily, and Nelson negotiated an Armistice with the Crown Prince. The agreement was signed on 9th April and was to last fourteen weeks in order to permit the British fleet to sail to attack Russia. Sir Hyde Parker to his credit viewed tolerably Nelson's disobedience, as Earl St. Vincent had done earlier at the Battle of St. Vincent.

Sir Hyde Parker continued to dally in the Baltic and engaged in an inconsequential action with the Swedish near Karlskrona, but on 6th May was relieved of his command. Nelson at once sailed for Reval, where he hoped to engage twelve Russian ships of the line which ice at Kronstadt had caused to remain in the harbour away from the main fleet. However, on his arrival at Reval no action took place, since Tsar Paul I had been deposed and murdered. Tsar Alexander I had no desire to continue the policy of war with Britain, which was not supported by Count Panin, his foreign minister. The league of Armed Neutrality was abandoned and British access to the Baltic and powers of search and seizures accepted.

3rd April 1367

The Battle of Navarette

In 1360 England and France signed the treaty of Bretigny, making peace at the end of the war in which Edward III had re-established English power in France. By the treaty Edward III gave up his claim to be King of France, but secured lands in south-western France including Gascony, Poitou and the Limousin. His eldest son Edward, the Black Prince, was made Prince of Aquitaine and in 1362 went to reside in his dukedom. After King John of France was succeeded by Charles V, the French fomented trouble in the English lands and around them, although unwilling to re-open the war. One sphere of troublemaking was northern Spain, and in 1366 an opportunity was taken to support the replacement of the King of Castile, Pedro the Cruel, by his bastard brother Henri of Trastamara. Led by the French commander Du Guesclin, an army made up of English marauders in France, mercenaries of various countries and French warrior knights entered Castile, and defeated and deposed Pedro, who fled to the Black Prince in Aquitaine. Edward III and the Black Prince, concerned at further French influence on the southerly borders of Aquitaine, and by the need to sustain the principle of legitimacy, agreed to assist Pedro to regain his crown. The campaign was delayed by the need to await the arrival of John, Duke of Lancaster from England, while some of the English with Du Guesclin were recalled to the Prince's army.

The Black Prince crossed to Castile by way of Navarre, where King Charles the Bad first supported the French, then accepted gold to allow the English over the passes of the Pyrenees, but finally had himself seized by the Aragonese so that he could pretend that he was unable to assist either side.

The Castilian army under Henri of Trastamara had advanced to the Ebro and blocked the English passage of the river. The Black Prince, in a manoeuvre carried out secretly, outflanked his army and arrived at the Ebro further upstream at Varna, crossing at Lagarno on the road from Pamplona to Burgos the capital of Castile. The Franco- Castilian army broke camp, re-crossed the Ebro and moved to block the Black Prince on the Burgos road. Their army established itself to the west of Navarette and east of Najira, leaving the River Najarilla at their rear. Huizinga in his 'The Waning of the Middle Ages' notes that actuated by the highest ideal of chivalry Henri of Trastamara abandoned the advantages offered by the configuration of the ground, since he desired at any cost to measure himself against the enemy in the open field.

At dawn on 3rd April the armies met in the open plain between the two towns. Each army arranged itself in three lines behind one another. The English army of about 24,000 seems to have numbered less than 12,000 lances, but was made up in equal proportions of both archers and men-at-arms. The Franco-Castilian army was overall in excess of 23,000, but an overwhelming element was Spanish infantry, comprising spearmen, cross-bow men and slingers recruited from the towns. In terms of men-at-arms the Franco-Castilian army were less in number. In numbers the armies appeared to have been closely matched.

The English vanguard comprised 3,000 dismounted men-at-arms and 3,000 archers on the wings commanded by the Duke of Lancaster. 1,200 of the men-at-arms were veterans led by Sir John Chandos. The centre, comprising three elements, was commanded by the Captal de Buch on the right, the Black Prince in the centre and Sir Thomas Percy on the left. The dismounted men were interspaced with and flanked by archers. The rear line of 3,000 lances comprised Gascons under King John of Majorca and the Count of Armagnac.

The Spanish vanguard, comprising the French men-at-arms and the Spanish knights, both dismounted, probably had cross-bowmen on the flanks. It was commanded by Du Guesclin; the centre was under the command of Don Tello (on the left), Henri of Trast amara himself in the centre and the Count of Denia on the right. The unreliable Spanish infantry made up the third line.

The vanguards of both armies first engaged and so great was the struggle of clashing arms that neither side gained or lost ground. The battle was evenly matched, only the cross-bowmen of the French line retiring under the impact of the English archers. Don Tello on the Spanish left and the Count of Denia on the right then endeavoured to outflank the English centre line, but the guarding archers insured that none of the horsemen came within distance to engage and to throw their javelins, and instead of engaging in battle, the repulsed Spaniards fled the field. The Captal de Buch and Sir Thomas Percy then turned their wings of the line on the flanks of the engaged Spanish vanguard, and the Black Prince advanced to assist his brother the Duke of Lancaster. Henri of Trastamara in his turn hurried to join the battle and brought up his centre and infantry. The latter fought bravely leading, his knights and armed men. The mass of infantry, disordered and struck down by the protecting English archers, fled the field. At this point King John of Majorca brought his reserves into battle on the left. The arrows flew thick and the Castilian, after fighting heroically, gave way. Henri of Trastamara retreated with his knights and men-at-arms, although Du Guesclin and the French stood their ground. At last they surrendered. About five hundred knights and men of arms had fallen on the Spanish side. The English were said to have lost two knights, (one the son of a baron, Sir John Ferrers) forty men-at-arms and twenty archers.

The Spanish infantry were decimated, since the River Najarilla was in flood and the masses blocked the narrow bridge at Najora. They are said to have lost 7,000 men.

Pedro the Cruel was restored to the crown of Castile at Burgos and thus in the short term the object of the campaign was won. However, two years later the Castilians rose again against their king; he fell into the hands of Henri of Trastamara and was murdered.

Du Guesclin was in time released and returned to serve the King of France and command his armies.

<h1 style="text-align:center">3rd April 1811</h1>

<h1 style="text-align:center">The Battle of Sabugal</h1>

The French Emperor Napoleon I commenced his intervention in Spain militarily in October 1807. From that date the British intervened in Spain and Portugal in order to protect the Portuguese and assist the Spanish to resist. The British and French had varying fortunes in the struggle, which affected most parts of the Peninsular. In 1810 Marshal Massena invaded Portugal with the 'Army of Portugal'. Wellington retired from the border and took up a defensive position at Bussaco. On 27th September the French attacked, but failed to carry the position taken up by Wellington. He however, to the surprise of Massena, retired to positions already prepared to the north-east of Lisbon, which provided a system of forts, defensive positions and redoubts on hills between the Atlantic and the River Tagus, known as the lines of Torres Vedras. The country outside the lines had been the subject of a 'scorched earth' policy and was substantially without population, food reserves, undestroyed villages and forage. The French advanced to the lines, arriving on 14th October, but found them impassable. Massena decided that to attack the lines was impractical and in November retired with most of his force to Santarem. He remained there in winter quarters, unmolested, Wellington deciding that his army was better served by rest and food and time for recovery. There were neither provisions nor forage to maintain the French, although they were reinforced by D'Erlon's Corps from Almeida, but that merely increased the problem of supply. In late February 1811 Massena decided to retire, the army leaving by way of the route on which he had come. By 4th March the French were fully in retreat and there began a one hundred and thirty-mile pursuit by the British army, marked by various rearguard engagements en route. However, after a short halt on 23rd March, Massena ordered a change of route, with a view to turning south to meet Marshal Soult in Andalucia. On 27th March, after the resignation of Marshal Ney, who viewed the plan as absurd, the French resumed their retreat direct to Spain. Finding that Wellington was on their flank, Massena retreated beyond the River Ebro with his left at Sabugal, comprising Reynier's Corps. Wellington and his force came up to them at that town.

For several days there had been rain and the morning of 3rd April was thick with fog. Wellington retained the 3rd and 5th Divisions of the army (of mixed British and Portuguese) facing across the Ebro to Sabugal. The Light Brigade, commanded by Beckwith and Drummond, was sent to outflank the left of the French and come up in their rear. In the dense fog they lost their way (possibly, having crossed the Coa, the battalions turned north too near to the river. That view is certainly to be found in Colonel Tomkinson's *Diary of a Cavalry Officer*). In the result they emerged from the manoeuvre in the middle of Reynier's Corps. Unprepared, the latter were driven back but French reserves appeared to back his struggling soldiers. A fierce struggle occurred but the fog clearing, Reynier became aware of the concentrated formations on the other side of the Coa. Retreat was ordered and his forces disengaged to join Massena and the main body to the north-east. Massena, having been outflanked, was forced to abandon the Coa River and make for Ciudad Rodrigo. His army was still a fighting force, but during the invasion of Portugal the Army of Portugal had lost 25,000 men, most of them victims of starvation and disease, all their baggage and most of their guns. Massena left a garrison of 3,000 at Ciudad Rodrigo but hurried on to Salamanca.

Tomkinson notes that Lt. Colonel Beckwith obtained great credit; having been hit by a musket-ball on the outside bone of the right eye, he kept going throughout the affair and did not miss a day of duty.

6th April 1812

The Taking of Badajoz

The Anglo-Portuguese Army of Wellington only took Badajoz at the third attempt. The town and castle was an important fortress on the Spanish-Portuguese border covering the routes into the interior of Spain and south to Andalucia. The Spanish held the town and fort, after the townspeople removed and killed the Governor in May 1808. In January 1811 Marshal Soult moved to besiege the town and on 9th March 1811 the weak Spanish Governor, despite being well provisioned, surrendered, to the surprise of the French. At that stage a British force was under way to its relief. The army had, however, no siege train save for twenty-three obsolete cannons, four dating from the seventeenth century. On 8th May under Sir William Beresford Badajoz was invested, but no attack was made until 12th May. Marshal Soult, who had left Badajoz, returned from his move to the south and Beresford retired. On 15th May the battle of Albuera was fought, where the Anglo-Portuguese army held the French and Soult had to withdraw. Badajoz was then invested for a second time; its French Governor was resourceful and without effective siege cannon, any siege had no real hope of success. Two assaults were beaten off on 6th and 9th June 1811. On 11th June the Army of Portugal under Marshal Massena approached and the siege was lifted. In the immediate area of Badajoz the second half of 1811 was used in limited campaigning and defensive action by both Wellington and the French, who were now commanded by Marshal Marmont. The army of Portugal was drained of men to meet threats to the French elsewhere in Spain and to provide soldiers for the armies, which were to invade Russia in 1812. A siege train had been sent from England and had come up to Almeida. In January 1812 Wellington besieged and took Cuidad Rodrigo. He then turned his attention again to Badajoz.

By the spring of 1812 Wellington had a formidable force on the frontier of Spain, comprising 60,000 men, with 58 heavy-calibre guns among the artillery. He split his force into three parts and with one part he arrived at Badajoz on 16th March. There was constant rain and the work to make parallels meant that parapets and revetments, (carried out under fire) were being washed away. The fortifications of the town had been greatly improved by General Philippon, the French commander, who had a force of 4,000. Its walls and bastions rose to thirty feet high and in the ditch abutting the south-east walls a twelve-foot deep trench had been dug, taking water from the adjoining rivers. Wellington decided to attack the town from the south-east. In order to secure his position it was necessary to take the Picurina fort outside the walls. Operations began against the fort on 17th March. From the first parallel dug, two batteries (10 guns in each) were brought up to direct against the fort. It took several days for all to be in place for the attack. By 25th March musquetry fire had silenced returning fire from the fort, since none dared to shew his head. Immediately after sunset the fort was attacked by 300 men in three columns – two with scaling ladders and one to enter by the rear door. The attack was successful and despite the rumour of a French counter-attack from the town the fort surrendered, largely undamaged. By 31st March, despite French fire from the city, three battalions of heavy guns were in place at the Picurina and bombardment of the city walls had begun. Three breaches of the walls were created but the energetic French set to mine the breaches with booby-traps and put *cheveux de frise* in place.

By 6th April, although in the view of the Engineers all was not ready, Wellington decided to order the assault, because of his worry that Marshals Marmont and Soult were on the move towards the frontier. The attack began at 10 am, by the 4th and Light Divisions. Secondary assaults were to take place on the San Vincente bastion in the north-west and the castle in the north-east of the city. The 4th and Light Divisions, who became entangled, moved towards the breaches, having to pass over the ditch and water-filled trench. The fierce defence inflicted heavy casualties; men drowned in the flooded trench; five hundred were blown up in the breaches by mines put there. Repeated attempts to enter the breaches were made: small parties even succeeded in the attempt. Attack followed attack; 40 times the bugles sounded and each doomed column advanced with a loud huzzah. After two hours Wellington called off the attempt.

Meanwhile, Picton had assaulted the castle. His troops had waited under fire in the ditch for the ladders to be brought. They climbed up the thirty to forty-foot walls; although ladders were pushed over and some broke under the weight of the soldiers, the top of the walls was reached. Once one soldier was on top, there was a hundred. A like attempt was made at San Vincente and for neither were there enough defenders. The town was taken and the British rushed through to take the breaches in the rear. General Philippon and the garrison laid down their arms, although all the troops in the castle were bayoneted. General Picton and General Kempt were wounded at the Castle and Major General Walker at San Vincente.

The troops entered the city and on the night of the 6th and on the 7th the whole city was put to the sword. Looting, drunkenness, rape, pillage and murder took place as the soldiers wreaked vengeance on the inhabitants. Muskets were fired at people in the streets; houses plundered. There was no respect for officers: even

Wellington was fired on by mistake. As Napier says in his Peninsular War: 'But the strong desire for glory was, in the British, dashed with a hatred of the citizens on an old grudge and recent toil and hardship with much spilling of blood had made many incredibly savage'. The death toll at the breaches was to quote Tomkinson 'the most shocking thing ever seen and thus perhaps a little plunder was necessary to drown the horror'. Order was restored by the use of the gallows and flogging.

Wellington went to visit the glacis and the breaches, where over three thousand men had fallen in the storming, and wept. In his letter to the War Minister he notes that 'the capture of the Badajoz affords as strong an instance of the gallantry of our troops as has ever been displayed. But I greatly hope that I shall never again be the instrument of putting these to such a test'

10th April 1814

The Investment of Toulouse

After the defeat of the Emperor Napoleon and the French at the Battle of the Nations at Leipzig in June 1813, the armies of Prussia, Russia and the Austrian Empire pressed westwards into France. Napoleon was forced to fight a delaying campaign, but by April 1814 the three allies were at or approaching Paris and Napoleon returned to Fontainebleau, south east of the city, from where negotiations began about the end of the war and the future of Napoleon and his family. On the 6th April Napoleon abdicated unconditionally and on 12th April a treaty was finally signed.

Meanwhile, the Duke of Wellington had pressed with the Anglo-Portuguese Army northwards from Spain into France. Bordeaux was against Napoleon and was taken with the help of the invading army. Bayonne had been bypassed. Marshal Soult and his army retired south-east towards Toulouse. This was the major French army depot in the region and heavily fortified with the old city walls, recently constructed redoubts and earth works. The city lay to the east of the River Garonne, with the suburb of St. Cyprian to the west of the river. From the Garonne north of the city the Royal Canal ran around the eastern boundary and away to the south-east. Beyond the canal east of the city existed a ridge, the Mont Rave, which overlooked the city, and beyond that to the east a waterlogged and marshy area towards the River Ers. The city therefore had strong natural and manmade defences.

Wellington commanded a force of about 49,000 with fifty guns by the time of this campaign, and the French army against him amounted to 42,000. Marshal Soult arrived at Toulouse on 24th March, pursued by Wellington. With great difficulty a pontoon bridge was constructed across the Garonne to the north of the city, and on 3rd April the British army began to cross to the east bank. When only 19,000 men, commanded by Marshal Beresford, had crossed, the river, swollen from the rains, swept away the crossing and this force was left isolated on the east bank. Four days passed before any effective communications were re-established. Despite the weakness of the British force, Marshal Soult chose to remain in the city and did not attack.

The plan to attack evolved by Wellington contemplated the main attack from the east, which necessitated the taking of the Mont Rave, with a feint made by Sir Thomas Picton with the Light and 3rd Divisions to the north in order to cover that movement, and a subsidiary attack on St. Cyprian, the latter to be made by Hill with 14,000 troops under his command. The eastern attack involved a two-mile march, skirting the marshy ground on muddy routes.

The action started at 5.00 am on Easter Sunday, beginning with Hill's attack on St. Cyprian. This continued all day and enabled Wellington to keep the garrison occupied with few casualties. Sir Thomas Picton, forgetful that his action was but a diversion, launched a fierce assault in the north, sustaining extensive losses, particular at Petit Granague and Pont Jumeaux. He was unable to force the Royal Canal and ultimately had to withdraw.

Beresford, commanding the eastern attack, because of the condition of the route, gradually fell behind and his artillery and infantry were separated. The artillery were ordered to bombard the hostile forces from where they were and, although the 4th and 6th Divisions were not in place, the Spanish corps, treating that as the signal for attack, endeavoured to storm the northern end of the ridge under the shadow of the Great Redoubt. They took shelter in a sunken lane but under a merciless bombardment from the French they retired headlong down the slope.

Beresford at last had his troops in place and attacked at the southern end of the Mont Rave ridge. As the troops mounted the slope, the French under General Tampin advanced in columns to meet them. That mass was therefore exposed to the British, whose rifle fire crashed into them, wreaking havoc and causing the French columns to retire. General Tampin fell mortally wounded. The French retreated down the western slope of Mount Rave towards the Royal Canal, where they were reinforced. Beresford did not immediately follow, wishing to have the guns on the ridge. In this interval Picton made yet another unsuccessful attack on the north. After a delay he pursued the French along the ridge, meeting continuous strong opposition. Despite heavy casualties from a strong attack by the French on the 42nd regiment the British fought forwards until they reached the Great Redoubt, where the Spanish corps had been savaged by the defenders resisting another heroic attack. The French held off the British while the guns were evacuated from the Great Redoubt across the Royal Canal.

Wellington's forces had suffered severe casualties in the attempt to encircle the city and he was not prepared, without regrouping his forces, to forward the attack with tired troops across the Royal Canal. The battle came to a standstill and, indeed, stopped entirely about six o'clock in the evening. Wellington had lost 4,600 men slain and described it as 'a very severe affair'. The French had 3,200 casualties.

In the night of 11th April Marshal Soult slipped out of Toulouse with his stores and guns towards Carcassonne and the south-east: Wellington was welcomed into Toulouse on 12th April by the inhabitants, who supported the Bourbon cause in France.

Neither side seems to have had news of the abdication of the Emperor Napoleon at Fontainebleau, first conditionally on 4th April and then unconditionally on 7th April. On 12th April the Treaty of Paris ended the war.

11th April 1809

The Naval Action in the Aix Roads

In January 1809, after the Battle of Coruna and the evacuation of the British army there, an army of ten thousand men remained in Portugal in order to defend Lisbon. The British Government of the Duke of Portland was concerned to secure the line of communication by sea with Portugal and on to the West Indies and Mediterranean. A strong French squadron was at Brest threatening the sea route, but the port was blockaded by the British commanded by Admiral Gambier. In an easterly gale in February the British ships were forced out to sea and the Brest fleet under Admiral Villaumez, failing to make L'Orient, ended in the Aix roads. There they were found by Gambier and the fleet, which anchored in the Basque roads on 7th March, nine miles out, to be ready to engage should the French emerge.

Admiral Harvey, who was second in command to Gambier, advocated that the anchored fleet should be attacked by fireships. Harvey was one of Nelson's band of Captains and the superbly gallant commander of the fighting Téméraire (see the Battle of Trafalgar, 21st October 1805). Admiral Gambier on the other hand was a commander who out of twenty-two years service had spent seventeen years at a desk in the Admiralty. He was a keen religious fundamentalist and imbued with the typical caution of the bureaucrat, averse to taking action since blame could seldom be attached to he who did nothing. He opposed alcohol and did not allow women on board in port, being known to his men as 'Dismal Jimmie'! In relation to the fireship suggestion, he wrote to Lord Mulgrave, the First Lord of the Admiralty that although the French ships were exposed to the operation of fireships, 'it is a horrible mode of warfare, and the attempt hazardous, if not desperate: but we should have plenty of volunteers in the service.' He added that if it were to be done, it should be done secretly and quickly.

Lord Mulgrave and the Government were anxious for political reasons to have a victory, and the First Lord remained committed to the fireship idea, setting in hand the conversion of twelve transports to fireships. He also had to hand in London a prospective commander of such a venture who could be relied on to relish a 'desperate' enterprise. Lord Cochrane, the son of the 9th Earl of Dundonald, a title dating from 1648, was a post-Captain aged thirty-four, who had had rapid advancement in the navy, successfully commanding the brig Speedy and the frigate Pallas in exciting engagements in the Mediterranean and Bay of Biscay, where his courage and adventurousness had brought success. In 1809 he commanded the frigate Impérieuse. Throughout his life he was interested in scientific innovation and technology. Asked about the fireships proposal and Gambier's letter, he recommended the construction of 'explosion' ships as a van to the fireships, making the attempt less risky. Mulgrave decided that, despite his lack of seniority, he should be given command of the fireship enterprise. Cochrane tried to refuse on the sound ground that such an appointment would not be warmly welcomed by those senior to him, but Mulgrave pressed it upon him. For the Admiralty, who disapproved of Cochrane, the appointment had the advantage that, were he to fail, they might be rid of him without embarrassment to the Admiral in command and, if he succeeded, a victory could be claimed, which would support the Government politically. On 19th March Gambier was sent the order directing him to permit Cochrane to attempt to destroy the French fleet with the fireships. Cochrane sailed from Portsmouth in the Impérieuse and arrived at the Basque Roads on 3rd April. He was accompanied by the twelve fireships and William Congreve with his rockets. The arrival of Cochrane in charge of the expedition to fire the French fleet incensed Admiral Harvey, who had urged the attempt on Gambier, and he visited Gambier in the presence of Cochrane to complain about being deprived of command. Harvey thought the arrangement an insult, and threatened to strike his flag and resign. In an explosion of invective he accused Gambier of being wholly unfit to command the fleet and of cowardice.

Admiral Villaumez had been replaced as commander of the French fleet by admiral Allemand, who after the arrival of the British started energetically to take measures to protect the fleet. The Aix Roads formed the access to the River Charente. They lay between the Ile d'Aix to the north and Ile Mad ame, just off the mainland to the south. The Ile d'Aix itself to the north of the river channel was the continuation of a promontory of the mainland on which the Fouras Castle overlooked the river channel. On the Ile d'Aix were three forts, the Citadel being on the south of the island Shoals extended northwest of the island and on its easterly side. The Ile Madame to the south of the channel was at the landward end of the Palles Shoal, which dried out at low tide and extended in a north-westerly direction. That in its turn, after a channel running north-west – south, was extended by the Boyart Shoal. The roads themselves and river channel were wholly exposed to north-westerly winds and sea swells from that direction. Allemand placed across the entrance a heavy nine hundred-foot boom, made of chains and timber and anchored to the seabed, just south of the Ile d'Aix under the shadow of the guns of the Citadel. Behind it were stationed three frigates and then in two lines, the first of five and the second of six, the eleven ships of the line which he had. Small boats were stationed near the boom to grapple and divert any fireships. By the time Cochrane arrived, therefore, protection for the French fleet was in place.

Immediately on arrival he began to reconnoitre the roads and take soundings. He discovered that the Citadel was much ruined, that the Channel had two miles of width and that southwards towards the Palles Shoal, incoming ships were out of range of the Citadel guns. There were soundings which showed that no rocky shoals as alleged were to be found in the channel between the Ile d'Aix and the Boyart Shoal. Cochrane also had the assistance of the standard French naval charts taken from the Neptune Francaise in 1806. He had in the tradition of Nelson at Copenhagen (see the Battle of Copenhagen 2nd April 1801) carried out his own survey ready for the attack. Gambier, in the four weeks that he had been off the River Charente, had had 200 soundings done of moment, only a few near the Boyart Shoal, and certainly never himself inspected the scene of the action. In terms of charts, he had charts drawn up by Thomas Stokes, master of the flagship Caledonia, and Edward Fairfax, master of the Fleet, but these were based on informal French charts taken from the Almeide. These showed the Channel at one mile. As Admiral Harvey in his denunciation had observed, the Admiral Lord Gambier had spent all his time organising and visiting ship's musters for the purpose of examination of the men's knowledge of the catechism, while the boats distributed tractarian pamphlets to the crews, at the neglect of proper survey work for the coming action.

Cochrane energetically had the fireships made ready. On deck were trails of gunpowder to carry the flame around the ship, whose ropes and sails were drenched in tar and resin. Turpentine and resin was poured all over the ship: air holes cut in the hull and grappling hooks and chains strung along the sides. In addition to the original twelve, another nine had arrived, making twenty-one in all. He had persuaded Lord Mulgrave of the feasibility of the action by describing to him his plan for 'explosion ships' to precede the fireships in. Three of these were produced. The floor of each vessel was packed tight with logs and firmed up with other substances. On the floor 1,500 casks filled with gunpowder were placed closely roped together. On the casks went shells and some 3,000 hand grenades, the whole compressed with sand into a solid mass. A fuse was set to ignite this huge mortar bomb after fifteen minutes. The plan was for the explosion ships to go in first, then fireships, and both would be followed up by frigates, which could pick up the returning seamen who had brought in the explosion and fireships. Pallas, Aigle and Unicorn were assigned this task.

On 10th April Gambier refused Cochrane leave to mount his attack citing danger to the crews of the explosion boats and fireships. On the 11th however, with the wind making north-westerly and all ready, he knew that he could no longer disobey the commands of the Admiralty and authorised Cochrane to make his attempt. On a mounting flood tide, under cover of the dark night Cochrane, on the Impérieuse, the explosion boat at his stern, led in the convoy of ships with the other three frigates and anchored just off the Boyart Shoal. About 8.30 he transferred with Lieutenant Bissel to the first explosion boat accompanied by four seamen: similar crews were in the others. In the second there was Midshipman

Marryat, later to become an acclaimed Victorian author. The strong wind and tide bore the boats down towards the boom: as the first neared, Cochrane, who in the darkness could not see the boom or French ships, at what he thought was the interval planned of fifteen minutes, left the explosion ships with his crew, and the seamen began to row energetically against the wind and sea, as they strived to outdistance the explosion. They had pulled hard for about nine minutes only, when in an ear-splitting roar of sound and rush of fire the explosion ship blew up. Cochrane himself described it as 'the grandest artificial spectacle.' Shells, rockets, and grenades flamed in the sky, and a great ring of water erupted and spread, almost swamping the gig in which Cochrane sat. Huge quantities of debris flew through the air and the sea convulsed.

Cochrane and his gig were saved from damage by the flying debris, as the short delay before explosion meant that the broken timbers and chains of the boom hit the water beyond them. A second explosion soon followed the first. The third explosion ship was less successful and drifted towards the Impérieuse with a fireship closing on it. Cochrane had by that time returned to his ship and he ordered Midshipman Marryat and a party of seamen to get the explosion ship to safety.

Behind the explosion ships the twenty-one fireships had been set on their way. These however were mismanaged and left by their crews after having been set alight four and a half miles out from the French fleet. They came down towards the French, however, in a flaming mass of lights, some nearer, others further away, all twenty-one of them, firing, burning and sparking in the night. The high roars and awesome impact of the explosion ships followed by the flame of the fireships over the sea panicked the French, who anticipated more explosion ships, unprotected as they had become by the destruction of the boom. With sails bent, they had, if they were to move quickly, to slip their cables, and many did. Only Foudroyant (80 guns) and Cassard (74 guns) remained at anchor. The frigates slipped behind the ships of the line, which as they cut their cables began to collide. Tonnerre (74 guns) and Patrick (74 guns), for example, collided: others in panic began to fire into one another. The chaotic fleet was carried off in the flood tide and north-westerly wind towards the south-east, some ships being swept along broadside. The fire boats, but for four, did not reach the panicked fleet, most, because of their early release, were blown off course and ended beached, burning themselves out. One of the four came up to the French flagship, L'Océan (120 guns) and set fire to the poop and then slid away along the starboard side without grappling the ship. L'Océan also was borne away on the sea and grounded.

When morning broke on 12th April, seven of the French ships of the line were to be seen lying beached on the Palles Shoal, carried there by the wind and now fast-flowing ebb tide. They included L'Océan, Aquilon (74 guns), Ville de Varsovie (74 guns) and Calcutta, a captured British East Indiaman (56 guns). Aground on their bilges and leaning, they were incapable of firing their guns. The seven ships were wholly at the mercy of the British and, had their exposed bottoms been riddled with shot, could have been destroyed. With dawn the guns of the Citadel on the Ile d' Aix started to fire on the Impérieuse and Cochrane moved out of range. Then, surveying the ships on the Palles Shoal, at 7 am Lord Cochrane signalled to Lord Gambier, nine miles away, 'All the enemy's ships, except two are on shore.' Only the answering pennant was raised and there was no reply. Cochrane tried again, 'The enemy ships can be destroyed.' The same answering pennant was raised. Cochrane tried again: 'Half the fleet can destroy the enemy'; again the answering pennant and the fleet remained motionless. The flood had begun to run and Cochrane signalled 'The frigates alone can destroy the enemy.' Eight and nine o'clock passed and the fleet remained as before, immobile.

With dawn the French had begun the work necessary to prepare the beached ships to heave off on the top of the floodtide, discarding onto the shoal their guns and stores. On board the Caledonia, the flagship, Lord Gambier called a council of his Captains and at last at eleven o'clock the fleet set sail toward Cochrane and the Aix roads. Meanwhile, guns from the Ile d' Oleron had tried to bombard the Impérieuse to no effect. To Cochrane's annoyance Gambier and the fleet came to a standstill and dropped anchor two or three miles off, out of range of the onshore guns. By this time having been lightened, the L'Ocean, the outer ship on the shoal, had managed to heave itself off. Cochrane, always courageous, ardent and fervent, and in despair at the lost opportunity, decided to go in himself, although without orders. In order to deceive Gambier, he weighed anchor and began to drift astern in the flood tide towards the Palles Shoal. At 1.30 pm he made sail to get up to the escaping French vessels. At 1.40 pm he signalled 'Enemy superior to chasing ship, but inferior to the fleet.' In reply there was just the answering pennant; at 1.45 pm in desperation he signalled, 'In want of assistance.' The request was not strictly true; although he was a lone frigate near some re-floated ships of the line, these were without guns, which had been thrown overboard. The Calcutta, still aground but upright, started to fire on the Impérieuse, which at two o'clock came to anchor and began firing its broadsides into the Calcutta, and with its forecastle and bow guns the Aquilon and Ville de Varsovie.

At 2 pm Gambier at last responded to the signal and sent in Valiant (74 guns and 1st of the name, Revenge (74 guns and 6th of the name), Indefatigable (44 guns), Emerald, Unicorn, Pallas and Aigle. Cochrane and the Impérieuse sustained their attack until 3.20 pm at which time the Calcutta surrendered. Cochrane forthwith put on board a prize crew. At 3.30 pm the detached squadron arrived. Impérieuse stopped firing. Indefatigable started to bombard the Calcutta and had to be told to desist since it had been taken. Captain Lafon and his crew had escaped out of the stern. The arriving squadron maintained the attack and by 5.30 pm Aquilon and the Ville de Varsovie had struck and were taken. By this time the Foudroyant and the Cassard had slipped anchor and sailed off towards the Charente estuary, going aground in the channel. At 6 pm the crew of the Tonnerre set fire to the ship and abandoned it; the Calcutta had been set on fire at about 5.30 pm and at 7 pm the Tonnere blew up and at 9 pm the Calcutta. The Aquilon and Ville de Varsovie still remained as prizes. Darkness settled and apart from desultory firing the action had come to a standstill.

At 4 am Gambier signalled by lights for the ships which had gone in to return. To Cochrane's annoyance the Aquilon and Ville de Varsovie were set on fire. He then proceeded to try to persuade the captains of the Indefatigable and the frigates to remain and join him in an attack on the L'Océan which was, although afloat, nearby. The Indefatigable's captain refused but Captain Seymour of the Pallas agreed. Four brigs, the Beagle, Growler, Conflict and Encounter also agreed to assist. The bomb ship Elma, protected by the brigs, began to fire on L'Océan, while Impérieuse was repaired, making good the damage inflicted by the Calcutta in the engagement the previous afternoon. As he prepared, Gambier hoisted the signal of recall. Cochrane ignored it once more, sending the signal 'The enemy can be destroyed.' A letter was then sent by Gambier repeating his order to return. Once more Cochrane took no notice and the recall signal was made by the flagship. A letter was then sent from Gambier relieving Cochrane of his command and ordering him back to the flagship. The action of the Aix roads was over. Three ships of the line had been destroyed and one East Indiaman. Two were beached and damaged beyond repair, but the opportunity to destroy the whole of the anchored fleet had been wasted. On 15th April Lord Cochrane was sent back to London with Gambier's despatch to Lord Mulgrave. With that despatch the political 'spin' would begin.

Lord Gambier's despatch reported that of seven ships on shore following Lord Cochrane's attack four were destroyed. He praised Lord Cochrane for his bravery and audacious action, but suggested that the boom had been destroyed by the fireship Mediator, which had 'led' the attack. He claimed that on learning of the night action he had proceeded at once to destroy the French ships. Lord Mulgrave indicated, the Government being politically in need of a popular victory, that votes of thanks to Lord Gambier would be moved by the Government in the two Houses of Parliament. Lord Cochrane was made a Knight Commander of the Bath. As the ships returned to port, gossip on shore began, indicating that maters had not been quite as described. The Times, obviously furnished with Cochrane's account of the delay and failure to bring in the fleet, began in its leaders to ask pertinent questions about 'the victory.'

Lord Cochrane was at the time of the Battle the Member of Parliament for the Borough of Westminster. That constituency had an almost complete manhood suffrage of about 11,000, unlike other Boroughs, where the electorate was in the hundreds or less. The constituency had returned to Parliament in

1784 the great eighteenth-century Whig, Charles James Fox and by 1809 returned with Lord Cochrane, the Whig Radical Sir Francis Burdett. Cochrane had the archetypal views of a progressive Whig, founded on the spirit and philosophy of the Glorious Revolution of 1688. He believed in universal suffrage and electoral reform, hounded corruption and abuses in the navy and was active with Burdett in submitting to the House of Commons the petitions of working men, who in the first decade of the nineteenth century were in want and poverty. He also had the Whig instinct for the protection of property nonetheless, campaigning for the right of navy captains and the seamen to their prize money and denouncing encroachments on it. One of his most famous interventions in the Commons was to denounce the level of naval pensions for those who fought and their families compared with the emoluments and rewards given to the holders of office in the Government and its civil service.

When Lord Mulgrave told him that there was to be a vote of thanks to Lord Gambier in the House of Commons, he told the First Lord that he would oppose it from his seat in the Commons. There then followed a number of attempts by Lord Mulgrave to dissuade Cochrane from that course, hinting that he would jeopardise his career and, when that had no effect, offering him a beneficial naval command. Cochrane however believed that the deception of the public by the untruthful story of the action of Aix Roads needed to be exposed. He remained undeterred. When Lord Mulgrave told Gambier, the latter demanded a Court Martial.

The Court Martial began on 26th July 1809. Having proclaimed a victory, the Government were clearly anxious to have a satisfactory outcome. The officers appointed to the Panel therefore knew where their duty lay as independent judges (and as inquiry chairmen also know today). The President was Admiral Sir Richard Curtis, the Commander in Chief at Portsmouth, a close friend of Gambier, Admirals Sir William Young and Sir John Sutton, with both of whom Cochrane had had difficulties, and eight captains. The charge was confined to that of failing on 12th April to attack, having had the signal that the enemy were onshore and could be destroyed and delaying for a considerable time or neglecting to take effective measures for destroying them. The evidence took eight days and ran to two hundred and forty pages. Gambier called twenty-five witnesses. Captains Maitland and Austen, who supported Cochrane, were not called, the former having been sent to sea.

The essence of Gambier's case was that to send in the fleet before the flood had mounted at two o'clock would have hazarded the ships in the shoals of the river under the guns of the forts. He relied, as did his witness, on the charts which had been prepared by the Master of the Caledonia and the Master of the Fleet. Cochrane and four others gave evidence to the contrary. Apart from the issue of the charts, Gambier's emphasis of the threat of the forts and guns was hardly persuasive, given that they did almost no damage to Impérieuse, which was exposed to them, and to the ships which went in on the afternoon of 12th April. Accepting Gambier's evidence and that of his witnesses, the Court Martial cleared Gambier of misconduct. The 'victory' remained intact: the fact that Gambier's action had allowed seven ships of the line to escape unnecessarily was to be overlooked. Had Nelson still been alive the outcome of the action of the Aix Roads as it occurred would have been inconceivable. Lord Cochrane refused to accept the findings of the Court Martial, accusing it of bias and alleging that the witnesses were perjured. In January 1810 the Government introduced the vote of thanks to Lord Gambier in the House of Commons and it was carried - despite large abstentions - by 161 votes to 39, being opposed by Cochrane and the progressive Whigs.

Lord Cochrane's life, although he was given no further naval command in the War, was to proceed full of excitement and incident. In a dispute with the Malta Prize Court, whose documents he had taken, he was imprisoned and escaped with the assistance of naval officers of the squadron. In 1814 he was prosecuted for criminal fraud in relation to a transaction of shares on the Stock Exchange. He, his uncle and a Mr Butt had contracted to buy shares and it was alleged that they had arranged that an acquaintance Mr De Berenger, dressed as an army officer, would bring news from Dover that the Emperor Napoleon was defeated and killed. Posing as Colonel de Bourg and dressed in a red uniform coat, the latter was alleged to have done that. Cochrane sold his shares, which went up in value on the news, and made a profit of £2,740. The others also sold. They were all indicted for common fraud and the case was heard in the King's Bench before Lord Ellenborough the Lord Chief Justice. Cochrane admitted that De Berenger had come to see him on the day on which the 'news' arrived but he alleged De Berenger was wearing a green uniform and not a red one. De Berenger constructed an alibi defence from his servants and an ostler. Lord Ellenborough summed up to the Jury in a wholly prejudiced manner against the accused. They were convicted and Cochrane was sent to prison for a year. He was dismissed from the navy, lost his KCB and ejected from the House of Commons. The electors responded by immediately re-electing him. It may be noted that Judge Henry Cecil, who wrote a book about the trial, was of the view that Cochrane was probably properly convicted.

In 1818 he left for South america, where revolts were in progress against the Spanish and Portuguese. He took his wife and family and went first to Chile, where he became Admiral in command of the Navy. On 22nd December 1818 he flew his pennant on the flagship, the O'Higgins. With his customary courage and boldness he set about attacking the Spanish fleet in the Pacific, using ruse and stratagem to get the better of them. His first attack, in February 1819 on Callao in Peru, where there was a Spanish squadron, attests to the spirit of his family. Before he left Valparaiso to waylay a Spanish treasure ship, Lady Cochrane and his family came aboard to see him off. The recall gun was sounded and Lady

Cochrane, going ashore, looked out of a window and saw her eldest son - five years old - on the shoulders of the Flag-Lieutenant waving his cap and calling hurrah. He had asked to be taken to his father. The O'Higgins sailed with the five-year old aboard. Cochrane turned him over to the sailors to care for him and a midget Midshipman's uniform was made for him. At Callao Cochrane prepared to attack during the Mardi Gras festival in order to surprise the Spanish ships in harbour. When on 29th February, under the protection of fog, the O'Higgins went into strike, Cochrane locked his son in the after cabin. Not liking that, the child climbed out of the quarter galley window and joined his father on deck in his uniform, refusing to go back below. There he busied himself handing powder to the gunners. As he was so employed, round shot took off the head of a marine spattering the boy with his brains. Cochrane went towards him, but he was unharmed and ran to his father, telling him 'I am not hurt, papa: the shot did not touch me: Jack says that the ball is not made that can kill mamma's boy.' Cochrane ordered him carried below, but so great was the struggle to resist made by the boy that he was allowed to remain for the rest of the action. There were of course no children's social service meddlers without commonsense to accuse Cochrane of want of care for his child, or to suspect the sailors who touched him and cared for him of abuse.

Lord Cochrane went on to support the independence movements in Peru and Brazil, assisting the son of the King of Portugal, Don Pedro I, to establish his Brazilian Empire. For his services he was made Marquis of Maranhao, a title still held by the 15th Earl of Dundonald. He became commander of the Greek navy fighting for independence from the Turks. In 1828 he returned to England and became 10th Earl of Dundonald in 1831. After King William IV, who, as Duke of Clarence, had served in the Navy, came to the throne, Cochrane was given a pardon, restored to the navy and reinstated to the Order of the Bath. In 1851 he became an Admiral. He remained fascinated with technology, using his own money to promote inventions ranging from convoy lamps, high-pressures engines, and screw propellers to new weapons such as gas. In the Crimean War against Russia in 1854 he pressed the Government to attack the Russian Fleet at Kronstadt with a weapon, 'stink vessels', involving 500 tons of sulphur and 2,000 tons of coke. In addition he suggested that huge naphtha balls should be used, ignited by potassium. He offered himself to command the attacking fleet, but his appointment was declined. The Admiralty had not forgotten or completely forgiven his tempestuous and independent character. The First Lord of the Admiralty told Queen Victoria, an admirer of Cochrane, that he might use the force under his command in some desperate enterprise, where the chance of success would not outweigh the risk of failure. Age, the Queen was told, had not diminished the adventurous spirit of Cochrane, which no authority could constrain.

He continued to press his innocence and wrongful conviction for fraud with vigour and acerbity for the whole of his life. He constantly suggested that Lord Ellenborough had been chosen to try him by the Government to secure his conviction and disgrace. Throughout the nineteenth century his family and that of Lord Ellenborough engaged in a war of print about the question. Cochrane died in 1860.

Admiral Harvey, for his accusation of cowardice and unfitness to command made so publicly against Lord Gambier, was court-martialled and cashiered. He was subsequently reinstated. Midshipman Marryat went on to become as Captain Marryat a successful novelist, producing sixteen novels, many about the sea. His first, *Frank Mildmay*, is said to be semi-autobiographical and that Peter Simple and Mr Midshipman Easy present insights into the navy of Marryat's time.

The 8th Lord Ellenborough was ejected from the House of Lords in 1999.

12ᵗʰ April 1782

The Battle of The Saints

The Battle of the Saints was one of the final incidents in the American War of Independence. After the Rebellion of the Colonies the French surreptitiously began to aid the rebellious colonists with armaments and money and by sending mercenaries, in the hope of reversing earlier defeats and losses to Britain in Canada and the West Indies. In 1778 France declared war on Britain and in 1779 they were joined by Spain. In 1779 an attempt to invade England came to nothing. In 1780 Britain declared war on Holland, which had been secretly assisting the French, and Britain conquered various colonies in the Dutch West Indies. The intervention of these powers extended the war to areas outside the thirteen colonies of North America. In October 1781, despite a victory at Chesapeake, Lord Cornwallis and the British were besieged in Yorktown. The French with a fleet of twenty-eight ships of the line entered the Chesapeake River and the British naval forces failed to disperse them. Cornwallis was therefore surrounded and forced to surrender. De Grasse then sailed south for the West Indies to join the Spanish. Despite the forces still in the thirteen colonies and the strong position still held, the House of Commons, tired of the war against the Americans, resolved (in March 1782) no longer to support the government in pursuing the war. The French and Spanish, however, remained a threat to the British sugar islands in the West Indies, a number of which had been taken leaving only Jamaica, Barbados, Antigua and St. Lucia. Hood and the fleet followed De Grasse south and the Government decided to send Rodney from England to join him.

George Bridges Rodney joined the navy at the age of thirteen. In 1759 he destroyed the invasion flotilla assembled at Le Havre as Rear Admiral in the Achilles. In 1780 he drove a Spanish squadron onto the rocks near Cape St. Vincent. By 1782 he was wracked with gout and grown prematurely old, but still the sailor most admired in the fleet. He left Plymouth on 10ᵗʰ January 1782 in the teeth of westerly gales in the Formidable (90 guns, launched in 1777 and second of the name) and eleven ships of the line. Off Ushant he recorded that the seas were so mountainous and high that they made a fair break over both Formidable and Namur. He reached Gros Islet Bay, St Lucia, in the first week of April, joining Hood to make a force of twenty-six ships of the line.

De Grasse had meanwhile been concerting plans to join up with the Spanish at Cape Haitren in San Domingo, in order to convey a force of 40,000 soldiers to invade Jamaica, where Britain had a garrison of 3500 men. If the fleets could join together, the combined fleet would amount to 50 ships of the line against Rodney's 36. The French fleet lying at Fort Royal on Martinque some thirty miles to the north of St.Lucia was fairly evenly matched to that of Rodney, totalling 2,526 guns carried in their ships to his 2,620 guns. The British advantage lay in seamanship, better gun technology and the use of carronades firing short-range shot. Frigates were laid out to keep watch on the French fleet. Troops were loaded on the French ships and at 8.00 am on 8th April the British frigates signalled the emergence of the fleet from harbour. The French were all at sea by ten. An hour later Rodney and the fleet left St. Lucia. It was the beginning of an action which with the light winds and persistent manoeuvring was to last for five days. The French transports preceded the battle fleet northwards and the latter did not become visible until 4 pm, when it was spotted from the Barfleur in the van. A fresh north-east – by east wind developed, falling off at midnight. The British fleet hove to at 2 am.

At dawn on 9th April, in a dead calm, the French were seen to be about six to twelve miles off, trying to weather the northern tip of Dominica into open water beyond the wind shadow of the island. At 7 am a sea breeze from the north-east carried part of De Grasse's fleet into the gap between Dominica and the islands called the Saints, which lay between the former island and Guadaloupe. The wind likewise carried Hood forward, separating the van of the British fleet from its centre and rear, which remained becalmed. De Grasse had fourteen ships in the channel to the windward of Hood with his eight ships, and he signalled his second in command De Vaudreuil to lead Hood to action. De Vaudreuil opened a long-range attack as ordered and circled the British ships, which kept to a close line. At one time Hood in Barfleur was under attack by seven ships. After three-quarters of an hour the French abandoned the action. The sea wind from the north-east had continued to lift the French and British fleets out of the wind shadow to the west of Dominica, and by noon about three-quarters of the French fleet had arrived on the scene. The head of Rodney's centre squadron, including the Formidable, had also arrived, although its rear ships and Drake's squadron were still becalmed. De Grasse renewed his attack with long-range firing and continued so for about one and a half hours, without pressing close. By that time the British rear had come onto the scene and De Grasse retired, working up windward towards the Saints. Rodney, in order to give time for repairs, reversed the line, putting Hood in the rear, and hove to, remaining so until daybreak on 10th April.

At dawn the French were seen to be some 12 miles away nearing the Saints, and Rodney began to beat up into the north-east breeze towards them. Both fleets spent the day beating up wind, the French gradually gaining slightly. On the morning of 11th April the French were out of sight but Rodney pressed on. Early in the afternoon two French ships were seen drifting to leeward towards the British, the Zélé (74guns), which had collided with another ship the Jason and lost its main topmast and the Magnanimic (74 guns) which had lost is foreyard while tacking. Rodney decided to give chase and the fleet nearest the weather drew on to them, inducing De Grasse to go about and bear down to save his ships. The British ships chasing the French were recalled, but De Grasse had lost much of the advantage gained over the previous days. Rodney resolved that he must bring the French to close battle by outmanoeuvring them under cover of the night. He turned therefore and bore south with the fleet until 2 am, and on a signal from Formidable the fleet turned and began to beat back. All fleet lights had been extinguished and signals limited. By dawn on 12th April he had drawn near to DeGrasse, who had no knowledge of the location of the British fleet. The wind blew south-easterly and Rodney steered on a starboard track east - north-east, which would keep the fleet in the gap between the islands. The French to the north-east were widely separated, at a standstill and out of formation about twelve miles away, although a small group was as near as eight miles.

Rodney came onto deck at dawn and his attention was attracted to two ships close by to the leeward. They were the Zélé and a frigate, the Astrée, which carried De Bouillé, the Commander in Chief of the French armies. In the night the Zélé had had a second collision with the flagship, the Ville de Paris, and De Grasse had ordered the Astréé to tow the Zélé from the fleet to San Domingo. Little progress had been made during the night. Rodney, seeing the nearness of the two ships, ordered four of Hood's squadron to intercept the ships and Monarch, Valliant (1st of that name), Centaur and Belliqueux turned towards them. The signal given, he went to breakfast with his officers. De Grasse, becoming aware of the attack likely on Zélé and the Astrée, signalled to make sail in line and close up on port tack on the Ville de Paris, thus bringing the whole fleet on to the British. The Ville de Paris with the nearest ships bore down towards the detached part of Hood's squadron. The latter were signalled to return to the fleet, but the manoeuvre had brought the French down to a point where battle could be joined and their fleet engaged. The British on the starboard tack were steering into the open waters of the channel between the islands whereas the port tack would ultimately lead the French into the wind shadow of the island of Dominica.

The French headed up and were going to cross the bows of the British fleet: the over eighty ships of the fleets glittering in the morning sun, slowly edged together. The British fleet closed up in line until only a cable length separated the ships of the line one from another; the French line remained strung out. At the point of intersection, which the French reached first, the French began a long-range bombardment. Little damage was done to British ships, which sailed on returning no fire. Marlborough led the line under Captain Taylor Penny from Dorset, sailing on silently to within one hundred and fifty yards of the French line, when opposite the fifth French ship the helm was swung over and the 74-gunner turned to port. No signal to fire had come from Formidable and Taylor

Penny sailed on until he reached the ninth ship, when the red battle flag appeared at the mast of the flagship. Each British ship in line followed the Marlborough into line amid the bombardment being made by the French. At the red signal the broadsides crashed devastatingly into the French fleet. Many, like Arrogant just behind Marlborough, fired three broadsides to every one of the French. Slowly the fleet slid along the French line towards the rear pounding heavily ship by ship, keeping the cable length gap and in line.

Rodney's squadron followed that of Drake. The second of them in line, the Hercules, a 74-gunner, held her fire until she came up to the Ville de Paris fifty yards away from her. Her Captain Henry Savage, a martyr to gout, had a chair placed on deck by the rail and sat there shouting abuse at the French as he passed each ship. After the double broadside into the French flagship, indifferent to the pain of gout, he leapt on a sea chest to roar a patriotic song. Resuming his armchair he was wounded, but having been bandaged, took his seat again to shout abuse as before between the rapid broadsides that crashed into the French. When the Hercules reached the end of the French line, he luffed up and fired his last broadside into the stern of the last ship.

Fourth in line was the Resolution (7th of that name, a third rate of 74 guns). The first on board to be injured was the Captain, Lord Robert Manners, who was hit by round-shot injuring both legs and his right arm. Subsequent to the battle, having had his left leg amputated, he died on the way back to England. The crew equally acted with the same fortitude as their Captain. The ships' surgeon told of a gunner standing at the ready beside his gun, when a shot came in at the port. It took off his leg at the knee: quickly he bound up his leg above the stump with his neck cloth. He then took up his lower leg and thrust it into the muzzle of the gun, which was instantly fired. 'My foot' shouted the gunner 'is the first to board the Ville de Paris'.

Some sixteen ships separated Marlborough from Formidable, which did not fire its first shot until after eight o'clock. By the time it came round in the line up to the French fleet, dark smoke lay over the sea and the hardly penetrable cloud masked the combatants. Each ship had to steer by the gun flashes of the one in front. At last the Formidable came up to the back of the Ville de Paris. The gunners redoubled their efforts and swept the French ship clear across the crowded decks. Only an irregular discharge was returned by the damaged vessel, as every British ship had reserved a broadside for the French flagship. The Ville de Paris shifted past and soon behind it came Glorieux, virtually reduced to a demasted hulk and drifting towards Formidable. Rodney ordered the breaches of the guns to be raised to fire into the Glorieux but as the order was given the wind shifted south. The wind change headed the French fleet and threw the whole line into disarray, with the heads to starboard. For the British the wind change was providential, sending them forwards and giving them an opportunity of sailing through the gaps in the French line. Rodney in Formidable seized the chance and turned between the Glorieux and Diadème, ordering firing to commence on the port side. The wind change had left three or four ships behind the Diadème in a group. The group forming the centre of the French fleet became an object attracting the most powerful 3-deckers in the British fleet - Formidable, Duke, Namur, St.Albans, Canada, Repulse (4th of the name) and Ajax (1st of the name). Each one as they passed fired into the Glorieux.

Elsewhere the French line had also been broken as a result of the wind veering south. Hood went through in the rear, led by Bedford, which sailed across a gap opened by chance between the Hector and the César, cutting off the French van. Both the Hector and the César were crippled as broadsides crashed out from the ten-strong squadron passing between them.

Towards the middle of the day the breeze gradually fell away as the daytime heat developed. Both sides lay becalmed, the French in total disarray. The British squadrons were together, but divided, about four miles to windward of the French, given the likely direction from which the afternoon wind would come. Around the ships, particularly the French, whose ships had been crowded with troops, the decks needed to be cleared of the dead by throwing the bodies overboard. These bodies attracted the sharks from around the islands and the seas boiled with them as they fell upon the dead.

Some time about one o'clock the breeze began to freshen. The British began to work their ships round to go downwind of the French, Hood having the Barfleur towed by his ships' boats into the wind. De Grasse for his part intended to go to leeward as far from the British as he could, even if it meant leaving the more damaged ships to their fate. The British caught the breeze first and sailed down on the French. The Glorieux, César and Hector fell first to the British. The Glorieux was too damaged to resist, but the César and the Hector put up a final resistance, the latter surrendering between five and six in the evening.

Meanwhile, the British fleet continued to sail on towards the rear of the French fleet where some eight ships had formed around the Ville de Paris. By half past five to six o'clock Rodney's ships were well up to this group. Hood with his squadron pushed on and steered to overlap the group, firing strongly as they came up. For a second time the battle flared up. The Canada went up to the Ville de Paris on its quarter and fired constant broadsides into it in order to cut away its rigging. The Russell then took on the task, until Hood in Barfleur came on the scene; by this time the Ville de Paris had lost her rigging, had an ineffective rudder and had lost a large part of her crew. De Grasse decided on Hood's arrival to surrender to him. The French second in Command, De Vaudreuil, seeing the surrender of the flagship from some distance, collected his dispersed ships and ordering them to put on full sail hastened to leave the action. Rodney after the surrender signalled to cease firing and for the fleet to heave to. The decision was probably an error of judgement, based on a failure to realise the size of the blow which he had given to the French, but the fleet, as he said had done handsomely. Night fell, but towards nine o'clock a sudden explosion illuminated the sky as the César blew up as a result of negligence by members of the French prisoners left on board. The attending British ships sent out boats to rescue the prize crew and the French, but the jostling pack of sharks which came immediately to the wreck prevented rescue. They snapped and tore at the poor wretches who clung to the fragments of floating debris. Some of the prize crew were saved but only a few Frenchmen.

A week later Hood took a further four ships. The French had lost 7,000 killed, wounded and drowned and 8,000 prisoners. The British reported a loss of 1,103 in all, including 337 killed. The light losses were attributed to the poorness of the French bombardment. The measure of the British attack at short-range can be judged by the fact that Formidable fired eighty broadsides.

The attack on Jamaica was abandoned. Rodney reached there as a deliverer. Before the news of his victory reached London the new Whig Government, following the resolution to end the American War, recalled Rodney, appointing Admiral Pigot in his place. The Admiralty tried on news of the victory to recall Admiral Pigot but he had sailed from Portsmouth before the message to recall him could be delivered. Rodney returned to public acclamation in the City of London for the victory which he had won.

The 10th Baron Rodney and 8th Viscount Hood were ejected from the House of Lords in 1999.

19th April 1587

The Singeing of the King of Spain's Beard

King Philip II of Spain, although having a pacific policy towards Queen Elizabeth I of England, was gradually roused to take action by Pope Sixtus V, who was promoting a crusade either against Algeria or England, the interference of English troops in the Spanish Netherlands to support the Dutch, and the depredations of Sir Francis Drake and his fellow buccaneers in the West Indies. Spain's leading sailor, the Marquis de Santa Cruz, prepared plans for an invasion of England in 1583, but Philip II moved slowly and Elizabeth was careful to give no outward provocation to him. The cruise of Sir Francis Drake in 1585 to 1586 in the West Indies finally roused him. In the course of his passage Drake sacked Santiago and Porto Praya in the Cape Verde Islands, captured and sacked San Domingo and ended by seizing, sacking and burning the Spanish capital in the Caribbean, Cartagena. He returned later with spoil and the fame of 'El Draque' spread across Europe. Elizabeth decided that she needed to restrain Drake on his return and she and her advisor Lord Burleigh tried to calm Philip II by diplomatic action disclaiming Drake's activities.

The preparations for an Armada against England now began to gather pace. Europe was scoured to provide ships and galleys, cordage, vessels, timber, tar guns and shot for Spain. The price of the first quality cannon rose to £22 per ton. The great fleet was being gathered at Lisbon and Cadiz. Queen Elizabeth for her part began to prepare; county militias were mustered, ships and the fleet put to right. In early 1587 Elizabeth was induced to act, and decided to commission Drake to lead a fleet with a view to hampering the Spanish preparations. On 15th March the Commission was given in wide terms 'to prevent or withstand such enterprises as might be attempted against Her Highness's realm or dominion,' permitting the fleet to raid Spanish and Portuguese harbours and make armed forays onto land. Drake was given four ships from the royal navy – the flagship, the Elizabeth Bonaventura, the Golden Lion, Rainbow and Dreadnought. He contributed four of his own and contracted for seven large armed merchantmen from London under Captain Flick. The Lord High Admiral, Lord Howard of Effingham contributed a large galleon. There was therefore a fleet of sixteen large ships, to which were added numerous pinnaces, which were small light schooner-rigged vessels.

Sir Francis Drake, having collected his fleet together, left Plymouth on 2nd April. In a letter to Sir Francis Walsingham he stressed the unity of his fleet, which had 'a more loving agreement than we hoped' one with another. 'I thank God,' he said, 'I find no man but as all members of one body to stand for our gracious Queen and country against Antichrist and his members.' Despite however the pledge of the Pope of monies to Philip II payable on landing in England, and Drake's belief that the operation was directed against him, the Antichrist, Queen Elizabeth decided that for diplomatic purposes she needed to dissemble her position. Thus, knowing that Drake had sailed, his Commission was changed on 9th April. He was limited to getting into his possession, avoiding as much as possible the effusion of Christian blood, the vessels of Spain coming and going to the West and East Indies. A messenger was sent to Sir Francis with the changed Commission by a pinnace. Needless to say the pinnace had difficulty catching up with him.

As Drake neared the end of the Bay of Biscay crossing, his fleet was hit by a spring gale and battered for five days, the vessels of the fleet being dispersed. He therefore did not arrive off Lisbon until 16th April. There he learnt from a captured small boat that Cadiz harbour was full of shipping and he decided to push on, arriving in the Bay of Cadiz in the afternoon of the 19th with the flood making and a light sea wind.

The town and fortress of Cadiz lay at the tip of the Island of Cadiz, a five-mile isthmus separated from the mainland only by the Rio Santi Petri. To the east of the town was the outer harbour forming the southern extension of the Bay of Cadiz. On the east this harbour was enclosed by land moving south from Puerto de Santa Maria to a jutting peninsula, which closed part of the south of the harbour, having on its point Fort Matagorda. Between the Fort and the isthmus of Cadiz was a limited access to the inner harbour, which connected to the River Santi Petri in the south. Shipping was at anchor in both the outer and inner harbours. In all there were about sixty ships of consequence. The main defence consisted of nine galleys and a galleon commanded by Don Pedro de Acuna and lay up towards the Santi Petri river mouth.

Drake, on arrival, in accordance with naval orders laid down by King Henry VIII that an Admiral must take council with his captains on his strategy and tactics before attacking a fleet or harbour, held such a council stating his view that an attack should be made at once. His Vice Admiral William Borough opposed that course but Drake overruled him and the fleet prepared to enter harbour with no flags flying. Two galleys came out to reconnoitre the approaching fleet. The flags were raised and broadsides were fired, the galleys quickly making off as Drake sailed in. A Genoese ship with thirty to forty guns under way was attacked, fired and sunk with the cargo of sugar and cochineal. As the English fleet moved in to the outer harbour under the shore guns from Fort Matagorda, panic took hold of the anchored ships and in the town. The anchored vessels began to slip their chains, collided with one another, drifted and grounded. The galleys under Don Pedro de Acuna moved quickly to the attack, rowed mightily by the galley slaves who, chained to the benches, powered them. Highly manoeuvrable and capable of turning rapidly, they could be a potent threat to sailing ships which were becalmed. Fortunately for Sir Frances Drake the light afternoon sea breeze enabled the flagship, the Elizabeth Bonaventura and the Queen's other ships – the Golden Lion, Rainbow and Dreadnought to turn and fire their broadsides of eight guns in sequence into the hulls of the galleys.

All was over in fifteen minutes; one galley was sunk and the others restricted to shelter under guns on shore. The English then proceeded to take the ships which were fully equipped and fire the remainder. In the town the sound of the guns, the burning ships and the confused and threatening movements of the vessels in the smoke put fear into the people of the city, who began to seek safety in the castle. In the mad rush to enter, twenty-two women and children were trodden to death. After the attack on the moored vessels and their destruction or capture, Sir Francis Drake decided once more to have a council with his captains. He had anchored out of range of the land guns and had to resolve whether to stay or go. He was determined to stay, the ships in the inner harbour being unmolested; once more the Vice Admiral William Borough again opposed action, but Drake had his way. As night fell the city was lit with pitch flares and drumming filled the streets where people surged about.

Just after dawn, as a light sea breeze made, probably north-westerly, Drake with the Merchant Royal and a flotilla of pinnaces boldly went in through the narrow channel to the inner harbour. There some thirty ships were fired and destroyed, including the large galleon belonging to the commander of the Spanish navy, the Marquis de Santa Cruz. The action concluded, Drake and his flotilla rejoined the fleet. Meanwhile in the night the Spanish had brought up on the land two demi-culverins with which they had begun to bombard the Golden Lion, which Borough had anchored further out in the Outer Harbour. The wind, which had began to die, meant that the ship had to be warped out of range, and the master set his sailors to do that, slowly edging the ship away. Borough, who had been visiting other ships, returned and ordered the master to continue. As the Golden Lion drew away from the main fleet, Don Pedro de Acuna, waiting close to Puerto de Santa Maria saw his opportunity to fall upon the isolated ship. On the failing gusty wind Drake sent the Rainbow and eight merchant men to protect the Golden Lion and the galleys were chased off. Borough and the eight merchantmen then left the fleet and anchored further out in the Bay of Cadiz.

As occurs on some sun-filled days in the Bay of Cadiz, the wind then fell and disappeared. Sir Francis Drake and the fleet were becalmed in the outer harbour. In such conditions sailing ships were very vulnerable to the oar-powered galleys. Don Pedro de Acuna once more tried to seize the opportunity given. The galleys sped towards the English ships. These had prepared for attack, put out boats and were ready to warp or pay out the heavy sailing ships so that the broadsides of the guns could be fired. Laboriously the sweat-drenched sailors bent under the sun to their task and the great English vessels were able to deliver their broadsides on the galleys, which were once more driven off. Further half-hearted attempts were made by the Spanish during the day, as the sea lay shining under the unmoving air.

In the middle of the afternoon the Duke of Medina Sidonia arrived in Cadiz with three thousand infantry and three hundred cavalry. New guns were to be mounted on land. Towards dusk the Spanish attempted to attack with fireships which had to be rowed out towards the anchored English. Once abandoned, the English small boats hooked up to them and moved them away from the fleet to ground them. The English position was however becoming more desperate and the land and sea were scanned for any sign of a making wind. The Bay of Cadiz is backed on land by a range of hills known as the Sierra de San Cristobel, and distantly by mountains visible from the bay, the highest of which is the Cabezo de Moro in the Sierra de Ronda. This configuration of the land affects the land wind, which often rises constantly with growing force after dark as the sea cools. At last darkness fell and the wind began to rise. At midnight Drake hoisted anchor and the fleet sailed out past the Castillo de San Sebastian, the northern tip of the Cadiz isthmus. He had been in Cadiz harbour for thirty-six hours and destroyed over sixty ships.

He then sailed first north to Lisbon, but despite a challenge made to the Marquis de Santa Cruz, the Spanish fleet did not leave the Tagus. Carried by a characteristic Portugal northerly, he next appeared at Cape St Vincent, rounding it and taking Sagres and its castle on 5th May, where he waited servicing his ships and resting the crews. He was stationed at a vital point where the Spanish fleets made landfall from the East and West Indies, and which lay on the routes from Portugal to the Mediterranean. Local shipping was attacked and forty-seven small cargo boats taken and sank. He also sank some sixty Andalusian fishing boats from which the Spanish fleet obtained their salt fish. He then made an attempt to take Lagos, but it was heavily defended and the operation failed. On 22nd May he left for the Azores; the fleet was however split up by storms and the merchantmen left to return to London. The Golden Lion, where Captain Borough was being held for insubordination after his arrest by Drake on 2nd May, also left the fleet: the crew mutinied against Captain Marchant and Borough returned to London. It is thought that Drake had had intelligence that a huge Portuguese carrack from the East Indies was nearing the Azores and he set out to find her. The San Philippe was packed with spices, silk, ebony, ivory, silver and jewels. When he came up with her, the ship was seized and probably in part looted. Nonetheless the prize on the return to London was worth £140,000, a share of which was paid to Queen Elizabeth. Sir Francis Drake returned to London with his prizes, arriving on 27th June. Not knowing of Drake's return, the Marquis de Santa Cruz and Don Juan Martinez Recalde went to sea to search for him in mid-July and did not return until October, the sailors wearied and sick and the ships worn by their time at sea.

Sir Francis Drake had proved at Cadiz that with skilled seamanship sailing vessels could be used against the quicker galleys, even in shallow waters, and drive them off. Thereafter, the use of galleys as men of war would begin to decline. He had by his action h ampered the Armada preparations and delayed the great expedition for one year. Philip II and the Spanish were demoralised in that they could not even protect their own shores from the marauding English. Sir Francis Drake was well aware of the limitations of his victory, although it foreshadowed things to come. His description of the affair that he had only, 'singed the King of Spain's beard' recognised that. He echoed the words of the Turkish Sultan, Selim, nicknamed 'the Sot' because of his drinking and his habit of spending his time in the seraglio. In 1570 the Turks had taken Cyprus from the Venetians, but in 1571 the latter with allied navies under Don John of Austria defeated and destroyed the Turkish navy at Lepanto. Selim remarked, 'When the Venetians sank my fleet they only singed my beard. It will grow again. But when I captured Cyprus I cut off one of their arms.' The following year the Turks had a new navy. Drake was aware of the forces which Philip II could command and wrote a firm recommendation to Government to 'Prepare in England strongly, and most by sea. Stop him now and stop him ever.'

Sir Francis Drake took part in the defeat of the Armada (see 29th July 1588) and continued his career at sea, finally sailing with Sir John Hawkins to the West Indies in 1595 to attack the Spanish colonies and Pan ama. In 1596 he died of sickness and was buried in a lead coffin at sea while off Portobelo in Pan ama. The myth of Drake sunk deep into English consciousness and that is reflected in a poem once read by all schoolchildren called 'Drake's Drum', written by Sir Henry Newbolt.

DRAKE'S DRUM
Sir Henry Newbolt

> Drake he's in his hammock an' a thousand mile away,
>   (Capten, art tha sleepin' there below?)
> Slung atween the round shot in Nombre Dios Bay,
>   An' dre amin' arl the time o'Plymouth hoe.
> Yarnder lumes the Island, yarnder lie the ships,
>   Wi'sailor lads a-dancin' heel-an'-toe,
> An' the shore-lights flashin', an' the night-tide dashin',
>   He sees et arl so plainly as he saw et long ago.
>
> Drake he was a Devon man, an' ruled the Devon seas,
>   (Capten, art tha sleepin' there below?)

Roven' tho' his death fell, he went wi'heart at ease,
    An' dre amen' arl the time o'Plymouth Hoe.
Take my drum to England, hang et by the shore,
    Strike et when your powder's runnin' low;
If the Dons sight Devon, I'll quit the port o'Heaven,
    An' drum them up the Channel as we drumm'd them long ago.'

Drake he's in his h ammock till the great Armadas come,
    (Capten, art tha sleepin' there below?)
Slung atween the round shot, listenin' for the drum,
    An' dre amin' arl the time o'Plymouth Hoe.
Call him on the deep sea, call him up the Sound,
    Call him when ye sail to meet the foe;
Where the old trade's plyin' an the old flag vlyin'
    They shall find him ware an' wakin', as they found him long ago!

The battle of Lepanto is commemorated in a fine poem written by G.K.Chesterton. Lord Burleigh's descendant the 8th Marquess of Exeter was ejected from the House of Lords in 1999.

23rd April

St. George's Day

St. George's Day is the feast day of the Patron Saint of England. St. George was one of the fourteen Holy Martyrs who held a special place in the Medieval Church. Intercessions could be made to these auxiliary saints directly, to whom God granted 'that whosoever shall involve their help with all his heart in all dangers he will hear their prayers, in all disorders whatsoever.' St. George was a popular saint for soldiers and his cult probably came to England from the men returning from the Crusades. Froissart in his chronicle refers to Kind Edward III resolving in 1340 to fight the French 'if it pleases God and St. George.' The banner of St. George is the red cross on a white ground, an emblem also used on their mantles by the Knight Templars, formed in 1118. Edward III embedded the cult of St. George at the heart of the monarchy by his foundation in 1348 of the Order of the Garter, whose emblems include the banner of St. George and the image of St. George and the dragon.

There is no known history of the saint, although he is thought to have been martyred in the reign of the Emperor Diocletion in 303 A.D. at Lydda in Palestine, which was a centre of veneration of the saint. The legend of his being a Knight of Cappadocia who rescued a maiden from a dragon at Silene in Libya has since mediaeval times been associated with St. George and could date from the sixth century.

In 1415 Henry V caused his festival to be raised to one of the highest rank and thereafter the flag of St. George was used as the flag of England until a Union flag was devised by King James I, incorporating the saltire of St. Andrew of Scotland. The navy has continued to use the flag of St. George with the union flag in the upper quarter. The flag of St. George remains the flag flown by the Church of England.

In 1416 the Emperor Sigismond of Luxembourg arrived in England. He was met at Dover by the Duke of Gloucester and once in London given a splendid and lavish entertainment. He was the first foreigner to be made a Knight of the Garter. As a gift he brought a sacred relic, the heart of St. George. England signed a treaty of friendship with him.

St. George's day should be a festival day to celebrate that historic fusing of duty, Christian humanity and courage, which has been so central to the people of England in the past.

May

3rd	The first Battle of Finisterre	1749
5th	The Battle of Fuentes de Onoro	1811
6th	The Breakthrough at the Medjerda Valley	1943
8th	V.E. Day	1945
16th	The Battle of Albuera	1811
17th	The Battle of Monte Cassino	1944
18th	The Conquest of Italian East Africa	1941
19th	The Battle of Barfleur-La Hogue	1692
20th	The Siege of Acre	1799
23rd	The Battle of Ramillies	1706
24th	Empire Day	
28th	The Sinking of the Bismark	1941
29th	Oakapple Day	1660
31st	The Battle of Jutland	1916

The First Battle of Finisterre

The first Battle of Finisterre was one of the last incidents in a war which opened in 1739, following the declaration of war by Britain on Spain on 19th October 1739. The first part of the war was known as 'the War of Jenkins's Ear'. Jenkins was a merchant captain who in 1731 had his ear cut off by the crew of Spanish guard ships in the West Indies during the boarding of his ship, and that war merged into a general European war triggered by Frederick II, King of Prussia, who invaded Silesia in 1740, known as the War of the Austrian Succession. Charles Albert, Elector of Bavaria, challenged the right of Maria Theresa, the daughter of the Emperor Charles VI, to succeed to the Hapsburg lands in Germany and to the position of Holy Roman Emperor. The French Government, desirous as ever of obtaining a dominant control of European affairs, supported Charles Albert against Austria. In 1742 they invaded Austria and seized Prague. The position of both France and Prussia in opposing the succession of Maria Theresa was in breach of a treaty made with her father, which Britain as a party decided to honour, the Prime Minister Sir Robert Walpole giving her a £300,000 subsidy. French and British armies took part in the campaigning in Germany, but only as allies of Bavaria and Austria respectively. War was not declared between Britain, France and Austria until March 1744.

At the outset of the War the British Army and Navy had been much neglected under the administration of Sir Robert Walpole, and were in no proper state to contest a war. The war was therefore characterised by few victories for British arms whether by land or sea, but had the effect of bringing about the strengthening and modernisation of the navy and army. By 1747 the aged commanders of the navy had gone and the fleets was better trained and maintained. Central to the improvement of the performance of the navy was George Anson, who in 1743 completed a three years and nine-month voyage around the world as commander of a squadron sent to Manila. He captured treasure worth £600,000 from the Spanish, and noted that the Falkland Islands would be a suitable base for the British fleet. The young officers whom he trained on the voyage became successful fleet officers, many of them admirals, including for example Keppel, Byron and Hyde Parker, who as an aged officer commanded Nelson at Copenhagen. In 1747 Anson was a member of the Board of Admiralty, when intelligence arrived that the French and Spanish were preparing their fleets for sea in the dockyards of the Atlantic coast. Anson was forthwith despatched to command the fleet watching the port with the object of destroying the French and Spanish fleet as they came out. April 1747 was spent by the British fleet cruising in the Bay of Biscay in training, practising forming a line and bearing down on the enemy. Previously in 1746 Anson had been given the western squadron in order to reorganise it as a strong force, with 17 ships of the line, six 50-gunners, four frigates and two ships. Of this fleet Anson, with Admiral Warren, had 14 ships of the line as they kept up their watch in the Bay off Biscay of Cabo Ortegal, just east of Finisterre. Anson had among his squadron the Prince George (the flagship), Devonshire (a 3rd Rate with 70 guns and 3rd of that name, launched in 1745) Monmouth (a 3rd Rate and 3rd of the name), Centurion (a 4th Rate built in 1732 with 60 guns and 6th of the name) Defiance (a 4th Rate of 64 guns rebuilt in 1695) Namur, Windsor and Yarmouth.

On 3rd May the weather was fair with a north, north-westerly wind when a French fleet under de La Jonquiére was seen with 9 sail of the line escorting convoys destined for Canada and the East Indies. The British fleet formed a line and soon bore down towards the centre of the French fleet. The French fleet broke away, veering away to the West South West. A general chase was ordered by Anson under full sail, engaging the French ships individually. Centurion reached the near-most ships of the fleeing French at four o'clock and engaged the Servieux and the Invincible. They were joined by Namur, Defiance and Windsor and the two French ships were disabled, allowing the British who had been engaged to set out to catch the French van. Among those attacking the Invincible was the Prince George (the Flagship). Six men-of-war and four of the East India men struck their colours; these included the Invincible (74 guns) and the Gloire (40 guns). Anson attributed the victory to the superiority of the British gunnery and discipline. The Servieux and Diamant were so damaged that they sank. Many prizes were taken from the convoy to Canada (the prize money amounted to £294,486 of which Anson was awarded £36,810) and only a small detachment of the ships destined for the East Indies reached Pondicherry.

Anson on his return was made a Baron and his descendant the Earl of Lichfield was ejected from the House of Lords in 1999.

5th May 1811

The Battle of Fuentes de Onoro

In November 1810 Marshal Massena, confronted by the line of Torres Vedras and having spent months in a country stripped of all food and supplies, decided to retire. Marshal Ney commanded the rearguard and a series of skirmishes took place in which Sir William Erskine on several occasions hazarded the Light Division. He had been forced on the Duke of Wellington by the Horse Guards, whose Adjutant General described Erskine as sometimes a little mad, but in lucid intervals was an uncommonly clever fellow. Massena at Guarda tried to save himself from being forced out of Portugal and moved towards Central Portugal. Without supplies and transport the attempt was futile; Marshal Ney, who opposed the move, resigned and returned to Paris. The attempt to go south was abandoned. Wellington caught the French Second Corps at Sabugal (3rd April 1811) and defeated them despite Sir William Erskine, who led the Light Division in the wrong direction in a mist. Finally only the fortress of Almeida remained in French hands in Portugal.

Before Wellington could develop a campaign in Spain he had to eliminate the threat to the advance of his army from the fortresses on the border of Almeida, which, although partly ruined, still had its formidable walls, and from Badajoz and Ciudad Rodrigo. He moved forward cautiously to cover Almeida. Meanwhile Marshal Massena had retired to behind Ciudad Rodrigo and in a fine feat of administration rebuilt his army with surprising quickness. He sent for reinforcements from Marshal Bessières, who commanded the 70,000 French Army of the North, but the latter had his own problems in the mountainous country of northern Spain and despatched only 1600 cavalry and teams of artillery amounting to 30 cannon. Massena in the end managed to muster 42,000 infantry, 4600 cavalry and 38 guns.

Wellington meanwhile had split his army and a force of 22,000, mainly Portuguese, but with two British divisions of infantry and a brigade of cavalry, had been sent south to the Estremadura under Marshal Beresford to besiege Badajoz. He was left with 35,000 infantry, 200 cavalry and 48 cannon. Two-thirds of this army was British, although with a two-hundred mile supply line to back the army there were difficulties over supplies and food and a high proportion of sick. In mid-April he galloped south to inspect the progress of Marshal Beresford at Badajoz, expecting Massena to be longer reconstructing his ravaged and weakened army. On 29th April he was back with the main army, which was encamped spread over a twenty square-mile area.

Massena moved quickly in an endeavour to placate the Emperor Napoleon who criticised his loss of Portugal and set out to relieve Almeida. In a position only to carry limited supplies however, a primary objective of his advance was to destroy the Allied army. On 1st May he drove back the outposts on the east side of the River Azava and on the 2nd moved across the river, forcing the cavalry and horse artillery to retire behind the Dos Casas river. Wellington in meeting the threat had two objectives to bear in mind, the first to prevent the relief of Almeida and the second to preserve his communications back to Portugal. He decided therefore to take up a position to meet the French army at Fuentes de Onoro, where both these objectives could be met, and ordered the army concentrated there.

The village of Fuentes de Onoro stood on the west bank of the River Dos Casas, a river running north to the Douro. To the east of the village beyond the river was open country to the nearby River Bimbre, which joined the Dos Casas about two miles north of the village. The river then entered a steep gorge one hundred and fifty feet deep as it ran northwards. At the southern end of the small plain formed by the rivers lay marshy land and woods and about two miles south of Fuentes de Onoro the small village of Pozo Bello. An eastwards road from Ciudad Rodrigo ran through Fuentes de Onoro mounting the southern end of a ridge which stretched 10 miles north to the Almeida road, connecting Wellington with his base in Portugal. From the village and bounding the north edge of the plain, the ridge ran north towards a ruined fort, the Fort of the Conception, on the road to Almeida, which lay about three miles north-west of the fort. To the west of the ridge ran a small river valley parallel with the River Dos Casas. The village of Fuentes de Onoro rose up the ridge from the river in a ragged patchwork of single-storey cottages, small gardens, boundary walls and farm buildings culminating in a square, where the church stood below ragged cliffs.

The Duke of Wellington, always conscious of the need to protect his troops and sparing of their lives and of ammunition, recognised the position as ideal to block the French advance and cover his line of retirement and Almeida itself. The topography of the country meant that the gorge itself over its four-mile length would impede attack north of the village. The key position was therefore the southern end of the ridge, which overshadowed Fuentes de Onoro, and to the south-west of the village the small plain. It was there just north-west of the village that he stationed the 1st, 3rd, 7th and Light Divisions. The 6th and 5th Divisions were deployed on the right beyond the gorge to cover the road to Fort Conception and Almeida. Forward in the village of Fuentes de Onoro there was placed a garrison of twenty-eight companies of British, Portuguese and German light troops. Pozo Bello in the South was covered by Spanish auxiliaries and a weak screen of cavalry, which was based to the rear of Fuentes de Onoro. According to Lt. Col Tompkinson there were two cavalry brigades (900) in bad condition.

Early on the morning of 3rd May the French debouched into the plain to see on the ridge and its rocky flanks a few skirmishers and guns. Marshal Massena, confronted by the obstacle of the northern gorge, decided that his only choice was to attack the village directly with concentrated force. The 6th Corps commanded by General Loison and the 9th Corps commanded by General D'Erlon, amounting to 29,000 men, were deployed to storm the village. The 2nd Corps of General Reynier (11,330) was disposed on the French right wing facing Erskine's 5th Division. The battle commenced with a strong feint by Reynier's 2nd Corps on the British left wing, and Wellington sent the Light Division to reinforce the 6th and 5th Divisions on the left. Between one and two o'clock in the afternoon General Ferey's Division of ten battalions scrambled across the river in three columns and attacked the village. The skirmishers and light troops between the cottages and gardens stalwartly resisted the onrush, but the French pressed on, only falling back after a counter-attack by Colonel Williams and his battalion. The French advance was renewed and the defenders were swept aside as the French pushed up to the square near the church through the alleys, along the roads and past the houses and gardens until they were under the hill where Wellington had his command post. At this point the Duke ordered forward from the 1st Division the 71st (Glasgow Highland Light Infantry) Regiment and the 79th (Cameron Highlanders) Regiment of Foot. The men had been without bread rations for two days but on the order the Scots regiments, holding their guns at the trail ran, at the double towards the village. Arriving there they gave three cheers, raised their weapons at the charge and swept into the French. Inexorably, alley by alley, house by house they pushed the French out of the village. In the confusion the French, who had among their number the red-coated Légion Hanovérienne, devastated them with friendly fire, thinking the Germans were the British. As night fell, the French were held at the west of the village and the struggle ebbed away, although skirmishing fire was heard until midnight.

On 4th May there was a lull in the battle. The British and French sought out their wounded in the village. There had been 650 French casualties, including 160 prisoners and 250 British and Portuguese. Troops on both sides rested and the armies mainly watched one another. The French occupied themselves with marching bands in sight of the British and bombastically played the martial airs of the Napoleonic era. The British soldiers played football. Marshal Massena and the Duke of Wellington both began to contemplate tactics for the morrow. The French cavalry reconnoitred the British line and Massena decided on a two-pronged attack, one on the British right flank through the village of Pozo Bello and the other a renewed attack in force on the village. The object was to outflank and break the British centre. Wellington, realising this risk, acted to prepare for an attack on his right. The Light Division was brought back to the centre. The Spanish Grenadiers of Julian Sanchez and the single battalion of the 7th Division at Pozo Bello were strengthened by the despatch of the division and cavalry to that village. The 7th, comprising both 2,900 British and 900 Portuguese was newly out from England and inexperienced. Colonel Tomkinson in his list of cant names for the army divisions says of the7th 'They tell us there is a 7th, but we have never seen them.' At Fuentes de Onoro they were visible.

In order to attack Pozo Bello, Massena shifted three infantry divisions from the 6th, 8th and 9th Corps and four brigades of cavalry, amounting to about 15,000 infantry in all (and the whole of the 4,000 cavalry) to the right. At dawn, out of the shifting light mist by the river, the troops began to emerge into the plain south of Pozo Bello along the edge of the marshy woods. The French Hussars and Dragoons swept over the plains towards the 7th Division stationed in and near the village. Sanchez's Spaniards were overrun. The British cavalry tried to check the onward rush, but within hours two battalions of the 7th west of the village were badly shaken and only saved by the Kings German Legion Hussars, who held the French cavalry. These two battalions began to move northwest and became separated from the rest of the 7th. Marchand's infantry from the VIth Corps meanwhile forced the 85th (Bucks Volunteers Light Infantry) Regiment and the 2nd Regiment of Caçadores out of the village. The 7th began to retire through the whirling cavalry in the plain, fractured into parts. At one point one of the regiments had to ford the rapid running stream of the River Turon up to their armpits and those who were through waited on the far bank to regroup. The British cavalry constantly harried the French particularly riding on their artillery to hamper cannonades from the guns. In the crisis that developed with the heavy weight of the French assault and the withdrawal of the 7th Division, Wellington repositioned the 1st and part of the 3rd Division along the southern crest of the ridge west of Fuentes de Onoro and ordered the Light Division under General Crauford down to the plain to shield the withdrawal of the 7th. The latter was retreating north-west harassed by the French cavalry and pushed by infantry: the Light Division moved south towards them and by deft manoeuvre and firepower reached the 7th, enabling its scattered parts to unite.

The French infantry turned north to meet the Light Division and General Montbrun led his cavalry on towards the British troops. As if on the parade ground, the Light formed squares as they drew back. Major Bull's artillery troops accompanied them, unlimbering their guns and limbering up after firing to deter the French artillery. Montbrun's cavalry, sabres extended, attempted to threaten the unmoving squares, which unlike other European armies, did not falter, break and run. The cavalry swirled around engaged in passing clashes. Lt. Colonel Tomkinson describes an encounter, for example, of two squadrons of the 16th Hussars charging and sabreing a French cavalry force twice its size. The costs were great: one hundred and fifty-seven of the cavalry were killed. At one point the French cavalry were seen broiling in a concentrated mass, from which there came a great English shout and Captain Ramsay's two guns were suddenly seen to burst out, the Captain at the head, sabre raised, the gunners and outriders on guard and the gun horses streaming at the gallop. Quickly squadrons of the 14th Light Dragoons and Royals went to help them and Captain Ramsay's guns were brought back safely. The Light had meantime reached the rocky ridge and began to regain safety. The 7th too had made good its retreat to Frenada: only three companies of the 3rd Foot Guards had been overwhelmed on the rise to the ridge, when they failed to form a square as the French cavalry went on.

Two hours after the flank attack began and the French were sweeping across the plain to Pozo Bello and beyond, Marshal Massena launched his new attack on the village of Fuentes de Onoro. In the north General Reynier and his 2nd Corps had been engaging in deceptive demonstrations of attack, to force the retention of the British 6th and 5th Divisions in the north in order to protect the road to Almeida and guard the British left. The 6th Corps and Grenadiers of the 9th Corps were to be committed. At first the soldiers of the 71st and 79th, who had held the village of Fuentes de Onoro on 3rd May were forced back fighting ferociously. One-third of their number was killed, including Colonel Cameron. Numbers were wounded, such as Lieutenant Blake who had a four-pound round shot hit his thigh and rode six miles to Castle Mondo before a Portuguese surgeon extracted the ball. The next day Surgeon Robinson amputated his leg but he died an hour later. As the French forced their way through the alleys of the village, Wellington sent in the 24th (2nd Warwickshire) Regiment of Foot and the Light companies of the 1st and 3rd Divisions. In a strong fight they managed to hold the upper part of village, the church and its graveyard. About noon General D'Erlon Commander of the 9th Corps launched his Grenadiers and they drove the defenders back, reaching the church.

General Mackinnon's Brigade, which had been held as reserve for the 3rd Division, on Wellington's order was sent to recover the village. Led by the 88th (Connaught Rangers) Regiment, they, the 45th (Nottinghamshire) Regiment of Foot and the 74th (Highland) Regiment of Foot marched down the hill with fixed bayonets, cheered by the remnants of the 71st and 79th scattered over the hill behind the village. Ruthlessly, the 88th in the lead, the Brigade pushed back the French in vigorous assaults through the alleys and streets, back towards the river, past the Scots dead with their gore-splattered kilts. By two o'clock the village was free and the flank assault had lapped away, confronted with the infantry ensconced on the ridge line to the west. The French had lost 2,100 men. Massena called off the attack. His ammunition and supplies were diminished. For want of provisions he was forced to utilise the supplies destined for Almeida for the army. His objective of sweeping aside the Allied army and of relieving Almeida had not been achieved. On 6th and 7th May the armies returned to watching one another. The British were put to work to fortify the ridge with earthworks. Massena decided to send three messengers to Almeida through the British lines ordering Lt. Colonel Brennier to break out. Two were caught and shot but one, Tillot, got through. The garrison was to fire three salvoes each at three-minute intervals to signal its breakout.

On the 8th and 9th May Massena began to withdraw the French army. On the afternoon of the 10th Wellington sent Sir William Erskine in command of the Fifth Division an order to move troops to intercept any attempted escape from Almeida at the bridge of Barba de Puerco, near the junction of the Rivers Dos Casas and Agueda. Erskine, who was at dinner, casually put the despatch in his pocket and forgot it. The message was finally passed on to Lt. Colonel Bevan of the 4th (The King's Own Royal) Regiment to intercept the French at the bridge. It was midnight before Bevan received the order, but he did not move immediately. Meanwhile late on the 10th Brennier had fired his signal and led his 1,300 men out of Almeida. They reached the bridge at Barba de Puerco at four in the morning of the 11th. Bevan and the 4th were still three miles off. Brennier was able to make good his escape back to the French army with nine hundred of his men. Erskine tried to cover his negligent conduct by telling Wellington that Bevan had been delayed by losing his way. Colonel Bevan challenged this version of events, but was confronted by the threat of a Court Martial because of his delay in moving off at midnight. On 9th July on the way south Bevan, haunted by the unjust accusation and the threat of Court Martial, blew out his brains.

Neither Wellington nor the British Government was enthusiastic about the victory marred by the escape from Almeida, and no vote of thanks was passed in Parliament. But Portugal had been freed and Wellington thereafter was to have a freer hand in formation of strategy in the Peninsula. Marshal Massena was recalled to Paris by the Emperor Napoleon and was never to hold active command in the field again. He was succeeded by Marshal Marmont.

<h1 style="text-align:center">6th May 1943</h1>

The Breakthrough at the Medjerda Valley

By the end of April the Axis army had retreated to their 'fortress' holding the passes which gave access to northern Tunisia. There were four passes – the Sedjenane in the north, south-west of Bizerta, the Medjerda Pass 30 miles south west of Tunis, the Pont der Fahs south of Tunis and Enfidaville on the coast north of Sousse. General Alexander in mid to late April re-organised the allied forces. The northern sector at Sedienane was manned by the 2nd United States Corps, comprising 1st, 9th, 34th Infantry Divisions and the 1st Armoured Division. The centre at Medjeb el Bab and south comprised the newly constructed 19th British Corps and the 5th Corps. The new 19th Corps was made up of the 4th Infantry Division, 201st Guards Brigade, 7th Armoured Division from the Eight Army, 4th Indian Infantry Division and the 6th Armoured Division of the First Army. On their right were the Free French and between them and the sea at Enfidaville the 8th Army. As before pressure was to be kept up along the whole one hundred and thirty-mile front, with attacks at Sedjenane and Pont du Fahs, but the main assault was to be along the Medjerda Valley. The entrance to the valley was dominated by a hill, Longstop Hill to the north, which the Germans still held. Throughout April, the British troops worked their way along the range of hills until they overlooked the hill. The Germans had strongly fortified it wth deep trenches and shelters, minefields and bunkers. The defences were such that the troops could remain underground during bombardment and fire their guns from below ground. There was no way to take the hill otherwise than by assault.

On 22nd April the artillery and air force pounded the hill and on the 23rd the infantry gathered under the mortar fire from the hill and when the guns fell silent at 1.30 pm began to climb up – the West Kents, Surreys and Argyle and Sutherland Highlanders. Some Churchill tanks gave support, but the men had to advance under the storm of machine guns, often to within thirty yards of those guns, before the Germans ceased firing and tried to surrender. Casualties were large but the positions as the men went up the rise to the crest were carried. The commanding officer of the Argyll and Sutherland Highlanders was killed and the command devolved on Major John Anderson. For five hours he led the assault uphill, rallied the dispersed men at the first objective and led them on to the second objective despite his leg wound. He stormed machine-gun pits and attacked a mortar position held by thirty Germans. When he reached the crest and the hill was taken, the force which he still had amounted to four officers and less than forty men. He was awarded the Victoria Cross. The Chaplains, as they ever did, went with the men forward under fire, comforting them, tending their wounds where they fell, administering morphine for the pain of their wounds and consoling the dying. By nightfall three-quarters of the hill was taken and it was finally totally occupied on 26th April. The Medjerda valley could now be entered with the threat from the northern hill removed.

The Germans held a narrow front across the valley of 6,000 yards and it was decided that the assault would be on a front of 3,000 yards on the southerly side of the valley. Ways through the minefield were to be made and as at Longstop Hill a heavy infantry assault was planned. Once the valley defences were taken the armoured columns were to stream through and race the thirty miles to Tunis. The 'blitzkrieg' approach used at 'Plum Pass' (see the Turning of the Mareth Line 27th March 1943) was to be replicated and close cooperation made between the heavy and light bombers, the fighter squadrons and the ground forces. On 5th May the air assault began, the line along its whole length being bombed. 2,146 sorties were flown over the front. From midnight the one thousand guns (one every six yards) began to play along the whole enemy line. At 3.30 am, under the umbrella of the crashing guns, the Royal Engineers crept out to lift the mines and cut the wire in front of the sector to be attacked. Behind them came the massed infantry divisions edging forward, as the night slid into dawn, and, when they were a hundred yards out from the forward line, they stood up in the wheat and charged up to the machine guns in a storm of fire.

Throughout, the air force flew constantly across the field giving protection to the advancing men; a thousand sorties were completed by 9 am. Soon after dawn the infantry were over a third of the way through the two mile-deep defences and by 11 am the sheer heavy power of their numbers involved on so narrow a front had taken the main defence. Despite the determined defensive fire, losses were quite limited and the hole punched let through the 7th and 6th Armoured Divisions, who began the race to Tunis. Accompanied by artillery, anti-tank guns and their Support Groups, the 7th Armoured (the 11th Hussars and Derbyshire Yeomanry) in the vanguard were in the middle of Tunis at 2.30 pm on 7th May. The German armies were split in half. On the same day the United States 2nd Corps took Bizerta. The German and Italian armies, like the French in 1940 began to dissolve; the command structures broke down and the troops began to make for Cape Bon, where they believed ships would be able to take them across to Sicily. The 6th Armoured was sent south from Tunis to occupy Hammamet and Hamman Lif which stood at the south and north ends of a range of hills astride the Cape Bon Peninsula. On 8th May the armoured division arrived outside Hamman Lif, and when the moon rose they advanced.

Within ten hours they had arrived in Hammanet, bypassing the German rear positions and supply and servicing depots, and cutting through the disorganised groups of troops with no clear orders or direction. There were no ships and on 12th May 1943 Feldmarschall von Arnim and General Messe surrendered. The prisoners consisted of 105,000 Germans, 90,000 Italians and 47,000 others. The war in North Africa was at an end.

8th May 1945
V.E. Day

Britain and Poland were the only countries at war with Germany for the whole period of the Second World War. The involvement of the British in war against the Germans, unlike the First World War, covered the continent, the Mediterranean area and North Africa. The oceans also experienced the struggle, particularly in the North Atlantic. The progress followed by Britain's war effort went through a series of distinct phases.

The earliest land action covered the 'phoney' war and the disaster in France (see the Deliverance of Dunkirk 2nd June 1940). There followed the Battle of Britain, where Britain and the Empire stood alone, aided only by the emigré governments of countries such as Poland, Norway and Holland, and repelled invasion (see the Battle of Britain, 15 September 1940). The ruthless determination of Winston Churchill and his Government to fight on, which persuaded President Roosevelt of the firm intent to do so, was made clear in the seizure and destruction of the French Fleet (3rd July 1940). Operations were maintained to sustain the fundamental interests of Britain and the Empire in the Mediterranean area, North and East Africa and the Near East, especially after Italy entered the war in June 1940. (see the Battle of Sidi Barrani, 15 December 1940; the Victory at Beda Fromm, 7th February 1941; the Conquest of Italian East Africa, 18th April 1941; the Surrender of Lebanon and Syria, 14th July 1941; the Relief of Tobruk, 10th December 1941). In June 1941, after Adolf Hitler attacked Russia, Britain and the Empire found a strong ally and the main German effort was diverted against the Soviet Union. There was no invasion of Britain as a consequence, and Britain was able to sustain itself with significant help given by the United States, even though America was not at war. When the United States joined Britain, after Adolf Hitler declared war on America in December 1941 in support of Japan, the operations of Britain and the United States in Europe were co-ordinated.

It was in the Mediterranean area that the fruit of co-operation was first seen (see the Turning of the Mareth Line 27th March 1943; the Breakthrough at the Medjerda Valley, 6th May 1943; the Conquest of Sicily, 16th August 1943; the Battle of Monte Cassino, 17th May 1944). By 1944 the two Allies were ready to invade Northern Europe and on 6th June in Northern France (see the Battle of Normandy 20th August 1944) the invasion took place. The Germans were gradually driven out of France and Belgium, after a separate landing in the south of France had also been made, and the Allies entered Germany (see the Crossing of the Rhine, 24th March 1945). After the encirclement of the German armies in the Ruhr, three general thrusts were made into Germany, the main one being directed across southern Germany towards Czechoslovakia. The United States 3rd Army took Kassel on 4th April, Weimar on the 11th, Jena and Chemnitz on the 13th and crossed the Czech frontier on 18th April. Further north the United States 9th Army reached the River Elbe south of Magdeburg on 11th April. The British thrust north was equally as expeditious. While the 1st Canadian Army cleared north-east Holland, the 2nd British Army under Fieldmarshal Montgomery crossed the River Weser on 5th April, reached Luneburg on the 18th and, by-passing Hamburg, were at Lubeck on the Baltic by the beginning of May, having crossed the Elbe on 29th April. The final collapse of the German land forces in the west was therefore outstandingly fast. Resistance was limited, indeed there was even a desire in the German army to be captured by the Allies rather than the Russians.

At sea at the beginning of the war Britain was not faced by a German Navy of substantial power, since its reconstruction in the nineteen-thirties had not been completed. There were two threats however, the first from the surface fleet comprising principally the new battle cruisers and the two battleships under construction, and the second from the submarine fleet designed not only to strike against the Royal Navy, but also the merchant fleet, which carried Britain's trade across the oceans. The threat of the large surface ships was to be as raiders sweeping the seas to sink the merchant ships found, since the German navy lacked the strength to take on the ships of the Royal Navy head to head. The danger of the U-boats (*Unterseeboote*) was brought home when on the first night of the war the outward-bound liner Athenian of 13,500 tons was torpedoed with the loss of 112 lives, including 28 American citizens. The point was underlined later in the autumn. On 14th October the battleship Royal Oak was sunk by U-47 in Scapa Flow. At the outset of the war, however, the German Navy's submarine strength was not more than sixty and the pocket battleships and cruisers were seen as a greater threat. The first success against them was at the Battle of the River Plate (see the Sinking of the Admiral Graf Spee 17th December 1939) and the fleet was to remain engaged to keep the others in port and out of the seas. There were three-others; Scharnhorst, Gneisenau and Lutzow (previously the Deutschland) renamed by Hitler after the Sinking of the Graf Spee. They were to emerge only on limited forays as the war went on such as in the Norway campaign of 1940, when the carrier Glorious was sunk.

After France deserted the Allied cause, Scharnhorst and Gneisenau made a foray in the North sea and fled back to Brest, where HMS Hood for a time blockaded them. Constant attempts were made to bomb them and one hundred and twenty-seven aircraft were lost in that task. Finally in April 1941 the Gneisenau was struck by a torpedo from a naval aircraft under the water line. In that spring the new battleship Bismarck ventured into the Atlantic on a raid, was pursued and sunk (see the Sinking of the Bismarck, 28th May 1941). Her companion cruiser Prince Eugen managed to regain Brest. The Fuehrer decided after the Gneisenau was repaired that all three ships should return to their home port and under air cover a successful secret dash was made up the Channel home. The next destination of Gneisenau and Scharnhorst was to Norway to join Bismarck's new sister ship the Turpitz. At Christmas 1943 Scharnhorst emerged to attack a convoy to Russia but was caught by British cruisers and the battleship the Duke of York and sunk. Gneisenau was not to be moved again. Constant attempts to damage or sink Turpitz in its Norwegian Fjord were made by air and other means. On 27th September 1943 Lieutenants Place and Cameron with their crews in two midget submarines, X6 and X7, penetrated the protective anti-submarines nets to plant explosives below the Turpitz on the hull. Before they could leave they were discovered, attacked and captured. Both were awarded the Victoria Cross. The Turpitz was severely damaged when the charges exploded. It was finally sunk by bombing on 12th November 1944.

The greater threat to the survival of Britain was the determined attack by the U-boat fleets, which was mounted under the active command of Admiral Doenitz. The campaign of 1917 in the First World War had already given a precedent as to how great the danger could be. In 1939 to 1940 strenuous efforts were made by Nazi Germany to build up the number of submarines which could be operational at any one time, and the fall of France gave Germany bases on the Atlantic and the ability to mount air attacks out to sea. The British response to the danger, as in the First World War, was to move merchant shipping in convoy through the North Atlantic with naval protection. Initially there were few escorts to protect the convoys and their range was limited. The 'leased' moth-balled destroyers handed over by President Roosevelt in exchange for bases in the Caribbean were at the time vital. Protection by air because of the range of aircraft could be given only to 15° west and from escorts to 17° west. Beyond that the convoys were vulnerable. The U-boats were organised into 'wolf-packs' of five or six, which could each cover in terms of observation a twenty-mile line and thus establish a cordon of over one hundred miles in mid-Atlantic. Others could be summoned by wireless to lay on the route of any convoy found. Because of the submarine's vulnerability on the surface and the advantage of surface attack, the U-boats tended to attack by night.

From June 1940 to June 1941 the U-boat fleet sank three million tons of shipping - air attack from France by the long-range Focke-Wolf Kondors and Kuriers one million tons. Surface vessels sank eight hundred and forty-eight thousand tons. The loss and the need to ensure the shipping lines were kept open led Winston Churchill, the Prime Minister in the House of Commons on 25th June 1941 to refer to the struggle as the Battle of the Atlantic. At that stage German U-boat losses were averaging two a month. The first response was to reroute convoys north so that escorts could refuel in Iceland, and some all-way escorts were also provided. The United States from July 1941 began to 'patrol' the convoy routes, becoming virtual escorts to mid-Atlantic. A new airborne radar was developed, which could identify the U-boat on the surface at night and within the range of aircraft the numbers sunk rose, but there still remained an uncovered gap in Mid-Atlantic. By November 1941 shipping losses were at the lowest since the spring of 1940. The average tonnage sunk by a U-boat per day was 100 tons, compared with a previous average of 400 tons.

The entry of the United States into the War brought a rich harvest to the U-boats, since the trade up and down the East coast of America to the Caribbean Sea was unprotected and the Americans had difficulties in introducing convoy systems and assembling sufficient escorts. In the North Sea to the Thames through which the merchantmen came, the Channel being effectively blocked, an intense struggle went on involving air attack and combat, motor torpedo boats and submarines. By July 1942 the United States had developed a convoy system to move near the East coast of America under air cover, and all U-boats were withdrawn but for nine in the Mid-Atlantic. By that time the operational fleet comprised some 140, and 120 were being built in the Baltic. The bulk were held in the Atlantic, with 20 in Norwegian waters and 20 in the Mediterranean. In 1941 the German Secret Naval Code was in the hands of intelligence and the ULTRA decoding system assisted the reduction in loss but in February 1942 the Germans changed their Enigma code for the submarines and it was not until December 1942 that the new code was de-crypted. The United States was beginning its immense programme of building quickly the prefabricated ships to replace the losses, the 'Liberty' Ship, for which there was a 7,000,000 ton construction programme, but 1942 was to witness the apex of the convoy U-Boat battle. From August to November 2,000,000 tons of shipping was sunk, reaching a high of 700,000 tons in the month of November.

The struggle stimulated the emergence of new measures of protection, better weapons to sink the submarines, extended air cover, escort carriers and technologies to locate submarines by searching for their wireless signals. The last six months of 1942 saw only 64 U-boats sunk. In December 1942, with the breaking of the new Enigma Code, the German naval instructions could be monitored again. In 1943 losses of shipping started to decline, although there was a peak in March, when 108 ships were sunk, mostly stragglers from convoys. The Germans began to lose U-boats at an unsustainable rate. From February to April 1942 the average was eighteen a month as against twenty on average built. In May their loss was forty-one and Admiral Doenitz decided to withdraw the U-boat fleet from the Mid-Atlantic. The battle for a safe passage from North America to Britain was to all intents and purposes won. The submarine campaign was to continue however both in the Atlantic, the North Sea and on the sea routes of the Artic convoys to Russia, but it was never again to achieve the success of 1942. At the end of 1943 losses had fallen to 80,000 tons per month, while 26 submarines a month were being destroyed. In 1944 and 1945 the U-boats had some resurgence with their new acoustic torpedo, but the convoys were generally safe. There were 60 U-boats at sea in April 1945 and a tonnage lost of 63,000 tons only. After the end of the war in May, 156 U-boats gave themselves up and 221 were scuttled.

One of the most controversial aspects of the war fought by Britain was the strategic bombing of Germany. In 1922 at the Washington Conference on the Limitation of Arnaments, Article 22, Part II, it had been agreed that aerial bombing for the purpose of terrorizing the civilian population, of destroying or damaging private property of non-military character or of injuring non-combatants was prohibited under the Treaty. Both Britain, France and Germany at the beginning of the war made declarations supporting the approach of the treaty. Aerial bombing was to be restricted to strictly military objectives or ones engaged in economic activities such as weapon, tank and aircraft production. The campaign of Bomber Command was initially conceived on that basis, the objectives being precision bombing of selected targets. Daylight bombing however resulted in significant plane losses, as the Germans found in the September of 1940, and the air attack was changed to one of night attack. In the opening period of the war the Royal Air Force Bomber Command was handicapped by not having a supply of heavy bombers, the length of the journeys to reach targets in Germany, the limited navigation aids – basically the sextant, map and the plotting of dead reckoning; and the fact that save on clear, moonlight nights targets were not clearly identifiable. There were significant losses for very limited results. The forces available for strategic bombing were further reduced by the call on Coastal Command to give air cover against surface naval sorties and the U-boats.

In 1940, after Churchill became Prime Minister, the policy as to air attack began to change. There began a shift towards 'area bombing' a method in which whole areas around military targets were bombed whether or not dwellings and non-combatant populations were affected. The policy was to be subsequently extended to cover whole cities. The justification for the change, in breach of the 1922 Treaty, was the Luftwaffe attack on London with its eight-month 'blitz' (and on other cities) and the fact that from May 1940 to 1944 the air bombing of Germany was the only principal means by which the war could be taken to the enemy. As the war in the air proceeded, there emerged better and heavier bombers. In the early phase of the war the British Blenheims provided the predominant part of the force. After them the main force was formed of the Vicker's Wellington, of which 11,461 were built, the Avro Lancaster (7,337 built) and the De Havilland Mosquito (7,781 built). With the new planes came better navigation aids and technology. Better techniques emerged such as were evidenced in the attack on 3rd March 1942, on the Renault factory at Billancourt engaged on tank production. The bombers followed a German tactic of being sent in three waves, the front dropping only flares to point up the target and guide the second and third waves in. The factory was put out of action for several months.

The effect of the early 'precision' bombing and the initial 'limited' area bombing achieved no significant result on German industrial production. After the coming of the United States Army Air force in 1942 with higher flying planes, strongly armed and with more efficient bomb technology, the day bombing which they carried out achieved no greater result. At the Casablanca Conference in January 1943 the objectives of strategic bombing were redefined – 'The destruction and dislocation of the German Military, industrial and economic system and the undermining of the morale of the German people to the point where their capacity for armed resistance is fatally weakened'. The latter objective inaugurated an area bombing policy in which whole cities and towns were attacked. While Sir Arthur (Bomber) Harris, in command of Bomber Command, was strongly for the policy of destruction to achieve the stated ends, in retrospect it was curious that Churchill adopted it so wholeheartedly in view of his remarks on air bombing in Spain in the Civil War and the experience of the 1940 to 1941 Blitz on London.

1943 was to see crushing attacks on German cities and towns by both the RAF and USAAF. Using incendiary bombs and high explosive on 28th/29th March, two hundred acres of the centre of the historic town of Lubeck was destroyed. In April seventy per cent of the city of Rostock was damaged. Sir Arthur Harris, pursuing the objective of striking economically and hitting at morale, conceived of the notion of a thousand-bomber raid. He had difficulty in assembling the aircraft but on 31st May 1943 bombers from 53 air fields led by 50 fighters attacked Cologne. 18,342 buildings were damaged, 500 people killed and over 5,000 injured. 60,000 people were rendered homeless. Already since March there had been a six-week attack on the towns of the Ruhr, with raids of four to five hundred aircraft, and on 13th May a specially-trained force with a purpose-designed bomb destroyed the Mohne Dam, flooding the towns and villages in the valley to the west. On 26th June 1,000 planes raided Bremen. From 24th July Hamburg was bombed on six successive nights and twice by day. The operation, launched first by incendiary attack, created fires throughout the city, aided by high-explosive bombs. The heat generated a tornado effect, rising one and half miles high and being fed on its edge by the winds created of thirty-three miles an hour. 500,000 acres of the city were destroyed, twelve and half square miles burnt, 300,000 dwellings demolished, 60-100,000 people killed and 750,000 rendered homeless. These bombing raids were described earlier in May by Deputy Prime Minister, Clement Atlee, the Leader of the Labour Party to cheering in the House of Commons as a 'military necessity'.

The continuance of this 'area bombing' policy was challenged by General Eisenhower in January 1944 after he became Commander in Chief for the Normandy invasion. He was of the view that strategic bombing policy should be revised to act in close support of the invasion of France. He was opposed by the British Air Ministry but a compromise was reached, in which he was to have control in the lead-up to the invasion and during it. Bomber Command

and the United States Strategic Army Air Force were under these arrangements in accordance with Air Marshal Tedder's orders to direct their efforts to the destruction of communications, principally by rail, and the reduction of the sources of oil supply. Their achievement in the period of the invasion in almost paralysing French rail traffic during the Battle of Normandy was followed as the Allies went west by the reduction of the capacity available for transport of coal from the Ruhr. In the Essen division the car replacements of coal had been reduced from 21,400 daily in January 1944 to 12,000 in September, of which only 3,000-4,000 were long haul.

By February 1945 there was a complete disappearance of coal loading and such as was loaded was taken by the Reichsbahn to fuel the engines of the trains. In terms of oil and petrol supply the bombing had equal success. German petroleum and diesel came either after from Romania and Hungary or from 18 synthetic plants. In August 1944 the Russians took the Ploesti oil fields and the German War effort had to be sustained by the eighteen synthetic plants. From May to July 1944 every one of them was bombed and production was reduced from 316,000 tons per month to 17,000 tons by September. In terms of aviation fuel the reduction was from 175,000 tons in April 1944 to 5,000 tons in September. The attacks had constantly to be continued to obstruct repair of these plants. The effect of these losses was drastic; at Baranov on the Eastern Front 1,000 tanks were immobilised by lack of fuel and gasoline. There were side effects for the manufacture of explosives and synthetic rubber tyres. Both these outcomes illustrate that, if strategic bombing is properly directed to military objectives and economic activities supporting the military effort, significant advantages can be gained.

RAF Bomber Command and the USAAF returned however to their habit of area bombing of cities and towns. In October 1944 the wreckage of Cologne was bombed for four days and in February 1945 the destruction of Dresden took place, on the excuse that it was a road and rail communications centre. During the night of 13th February, 800 Royal Air Force bombers dropped 650,000 incendiaries on Dresden, backed by 8,000 and 4,000 pound bombs. On the 14th and 15th the USAAF with a force of 1,350 bombers and 900 fighters continued to pound the city. 25,000 people were killed, 30,000 injured, 27,000 dwellings were destroyed and six square miles of the city left in ruins. Thus, the bombing air war came to both a climax and an end, although assistance was given to the Russians in their attack on Berlin, the measure of the cost of which can be seen in the numerous graves for those killed in March 1944 in the Royal Air Force cemetery in Charlottenberg. The question of the benefit from this air bombing campaign in the war has been constantly debated. The air attack required Germany to keep half its aircraft for the defensive and drove production to supplying more fighters than bombers; it kept personnel amounting to one million men on air defence and prevented the dispersal of the anti-aircraft guns as anti-tank weapons weakening the artillery defence in the battlefield. It did not affect armament and aircraft production significantly: indeed by the end of the war some of that was being carried on in large underground bunkers, enlarged caves and disused railway tunnels. It did in 1944, when specially targeted, achieve useful advantages. The human cost was one million people killed and wounded, 7.5 million made homeless and 3.6 million dwellings destroyed or damaged, together with the supporting infrastructure of the cities. In 1947 in Cologne and Hamburg, the trams still jangled through the streets of piled rubble edged by the skeletal fragments of buildings; habitation was marked in winter by wisps of smoke from galvanised pipes embedded in the piled waste of broken bricks, fractured concrete, dust and earth, where families were huddled in cellars beneath the ruins.

There can be no doubt that the survival of Britain owes much to the agony of Russia. Adolf Hitler envisaged a short campaign leading to the collapse of the Soviet Union, after which he said he would return to the problem of Britain. The staunch Russian love of country and its expression in a persistent fierce defence did not give Nazi Germany its quick victory. For over three and a half years the Russians were subjected to a war and occupation of unbelievable barbarity but ultimately, based on their own strong resources and the aid brought through the Artic convoys and across Persia from Britain and the USA, the Russians drove back the Germans. On 17th April 1945 the attack on Berlin was launched in a pincer movement across the River Oder and from Silesia and by 22nd April the Ring Autobahn had been reached. On the 25th Berlin was completely surrounded and the Russians began to fight their way, street by street, into the centre where stood the Reichstag and Hitler's Chancellery. As they neared, Adolf Hitler in his bunker shot himself, transferring the powers of the Reich Government to Admiral Doenitz in Flensburg on the Baltic. Under his authority, on 3rd May Feldmarschall Keitel in Berlin sent a delegation comprising Admiral Friedeburg, General Kinzel and Rear-Admiral Wagner to negotiate terms of surrender to tactical headquarters on Luneburg heath. Montgomery told the Germans when they arrived that he would only accept the surrender of the armed forces in Holland, Denmark and North-West Germany, but not for all northern Germany as the delegation wished. After negotiations, Friedeburg and Keitel arrived to sign the terms agreed for surrender as from 4th May. A General Capitulation of all armed forces in the west was to follow and that was signed by Admiral Friedeburg and General Jodl with General Eisenhower at Rheims on 7th May, hostilities to cease at midnight on 8th May. The arrangements were ratified in Berlin on 9th May and the war on the eastern front ended that day.

Compared with the First World War the losses of the British Armed forces were moderate. 264,443 people in all were killed, 41,327 missing and 277,077 wounded, amounting in all to 582,327 on all fronts including the war against Japan. The greatest losses were in the army and there were 172,592 people who were prisoners of war.

16th May 1811

The Battle of Albuera

The town of Badajoz and Cuidad Rodrigo lay upon the route from Portugal to Spain. After the retirement of Marshal Massena from his positions around Santerem the way was open to envisage carrying the war in the Peninsula into Spain. Both the British Government and Wellington wished to use the campaign of 1811 to support their Spanish allies. In January 1811 the Spanish still held Badajoz, but in that month the town was besieged by Marshal Soult with an army from Andalusia. Marshal Beresford was dispatched to its relief but surprisingly the Spanish Governor, despite adequacy of provisions, capitulated on 9th March. Leaving a French garrison to refortify the town, the French retired back to Seville. Beresford arrived at Badajoz on 8th May. He lacked an effective siege train, having only some old and ineffective guns from Elvas. Four dated from the seventeenth century and their varying sizes presented a problem in finding ammunition. By 12th May the siege had begun, but news was brought that Marshal Soult, with a French army of 24,000, was returning north to the relief of Badajoz.

Gathering up his own army and calling together the Spanish forces in the Estramadura, which comprised two armies and another brought from Cadiz and recently in Lisbon, Beresford began to move south-east on the Seville Road. Soult, coming north across the Sierra Merina, and Beresford were to meet at La Albuera on the River Albuera, fourteen miles south east of Badajoz.

The village stood on the west bank of the river on the direct road to Badajoz. Just east of the village the road from Seville split, a southern branch leading to Valverde and Jerumenha, where there was a crossing over the River Guadiana, which would have to be used if the Allied army had to retreat. South of the village the river split into the Arroyo Nogeles, following the line of the Seville road, and the Arroyo Chicapierna, which ran down a shallow valley to the west. West of Albuera and the Arroyo Chicapierna lay a long ridge, crossed in the north by both roads and stretching over a distance of three and half miles. The ridge was featureless grassland rising to one hundred and fifty feet at its highest and sixty feet at its lowest. At its southern end, about one mile and a half south of the road to Jerumenha, there was a depression in the ridge before there began a further ridge stretching south. To the west of the ridges the small stream of the Arroyo de Valdesvilla ran northwards through a plain. On the east of Arroyo Chicapierna the east bank of the valley, covered with olive and ilex trees, rose shallowly towards the Seville road.

Sir William Beresford arrived with part of his army at La Albuera on the morning of 15th May. He had accompanying him only the 2nd Division, the Portuguese and King's German Legion. The 4th Division and the Spaniards were not expected until later in the day. Sensibly he anticipated that Soult and the French would come up the main road to cross the river and he deployed his troops to cover the position. Outposts of Brigadier-General Colborne's 2nd Division were stationed east of the river; the King's German Legion occupied the village and the rest of the 2nd Division on the ridge straddled the road to Jerumenha, protecting the route of retreat. Major General Hamilton's Portuguese, comprising two independent brigades and the Portuguese cavalry, were posted behind Albuera on the ridge covering the route to Badajoz. During the day the French army began to come up and drove into Colborne's outposts, reaching the river. In the afternoon Lieutenant-General Cole's 4th Division arrived and took up position in the shallow plain west of the ridge on the Jerumenha Road. The Spaniards did not arrive until night had fallen and spent the night moving into position on the right along the ridge southwards. They comprised in the centre General Lardizabel's Division, then that of General Ballestoros and on the far right that of General Zaya. The Spanish were still slowly taking position when dawn broke.

Mashal Soult with his limited army, comprising mainly the Vth Corps, had decided to strike as soon as possible before the Allied army and the Spanish had joined up. At Albuera he made his dispositions on the basis that the forces had not met up. Beresford's force on the ridge was largely stationed on a reverse slope and the combined force was not visible. He decided to avoid a direct full frontal attack at Albuera village, but to rely on a flank movement as his principal tactic up the south end of the ridge, which could take the allied army on its right flank and rear. An assault was to be launched first at the village to deter any movement by the Allied army south.

At dawn General Goudinet attacked the King's German Legion in strength at the village, and General Werle's division came out of the wood supported by cavalry immediately to the south opposite the Spanish. At the same time the Divisions of General Girard and Gazon, having come out of the olive trees and crossed the Arroyo Chicapierna, began the attack in the south. Girard on the right climbed towards the top of the ridge at the end of the east-west depression and Gazon mounted the ridge south of the depression. General Zaya's Spaniards, seeing the French in column marching on their flank, tried to turn to face the French. While brave individually, the Spanish troops were badly trained and undisciplined; their drilling was ineffective and they had the greatest difficulty in executing manoeuvres on the field of battle. Only four battalions of General Zaya's Division managed to turn to face the French, while the rest fell into confusion. It took the French some time to change from column of march into mixed columns with outlying *voltigueurs* to advance to battle. Beresford, seeing the threat in the south, ordered Major-General Stewart's 2nd Division to move south to hold the major French attack. Hamilton's Portuguese were to be moved to support the King's German Legion in Albuera. In the lead south was Sir John Colborne's Brigade, comprising the 3rd (East Kent – the Buffs) Regiment of Foot, the 31st Regiment of Foot, part of the 48th (Northamptonshire) Regiment of Foot and the 66th (Berkshire) Regiment of Foot. These moved across the Spanish front obliquely uphill, and then through the Spanish Divisions, to supports Zaya's four battalions on the right.

As they marched the French guns thundered at them across the valley. Zaya's Spaniards, with fierce heroism had stood resisting the oncoming French of Girard's Division with musquetry and artillery fire. As the French came up the ridge though the depression in mixed column of three diverse battalions and accompanied by artillery between the columns, the Spanish began to give way slowly. Coming up as they wavered, Colborne committed his brigade in their support. The troops formed line abreast and, passing Zaya's fighting troops, having veered to the left, began to enfilade the French on the flank. Girard's troops began to crumble as they tried ineffectively to turn to meet the violent musket fire while the British regiments fixed bayonets to charge. Colborne's regiments had, however, no cavalry protection, two regiments of Heavy Dragoons already having been put to flight. As the men fired and continued to form up to the centre as they advanced on the French ready to charge, Polish Lancers and Hussars crashed through their lines from the flank and rear. Blinded by rain and a hailstorm, there was no time to form squares, only the 31st succeeding in doing so.

The Polish rode down the regiments savagely, lancing the wounded and trampling the dead under foot. The rampaging French cavalry swept away Beresford and his staff forward on the ridge, and they had to defend themselves with their sabres. Of Colborne's brigade 1,300 men were killed, wounded or made prisoner out of 1,600. Both Brigadier-General Hoghton's and Brigadier-General Abercrombie's brigades had by this time come up, the latter on the east of the ridge under artillery fire. The two formed up in line across the ridge, Hoghton's brigade on the right and Abercrombie's on the left behind Zaya's battalions, around whom the Polish Lancers swirled. Soult, seeing Girard's Division halted, ordered General Gazon to his support and his columns moved down from the ridge beyond the depression and crossing it began to mount the hill, pressing on Girard's columns, so that they almost seemed to coalesce. Hoghton's brigade was formed from the 29th (Worcestershire) Regiment of Foot, the 48th (Northamptonshire Regiment of Foot (less that with Stewart's brigade) and the 77th (East Middlesex) Regiment of Foot, and Abercrombie's from the 28th (North Gloucestershire) Regiment of Foot, the 34th (Cumberland) Regiment of Foot and the 39th (Dorsetshire) Regiment of Foot. Early on Soult had moved Werle's Division and the detached cavalry across the front, and they now waited as a reserve behind Girard's and Gazon's Divisions.

The two brigades of the 2nd Division began to fire on the Polish Lancers (killing some of Zaya's Spaniards by friendly fire) but the Lancers were driven off. They began determinedly to advance through Zaya's battalions. Inexorably, with steady pace, closing to the centre, they marched on towards the French firing devastating volleys, to which the French replied. Girard's leading column began to disintegrate, but Gazon's Division, on its way down into the depression, was able to wrack the British brigades with musket fire, the centre column firing over the heads of the van. The odds were three to one, so great was the preponderance of numbers held by the French. Despite the fierce volleys, the 2nd Division walked forward, dead and wounded falling in their places facing front, and the French were held. In the advance General Hoghton was killed and Major General Stewart wounded. Colonel Duckwoth of the 48th was killed, Colonel White of the 29th wounded. Colonel Inglis of the 57th, lying wounded and dying, cried with his last breath 'Fifty-Seventh Die Hard!' Thus he gave the regiment its name.

Marshal Soult had become aware that the Allied and Spanish armies had joined, but having real contempt for Spanish armies, he decided that to break through with his flanking movement he must commit General Werle and his reserve Division and deploy the cavalry in the western plain. Although Beresford had moved the 4th Division south into the plain west of the ridge, it stood waiting. At La Albuera the troops of Goudinot had forced the King's German Legion to evacuate the village and they were being held only by the steadfastness of the latter and the support of Hamilton's Portuguese. As Beresford saw the slaughter of the 2nd Division in the furnace of the mutual infantry fire, he worried about his communications; he was uncertain whether to send the 4th Division into the conflict. He tried to move Portuguese troops to the right, but could not decide on the best course. General Cole, observing the fight, sent an aide-de-camp to Beresford seeking orders, but the aide-de-camp was killed on the way. Major Henry Hardinge (26 years old) a staff officer with the Portuguese, hurried over to Cole and persuaded him to advance to support the 2nd Division. Cavalry support was promised to Cole but was not forthcoming.

On his own responsibility he moved forward. His strength was down as Brigadier-General Kemmis and his brigade had been left behind by mistake. The Division comprised 3,000 Portuguese under General Harvey and two British Fusilier Regiments – the 23rd (Royal Welsh Fusiliers) Regiment of Foot and two battalions of the 7th (Royal Fusiliers). Cole formed lines of the Fusiliers across the valley with the Portuguese as a covering wing. On the march they were attacked by four regiments of General Latour-Maubourg's cavalry, but the intense musket fire of the Portuguese drove the cavalry off. The 4th wheeled left and caught Werlé's division as it stood parked in dense columns struggling from the depression to the top of the ridge. The deployment of Werlé's column was such that only the troops on the edge had freedom of fire and the 4th Divisions infantry swept away the massed troops with the intensity of their fire as they tramped on towards them, startling the French as they emerged from the smoke. The French retaliated with a heavy fire and tried to redeploy but the Fusiliers, the 23rd and the remnants of Stewart's brigade which had joined them marched on. The van of the leading French formation had their heads shot away and finally, in incredible confusion, the French divisions broke. With deafening shouts the British pushed them helter-skelter down the ridge.

The battle had reached a sudden impasse. Both Beresford and Soult were stunned by the casualties. Colborne's Brigade was reduced to a quarter, Abercrombie's to three quarters, and Hoghton's to a third, one regiment being led off the field by a junior Captain. The Fusiliers lost over 1,000 (half their number) and the Portuguese a third. The total Allied loss was 5,916 out of 35,000, the British infantry losing 4,407. The French lost nearly 7,000 out of 24,260. After the attack of the 4th Division the French crossed back to the east of the Arroyo Chicapierna and Goudinot retired from La Albuera. Apart from desultory firing, the battle had come to an end.

Marshal Soult lined up his remaining infantry reserve, cavalry and guns on the east of the valley but did not attack again. Beresford, in no position to attack, waited. Having assessed the situation it was clear to Marshal Soult that, having lost almost one-third of his army and still facing a united force of 30,000, the chance of reaching Badajoz successfully was remote. He decided therefore to retire south to Seville. The French thus abandoned their campaign and retreated, pursued by Lumley's British Cavalry. Wellington was invariably scathing about the cavalry because they always went out of control in a charge, as if fronting the field out foxhunting. However, at Usagre on 24th May in the course of their pursuit of the French, the 3rd, 4th and 13th Dragoon Guards ambushed three Regiments of Dragoons and defeated them, killing 30-40 and taking 78 prisoners. Many such actions characterised the Peninsular War. Beresford returned to Badajoz to continue the siege.

On 21st May Wellington visited the site of the battle and was moved as he saw the soldiers from the famous regiments involved 'literally lying dead in their ranks as they stood.' After the battle Beresford was in a mood of despondency and wrote a depressing report of it, even though Soult had been forced to withdraw. When Wellington received it, he told his aide-de-camp, 'This won't do: it will drive the people of England mad. Write me down a victory.' A year later the hill remained white with bones, where the bodies had been picked clean by kites, wolves and rats.

Sir John Colborne recovered from his wounds, commanded the 52nd Regiment of Foot at Waterloo and rose to become a Field-Marshal, in 1860 being made the 1st Lord Seaton. Major Henry Hardinge was wounded at Vitoria in 1813; became British Liaison Officer to Marshal Blucher at Ligny in 1815, Governor-General of India and a Field Marshal. He was made a Viscount.

In his poem *Childe Harold's Pilgrimage*, Lord Byron includes reflections on his visit to Spain in Canto I. While lauding the spirit of Spain to resist the French and Buonaparte, his verses on the site of the Battle of Talavera (see 28th July 1809) have an anti-war bias. (Stanzas XXXVIII – XLII). Stanza XLIII comments on the Battle of Albuera with a similar ambiguity.

> Oh, Albuera, glorious field of grief!
> As o'er thy plain the pilgrim pricked his steed,
> Who could foresee thee, in a space so brief,
> A scene where mingling foes should boast and bleed!
> Peace to the perish'd! may the warrior's meed
> And tears of triumph their reward prolong!
> Till others fall where other Chieftains lead
> Thy name shall circle round the gaping throng;
> And shine in worthless lays, the theme of transient song!

The 6th Viscount Hardinge was ejected from the House of Lord in 1999.

17th May 1944

The Battle of Monte Cassino

After the fall of the Italian Dictator, Benito Mussolini, on 25th July 1943 the new Italian Government, presided over by Marshal Badoglio, tentatively sought to enter into an armistice with Britain and the United States, and talks began in Lisbon on 3rd August. The final conquest of Sicily (16th August 1943) opened the way to the next stage of operations in the Mediterranean, an invasion of Italy. Whether there should have been such an invasion was a matter of disagreement between Britain and the Americans, but the latter had reluctantly agreed after a definite date had been fixed for the invasion of France, and the British had agreed to the transfer of four United States and three British Divisions to the Normandy Campaign.

The character of Italy as a long sea-girt peninsula gave the opportunity in theory for a seaborne attack to be made along its length; and the character of the terrain argued for an invasion as far north as possible. Any invasion in the south had the disadvantage that the invading army would have to move north on a front which, outside narrow coastal plains, comprised a mountainous backbone from which rivers ran across the invasion route to the sea. It was an ideal country for the creation of successive strong defence lines one after another. Because there was an inadequate backing force of aircraft carriers and a shortage of landing craft, General Eisenhower decided that no landing could be made north of the range of effective air cover. The consequence of this strategy implied an amphibious landing south of Naples and the Bay of Salerno was chosen. The plan conceived that the British 8th Army commanded by General Montgomery would cross the Straits of Messina into Calabria with the object of drawing the Germans south, while the 5th United States army under General Mark Clark (Operation Avalanche) would land at Salerno. The 8th Army would move north and the Salerno landing was designed to encourage a German retreat or even bar it, taking the Germans in the rear. General Clark's 5th Army was to comprise the 6th United States Corps under General Dawley and the 10th British Corps under Major-General McCreery, together with units of US Rangers and British Commandos.

It was not until 31st August that an armistice was signed between Marshal Badoglio and the Allied Governments, the negotiations having been bedevilled by the demand for unconditional surrender. It was to be announced simultaneously by the Italians and by General Eisenhower, the overall Commander in the

Mediterranean. Adolf Hitler, from immediately after the arrest of Mussolini, was suspicious that the Italians would seek a separate peace, and ordered army units to cross the border into the country. Feldmarschall Kesselring was therefore reinforced in the period up to the armistice with sixteen extra divisions. The announcement of the Armistice was made on 3rd September and that night King Victor Emmanuel and Marshal Badoglio fled Rome. That same evening the coast at Reggio di Calabria was the subject of a blistering aerial and naval bombardment and the British 8th Army then landed on the Italian mainland. They were unopposed and began the movement north hindered by bridges over the rivers demolished by the Germans on their retreat. The German armies in Italy had busied themselves arresting and disarming the Italian forces, and on 8th September rescued Mussolini from his mountain prison to establish him as dictator of a new Italian Social Republic in the north of Italy. The Italian desire to escape from the war was thus thwarted.

At 3.40 am on the morning of September 9th, the 5th United States Army landed on the beaches at Salerno. The landings covered an extensive front, the Rangers and Commandos to the east of Salerno, the British 10th Corps under Lieutenant General McCreery on the left and the 6th United States on the right, on a twenty-mile front between Salerno and Paestum. The front was bisected by the River Sele and the small coastal plain was overlooked by hills. The British 10th Corps was constituted by the 46th and 56th Divisions and the 6th US Corps had four divisions. The expectation of the troops in view of the Armistice was that there would be little opposition, but decoding by ULTRA of German army messages showed that General Hube and 16th Panzer Division, brought up from Calabria, were in the area. In fact the landings were strongly opposed, but by sunset on the 9th the beaches were cleared and on the 10th a bridgehead established. Feldmarschall Kesselring soon added to the German defence the 76th Panzer Division from the south and a Panzer-Grenadier Division from Rome. By the 11th the Germans were ready to counter-attack. Little artillery was ashore (indeed because of shortage of shipping the heavy artillery was not brought up until 14th September) so that the protection of the beachhead was dependent on air and naval support. The beachhead was of course exposed to German artillery in the hills. 627 ships and landing craft were involved in the operation, including parts of Force H from Gibraltar, while Force V comprised an aircraft carrier and six escort carriers. The latter were able to give constant local protection, since fighter sorties from Sicily were subject to the limitation that aircraft could only spend fifteen minutes on any sortie over the battlefield.

The German counter-attack on 11th September, supported by the Luftwaffe, struck heavily at the hinge between the British and American forces and thrust forward, pushing into the beachhead. The Luftwaffe brought into use a radio-controlled glider bomb and the American ships U.S.S. Philadelphia and U.S.S.

Savannah were severely damaged. Baltipoglia was retaken and the German thrust was moving towards the beaches. On the 12th the Germans continued to enlarge their bulge and, there being no reserves with the landing forces, two battalions of the 82nd U.S. Airborne were dropped into the beachhead. The cruisers Eruyalus, Scylla and Charybdis were to bring another 1500 troops from Tripoli. The white painted 'red cross' hospital ship Newfoundland was bombed by the Germans and sunk with heavy loss of life. On 13th September the situation was reaching a critical point and the 6th U.S.Corps began to give ground. Vice-Admiral Hewitt (USN) began to worry at the naval losses. The naval support was crucial since, in the absence of heavy artillery, only the naval guns gave protection to the troops in the bridgehead, although air cover and bombing inhibited German progress. On 14th September the whole Mediterranean Tactical Air force was switched to attack the German drive at Salerno, and their troop concentratrations and columns were mercilessly bombed.

The battleships Warspite and Valiant arrived and from 21,800 yards out at sea the massive shells were sent onto the German positions. On that day General Mark Clark raised the question whether part of the force in the northern part of the bridgehead should be embarked and landed in the south. Commodore Oliver, the British naval commander, and General McCreery were opposed to this proposal, which they regarded as impractical. Their task, they thought, was to keep the beaches open on the twenty-mile front and the flanks firm, while re-embarkment and landing would be hazardous. Warspite was hit by a glider bomb and severely damaged, her boilers filling with water so that steam could not be made. She was towed back to Gibraltar. On the 15th the German drive had stalled and on the 16th Kesselring began to withdraw. The naval guns and air support had saved the landings – V Force, for example, in three and a quarter days flew 713 sorties.

The US 6th Corps patrols and General Montgomery's forward troops met on 16th September, forty miles south-east of Salerno. Kesselring continued to make short stands to oppose the advance but on 1st October Naples was taken. The Germans stood on the River Volturno but in mid-October moved north to a line across Italy from the River Garigliano in the west, past Cassino at the entrance of the Liri valley over the mountains and along the River Sangro on the east. This line, the 'Gustav Line' had been prepared by General Bessell pursuant to the policy of holding on to as much territory in Italy as possible. After Salerno Adolf Hitler had considered withdrawing to south of the River Po in the north, but Feldmarschall Kesselring had persuaded him that holding a series of defensive lives would bleed Allied resources, which would not be available elsewhere, and that a northern line would allow Allied bombers in the south to operate more closely against the Reich and Central Europe. The scene was set for the protracted struggle around Monte Cassino.

The town of Cassino was the focus of the line west of the Abruzzi Appenine Mountains, lying on the route to Rome, and was over-shadowed by the mountain hill of Monte Cassino, upon which the large Benedictine Abbey stood, first established in the 6th century A.D. Kesselring had entrusted the defence of this sector to Lieutenant-General Fridolin von Senger und Etterlein, a former Rhodes Scholar at Oxford, devout Roman Catholic and as a young man a lay Benedictine. He had been part of the relief force sent to liberate the German army at Stalingrad. He was to prove a resourceful and doughty opponent. There were to be four battles at Monte Cassino between January and May 1944.

General Eisenhower and the Allied Command decided that the flank of the Gustav Line should be turned, and that could only be achieved by another amphibious operation. It was decided therefore that a landing should be made behind the line at Anzio, some thirty miles south of Rome, to coincide with a frontal attack on the line itself in the Cassino sector. Before the operation could be executed the commanders in the Mediterranean were recalled and on 24th December General Eisenhower, General Montgomery, Air Marshal Tedder and General Omar Bradley all left for England. Their Commands were taken over by General Sir Henry Maitland-Wilson, General Sir Oliver Leese and General Ira C. Eaker. General Alexander remained as commander of the Ground Forces and General Mark Clark as Commander of the 5th U.S. Army. The latter, following Salerno, had become even more self-obsessed and paranoid, determined not to have his 'glory' stolen, particularly by the British. He took with him to the next operation nearly fifty public relations people, and insisted that every release should mention him three times on the front page and once on every page thereafter.

The task of the landing force, having established a bridgehead, was to strike into the Alban Hills aiming for Valmontone, a town astride the road from Cassino to Rome, with the object of cutting off the retreat of the German Army. The force employed was commanded by Major-General Lucas of the 6th Corps of the 5th Army. It comprised only, when put ashore, the British 1st Infantry Division and a Commando Brigade and the 3rd U.S. Infantry Division, supported by tanks and Ranger battalions. The British were to be landed north of Anzio and the Americans south. The operation was therefore more limited than that at Salerno and, while it had Tactical Air Support, the naval back-up was less extensive. The landing on 22nd January went largely unopposed. General Lucas, advised by Mark Clark, decided to establish a defensible bridgehead and lingered on the beach, unwilling to move inland until reinforcements arrived. Considering the smallness of his force there was a certain sense in this course. However, it allowed the Germans to surround the bridgehead with ruthless swiftness, and Kesselring had General von Mackensen's 14th Army of six divisions quickly in place to seal a ring round the bridgehead. Attempts to break out of the perimeter failed and by 30th January there were 3,000 casualties, 2,100 of them British. On 16th February the Germans launched a counter-attack but, warned by the intelligence obtained by ULTRA, a combination of air cover and artillery concentration halted the attack by 20th February. Although the attack was held, General Lucas was replaced on 22nd February by his deputy General Truscott. Thereafter the Germans directed their attention to keeping the perimeter sealed.

The first battle of Cassino had commenced prior to these landings on 11th January. To the north-east of Cassino, the first line rested some four to five miles in front of the Gustav line itself. It was decided that an attempt should be made to outflank Cassino through the mountains to take the Alina bastion. A French Expeditionary Force made up of troops recruited in Algeria and Morocco from the settlers and native Arabs was to move forward in this attempt. They were familiar with mountainous terrain and thus adapted to the type of warfare involved. In a strong push the Germans were forced back to the Gustav line, but it could not be penetrated.

The autumn and winter rains, falling torrentially, had turned the country and roads into endless swamps of mud. Conditions for the troops were bleak and cold. Axle-vehicles were embedded in the mud and the conditions replicated those of the campaigns at Ypres in the First World War. Attacking a fortified and defended line re-introduced into the war the factor of attack and success by attrition and the series of Monte Cassino battles were in that sense a throw back to the past. General Mark Clark conceived the first battle as a movement to turn the flanks at Cassino. The British were to attack across the lower River Garigliano and proceed forward to take the Ausonia defile into the Liri Valley about three or more miles behind the Germans positions. The Americans were to attack round Cassino and across the Cassino Massif crossing the Rapido River. The British 5th Division was near the coast, the 56th in the centre and the 26th on the right. General McCreery planned for an attack by the 56th preceded by heavy bombardment, but not for the 5th. The task of crossing was formidable since the river was swollen, and the German lines were protected by 300 yards of anti-personal mines, a flat open plain and 15 yards of barbed wire before reaching the posts and bunkers at the foot of the hills. The 46th was to cross higher up to secure high ground as a protection to the forward move of the US 34th Division over the Rapido River.

On the 17th the attack began and the British crossed the Garigliano, establishing bridgeheads around Mintorno and Castleforte across the river which by 30th January were linked. On 19th January the 46th however failed to cross at San Ambrogio. The 36th Texan Division carried an assault across the River Rapido to the north on 20th January but fog reduced visibility and the assault boats were not successfully launched on the swollen, rapid stream. The troops faced (as had the British) fields of mines and entanglements of wire. After but small success, the Germans and Americans called a truce to collect the dead and wounded. The Americans had 1,300 dead and others wounded. The Germans lost only 64 killed and 179 wounded. Nothing had been achieved. Clark was now to turn to a separate thrust north of Cassino with the US 34th Division. The first objectives were a barracks two miles north of Cassino and a hill denominated Hill 213. The defences were again formidable – the band of anti-personnel mines, a flat open area, yards of mines, machine gun posts and foxholes at the base of the hill. On 24th January two battalions of the 133rd Brigade crossed the Rapido supported by tanks, but due to rain and mud tank movement was difficult. By midnight on 25th January a small bridgehead had been established and on the 27th the 168th Regiment crossed with tanks, only four of which were to come into battle and all of which were knocked out by 11 pm. The men were forced to retire and a general withdrawal took place. On the 29th a new attack was mounted towards Caira village.

Following the failure of the attack by the 36th Texan division, Clark ordered General Juin and the French Expeditionary Force to attack a height known as Monte Belvedere, north-east of Cassino, to guard against pressure on the U.S. flank. Juin correctly described it as an 'eccentric command'. It was at the least accessible point of the Gustav line and necessitated crossing two rivers with an eight hundred-metre climb over bare and open rocks to pierce the defences. Nonetheless the colonial French took the impossible heights aimed for in their attack, although they were driven back from the extreme outposts. Juin tartly wrote to Clark on 29th January that his force was now in an exposed salient unless the 34th U.S. Division could make progress. Gradually the Americans made progress on the Cassino Massif, reaching almost to the summit by 6th February, where they were at Monte Castellone and Snakeshead Ridge subject to counter-attack. The last days of the attack had been carried out on the heights in bitter winds, freezing rain or snowstorms. Clark still tried to order his men into the Liri valley, but the push had effectively reached a standstill, the situation dominated by bad weather and exhaustion. Meanwhile Major-General Ryder, who appreciated the courage and endurance needed to take Cassino, at last on 1st February took the barracks and his 133rd Regiment edged their way into the north of the town to face direct street-to-street fighting, where General von Senger had strengthened the defenders with two battalions of Panzer-Grenadiers. The Gustav Line had not however been pierced or Anzio reached, and the outcome was a defensive victory for the Germans. The cost had been excessive – five divisions had been deeply weakened (two British, two American and one French) by the losses. Clark had hoped to be at Rome by the end of January and public opinion and the Allied Command were restless.

A second battle of Monte Cassino proved in retrospect to be one of the most controversial episodes of the Second World War. The town was overlooked on the north by the monastery of St Benedict, which crowned the hill on which it stood and dominated the landscape over an extensive area, including the entrance to the Liri Valley. The monastery had been founded by St Benedict in 529 AD, and an urn containing his remains was kept under the high altar. It was an extensive, richly decorated historic building in the Classical and Baroque style, with a library containing illuminated books from the twelfth century. While in January, during the first battle, isolated shells had struck it, both the Germans and the Allies had given instructions that no attack was to be made on it. There is no reason to believe that because of his past the Germans under General Fridolin von Senger und Etterlein had any intent to occupy it. It had been fenced off and guarded and the crowds of refugees who had arrived there evacuated. In February 1944 only Abbot Diamare and six monks still remained and its portable books and art treasures had been removed. Its unavailability as part of the German Gustav line was not however totally clear cut, for out-buildings had been demolished to clear areas of fire, ammunition was stored in a cave under the abbey and outposts were close up under the walls.

Because of the earlier failure to penetrate the line and the penning down of the Anzio bridgehead there was pressure to break the stalemate, and General Alexander decided to replace the mauled and exhausted United States divisions by crack forces from the 8th Army. There was therefore transferred to the Garigliano front the 4th Indian Division under Major General Francis Tuker, the 2nd New Zealand Division (which included an armoured brigade) now under Brigadier Kippenberger, and the 78th British Division. The whole was placed under the command of Lieutenant-General Sir Bernard Freyberg, VC, as the New Zealand Corps. Mark Clark was to complain that with the withdrawal of the United States troops he had under his command only five corps, of which two were American and both at Anzio. The basic tactics were to repeat the thrusts of the American 36th and 34th Division which had stalled. The New Zealanders were to attack again at Cassino and the 4th Indian Division from the positions on the Cassino Massif towards the abbey, and having cleared the ground pass into the Liri Valley. Both Freyberg and Tuker inspected the battle terrain on arrival. It was Tuker's view that there could be no attack forward without overwhelming aerial bombardment which would remove the abbey, which he saw as a modern fortress because of its construction and position. Tuker asked for consent for such bombardment, since General Alexander had ordered that no strike on the monastery should be made without consent. General Mark Clark was not disposed to give his consent and it was only after the intervention of Freyberg on 12th February that Alexander gave his permission. Freyberg had represented that the destruction of the monastery was a 'military necessity' to prevent a potential loss of life. Sir Henry Maitland-Wilson, the overall commander, moreover thought on a scant basis that there was 'irrefutable evidence' that the Germans were in fact using the abbey for observation and sniping purposes.

Through information gleaned by ULTRA that the German counter-attack on the Anzio bridgehead was due on 16th February, efforts were made to hurry forward the new attack on the Gustav Line, but the arrangements for putting the 4th Indian Division into the positions on the Cassino Massif left by the 36th U.S. Division were slowed by the need to pass up the mountain with ammunition and supplies in narrow, muddy and confined defiles, and hampered by a shortage of mules. The raid on Monte Cassino was fixed however for 15th February in order that maximum airpower would be available for meeting the German attack at Anzio the next day.

The Tactical Air Force came in two waves, the first of 142 Flying Fortresses (B17), which dropped some two hundred and fifty-three tons of bombs on the monastery and hilltop, and the second of twin-engined Mitchell's, which dropped one hundred tons. The high walls of the abbey and the towers were smashed but the residue was to be destroyed by artillery bombardment, until there remained of the great monastery nought but heaps of waste and rubble. Some of the hundred refugees left were killed and injured but the Abbot and his monks escaped. General von Senger had them conveyed to Rome, where en route to a new monastery, they were seized by the Gestapo and the Abbot forced to make a broadcast which was used by Dr Goebels and the Nazi propaganda machine to denounce Allied barbarism and indifference to the heritage of Europe. The German army in the next two days was to occupy the rubble and begin to turn the ruins into a fortified place.

In order to reach the site of the monastery the 4th Indian Division had to move along the lower slope of the Cassino Massif under the guns of a German defensive post, on the end of a high ridge known as Point 593, and then attack two others, Points 444 and 445. The position of Point 593 was such that until it was taken the route was wholly exposed to enemy fire. The 1st Royal Sussex battalion on 15th February therefore attacked along Snakeshead ridge with a view to taking it. The fierce German resistance drove off their assault and on 17th February at midnight the 4/6th Rajputana Rifles renewed the attempt. There were many casualties along the ridge and one company who became entangled in gorse scrub which had been mined and booby-trapped was almost to a man killed. On 18th February the 1/9th Ghurkhas renewed the attack up hill on both Points 593 and 569, while the 1/2nd Ghurkhas worked their way forward to Point 445. In withering fire they fought their way up but with daylight the attacks were called off. It had been an expensive defeat in terms of lives lost, in total some 469 men killed, wounded or made prisoners of war from a division previously so successful. The Germans still held their strong points.

At Cassino, where the Rapido Valley had been flooded, a virtual moat protected the town. General Freyberg was therefore forced to plan an attack which could take the attackers and their tanks into the town across the water and swampy areas. The point of assault chosen was from the south along the line of the railway embankment into Cassino railway station. The embankment had been mined and in places blown up so that repair was needed before tanks could cross. It was decided to take the station and hold it while the engineers made good the embankment to allow the tanks to cross. The 28th Maori battalion was chosen for the task. The battalion was organised on a tribal basis and were efficient and fierce fighters. At 8.45 pm on a black, cold night the troops began to move forward through the sodden swampy ground, the mines, and the wire and were subject to fire by the mortars, but by 10.30 pm they had taken the railway station. The engineers went to work on the embankment to let the tanks in. They were not able to complete their task before dawn and, exposed in the open, had to retire. The Maoris were left holding out in the station under growing and constant assault on three sides. Despite supporting fire and the making of smoke screens, by the early afternoon, when German tanks were brought up, and there was little ammunition for the bazookas, they started to withdraw under heavy fire. The operation had failed with heavy casualties.

Despite the failure of both these attempts, Freyberg was keen to make a new thrust on a different axis. General Alexander insisted that he must wait for better weather and three dry days so that the 400 waiting tanks did not bog down in the mud leading into the Liri Valley. Freyberg's plan was to flatten the town of Cassino by bombing and artillery bombardment, allowing the New Zealand Division to move through to open the valley route. The 4th Indian Division would go forward from Castle Hill up the winding route to the abbey and take Point 435, within three hundred yards of the walls, thus clearing the way through the town from gunfire. On 22nd February the New Zealanders took over the north east corner of Cassino won by the Americans and were replaced on the Rapido River near Saint Angelo by the 78th British Infantry Division. On the 23rd, however, it began to rain and it was to continue to rain for three weeks. On the heights, where the Ghurkhas and the Indian battalions occupied positions overlooked by the Germans, there were blizzards and snowstorms but nonetheless they had to sit out the weather. The Germans were to spend their time enhancing their defences, while the troops shivered in the slit trenches.

The new attack in the Third Battle of Monte Cassino predicated a line of attack from the east along a narrow road, Cassino Road, entering the town and gaining access to Route 6 (the main route to Rome) running through the town. It was necessary therefore to take the town. The town itself was overlooked to the north-east by a steep but low hill upon which the castle stood, Castle Hill. The castle had been turned into a German strongpoint, Point 193. From the town a sinuous curving road ran up the mountain to the north of the town, upon which stood the monastery. On the bends of the road further strong points had been placed at each curve – Point 165 above the Castle hill, Point 202 on the next bend north of the town, Point 236 on the east further above the Castle Hill and finally Point 435, Hangman's Hill, on the last bend before the abbey some three hundred yards from its walls. East of the monastery ran high ground leading to Snakeshead ridge. Between the abbey and the ridge lay strong points 444 and 445. The two-pronged thrust was to climb to Hangman's Hill and the Abbey by way of Castle Hill and press into and through the town, the intention being that by taking the castle and abbey hills, the overlooking of the drive into the Liri valley by artillery and mortars would be prevented.

General Freyberg was determined that the attack should be preceded by a colossal bombardment which would destroy the town and the ability of the defenders to hold it. The town was occupied by the motivated elite troops of the German 3rd Regiment 8th Parachute Division, young, indoctrinated, fit and experienced. The 2nd New Zealand Division was entrusted with the assault through the town. The 4th Indian Division, containing units of the 1/4th Essex, the 4/6th and 1/6th Rajputana Rifles, and 1/9th and 2/7th Ghurkhas, were to be responsible for the assault up to the abbey. The bad weather yielded on 14th March and on the 15th the waiting heavy and medium bombers began to strike the town at 8.30 am, the New Zealanders being withdrawn from the north-east corner which they held. Some 575 heavy and medium bombers took part and 200 fighter bombers. The bombs rained down wave after wave until mid-day, dropping 1400 tons of bombs on one square mile. Not all were dropped with accuracy – some destroyed the French Headquarters twelve miles away since as the smoke, which rose high, smothered the town, the target was obscured. During the whole operation the ruins were subjected to dive-bomber attack and heavy artillery fire. Behind the barrage, troops of the 24th New Zealand Battalion began to press along the Caruso Road from the east of the town with elements of 19th Armoured in support, their job to enter the town and turn to attack Castle Hill. The entry road was in fact a narrow corridor overlooked by the Germans and with the ruined buildings, crater holes and piled rubble, was a narrow funnel through which to pass. The troops gained their old positions, but in the town about half the defenders survived protected in the ruins in broken house cellars and behind fractured walls and debris.

Intense hand-to-hand fighting was to break out as the 25th and 26th New Zealand battalions were to join the struggle. The 19th Armoured did not progress easily, being prevented by the large craters and the flooded areas which obstructed roads. The mobile heaps of rubble in which the Germans lurked were often twenty feet high and the craters up to sixty feet wide and ten feet deep. The New Zealanders and the German paratroops at times even found themselves in the same buildings, as the hand-to-hand fighting pressed through the town. The 26th New Zealand Battalion reached the station and by the end of 16th March, half of Cassino was taken. Torrential rain began to fall which began to fill the craters. After close fighting on Castle Hill the 25th New Zealanders took the Castle, but had to await the contingents of the 4th Indian Brigade, who were to use it as a base to push up the hill to the abbey. They were relieved by 1/4th Essex Battalion.

The next hours and days were filled with the attempts of the 4th Indian Brigade to progress up the monastery hill and hold on. The 1/9th Ghurkhas reached Hangman's Hill and lay in an open, exposed position near the ruins of the abbey. There was a need to reinforce them and push up from the Castle. The lowest Point, Point 165 was taken, lost and retaken by the Essex battalion. The Castle was the subject of sustained struggle. A and C companies of 1/4th Essex were in the Castle and were to be relieved by B and D companies in order to enable them to join the Ghurkhas at Hangman's Hill. The Castle was however the subject of sustained counter-attack by the paratroops of the 4th Regiment who, although beaten off, mounted some five attempts to retake it. In the last, one of the buttresses was exploded and the Germans entered the courtyard, to be driven out by fierce hand-to-hand combat. On 16th May above the Castle 1/6th Rajputana Rifles made three attacks to gain Point 236 but were driven off. On 19th March B and D companies of the Essex tried to reach the Ghurkhas on Hangman's Hill but only 70 men succeeded in doing so. Point 202 on the road up monastery hill was also taken by the 1/6th Rajputana Rifles and held by the New Zealanders. A tank thrust was made from Snakeshead Ridge on 19th March, shooting up Point 593 which overlooked that section of the massif, but after twelve tanks were lost the column withdrew. In the town the Germans turned two hotels in the north on the lower slopes of monastery hill into strong fortresses and although at one point almost surrounded, sustained their defence. By 20th March the forward advance had stalled; the Ghurkhas and Essex men on Hangman's Hill were penned down under overlooking fire; the German were still entrenched in the town. Front line conditions were intolerable: everywhere there were dead men, fouled bunkers and cellars, the open ground in daylight subjected to mortar fire and snipers. On the 24th Freyberg decided to withdraw from Point 202 and Hangman's Hill and after dark the men were brought down. The assault had again failed; a new defence line had been established taking in two-thirds of the town and the Castle Hill, but the way to Anzio and Rome remained blocked. There followed a vicious war along the front line while the stalemate lasted and the Tactical Air force concentrated on bombing the German communication links.

The fourth battle of Monte Cassino represented the final and successful attempt to break through the Gustav Line. General Alexander was determined that the attempt should not be started without detailed planning and an overwhelming superiority over the German defenders in aircraft, artillery and men. He desired a three to one advantage in troops, which implied an extra seven- and a half divisions to those already engaged. The strategic objective of the attack, Operation Diadem, was (together with a break-out from Anzio) to surround and destroy the German 10th Army. It did not have as an objective the taking of Rome. The need to have the overwhelming preponderance of troops caused Alexander to collect divisions of different nationalities from along the Italian front line in order to assemble them on the twenty-mile front of Cassino. The salient over the River Garigliano won by the British in the first battle in January 1944 was to be the launching point of the United Sates 2nd Corps, nearest the coast, with the French Expeditionary Force on their right up to the south bank of the Liri

River. The British 13th Corps occupied the front north of the Liri River, the part of Cassino taken and the lower slope of the Cassino Massif. There in the high salient were placed the Polish Corps. The section of the Gustav Line was left with two Indian divisions, while New Zealanders stood on the Appenine mass. It was of the essence of the plan that the attack should be launched over the whole Cassino front simultaneously and that the element of surprise should be kept. To this end information was disseminated that an amphibious landing was planned north of Rome and seaborne exercises for troops were carried out south of Naples. Feldmarschall Kesselring was sufficiently persuaded to retain two strong divisions north of Rome.

To obtain weapon superiority 3,000 aircraft were designated for the attack, with 1,600 guns and 2,000 tanks. The armour and artillery brought in was carefully camouflaged and put in place at night. Bombing and an artillery barrage was to precede the attack and a key to the forward movement of the British 13th Corps was to be the immediate construction of seven bailey bridges across the Rapido River so that the infantry crossing could be backed by tanks and artillery once across, one of the failures of the earlier battles. Three were planned on the front of the 4th Division – Amazon, Blackwater and Congo and four on the 8th Division front – Cardiff, London Oxford and Plymouth. Infantry were to pave the way, crossing in rubber boats to establish bridgeheads for the engineers to place their bridges. The 7th, 59th and 225th Field Engineering Companies attached to 4th Division were to play a crucial role in the success of the battle. To prepare them, practice exercises were carried out on the River Volturno. Immediately prior to the battle the engineers were employed by night creating tracks through the minefields up to the river, covering them by day with brushwood, clearing mines and sending parties to inspect the bridge sites, including the measuring of the river's width – plunging in and swimming with a measuring tape to the German side. All these activities involved great risk.

Limited objectives were defined for the first day of the assault, but each Corps involved was proscribed an overall strategy. The 2nd United States Corps on the coast, comprising the 85th and 88th Divisions, were to take first Santa Maria Infante and then push on into the Arunci mountains towards Monte Petrella and Formia on the coast. On their right the French Expeditionary Force of four divisions – 3rd Algerian, 2nd and 4th Moroccan and the 1st Division de Marche together with the Goumiers – were to take Monte Maio and Monte Faito and move on to Ausonia, then making for Pontecorvo in the Liri valley. The British on the seven-mile front at the head of the valley comprised the three Brigades of 8th Division on the left – the 17th, 19th and 21st Indian Brigades – and those of 4th Division on the right, the 10th, 12th and 28th. These two divisions were backed by a Canadian Division on the left (1st, 2nd, 3rd Canadian Brigades) and the 78th Division on the right comprising 11th, 36th and 38th Brigades. 1st Armoured Brigade were held to the rear to break through once the bridges were in place. The objective of the British Corps was to push up the valley outflanking the town to take Route 6 west of the town and move towards Aquina and Piedimonte. The Polish Corps had by far the most difficult task: to break out of the salient on the Cassino Massif, move along the heights to Points 593, 505 and 601 on Colle San Angelo, outflanking the monastery and moving on and down to Route 6 behind Cassino. The Polish Corps under General Anders was made up of two Divisions – the 3rd Carpathian Infantry Division of two brigades, the 5th Kresowa Infantry Division made up of the Wilkenska Brigade and the 6th Lvov Brigade and the 2nd Polish Armoured Brigade. Anders welcomed the test for his Polish troops as a way to re-ignite national feeling and raise morale in Poland by showing that the traditional enemy could be beaten even in his most formidable strongholds. Among the British, the Poles had a reputation as sophisticated, reckless and brave. The Poles in their turn regarded the British as too casual.

The 11th May was fixed as the day for the attack. On the 10th on the Rapido front the rubber boats for the infantry had been taken up and left camouflaged near the river. The 11th itself was hot and sunny and events followed the daily pattern, a morning and evening bombardment which by 10 pm fell away into silence. At 11 pm the night dissolved in the firing of the 1,600 guns behind the front. For forty minutes the bombardment moved over the German positions, the flashes filling the darkness with constant bursts of light. For forty minutes the guns crashed on. Thereafter a tactical firing pattern would be used, moving forward in front of the attacking troops and with which they were in the event to fail to keep up. The Germans could emerge from their foxholes and bunkers to man their line.

The American 83rd and 88th were the first to attack on the coast. The 88th was the first all-conscript division to go into battle. It had no experience and its morale was affected by the devastation they saw in the Garigliano sector – the burnt-out equipment, rotting dead bodies out in the open and the constant toll of casualties. There was a pre-battle focus on the division as one of conscripts because General Mark Clark had now insisted that every division should have public relations men and all press releases should be released as from General Mark Clark's Army. The night had become foggy which added - with the smoke of the shells - to the confusion. The 85th gained one objective, but some were surrounded and taken prisoner. The 88th took the southern slope of Monte Damiano but the attack on Santa Maria Infanta failed and the advancing troops on the Mintorno road were shelled from the hills, one of which was partly taken. There were many casualties and the inexperienced troops, when they lost their officers, tended to be paralysed, not knowing which move to make.

On their right the French Expeditionary Force moved off forty minutes after the United States Division towards their first objectives, Monte Faito and

Monte Maio. Their attack was met furiously from the gunpoints and pill-boxes of the German line and they had to cross the minefields, but the Germans had less strongly defended the front before the Arunci Mountains. The Moroccans however struck through, inflicting heavy casualties with the artillery in support on German reserves and communications and just after midnight took, climbing steep slopes under fire, the heights of Monte Faito. On their left the armoured force moved slowly across the mountains and by the end of 12th May had taken half of Castelforte. The level of casualties was nonetheless great and General Juin had to stiffen troop morale with his personal encouragement.

Affairs did not progress so well along the British front where the Germans were heavily entrenched behind minefields on the west side of the Rapido River, which was at least sixty feet in width and fast running. The attack was much hampered by the thick fog which had descended over the river, although that gave protection from the guns which the Germans had overlooking the sector. The fog prevented troops being clear about the positions reached and some confusion resulted. To the left the 8th Division crossed either side of St Angelo. Parts of the 17th Brigade north of the town were across within two and half hours and the Royal Fusiliers and Frontier Force tried to move forward in the fog against intense German fire. At 4 am the Royal Fusiliers were to halt, pinned down in a two-foot drainage ditch where they lay head to toe under constant fire. The Frontier Force was also stalled. All but two boats were destroyed or swept away in the river. The 19th Brigade was also thrown out by the fog, but although the Sikhs had great difficulty in forming up in dense mist and although impeded by the irrigation ditches, they managed to get through the German wire and dig in.

Sepoy Kamal Ram of the 3rd Battalion, 8th Punjab Regiment was to exemplify the courage of his fellows. The company advance was stopped from four machine gun posts. Kamal Ram volunteered to go behind the lines to try to take out these posts. He crawled round through the wire to the rear right post, shot the machine gunner, killed a second German with the bayonet and an officer with a revolver. Quite alone he went on to the second post, killed the gunner and lobbed in a grenade; the remaining enemy surrendered. He then joined a havildar reconnoitring the third post and attacked and destroyed that. The company were thus able to charge and take the ground needed for the bridgehead to allow work on the bridges. Sepoy Kamal Ram was awarded the Victoria Cross for his initiative and fearlessness.

The Brigade too was pinned down but had the advantage that on the far left one bridge across the river was built in the night and survived. Of the other three on this sector, one was built and then destroyed by shelling and the others abandoned. By morning four squadrons of tanks were across and while some were bogged down in the swampy land the others moved north towards St Angelo. The British 4th Division nearer to Monastery Hill also failed to make significant progress. The 28th Brigade on the left was late in crossing because of the fog, and encountered heavy casualties from the gunfire and the minefields. By daylight only 250 men were entrenched on the far bank of the river. The 10th Brigade to the right had more success: part of all three battalions succeeded in crossing and the 2nd Bedford and Herts moved forward half a mile. The Germans mounted seven counter-attacks, but three failed under the screen of heavy gunfire. During the night the Royal Engineers struggled to put in place the three bridges designed to serve the 4th Division and the armoured thrust, but once more the fog and German machine gun fire and artillery prevented success. Casualties were large, the engineers being subjected to machine gunfire from the opposite bank, and they were finally forced back.

The Poles on the Cassino Massif did not begin their general attack until 1 am after a devastating bombardment of Phantom Hill. They were to move along Snakeshead Ridge towards Point 593 and Point 569 and follow through towards the abbey: they were further ordered to press on through a gorge between Snakeshead Ridge and Phantom Hill, while a separate attack on the latter hill was to be made. The Carpathian Division pressed through the gorge, shelled by German artillery on the heights, and their 1st Brigade mounted an attack on Point 593. That was taken after the barrage, before the Germans could re-occupy it. The troops mounting the gorge were heavily fired on by snipers, some under cover of tanks abandoned in the third battle. The Kresowa Division pressed onto Phantom Hill and achieved an advance along it, to be met by ruthless hand-to-hand fighting before they came to a halt. In the end, like the other attempts to breach the line, the Polish advance came to an end. The Poles had had by far the most difficult task, facing the problems inherent in a mountainous, gorge-ridden landscape of open rock and scrub with their assault overlooked by strong German positions.

After first light on 12th May the drive forward paused. The Germans had to re-organise following the impact of the constant and heavy bombardment and were not able to mount a forceful counter-attack. The allied troops had the problem of hanging on to the gains made, like the Royal Fusiliers of 17th Brigade who were pinned down in the open. Monastery Hill was actively battered with smoke shells in an attempt to hamper the German guns and mortars overlooking the way forward. For Lieutenant-General Sir Oliver Leese commanding the 8th Army Division, the problem was to get across the river, which was the key to the breakthrough. In the sector of the 4th Division the decision was made to concentrate on the construction of an 'Amazon' bridge nearest to Cassino and Route 6. The British force was to be regrouped so that the bridge could be used by 12th Brigade and the tanks of 6th Armoured Division. Careful reconnaissance of the sites was undertaken under fire, resulting in losses among the officers of the engineer companies of 4th Division. There were three companies, the 7th, 59th and 225th. The plan was for them to work in sequence through the night on the bridge and the work was to be covered by a special artillery programme and by laying a smokescreen. Only volunteers were sought for the task, the completion of which was the key to the battle, since without a bridge tank and artillery support could not strike through and into the Liri Valley by-passing Cassino.

At 5 pm smoke was made over the river at the Amazon site and the 225th company moved up. A bulldozer was brought up to shape the bank and although there was sniping the driver was not hit. The work gang pressed on shaping the approach. The lorries bringing the bridge went forward towards the site and at 7.45 pm the 7th company moved up to relieve the 225th. The rollers for the bridge had to be laid under the continuing fire while the bridge parts were unloaded. That task was completed by 9 pm for all but two lorries, but the large bulldozer had been damaged and was out of action. Three quarters of an hour later the 59th went in. It was impossible because of increasing sniper and mortar fire to get across the river to prepare the far bank. Later eight men of the 59th tried taking hand tools but four were killed and the other four wounded. Casualties were continuous, the German fire becoming gradually more accurate. At times flares were put up in the night to silhouette the engineers assembling the bridge. At 1 am the advance units of the armoured division came up noisily to the front led by the 17/21st Lancers and stopped two hundred yards behind the bridge. Near the working engineers, a shell exploded a lorry loaded with smoke shells, which blew up, igniting a blazing fire spreading to adjoining trucks.

The presence of the tanks brought an increased rain of gun fire. About 2.30 am a machine gun started to fire down the line of the bridge as the construction went forward. It was not until 4 am that the bridge would be ready to be pushed on to the rollers laid down to take it across the river. Men started to heave and push the bridge forward, but they lacked the impetus which came from the necessary bulldozer. The officer in charge, Lieutenant Boston, asked the leading tank under the command of Lieutenant Wayne to help. Cranking forward, the tank began to push the bridge and it shifted on, coming off the rollers without damage, falling on its plates. Still under fire the approaches were made, and just before 5 am the tanks of the 17/21st Lancers led the tanks and the men of the 12th Brigade across. The Germans continued to fire at the bridge as the column rolled forward. The men of the 6th Black Watch marched across to the skirl of the pipes. The engineers paid dearly for their heroism with about forty per cent casualties. As the troops and tanks took the west river bank the other bridges were built.

On 13th May the attack along the line was renewed. The 88th Division of the United States 2nd Corps advanced once more to endeavour to take Santa Maria Infante. The 351st Regiment, whose Colonel had led them from in front, stalled in the ferocious defence made and called up tanks, which came to a standstill in the road. Accurate shelling began to disable the tank column and the assault came to an end. The Germans kept the village. However, with the Moroccan drive on the right, on the 14th the Germans abandoned Santa Maria Infante. On the right the Moroccans of the French Expeditionary force fought forward from Monte Faito to Monte Maio. Despite artillery fire they went on bunker by bunker until the German defence, which lacked depth, was driven back. The summit was taken and an observation post established to direct the artillery on to the retreating Germans. The German line had been pierced and apart from the taking of isolated posts, which had been bypassed, the Moroccans, urged on by General Juin, were to press their advance forward towards Castelforte, which was taken on 4th May, and Ausonia. On the front of the 8th Indian Division forces continued to move over the bridge built and the Ghurkhas and tanks took St Angelo. The 17th Brigade was ordered to attack the German line, but made little progress at the expense of heavy losses. The Royal Fusiliers managed a few hundred yards to come to a standstill sheltering in a more forward irrigation trench system, from which they soon had to withdraw. The taking of San Angelo and the arrival of the tanks resulted in a German withdrawal on their front. The 4th Division, faced by hard resistance, fought their way forward throughout the day and on the 14th the 12th Brigade had reached the road south from Cassino to Pignetaro and established a salient over a mile and a half in depth. The Poles on the heights continued to exchange fire with the Germans but were not to launch further major attacks until early on 16th May.

The next days saw bitter, hard fighting as the Allies edged forward, subject always to counter-attack. The well-designed Gustav Line meant constant individual attempts to besiege, overwhelm and destroy the network of artillery position, pill-boxes, bunkers and strong points of which the line was made. It was a persistent test of the skill and courage of those involved, like Fusilier Francis Jefferson of the 2nd Battalion Lancashire Fusiliers, who on 16th May, when the tanks were held up by an anti-tank obstacle and his battalion had to try to dig in without support on an exposed hillside, destroyed one approaching German tank with a PIAT and chased off another. To do so he ran forward and stood up twenty yards from the leading tank to fire his weapon. He was awarded the Victoria Cross, since his action resulted in the failure of the counter-attack on the battalion. The 78th Division and the 1st Canadian Corps were brought up from reserve and determinedly and deliberately the Germans were pushed out of their positions in the Liri Valley. On the German right the rapid advance of the French had thrown their right flank into confusion. By the evening of 16th May the 11th Brigade of the 78th had reached Route 6 and the 36th Brigade were pressing towards it, while the Moroccans had succeeded in passing through the mountains to come down to Route 6 further west. On the heights the Poles renewed their attack. The 6th Lvov Brigade took the Colle San Angelo and the 1st Carpathian Brigade Point 593. The high ground around the monastery was progressively occupied.

The constant move forward on the front to the south of Cassino and the arrival of the Moroccans and the British on Route 6 meant that Cassino had been outflanked and the Allies were behind the Gustav Line. The Moroccans had burst through the improvised Hitler Line to the rear and the British with their mass of tanks, artillery and infantry were entering the open Liri Valley. Consistent with his policy, Feldmarschall Kesselring decided to abandon the Gustov Line and ordered a retreat to be signalled at midnight on 17th May by the bombing of the station. That night the Germans began to flow back in an organised fighting retreat.

On the morning of 18th May a white flag was raised over the ruins of Monte Cassino Abbey and at 8 am Lieutenant Gurbiel of the 12th Podolski Lancer Hussars was ordered to lead a patrol to the ruins. He found there seventeen men and three wounded, the remainder of the garrison having slipped away. By 9.50 am he had raised an improvised pennant of the Podolski Hussars made with a red-cross flag and a blue cloth. A bugler sounded the Krakow Hejnel. On the 18th General Anders ordered that the flag of Poland and the Union Jack be flown over the ruins. The Germans left were driven from their last positions on the Cassino Massif and in the town the Guards were able to emerge from their defensive points.

As the Allies followed after the retreating Germans, who remained on the defensive, a break-out took place at Anzio, which had been reinforced by the 36th United States Division. At first in accordance with the overall plan as ordered, the Americans struck north towards Valmontone to take the retreating 10th Army in the rear with a view to its annihilation, but on 27th May General Mark Clark ordered the American Army to turn north for Rome. He was determined to obtain the 'glory' of taking Rome and even threatened to fire on the British if they sought to reach Rome first. Through this act of disobedience to the orders of the overall Ground Forces commander General Alexander, the German 10th Army was allowed to escape. Kesselring was able to save his army to fight on other lines further north in Italy. On 2nd June the Americans entered Rome and on the 5th Clark had himself photographed under a sign marked Rome for general distribution to the media. His disobedience to orders for his own glory was far more momentous than the error which led to Admiral Byng being shot for his mistakes at Minorca in 1757. General Omar Bradley was vindicated however about Clark, for on his appointment he had doubted whether he was the right person to command at Anzio, noting that 'he seemed false, somehow to eager to impress, too hungry for the limelight, promotions and personal publicity.' Clark was not however censored; indeed, consistent with the dawning age of celebrity and populism, he was to succeed General Alexander as Army Group commander in December 1944 and be made a five-star General in March 1945. The troops, who remained in Italy and whose victory of annihilation was stolen, were to have to fight the same troops again in the north when the Germans came to rest on a fortified line north of Florence, the Gothic Line running from south of Spezia, through Luccana south eastwards along the Appenines and across south of San Marino to Pesaro.

The Germans were not strongly attacked again until September 1944. The Allied Army in Italy had been weakened by the diversion of six divisions and the Moroccans and Free French to the invasion on the Riviera in August, but the British did attack on the Adriatic, pushing the Gothic line back and entering the plains of the Romagna. Winter set in and in February after the Yalta Conference General Alexander, as overall commander, was ordered not to mount further attacks on the German line. The character of the army had moreover changed, there being among the Allies both Italians and Brazilians. The object in Italy had become the need to hold down as many German divisions there as possible. At the end of April 1944 movement forward across the Serio River began and on into the Po Valley. On 2nd May Feldmarschall Kesselring signed an Armistice and the Italian campaign was over. There were 123,254 casualties suffered by the 8th Army, 188,746 by the United States 5th Army and it is thought 434,646 (including the missing) by the Germans.

The Conquest of Italian East Africa

Italy was united only in 1870. Eritrea was acquired as a colony in 1885, and Italian Somaliland, centred on Mogadishu on the west African coast. Ethiopia lay between the two countries and in 1895 the Italians endeavoured to seize it, but were decisively defeated at the battle of Adona. In 1911, when Turkey was involved in conflict in the Balkans, Tripolitania and Cyrenaica were siezed from them. Italy had a pro-active colonisation policy so that by 1940 there were a quarter of a million Italians in the African colonies. In 1934 Ethiopian guerrilla gangs attacked the Italian consulate at Gondar and in December regular Ethiopians troops attacked Val. Such attacks re-awakened in the Duce, Benito Mussolini, the Italian leader, the idea of taking Ethiopia and of adding it to the Italian empire. Preparations began and, despite protests and a discussion in the League of Nations for three weeks on whether economic sanctions should be imposed on Italy, on 2nd October Mussolini announced to crowds on the squares of Italian towns by radio and loudspeaker his intent to take Ethiopia, because of the poor outcome of the Treaty of Versailles for Italy. On 3rd October Italian forces crossed the frontier. The campaign was to last until the following May. Under its Emperor Haile Selassie the Ethiopians fiercely resisted the attacks from Eritrea and Somaliland. The League of Nations voted for sanctions, but none of the governments had any real intent to apply them. Britain tried to encourage their enforcement, but Germany and Russia, who did not belong to the League, would not apply them. Even Switzerland continued to supply the Italians with arms.

As the Italians gradually took the country, they abolished slavery, and started to build roads and facilities. Ethiopia had of course never been colonised by any European power and slavery, as it had formerly in most of Africa, still persisted. Pitched battles were fought until the Emperor was left with one army which, was defeated at Dessie. Haile Selassie on 2nd May fled into exile and on 9th May in Rome Mussolini proclaimed the reborn Roman Empire to enthusiastic crowds. In July sanctions were abandoned. In 1937 the Duke of Aosta, a cousin of King Victor Emmanuel II, the Italian King, was made Governor-General and viceroy of Italian East Africa and in 1939 its Commander in Chief. He was a man of chivalry and sophistication, appreciated by the English, whom he met, and that character was to imprint the war in East Africa with a humanity and conformity with the rules of war not found elsewhere in the Second World War. The attitude of the Duke to the war is a matter of speculation, but he was the object of Mussolini's suspicion. Certainly he was influenced by his position, wholly isolated from Italy and incapable of being reinforced or re-supplied, so that any defence could only be a holding one, and the lives and safety of the troops needed to be a prime consideration.

Soon after Italy declared war the Italian armies took some Sudanese border towns including Kassala, and Moyale in Kenya; and in August they took British Somaliland with its port of Berbera. The Italians invaded the latter with overwhelming force against a British garrison of fifteen hundred. Access to Berbera was obtained through the Tug Argan gap, where the few British established a defended position, a principal element of which was 'Observation Hill.' That position was attacked on 11th August and briefly defended by the Somaliland Camel Corps In the course of the action a Victoria Cross was earned by Captain Wilson of the East Surrey Regiment, who, although wounded seriously, kept his artillery firing over four days, wounds untended, until his position was overrun on the 15th and he was taken prisoner. At that time the Italians had in East Africa some 90,000 Italian troops, 250,000 in local forces, and 223 aircraft, with a naval contingent at Massawa of 9 destroyers, 8 submarines and various small ships. The British land forces comprised some 90,000, mainly local levies with 100 aircraft, many of which were obsolete. In July the Emperor Haile Salassie moved to Cairo to establish a movement for national liberation in his country, and in October the Emperor, the Secretary of State for War, Mr Anthony Eden, General Smuts from South Africa and General Wavell, the Commander in Chief, met to evolve a policy for retaking Italian East Africa. Meanwhile, Britain built up its forces in the area with troops from India, South Africa and West Africa.

After the invasion on the borders the Italians came to a standstill. Guerrilla activity, particularly in the west of the country round the source of the Blue Nile, grew and progressively the Italians had to disperse their forces throughout the country, since they faced a similar problem to the French in Spain in the Peninsula war. By the end of 1940 both the Sudan and Kenya had been reinforced and General Smuts urged the use of the troops in Kenya in action. In December General Sir Archibald Wavell, Lieutenant-General Sir William Platt (the Kaid of the Sudan) and Lieutenant General Sir Alan Cunningham (the Commander of the Kenya forces) met and resolved on a strategy. It was to further insurrection in Ethiopia and to embark on limited campaigns in the north from the Sudan and in the south from Kenya simultaneously. The two armies had bases over a thousand miles apart. In early January General Frusci abandoned his border conquests, including Kassala, on the orders of the Duke of Aosta, who was influenced by the success in North Africa of the British troops and wished to concentrate his forces.

The northern offensive commenced on 19th January, when General Platt's troops crossed into Eritrea. They consisted of the 4th and 5th Indian Divisions, which were an amalgam of two Indian battalions and one British or Ghurkha battalion, and the Sudan Defence force. They pushed General Frusci into Eritrea, defeating him at Agordat. He was then ordered to take a stand at Keren, where the pass pierced mountains 6,000 feet high which overlooked the western plain. The position could not be outflanked and could only be taken by frontal assault up the slopes. Two Italian Divisions held the front, one of which was the crack Salvia Division despatched by the Duke of Aosta. The air cover for Platt's armies was exiguous, even old-fashioned Vincents being used as dive-bombers. The supply route for the invading forces was a single road, under bombardment, to a railhead one hundred and fifty miles away. Early attempts were made to take the Keren position in February 1941 but the defenders had the advantage of position and numbers. Fierce attacks were however made, like those on 7/8th and 12th of February by a leading company of the 6th Rajputana Rifles. In the action on the 7th Subadur Richpal Ram, after the death of his company commander, urged on the men to take their objective, and with 30 men rushing the objective, it was taken with the bayonet. Six counter-attacks were made but this small group held on and when ammunition ran out, fought their way back to safety through the enemy. On the 20th Richpal Ram again led his men forward and until the end urged on his company, even after his right foot was blown off. For his leadership and courage he was awarded the Victoria Cross. Preparations were needed to dislodge the Italians at Karen and six weeks was to elapse before the main assault on the position was to begin. A propaganda war was waged: Viscount Coverdale, the heir of the late Prime Minister, Earl Baldwin, trained loudspeakers onto the Italian lines broadcasting snatches of opera and news of Italian defeats. Meanwhile in the mountains in Gojjim province, the guerrillas, fortified by a small force led by Brigadier Stanford and Colonel Wingate, took control of wide area to which on 20th January the Emperor Haile Selassie returned to fuel the insurrection.

In the south the campaign did not commence until February. General Cunningham had 77,000 troops in Kenya of which 33,000 were from British East Africa, 9,000 from British West Africa and 27,000 from South Africa. The campaign was to involve movement over vast distances. On 11th and 12th February African Divisions from East Africa with the 1st South Africa Division crossed the Kenyan frontier into Italian Somaliland and recaptured Moyale in the west. On 14th February the port of Kismayu was taken. The Italians had entrenched themselves just north of the town on the opposite bank of the Juba River with a strong force of six Italian brigades and six brigades of local troops. On the 22nd the British force mounted a three-pronged attack across the river, one on each flank of the Italian and one in the centre. There was stern fighting but on the 23rd the river had been crossed. The Italian force of 30,000 had given way, killed, wounded, captured and dispersed into the bush. With the consent of General Wavell, Cunningham pressed on 275 miles to Mogadishu, which was entered on 25th February. On the airfield lay 21 Italian planes and supplies were found of

35,000 gallons of motor petrol and 80,000 of aviation fuel. Further advances were made possible and consent was given to a push north to Jijjiga and Harar, 774 miles away to the north-west. On 1st March the motorised force set out, reaching Jijjiga on 17th March. There was little resistance. On the previous day, under air cover from Aden of four squadrons, two battalions of troops landed at Berbera and moved to unite with the force from Kenya liberating British Somaliland. The Italians were to make a stand on the Jijjiga-Harar road at the Marda Pass, which lay through steep hills commanding the approach to it. The position was fortified with a honeycomb of trenches, machine gun points and obstacles, while its guns could fire over a range of ten miles. There was to be no frontal assault and the position was taken by being outflanked. On 26th March Harar was taken. The Kenya force had advanced 1,054 miles in 30 days, an average of 35 miles a say.

At this point the control of eastern Africa by the Italians had been reduced to the area of central Ethiopia and Eritrea. Platt's forces still stood at Keren and Cunningham was within 300 miles of Addis Ababa: the western province of Gojjim was in Ethiopian hands. On 15th March the 4th and 5th Indian Divisions began the assault on the Keren position. The drive uphill was resisted stubbornly and desperate mountain fighting took place. A squadron of Hurricanes from South Africa gave air cover. For three days the initial push went on and the Italians counter-attacked. After a pause on 25th March the position was finally taken and the pass was opened. In his message to the Viceroy of India, Winston Churchill paid tribute to the ardour and perseverance of the Indian troops in scaling the heights. The Italians retired east to Aswara, the capital of Eritrea, and then south to a strong position at Amba Alagi. After the loss of Keren a member of his staff is on record that the Duke of Aosta thought the military position in East Africa for Italy untenable, despite the constant exhortations from Rome for the Italian armies to keep fighting. In Khartoum the Bishop ordered the bells rang in the Anglican Cathedral. Despite the fierce fighting the British losses amounted to 536 killed and 3,229 wounded, many of the latter by 3" mortar shells used by the Italians, which caused festering wounds. The Italian dead totalled 3,000. On 1st April Aswara was taken and a mixed force from the Indian Divisions and Free French moved on to Massawa on the Red Sea. As they approached, six Italian destroyers left to raid Port Sudan but four were sunk and two scuttled. Massawa fell on 8th April. The 4th Indian Division and the air squadrons were then sent on to Libya.

In the south Cunningham reached Diredawa on the 29th and he received there from the Duke of Aosta a naval attaché, who indicated the Duke's desire to treat Addis Ababa as an open city, and on 4th April the Italians abandoned it and moved north. On the 6th the city was taken. Only a small garrison was left as the pursuit of the enemy army went on and that was outnumbered by the Italians taken by ten to one. There were 7,000 Italians in the city including women and children, and the garrison was hard pressed to guard them all from the Ethiopian tribesmen, who thought that one of the fruits of victory was the slaughter of the defeated. The southern pincer force had captured thus 50,000 prisoners and taken 360,000 square miles of land at the price of 135 men killed, 310 wounded, 52 missing and 4 captured. In the west on 6th April the irregular forces (the 'Golden Force') with Colonel Wingate, occupied Debra Markes, taking the surrender of an Italian army of African troops.

Spearheaded by the 1st South African brigade the troops who had taken Addis Ababa set out to open the road north to Aswara. On 13th April they engaged in the Cumboleia Pass in a five-day battle with the Italian rearguard, in which 10 men were killed and 8,000 prisoners taken. On 20th April Dese fell, 450 miles north of the capital. The Duke of Aosta and the main Italian army were now threatened from north and south at Amba Alagi, a conical mountain rising to 10,000 feet above sea level and overlooking the road between Aswara and Addis Ababa. On 15th May the 5th Indian Division and 1st South African Brigade launched an assault on the mountain peak. The next day the Duke of Aosta opened negotiations to surrender and did so on 17th May. 5,000 troops emerged with arms to march past a guard of honour before being disarmed. The Duke of Aosta became a prisoner, dying in Nairobi in 1942. Not all the Italian generals accepted his unconditional surrender and fighting was to continue until November at isolated places such as Gondar, which held out until 27th November.

After the taking of Debra-Markes the Emperor Haile Selassie returned to his capital on 5th May. With the fall of Gondar the campaign in East Africa ended. Italy had lost an army of 220,000 men and its empire in East Africa. The Red Sea route was no longer threatened. There were notable features to this local war. The bombing and killing of the civil population of the countries was largely avoided, the towns and villages not wantonly destroyed and the Hague Convention on war observed. It was notable however primarily for the speed and distance covered by Cunningham's army in so short a time; from the Kenya border to Amba Alagi, some 2,000 miles in three months.

General Sir William Slim, who commanded the 10th Indian Infantry Brigade in East Africa and an Indian Division in Syria, was to go in 1943 to fight in Burma, ultimately as Commander of the 14th army, defeating the Japanese at Arakan and Imphal. After the war he was promoted to Fieldmarshal and from 1953 to 1960 was Governor-General of Australia. In 1960 he was made a Viscount. Colonel Wingate also was posted to Burma where he was to become a Major-General. He organised an irregular jungle force, supplied by air, behind Japanese lines known as the 'Chindits' harrying their supply routes. He was killed in an air crash in March 1944.

The 2nd Viscount Slim was ejected from the House of Lords in 1999.

19th May 1692

The Battle of Barfleur-La Hogue

On 14th September 1688 Louis XIV of France launched his armies against the countries on the middle Rhine, as a pre-emptive strike before those who opposed him could organise themselves. The pretext for this attack was the League of Augsburg, led by the Emperor of Austria and the King of Spain. The French devastated the Rhineland and the Palatinate, invading Heidelberg twice in 1689 and in 1693, on the latter occasion putting the castle to the torch and leaving it a ruin, which can still be seen today.

King William III as Stadtholder of Holland had been active in rallying the alliances against the French, and in February 1689 Holland declared war on France. In the autumn of 1688 William and his wife Mary had became King and Queen of England, ejecting King James II, who fled to France and was well received there by King Louis XIV. The latter gave his support to the exiled English king with money and armies, in the hope of his being able to regain the crown with the support of the Catholics of Ireland. In April 1689 Louis XIV declared war on Spain and in October the Dutch agreed with the Emperor of Austria and the Kings of Spain and England to work together in order to restore the territorial holdings of the powers and princes as established under the Treaty of Westphalia in 1648. On 7th May 1689 William III declared war on France, with the object of preserving the Glorious Revolution settlement of 1688, which had established the constitutional monarchy and parliamentary government.

As on other occasions, at the outset of a war the Navy was ill-prepared and disorganised. There were divided councils, an inadequate number of ships of the line, with too many diverted to commerce protection, and they were under-manned. The French were able to transport James II and a convoy of troops to Ireland. In 1690 there came the disaster of the Battle of Beachy Head, where the French severely disabled the Anglo-Dutch fleet. The Earl of Torrington was court-martialled, although he was subsequently acquitted. Uproar and consternation swept the country, not much tempered by the news of William III's decisive victory at the Battle of the Boyne. Parliament in December 1690 voted £570,000 to build twenty-seven men-of-war, a new yard at Plymouth and a dry dock at Portsmouth. Naval hospitals were improved and new instructions were issued abandoning the manoeuvre of breaking the line, unless there was a gap. The rebuilding and revival of the navy resulted in the emergence in 1692 of a proposal to invade France, and preparations for that were hurried forward.

For his part Louis XIV also contemplated an invasion. The supporters of James II persuaded Louis XIV that there was disaffection in England, indeed the Earl of Marlborough was suspected of going over to James II and was sent to the Tower of London. The Navy was said to be sympathetic to the Jacobite cause. A force of 20,000 soldiers was collected and sent to La Hogue on the Cotentin peninsula, with a view to crossing to invade at Torbay. It included James II's ragged Irish army, who arrived following their expulsion from Ireland. The French Commander, Admiral de Costentin Tourville, warned Louis XIV that the invasion was unlikely to succeed, but he was nevertheless ordered to undertake it.

Meanwhile in England, actions was being taken to meet the threat and to unite the Anglo-Dutch fleets into one force. Sir Edward Russell was placed in command of the English fleet, flying his flag as Admiral of the Red, the centre squadron, in Britannia. Before 1689 he had not commanded anything larger that a single ship, but he was a devoted Whig, who had been sent by the disaffected Whig aristocrats as their messenger to William of Orange in the Hague in 1688 to invite him to England. Queen Mary, not without reason, as later events showed, had no great opinion of his abilities as an admiral, but the Government took the view that a Whig Commander was necessary out of suspicion of the Navy's loyalty. Sir Ralph Delavel was on Royal Sovereign as Vice-Admiral of the Red, Sir Clowdisley Shovell as Rear-Admiral. Sir John Ashby commanded the Blue Squadron with Admiral Rooke (Vice-Admiral) and Admiral Carter (Rear-Admiral). The White was to comprise the Dutch under Admiral Philip Van Almonde. In all there were over 90 warships, 38 fireships and 40,000 men in the combined fleets. The first need however was to unite the fleets for the spring campaign.

In France Admiral Tourville was ordered to sea from Brest on 2nd May with instructions not to enter the Channel. He left with 39 ships of the line and was joined later by five from Rochefort; 20 ships had been left behind because of the problem of manning and the state of repair. The Toulon fleet under Admiral D'Estrées with 12 ships of the line was expected to join him, but due to contrary winds failed to arrive in time for the battle. The English and Dutch fleets joined up in early May and news of that reached Paris on 12th May, when the Marine Minister, the Count of Pontchartrain, sent a messenger to warn Tourville that the fleets had combined and to order him to return. The message was not delivered, the messenger being hampered by fog, until the battle had commenced.

On 15th May Tourville was off Plymouth with his 44 ships of the line. Without knowledge that the Anglo-Dutch fleet had combined, he continued to patrol the Channel mouth. On 19th May the French frigates Perle and L'Henry met the Chester and the Charles; the exchange of gunfire alerted the fleets to the presence of one another and they came into touch early about twenty miles north-east of Barfleur. The morning was foggy, the sea scarcely stirred by a feeble south-westerly wind. Russell ordered his fleet into line with the Dutch in the van. The French and Anglo-Dutch were both on the same track south, the French having the weather gauge. Touvier decided to attack, a decision much discussed since. This inferiority, 44 ships of the line to over 90, made the decision in terms of naval warfare scarcely rational. Some have suggested that he was unaware of the size of the fleet in the morning mist and others that he allowed the slight, which he saw in the orders of Louis XIV about his courage in attacking the enemy, to lead him to challenge the combined fleet. Early after 8 am he ordered the French to put about and bear down on to the enemy fleet. At a slow pace because of the feeble wind, he came down towards the Anglo-Dutch centre. Russell responded by ordering the Dutch in the van to go to the west of the French around their south flank and the Blue Squadron, which was some way astern, to the north of them with a view to encircling Tourville. The wind however dropped and the manoeuvre became impossible. On the starboard flank of the French fleet Capitaine Perrinet on Le Bourbon, covered by Le Monarque of 82 guns, perceiving the Dutch attempt, took on four Dutch battleships at the rear of the squadron.

When the wind fell, Tourville and the French fleets and Russell with the Red Squadron were immobilised at about the distance of musket fire. Before either commander could order the fleets to engage, a Dutchman launched a broadside on the Saint-Louis. The engagement then became general. The Soleil-Royal (90 guns) with Tourville on board, commenced battle with the Britannia. The two ships fought fiercely for an hour and a half, with the English firing faster. Each tried to board the other twice and Tourville fought in helmet and cuirass. The Soleil-Royal found itself confronted by the London and St. Andrew as well as Britannia and battled on. Towards 1 pm the wind started to return from the north to north-east and Tourville was given help and protection by five ships under Admiral D'Ambreville. By late afternoon the battle had became a general melée with the Dutch to the south and the Blue squadron to the north almost encircling the French. The ships of both sides were severely damaged: the Anglo-Dutch fleet had some twenty dismasted and the French showed similar damage. Admiral Carter had been killed and Sir Clowdisley Shovell's ship the Royal William disabled. About 4 pm the fog started to settle on the sea and the battle came to a standstill. Russell drew off and the fleets anchored. The night remained foggy with scarcely any wind.

At 1pm on 20th May Tourville, having carried out running repairs, ordered the fleet to weigh anchor and the French began to slip away to the west in the light breeze. The Soleil-Royal joined D'Ambreville with 27 vessels about 7 pm and the fleet took course towards the Cotentin peninsula with a view to gaining safe anchorages either there or at St Malo. The Soleil-Royal slowed the French fleet but Tourville refused to abandon her. When the fog lifted, the Dutch and the Blue squadron pressed on, chasing the French home. Russell had ordered a general chase, but the Red Squadron, who had born the brunt of the fighting, lagged. About midday the wind changed to southwesterly and at 4 pm the fleets converged off Cherbourg, stopped by the tide. Three French ships were beached at Cherbourg – the Soleil-Royal, Le Triumphant and L'Admirable – with a view to saving them. A few hours after they went aground, Sir Ralph Delaval arrived with the Saint Albans, the Ruby and two fireships close in, in order to attack the beached vessels; while 15 ships of the line hovered at a distance. The Soleil-Royal resisted their attack, which was not fully pressed. On the next day the Anglo-Dutch squadron returned to assault the beached ships with small ships suitable as escort to the fireships. The Soleil-Royal gunfire destroyed the Hind, but the Blaze crashed the three-decker, which went on fire. The Wolf destroyed Le Triumphant and the L'Admirable was fired by accompanying small boats.

D'Ambreville with 27 ships decided to brave the Alderney Race and the strong tides around the Channel Islands to gain St.Malo, but 12 ships decided to secure refuge in the bay at St.Vaast La Hogue, where the invasion army was assembled and where they would have the protection of Marshall de Bellefonds and his guns. Russell arrived and began to lie off the Bay in order to blockade it. The anchorage of the French vessels was altered on the next day, 23rd May – six were anchored near the Isle of Tatitou and six behind the point of La Hogue. This operation was carried on in great confusion and the six sheltered by the Isle of Tatitou were left unmanned and so easily put on fire; James II watched the operation impassively from the shore. In the afternoon two hundred longboats, and cutters and other small ships escorted the fireships towards the other six behind the Point of La Hogue. The Jacobite and French army and its artillery gave little protection despite the fact that some of the boats coming in were so close that in one the boathook held by a sailor was grasped by a cavalry man on shore. The fleet of fireships brought in set alight the remaining six and some of the convoy ships before the attacking force retired.

The result of the battle was the loss to France of 15 ships of the line, pursued in flight to a relatively unprotected coast and anchorage. The planned invasion of England was abandoned, so that, although no French ships of the line were sunk in the battle itself, the security of the sea was kept. Want of money caused the French subsequently to neglect the fleet and to turn to a policy of encouraging mariners to strike at commercial vessels.

Sir Edward Russell, despite persistent urging by the Queen, failed to use the advantage of the battle, complaining constantly of the difficulties of attacking France, refusing, for example, to attack St. Malo when ordered on 6th June, and of the unreasonable nature of the rough Channel weather. The English nonetheless acclaimed the victory; on the news arriving in London, church bells were rung all day. Queen Mary ordered £30,000 to be distributed to the officers and men. A gilt medal was struck in Holland, having on one side a bunch of withered French lilies and the motto 'non semper lilia floreat'.

Despite his foolhardy and ill-considered attack, Admiral Tourville and his fleet had fought with courage against extreme odds. He had showed undoubted heroism and persistence in battle. He and his captains had done wonders and, had there been no destruction at Cherbourg and La Hogue of the French fleet, Barfleur might be regarded as a French triumph. Louis XIV was fully conscious of the effort made by Tourville and remarked, inquiring how it had gone with him, 'Ships, one can replace, but it would be impossible to replace a man like Tourville.'

20th May 1799

The Siege of Acre

After General Buonaparte was recalled from Italy in 1797 and the Peace of Campo Formio was signed with Austria, the French republican Government, the Directory, asked him to consider the strategy needed in order to secure the defeat of Britain. He regarded invasion as impracticable without command of the Channel, and an attack on Hannover as likely to ignite a war in central Europe. As an alterative he recommended striking at England in the Mediterranean, to disrupt her commerce and links with India. Urged on by Talleyrand, the Foreign Minister, who thought that Egypt would be a worthwhile new colony, the Directory accepted the recommendation and in March and April 1797 empowered Buonaparte to take an army to Egypt. The government of the Ottoman Empire, the Sublime Porte, was to be told that the expedition was in support of the power of the Sultan in Constantinople (Istanbul) restoring his control over the Mamelukes, who effectively ruled the country under the Viceroy. The French eluded Lord Nelson and the Mediterranean fleet, landing and taking Alexandria. Buonaparte proceeded inland and defeated the Mamelukes at the Battle of the Pyramids (21st July 1798). Nelson however found the French fleet at Aboukir Bay and destroyed it at the battle of the Nile (1st August 1798). Buonaparte was isolated in Egypt and could not be supplied unless the French fleet could burst through the control of the Royal Navy over the Mediterranean.

The British Government, exercised by the threat of the French in the near east, decided to send a delegation to the Sultan, Selim III, comprising two brothers, Spencer Smith and Sir Sidney Smith, to act as representatives on their behalf. Sir Sidney Smith had entered the navy in 1777 at the age of thirteen and had led an active naval career, including a period in the Swedish navy, by whose King he had been knighted. He had been thrown into the Temple prison in Paris and had escaped, gaining him a certain notoriety. His position at Constantinople was to some extent invidious, since as the Government's representative he had an authority of his own, but as a naval officer in command of a squadron in support of the Turks he was supposed to take his authority from Lord Nelson and Captain Trowbridge. Commanding the squadron, he called himself 'Commodore' of the squadron, although he had not been so appointed by the Admiralty, engendering a scathing attitude toward him by Lord Nelson. On arrival, he and his brother signed the Treaty of Alliance with the Sublime Porte, and the Sultan gave him command of all military and naval forces to fight the French. The Sultan, not convinced by the French assurance that they came to support the Sublime Porte in Egypt, had declared war on 9th September. Together with the Sultan, Smith planned a strategy of attack on the French aimed at harassment of the French by gunboats and an attack on Egypt by two armies – the Army of Damascus south through Syria, and the Army of Rhodes to join with that by sea or go on to invade Egypt. The Turks were trained by shipwrights to build cutters capable of carrying guns in order to make raids on shore and in the Delta of the Nile.

In October the Sultan issued his *firman* declaring Holy War on the French. Sir Sidney Smith used his position with the Sultan to secure the release of thirty French prisoners of war from the galley dungeons and he sent them back to Marseilles by brig. After the destruction of the French Navy, Buonaparte's position in Egypt became increasingly difficult, although the country was progressively subdued. By October fifteen per cent of the army was sick and in December bubonic plague started among the troops. There was no hope of new supplies. He resolved that the only viable course would be to go north through Syria to destroy Turkish power, make the Sultan change his policy, and perhaps reach Constantinople and the Balkans. He tried to prepare the way by tempting Ahmed Djezzar Pasha, (called 'the Butcher') the Bey of Acre, to join him, and made overtures to the Druze in the mountains of Lebanon. He embarked on a propaganda campaign, appealing to different communities for support in the skilled mode of modern political leadership, in which he gave out to the Muslims that he was the protector of Islam and to the Christians that he had come on a new crusade. Despite his blandishments Djezzar Pasha did not go over to him, and the Druze said that they would await the outcome of his campaign, until the French were north of Acre. Sir Sidney Smith was to counter this propaganda by putting copies of all the leaflets together and having them put into circulation. Preparations were made in Egypt to march and by February 1799 the French were ready to move north.

The French army marching into Syria comprised four under-manned divisions of infantry, 800 cavalry men under Murat and 1,755 sappers and artillerymen, amounting to 13,000 men. The force was supported by mule trains and ambulances, but the siege guns were to be carried up the coast on offshore craft. On 6th February General Reynier left Katia. The first part of the march was across the Sinai desert, barren and waterless, but the march was held up at El Arish. The village and camp were garrisoned and there was a strong masonry fort, the total force being 600 Mamelukes and 1,700 Albanians. The French had not realised however that there was a fort there. By 9th February the village and camp had been taken but the fort held out. General Kléber arrived with his division, but apart from dispersing a Turkish relief column, he had no success and the fort continued to hold on. Buonaparte did not appear until the 17th, when he ordered the guns and mortars to bombard the fort. On 19th February the 900 surviving defenders surrendered. Acre was still 140 miles away. The delay had reduced the ration supply and the Syrian frontier had not been crossed. There was no problem at Gaza and the French were welcomed by the Christians at El Ramle. Jaffa was reached on 3rd March and stormed on the 7th by General Lannes and his division, the defenders being killed, the women raped and the children shot. Buonaparte was to wait seven days at the town.

After the initial storming, some 3,000 Turkish troops still remained on defence the following morning in a *caravanserai* in the town. Two French officers approached them, one of whom was Eugene de Beauharnais, Buonaparte's stepson and aide-de camp, and undertook that, if they surrendered, they would not be put to the sword. On that basis they surrendered. The next morning a large group were brought to a parade ground in full view of Buonaparte and in breach of the promise made, shot. A further group were bayoneted to death (in order to save bullets, on the General's orders) and driven down to the sea where the slaughter continued. In all, with prisoners already held, the French slaughtered 4,400 prisoners. The army, while in Jaffa, began to be decimated by plague and to restore morale Buonaparte visited the pest houses of the sick. A picture was painted in France to record this act; but none of the General sitting writing at his table, while the prisoners were slaughtered before him on his order. General Kleber had his reservations as to the wisdom of the executions, but Buonaparte wrote to General Marmont in Egypt to the effect that the capture of Jaffa was a brilliant affair. Bourrienne, Buonaporte's secretary, tries to justify this 'success' as a horrible necessity. Captain Trowbridge, on Lord Nelson's order had meanwhile summoned Sir Sidney Smith to bring his squadron from Constantinople to off Alexandria, where in early March Smith and Trowbridge met and Trowbridge handed over Thescus and Lion to him. While there on the 7th he received a message from Djezzar Pasha's Chief of Staff requesting him to come to the assistance of Acre. Captain Miller on Theseus was at once despatched there, taking Colonel Phélippaux, a military engineer. He arrived on 13th March and began inspecting the defence. Two days later Sir Sidney Smith arrived in the Tigre.

The town of Acre constituted effectively a strong fortress. It was built on a peninsula into the sea with high masonry walls; two-thirds of the city's wall was lapped by the sea and it was only approachable from the east and north-east. The landward wall was strengthened in the middle by a strong keep-like tower, the Devil's Tower. There was a small harbour protected by a mole, but it was silted up and Smith had to anchor at sea. In the event of a westerly storm, ships had to shelter at the south end of the bay of Acre in the lee of Mount Carmel. Water was brought to the city by a large aqueduct. The condition of the walls and fortifications was crumbling and ill-repaired. One section of the curtain wall on the landward side was abutted by Djezzar Pasha's palace, mosque and seraglios. Djezzar Pasha, who was sixty-six, was of Bosnian origin and had gone as a slave to a Mameluke voluntarily, where with his ruthlessness and drive he had risen to become ruler of the Levantine province round Acre. He had a reputation for cruelty. General Berthier, the French Chief of Staff, said that he flayed faithless wives and personally beheaded disloyal courtiers. The garrison comprised 4,000 men of mixed nationality - Turks, Syrians, Bosnians, Kurds and Albanians; the latter were deputed in the siege to guard the outer wall of the seraglio.

Until Smith arrived, Djezzar had become fatalistic, but Sir Sidney soon galvanised the garrison into action. He had sent on his friend Colonel Phélippeaux, who had aided his escape from the Temple in Paris. The latter had studied in the same class as Buonaparte at the military academy in Paris but was a Royalist and an engineer. He set to work to restore the strength of the defences. Gangs were formed and ordered to fortify places of weakness. The few guns were facing the sea. Sir Sydney Smith landed 800 marines and sailors with guns from the men-of-war, which were placed along the land wall with particular concentration round the Devil's Tower. Tigre was moved to east of the town on its south side where together with four gun boats it could enfilade the approach from the east. The Thescus under Captain Miller moved north to fulfil a similar role for the north-west flank of the landward wall. Phélippeaux pressed on with his work and the defences were in tolerable condition by the time the French arrived.

On 15th March General Buonaparte arrived at the southern end of the Bay of Acre at Haifa. From there he could see the condition of the town and apart from the two men-of-war riding at anchor there was little to concern him. His supplies had been enhanced by stocks of grain, rice and biscuits taken at Jaffa and there was no alternative to the subjugation of Acre. It stood astride the coast route north and could not be left as a threat to the rear of the French army as it moved on to Aleppo and Damascus. The old walls of the town, which seemed little changed since the age of King Richard the Lionheart, would not withstand heavy siege guns and a swift advance was necessary. The vanguard was soon ordered out of Haifa and being observed by Sir Sidney Smith was attacked from the sea by a gunboat mounting a 32-pounder carronade. The French were forced to march inland by the Nazareth Road. On the army's arrival at Acre, camp was established to the north-east of the town beyond the range of guns on the men-of-war and gunboats, which could enfilade from the sea the approaches to the walls. Their ability to sweep away troops going up to the wall limited reconnaissance and Bonaparte had to inspect the defences by night. He was awaiting his siege guns, but learnt from coasters arriving at Haifa that the flotilla carrying them had been taken by the Royal Navy. Sir Sidney Smith on Tigre had sailed south and the whole flotilla of a corvette and nine gunboats were chased. The corvette escaped but the rest were taken with their cargo of 32 guns, ammunition and battering equipment; on their arrival at Acre Sir Sidney Smith had the guns mounted at the Devil's Tower.

Buonaparte needed to send to Egypt for more guns but, impatient, decided that his twelve-pounders would suffice and on 26th March opened fire on the curtain walls. The French also began the time-consuming task of digging trenches and parallels towards the walls as shelter for the assault. On the 26th bombardment began to establish a breach and on the 28th the first assault was made. The breach made had been blocked by Colonel Phélippeaux and his men with wood and stones, but at noon the French engineers and Grenadiers advanced, their drums incessantly beating. Turks on the wall abandoned their posts but the British Marines and seamen stood waiting unmoved. Suddenly the French halted abruptly. They had come upon a dry moat 15 feet deep and 20 wide, which early reconnaissance had not discovered. After it was negotiated they found that their scaling ladders could not reach the top of the wall. From the top the attackers were peppered with grapeshot by the naval guns of the seamen and the storming party retired. As they went the Turks emerged to cut off the heads of the fallen Djezzar Pasha had rallied his men and they had returned to the wall, but after the retreat he sat waiting for them to come back to him in order to reward them for every infidel head brought.

At the end of March a westerly gale rose, blowing hard on the Syrian shore, and Sir Sidney Smith had to take Tigre, Theseus and the armed store ship, Alliance, which he had commandeered on the 24th March, preventing its return to Captain Trowbridge, to shelter in the lee of Mount Carmel. Djezzar Pasha took advantage of his absence in order to amuse himself. Some thirty French prisoners, including Captain Mailly, who having been taken under a flag of truce considered himself safe, were tied in pairs alive, put into sacks and thrown into the sea. Some of the sacks were to be washed up in the Bay and were found by the French. In Smith's absence, on 1st April, another assault was made, but all the French were killed or wounded.

Sir Sidney Smith returned on 3rd April to find that in the absence of the protecting force from Tigre and Theseus over the approaches to the walls the French had been able to press forward their siege works to within pistol shot of the wall, from where mines could be driven under the walls. One of the mines was directed at the Devil's Tower and there was a problem about attempts to countermine in this location because of deep and heavy foundations, apart from a shortage of pickaxes. It was decided to attack the mine with a sortie and Major Oldfield of the Marines and Lieutenant Wright of the Theseus led the party. Instead of a quiet move forward, the Turks began to yell, alerted the French, and resistance was met. The attack however reached the entrance of the mine and Lieutenant Wright and his party collapsed the roof of the tunnel, but Major Oldfield was killed and Lieutenant Wright wounded. The Turks returned with 60 heads for Djezzar Pasha.

At this point Buonaparte's attention was directed inland, for the Army of Damascus had moved south into Galilee and posed the threat of attack to the besiegers in the rear. First, General Junot was despatched with cavalry to Tiberias, meeting a small body of Turks at Canaan on 11th April and routing them. Kléber, with 2,000 infantry, followed. The Pasha of Damascus had come however with an army of 25,000 cavalry and 10,000 infantry. On 16th April the armies met at the foot of Mount Tabor. Buonaparte had heard by message on the 15th of the presence of the Pasha's army and had set out to the support of Kléber. All day Kléber's small force formed squares and resisted the Turkish cavalry. Late in the day a distant gun announced Buonaparte's arrival. He came up, fired from the guns two shots with successive volleys from his infantry, who had formed squares, and the Turks retired, scattering in the hills. The threat to the rear had been averted and Buonaparte returned to the siege. Morale in the army was low, with 270 plague cases. Shot was in short supply, but on the 15th the flotilla bringing the new siege guns had arrived at Jaffa. They were unloaded and slowly heaved and humped overland. On 24th April, before their arrival, a mine was blown at the corner of the Devil's Tower, but it scarcely rocked the masonry. The assaulting force was repulsed with grenades, rocks and 'Stinkpots', a missile containing sulphur and gunpowder whose smoke had a suffocating effect. By 31st April the huge guns were in place. In the next ten days constant bombardment and assault in order to take Acre were to follow. There were unsuccessful night assaults on 1st and 4th May and on the 6th the French were driven off by a line of Turks backed by British Marines and seamen from a breach in the wall. The climax was to come on 8th May.

During this part of the siege, Sir Sidney Smith was to be found everywhere organising defence, urging the repair of breaches, encouraging the defenders and directing fire. Colonel Phélippeaux, who had striven throughout April to repair the defences after bombardment, had died of sunstroke and fatigue on 2nd May and his tasks had devolved on Smith. At the beginning of April Smith had sent for the assistance of the Army of Rhodes, and on 7th May the sails of the large fleet bringing them appeared on the horizon. Buonaparte immediately recognised their arrival meant that the besieged could last out a longer time than could his attacking army. The bombardment was intensified materially on the area of the Devil's Tower and the curtain wall of the seraglio, where only 200 of the 1,000 Albanians posted there now survived. Earlier, the aqueduct to the city had been blown and at that point and at the point of breach the moat had become filled with rubble mounting up the wall. On the night of the 7th the sides of French parallels and trenches had been raised by sand bags, sometimes with bodies mixed in, so that the assaulting parties could not be seen and were shielded from the grapeshot of the naval guns. In previous assaults the visible troops moving forward had to advance through the withering grapeshot fired from the sea. Sir Sidney Smith, realising the need to place defenders at the seraglio wall, persuaded Djezzar Pasha to allow there the Chifflick Regiment, a European-trained Turkish force, newly arrived on the convoy from Rhodes.

Before dawn the French advanced towards the Devil's Tower, whose top had been reduced in the bombardment. The Turks and French met across the piled rubble firing on one another, and the French planted their flag on the corner of the tower. Sir Sidney Smith with a small British party hurried there to stiffen resistance. Djezzar Pasha, concerned for his safety, tried to pull him away saying that 'if harm befall his English friends, all would be lost.' The breach held however and the French were driven off. That same day a further attempt was made before sunset on the breach in the seraglio wall. The Chifflicks firmly withstood the attack and the French retired, hotly pursued by them to the extent that they took French trenches and established a salient in their line.

Buonaparte decided on one more try. General Kléber, whose division was guarding the Jordan, was recalled and 9th May was spent bombarding the seraglio wall, opening the breach until it was said fifty men could pass through. On the 10th the Chifflick Regiment in their salient were forced back from the trenches taken through the breach. The column came on and its van broke through into the garden. The French however were unprepared for the trap laid. There was an inner line and the Turks fell upon them with their scimitars, for which the bayonets were scant protection. The fierce wounds made and slaughter done caused the French quickly to retire to their trenches. Djezzar Pasha, seated with money at hand, was to hand out so many rewards that day of fifty piastres that, as an English sailor said, the pile of heads before him looked 'like so many cabbages at Covent Garden'. Despite their rout Kléber's men tried again, but this time they were stopped by a huge roaring explosion as they went forward which brought them to a standstill. The attack was called off. The siege had lasted for 63 days and there had been eight costly assaults but with the reinforcement supply from the sea there was no realistic hope for the French of taking Acre.

Buonaparte did not retreat immediately but ordered his guns to bombard the civilians in the city. It was not until 20th May that his columns left. The campaign had left half his army dead, wounded or sick. The latter posed a problem for the long retreat back to Egypt. Admiral Pérree with his small flotilla at Jaffa refused to take the worst on board his ships. Buonaparte therefore suggested that the hopeless cases should be shot, but was deterred from that course. Harassed by Turkish horsemen, the retreating army reached Jaffa on 24th May. In Egypt a victorious proclamation was ordered to be issued, referring to the triumph at Mount Tabor and reciting the destruction of the fortifications of Gaza, Jaffa, Haifa and also, despite the facts, of Acre.

At Jaffa there was a four-day halt and it was ordered that those capable of walking among the sick and wounded should do so. Others who could not were placed on ships and were pleased to be taken by Royal Navy Vessels which intercepted them. At Jaffa the hopelessly wounded were poisoned. Admiral Pérree's flotilla lost however one opportunity. On the way south to Jaffa a sailor on the Theseus removing a charge from a French shell caused it to explode and it resulted in an explosion of twenty 36-pounder and fifty 18-pounder shells on the poop. The American Captain Miller was killed. The whole of the poop, the after-part of the quarter-deck and the booms were shattered. Fire broke out in the ship, but with manful effort it was put out. With Theseus in that condition, it would have been a not too dangerous target for the three French frigates. It was not until 3rd June that the French reached Katia, their starting point, after a four-day trek through the beating sun and sand of the Sinai desert. Leaving the wounded and sick, Buonaparte went on to Cairo where on 14th June he entered the city staging a triumphant march of victory. Buonaparte's secretary Bourienne records that Buonaparte on his entry into the capital issued one of his typical lying bulletins. 'I bring with me,' he said, 'many prisoners and colours – I have raised the palace of Djezzar, the ramparts of Acre – there no longer remains one stone upon another, all the inhabitants have left the town by sea – Djezzar is dangerously wounded'. It seemed to matter not to him that his failure to take Acre left him still imprisoned in Egypt by the Royal Navy. He had however decided to desert the army and on 21st June he secretly ordered Ganteaume to prepare two frigates for his departure. Sir Sidney Smith ensured Bonaparte was informed of events in Europe by having smuggled inshore newspapers designed to fall into the hands of the French, and Buonaparte was aware of the course of events in Germany and Italy, where Prussia, Russia and Austria were stirring. In July Buonaparte hurried to Aboukir, where the British had landed the Army of Rhodes, and on the 25th defeated it. Back in Cairo he received more information from the newspapers thoughtfully sent in by Sir Sidney Smith and on 17th August he resolved to sail home. His departure was kept a total secret and he took only his intimates – notably Generals Berthier, Lannes and Murat, his household, his aides-de-camp, secretary Bourienne, Mameluke servant Roustam and Generals Andréossy, Marmont and Bessieres. Two hundred Guides were taken for protection. Of those taken most were to figure conspicuously in Buonaparte's future history. On 9th October Buonaparte landed at Fréjus.

Sir Sidney Smith sent an account of events to Lord Nelson at Palermo by Midshipmen Boxer on one of the French gunboats taken. Nelson read the message and was delighted. Nelson offered to make Boxer a Lieutenant with immediate effect, but the young man had to stammer out that he had not passed the exam. Nelson told him to write to him when he had. Lord Nelson, forgetting his previous reservations about Sir Sidney Smith and their disputes, wrote to him immediately a warm letter of congratulation for his notable service in defending the city of Acre and protecting the Ottoman Empire. In London, when the news arrived, there was satisfaction at the defeat of Buonaparte. Motions were passed in both Houses of Parliament thanking Sir Sidney Smith and those whom he had commanded for their success, and Smith was granted an annuity of £1,000 a year. Sir Sidney Smith had achieved a unique victory for the Royal Navy. He had used his ships, seamen and marines to win a land battle against the most formidable general in Europe. The victory was at relatively small cost; 22 were killed including 5 Midshipmen, 66 wounded, 4 drowned and 82 prisoners. There is a statue of Smith outside the National Maritime Museum of Greenwich and a monument in St Paul's Cathedral.

Talleyrand, the Directory Foreign Minister, who had urged Buonaparte to go to Egypt and supported him, served him as Foreign Minister when he became First Consul and subsequently Emperor of France. He became Prince Talleyrand de Perigord, reviving in his title his aristocratic family name, and was dismissed after he disagreed with the attack on Spain in 1808. While he continued to hold rank at court under Napoleon, after 1814 he served the restored Bourbon Kings as Foreign Minister and under King Louis Phillipe he became Ambassador to London from 1830 to 1834. Talleyrand was lame from birth and there is a special rail fixed to the top of the balusters on the staircase at the Traveller's Club in Pall Mall to assist his going up and downstairs while he was Ambassador in London.

23rd May 1706

The Battle of Ramillies

Charles II, King of Spain, was simple-minded and did not succeed in producing an heir. Since Spain was a country containing Spain itself, part of the Netherlands equivalent to Belgium, Milan, Naples, Sardinia, Sicily in Italy, colonies including Central America, and large parts of South America, the question of who should be his heir exercised the minds of most of the rulers of Europe, who would be affected by the succession. Two attempts were made to settle the matter by Partition Treaties, which would divide the lands held by the Spanish Crown between the two claimants, both young men and referred to by the Earl of Peterborough as the 'two louts'. These claimants were relations of Charles II connected by marriage and family descent. One was the candidate of Louis XIV the King of France, his grandson Philip, Duke of Anjou, the other was the Archduke Charles, the younger son of the Emperor Leopold of Austria by a second marriage. The realm of the latter covered Austria, Hungary, parts of Czechoslovakia, parts of Italy and the Adriatic coast in Slovenia and Croatia. A principle concern of those involved was to prevent the crowns of France and Spain becoming joined in the future to create an over-whelming superpower. In January 1701 Charles II died leaving a will which had been suggested to him by the Pope in Rome. That left his crown to Philip of Anjou, with all his lands.

Louis XIV promptly ignored the second Partition treaty and occupied the throne for his grandson. He compounded this breach of treaty by seizing the fortified towns in the Spanish Netherlands (equivalent to modern Belgium) and recognised the son of James II (the Old Pretender) as King of England. Austria went to war in 1701, but it was not until 15th May 1702 that Britain declared war on France as a riposte to the seizure of the Spanish Netherlands, which threatened the security of Britain's trade and existence in the North Sea, and to the backing given to the Old Pretender's son, contrary to the Treaty of Ryswick in 1697. Marlborough was given charge of the military resistance to France in support of Holland, and acted as King William III's agent there. A Grand Alliance was formed in order to obtain the renunciation of the succession to the French throne by Philip of Anjou, and the Archduke Charles of Austria was recognised as King Charles III of Spain. A succession of summer campaigns were fought by the belligerents in the low countries, Germany and Italy. Ramillies opened the campaign in 1706.

The Duke of Marlborough was to command for the summer campaign a mixed force of British, Dutch and Danish troops. The Prussians did not arrive to participate in the Battle of Ramillies, since King Frederick I was sulking over the non-payment of a subsidy. By 20th May the army was concentrated south-east of Louvain between Borchiem and Corswaren, comprising 74 battalions of infantry, 123 squadrons of Cavalry and 90 guns and howitzers.

Marshal Villeroi encamped to the west of the River Dyle with some 60,000 troops - about the same number as that of Marlborough, but with fewer guns. It was the aim of Marlborough to tempt him out to battle, but the Marshal was loath to expose the army. However, Louis XIV, who was embarrassed by a bankrupt treasury, decided that he needed a victory in order to negotiate a suitable peace. He therefore ordered Villeroi to take the offensive. The French moved across the Dyle and took up position in open country along a ridge between the River Mehaigne in the South and the village of Autre Eglise to the North. The centre of the position hinged on the village of Ramillies; the left wing stretched to Autre Eglise in the north, to some extent being covered by the River Gette to the east, and the right reached to Taviers and Francqnée in the south. The land to the east of the ridge lay in shallow valleys and folds and from Ramillies the right wing in the villages of Taviers and Francqnuée could not be seen. The French army moved up, glittering in new uniforms with the gold and silver lace of the Maison du Roi – which included the Garde du Corps, Gens d' Armes and the Mousquétaires. Villeroi disposed of 100 of the 130 squadrons of cavalry, interspaced with infantry, on the right between Ramillies and Taviers; 20 battalions of infantry were stationed in Ramillies. The left was therefore short of cavalry and relied on a strong infantry screen along the ridge to Autre Eglise.

The ridge upon which the French had stationed themselves had been identified by Marlborough as a battle site, but he did not move through the open countryside to occupy it until the French had started to come forward. Movement of his forces began at 4 am in eight columns along roads made muddy following the rain. Previously the Quartermaster General, the Earl of Cadogan, had been sent ahead to reconnoitre the ground, but he was hampered by a heavy mist. He did not come upon the French until he met their patrols in the mist. An aide-de-camp was sent back and two hours later, in advance of the troops, the Duke of Marlborough arrived. Unlike the position at Ramillies where Marshal Villeroi was stationed, the whole field including the villages of Taviers and Francqnée were visible from the plain once the mist lifted. The troops gradually came up, including Danish cavalry, whose pay Marlborough himself guaranteed. Marlborough positioned the Dutch cavalry on the left, opposite the Maison du Roi, backed by infantry and the Danish cavalry. The Dutch general, Overkirk, was put in charge of the left wing. Red John of the Battles, the Duke of Argyle, commanded the centre opposite Ramillies and the Earl of Orkney the British and Danish infantry on the right. It took three hours for the troops to position themselves with bands playing. At 1 pm the guns took over.

The order given, the British infantry on the left of Orkney's command (the Guards, Royal Scots, Royal Welsh, Cameronians and the 16th Foot) began to go forward through the marsh and the River Gette and determinedly up the ridge, despite the fire from the French infantry. The village of Offus to the south of Autre Eglise was strongly contested. Villeroi, convinced this was the main attack, transferred reserves from the centre and right to resist it.

Meanwhile, the Dutch General on the left attacked the southern flank of the French at Taviers and Francqnée. The Dutch Guards took Taviers and opened up space for the cavalry to attack and the guns to harry the French right flank. Seeing the success at Taviers, Marlborough sent an A.D.C. to instruct Orkney to call off the attack in the north. At first Orkney refused to retire, until the Earl of Cadogan came with Marlborough's direct command. The British regiments then retired to the starting point beyond the River Gette. 18 cavalry squadrons were transferred from Orkney to the right wing at Taviers.

At Ramillies itself the 12 battalions of infantry facing it, largely of Scottish troops, fought their way into the village and led by the Duke of Argyle, who was struck by three bullets, took it. While that attack was made, the success of Overkirk at Taviers had opened the French southern flank to attack. The Danish Cavalry were launched and crashing forward at the trot engaged the enemy cavalry. The fighting squadrons were entangled, but the Bavarian and Walloon cavalry broke and fled. The Maison du Roi then advanced and the allied squadron started to recoil. The Duke was at a point where a breakthrough threatened. He rallied the Dutch infantry and led them back into the fray. The French recognised him by the Garter sash and pursued him. His horse fell at a ditch and the Duke had to run towards two infantry battalions sent to his rescue. A new horse was brought and Colonel Bringfield, his A.D.C., was assisting him to mount when a cannon ball took off the latter's head. On the left meanwhile a vast superiority was built up and finally at 4 pm the Duke launched a general advance. The Danish cavalry turned the right flank of the French who broke and fled, in disorder.

The Allied cavalry followed in hot pursuit to the gates of Louvain. The French army was destroyed as a fighting force: 13,000 troops were lost, along with 80 standards and all the artillery. The Duke's army had casualties of 1,066 killed and 2,500 wounded. On 28th May the Duke rode into the Grande Place in Brussels where Charles III had been recognised as King of Spain. By the end of the year Marshal Villeroi had abandoned most of the Spanish Netherlands including Louvain, Brussels, Antwerp and Ghent.

On the news of the victory of Ramillies reaching London, Queen Anne, with the Lords and Commons attending, ordered a thanksgiving in St.Pauls. The Dean of Canterbury preached on the text 'Happy Art thou, O Israel. Who is like unto thee; O people saved by the Lord'.

At Versailles, on his return, King Louis XIV, well known for his courtesy, greeted Marshal Villeroi with generosity. 'Ah!' he said, 'at our age, M. le Maréchal, one is not lucky.'

The 12th Duke of Argyll, the 11th Duke of Marlborough and the 8th Earl of Orkney were all ejected from the House of Lords in 1999.

24th May

Empire Day

The 24th May was the birthday of Queen Victoria. Until the Second World War it was celebrated widely throughout the Empire. At primary schools in the 1930s, special assemblies took place at which the children heard about the Empire upon which the sun never set, thus emphasising its worldwide character from the Pacific islands to the Caribbean. The day was observed in Australia as much as in England and Canada. The Empire may have passed into the shadow which is the Commonwealth, but 24th May should still remain the day on which the builders of the Empire should be recalled, their triumphs and their sacrifices, the civilisation, law and liberties that they spread worldwide in the British Imperial achievement, which created a global civilisation whose results are still apparent now.

The Empire rested in the last analysis on the basis of government by the Crown in Parliament as established in the Glorious Revolution of 1688. That implied representative government, no taxation without representation, a system of law supporting liberty and tolerance of opinion and of minorities. The structure therefore carried within it the seeds of its own destruction. Representative government was granted first to Canada under the Canada Act of 1867 and the precedent was followed in Australia, New Zealand and South Africa. Ultimately self-government extended in the twentieth century to the whole Commonwealth, an unparalleled extension of parliamentary government and the rule of law throughout the world.

The conduct of the peoples of the Empire in the World Wars of the twentieth century was an example of heroism, sacrifice and loyalty, particularly from the old Dominions. All however played their part, the Indians, for example, in East Africa, the Near East and Burma, who fought with courage and determination for a cause which was not their own.

27th May 1941

The Sinking of the Bismarck

The end of May 1941 saw Britain in the lowest pass since France had deserted its allies in June 1940; Crete was under severe attack and Feldmarschall Rommel had just reversed the earlier capture of Cyrenaica and chased the British army back to the Egyptian border. On 21st May news came that the Bismarck (42,000 tons with eight 15-inch guns), the newest and strongest warship built by the Germans, had sailed with a large escort from the Baltic Sea. She was accompanied by a battle cruiser, the Prince Eugen, with 8-inch guns. The passage of these ships to the North Sea and possibly the Atlantic posed a profound threat, should both enter the North Atlantic, to the convoy links from Iceland to Russia and from America to Britain. The Admiralty, alerted, viewed it as essential to discover the whereabouts of Bismarck and Prince Eugen, so that proper measures could be taken to bring these ships to battle. On the same day about 1 pm a spitfire found the two ships in Grimstad Fjord. The following day about 7pm a coastal command Catalina, flying low under clouds found the fjord empty, as was the fjord at Bergen. The Bismarck and Price Eugen had gone to sea. If they were to reach the North Atlantic, they needed to pass through one of three passages north of Britain; the cruisers Norfolk and Suffolk were ordered to be on guard at the Denmark Straits west of Iceland, and Manchester and Birmingham were to patrol the passage from Iceland to the Faroes.

Just after first light the Prince of Wales and the battle cruiser Hood with six destroyers left Scapa Flow to cover the Suffolk and Norfolk. Repulse and the aircraft carrier Victorious, which were attached to a southbound convoy from Liverpool, were transferred to the Commander in Chief of the home fleet, Admiral Tovey. At 8 pm, on 22nd May, Tovey despatched the King George V, four cruisers and seven destroyers together with the Victorious to a central position in the West Atlantic and they were joined by Repulse on the morning of 23rd May. The whereabouts of Bismarck and Prince Eugen remained unknown but it was thought that they had headed for the Denmark Straits between Greenland and Iceland, where the ice had narrowed the strait to less than eighty miles wide. The weather remained bad – low clouds, heavy seas, rains and in places sea fog. The mountainous seas in the Atlantic south of Iceland were whipped up by gale force winds, strengthening as the chase went over the succeeding days. On the evening of 23rd May the cruisers Suffolk and Norfolk spotted two warships skirting the ice as they entered the Straits. Orders were given to Hood and Prince of Wales to change course to intercept Bismarck at the south of the Straits, and King George V was ordered to speed to the west. At 2 am on 24th May Force H left Gibraltar to go north. Force H comprised Renown, the aircraft carrier Ark Royal and the cruiser Sheffield. Light was breaking on the 24th when Bismarck and Prince Eugen saw the Hood and the Prince of Wales on their port bow. Bismarck began to fire and the battleships engaged at 5.52 am at about 25,000 yards. At 6 am Bismarck fired a fifth salvo which hit the Hood. Its lack of modern armour, as it had not been modernised, and the plunging fire from Bismarck, combined to make Hood vulnerable and suddenly with a vast explosion amidships, it blew up.

A pillar of dense smoke arose from the ship and when it cleared, Hood had disappeared. Only three out of its total complement were saved. The Prince of Wales changed course, to avoid the wreckage of Hood, but it was itself heavily hit, its bridge wrecked and there was an underwater hit aft so that Captain Leach decided to break off the action and turned away under a smoke screen. Bismark was damaged and had been struck under water in the bows by two shells, one of which pierced an oil tank. She began losing oil. In all about 200 tons were lost and as the ship proceeded south-west an oil slick trailed behind it. Admiral Wake-Walker on Norwich decided not to continue the action; but Norfolk and Suffolk proceeded with their shadowing role of Bismarck. At 6.40 pm, Bismarck turned to challenge its pursuers in order to enable Prince Eugen to return home (it arrived in Brest ten days later). The combined forces were closing on Bismarck from all directions – but could not arrive on its course to intercept until the morning of 25th May. The Victorious however was within aircraft range of Bismarck, about 150 miles away. It was newly commissioned and the pilots inexperienced, but it was decided that an attack should be launched and thus in the evening about 8 pm 9 Swordfish were sent out to strike the Bismarck. Despite intense anti-aircraft fire and the poor weather conditions, the aircraft went in and hit the warship under the bridge. In pitch dark and heavy seas they landed back on the carrier guided only by signal lamps on approach. All landed safely.

During the evening Bismarck turned south and at midnight in the fog turned to port for Brest, putting out a smokescreen. She was lost to Norfolk and Suffolk and began proceeding towards Brest, making speed at 25 knots. The Home Fleet was still battling its way through the heavy seas towards the last known position of Bismarck. All were to converge to carry out the urgent instruction of the Prime Minister, Winston Churchill to the Admiralty, 'Sink the Bismarck'. Had it escaped, the propaganda value of its incursion into the Atlantic would have been influential worldwide, having regard to the exchange in the Denmark Straits and the loss of the Hood, striking a mortal blow to British naval prestige. After Suffolk lost contact, King George V made a cast to the west and then turned north-east towards the North Sea. The admiralty however, thought Bismarck was making for Brest, and thus ordered the fleet on to a more southerly course early on 26th May. By the end of the day Bismarck was well east of King George V and Rodney, with its 16-inch guns which had passed to the north of Bismarck's course. The battleships were short of fuel and speed had to be reduced. Meanwhile, far to the south Force H was hurrying to intercept the course of Bismarck.

At 10.30 am a constant search by Coastal Command resulted in a Catalina aircraft finding the warship 700 miles east of Brest. Despite anti-aircraft fire the Catalina was able to signal to the Admiralty giving the position and escape into the clouds. Later in the morning a second sighting of Bismarck by two Swordfish from Ark Royal was made. Bismarck was still well away from air cover by the Luftwaffe in France, which they were likely to gain on 27th May. Renown needed to wait for Rodney and the King George V to come up. Sheffield however began to close up towards the Bismarck. Ark Royal prepared to strike by its Swordfish complement. The seas were mountainous: when the carrier turned into the wind, there was a rise and fall of the deck of fifty feet. Despite the difficulties the Swordfish took off. Unhappily they had not been told of the presence of Sheffield and thought that only Bismarck was in the area. They flew on and seeing the cruiser began to attack. The latter dodged and did not fire back. Warned of the presence of Sheffield, the aeroplanes discontinued the action and returned to Ark Royal. With only one hour of daylight left a second attack was mounted. The Swordfish, under heavy fire, attacked from the port side. Two torpedoes hit the Bismarck: one in the bow and a second in the stern as the warship turned to port. The latter stopped the port propellers, which were jammed: the steering engine was put out of action and the hand rudder jammed. The Bismarck turned in two tight circles and started to head north. Its speed appeared reduced to 10 knots and it was headed towards the Rodney. It was still 170 miles from air cover. At 12 pm the German Admiral Lutjens telegraphed Berlin – 'Ship unmanoeuvrable. We shall fight to the last shell. Long live the Fuehrer'. Bismarck was 400 miles from Brest.

In the night Captain Vian in Cossack with four other destroyers (one Polish) arrived to harry Bismarck and a flowing engagement followed as the destroyers appeared and reappeared on both port and starboard of the Bismarck. The high seas threw them about and they rolled as they fought the huge waves breaking over them.

When daylight arrived on 27th May, the King George V and Rodney had arrived. Daylight broke in a Beaufort Force 8 North-westerly gale. At 8.47 am Rodney opened fire and a minute thereafter King George V. The range was 25,000 yards. Rodney's second salvo began to land on Bismarck and its radar room was put out of use. Bismarck returned the fire but it became erratic. The second turret forward was hit and fragments swept the bridge. A Swordfish from the Ark Royal observed the rain of shells on Bismarck as it lay under a pall of black smoke and flames. The after-turret remained in action after the others had ceased. The

King George V and Rodney began to turn away as they were short of fuel. Ships carrying torpedoes came in and Dorsetshire at two miles fired two torpedoes which scored hits. The Bismarck rolled over and sank, leaving hundreds of its crew in the sea. A rescue was attempted by the British ships present and 110 of the crew were rescued. The rescue was interrrupted by the arrival of a U-boat and the British withdrew.

Admiral Tovey reported that Bismarck 'had put up a most gallant fight against impossible odds... worthy of the old days of the Imperial Navy'.

The sinking, despite the loss of life, had important consequences for attitudes formed by nations watching Britain's lone struggle, and clearly maintained the supremacy of the fleet in home waters and its worldwide reputation.

29th May 1660

Oakapple Day

Samuel Pepys records in his diary in 1660 that Parliament ordered the twenty-ninth of of May to be forever kept as a day of thanksgiving for our redemption from tyranny and the King's return to his government. The day was both the birthday of King Charles II and the day of his return from exile to London. Oakapple Day was regularly and enthusiastically celebrated for two centuries; even the naval mutineers as Sheerness in 1797 fired salutes and dressed the men-of-war with the Royal Standard on the fore and the Red Flag on the main. The reason for general public rejoicing lay in the release of the people of England from the interference of the Puritan government in their lives. They had cut down Maypoles, forbade Sunday games, employed soldiers to enter homes to see that the Sabbath was being kept and fasts set by Parliament observed, even taking away meat found in kitchens. Theatres and race meetings were proscribed. People were told and ordered how to live their private lives.

The abandonment of Oakapple Day at the end of the nineteenth century has no apparent reason, but it is possible that the Victorians believed that freedom from interference in people's lives was secure. For the present generation such a view can be seen to have been naïve. The modern puritans, driven by ideas derived from sociology, of levelling and the social rebuilding of society, and zealots of health care and safety, are alive and well. To their numbers may be added the proponents of political correctness and multi-culturalists who at the extremes deny freedom of thought on the basis that no offence should be given. Much of the motivation stems from a feminine impulse to infantilise grown adults in society. The litany of interference is growing and endless. There is the banning of private amusements like foxhunting; the interference with smoking by banning it even in private clubs; the lecturing on eating, banning chips being eaten in schools; the emerging attack on drinking; the interference under the cover of health and safety considerations of age-long childish traditions like conkers; the ban on smacking one's children. The ingenuity of the mini-dictators on local councils and their officers defies imagination but has become ever present. Political correctness has extended to the banning of the symbols of the Christian order: Christmas decorations have come under ban in places for fear of offence to people of other religions. Jokes and humour are censored by fear: no newspaper or magazine in Britain was prepared to publish the caricatures of Mohammed produced in a Danish magazine, which gained so much notoriety. Freedom of speech however was once always robust and offence inevitable: offence may go to good taste and courtesy, but as a criticism of liberty of speech it destroys freedom.

Oakapple Day needs to be revived with enthusiasm in twenty-first century Britain in order to recall the lost past and challenge the inexorable march of interference with people's private lives. Smoking, drinking, over-eating and the treatment of children by their parents is a matter for the adults involved in a free society, and they should be left to make their own choices, however detrimental, so long as there is no provable significant harm to others.

The name of the day celebrated the story of King Charles II on his flight from the Battle of Worcester, hiding from Cromwell's Puritan soldiers in an Oak tree.

31ˢᵗ May 1916
The Battle of Jutland

Observed at the Carlton Club one summer evening in the late 60s was a party of different ages, one of whom wielded a beautiful horn ear-trumpet. Across the table an enthusiastic young man, in a sudden silence which fell on the dining room shouted; 'And what, General, did you say on getting the news of Jutland?' That question still hangs over the Battle of Jutland: was it a victory? Put in the context, however, of Karl Von Clausewitz's Theory of war, it was; and thus it is included.

Prince Von Bismarck, the creator of the German Empire in 1870 by the unification of the German states, pursued a policy which ruled out the construction of a significant navy in order to avoid a challenge to Britain. In 1890 he was dismissed by the young Kaiser William II, a grandson of Queen Victoria, who was both clever and unwise. He admired the British Navy, and encouraged by German commercial interests and by Admiral Von Turpitz, an Anglophobe, decided to build a navy large enough to ensure that the danger for the greatest sea power would be such as to imperil its position in the world. In pursuit of this objective in 1898 the Imperial Parliament passed the first Navy Law, authorising the creation of a navy. In 1898 Wiesbaden was launched. On 18ᵗʰ October 1900, on the launch of the Karl der Grosse, the Kaiser declared that there was a 'bitter necessity for a powerful German fleet'. In the same year a second Naval Law was passed to meet Von Turpitz's objective of having 38 ships of the line.

The challenge to Britain which the naval programme presented, reinstated the need to modernise the British Navy. In 1904 Lord Fisher became First Sea Lord and in 1906 an entirely new type of battleship, 'the Dreadnought' was launched. The innovative design of this ship, with its ten 12-inch guns, rendered obsolete earlier designs and led to navies worldwide being rebuilt. Fisher believed in submarines, aircraft and destroyers but in addition, created a new class of battle cruiser, less heavily armoured, faster and with greater firepower than ordinary cruisers. These were built secretly and three were launched in 1909 – the Invincible, Inflexible and Indomitable. Fifteen were built in all. By 1914 the British had 29 'Dreadnoughts' and the German navy 18.

Both combatants at the outset of the war were cautious in the use of their fleets in North Sea waters. The British fleet under Earl Jellicoe was stationed at

Scapa Flow in the Orkneys where it could be protected from submarines. The 5th battle squadron under Rear Admiral Evan-Thomas, comprising Barham, Valiant, Warspite and Malaga was at Rosyth, and in the south a mainly destroyer force under Commodore Tyrwhitt at Harwich. The battle cruiser fleet under Vice Admiral Sir David Beatty on Lion was put with Evan-Thomas and his 5th Battle Squadron. The main threat to the ships of the Grand Fleet was the threat of being torpedoed from destroyers or submarines, and Jellicoe was fully conscious of this risk and the fact that, as Winston Churchill said, 'he was the only man on either side who could lose the war in an afternoon'.

On the German side the preponderance of the British navy in ships and firepower made the naval commanders unwilling to risk the High Seas fleet against the Grand Fleet, until the British navy had been weakened by the use of submarines and destruction by mines, thus giving fair odds in any fight. There was the further consideration that Kaiser William II was reluctant to put the new battleships on trial and perhaps have them lost. In many there had been included luxurious cabin space for him, in which were fitted special toilet apparatus by his old body servant, Schultz. Von Bulow, Germany's chancellor, said that the Kaiser's heart sank at the thought of having to sacrifice even one of these toys.

By 1916 the British navy had 37 battleships and battle cruisers of the Dreadnought type to Germany's 23, 34 armoured and light cruisers to 11, and 80 destroyers to 63. In firepower the British had 344 major weapons to 244, with a bore varying from 13.5 inches to 15 inches. The German Navy guns were mainly 12-inch, but as the battle was to show, the accuracy of German gunnery was better than that of the British.

In January 1916 Admiral Von Pohl was superseded by Admiral Von Scheer as Commander of the German High Seas Fleet. He advocated a more aggressive policy for use of the fleet and in May conceived an incursion into the North Sea to draw out the Grand Fleet from Scapa Flow. The battle cruisers were to bombard Sunderland, attracting out the Grand Fleet onto mines and waiting lines of submarines, to where the High Seas fleet would be ready to pounce. The scheme was put in train but the submarines exhausted their sea-going time, and Zeppelin air cover to search out the positions of the British Grand Fleet proved impossible because May was too foggy; thus, the scheme was abandoned. An alternative plan was evolved to send Admiral Hipper with a force of battle and light cruisers north towards Norwegian waters, while the rest of the High Sea Fleet followed out of sight about fifty miles behind.

The British had the advantage that they had the cypher and signal code of the German Navy, which had been recovered by the Russians from the sinking of the Magdeburg and passed on. Captain Rounds had established listening stations in the East of England and an unceasing watch was kept on radio traffic, which at the time of Jutland was centred on the Bayern for messages affecting the High Seas

Fleet. The Admiralty thus learned on 29th May that Hipper was ordered to sea on 30th May, carrying his flag on Lützow with Derflinger, Seydlitz, Moltke and Von der Tann. The Bayern also moved down river from Wilhelmshaven into the Jade estuary. That movement led the First Sea Lord to order the Grand Fleet to sea on 29th May. Hipper's squadron was to be accompanied by eight cruisers and destroyers and submarine activity increased. As Jellicoe plunged east towards the Skaggerak, Scheer and the High Seas Fleet steamed north. On 30th May Beatty left the Firth of Forth with 6 battle cruisers, 4 dreadnoughts, and 29 destroyers in three flotillas, and the aircraft-carrying ship the Engadine. Gradually the fleets closed together.

On 31st May at 2 pm an incident involving the stopping by two German destroyers of a merchant ship, thus giving rise to a smoke column, attracted the Galatea and there she discovered the van of the German fleet under Admiral Von Hipper. At 2.20 pm Galatea signalled, 'Enemy in sight'. The destroyers abandoned the merchant ship and returned to the Elbing, a light cruiser on Hipper's Flank. At 2.36 pm Galatea signalled *en clair* the position; that there was considerable smoke there with 7 ships, which turned north. Beatty ordered a change of course to the south-east and Jellicoe, two hours away, ordered fresh speed. At 2.52 pm the Galatea was shelled by Elbing.

The Engadine had launched its observer aircraft and at 3.20 pm the presence of a large fleet had been found. At 3.25 pm Captain Chatfield on board Lion informed Beatty that the enemy were in sight on the starboard bow. Beatty, anxious to engage, ordered 25 knots. Evan-Thomas's battle squadron was left behind as it was slower and at a stroke Beatty deprived himself of his superiority of two to one against Hipper's squadron. At 3.47pm Beatty's and Hipper's fleets were twelve miles apart and Hipper opened fire. The first of the phases of the Battle of Jutland had begun. The fight between the battle cruisers, which went on intensively for about two hours, had commenced. At 4 pm a shell from the Lutzow penetrated the Q. turret of the Lion. Major Harvey of the Marines, commanding the turret, despite severe injuries to his legs, ordered the ammunition magazines below to be flooded, thus saving the ship. He received a posthumous Victoria Cross. The explosion was seen from the Nicator and as Lion emerged from the smoke with her other guns firing, the crew raised a cheer. The Indefatigable engaged in a bout with the Von der Tann and was hit by a salvo of three shots on the upper deck near the rear turret: a small explosion occurred and she swung out of line, sinking by the stern. A further salvo hit the ship and she rolled over and sank. At 4.20 pm the Queen Mary, the newest of the battle cruisers, mounting 13.5-inch guns and having a top speed of 32 knots, was duelling with two of the enemy.

Suddenly buffeted by salvoes from the High Seas Fleet there was an explosion, smoke hid her and she began to list heavily. In moments she was gone with 1,266 officers and men. Beatty on Lion turned to Captain Chatfield and morosely remarked 'There seems to be something wrong with our bloody ships, today,

Chatfield'. While the battle cruiser action raged from 4.15 to 4.43 pm, Evan-Thomas's 5th Battle Squadron tried to engage the rear of Hipper's fleet from long range, without great success. The light cruisers and the destroyers were active during this phase of the battle and the sea in the battle area was a heaving volcano of exploding shells, turbulence and gunfire. For example, the light cruiser Chester was engaged by three enemy ships of similar size and firepower. On board her was John Cornwall, aged sixteen from Walton Road School in London who had enlisted as 'Boy First Class'. He was serving in the crew of a 5.5-inch gun, when a shell exploded near the guns. He was the last survivor. Mortally wounded, he struggled to load the gun and slam the breech shut. The shell hit the Wiesbaden and contributed to the damage already done. He did not live to see her sink. He was awarded a posthumous Victoria Cross.

About or just after 5pm Beatty veered to the north-east to join with the Grand Fleet in order to 'cross the T' and with Jellicoe entrap the High Seas Fleet within a cordon in which full fire-power could be brought to bear. A rearguard action was fought but by 6 pm Jellicoe, with a seven-mile line of ships, appeared to the surprise of Scheer who had been unaware so far of their presence. At 6.01 pm Jellicoe sought a current position from Beatty and information to establish a course. The uncertainties of position made firing by the Grand Fleet imprudent as the fleet manoeuvred, and there was confusion among the 100 ships because there was no effective method of signalling in the carnage and with smoke lying over the sea. In the melée disasters occurred. The Defence from the First Cruiser squadron was destroyed by German battle cruisers. Invincible, which was accurately pounding the Derflinger and which was part of Sir Horace Hood's Battle cruiser Squadron, was hit at 6.15 pm and the watchers saw a tower of smoke and flame. The ship blew up with only 6 people saved. Jellicoe continued, uncertain whether the High Seas Fleet was to starboard or ahead, but at 6.30 pm he ordered the Grand Fleet to form line of battle. The battle formation developed into a long line with only the centre and rear of the line firing and the course chosen was east south-east following a turn to starboard. Beatty, whose force had joined up with the Grand Fleet, and Jellicoe thus succeeded in 'crossing the T' and Hipper and Scheer were steaming into the cordon of the Grand Fleet.

Scheer, perceiving the danger, had no intention of fighting the whole Grand Fleet and brilliantly executed a manoeuvre to turn home. He first feigned to go to the west, where he thought that the Grand Fleet were trying to drive him away from his bases: then, he executed a starboard turn to change course to the south with a view to escaping the battle line of the Grand Fleet. At about 9.12 pm the order was given for Hipper's battle cruisers and destroyers to close with the enemy. Derflinger, Seydlitz and Von der Tann turned south-east. Derflinger came under heavy fire. Lützow too was on fire and sinking so Hipper transferred his flag to another ship. The darkness fell and the battle continued between the destroyer fleets. The High

Seas Fleet steamed south initially and did not turn south-east until about 9.30 pm, heading for Horns Reef and the swept channel into Wilhelmshaven. The battle cruiser fleet and the Grand Fleet shadowed them to the east until on their south-east course the High Seas Fleet pressed through the track of the British fleet. In this period of the chase desultory actions took place as the Germans tried to go east. Beatty's battle cruisers covered the course of the German fleet in advance of them between 9 and 10 pm. At 10.20 pm the Frauen sank after having been torpedoed by the Southampton, a light cruiser. The convergence of the Grand Fleet and the High Seas fleet at 11 pm with the latter succeeding in crossing to the east, brought the fleets together. Their closeness resulted in the First Cruiser Squadron wandering into the centre of the High Seas Fleet and the glare of searchlights; Black Prince was destroyed and sank. After midnight the fleets steamed on diverging courses and the battle subsided, the last incident being a torpedo attack by the 12th destroyer flotilla on the Pommern, an ageing battleship of 13,000 tons. The torpedoes fired resulted in the explosion of the ship, spreading fire fore and aft, and the ends rose as if the back were broken. The Pornmern then disappeared from sight. At 3.00 am Jellicoe and Beatty turned north to return to home. The nearer he came to German waters the greater had become Jellicoe's concern about waiting submarines and destroyers. He felt that he did not have enough destroyers for safety. Ironically Sir Robert Tyrwhitt, with the destroyer force at Harwich, had departed of his own volition from Harwich early in the day, but was recalled by the Admiralty at 6 pm. At 4 am the German High Seas Fleet re-entered the Jade River and were home. So ended the Battle of Jutland without a final meeting between the great battle fleets.

There is no doubt that the British fleet suffered the greatest loss of ships, due to the defective design of the battle cruisers, which had insufficient armour and no proper flash control to protect the magazines. Critics have argued that Beatty was too impetuous in attacking without the cover of Evan-Thomas's warships and that Jellicoe was overcautious, particularly in not acting with vigour on a signal which he received that the High Seas Fleet had been ordered home at 9.14 pm on a course south south-east. The British gunnery was also poorer than that of the Germans and the large warships were vulnerable to the attack of the submarines, unless protected by destroyers. Initially Kaiser Wilhelm II called Jutland a victory, although in later life he admitted that from a German point of view it was inconclusive. From the British point of view, first, German ships had been sank – the Lützow, Wiesbaden, the Pommern, the light cruiser Elbing, - and others damaged, and second, after this battle the High Seas Fleet was to remain tied up in port for the rest of the war. Only on three occasions did it re-appear at sea – on 18th August 1916, 10th October 1916 and 24th April 1918. In justification of Jellicoe's caution, reliance can be placed on the words of Samuel Pepys, the Clerk of the Acts in the Navy Office, who wrote in 1666: 'This is all, only we keep the sea, which denotes a victory'.

On 19th August 1916 a plan was put into effect by Scheer to attract the Grand Fleet out of Scapa Flow on to four lines of submarines laid in the North Sea off the coast of England which, by destroying the warships, could weaken the fleet and allow another attempt by the High Seas Fleet to attack it. The High Seas Fleet was to be the bait, setting out to bombard Sunderland. Reconnoitring Zeppelins – 8 in number – were to cover the North Sea and keep the Germans informed of British naval movements. The High Sea Fleet was observed by participating destroyers from Tyrwhitt's Flotilla squadron leaving the Jade River. Torpedoes were fired and the last ship, the Westphalen, was crippled, returning home. By coincidence, following the report of large submarine activity on 18th August, Jellicoe had ordered the Grand Fleet out to make a sweep of the North Sea, so that the British were already at sea before the Germans left Wilhelmshaven. The two fleets manoeuvred around the North Sea, the one, the British, searching to make contact with the other, the Germans, seeking to avoid it. Scheer changed course on receiving information from Zeppelin L13 away from Sunderland, in order to go south to attack Tyrwhitt's force: however, thunderstorms caused the shadowing Zeppelin to lose touch with Tyrwhitt's fleet and contact was never regained. Scheer, knowing that the Grand Fleet was at sea and forty-two miles to the north, turned south south-east for home. Tyrwitt's force came up with the High Seas Fleet after dark on a parallel course, but Scheer decided not to send light cruisers after him. Tyrwhitt thought it too short a night to attack. Thus the battle never took place. The lines of submarines showed their value. The U66 met HMS Falmouth 50 miles north east of Flamborough and damaged it with two torpedoes. It was taken in tow, hit again by two torpedoes, but foundered before reaching Hull. As Inflexible on its return crossed the first submarine line running north-east – south-east off the Northumbrian coast, thirty miles north of Sunderland at 7.00 pm, U65 attacked it with two torpedoes which went astray and missed.

The use of submarines was a significant outcome from the Battle of Jutland. Scheer on his return, reporting to the Kaiser, stressed that the fleet was not able to force peace on England and he recommended that the resumption of unrestricted submarine warfare was the sole way of attaining a victory within a reasonable time 'even at the risk of war with America'. Despite resistance from the Kaiser and the Chancellor, that course was adopted and late in 1917 the United States entered the war. Incidentally Von Hase, the gunnery officer of the Derflinger, thought that Jellicoe had wisely turned home in order to keep the fleet in being; that had been achieved.

Sir John Jellicoe was made a Viscount in 1917 and subsequently an Earl. Sir David Beatty was made an Earl in 1919. The 2nd Earl Jellicoe and the 3rd Earl Beatty were ejected from the House of Lords in 1999.

June

1st	The Glorious First of June	1794
2nd	The Deliverance at Dunkirk	1940
3rd	The Battle of the Gabbard Bank	1653
	The Battle of Lowestoft	1665
17th	Cornwallis's Retreat	1795
18th	The Battle of Waterloo	1815
21st	The Battle of Vitoria	1813
24th	The Battle of Sluys	1340
28th	The Battle of Dettingen	1743

1ˢᵗ June 1794

The Glorious First of June

O n 31ˢᵗ January 1793 the French Convention declared war on Britain and Holland. Once more the French were to embark on their traditional objective of dominating west and central Europe. In 1789 the Revolution had broken out, and the politics of France moved from establishing a constitutional monarchy under Louis XVI to a radical Convention, dominated by a Jacobin minority, which on 21ˢᵗ January 1793 executed the King. War had already broken out when Louis XVI was forced to declare war on the Austrian Empire on 20ᵗʰ April 1792. The British Government throughout this period of revolution in France leading up to war had tried to remain neutral, and the policy of the Prime Minister William Pitt was to maintain the peace. In August 1792 Robespierre and Danton took power and in September France became a Republic. After an initial success, the army of Austria and Prussia taking Verdun, the French armies defeated the forces against them at Valmy and Jemappes and began to advance. The French seized Savoy and Nice, entered Mainz and Brussels. The Convention, excited by its desire to spread French 'Liberty' to the peoples of Europe, adopted resolutions declaring that all nations were enemies of France who had princes and privileged classes; that their armies should follow their fleeing opponents across borders into other countries and that the navigating rights on the Scheldt should be open to all nations. The latter had been guaranteed to Holland under the Treaty of Westphalia 1648 and successive treaties. The mission to bring freedom to all Europe was resolved upon against a background in which Robespierre and the Convention were engaged in a bloody reign of terror, guillotining thousands as enemies of the state. In this context General Dumouriez was pressing to annex Holland in addition to his seizure of the Austrian Netherlands.

On 13th November 1792 Pitt pledged that Britain would support the United Netherlands (Holland) if France invaded. On 28ᵗʰ November Antwerp fell and the French demanded of the Dutch the right to pass to the fortress of Maastricht. Between 29ᵗʰ November and 2ⁿᵈ December Pitt warned the French representative in London that any action against Holland would mean war. On 1ˢᵗ December Pitt called out the militia (the territorial army of the time). On 13ᵗʰ December the Whigs under Charles James Fox divided the House of Commons on a Government motion to strengthen the forces. That encouraged the Convention, who thought that conquest of Holland was a revolutionary interest which would enable the taking of the wealth of Holland to fund their treasury. They resolved to raise 17,000 more soldiers and 9,000 Seamen. The French Navy was to be strengthened by thirty ships of the line and twenty frigates.

News of the execution of the King reached London on 24th January 1793 and public opinion was so outraged that enthusiasm for war began to be raised among people in Britain. On 30th January the convention resolved unambiguously to annex the Austrian Netherlands (Belgium). Pitt persisted to the end in trying to save the peace but the aggression of the French drove him towards war, which France declared.

The outbreak of war necessitated a need to reinvigorate the Navy. Major objectives were of course to secure the western approach to Britain and to maintain a blockade on France. Although the French Navy was large – 80 ships of the line with 30 in commission, its discipline and effectiveness had been destroyed in the Revolution by the killing of the officers, and mutinies and riots. A large Channel squadron was created by the British Government, which had its base at Spithead. Earl Howe was appointed to the command.

Earl Howe was sixty-eight and a favourite of King George III, who pressed for his appointment. He was born in 1726 and was a grandson of the Countess of Darlington (a German) who herself was the mistress of George I, a couple whom irreverent courtiers referred to as the Elephant and Castle. He held an Irish Viscountcy inherited from his brother, and was in Parliament for Dartmouth for twenty-five years. He sailed round the world with Anson and fought in the Seven Years War. Known within the fleet as 'Black Dick' he was taciturn, of forbidding demeanour and countenance. He was nonetheless well loved in the fleet for his concern for the crews of his ships; as Dr Trotter wrote 'the health and comfort of his people were his first object (sic)'. He established regular patterns of shore leave and would visit the wounded on his ship, providing them with food and wine from his own supplies. He re-organised the navy, producing among other changes a standard signal book.

By July 1793 he had succeeded in getting a Channel Fleet to sea of 15 ships of the line, but the French fleet were never brought to battle and only seen distantly. Howe did not believe in close blockade of the French ports and therefore the fleet was kept at home. Frigates were used to watch the French along the coast in 'open blockade'. These interrupted the French coastal trade and their exploits appealed to the British public in the absence of major action. One such occasion was the engagement in June 1793 between the Nymphe commanded by Sir Edward Pellew and Le Cléopatre. Nymphe was the slower boat but Pellew bore down upon Le Cléopatre, bringing his ship up gradually on the starboard quarter. The French Captain, Capitaine Mullen, prepared to fight and as the Nymphe drew up came to the rail to exchange courtesies with Captain Pellew: he raised his cap of liberty and it was then placed by a seaman at the mast top. A furious cannonade then commenced, which lasted 15 minutes. The French mizzen mast fell, severed about twelve feet above the deck, and the wheel was shot away. Le Cléopatre began to swing, Nymphe following her movement until both ships became entangled. Pellew ordered the crew to arms and they scrambled aboard the enemy ship. While they fought to control the Frenchman, Pellow attended to an attempt to free the swinging Le Cléopatre in order to prevent injury to his mainmast. On the British reaching the quarterdeck of the French ship, the Second Lieutenant surrendered his sword and the Tricolore was hauled down. Capitaine Mullen lay seriously wounded on the deck, trying to swallow a paper which he thought was the secret coastal signal code but was in fact his commission. The code was recovered by the British. Heavy casualties were suffered by both ships. Capitaine Mullen died and Pellew, having put a prize crew on board the French ship, returned on 21st June to Portsmouth. The news of his success was given to King George III at the opera and he announced it to the audience, who received it with great enthusiasm. Pellew received his knighthood for this engagement and the purchase money paid by the Navy to take the captured ship into service, of which a substantial sum was sent by him to the widow of Capitaine Mullen.

In spring 1794 Paris was near starvation and Robespierre and the Convention anxiously awaited a grain convoy from North America. The Navy had two duties; first to secure the safety of a British convoy out of the Channel and second, to intercept the French grain convoy. Earl Howe left Spithead on 8th May, designating eight ships of the line to escort the British convoy to Finisterre. Admiral Montagu, after doing his convoy duty, patrolled the Bay of Biscay from Cape Ortegal to Belle Isle. Howe reconnoitred Brest and returned there on May 19th. The French Admiral De Villaret-Joyeuse had left with twenty-six ships of the line. Before leaving he had been warned by Robespierre that he would be guillotined if the grain convoy was lost. Howe tracked the ocean west of Brest, but in vain, until he came up with the French fleet on 28th May about four hundred miles west of Ushant. A fresh south-westerly was blowing and there were heavy showers and a great Atlantic swell. The French were close up to the wind in order to keep the British from the weather gauge. The Queen Charlotte, the flagship, with double-reefed topsails, still split her jib in the heavy weather. The British held on and by evening Admiral Pasley was within shot of the rear of the French. On 29th May the fleets had moved out of range about six miles apart as they headed north-westerly. Rain and fog alternated; now and then the French were detected as the chase went on for the next forty-eight hours. Most of the British fleet had some damage done in the weather that prevailed, but in this period Earl Howe succeeded in crossing the track of the French and securing the weather gauge. On 31st May both fleets held a parallel course under heavy sail. The first of June arrived fine and clear; the wind a moderate westerly with a long swell on the sea. Earl Howe had decided to bear down slantwise and to take individual ships of the line one to one going through the line, in order to bombard the French ships on both sides and in the stern.

At 9.00 am the French were eight miles to leeward and Howe began his approach, coming up at a slow pace of about five knots. At 10.00 am the fleets came together and the bombardment between the ships began. Not all the captains of Howe's fleet seem to have fully understood his orders and the leading ships were held up by the Caesar in the van, because there was no gap. The Queen Charlotte, aiming for the centre, sailed towards the Montagne, the flagship of De Villaret-Joyeuse, which had the Jacobin to its lee. Under fire from the Vengeur du Peuple and the Achille it passed through the line firing into the stern of the Montagne, killing 300 and wrecking it. So narrow was the gap that the fly of the ensign brushed the Frenchman's shrouds. Seven out of 26 pierced the line and everywhere there was a melée of individual battle engagements. The 19 ships still to windward ranged the enemy with strong salvoes. The Queen Charlotte became engaged with two French opponents: the main topmast, mainyard and fore topmast were lost and, while the Queen Charlotte was engaged, the Montagne drew away. The Juste struck to the British flagship.

The Brunswick, next astern, engaged the Vengeur du Peuple. The starboard anchors of Brunswick locked into the French ship's fore shrouds and the interlocked ships fought fiercely. Brunswick raised and lowered its guns, wreaking havoc into the hull of the Vengeur. About an hour after this fight began Brunswick forced the Achille, who was also attacking her, to strike her colours. The two locked ships drifted away and remained locked until 12.45pm. Ramillies and other ships joined in and Vengeur, with a large hole in her counter and the mast split, surrendered. Later in the day she sank with half her crew. Brunswick had to make sail away because she was so damaged.

Among the other ships engaged the Marlborough distinguished herself, dismasting the Impétueux and Mucius. Both she and Defiance were totally dismasted. The French however, had suffered the worst of the exchange by reason of the superior British gunnery and seamanship. About 12 French ships had been wholly or partially dismasted and left crippled. About five made to get away and were being pursued by Thunderer and Orion when they were recalled by Earl Howe. The British secured six ships as prizes, but five which were unsecured succeeded in escaping. Meanwhile De Villaret-Joyeuse had collected his van and sailed off towards the north-west.

By the time the battle was fought Earl Howe, despite his age, had been awake for five nights and was exhausted. The British had suffered substantial damage, for example, like Bellerophon, which had lost its rigging and boats. Howe did not order a general chase.

Admiral Montagu failed to find the French convoy in the Bay of Biscay and De Villaret-Joyeuse had achieved his strategic purpose of drawing the Home Fleet away from that convoy. The remains of the French fleet met the grain convoy and entered Brest together. Earl Howe returned to Spithead with his prizes. On

9th June his dispatches reached London. The news of the victory over the French fleet was welcomed with joy: at the Opera the audience interrupted to sing Rule Britannia and the soprano sang God save the King. On 13th June George III and his daughters joined Earl Howe in the flagship to dine. None of his captains was asked to join the dinner despite their achievements and their demonstrable skill, which had resulted in the victory. Thirteen of these captains became future Admirals.

The fact that five ships escaped led Lord Nelson, who believed in annihilation, to refer disparagingly to engagements with no conclusive outcome as a 'Lord Howe Victory'.

2nd June 1940
The Deliverance of Dunkirk

The politics of British Foreign Policy leading up to 1939 was dominated by two realities; first, the problem of how to deal with the revision of the peace of 1918 by a resurgent Germany under Adolph Hitler and second, an ambiguity of attitude to Russia, which at the same time was feared for the threat it posed by the spread of Bolshevism, and yet was recognised to be an important element in maintaining the peace of Europe. The problem of the revision of the Treaty of Versailles and the Treaty of St. Germain itself involved ambiguities for the British because on the one hand revision was seen as just for a treaty too much based on the revenge of France but too little on President Wilson's Fourteen points, the basis of the Armistice, and yet revision destabilised the peace of Europe by undermining the collective security given by treaties of alliance made by France with states to the east of Germany. The British Prime Minister Stanley Baldwin exemplified the approach taken after Hitler came to power in 1933 by adopting a policy of drift to the emerging questions while at the same time tentatively embarking on the policy of rearmament. In May 1937 he was succeeded by Neville Chamberlain, who was determined to arrive at a settlement of European problems on the basis of peaceful agreement. In his tribute to Neville Chamberlain on his death in November 1940 the Prime Minister Winston Churchill movingly summed up the objects for which Chamberlain had worked – 'the love of peace , the toil for peace, the strife for peace, the pursuit of peace, even at great peril and certainly in utter distain of popularity and clamour'. That policy led in November 1937 to the Foreign Secretary, Lord Halifax, telling Adolf Hitler at Berchtesgaden that alterations to the treaties might be possible with time in relation to Austria, Czechoslovakia and Danzig, all of which had German populations, with some 3 million Germans in Czechoslovakia and 350,000 in the city of Danzig.

The peace and revision of the treaties policy led Chamberlain down the road to appeasement, first over the Anschluss taking Austria, and second over the Sudentenland at Munich, where Czechoslovakia was forced to transfer areas along its borders to Germany. The Munich crisis and its resolution divided British public opinion and appeasement as a policy was increasingly savagely attacked. Chamberlain had returned from a meeting with Adolf Hitler with a signed undertaking that all questions arising between Germany and Britain would be resolved peacefully. On the evening of his return on the balcony at Downing Street he unguardedly said that he had returned from Germany with peace with honour again, a reference to Benjamin Disraeli's return from Berlin after the congress there in 1878 to settle problems in the Balkans. Adolf Hitler however was no

Prince von Bismarck, who ably preserved the peace until his policy was torn apart by Kaiser Wilhelm II. These words were to haunt Chamberlain throughout 1939, after Hitler marched into Czechoslovakia in March, establishing an independent Slovakia and annexing Bohemia to Germany.

The month following these events Chamberlain and the British Government gave a guarantee to Poland on behalf of themselves and France, which had not been consulted, that if any action were taken which clearly threatened Polish independence, the two governments would at once lend them all support in their power. The guarantee was unqualified and did not take account of the continuing problem of the Germans in the city of Danzig, which was to act as the trigger of war. It is probable that Chamberlain's motive in giving the guarantee, quite apart from his sense of betrayal, was a warning to Adolf Hitler, since the British Government remained disposed to negotiate over Danzig. They had reckoned however without Colonel Josef Beck, the Polish Foreign Minister, who was determined to give way to Germany neither over the Polish Corridor nor Danzig.

For Hitler with his policy of securing 'lebensraum' for the German people in the east of Europe, the position of Poland was an obstacle to his moving against Bolshevik Russia. Hitler however was always opportunistic in his foreign policy up to the war and right up to its outbreak pursued a dual policy to Poland, first to secure Polish co-operation by agreement similar to his alliance with Italy, and second, if opposed, to crush Poland by force. It is improbable that he seriously cared about Danzig, since there are indications that he would have bargained it away to the Poles as the price of agreement. In October 1938 he began by seeking agreement with the Poles and in January 1939 had discussions with Beck, who would not enter any arrangement, even though offered a share of the Ukraine in the future. Thereafter he embarked on a war of nerves to induce Britain and France to make Poland give concessions on the issue of Danzig and the Corridor. It is also probable that he hoped by dividing off the western powers from Poland, that Beck and the Poles would then accept the alliance he offered. The corridor was that area of land between East Prussia and Brandenburg given to Poland in 1919. It had a Polish majority population but had been part of Germany since the eighteenth century and its loss isolated East Prussia from Germany. Danzig was not Polish, but administered by a High Commissioner appointed by the League of Nations as international territory. Its Senate however was in the hands of the Nazi Party. As a port for Poland its importance was diminished since 1919 by the growth of Gdynia. Hitler's original request to Poland was for a transport route across the Corridor and not for the Corridor itself, and even in August 1939 he demanded not its cession but a plebiscite. These approaches were calculated to appeal to the governments of Britain and France, who wanted a settlement by negotiation. Chamberlain however was to an extent the prisoner now of public opinion and had to use care.

The Government began to try to negotiate a pact of mutual support with the Soviet Union, enthusiastically abetted by France, but Beck and the Poles would concede nothing. On 8th April Hitler ordered as a precaution the preparation of a plan to invade Poland. On 23rd May, as part of the war of nerves he addressed the German High Command stating that there could be war, but that he wished no conflict in the west, knowing that the generals, who mistrusted him, would leak his comments to Britain. The next months saw general activity by the powers to try to keep the peace. Britain, France and Italy did not think Danzig worth fighting for, but the British Government had to move by stealth. The Poles showed no sign of giving way and Chamberlain with reluctance negotiated with Moscow, hoping that with an Anglo-Soviet agreement the Poles could be forced to concede. On 17th August the talks failed when the western powers' representatives could not answer the question whether Poland would consent to the passage of Russian armies to fight Germany. Britain and France could give no answer. On 19th August Russia agreed to a negotiator being sent from Germany to Russia to arrange a mutual pact of non-aggression. On 23rd August the German Foreign Member, Von Ribbentrop, arrived in Moscow and the treaty was signed. It included trade provisions and a secret clause partitioning Poland and handing over the Baltic states to the USSR. These arrangements also revised the settlement established after the First World War. Hitler was radiant: he now believed, as did Stalin, that Britain and France would force the Poles to accede to Germany's requests. Based on Munich, he thought there would be no will to war and with the collapse of the possible alliance with the USSR, a positive drive for peace. He postponed his proposed attack on Poland on 26th August to 1st September to allow for negotiation. The British Ambassador in Berlin and a Swedish businessman, Dahlerus, sponsored by Reichsmarschall Herman Goering, hurriedly tried to arrange a compromise. Bonnet, the French Foreign Minister, tried to persuade the French Cabinet to slide out of their undertakings to Poland. Britain, however, on 25th August signed a formal alliance with Poland to give effect to the guarantee, having sent a warning to the Germans of the likelihood of war were Poland to be attacked. The moment came, however, when the Fuehrer had to gamble whether to invade Poland and risk war or hold back. It was 12.40pm on 31st August before Hitler ordered the attack to be made at dawn the next morning. That day, 1st September, the 'blitzkrieg' by air and land was launched on Poland. Mussolini, who had told Hitler that Italy would not be ready for war until 1942, suggested another 'Munich' conference. The British issued a warning requesting Germany to withdraw its forces. On 2nd September Chamberlain faced a tumultuous debate in the House of Commons opposed by some of his own party. L.S. Amery called on the Labour front bencher, Arthur Greenwood, to 'speak for England'. That night the Cabinet, led by Sir John Simon, warned Chamberlain that the Government would fall without an ultimatum to Germany. Chamberlain authorised its delivery and at 9 am the Ambassador delivered it to the German Foreign Office: it called for an undertaking by 11 am to withdraw the German forces from Poland. It was rushed to the Fuehrer and read to him. He sat with glazed expression listening to it and then turned after an interval of silence to von Ribbentrop, standing by the window and asked 'what now then?' Reichsmarschall Goering turned to his companions and said, 'If we lose this war, then God have mercy on us!' War was declared by Britain on Sunday morning, 3rd September at eleven o'clock.

Chamberlain throughout this period had persisted with a policy of re-armament, but on a limited scale, equipping the forces with new weapons and furthering projects such as radar. Compulsory military service was introduced in April 1939 on a limited basis, gas masks provided for the population and plans for the evacuation of women and children from the towns and cities to the countryside made. On 1st September members of the territorial army were called up and evacuation was begun. Trains, buses and even ships were employed to move thousands of children: one group sent to Lowestoft by the Thames Pleasure Steamer, the Royal Daffodil, was to hear the eleven o'clock broadcast by Chamberlain out in the waters of the North Sea, a curious route to safety. The British Expeditionary Force for France was organised and prepared. Its Commander was General Lord Gort, 6th Viscount Gort, a straightforward common sense soldier, whose bravery could not be doubted, holding as he did a Victoria Cross, Military Cross and Distinguished Service Order with bars, and he was sent initially to France with four divisions, comprising General Dell commanding the 1st Corps and General Brooke the 2nd Corps. Each corps had two divisions. To protect the landing of supplies and disembarkation from air attack the bases were fixed at Le Havre, Cherbourg, St Nazaire and Brest. By the end of October the BEF was in place on the French frontier in the area north of Lille between General Blanchard's 1st French Army on its right and General Girard's 7th Army on its left, which lay between the BEF and the coast. Lord Gort was made subordinate to the French General George, who commanded the Armies of the North East. Sir Leslie Hore-Belisha (after whom the traffic crossing beacons were named), the Secretary of State for War, was to declare that the army was probably 'as well if not better equipped than any similar army,' but in fact it was woefully supplied and inadequately prepared for a modern technological war. As General Brooke pointed out, its tanks were only light ones, with few heavy Mark I tanks; there were too few anti-tank guns; ammunition for the dual-role Bofors gun was lacking; there was no tracer ammunition for defence against low flying aircraft and poor air cover. Artillery guns of all types were inadequate in quantity and quality. Weapons often had essential pieces missing. Throughout the winter the army numbers were to be built up. In December the 5th Division was to join the 2nd Corps and between January and March there arrived the 48th (South Midlands) Division, the 50th (Northumbrian) and the 51st Highland. In

April a 3rd Corps was formed under Lieutenant General Adam with the 42nd (Lancashire) and 44th (London) Divisions. Three divisions, the 12th, 23rd and 46th arrived in April but without artillery, little training and inadequate equipment. The one regiment of Mark I tanks (4th Royal Tank Regiment) was joined in April 1940 by the 7th Royal Tank Regiment with 27 Mark I heavy tanks and 23 Mark II's (Matildas).

The period which was to become known as the 'Phoney War', until May 1940, was to be spent by the British and French on the western front in an inactive defensive posture. Initially the Germans had 56 of their divisions in Poland out of 98 and out of the other 42 only 11 regular divisions were on the Western front. The 'Siegfried Line', the German answer to the 'Maginot' Line, was little more than a building site, while the French had mobilised 110 divisions in addition to the 4 British. The French military strategy was entirely defensive, dominated by confidence in the Maginot defence line built in the 1930s from the Swiss frontier to Longwy on the Belgium border. Out of sensitivity to the Belgians it ended there, and the Belgian frontier was open. The German High Command (ORH) worried endlessly during the six week campaign in Poland about an attack in the west. They need not have worried: the British and French Government's attitude to the war was enervated, typified perhaps by the attitude of Sir Kingsley Wood, the Secretary of State for Air, who said that bombing was unacceptable as it damaged private property and the Cabinet agreed that, in relation to a raid over the Black Forest in order to eliminate ammunition supply dumps, leaflets were to be dropped instead over Germany. On 6th October Adolf Hitler offered a negotiated peace with Britain and France on the basis that the Polish problem had been solved and that he had no argument with the west. The call went unanswered. He then issued Fuehrer Directive 6, preparing for the invasion of Holland, Belgium, Luxemburg and France as soon as possible. The first dates fixed were 25th October and then 12th November. Feldmarschall von Brauchitsch, the Army Commander in Chief protested that these dates could not be met and so 17th January was adopted. Just before the due date an Army Officer, Major Rheinberger, carrying the plans, came down in Belgium in a fog. The plans were taken by the Belgian police before destruction and passed on. The campaign was again postponed.

The BEF on the frontier spent the winter, which became unusually cold, in digging trenches, bunkers and other fortifications parallel to the Belgian frontier. Their conditions of existence were often poor as they had been housed in derelict warehouses, broken down barns, even disused pigsties. Many were open to the snow and the wind: the beds provided were often of straw. Cheap wine and spirits in the bars entertained them and in the streets, drunk, they fought with fists as they had in Aldershot on Saturday nights. Like all the working people of Britain they had the courage, strength and combativeness of 'the hooligans' so often condemned, and which made them in war indomitable. Venereal disease numbers grew and General Montgomery was almost dismissed by Gort, when he advocated clean rooms for every company for treatment, in order to reduce its incidence. He was saved by General Brooke. The troops had other entertainment apart from fighting; sports were organised, concerts and entertainments with such performers as Gracie Fields and the comedians George Formby and Will Hay. There was not much training done and supplies of ammunition and fuel were slow in appearing.

Winston Churchill throughout the events of 1940 seemed not to comprehend entirely the moral collapse of the French Government and the inadequacy of their army and its fighting abilities. That no doubt stemmed from his thirty-year commitment to the cause of Anglo-French solidarity, of which he wrote in 1938, and his belief in the 'solid strength and quality of the French army' and the sober confidence of its leaders as shown in the efficiency of the mobilisation of September 1938. Others on the spot in Northern France and Belgium were not so confident of its qualities. General Brooke, Commander of 2nd Corps, early on had doubts about the French and was shocked at an Armistice Day Service on 11th November 1939 at the slovenliness and ill-discipline of the French soldiers on parade. They were unshaven, their uniforms unkempt, the horses ungroomed and vehicles dirty. On being ordered to turn eyes left, few obeyed. There were French troops who fought bravely as their defence of the perimeter at Dunkirk was to show, but the general condition of the army did not inspire confidence. Even at the highest level, General Gamelin, the Commander in Chief, a dapper sixty-seven year old, despite his attempts prior to the war to reform and reinvigorate the army, sat at his headquarters at the fort of Vincennes without radio means of communication with the French armies and as General de Gaulle said 'completely insulated from current events.' The French political élite were not reconciled to the war into which they thought they had been dragged by the British, and their resentment was often perceptible to those who visited Paris. The Prime Minister, Paul Reynaud, from January 1940, had for example a mistress, the Countess de Pourtales, who was about him always and fiercely anti-British. Later even some of the cabinet like Chautemps were to side against Reynaud with Marshal Petain in desiring an armistice.

In April the Fuehrer struck against Denmark and Norway and Chamberlain despatched on the 16th a force to Namsos and on the 18th to Andalsnes. They were both diversions to allow a main attack by sea on Trondheim with its airfield. That attack was abandoned and by 2nd May the troops had to be withdrawn. On 7th May a debate in the House of Commons led to a vote on 9th May in which large numbers of his own supporters deserted Chamberlain. The Government narrowly won and Chamberlain resigned. Lord Halifax refused the office of Prime Minister offered to him and Winston Churchill succeeded Chamberlain as Prime Minister.

By 9th May both sides in the war had made ready their plans. Feldmarschall von Manstein had evolved a plan of campaign which allowed a simultaneous strike on Holland and Belgium and through the Ardennes on France. The main attack was to be the latter and that through Belgium more of a feint. The British and French for their part had decided that in the event of an attack on Belgium the armies on the Belgian frontier would move up to the River Dyle, east of Brussels, as the main line of defence, while the Belgians stood in the east based on the Albert Canal. The Allied order comprised the French 7th Army on the coast, the BEF, the French 1st Army, and the French 9th Army under General Corap up to the Maginot line, which was manned by 26 divisions under General Prétalet. There was a further army in the Alpes Maritimes of 36 divisions. The move forward to the River Dyle was only to be made if Belgium was attacked, since the strategy was defensive. It was the view of Marshal Petain and others that the Ardennes front was impregnable, since the hilly country and winding roads would not lend themselves to tank and motorised warfare. On that section of the frontier from the River Sambre south to Sedan, the 9th Army was stationed on a 64-mile front, comprising two regular divisions and seven reserve or fortress divisions made up of elderly, untrained and ill-armed troops. The German dispositions comprised the 4th Army under General von Kluge just south of Aachen, the 12th under General von List and then the main army group from Monthermé to Sedan under General von Kleist. The latter had two Corps, the northern containing two Panzer Divisions under General Rheinhardt and the southern under General Guderian with three Panzer Divisions. Rommel had an independent Panzer Division to the north of the Monthermé section of the front. The weight of the army was thus focussed on the section of the French front occupied by the weak French reservist divisions. To the south of von Kleist the 16th Army under General Busch was to act to protect the flank of the latter's advance. The blitzkrieg technique of attack had been perfected in Poland, co-ordinating preliminary bombing, movement of armoured forces in divisions, which were miniature armies in themselves with infantry, artillery and logistic support, air attack on the enemy in direct support and air cover for the ground force. The columns were assembled in early May and stretched 60 miles back from the point of attack in some cases. General Guderian, the main Panzer Commander, had been an active promoter of armoured warfare in the army, inspired by the creation of the British Tanks Corps in 1922 and by the writings of the British Major-General J.C. Fuller, who was responsible for the formulation of much of the concept underlying tank warfare.

At 3.30 am on 10th May the combined attack on the whole front was launched. Bombing began on headquarters, installations and airfields. By 4.30 am General Headquarters of the BEF at Arras was being attacked. At 5.30 am General Billotte, the overall commander, ordered the move forward to the River Dyle in accordance with the plan. The 7th French Army under General Giraud, which was motorised, was ordered north along the coast and on towards Breda in west Holland; the section from Antwerp to Louvain was to be occupied by the Belgians. On their right the BEF held the line south to Wavre with three Divisions in the line and a reserve of three divisions, and on their right south to the River Sambre at Namur was the 1st French Army. From Namur to Sedan General Corap's 9th French army was to go into place, the two regular divisions on the Meuse south of Namur on the left and the unreliable reserve divisions in the centre and right as far as Sedan opposite the Ardennes. To their south were General Huntziger's 2nd Army divisions. The move forward of the BEF was greeted by the Belgians with waving flags, cheers, and gifts of flowers and wine. The first motorised troops completed the 75-mile journey by nightfall and the remainder were in position by the end of the next day. Lord Gort, concerned at the weakness of his armour, asked the war office for the 1st Armoured Division. As the British moved up, there was no attack on them by the Luftwaffe, a fact which General Brooke thought suspicious, but was entirely consistent with the German strategy of leading the British and French armies into a trap in Belgium.

The Luftwaffe had an overpowering force to complement the 2,574 tanks which the Germans had to employ. In May 1940 the air force amounted to almost 4,000 aeroplanes operating from 400 airfields, compared with 89 airfields usable by the RAF. This huge air force was the cutting edge of the blitzkrieg with Holland and Belgium. Airfields were bombed, and communication centres. The Dutch lost 62 out of 125 aircraft on the ground on 10th May and the Belgians had similar losses. Parachutists of the 22nd Airborne Infantry Division and 7th Air Division were dropped to seize bridges over the rivers and canals into Fortress Holland, to which the German columns drove west. Luxemburg was overrun in four hours. The Belgian army, which was larger than the Dutch, waited on the Albert Canal and the Meuse River. On the 10th three bridges were taken by the Germans on the canal and the main fortress of Eben Emael built in the 1930s, was captured by a one-hundred man force of parachutists brought in by glider, who overwhelmed the 1,200 defenders at the cost of six dead. The taking of the fort and bridges meant that the defence line began to crumble.

In the south, as the British and French moved north, the German forces in the Ardennes under General von Kluge and General von List began to roll south-west towards the sector Namur to Sedan. By midnight the next day three Panzer Divisions had arrived within ten miles of Sedan and Rommel with his 7th Panzer Division on the right was the same distance from Dinant. In 36 hours the Germans had gone 50 miles. Behind the shield of the bombers and Stuka Junker 87s, the armour made up to the river on the east side, taking the whole east bank from Namur to Sedan by the 12th. On the 13th from early morning to 3 pm the Luftwaffe and the artillery pounded the pill-boxes and defence points on the west side of the Meuse. At that point under covering fire at Donchery and Bazeilles either side of Sedan German engineers began constructing pontoon bridges across the river; by one o'clock in the morning of the 14th the bridges were ready and the armoured columns began to pound across. There were no concentrated tank formations of size in the French army sufficient to withstand these divisions and despite the promise of reinforcements General Corap's 9th Army began to disintegrate. From that day the Panzer Divisions under General Guderian were to run helter-skelter through France. Sedan was abandoned. Similar pontoon bridges after crashing bombardments were pushed over the River Meuse at Monthermé, Dinant and Givet. The RAF bombers tried relentlessly to destroy these bridges without success.

In front of the German advance in Belgium and France the roads began to fill with refugees of all ages - young, very old and children, struggling with their baggage in every type of vehicle, broken-down cars, lorries, traps, farm vehicles and handcarts. Among them as they passed the Dyle line in the north were groups of terrorised Belgian troops fleeing from the Albert line. General Brooke became nervous of the Belgian troops on his left and of their fighting capacity. On the 11th the 3rd Division led efficiently by General Montgomery, had taken over the line from the Belgians east of Louvain, which on that day was ruthlessly bombed. The BEF was however subject to air attack and on Sunday the 12th troops were machine-gunned at an open air service, which continued, the men merely putting on their tin hats. The Rev. Ted Brabyn, who was bald, felt he should remain bare-headed, but was heartened when the hymn was sung which contained the words 'Cover my defenceless head with the shadow of thy wing'. The Germans had not come up to the Dyle on the 12th but Lord Gort warned London that the RAF support was reduced to 60 aircraft, 10 squadrons of Hurricanes having lost half their aeroplanes, and that there were no aircraft available for tactical reconnaissance. The 12th Lancers, carrying out a reconnaissance to the east of the Dyle, first made contact with the Germans and retired to the line. The Germans were advancing closer. In Holland the armed sweeps pierced the defensive lines and on 13th May the Dutch Government and Queen Wilhelmina left for London. The French 7th Army, realising that it could not sustain the Dutch, drew back to the Antwerp-Louvain line. Continuing resistance in west Holland led the Germans to bomb Rotterdam savagely, destroying 20,000 buildings and killing a thousand people. The Dutch Commander-in Chief was driven to ask for an Armistice.

Despite the limited time which the BEF had had, they had organised their front, taking up position along the railway line east of Louvain, since the river there ran through the middle of the town. On the 14th the town was viciously bombed. Along the Dyle front the British had blown six bridges so that the Germans had a real obstacle to cross. General von Reichenau's 6th Army was to find they were strongly opposed and held. The first Victoria Cross won by the army in France was awarded to Captain Richard Annand of the 2nd Battalion Durham Light

Infantry, who attacked a German bridge-building party with his platoon, and advanced alone in open ground with grenades when the ammunition ran out, hurling them at the Germans. Although wounded, he carried on and after being ordered back, returned to rescue his wounded batman under fire, bringing him to safety in a wheelbarrow. Despite heavy casualties regiments like the Coldstream Guards remained stalwart, and the line, despite passing encroachment, was held. To the south of the British between Wavre and Namur a mass attack fell on General Blanchard's 1st French Army, piercing the front. The Belgian's on the left to the north were, General Brooke thought, shaky. The disintegration of its flanks meant that the resistance and success of the BEF was compromised. In the evening of the 14th General Billotte, the overall commander planned a phased retreat of the armies, first to the line of the River Dendre and then the Escaut. On the 15th and 16th the struggle on the Dyle continued, although the French 1st Army had given way. The latter's withdrawal threatened the BEF's First Corps and its commander became anxious to withdraw. It was however to be action further south which was to dictate the course of events.

It was on 12th May that General Georges had informed General Gamelin of the break through on the Meuse, but Paul Reynaud, the French Prime Minister, did not inform Winston Churchill until 7.30 am on the morning of 14th May. The Prime Minister at once arranged to go to France and was to travel there on the 16th. During the course of his visit he was pressed by the French to send fighter squadrons to French airfields for support of their armies and he moved to order first six and then ten squadrons to go to France. This was obstinately opposed by Air Chief Marshal Sir Hugh Dowding, who regarded a minimum of 25 squadrons as necessary for the defence of Britain. In the end Churchill was not to persist. The French demand for fighters was to continue to bedevil relations with the French until their collapse in mid-June. When Churchill had arrived in Paris, the foreign office officials at the Quai d'Orsay were to be seen under the conference room windows burning secret papers brought out from the office in wheelbarrows. The gap made in the 9th and 2nd French armies now extended to a 50-mile front. The Panzers were at Rozoy, 25 miles west of Donchery by 8 pm. On the 15th General von Kleist and the German High Command had had doubts about the risk to the speeding tank columns moving forward in a narrow probe and ordered a halt, but after argument Guderian was permitted to continue forward 'on reconnaissance'. A similar disagreement was to occur on the 17th but Guderian's reconnaissance remained an unchecked advance flanked on either side by motorised infantry support.

The Panzer Divisions, with Rheinhardt on the German right, driving onto the bases of the BEF which they had left when they moved forward, were lapping the flank of the First Army. In their drive forward to divide the Allied armies towards Amiens and Rheims, the columns at times refuelled at the French filling stations, when their supply tankers lagged. The French Prime Minister had nerved himself to dismiss General Gamelin, who was replaced by General Weygand on the 16th. He had retired in 1935 and had never commanded armies troops in battle. At the conference with Churchill, to whom the deteriorating position was explained, he asked Weygand, 'Ou est La Masse de Manoeuvre? To which the reply came 'Aucune'. There was no mobile reserve left: the 7th Army had gone to Holland and 26 divisions stood immobile in the Maginot Line. Despite this reply Churchill, the Cabinet and the War Office were to persist in demanding from Lord Gort an attack south by the BEF to rejoin the French. The French were dependent principally for movement on the railways and these the Germans persistently bombed. Road movement was impeded by the streaming refugees, hurrying in terror as they were machine-gunned from time to time, while damaged vehicles prevented passage along the roads. The 1st French Armoured Division, for example, had been ordered to move and, as it groped along the crowded, over-flowing roads, ran out of petrol halfway.

By the morning of the 17th General Rheinhardts's Panzer Divisions had reached Landrecies and at 6.30 am were at Le Cateau. The previous night General Billotte had issued orders to retire to the Escaut line. It was time enough for that: that day Brussels was occupied, while the British, division leap-frogging through division, began an orderly retreat. On the German left flank, General de Gaulle had a transient victory in an armoured fight near Laon, but had to retreat for want of infantry back-up. As the Allies in Belgium moved back, the Panzer Divisions and the German army pressed on, arriving at Cambrai and St Quentin on 18th May. Where they came up to the trudging refugee columns, they passed them by and French troops, muddled in among civilians, threw down their rifles. In one place Rommel captured fifteen undamaged French tanks and incorporated them into his division, using the French drivers. Defection on the roads was paralleled by defection in Government and Marshal Petain became Deputy Prime Minister, carrying despondency into the power centre of France. Among the retreating British, without two-way radio, communication became difficult, dependent on personal contact and despatch riders, but a sense of proportion and order remained. Lord Sysonby of the Queen's Royal Regiment received a 'most secret and urgent' message cancelling the meeting of the Old Etonian Society of his division. One private was handed two letters from home, one from the Inland Revenue and the other from the police asking for a donation to a police charity.

In a change of tactics the Luftwaffe had started to bomb the retreating BEF on 18th May and the 48th Division, caught in the open, suffered many casualties. Retreat was hampered by the bombing of towns such as Tournai and the refugees, ever more pitiful and chaotic, as the lunatics were released from asylums, while there appeared in one place elephants escaped from the circus. Dead children, women and old people lay killed by air attack beside and on the roads and tired, thirsty and worn out people sat with their few belongings on the margins. Congestion was everywhere around Lille, Roubaix and Tourcoing. On the 19th the army was back on the River Escaut, having travelled 150 miles in nine days, and it began digging trenches, which they were not to use. On the way bodies of men, both large and small, had become isolated or left behind: the rear of the 3rd Brigade of the 1st Infantry division had to swim a canal, when it arrived after bridges had been blown.

The 19th May brought news that Guderian's Panzer Divisions had reached Amiens, where the RAF Hurricanes took off from their airfields as the tanks reached the perimeter. The Germans were thus 60 miles from the Channel coast. Lord Gort and General Headquarters of the BEF formed the view that plans should be put in hand for an evacuation from Dunkirk. The War Office was informed that in a 'last resort' the army would need to retreat with a view to re-embarkation back to England. Gort realised that with the Germans advancing from north and south the BEF was in danger of encirclement. Winston Churchill in response adhered to the idea of a push south to break the German rear and re-unite with the armies in France proper, which were to move forward north in accordance with a strategy devised by General Weygand. The Royal Navy for its part moved to put into preparation 'Operation Dynamo' under the command of Admiral Ramsey at Dover. That operation involved the gathering under the protection of destroyers, minesweepers and motor torpedo boats of sufficient vessels to lift the army away from Dunkirk, including small inshore boats for beach work. Adolf Hitler at his headquarters told General Jodl that victory and peace was within his grasp.

Worried by the warnings given by Lord Gort, the Chief of the Imperial General Staff Sir Edmund Ironside hurried to France to see for himself the position and met Gort, who firmly refused to turn the army south to break through on the ground that it would endanger the BEF on both sides, subject as they were to strong attack by General von Bock's army group, and leave the flank of the Belgian army, which was already shaken and unnerved, exposed, leading to disaster. Ironside then went on to visit General Billotte, whom he found despairing with broken morale. Exasperated, the six-foot four-inch Ironside took hold of the small French general by his tunic, lifted him and shook him. The reaction which Ironside had to his visit was clearly put – 'God help the BEF, brought to this state by French incompetence'. Nonetheless he pressed the Government order, made without regard to the state of the French army and its partial dissolution, to advance south at Arras. So great was the confusion in the French army as it retreated that on 20th May, General Girard, who had replaced Corap on the 16th, while searching for some of his units and their command posts, drove into men of the German field kitchen attached to 6th Panzer Division and was captured. Lord Gort, knowing that his first responsibility was to protect and preserve the army, did not give full effect to the order to push south, but prepared nonetheless for a stand and limited attack on the Germans at Arras.

On the 20th a force under Major-General Petre to be known as 'Petreforce' was stationed in Arras to hold the town. It comprised only the 1st Battalion of the Welsh Guards, the 5th Battalion Green Howards, 8th Battalion Royal Northumberland Fusiliers and mixed troops from the Pioneer Corps, engineers and military police, a few light tanks and limited artillery, having only one battery of 25-pounders. Supplies and water were limited and the town was being shelled. The southern attack was made on the morning of the 21st from a position near Vimy Ridge to the west of Arras and went south. It comprised 74 tanks of the Royal Tank Regiment of 1st Armoured Brigade, which still remained serviceable after the 120-mile round trip to the River Dyle, of which 58 were Mark I's and 16 Mark II's with their 2-pounder guns. These were supported by two territorial battalions of the Durham Light Infantry from the 50th Division and troops from the 5th Division. The spearhead of the 7th Panzer Division had just passed by and they fell upon a lorry convoy of the SS Totenkampf Division, whose anti-tank shells bounced on the Mark II tanks. The SS troops broke and 400 were taken prisoner by the Durham Light Infantry. General Rommel was however to come up and using the 88mm anti-aircraft guns wreaked havoc on the tanks, some 46 being lost. The Junker 87 Stukas came unopposed to attack the infantry which was returning, and thus ended the probe south. The French had told Lord Gort that they were unable to be ready for the push and no assistance came from the south. After this attack, shelling and bombing became ever stronger on Arrras and the pressure intensified, and on the next day Arras was in flames. Finally, after three days' resistance, Gort ordered the garrison to retire at 1.30 am on 24th May. The shock of the Arras attack again caused the German High Command to hold up Guderian and the Panzer Divisions as he went north from Etaples. Evacuation of Boulogne had begun on 19th May and by the 22nd fighting had begun there, with the port being evacuated on the 23rd. 700 Irish Guards were rescued but three companies of Welsh left.

That same day Calais was surrounded by the speeding Panzer Division and at the moment of their stopping by Feldmarschall von Rundstedt they were within ten miles of Dunkirk. The following day the decision was endorsed by Adolf Hitler. Their line on the south flank of the BEF and the French ran from Gravelines to St Omer, Aire, Béthune and La Bassée. Winston Churchill ordered for Calais a defence to the end in the 'interests of allied solidarity' and strengthened by the Rifle Brigade sent by Gort the town held out until 26th May. The reason for the order given by von Rundstedt and confirmed by Hitler has been debated. The German High Command and the Fuehrer had consistently worried about the velocity of the mobile probe through France but by the time Calais was reached only fifty per cent of the tanks remained serviceable in the Group Commanded by General von Kleist, and thirty per cent in that of General Hoth. The Panzer Divisions were needed moreover for the strike south into France and the thoughts of the military planners were turning to that task. Their renovation and conservation had become issues of importance. Hitler in any event had served in the Flanders area in the First World War with its waterlogged land, mud, streams and drainage canals and was likely to have felt that the area was not one where the cherished Panzer Divisions should be used. Whatever the reason, the two-day delay enabled the evacuation of the BEF to be carried out.

Lord Gort, however, remained under pressure. Winston Churchill seemed incapable of hearing the messages transmitted from the BEF of their plight and, in line with his thirty year-old commitment to the French, tried to order Gort again on the 23rd to organise a drive south to unite with the French. Lord Gort and the Chief of Staff, General Sir Henry Pownall, thought given the situation that the man was mad. Gort pointed out to London that while there was plenty of fuel, there were only three days of food and ammunition left and the army was cut off from their bases in Normandy and Brittany. The front, moreover, being held with an army of 200,000 men, was 100 miles long out of a total of 130. The scarcity of food and ammunition was solved by General Montgomery with his usual flair and audacity, for the 3rd Division, by collecting and moving with a herd of cattle and removing the ammunition being carried on a motionless train left bombed and stationary. The order from Lord Gort to withdraw from Arras was executed throughout the night. In one incident as the transport was withdrawing, Lieutenant Furness, son of Lord Furness, the 1st Battalion the Welsh Guards, was ordered to accompany a convoy of forty lorries with his platoon of bren-gun carriers. The Germans reached the road being used and began to fire on the column with anti-tank guns. Although wounded previously, Furness with three of his carriers advanced, despite no support from some light tanks, which were put out of action, towards the guns in the enemy position. A Welsh Guardsman, known in the Regiment as Williams 17, insisted on travelling on the carrier with his machine gun, even though lying outside the light armour. The three carriers reached the enemy position and circled at close range, inflicting heavy loses on the Germans. Even when the carriers were put out of action, and their three-man crews, including Williams 17, were wounded and killed, Furness continued single-handed until he was killed. The enemy withdrew and the convoy proceeded. Furness received for his bravery the Victoria Cross.

On the same day General von Bock's army group fell on the Belgians on the left wing near Courtrai and advanced towards Menin. He had the potential as the Belgian army fell back of pushing across the 1914-18 battlefields from Ypres to Hazebrouck and of splitting the main British formations, which were defending a line north-east of Lille from Dunkirk. The Allies were now becoming pressed into a 50-mile 'sausage-shaped' corridor to the sea from Douai, to which the

Arras garrison had retreated. On the 25th the Belgians offered varying resistance to the Germans, but their poorly-armed army was dissolving, and as it did, the threat grew on the left (the north) side of the corridor. The new Chief of the Imperial General Staff, Sir John Dill was at last able to persuade Churchill of the serious plight of the BEF and the truth sank in. Lord Gort was able now to order a fighting retreat to the 25-mile Dunkirk perimeter, since he could no longer execute the orders of the Cabinet and the French High Command to go south. The dissolution of the Belgian army resulted in the Belgian Government trying to persuade King Leopold II to leave for London, but he said that he intended to stay with his people.

Admiral Ramsay had seen the flashing guns across the Channel from his Dover office as the Germans reached Bologne and Calais and, given the decision to evacuate, sent Captain Tennant with a dozen officers and 120 ratings to organise the landward arrangements. He reported to the French Commander at Dunkirk, Admiral Abrial, entombed in his Headquarters in Bastion 32 under thirty foot of concrete, where he was to remain during the action, and then proceeded to assess the situation. The beaches to the east of Dunkirk were at low tide one mile wide, backed by sand dunes, and while usable by little boats were not directly accessible by large ones. The docks were devastated by bombing, and from the oil storage tankers rose a column of black smoke towering above the town. Leading into the harbour there were however two moles capable of berthing larger ships. The west mole of stone was unusable by reason of the oil depot fire but the east mole, stretching a mile out to sea, could be used. It was made of wood planking and was wide enough for about four men abreast. It disadvantage was a high tidal rise and fall of sixteen feet, and a rip tide which did not render berthing easy. Tennant recommended the use of the mole and from it the evacuation was to begin. Ramsey had on becoming Flag Officer at Dover worked to restore the harbour and build up the destroyer and minesweeper force there.

Larger ships were collected to carry troops and on 13th May the requisition had been ordered of all vessels between 30 and 100 feet in size which had not been offered for the evacuation. Ferry boats were assembled from the Channel routes, the crossing to the Isle of Wight, the west coast and the Isle of Man. The fleet of Thames pleasure boats, mainly paddle steamers of charm, with names like Crested and Golden Eagle and Royal Daffodil were called in. Port of London tugs were collected, the London County Council Hopper craft and the London Fire Brigade's tender Massey Shaw, named after the Victorian fire-fighter hero. Trawlers and drifters were to come too. The extensive coastal shoals of France limited the sea routes to three; the longest took the ships north to the Kwinte Buoy off Ostend and round the North Goodwin and was 87 nautical miles (Route Y), the next was a mid-route of 55 nautical miles north from the coast between

Gravelines and Dunkirk and then to the North Goodwin buoy (Route X), and the last (Route Z), the shortest at 39 nautical miles, along the coast and direct across the channel to Dover.

By 25th May the German drive against the Belgian army had reached Menin and the BEF was scattered in a rough circle from north of Aire and Béthune in the south, to south and north-east of Lille in the vicinity of Roubaix. The collapse of the Belgians meant that a void was opening west of Ypres towards the sea. The British Divisions, in order to meet the fluid situation, had to be moved and used to defend new parts of the corridor line as the Germans came on and their allies gave way. At the vital Comines end of the Ypres-Comines canal, where the Belgians had been pressed back through Menin, the 50th Division, under severe attack, stood firm. On their left in the void was to move Montgomery's 3rd Division. The 5th Division was brought up from south of Lille to the perimeter south of Ypres. All these changes meant long and forced marches at night. The shift made by Montgomery on the night of 27th May for example, was made close up behind the front line in total darkness and by the morning of May 28th he was in position. The problem of Belgian collapse was to become acute when King Leopold II asked for an armistice at 5 pm to take effect by midnight on 27th May. The French 1st Army was still holding in part east of Lille, but French soldiers were joining the refugees and moved back towards the coast. The River Iser and the Ypres-Comines canal line was a vital defence while the strung-out divisions moved back on Dunkirk. It was held with bravery and fierce determination, some units such as the 3rd Battalion of the Grenadier Guards counter-attacking.

In the south the 3rd Corps, which had been spread out, protecting individual towns like Cassel and Hazebrouck, fell back but continued to hold open the eastward section of the corridor against the 5th and 7th Panzer Divisions from the south. Even on the 27th however, Churchill was suggesting to Lord Gort to make a counter-attack towards Calais. Whitsunday (26th May) was to be a sombre day in Britain, as the public began to be told of the disaster occurring in Belgium and France. Churches were full for the National Day of Prayer and King George VI attended the service at Westminster Abbey which was packed by its overflowing congregation, while 2,000 people waited outside. The War Cabinet approved Lord Gort's decision to retire and the Government was told that the greater part of the army would be lost, it being anticipated that not more than 45,000 could be evacuated over two nights. The French Prime Minister, Paul Reynaud, was told of the decision and, as recorded by General Spears, Liaison Officer to the French Government in Paris, General Weygand sarcastically remarked that the British could not withstand the call of the beaches.

The capitulation of King Leopold II and the Belgians made the safe retreat to Dunkirk of the army even more essential and starkly urgent. The order was given to the troops making for the defended perimeter on 28th May to destroy all weapons, equipment and stores being abandoned. The aim of the evacuation was so constrained by the danger threatened that only men were to be lifted away. Everything was to be destroyed and the army began to smash the radiators of its vehicles as they were left, crush or immobilise land weapons, burn and destroy all supplies, even down to maps and blow up or mangle the tanks and the guns. For regular soldiers long schooled to cherish their arms, the execution of this order was soul searching. A gunner, for example, of the 2nd Royal Artillery Medium Regiment, ordered to destroy his gun and having done so, collapsed on the ground sobbing bitterly and had to be carried away to the lorry taking him to Dunkirk. Lord Gort went to Blanchard, the French Commander of the Ground Forces who had succeeded General Billotte when the latter was killed in a car crash, and informed him of the order of evacuation. Blanchard was horrified: the French conception was that Dunkirk would be held as a fortress and defended.

The split between the French and English views was to be a source of tension in the ensuing days, although nonetheless the French put their surviving troops to work to defend the place and its perimeter with intent to hold it. By 28th May the BEF was drawn back to Armentieres, while its northern flank still held and, as it retreated, the troops marched into the Dunkirk area or found their way across country. The retreat continued, hampered endlessly by the destruction of the towns and villages and the teeming refugees. Poperinghe, a crucial village on the route from Ypres, became choked, the main street blocked. The Coldstream Guards were led through along a side street by a team of Belgian boy scouts. As they moved back, the low-flying Messerschmidts and Stukas harried the troops. There were no anti-aircraft guns and any reply was only by rifle or Bren gun. Brigadier Martin Beckwith-Smith told the 1st Guards Brigade that, when they used their guns, to shoot high like taking a pheasant. As they marched the men sang, joked and moved without haste – those that fell from want of sleep were lifted and dragged along by their mates. General Brooke described the troops as having an 'indescribable quality of detachment and staunchness.' The British solder, he said could 'sympathise with misery, he can rub shoulders with demoralised allies and suffer on that account: he can be subjected to untold fatigue and hardship in the face of disaster, and yet none of these factors affect his balance'.

Units tried to keep together, carrying their unit flags and mascots: a signals unit entered the Dunkirk perimeter with a large underground railway sign from the Angel Station in London. By 30th May the army was within the perimeter defence. Land outside the perimeter had been opened to the sluices and was flooded in places to depths of three feet. At the western end the French 16th Corps held the line south-east to Bergues, the 1st and 46th Divisions with the 126th Brigade of the 42nd Division held the west of the line along the Bergues-Furnes Canal, the 50th, 3rd and 4th Divisions the eastern sector to Nieuport. The 3rd Corps was held towards the beach, where its evacuation was planned first. They were to be followed as the perimeter contracted by the 2nd Corps of the 3rd, 4th and 5th Divisions and finally by the 1st Corps holding the western sector. Lord Gort established his headquarters in the Belgian King's villa at La Panne, which had a telephone line to London, although he could no longer get into touch with Paris.

The Royal Naval operation had commenced on 25th May. The first ship away loaded with 1,000 troops was the Queen of the Channel, a ferry boat. On the way back from Dover it was bombed, but its crew were rescued. The ships started to come in a stream to the East Mole, Naval vessels by day and passenger and other vessels at night. There were 40 destroyers out of 202 available for the Dunkirk operation and it had not originally been intended that they should carry men, but it was almost immediately obvious that they needed to do so. Apart from the East Mole they were to stand off the eastern beaches, while the small cutters and craft went in to bring the men out to them and any passenger ships. There was no food and water on the dunes, but the sand gave the waiting men a limited protection from bombing and machine gunning, since its softness damped down the effects of the explosive. On the 27th 15,000 bombs and 60,000 incendiaries were dropped on Dunkirk. The east mole was hit and a wide break was made, which had to be bridged by planks. The Royal Air Force, contrary to the view of the soldiers on the ground, was engaged at Dunkirk but in order to make best use of the fighter squadrons they were massed together and thus there were long intervals between their appearances. The beaches from the sea looked as if they were covered with lines of woods stretching in from the water, as the men patiently queued under the control of the naval shore parties to be taken aboard, dispersing and diving into the sand when the Luftwaffe came over.

Access to the boats on the beaches depended on wading out in the sea, often with torn and missing uniforms, although some tried to go out wearing their greatcoats and carrying their rifles, only to be swept away by the surf. Access along the mole in the slow-moving columns meant waiting under fire, struggling across the planks bridging the bomb gaps and at low tide dealing with the 16-foot drop down. A small number of the army behaved badly: some military policemen in the early days tended to desert their posts and go on board, as did some Royal Army Service Ambulance Drivers after they had threaded their way with the wounded through the town. One Lieutenant who jumped a queue on the beach had to be shot by a naval officer. The numbers taken increased daily. On 28th May Captain Tennant signalled Dover that more ships were needed as the stream of troops became ever more limitless. On the 28th a greater effort was made – eleven destroyers becoming involved. The Sabre made three trips backwards and forwards that day, the Montrose carried 1,200 on one trip, including wounded, and served tea and biscuits. Quite apart from attempts to rush the queues, the naval parties had trouble with the small boats being rushed in the shallows and with attempts to take personal baggage on board. On the 28th the naval operation embarked 18,527 men. That day and on the 29th cloudy skies made the Luftwaffe attacks difficult, but shelling by artillery from the perimeter continued.

In the night on Route Y at Kwinte Buoy, the Wakeful was torpedoed by the German Motor Torpedo boat, Schnellboot 22, while the Grafton was damaged by the U32. 640 soldiers were lost in the Wakeful, which sank in fifteen seconds. Confusion among the ships present led to the Lydd opening fire on the Grafton, which sank. Dover command was on the 29th to collect a maximum force, sending all the destroyers and larger vessels. At 3.30 pm the first German raid came, when present at the mole were the destroyers Jaguar and Grenade, six trawlers, the paddle steamer Crested Eagle and two troopships, Fenella and Canterbury. At 4.30 pm a further attack was made disrupted by the RAF. Jaguar had left before the third raid at 6 pm damaged the Grenade. The crew climbed out astern and the burning Grenade was towed to sea on fire, where it exploded. Fenella went down at its moorings. Crested Eagle pulled away, but was hit as she steamed away and drifted into the eastern beaches burning. 300 soldiers were lost. Jaguar was bombed, as was Canterbury, and both limped back to Dover. The list of losses for the day grew – including Gracie Fields whose engine room was hit by a bomb, exploding and scalding soldiers and crew, the Normania, Lorinia and Mona Queen. The carnage led Admiral Ramsay to remove the eight modern destroyers from service in the evacuation.

However, 50,000 troops were lifted that day from the jetty and the beaches. Lord Gort and Admiral Abrial met and once more the issue of full evacuation of the BEF was the subject of bitter discussion. Gort was in touch with London and told Sir John Dill, the C.I.G.S, that he was responsible to save the BEF and every Frenchman taken displaced a British soldier. Churchill reminded him that it was joint operation and the French should be evacuated: this Gort thought amounted to unhelpful political interference. Thousands of British troops remained in depressions and foxholes in the sands, waiting while being machine-gunned, as the German fighters moved along the beach, even machine-gunning wounded collected round a Red Cross flag. The need for more space in ships led Admiral Ramsay to seek to recruit more ships. At nine o'clock that evening on the BBC News the appeal went out for the small ships not already taken and volunteers to man them. Ramsay thought too that Tennant needed his authority bolstering and sent out Rear Admiral Wake-Walker at 8 pm on the Esk. Throughout the next day Wake-Walker inspected the mole and beaches, changing his flag between six ships, finally ending on the Keith. That night he dined with Lord Gort at La Panne, his uniform soaked from his wade in, on champagne and tinned fruit salad. He was to spend the next three days tirelessly and indefatigably organising the ships to remove the troops, deploying them along the beaches. A large-scale attack organised by the Germans massed along the Yser was broken by a Royal Air Force bombing attack by eighteen Blenheim bombers and six Fleet Air Arm

Albatrosses, while the 50th Division withstood attack along the Bergues-Furnes canal. With the need to speed the pace of withdrawal the creation of sea jetties was improvised around La Panne. Ten were made. At low tide vehicles were driven out across the sands and then abandoned in lines. The Royal Engineers roped them together firmly and stood by to keep them in being until 1st June.

On the 30th the 'little ships' previously collected at Sheerness arrived to begin their work, which has gone into legend. They had both naval and civilian crews, many owners volunteering to take their prized boats to the war. There were eleven Skylarks, nine Port of London tugs, cockle boats from Canvey Island and the Thames, drifters, yachts and motorboats with names like Gladys and Dumpling. Some came poorly equipped for sea without compasses. The volunteers were of all ages and occupations. Sir Thomas Lipton's great racing yacht Endeavour was there. On a 58-foot power cruiser came Captain Lightoller, made famous as the courageous Third Officer of the Titanic, who acted to save so many, when the liner hit the iceberg and sank in the Atlantic in April 1912. He was aided by his son and an eighteen year-old sea scout. There were boys of fourteen as crew like Albert Barnes, the galley boy on the Thames tug Sun 12. They all came across a calm sea to brave air attack and gunfire to save the men who fought for Britain, spurred not by ambition but deep love of country. In and out of the beaches went the small boats, delivering their loads to larger vessels, or in some cases returning to England, only to return again. At the end of the first day 53,828 troops had been rescued, of which 29,512 were taken off the beaches. The ferries which had worked for two or three days non-stop had crews who had become dispirited and exhausted and they began to refuse to return. They were seized and naval crews put on board. Nineteen RNLI lifeboats took part but the Hythe crew refused to go. The Dungeness, Hythe and Woolmer boats were taken and the Hythe crew subsequently dismissed.

On the 31st Lord Gort was ordered home as the Government thought it unsuitable for him to be captured. With him were to come General Brooke, General Montgomery and General Leese. He was to be succeeded by General Alexander, who was to command the rearguard which by the end of 1st June was to amount to no more than 5,000 British soldiers. 60,000 British troops were taken off between 30 May and 1st June. Gort, like all others, was allowed no baggage and was to be seen stripping off the Victoria Cross, Military Cross and other ribbon decorations from his abandoned uniforms. He went aboard the minesweeper Hebe, which waited to pick up men and afterwards boarded a Motor Torpedo Boat, arriving in Dover in the morning at 6.20 am. General von Knechler had been given the task by the German High Command to push back the British; he had ten Divisions. The British 3rd, 4th and 5th Divisions retired for evacuation from Nieuport and the 50th took their place further west on the new frontier line. La Panne was abandoned and the troops moved along the beach as the Germans shelled the coast and the La Panne Road. The canal where the 1st Division and the 126th Brigade of the 42nd Division were left was attacked. By dawn on 2nd June there were only 4,000 British troops left, armed with seven anti-aircraft guns and twelve anti-tank guns.

Winston Churchill met Paul Reynaud on 31st May and, although the French had opposed evacuation, wishing to hold Dunkirk as a fortress, and had further made little effort to provide shipping, the latter demanded to know why so few French had been evacuated, some 15,000 only as compared with 150,000 British. Churchill assured him that he would give orders that henceforth the troops taken would be divided half and half. Alexander visited Admiral Abrial in his Bastion with little better result than had been achieved by Gort, and told London that he expected to close down the evacuation on the night of June 1st to June 2nd. The bombing and machine gunning persisted all day as the troops moved on to the beaches. 31 ships were sunk and 11 damaged. The Keith sunk in shallow water with her mast showing, the crew swimming round her awaiting rescue singing 'Roll out the Barrel, we'll have a barrel of fun'. 61,557 were taken off on 1st June, the predominant number - 35,013, being French. That day the destroyers Havant and Basilisk were sunk and Worcester, Ivanhoe and Vivacious damaged. The RAF were not much in evidence on 1st June. Sir Hugh Dowding was worried about his need to preserve a force for the defence of Britain and he was reluctant to send his valuable Spitfires and Hurricanes in large numbers to do battle. Losses had not been insubstantial: in the nine days of Operation Dynamo 145 planes were lost overall, 99 from Fighter Command, including 42 Spitfires.

The rescuing crews were not wildly enthusiastic about taking on board 'the frogs' as they called then, who tried to bring aboard vast quantities of luggage and personal possessions. Argument was heated as they were forced to abandon them. On 2nd June the Royal Navy did not think a day operation sustainable. Rear Admiral Wake-Walker was in Dover to discuss with Ramsay the arrangements to abstract the rearguard. A large collection of small craft were to embark soldiers from the beach and the larger vessels, the cross-channel steamers from the moles. At 7 pm he was in Dunkirk, having travelled on a motor-anti-submarine boat flying his flag made from a cleaning cloth painted with red paint, where he met Captain Tennant, whose helmet had stuck upon it in silver paper S.N.O. (Senior Naval Officer) with sardine oil. Wake-Walker met the ships coming in and directed them to their picking-up points. The embarkation began after dark, about 9 pm and the remainder of the BEF boarded, the last troops leaving being mainly from 146th and 126th Infantry Brigade and the remnants of 1st Division, which had been on the Bergues-Furnes Canal. The 2nd June had been a fine Sunday and a service was held for the troops on the beach among the dunes at Malo-Les Bains, the congregation being dispersed by dive bombing. Two hospital ships were sent that day for the wounded, painted white with conspicuous red crosses, the Worthing and the Paris. The Worthing was attacked by twelve Struka dive bombers and had to turn back; the Paris was later sunk off the French coast. General Alexander waited himself to the absolute end, wishing to ensure the British under his command were evacuated and that all stragglers were collected. The last to come marching in were 300 or so Scots who boarded the destroyer Codrington. At 11.30 pm on 2nd June, as Alexander and Captain Tennant left, the latter signalled to Dover 'BEF evacuated'. Operation Dynamo was officially over.

Part of the 1st French Army had been surrounded east of Lille on 29th May, but about 40,000 French troops remained within a shortened perimeter at Dunkirk. The number of French boarding on the night of 2nd June was limited and part of the rescue fleet went away empty. It was decided that on the night of 3rd June one more attempt should be made to rescue them. The crews of the naval ships and the civilian vessels were at the limits of endurance and Admiral Ramsay felt that he could not order them to go. He called for volunteers and ten transports, six destroyers, twelve mine-sweepers, two yachts, a gunboat, ten drifters, five scouts and one tug offered themselves, as did a large numbers of boats and small craft. The embarkation was complicated by large numbers of French small craft blocking the harbour but before daylight 26,746 men had been lifted. The delays meant that it was almost daylight before the British ships finally left, but they were able to make their way safely to Dover in the fog. By 3 am the Germans had started to enter the town and on 4th June it surrendered.

In all 224,320 British troops had been evacuated and some 68,111 killed, wounded or made prisoners of war, including 900 of the 51st Division, which had been sent to the Maginot Line and were trapped in France at St Valery-en-Caux on the coast after the German breakthrough on the Somme. 63,879 vehicles were lost: 2,472 guns, 76,000 tons of ammunition and half a million tons of supplies and stores. The British army had suffered a huge disaster, but it was still an army in being. It had not been destroyed. The Royal Navy could look with pride on the success of Operation Dynamo. The instinct of the British people was sound in that, when the returning troops came shame-faced home fearing public resentment, they were greeted as the trains steamed back from Dover to the bases with flags, cheers, tea and buns at stations like Paddock Wood, when the train stopped. At no time had the British not defended their front and given way. They had showed their mettle. Feldmarschall Keitel was to remark as a result that every division of the BEF was worth three or four French. Of the total of 693 British ships engaged, 226 were sunk. 6 destroyers were lost and 19 damaged, 7 minesweepers sunk, 8 personnel ships and 5 hospital carriers, 7 tankers and drifters and 170 small craft.

In his statement to Parliament Churchill was at pains to make the point that 'We must be very careful not to assign to this deliverance the attributes of a victory. Wars are not won by evacuation.' Even he thought, however, that there was a victory in the success of the RAF which it was thought had destroyed four times the number of aircraft shown in German records. In fact it is reasonable to assign to the whole the attributes of a victory, for if the object of war is to achieve some military or political objective, the Germans failed to achieve either the one or the other. The combined operation of staunch defence and daring evacuation meant that the army was not destroyed and the loss of its weapons did not force Britain to make peace. The contribution of Lord Gort, that 'brave, honourable simple' man as General Brooke called him, should not be discounted. He held to the need to save the BEF and resisted the political interference urging on him courses which he knew lacked reality.

Subsequently in June the force of events was to rush forward in France. Once the BEF was driven from the continent, the object was to force France out of the war. 113,906 non-British troops had been evacuated, the vast majority being French who returned to France. South of the Somme, Laon, Rethel line there still remained about 140,000 British troops, including the 57th Division. The German attack began on 5th June, spearheaded on the Somme section of the front by Generals von Kluge's and von Reichenau's Panzer Divisions. The period to 17th June was to witness the progressive collapse of the French Government. There were already many defeatists among the political elite of France, some indeed who looked forward to a society on a Fascist basis, but the infection was to spread to the Government urged on by the Commander in Chief of the French army, General Weygand. The Germans were to continue their blitzkrieg tactics on the fighting troops, but were restrained in bombing factories and towns, although they attacked the car factories in Paris. The French had lost their prime industrial areas, save the coal and iron-producing area around Metz. Much of the air force had been destroyed on the ground. On 4th June Prime Minister Reynaud had forwarded a request from General Vuillemin, the head of the French Air Force, asking for half the fighter force based in England to be sent to France.

Anxious as Winston Churchill was to help, and strongly as he was committed - almost blindly - to France, it was a request to which he could not accede. He had already received from the joint Chiefs of Staff a memorandum to the effect that while the air force was in being, the Royal Navy and the air force would be able to prevent a sea-borne invasion of Britain, but that the crux of the matter was air superiority. Churchill was content however for the British fighters based in England to assist the French at the front. For example, 144 fighters were engaged on 6th June and bombers made 59 sorties over objectives determined by French High Command. On the 7th two squadrons of fighters were added to the three already in France south of the Somme. Given the requirement specified by Sir Hugh Dowding to retain the core fighter force, and the losses at Dunkirk, this was the limit of support possible.

On 11th June, the French Government being retired to Tours, Winston Churchill flew to meet the French Cabinet. The Germans on the 9th had penetrated the lines at Rethel and made progress in the Argonne. The meeting with the French was uneasy. Churchill reiterated the determination of Britain to fight on; apart from Reynaud the atmosphere among the French was pessimistic. Weygand delivered a report with the heavy implication that the battle was lost. The Germans were penetrating the defence line east of Paris based on the Lower Seine, breaking through elsewhere and there were no reserves. He ended by adding 'C'est la dislocation' – the break-up. The French demanded that the British send in troops and there was the familiar demand for the airforce to be brought to France, Weygand asking for every British fighter plane to be sent. Churchill was not prepared to deliver the precious fighter squadrons, saying that in any event eight to nine were in action everyday. The troops were not available, as the British army had lost all its equipment.

Three divisions were to be sent however, the 52nd Division, which in fact had landed already at Cherbourg, the 1st Canadian Division and 3rd Division. Reynaud told Churchill that if the defence line broke a political decision would need to be made. There was to be another meeting on the 12th before which the British learned that, despite a joint decision to attack Italy including by air bombing, General Vuillemin had ordered the French air force to block the runway of an aerodrome in the south of France with lorries, where Blenheim bombers were taking off to bomb Turin and Milan in reprisal for the bombing of Malta. General Vuillemin, who consistently pressed for more planes to be sent from England, was to be highly decorated by the pro-German Vichy Government of Marshal Petain. At the meeting Air Marshal Barrett explained that he had six squadrons of bombers in France and five of fighters, but only 70-80 bombers were fit for operations and 50-60 fighters. The decision on sending more aircraft was again raised, but Churchill firmly stressed that it would be a fatal act of folly to deprive Britain of the force essential for its defence. It was agreed to ask the United States for help. Churchill also asked to be immediately informed of any change in the position.

On 13th June Churchill came again to France, having returned to London, to meet Reynaud at Tours. The Prime Minister was asked, in view of the Anglo-French treaty not to make peace separately, what might be the attitude of the British to an armistice sought by France. First, Churchill indicated that Britain could not help because of the reverse in Belgium, which resulted from the BEF following the strategy adopted by the French High Command of advancing to the River Dyle. He again stressed the resolve to fight on. He avoided however giving his consent to an armistice and suggesting awaiting the outcome of the appeal to President Roosevelt. On 13th June the French Government prepared to move to Bordeaux; on the 14th June Paris was occupied. On the 13th in the French Cabinet Marshal Petain supported Weygand's demand for an armistice. On the

14th Churchill sent Reynaud a pledge to fight on in indissoluble union until the war was won. On the 15th the Germans had reached Le Havre in the west and attacked in the east towards Metz and Nancy. Reynaud asked Churchill again to consent to an investigation with Germany and Italy as to the terms of an armistice and Roosevelt answered Reynaud pledging supplies of weapons and support, but indicating that there would be no armed intervention.

The climax was reached on Sunday 16th June. The French Cabinet argued about whether to fight on in the Empire and how to resolve the problem of the future of the French Navy - whether to order it to leave France. In the afternoon Churchill sent Reynaud an offer approved by Cabinet for the 'indissoluble union' of Britain and France, of its Government, Parliament, institutions, defence forces and people for the period of the war. In order to give Reynaud support, Churchill had allowed his commitment to France to go beyond the practicalities of reality. Even the Ambassador and General Sir Edward Spears, as he admits in his memoirs, doubted at the time the reality of a joint Anglo-French Government, but the idea of a joint Parliament reduced them to irresistible laughter.

That day Reynaud resigned and Marshal Petain became Prime Minister. On 17th June, the Germans had reached a line running from Caen to Le Mans, Orleans, Le Creusot and Chalons. The army had in many places become a rabble trudging south. British officers arriving at Bordeaux had seen army ambulances carrying drunken women, soldiers without arms and without officers, most of whom seem to have vanished leaving their men. Marshal Petain's request for an armistice was agreed and signed on 25th June at Compiegne in the same railway carriage in which the Germans were forced to sign the 1918 armistice. The carriage was taken away to Berlin, where it was destroyed in the war, and the French have put a replica in its place. Hitler was present for the signing and the cameras caught him in a little jig of exultation. The north of France and the west coast were occupied; the French navy remained in its ports, and Marshel Petain went to Vichy to establish his government. The army laid down its arms, although units fought on in the Maginot line until 22nd June.

Sir Alan Brooke had foreseen the debacle on 13th June and the 1st Canadian Division and 3rd Division were not sent on to France. Churchill however resisted the embarkation of the British still in France until the night of the 14th, when he was persuaded by General Brooke of the need to do so. He wanted the 52nd Division to remain for moral support to the French and Brooke told him frankly that it was impossible for a corpse to have feelings and that the French army was to all intents and purposes dead. Nonetheless in the planning of the evacuation there was interference from London. It was not for example, until the morning of 16th June that the waiting two brigades of the 52nd Division were permitted to take ship at Cherbourg. Brooke tried to organise his commands at the Brittany ports to hurry the evacuation. One of the brigades of the 52nd Division was with the

French 10th Army and was told by Brooke to retreat to Cherbourg. The supporting troops – 7,000 at Le Mans, 65,000 at Nantes and 20,000 at Rennes, were ordered to the ports. Brooke was not told of the request for an armistice by the French on 17th June, and only learnt of it from London. The French abandoned the British forces to their fate and left them to extricate themselves. As Brooke said 'they never even had the decency to inform me officially'. The Royal Navy pushed on with loading the troops. A disaster occurred off St Nazaire that day when the Cunard liner Lancastria was bombed and sank in twenty minutes. It had taken aboard 9,000 British personnel, most of whom were lost. The effort continued. Brooke and his staff had to wait for a convoy from the Bay of Biscay being escorted by HMS Cambridgeshire and spent 18th June waiting in a tug, the Sun. The evacuation was to take from 16th to 24th June and 163,225 troops reached safety, including nearly 19,000 Poles. Despite the disaster it was greeted in Britain with relief. King George VI wrote to Queen Mary to the effect that personally he felt happier now that we had no allies to whom we had to be polite and whom we had to pamper, and Air Chief Marshal Sir Hugh Dowding told Lord Halifax, 'Thank God we're now alone.' There could be no more pressure on him to yield up the Royal Air Force.

There is no doubt of the brilliance of the victory over France achieved by the German Army. They had used the full integration of ground and air power to win and had fought with their armoured forces a campaign marked by its velocity. They suffered for the conquest of France, 27,074 dead, 18,384 missing and 110,034 wounded, a figure so limited as to be part of their achievement, if compared with their losses at Verdun alone in the First World War. Despite the French complaints about the contribution of the Royal Air force to the fighting, the air force from 10th May to 16th June lost 959 planes, of which 453 were fighters, 386 Hurricanes and 67 Spitfires. In manpower 1,382 men were lost, killed, wounded or captured, including 534 pilots.

General Viscount Gort went on to be Commander in Chief in Malta in 1941 while it was under severe attack. He was made a Fieldmarshal in 1943. General Brooke in December 1941 became Chief of the Imperial General Staff. He was promoted Fieldmarshal in 1944 and became Baron Alanbrooke in September 1945 and later was created a Viscount. General Alexander went on to command in Tunis and Italy. In 1944 he was promoted Fieldmarshal. In 1946 he became a Viscount and until 1952 Governor-General of Canada, when he became Earl Alexander of Tunis. General Montgomery was to command at El Alamein, in Tunisia and Sicily, Normandy and in Germany. He became a Fieldmarshal and a Viscount as Viscount Montgomery of Alamein.

The 3rd Viscount Alanbrooke, the 2nd Earl Alexander of Tunis and the 2nd Viscount Montgomery were all ejected from the House of Lords in 1999.

3rd June 1653
The Battle of the Gabbard Bank

After the execution of King Charles I in January 1649 Parliament embarked on the rapid creation of an effective Navy. Between 1649 and 1651 41 new warships were added to the fleet, which had numbered only 39, and about half of the income of government was devoted to naval expenditure. The ships built celebrated the triumph of the Puritan Parliament in the Civil War; and the Naseby, the flagship, for instance, had a figurehead of Oliver Cromwell on horseback trampling under foot, according to Evelyn the diarist, the nations of England, Scotland, Ireland, France, Scotland and the Netherlands. By 1660 some 221 ships had been built. The Navy was built under the impulse of the need to protect England from invasion, and to secure the ability to forward the security of its commercial sea-borne commerce. In 1648 the Treaty of Westphalia had ended a thirty year-long continental war and freed the combatants to pursue other interests. There was a threat of a war with Sweden but the main challenge was the Dutch. There were a number of issues which arose (see the Battle of Portland, February 20th 1652) culminating in an inconclusive engagement off Dover between Blake and Tromp, in which Blake had probably fired first. War was declared on 8th July 1652. That summer and autumn the two fleets were involved in a number of engagements, which gave no real advantage to either side. The English government decided that the navy should be made more efficient and in December 1652 published the first Articles of War regulating food, pay, prize money and other matters. A 'General at Sea' was appointed to succeed the position of 'Lord High Admiral' and was put into a commission of three – Edward Popham, Richard Deane and Robert Blake. These issued instructions for the warships to attack in 'line ahead', and that was made obligatory.

In May 1653 the Dutch left port, firstly to escort a large convoy of merchantmen north around Scotland, and second to seek out the English fleet. The command was in the hands of Tromp, a skilful sailor and courageous fighter. His seamanship and tactical grasp had been expertly shewn at Cap Gris Nez in the Battle of Portland, and he knew how to save his fleet in any engagement, where needed, to fight another day. The excursion into the North Sea embodied the conflicting objectives of Dutch policy, namely, to give protection to the convoys and yet to destroy their opponent's navy, objectives which were, given their resources, incompatible. Tromp believed in the latter.

Blake was ill ashore when the English fleet set out to search the North sea for the Dutch. Command was therefore given to Deane and General Monk. Monk, who was born in 1608, knew nothing of seamanship, but was a successful general well experienced in the use of gunnery and both cavalry and infantry, knowledge which was of use while naval battles still involved the boarding of ships and hand-to-hand fighting. At the outbreak of the Civil War in 1642 he was a soldier, but would not fight the King, and spent three years in the Tower of London. After the King's execution he was willing to take up arms for Parliament. Oliver Cromwell appointed him to command his regiment and he distinguished himself at the Battle of Dunbar, going on to take Perth, Stirling and Dundee. The regiment took part in the restoration of King Charles II in 1660 under Monk, who was a principal actor in that event. Monk was then created Duke of Albemarle and the regiment joined the Royal bodyguard as the Coldstream Guards. Monk was described by the Earl of Ailesbury as 'naturally of heavy parts and illiterate'. He did have real physical courage, visiting pest houses in London, where he remained during the plague in 1665. When at sea and his ship beached, he terrified James II's gentlemen volunteers on board by threatening to blow up the magazine if there was a threat of capture by the Dutch. He married a seamstress while in the Tower, Nan Clarges, whom Samuel Pepys, the diarist, traduced. After a visit to Albemarle's house, Pepys noted: 'The Duke has sorry company, dirty dishes, bad meat and a nasty wife at table'.

For a week the English fought the Dutch in the mists of the North Sea and finally sighted them at twilight on 1st June. Tromp was found at the southern end of the Gabbard Bank about 40 miles east of Harwich: he had 98 ships and five fireships. Monk had one hundred and five. At daylight on 2nd June in a light northerly wind Monk and Deane, on the flagship Resolution, began to bear down with the fleet towards the Dutch. The plan was to come upon them on a tack and at a two cannon-shot distance put themselves in line in order to close at half-cannon shot. At 11 am the Dutch fleet was finally within range and a savage bombardment began. General Deane was almost immediately killed by a chainshot, a weapon comprising two cannon balls linked by a chain. Monk took off his cloak and had the mangled body carried away. The battle fleets became engaged in a running melée all afternoon until six o'clock when Tromp began to use the wind to disengage. The Dutch had lost two ships and many were seriously damaged. Frigates shadowed their fleet and the English used the time to effect repairs. During the evening Blake joined the fleet from the Thames with 20 ships.

On the morning of 3rd June Tromp was in a difficult position, low in ammunition and faced by superior forces. He tried to get to the west in a slight change of wind, but it died away and he was left with flapping sails. At noon the fleet re-engaged, firing at long range. The English had therefore an advantage, as their guns were superior to those of the Dutch. The Dutch were scattered, but the action was confused in the pall of smoke lying on the sea. Tromp, indeed, could not detail (in his report) the battle because of the smoke. For four hours the fight went on but the wind turning west south-west, Tromp was able to extract himself and make for Wielings, where the English heavier ships could not follow, and home. The Dutch had lost 19 ships, 11 taken and six sunk and had some 3,000 men killed. The English lost one ship, a captain and 200 seamen. The English fleet followed the Dutch and began a blockade of the Flei and Texel.

The war and the interruption of trade had seriously affected Holland: commerce was stilled and there was a shortage of corn and herrings, a staple diet. After the Battle of the Gabbard Bank, the States-General sent delegates to London to discuss peace. Oliver Cromwell was in favour of peace, but the anti-Dutch party in Parliament was opposed to any settlement. Led by Praisegod Barebones, a leading Puritan member, they resolved that 'the seas should be secured ... in order to prepare for the coming of Christ'. After another closely-fought sea battle, peace was finally made in April 1654 by the Treaty of Westminster.

3rd June 1665

The Battle of Lowestoft

In 1660 Parliament in concert with General Monk entered into the Treaty of Breda providing for the restoration of the King after the Civil War, and the Commonwealth. Edward Montagu, a Parliamentary General, brought Charles II to England from Holland in the Naseby, renamed the Royal Prince. The voyage was attended by great festivities and Montagu was created first Earl of Sandwich. A new Parliament was elected and Charles II had for want of money to pursue a policy of retrenchment. Ships were laid off and seamen discharged. By August 1664 the Navy had only limited warships active; indeed, Samuel Pepys, the diarist, who was Clerk of the Acts in the Navy Office, worried that there were only eight warships at anchor in the Downs, which the Dutch could easily eliminate.

Despite the running down of the fleet, the Navy did see improvement and reorganisation under James, Duke of York, the King's brother and afterwards King James II. He had in 1660 been appointed Lord High Admiral, a post which was revived. The Navy Board was re-established. The title of Admiral was brought back and James established a scheme of gentlemen volunteers in order to improve the officer corps. To deal with the protection of the ships and to strengthen the capacity to fight hand to hand, the 'Admiral's Regiment' was created, the forerunner of the Royal Marines. Charles II, a keen sailor with an interest in navigation, had the Articles of War revised. The Preamble recited that 'It is upon the Navy under the good Providence of God that the safety, honour and welfare of this realm do chiefly depend', a reality that remained until 1940 when that function came to be shared with the Royal Air Force. The squadron system was refined with the division of the three squadrons – the red (the centre), the white and the blue – into three sections, van, centre and rear, the former under a Vice Admiral and the latter a Rear Admiral. The command structure was thus improved with a clear definition of seniority, so that the captains of ships could know their assigned parts.

The underlying competition of the English and Dutch for control of worldwide commerce had not been settled by the First Dutch War (1652 – 1654) and in the early part of Charles II's reign the two nations became ever more antagonistic. De Witt had reconstructed the Dutch fleet after that war and had created a fleet with purpose-built warships. Competition between England and Holland developed in the Mediterranean, the East Indies, West Africa and North America. The Duke of York with others established the Royal Africa Company which acquired trading sites on the West African coast, an area which the Dutch regarded as their own sphere of influence. By April 1664 the City and Parliament, concerned to protect the nation's commercial interest, began to press the King to make war upon the

Dutch. War fever rose and Parliament voted the largest subsidy ever up to that time so that Charles II could go to war - £2.5 million. Each side spent the year building ships, refitting and raising crews. Clashes between the two countries became more serious. Sir Richard Holmes, an impetuous and dashing sailor, was sent with a squadron to West Africa to protect the settlements of the Africa Company, but in ill-judged enthusiasm pursued his task by attacking the Dutch trading posts. On 7th September 1664 the colony of New Amsterdam was captured by Colonel Richard Nicholls and renamed New York, following the grant of a charter company for its exploitation to the Duke of York. In November the Dutch seized a Swedish ship carrying ship masts to London for the Navy's largest shipbuilder. Admiral Toddiman brought into Dover a Dutch convoy of merchantmen trading with Bordeaux. On 19th December an attack was made unsuccessfully by the English on the rich Smyrna convoy bringing spices from the Levant. The City worried about its trade and merchant ships, but the nation's eyes were fixed on war. On 4th March 1664 war was declared. The English had built up the fleet and had 160 ships with 500 guns: the Dutch had 130-140, some heavier and stronger than in 1654, with brass guns.

On 27th March 1665 the fleet, including 30 warships, lay off the Gunfleet sands commanded by the Duke of York, Prince Rupert and the Earl of Sandwich. It departed to cruise for a few weeks and then, needing revictualling, it returned to Gunfleet where it lay for a week, while two boatloads of ladies came each day to entertain officers. The Duchess of York paid a visit and merriment prevailed. On 23rd April the fleet, now numbering 180, departed to blockade the Texel. The blockade was soon lifted through lack of victuals. The fleet reverted to searching the North Sea.

On 1st June, having weighed anchor at Lowestoft, the fleet of 88 ships sighted the Dutch about six miles off Southwold. The wind was a light easterly, thus giving the Dutch the weather gauge. The Dutch had 113 ships and were commanded by the Heer Van Opdam, a cavalry officer, who had secured a naval victory over the Swedes in 1658. The Dutch fleet was organised in seven squadrons, each with three admirals, controlled by five different admiralties of five of the states which made up Holland (the United Netherlands): the English were arranged in squadrons - the Red, commanded by the Duke of York, advised by Sir William Penn on the flagship, the Royal Charles; the White, commanded by Prince Rupert and the Blue by the Earl of Sandwich. The Duke of York conferred with his commanders, provided that the flagships should be escorted by warships, fore and aft, and required that no ships of the line should leave the line to take prizes or assist others in difficulty.

The Dutch, despite their advantage, did not attack. On 2nd June nothing happened, but in the night the wind changed to become a fresh west south-westerly, giving the weather gauge to the English. The two fleets first passed by on opposite tacks at long range: the English then tacked and began to bear down on the Dutch, a manoeuvre which took until 2 pm. They approached as ordered in line, but soon became to some extent disordered. A fierce general engagement ensued: rigging, sails and the hulls of the ships were shattered, or shot away; the Duke of York on the Royal Charles engaged the Dutch flagship, the Eendrecht in a bloody fight. The Prince was with three friends, the Earl of Falmouth, Muskerry and a Mr Boyle, when they were killed by a cannonball, splattering the Duke of York's face with blood and brain. The gunners had been ordered to fire into the Dutch Flagships tier by tier and they were engaged in that task, when suddenly the Eendrecht blew up in a tower of smoke and flame, only five of her crew being saved.

Meanwhile the Earl of Sandwich, seeing an opportunity, his Blue Flag on the mizzen, led his squadron through the Dutch fleet containing thus a section to the east, while Prince Rupert bore down and took the west. The explosion of the Eendrecht spread confusion through the Dutch, four ships collided and the Admirals of several state's fleets started to withdraw, their retreat being covered by the son of the great Admiral Tromp, Cornelius Tromp, who distinguished himself.

The English began a pursuit as the Dutch headed home, the latter having lost 18 ships taken and six sunk. Pepys recorded that they lost 8-10,000 men killed and wounded. In the night the pursuit was abandoned. The fleet had suffered damage, but the ending of the pursuit came about as a result of a deception carried out in the night by a cowardly Member of Parliament, a Mr Brouncker who, fearing for his life, told the captain of the Royal Charles that the Duke of York had ordered the ships to slow and not press on. The Duke was asleep but he pretended to consult him and repeated the order. The fleet slowed and 43 Dutch ships reached the Texel and others elsewhere. On 16th of June the Duke of York returned to London and Pepys went to court to see him and his courtiers who had been at the Battle. They had returned, said Pepys 'all fat and lusty, and ruddy by being in the sun'.

On 20th June a Thanksgiving was given for the victory. Pepys records that he attended a church service in the morning and listened to a bad sermon by Mr Mills. He had dinner at the Dolphin Tavern with some of the captains and the Commissioners of Ordnance, at the huge expense of 34 shillings a head; went to Whitehall and afterwards visited his mistress to cover her with kisses and fondle her breasts, which, as he recalls, gave him great pleasure. He then returned home to his wife, to supper and to bed.

When the fleet returned, the plague was raging in the seaside ports and in London and great difficulty was experienced in finding places for the prisoners, who were scattered throughout the towns and villages of Kent. The plague meant disorganisation for the fleet and, although an operation under the Earl of Sandwich was sent to Bergen in July to capture the Dutch convoy sheltering there, an enterprise which did not succeed, the two countries were too exhausted to continue to make an active struggle. The Dutch on their return had to face the need to deal with the flight of their ships from the fleet action without justification and four captains were shot and four cashiered. The Duke of York was painted by Lely with his sea captains around him.

The war continued with varying fortunes, the Dutch in June 1667 taking Sheerness, and proceeding up the Medway. The Royal James, the Royal Oak and the Loyall London were burnt and the Royal Charles taken back to Holland, where her stern carving remains in the Rijksmuseum. Peace was made in that year, the English retaining New York and New Jersey.

The Duke of York became King James II in 1685. He lacked political tact and was driven from the throne in 1688. His previous history, however, showed him for the generous, courageous, hardworking, straight-forward man which he was.

The Earl of Sandwich after 1665 returned to court and did not command the fleet again until 1672 in the third Dutch war. He died at the disastrous battle of Sole Bay on 28th May 1672. On this occasion the Dutch did not make the error of the one made at the Battle of Lowestoft. They caught the English fleet unprepared in the bay and bore down on them together with their fireships. The Royal Prince, the flagship of the Earl of Sandwich, fought stubbornly, but went on fire. The Earl with a few companions stayed to the end, as fire raged through the vessel, before abandoning ship. His body was washed up on the beach at Harwich two weeks later and he was buried in Westminster Abbey.

At the battle of Sole Bay John Churchill, the future Duke of Marlborough, commanded (as an ensign) the contingent of Admiral's guard on board the Royal Prince and remained on board to the end. He was afterwards promoted two ranks in the army. Notable also was the recapture of the Royal Katherine, which the Dutch had taken. Led by a seaman called Small, a sober and quiet non-conformist, who was armed only with a whistle which he blew, the survivors of the crew retook the ship.

The 11th Earl of Sandwich was ejected from the House of Lords in 1999.

17th June 1795

Cornwallis's Retreat

In spring 1795 a Breton nobleman, Count Puisaye arrived in England and persuaded William Pitt, the Prime Minister of the Coalition Government formed by the Tories and the Duke of Portland's Whigs, that if western France were invaded, there would be an opportunity to check the advance of revolutionary France. Many thousands of Frenchmen had been captured and he suggested that, given an army, the Royalist Bourbon course could be advanced by the invasion of Brittany. The Government was attracted to the scheme since such an invasion could threaten Brest, the base of the French fleet, and hamper any project for the invasion of England. Money, uniforms, and arms were provided and 4,000 men, many from among the prisoners, were collected to sail by convoy to France. The fleet were to have the duty of protecting that convoy.

Earl Howe had retired as Commander in Chief from active command to Bath, where he took the waters, issuing orders to his second in command, Lord Bridport. The Admiralty also continued to give the latter directions, resulting in poor co-ordination of naval operations. In late June 1795, in order to cover the movements of the French fleet and protect the invasion convoy, Bridport himself remained in the Channel but sent a squadron under the Hon. William Cornwallis to sweep the sea between Ushant and Belle Isle. He sailed with five ships of the line, the Royal Sovereign, his flagship (4th of that name with 100 guns), Bellerophon, Triumph (5th of that name with 74 guns), Brunswick and Mars. In addition there were two frigates – Pallas and Phaeton.

On 17th June at daylight the frigate Phaeton, scouting ahead, espied the French fleet, which had set out from Belle Isle for Brest. It was made up of 12 men-of-war, frigates and other ships totalling 29 and was thus vastly superior to the British force. The signal was given just as the men had finished washing the decks, a daily task which always surprised the French whose ships were left filthy. The crews were rallied and the fleet prepared for combat, the guns run out. The overwhelming superiority of the French caused Cornwallis to act with caution and in touch with the French fleet he decided to go about, putting the slow Brunswick in the van, and designating Bellerophon (7th of the name and the fastest man-of-war in service) as a reserve. He summoned the crew on the Royal Sovereign telling them, 'Remember, men, the Sovereign's flag and ensign are never to be struck to an enemy. She goes down with them flying'. The French fleet began to envelop the English squadron on port, starboard and astern. A fierce interchange commenced, which lasted most of the day. The three-tiered Royal Sovereign savaged its opponents with double shot; Triumph and Mars were attacked and the latter disabled. The Royal Sovereign bore down to protect them and the French were held off.

Meanwhile Cornwallis gave orders to the Captain of the Phaeton (the Hon. H. Curzon) to cruise on the horizon and at a given signal to let down his topgallants and fire a signal gun. This was the internationally acknowledged signal that a fleet was drawing near. Coastal ships passing on the horizon looked like specks on the western sea. De Villaret-Joyeuse, seeing the signal and thinking that Lord Bridport was near with the main fleet, put about immediately to make back for France.

The convoy to invade France had left England on 17th June and was escorted to the Quiberon Peninsula where the emigré army was put ashore. Lord Bridport joined up with Cornwallis's squadron and they sailed once more into touch with the French fleet. The latter however turned to put into L'Orient, but lost three men-of-war on the way.

The Quiberon expedition proved a disaster. Although on 3rd July the fort of Quiberon was taken and the Breton peasantry welcomed the invaders, dissension and treachery allowed the fort to be retaken on 19th July. The prisoners taken by the revolutionaries were massacred, although Count Puisaye was taken off to return to England.

The tactics of Admiral Cornwallis in shrewdly diverting the French away from Brest were plainly of vital significance in securing the Channel passage of the convoy. The stand against a French fleet four times superior in numbers was heroic and determined. In his official dispatch, writing of his ships' crews, Cornwallis said; 'Could common prudence have allowed me to let loose their valour on the enemy, I hardly know what might not have been accomplished by such men'. Parliament thanked Cornwallis for his action and ordered a Naval Medal struck. Every seaman in the fleet was re-ranked as AB, thus receiving higher pay. The action was wholly consistent with the definition in Falconer's Naval Dictionary of 1789 – 'Retreat- the order or disposition in which a fleet of French men-of-war decline engagement, or fly from a pursuing enemy'. The action was commemorated in a contemporary seamen's song, 'Billy Blue', the nickname in the fleet for Admiral Cornwallis.

18th June 1815

The Battle of Waterloo

After the Treaty of Paris in 1814, the Emperor Napoleon I of France was given the Isle of Elba by the victorious powers which had defeated him, as a principality for his own use. While he was to be ruler of this tiny island, eighteen miles by twelve across, he was also to stay there as a virtual prisoner. The Emperor of Austria did not permit his daughter, Napoleon's wife, and his baby son to join him. Louis XVIII became King of France, restoring the House of Bourbon expelled by the Revolution. The returning émigrés were not popular with the people of France, who remained substantially loyal to Napoleon. The powers – Britain, Prussia, Austria, France and Russia and smaller states – gathered in Vienna to arrange the restoration of a Europe of order and legitimacy after the tumult of the Revolutionary and Napoleonic period brought about by the French. They were still engaged in that task when in March 1815 news came that Napoleon I had evaded the patrolling British frigates and had arrived in the South of France.

On 1st March 1815 Napoleon landed with 400 infantry and 100 Polish Lancers at Golfe Juan near Cannes. On 7th March he reached Grenoble and entered Lyons on the 10th . Marshal Ney, the Bourbon Commander in Chief, promised Louis XVIII to bring him back to Paris in a iron age. However, the regiments of the French army acclaimed him and joined him. On 19th March he slept at Fontainebleau and entered Paris to be carried shoulder-high into the Tuileries on 20th March. Louis XVIII with his brother the Duke of Berry had fled to Ghent. Many members of the French ruling classes welcomed him, including Marshal Ney, who returned to his former loyalty. The Congress of Vienna declared him an outlaw, a disturber of the peace and agreed to mobilise their armies to invade France. The Duke of Wellington was to be Commander in Chief in the Low Countries, commanding the combined British, Dutch and Belgium forces. Prussia was to provide a force under Marshal Blucher to co-operate with him on the Lower Rhine. Austria and Russia were to move into France from the upper and middle Rhine.

Napoleon exhibited all his genius and energy for government, re-organised the finances of the government and set about raising and arming a huge army for the defence of France. By the end of May he had achieved a fighting force of 280,000. 75,000 veterans returned to the tricolore, 15,000 volunteered and the national guard was mobilised. He had an effective force of 128,000 to take to the northern frontier, many of them veterans. He was under pressure to act

249

expeditiously, because the longer he waited the worse his position would be. The allied powers had far greater resources and were planning to have over 600,000 troops on the French borders by mid-summer. Typically, he devised a sound strategy of preventing the juncture of the British and Prussian forces in Belgium, by striking at the gap between the armies and of defeating each in turn.

The Duke of Wellington assembled his forces in Belgium in April and May, but his strategic view was dominated by the idea that Napoleon was most likely to attack his right flank with a view to cutting him off from the sea. His forces were therefore dispersed around Mons to the west of the Brussels-Charleroi road. The Prussians under Marshal Blucher, pivoting on Liege, were moving towards France to the east of that road. There were reports of French troops moving south of Mons but in fact Napoleon concentrated his army near Beaumont, south of Charleroi. The movement of troops to the rendezvous was done with the utmost secrecy, all borders being closed on 7th June. Napoleon reached this base on 14th June. 89,000 infantry, 22,000 cavalry, 11,000 gunners and engineers and 366 guns had been collected there.

At 2am on the morning of 15th June the French forces were roused ready to move forward to Charleroi. Wellington was not aware of the concentration at Beaumont and only received a message at 3 pm from the Prussians that they had been attacked at Thuin. The Prussians retreated before the three corps of the French army and Napoleon, falling asleep on his horse, carried out a review of his troops at 12pm in Charleroi. Wellington alerted the army to move to the east and to concentrate at the crossroads of Quatre Bras, where the east-west road linking him to Blucher and the Prussians crossed the Charleroi-Brussels road, and went on to Nivelles. Wellington and Blucher had met and agreed to co-operate in their troop movements. Blucher brought the Prussian army forward to make a stand around Sombreffe, north-east of Charleroi.

Wellington, in the days preceding Quatre Bras, had participated in the active social life of Brussels, attending a cricket match, playing with his host's children and attending balls and parties. Having given orders to concentrate the army at Quatre Bras, he went to the Duchess of Richmond's ball, where the principal army officers, the Prince of Orange and the Duke of Brunswick were present. Among the chandeliers, roses and champagne, the message came that the Prussians had been defeated on the Fleurus road and were retiring to take up position at Ligny. A Dutch and Belgian force of 4,000, under Prince Bernhard of Saxe-Weimar, were stationed at Quatre Bras and, although no attack had been made, the French had come up under Marshal Ney. Wellington therefore suggested to the Prince of Orange to leave for the troops. He then went into supper. After supper he asked the Duke of Richmond for a map, studied the plan and sent off aides-de-camp to attend to dispositions. He told the Duke that Napoleon had humbugged him and said that, if Quatre Bras could not be held, he would stand at Waterloo.

Up early, Wellington left with his staff for Quatre Bras at 8.00am and arrived there at 10.00am. Reille's corps two miles away at Frasnes already outnumbered the Prince of Orange's troops: the French had 20,000 men with sixty guns as against 7,000 with eight guns, but because the latter were shielded by woods, Ney did not realise how few there were. Wellington knew that his army could not be fully in position until the afternoon and Ney showed no sign of attacking. He therefore rode over to Blucher, six miles away. The two Field-Marshals conferred, reinforcing their intention to keep in touch so that the armies could join up. As he departed, having seen the Prussians drawn up on the forward slope of the valley of the River Ligny, he expressed the view that they would be damnably mauled. Napoleon had 68,000 infantry and 12,500 cavalry confronting Blucher with his army of 84,000.

By the time Wellington returned to Quatre Bras, the French attack had begun and they were moving forward. As the battle continued in the afternoon the British infantry and cavalry had progressively come up and been deployed. Ney launched continuous assaults, but the thin red line of British infantry held: as each gap was made it was stoically filled. Ney called for support from D'Erlon's corps of 20,000, but contradictory orders from him and from Napoleon left it marching back and forth between Quatre Bras and Ligny. In Ney's second attack the young Duke of Brunswick was killed by a ball in the stomach. The Dutch-Belgian troops in Bossu wood fled and the Duke and Lord Fitzroy Somerset had to gallop for their lives. The Gordon Highlanders saved the day, rising up out of the rye and shooting down the French cavalry. In the late afternoon Kellerman and his cavalry attacked the British infantry, which formed squares, apart from the 69th (South Lincolnshire Regiment of Foot), who were consequently cut down. The 30th (Cambridgeshire Regiment of Foot) and the 73rd (Perthshire Regiment of Foot) devastated the cavalry with musket fire and the 92nd (Highland Regiment of Foot) utterly levelled the field, firing from thirty yards away. The French cavalry however persisted. The square of the 78th (Highlanders Regiment of Foot) began to balloon. Sir Thomas Picton, fighting in his top hat, rallied them: 'Remember Egypt' he called. Only the 33rd (1st York West Riding Regiment of Foot) succumbed to the onslaught. At this stage the Guards came up and at 6.30pm the advance was sounded and the Bossu wood and the crossroad farms were retaken from the French. Few cavalry took part in the battle at Quatre Bas, although their role was to prove indispensable on the next day. At 9 pm the battle died away with both sides still in place where they had stood at the start.

Meanwhile Napoleon directed the attack at Ligny against the Prussians, starting with a cannonade at 2 pm. The indomitable Prussians stood and accepted a terrible bombardment throughout the day, as predicted by the Duke of Wellington, until the Ligny stream ran with blood. They withstood the assaults of the French but were gradually forced back. Late on Marshal Prince Blucher himself led the Prussian cavalry in a charge, in the course of which the great grey given him by

Wellington was brought down by a bullet. Blucher was at this time seventy-three years old. He had first joined the Swedish army at the age of twelve in the Mörner Hussars and transferred to the Prussian Black (Death's Head) Hussars. He spent some time as a farmer in Pomerania having resigned, and his military career only blossomed after 1793. He was distinguished for his heroism and fighting spirit, which was recognised by his steady promotion. When the grey fell, it rolled on him and, as he lay pinned down, French cavalry rode backwards and forwards around and over him: finally he was extricated and returned to Mellery where he stilled his aches and pains with schnapps, rhubarb and garlic. The next morning he rose to wash his bruises with brandy and after a generous tot of schnapps departed to Wavre, to which the Prussian army was retiring. An eccentricity of his old age was to believe himself pregnant with a baby elephant.

The fighting had ceased at Ligny about 9 pm and the Prussians began to withdraw in the direction of Wavre, but in an ordered fashion and with regularity. The corps present at Ligny was reformed and Bulow's Corps, on Blucher's orders, began to move towards Wellington, whom he was determined not to fail despite the opposition of the Chief of Staff, Count Gneisenau.

On 17th June Wellington waited at Quatre Bras for news of the Prussians. At 7.30 am a messenger arrived with information concerning the retirement of the Prussian army on Wavre. Wellington realised his position was untenable. 'As they have gone back, he said, we must go back.' He had already found the Waterloo site and picked it for a stand on the road to Brussels. It was at a focus where communications could be maintained to Nivelles and towards Wavre. At 10.00 am the retreat began, the infantry preceding the rest of the army. The cavalry and artillery, with a screen left at Quatre Bras, protected the infantry retreat. Ney made no move during the morning and was joined by Napoleon at 1 pm. It was then realised by them that Quatre Bras was almost abandoned. By 2 pm the Guards finally departed. The artillery still there began firing at the French as they came up the road towards the crossroads. As they did so, the heavy black clouds, which had built up in the day, broke in overwhelming peels of thunder, and torrential rain began to fall which lasted into the night. In sequence the infantry retired to redeploy on the ridge of Mont St Jean to the south of the village of Waterloo; the cavalry gave the army cover, moving up the main road with skirmishes as they went, for example, at Gemappe, where Lord Uxbridge ordered the 7th Hussars to charge a body of Lancers and Life Guards to clear the village. The route to the side of the road was so poached by the mass of horses that off the road itself the land was impassable for cavalry and artillery. The cavalry went though the infantry on the ridge of Mont St Jean to station themselves a mile or so in the rear. It never ceased to rain and bivouacs for all the troops were veritable seas of mud.

The commissariat had not been effective, suffering the same impediment from the rain as the army, so that the troops were many of them without food and adequate water. There was a shortage of firewood; the bivouacs were without heat and had no means of cooking. In these grim conditions the army paused for the night protected only by their uniforms and cloaks. The French army, which came up behind, spent the night taking up position opposite the Mont St Jean ridge on a line to the fore of a farm called La Belle Alliance, to the south.

The position chosen by Wellington to fight was the product of his shrewd military skills and eye for country. The crossroads of Mont St. Jean on the Brussels road lay on the top of a long plateau ridge and were at the centre of the position. In advance of them down the road on the west side was a farmhouse, giving a little cover to a body of troops, La Haye Sainte, to the east of which was a gravel pit. Along the ridge there ran a road from Hougoumont in the west towards Ohain in the east, passing the farms of Paplotte and La Haye. The centre right of the position pivoted on the orchard and Chateau of Hougoumont, with its garden wall standing slightly in advance of the line of the position which ended by a ravine near Merbraine. In order to reach the ridge and the road along it, it was necessary to mount the slope leading up to the ridge line through ground which was uneven, falling in small hillocks to the valley lying between Mon St. Jean and La Belle Alliance, which was itself on a hill. The shallow incline of the slope lay between Hougoumont and La Haye Sainte. The road along the ridge was in part sunken and in part a shallow way bounded by hedges of varying thickness

The total force which the Duke of Wellington had at his disposal amounted to 67,661 men and 150 guns. That total however comprised a mixed force army of doubtful reliability, as conduct in the battle was to prove. Colonel Tomkinson in his Diary of a Cavalry Officer thought that the effective force of infantry amounted to 17,500 British, 5,600 of the King's German Legion in British pay and 8,800 Brunswickers and Nassauers out of an infantry force of 50,300: The remainder were Dutch and Belgium, including militia. In terms of cavalry there were 49 squadrons of British amounting to 5,220 men and 16 squadrons of Germans in British pay of 1730 amounting to 6,950 men, which were regarded by Tomkinson as effective. There were additionally cavalry from Holland, Belgium and Hanover. Some of the former never reached the field, but according to Tomkinson, engaged in plunder of the baggage, the 1st Dragoon Guards losing all of theirs.

At 6 am on 18th June Wellington gave orders for the disposition of his troops and the army moved to its positions. The weight of troops was posted to the west of the Brussels road on the right centre and flank. The wood at the Chateau of Hougoumont was occupied by Brunswickers and Nassauers and three battalions of Coldstream Guards within the château. The British infantry were mainly scattered along the ridge between the latter strongpoint and La Haye Sante, which was occupied by the King's German Legion under Major Baring, while the sandpit was garrisoned by the 95th regiment. To the east of the road on the left stood the reserve division of Sir Thomas Picton and two brigades of the 6th division. On the far left were stationed Vivian's and Vandelour's cavalry and troops from 1st Corps commanded by Prince Bernhard of Saxe-Weimer. Otherwise the cavalry were placed down the reverse slope in a position to the rear of centre. The troops were stationed behind the ridge apart from Bylandt's brigade of Dutch-Belgian troops, who stood on the slope facing the French, much as the Prussians had done at Ligny. 156 guns were stationed along the line. As the troops formed up, Wellington visited the lines, riding his chestnut Copenhagen and dressed in a blue topcoat and white breeches.

Napoleon breakfasted at his headquarters at Le Caillou. His Chief of Staff, Marshal Soult suggested, having fought Wellington in Spain, that he should recall the corps under Marshal Grouchy (33,000 men) who were in pursuit of the Prussians. His arrogant reply was, 'Because you have been beaten by Wellington, you consider him a great general. And now I tell you that Wellington is a bad general, the English are bad troops and this affair is nothing more serious that eating one's breakfast'. Napoleon had not of course himself fought a British army on the field of battle. Count Reille, commanding the IInd corps on the left, joined the party and re-emphasised that the British were as well posted as Wellington knew how, and that English infantry were unshakeable. Napoleon ignored his advice and continued with his plan to drive in the British front with an assault on the centre and a first attack at Hougoumont. With equal arrogance he could not believe that the Prussians were not in disorderly retreat, having of course beaten them decisively at Jena in 1807, and he thought them incapable of joining up as an effective force with the British. Marshal Soult had given orders for the disposition of the troops at 5 am to be ready by 9 am, but it was much later before the French were in place. The French had on the field some 71,947 and 246 guns. All were packed with the British into a small battlefield of three square miles with a constricted front to attack. Count Reille was placed on the centre left with his corps with infantry under the command of Prince Jerome Bonaparte and Kellerman's cavalry. Count Lobau was stationed to his rear. On the right was the First Corps under Count D'Erlon with cavalry commanded by Milhaud and Lefebvre-Desnouettes. The guard was held in the rear near La Belle Alliance. The French army with their rich uniforms, pennants and bands presented a formidable spectacle from the British lines, where few troops were visible, hidden as they were below the ridge.

At 10 am Napoleon rode through the lines to military bands playing marching tunes such as *Pas Accéléré*, *Veillons au Salut de l'Empire* and the *Salut des Aigles*. As he passed through the lines, cries of 'Vive L'Emperor!' echoed across the valley. He had intended to start the battle in the morning, particularly as he needed to defeat the British before the Prussians could arrive, but the mud on rain-sodden fields would severely hamper cavalry and the commencement was fixed for 1 pm. Anyone who has rode over heavy wet clay can appreciate his concern and knows the effect on the pace of the horse and the strength, which it needs, to persevere forward, particularly uphill. Just before the review he sent an ambiguous message to Marshal Grouchy ordering him to pursue the Prussians to Wavre and at the same time draw close to him on his right.

At 11.25 am the French guns opened at the Hougoumont position on the British right. Four regiments of veteran infantry preceded by skirmishers were launched against the orchard and the château by Prince Jerome Bonaparte. The wood and orchard were taken but a devastating fire from the château, where the Coldstream Guards under Col. James Macdonell of Glengarry were stationed, felled the French in heaps. Directed by the Duke of Wellington, British howitzers fired shrapnel over the château on the besiegers. Allied infantry attacked and shattered the French and the wood was recaptured. Prince Jerome, oblivious to the fact that the attack was supposed to be a feint, mounted a second attack and this time French infantry managed to force the gates open, led by a gigantic subaltern named Le Gros and nicknamed the Smasher. Desperate hand-to-hand fighting took place, but Macdonell, three other officers and a sergeant threw themselves against the gates and pushed them back against the soldiers outside. Of the French inside the courtyard none survived save a drummer boy.

Prince Jerome's response was to throw in more troops from Foy's division. Wellington responded by sending four further battalions of Coldstream Guards. The woods had once more been taken, but the château, protected by its loop-holed walls, stood firm. A further effort was made by the French, but Hougoument survived, although fighting continued there for a great part of the day.

At 1 pm Napoleon perceived a dark shadow against the woods at Chapelle St. Lambert in the east and at first thought it was Grouchy and his corps returning. He soon learnt that it was Bulow's corps of Prussians. At the same time as the bombardment began on the British front line at 1.30 pm, Lobau was ordered to move the VIth corps, with two cavalry divisions, towards the south-east on the French right flank in order to resist any Prussian advance. The 80 guns opened at La Belle Alliance and pounded the centre, but the British were protected by the ridge from direct fire where they were lying down on the reverse side. Only Bylandt's division was seriously mauled. The deep mud meant that many of the projectiles and shot did little harm as they buried themselves in the ground.

Marshal Ney had effective command in the field, having only returned to the army on the day previous to Waterloo. The 'Bravest of the Brave', he was known for his outstanding courage and determination but lacked tactical skill. He was ordered by Napoleon to launch D'Erlon's Corps, supported by cavalry, on to the British centre. The French force of 30,000 men descended into the valley: the cannonade fell off and the French troops began to come up the hill towards the ridge. Strangely they came on in a formation of three or four close phalanxes, 200 files wide and 24 to 27 men deep, which made them peculiarly vulnerable to artillery and musketry fire and were formations which on the narrow British front made it difficult to deploy.

As the French mounted the ridge, swathes fell as they were shot down by the guns and musketry fire. Nonetheless, they reached the ridge. The garden at La Haye Sainte was taken and the King's German Legion surrounded in the house by teeming French. Bylandt's Dutch-Belgian brigade was swept away, the Cameron Highlanders booing their retreat. Napoleon watching from afar thought that the front was giving way, but Sir Thomas Picton was waiting and gave the command to Pack and Kempt with their divisions to move forward – '92nd you must advance' shouted Sir Dennis Pack, and the Gordon Highlanders, the Black Watch and the 44th (East Essex Regiment of Foot) flung themselves upon the French. Kempt's brigade fired close volleys into the enemy and Sir Thomas Picton led that brigade from the front. 'Charge' he said, 'Hurrah, Hurrah, Rally the Highlanders'. At that moment a bullet struck his top hat, which he always wore, and he fell dead.

Lord Uxbridge, observing the threat to the centre and the seriousness of the situation decided to bring up the heavy cavalry from the rear and he called up the Union Brigade, commanded by Sir William Ponsonby and the Household Brigade, commanded by Lord Edward Somerset. The Duke of Wellington, seeing that Picton's counter-attack might be overwhelmed by numbers, put himself at the head of the Household Brigade to lead them forward. The bugle sounded the ten blasts for the advance: as the Scots Greys galloped past the infantry, the Gordon Highlanders raised the cry 'Scotland for Ever'. The heavy cavalry, sped by the downhill slope, crashed into the French, who broke. The Life Guards and Royal Dragoon Guards with the heavy strong horses, fresh from England, were able to sweep away the more lightly-horsed cuirassiers supporting the French infantry. Acts of individual heroism were legion. Sergeant Ewart, for example, of the Scots Greys, six foot four inches tall and strong, struggled with two French cuirassiers and captured the Eagle of the 45th, carrying it back. Lord Uxbridge, as the French fled ever on to their own lines, tried to sound the Rally, but the heavy cavalry moved on, no doubt in thrall to the ecstasy which can be experienced in the hunting field in going away from a cover and which men and horses communicate to one another, as in a thundering mass they rush forward. Up to the French lines and guns, they went, riding along the front sabreing and silencing some 30 guns by cutting down the gun crews. But they were outnumbered; the French soon overcame the squadrons whose temerity had taken them on. Casualties were high: two in three of the heavy cavalry were lost, including Sir William Ponsonby and his aide-de-camp. At three o'clock however the field was cleared, and time was not on Napoleon's side as the Prussians came ever nearer.

Marshal Ney was ordered at this juncture by Napoleon to take La Haye Sainte as a base once more to break the centre. By this time smoke from gunfire hung over the field and on the ridge visibility between the bodies of troops had become limited. However, as he prepared to execute his orders, Ney thought, in the course of an infantry attack by the brigades of D'Erlon's corps, which had rallied, that he saw the lines on the ridge broken and the signs of retreat – wagons and men moving away in the Brussels direction. His impetuosity and want of judgement were known to Napoleon, but nonetheless no specific orders were given. Of his own volition, deciding that the British appeared to be in retreat, he ordered the cavalry to go in unsupported to speed up the retreat. It was contrary to the tenets of battle to use cavalry without infantry support where an infantry line was unbroken. In fact the British were re-organising themselves and still using the shelter of the ridge, its sunken road and hedges. Meanwhile, at Hougoumont the struggle continued and Prince Jerome was ordered to fire on the position with howitzers. The château was set on fire but the defenders continued to resist.

Marshal Ney ordered Milhaud's brigade of cuirassiers forward and their movement drew in the other brigades in the excitement of the moment. Lefebvre-Desnouettes on his own initiative added his light cavalry and by 4 pm 4,000 French cavalry were coming up the slope at slow trot, dictated by the deep-poached mud which they had to cross. The British infantry formed squares with artillery stationed between and the French cavalry advanced up the slope into a torrent of gunfire, grapeshot and musketry fire. Large numbers fell but heroically they came on. As they reached the ridge the gunners, on orders from Wellington, left the guns and entered the squares. The cuirassiers and light cavalry swept along the ridge and round the squares without success, harried by volley after volley of musketry fire. They came and went through the smoke unable to sabre or break the infantry. As Captain Mercer of the Horse Artillery describes, even the Brunswickers, who had broken at Quatre Bras, stayed firm, encouraged by Mercer's battery of gunners, who kept their place and did not enter the squares adjoining them. The battery continued to fire at times at 50 to 60 yards, into the massed cuirassiers, and wreaked a havoc not seen elsewhere along the line. The cuirassiers were driven off the plateau; the gunners returned to their guns, which the French had neither been able to spike as they carried no tools, nor to take away since they brought no horses. The squares were now full of dead and wounded, with spent ammunition and the debris of war, still standing firm in the swirling smoke. The Scotch squares lived up to Tomkinson's judgement in his Diary of a Cavalry Officer that in resisting cavalry they showed 'steadiness, coolness and obedience to orders'.

At the bottom of the slope, Marshal Ney reformed his cavalry and ordered Kellerman and Flahaut to join them. In the general excitement Guyot with the Guard cavalry also joined in; 9,000 horsemen were sent on after a cannonade, but their impulse was slowed, not only by the ground but also by the dead and wounded cuirassiers and horses which lay around the squares. Once more guns and musketry fire shattered their ranks and as they retired, having circled the squares, Lord Uxbridge launched a cavalry counter-attack, which helped to drive them back to their starting point. The French persistently reformed after each of their retirements and charged over and over again; how many times is uncertain but there were probably at least five to eight attempts. The Household Brigade counter-attacked: their heavy horses and men cutting down the French, in one case a Life Guard sabred off the head of cuirassier and the headless horseman was carried away seated in the saddle. They were not supported by the Dutch/ Belgian cavalry, who retreated down the reverse slope, while the Hannoverian Cumberland Hussars fled. The squares themselves suffered severely. That of the 73rd (Regiment of Fort, predecessors of the Black Watch) for example, was targeted by guns and many men fell by the dozen. Sergeant Morris records that in one instance seventeen were killed by one shell. When the advance came at the end of the battle, one regiment on the ridge did not advance, the 27th (Inniskillen) (Regiment of Foot) who lay dead in their square. At the end of this phase of the action, most of Lord Uxbridge's cavalry had been expended and there were only remaining Vivian's and Vandelour's brigades on the left flank. By the end of the cavalry attempt, Ney called on Reille's corps, where there were 6,000 infantry who had not fired a shot. These he called up, but they could not endure the withering fire from the ridge top, loosing 1,500 men in ten minutes.

Meanwhile at 5 pm the 2nd Corps of Prussians commanded by Von Bulow had come up to attack the French at Plancenoit on the far south-east of the battlefield. Behind them were two further corps, only Thielman's Corps having been left to fight Marshal Grouchy at Wavre. Marshal Blucher had marched eleven hours himself to reach the battlefield, encouraging his artillery along the muddy roads and valleys. To meet the attack Lobau and his corps were sent by Napoleon to confront Bulow. The Prussians however, drove him back and captured Plancenoit.

Napoleon realised at this point how critical it was to capture the forward stronghold of La Hay Sainte in order to use it as a base to smash Wellington's centre. During the cavalry attacks, as the horsemen whirled round the farm, Major Baring and his King's German Legion had held fast, but ammunition was running low and his losses of men had mounted. Supplies of ammunition for the army were few and the farm difficult to reach. Ney was ordered by Napoleon again to take the farm. About 6 pm he went forward to the attack on this occasion with Douzelet's infantry and a handful of cavalry and guns. Major Baring and his men strongly resisted, fighting with bayonets when the ammunition was gone. They were dislodged and the survivors struggled back to the frontline. Only Major Baring and 41 men escaped of the original 379 of the Legion which had occupied the farmhouse. Having captured the farm, Ney positioned guns there, some 300 yards from the front line, and began to bombard the British troops. The line began to crumble: Lord Fitzroy Somerset, while next to the Duke of Wellington, lost his arm. Brigades commanded by Ompteda and Kilmansegge were virtually eliminated and dissolving. Ney, perceiving the opportunity, sent an urgent message to Napoleon to send more infantry. Fourteen battalions of the Imperial Garde stood at La Belle Alliance. Zieten's Corps of Prussians was not two miles away, in force on the Ohain road. A decisive moment had come. Napoleon, worried about the Prussians, refused Ney and the opportunity was given to Wellington to reorganise his front. Reserves were brought to the centre, Chassé's division in the west at Merbraine was ordered up. Seeing Zieten's Prussian corps, the cavalry brigades of Vivian and Vandelour were moved up behind the centre as the Prussian cavalry came on. Wellington rode along the line encouraging the troops and steadying the Brunswickers and Nassauers in order to prevent them from giving way.

Napoleon, on the news that the Prussians were advancing, had sent the Young Guard to resist them and they retook the village of Plancenoit only to be driven back again by the Prussians as their numbers rose. Two battalions of the old Guard were sent to achieve the recovery of the village but the Prussians fought back. However by 6.45 pm the position there was stabilised.

When Napoleon also perceived the Prussians on the Ohain Road moving up to the British he decided to have a last attempt to drive into the British line. Napoleon, the French hearing booming guns on the flank to the rear, sent riders to deceive his soldiers that Grouchy had arrived and thus for the moment encourage them. He then decided to launch the Imperial Guard to attack. The details of the attack are unclear but the British troops were told to lie down to wait behind the bank to the Ohain road. Leaving La Belle Alliance at 7 pm, where they were drawn up, Napoleon led them towards the front lines on his grey, the troops calling out 'Vive L' Emperor!' as they went. They were supported by the rallied infantry of Reille's and D'Erlon's corps. On their advance the Guard separated into two columns, deviating from the road. On they came, led by Ney, the tall men in the looming bearskins stepping regularly in pace with insistent drums. In no battle had they failed. The grenadiers were to the right of the chasseurs. As they mounted the rise, the artillery battered their ranks as they came out of the smoke.

They came within 60 yards of the Ohain road, before Wellington gave the order 'Maitland your turn! Stand up, Guards'. 1,500 men sprang up. The Imperial Guard hesitated; the French were hit by 400 men firing at 20 yards. 300 fell in the first volley. The other column had turned and that in its turn was fired on in the flank by Halkett's brigade. The Light Brigade joined the attack. Volley after volley struck the two columns of Guards and Wellington ordered an attack on the flank. The Imperial Guard dissolved and recoiled. The mass of French troops, seeing the failure of the Guard, took up the cry 'La Garde recule'. It spread like panic through the troops and the army disintegrated in flight from the field. Wellington, seeing the retreat at 7.45 pm, waved his hat three times and ordered the advance, led by Vivian's and Vandelour's cavalry. Zieten's Corps of Prussians at this time drove a wedge between D'Erlon and Lobau on the British left flank and the French came under crossfire. The cannonade started to die away, but at almost the last moment shots from a battery in fields near La Haye Sainte sent a ball flying over the Duke of Wellington and smashing Lord Uxbridge's knee. It is said that the latter remarked on looking at his leg 'By God I've lost my leg'. 'Have you by God?' said Wellington, looking coolly at it and galloping away.

Napoleon endeavoured to steady the army using four battalions of the Imperial Guard in squares near La Belle Alliance, but the fleeing troops pushed past in disorder, flowing down the road to Gemappes and Quatre Bras. In the end he abandoned the attempt and retired himself in the hope of steadying and reforming his army. Wellington and Blucher met at 9 pm near La Belle Alliance, where it was agreed that the French should be pursued by the Prussians.

The British losses amounted to 15,000, the French 25,000 killed and wounded and the Prussians 7,000. There were 8,000 French prisoners and 220 guns taken. Many thousands of wounded lay that night on the field, a crisp night, without water or relief and the night echoed with cries of agony. They were without food and water and the local Belgian peasants began to plunder the field, taking the clothes and boots of the dead and dying and any objects of value. The British on the 19th tried to relieve the wounded, both British and French, and Brussels gave the wounded troops its hospitality. Lord Uxbridge was carried back to a house in Waterloo. The surgeons took the view that he was in imminent danger of loss of life, if his leg were not amputated. He calmly accepted their advice, discussed the action with his staff and had the amputation done. During its course he never moved, or complained although he thought the instruments not very sharp. His pulse never altered. Later that evening he showed the severed leg to Vivian, who thought it best off. The leg was buried under a tombstone in the house which he had used, and he devised and had made a wooden leg with a moving knee, which can still be seen at Plas Newydd in Anglesey.

The French army continued its rout to Philippeville where it stopped and reformed. There it was joined by Marshal Grouchy and his corps who had carried out an ordered and brilliant retreat from Wavre. Napoleon left for Paris and at 6 am on 21st June he re-entered the Elysée. He tried to save the Empire but was unsupported and finally sought refuge on a British ship, the Bellerophon. The victorious powers resolved on his banishment to St. Helena, the Governor of which was to be Sir Hudson Lowe. Wellington had been offered him as Quarter-Master General for the Waterloo campaign but refused, for he regarded him as both dull and stupid. Napoleon died in 1821 and his remains were returned to France in 1840, where they were buried in Les Invalides in Paris. Under pressure from the British the other powers agreed to the restoration of Louis XVIII and with his brother Charles X, the dynasty survived until 1830. The Duke of Wellington returned in acclaim to London and pursued a career as a politician, becoming Prime Minister. He died in

1852 and was buried in St. Pauls Cathedral. Lord Uxbridge was created Marquis of Anglesey. Lord Fitzroy Somerset ultimately became Lord Raglan and commanded the British Army in the Crimea in the 1850s.

Marshal Ney hoped to retire after Napoleon abdicated on 22nd June, but in August 1815 he was arrested by the Bourbons, tried by the House of Peers and shot on 7th December, insisting that his eyes were not covered. Marshal Soult, after an exile to Dusseldorf, returned to France and held various government and ministerial appointments under King Louis Phillippe between 1830 and 1848. Marshal Grouchy retired to Philadelphia but returned to France in 1831, when he was reinstated as a Marshal and Peer of France.

The 8th Duke of Wellington, the 7th Marquess of Anglesey and the 5th Baron Raglan were ejected from the House of Lords in 1999.

21ˢᵗ June 1813
The Battle of Vitoria

The year 1812, which had opened with the storming of Ciudad Rodrigo in January, was a year of success for the Duke of Wellington in the Peninsula. The Anglo-Portuguese army advanced and the Spanish and the guerillas became stronger. Wellington took the border fortresses, Salamanca, and in August advanced to Madrid, which King Joseph Bonaparte had abandoned, retiring towards Valencia. 1,000 guns had been taken or destroyed and 20,000 prisoners sent to England. This very success enjoyed by the British put the army at risk. Marshal Soult abandoned Andalucia and moved to join King Joseph and unite his army with the troops under Suchet in the south-east. In the north the attack on Burgos was threatened by the French armies of the North and Portugal with 50,000 men. The Spanish in La Mancha had failed to prevent Soult from joining King Joseph, who together had a combined army of 60,000. Wellington was in danger of being caught with only limited forces in Madrid, because he had detached three divisions to guard the Tagus and so on 31ˢᵗ October Madrid was abandoned. The attack on Burgos was called off and the army retreated to Salamanca, where the divided forces joined. The French showed no disposition to attack him there, but Marshal Soult commenced an enveloping movement on the southern flank, to cut the communications with Portugal. On 15ᵗʰ November the order was given to retreat to the Portugal frontier. For four days the army marched back in equinoctal gales with unprecedented cold and rain. Streams were in spate and there were no rations. The army halted on the Agueda exhausted, sick and demoralised. Wellington immediately began the task of rebuilding the army ready for the spring campaign. The fortress of Cuidad Rodrigo, Badajoz, Almarez and the Alcantara remained in British hands: just as importantly Santander provided a new base in the north, having been seized by Admiral Sir Home Popham and the guerillas in July 1812.

Just as Napoleon I had plundered Spain for troops to strengthen his armies for the attack on Russia in early 1812, he was faced again by the requirement to recall troops following the disastrous campaign into which he had entered with 450,000 troops and returned with 25,000. New armies were needed to defend his position in Germany against Austria, Russia and Prussia, who were beginning to threaten the French hegemony in Central Europe. The Imperial Guard were entirely recalled and the regiments stripped of veterans, reducing the French armies to less than 200,000. Spain itself was in total insurrection, with guerrillas conducting savage attacks upon French troops, who had to garrison villages even after turning them into fortified positions. Single messengers required battalions of troops to accompany them. The French and the guerrillas pushed their conflict with all the violence and inhumanity which is shown in the drawings of Goya. In March Napoleon ordered King Joseph to leave the capital and he did so, with part of the French army, for Valladolid. The court, its treasure and retainers accompanied him. By spring 1813 the French retained little of Spain under effective control but for the immediate area controlled from Valladolid, Catalonia and Valencia, apart from Tarragona. Many of their forces were occupied in dealing with the guerrillas in the valleys of Biscaya and Navarre.

By April 1813 the combined army under the Duke of Wellington was ready to move: he commanded 52,000 British, 29,000 well-ordered and experienced Portuguese and 21,000 Spaniards. Sir George Murray had seen to the proper provisioning of the army with ammunition, military supplies, tents and rations and discipline was restored. Having Santander as a new potential base Wellington conceived the notion of outflanking the French in Valladolid and moving north towards his new base with the ultimate aim of severing the link to France northwards to Bayonne. For the forces stationed fifty miles to the west of the plain of Leon the concept involved a march across rugged country thought largely impassable by the French, and the covering of a distance of about 2 to 300 miles. At the same time a force was to be sent under Sir Rowland Hill towards Salamanca. The flanking march would have the advantage of turning the defensive position of the French on the River Douro.

The spring attack was delayed by the inclement weather; that winter the Thames in London had been frozen for eight weeks; but in the second week of May the army started on its long walk. Sir Thomas Graham was to lead this flank movement with the 1st, 3rd, 5th, 6th and 7th divisions, the cavalry brigades of Anson, Ponsonby and Bock, and Pack's and Bradford's Portuguese infantry. On 22nd May Sir Rowland Hill, who was joined by the Duke of Wellington, moved on Salamanea, which was taken on the 25th after the French division there withdrew across the Douro. On the Tormes River, Hill and Wellington waited a week to allow Graham to come up on the French flank. On the 29th and 30th Graham crossed the Esla, which was in spate, by means of pontoons and fords, the troops having to wade up to their chins. On 2nd June after Zamorro was taken the French retreated from Toro and the two wings of the army joined, Hill crossing the river with 30,000. The army was now north of the Douro. The French evacuated Valladolid on 2nd June. After the meeting at Toro, Wellington turned north-east and did not follow the French along the main road to Burgos, the army covered by a cavalry screen between it and the retiring French. For ten days the army marched across the fertile green plain of Leon passing through Palencia, when among the welcoming crowds, nuns from the upper window of a convent showered the army with rose petals. The French had left the town on 7th June and evacuated Burgos on the 12th. In the morning of the 13th a thunderous explosion was heard at 4 am, caused by the French blowing up the citadel of the town. The river Pisuerga was crossed and only the Ebro remained as a barrier. The Anglo-Portuguese army went north-east to cross the Ebro over the headwaters, once more going across formidable country where at times the guns had to be manhandled. Wellington crossed between Rocamonde and Puerta Arenas, which was reached on 15th June. The French once more had had their defensive position turned and Wellington thrust out his left wing to go north of Vitoria in order to cut the Bilbao Road. For his part he with the rest of the army moved on Vitoria.

King Joseph and his Chief of Staff Marshal Jourdan had decided to make a stand at Vitoria, which was without doubt a good defensive position. Wellington approached it from the west.

The town of Vitoria was sited on an eminence in a small plain between mountains shaped like a diamond, twelve miles long by seven wide. The golden-spired church, which dominated the town, was the signpost for a number of roads, to Madrid in the south-west, Bilbao in the north-west, Bayonne to the north-east, Salvatierra and Pamplona in the west and Lograno in the south. The plain was abutted on all sides by mountains – the range in the south being the Puebla Hills, which enclosed the right side of the River Zadorra at its west end. The River Zadorra ran through the plain, which had a hilly character, being a twisting river through the western end and for most of its length moving west - east through the plain. At the western end of the plain beyond the river to its south stood a pre-eminent height fringed by poplars, the Monte Arinez, protecting the village on the Royal Road to Madrid, which ran along the Zadorra valley. The river was crossed by twelve bridges. A string of small villages bounded the river – in the west Nanclares, Villodas and Tres Puentes; in the north Mendoza on the north side of the river, and Margarita, Lermanda and Crispijana. The roads from Vitoria to the north-west to Bilbao were guarded by Yurre, and Abechuco; those in the north-east by Gamarra Mayor and Durana. Halfway along the plain on the Madrid road was Gomecha and to the south of it Esquivel.

King Joseph and Marshal Jourdan drew up the French army in three basic lines initially across the valley, expecting as they did that the Duke of Wellington would come from the west. The front line comprised the Corps of General Gazon, the second that of General D'Erlon and the third that of General (later Marshal in 1847) Reuille, as a reserve. Some guns, the stores and wagons, and the mixed carriages and wagons of the court were left to the east of Vitoria and King Joseph had stands erected in the town to permit the battle to be viewed. Wellington, who had advanced through the hills north of the Royal Road, positioned Sir Roland Hill's division on his right, Sir Thomas Picton's in the centre between Nanclares and Mendoza and Sir Thomas Graham's on the left. Graham was ordered to

move north-east of the town of
Vitoria to secure the Bayonne
Road in order to impede any
retreat to France. In fact he
was delayed and crossed the
Bilbao, road joining up with
Longa and a Spanish guerilla
army, who blocked the road to
Bayonne.

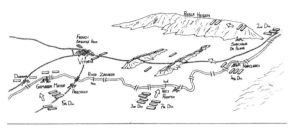

The 21st of June opened cold and drizzly, with a mist. Hill crossed the Royal
road and the River Zadorrra about eight miles west of Vitoria and then moved up
to the Puebla Hills which the 21st (Highland Light Infantry) were ordered to take
in order to enfilade Gazon's line from the south, while Spanish infantry took the
ridge of the hills. The attack began at 8.30 am and against fierce resistance Hill's
troops pushed forward – Generals Maransin, Couroux and Daricou could not
stem the tide, King Joseph and Jourdan responding by sending part of General
Billette's division to strengthen the left flank. While this was being done, cannon
fire was heard at the east end of the valley, where Graham had emerged, requiring
General Reuille on the French right to protect the rear of the army and the town
of Vitoria, but although Graham had lagged behind because of the difficulties of
his march, his appearance gave little time for the French to respond. The main
attack in the valley did not, however, begin until about mid-day.

Wellington's right pushed on and elements of Kempt's Light Division took the
undestroyed bridge at Tres Puentes. It was lightly defended, a fact made known
to Wellington by a peasant informer, who was decapitated by a cannonball as the
troops took the bridge. The bridge at Villodas was also taken and General Laval
fell back. Meanwhile, Sir Thomas Picton opposite the French centre launched an
attack at Mendoza on the village and its bridge. He had been ordered to wait for
Lord Dalhousie's 7th Division, but the latter had not come up in time because
the division had lost its way and Picton became impatient. Raging and fuming
he gave the order to charge – 'Come on you rascals! Come on you Fighting
Villains!' Led by a cursing Picton, the 3rd Division dashed on through grape and
round shot and towards the hill of Arinez; on they went, the 45th (Derbyshire
Regiment), the 88th (Connaught rangers) and the 74th (Highland Light Infantry)
on the left. Both sides were involved in an unending bombardment. The whole
front along the Zadorra was now in action. Fierce fighting flowed too also around
Yorre, Abecheco, Durana and Gamarra Mayor – where Graham's first division
was embroiled with Reuille's Corps. Hill was still pushing along the Puebla Hills
and from the villages in the west where the river had been crossed. Wellington,
with two infantry brigades, moved with troops from Dalhousie's 7th Division to
support Picton, and by 3pm a huge hole had been rent in the French centre.

The hill of Arinez was taken, and the village beyond. Vandelour's light brigade took Margarita – and Gazon's Corps began to crumble as it saw itself outflanked by Hill and Morillo's Spaniards on the French left. King Joseph and Marshal Jourdon endeavoured to re-establish a new line to the west of Vitoria from Crispiljana on the river south to Esquivel, using six infantry divisions backed up by 4,000 cavalry and seventy-five guns. General Gazon however, troubled by Hill on his flank, began to withdraw his divisions and the line never stabilised. In the north-east, despite Count Reuille's fierce defence, the villages began to fall. Gamarra Mayor was taken by the Second Brigade of the 5th division – 4th (Royal Lancashire), the 47th (North Lancashire) and 59th (East Lancashire), the 4th bearing the brunt and taking 2,000 prisoners. The 1st Division and Bradford's Portuguese brigade, with Halkett's light German infantry, stormed Abechuco, with artillery support.

The hills on the far left near Durana were taken by General Longa supported by the 5th Division, particular distinction being won by the 4th Regiment of Cacadores from the Portuguese Brigade, who charged the enemy downhill with their bayonets. The collapsing centre and the taking of the villages in the north-east created a move to retreat, the French abandoning their guns. Reuille's division had prevented complete encirclement, although the main road to Bayonne had in the hands of the Spanish guerilla army become unusable; thus only the poor road to Pamplona remained to the French. Already clogged with civilian and other transport, the route did not provide a road along which formations of the French army could entirely be held together.

By 5 pm King Joseph had ordered a general retreat and the move back to France began. Only General Reuille's Corps retired in any sense of order: the French army had disintegrated into a flowing rabble, mixed with fleeing courtiers, women, and Spanish supporters of King Joseph. The King himself was almost captured in his state carriage by the 18th Hussars, and had to make his escape on horseback. Carriage and baggage wagons cluttered the road as the refugees took out the horses for their own use. The temptation to the troops of plunder was too much: pursuit was intercepted as the abandoned wagons were looted. One contained the treasure of the Kingdom; others, silver and gold artefacts, fine cloth, military uniforms, wine and brandy. The Duke of Wellington estimated that over half a million pounds' worth of booty fell to the soldiery. Not all of it went to ordinary soldiers. Officers had their part: the 14th Light Dragoons acquired, for example a silver chamber pot from King Joseph's carriage for their mess, and Sergeant Blood returned to the 16th Regiment of Light Dragoons with 6,000 dollars. The boys in Portuguese regiments could be seen dressed in French officers' uniforms.

The carriage containing the Bonapartist Spanish archives and secret papers, to Wellington's annoyance, had the papers scattered to the winds by the failure of the 18th Hussars to guard it. Many of the court ladies and others were taken: for example, Madame Gazon, the general's wife, who was returned to the French.

The exhausted British infantry, after their 200-mile march and struggle at Vitoria, paused. The cavalry was ill managed and the pursuit was not pressed. 50,000 Frenchmen escaped to France, but by 25th June Sir Thomas Graham was in the Bidassoa Valley on the borders of France. The Emperor Napoleon put King Joseph and Marshal Jourdan under house arrest and on 11th July ordered Joseph to retire from the Kingdom. Marshal Soult was sent to re-organise the routed armies and defend the south-west of France.

The Battle of Vitoria, because of the absence of immediate pursuit by the cavalry, did not achieve the destruction of the French army in north-west Spain, but it was nonetheless one of the greatest, if not the greatest, of the Duke of Wellington's victories. The brilliant strategic march from the Portuguese border, carried out with careful organisation and consummate skill, itself resulted in the liberation of much of Castile and Leon. Vitoria for its part secured the clearing of the French from the whole of northern Spain (apart from Catalonia, which Marshal Suchet held, and the isolated fortresses of San Sebastian and Pamplona). The army, moreover, had captured all the French baggage, wagons and equipment, including 5 million French francs. 152 guns were taken and 415 wagons. The French lost 8,000 men – killed, wounded or captured. The casualties suffered by the allied army were 4,910, of which 3,308 were British, with 501 killed. Wellington stayed the army on the passes to France, because of the uncertain situation in Germany, where Napoleon was having treaty talks with Austria, Russia and Prussia. Marshal Soult later in the summer was to launch an assault on his position in the passes, which met with some initial success.

24th June 1340

The Battle of Sluys

When King Edward III began his personal rule in October 1330 his realms included part of modern France – Guienne and Aquitaine in the south-west. In 1331 his grandfather King Charles IV of France died, leaving his mother Queen Isabella as the only surviving child of Philip the Fair. The French in the past had adopted a practice that a female heir could not take the throne, but there was no principle that a grandson could not succeed his grandfather. The nobles of France were less than enthusiastic at the idea of an English King, so they crowned Philip de Valois, a great-nephew of Philip the Fair. As King Philip VI he and Edward III became entangled in futile disputes over the relationship between them regarding Guienne and Acquitaine, both of which Philip VI would like to have acquired. In 1338 Guienne was attacked unsuccessfully and covert support was given to the Scots, with whom Edward III was at war. In response to those provocations, King Edward III made his claim, as the son of the eldest Valois, line to be King of France. To some extent he was impelled to that course by the Flemings, who would only support him if the claim were made. From then until the reign of George III the royal arms bore the quarterings of the lilies of France.

In 1338, on 24th March, under the command of Bechuchet, the French, reinforced by 20 galleys from Genoa under Ayton Doria and 17 sent by the Grimaldis at Monaco, sacked Portsmouth, burning the hospital and church. The galleys were particularly adapted to this coastal plundering and incursion because of their shallowness and manoeuvrability, although not significantly effective in the open sea, where the sailing vessels, 'the cogs' had the advantage. Guernsey was attacked on the way back to France. On 23rd September the recently-appointed Admiral of France, Hue Quiéret, Seneschal de Beaucaire, seized off Walcheren five large English ships, which had recently brought King Edward III to Flanders, including the cogs Edward and Christopher. On 5th October Southampton was burnt.

1339 saw the same type of sea-borne war. Jersey was besieged but not captured. The English attacked towns at the mouth of the Gironde and sacked Treport. In May Hastings was burnt and destroyed. At the end of the year, however, for want of pay from King Philip VI, the Genoese mutinied and part of their galley fleet returned home, the other part suffering badly from a storm at Sluys. The Grimaldi galleys also returned to Monaco. In January 1340 the English, covered by a fog, attacked Boulogne and destroyed 18 galleys and 24 merchantmen, burning the lower town. Edward III returned home and set about collecting a fleet to transport an army back to the Low Countries, where the French were invading. With great energy Philip VI put together a fleet of some 200 ships and

268

sent them to the estuary of the Zwyn, part of the River Scheldt system, in order to intercept the English arriving in Flanders. This French fleet anchored off Sluys on 8th June. Philip's ultimate aim had been the invasion of England, but the first need had been to prevent reinforcement of the allied army against him. Under the command of Admirals Quiéret and Béhuchet the fleet was drawn up in three lines, their bows to the sea: the first seaward line were the vessels from Flanders and the Lower Seine, the second from Dieppe and Picardy and the innermost from Normandy. In front of the seaward line where the Genoese Barbavera was stationed with his four galleys, were the four large ships taken from the English – now renamed – Christophe (carrying archers), L'Edward, La Katherine and La Rose. Each had had mounted on them four cannons. The three lines of vessels were joined by heavy chains interspersed with rowing boats and barges. The formation replicated a great fortress floating on the sea, but that was achieved at the expense of mobility.

The English fleet met Edward III in the River Orwell on 21st June. He flew from the mainmast of his ship, the Thomas, the Royal banner of the quartered arms of France and England. The English had upwards of 160 ships. Froissart in his chronicles, in a great roll call of chivalry, recites the lords and knights on board – for example the Earls of Pembroke, Huntingdon and Gloucester, Lord Percy, Lord Delaware, Sir John Chandos, Sir John Beachamp. Each flew their vivid pennants at the mast heads of the cogs which had been provided with fore and after castle and a mast head castle, the 'castles' being painted with golden lions. A party of ladies of the court, desirous of returning to the Queen in Ghent, were on board some of the ships. About 1 pm on 22nd June, followed by a north-east breeze and fine weather, the fleet sailed for Flanders, the King leading in the Thomas. At mid-day on 23rd June the Flanders coast was in sight and the fleet came up near the dunes at Blankenbourg. The large ships anchored there and the small were drawn up on the beach. Edward III had already had some pre-knowledge that the French were at Sluys, but he sent out horsemen to discover their precise disposition. By evening these had returned and reported. The King decided to attack the next day, the feast of St John the Baptist. The Genoese commander Barbavera, seeing the mass of sail arriving on the coast, had warned the French admirals that their ships linked together and immobile they were like a mouse in a trap, and he advised them to make out to sea. This advice was ignored.

At 5 am on 24th June Edward's fleet moved into its dispositions, pennants flying and sails raised. It was high tide; the wind was blowing towards the French fleets. He manoeuvred the whole fleet out to sea and northwards with the intent that it should be taken down on to the French by the wind and incoming tide with the sails set for a starboard course, in order to shield the massed ranks of soldiers and archers as much as possible from the sun. Thus, the French initially enjoyed the illusion that the English had turned and fled. The fleet, however, as the day wore on, turned and came down rapidly on the French line on its left, where King Edward had stationed the biggest boats and most skilled captains. These sea-born 'castles' at a signal from the Thomas came down towards Le Christophe, the ship captured from the English. One to one they engaged in combat. The English Archers began their fire, longer in range and three times as rapid as the French, whose men in consequence fell on deck long before the grappling irons, ship for ship, enabled hand-to-hand fighting to begin. The whole weight of the English fleet pressed down on the first line, which the rear lines could not resist.

A general mêlée ensued, sword to sword, with lance and bow, the English boarding the French ships. As the vessels were each taken, the victors threw those who had fought, dead and alive, into the sea. The French cannons had been ineffective, although the Thomas was itself damaged. The four great ships were all taken. Admirals Quierét and Bechuchet were killed: the latter's body was hauled to the top of the mast of the Thomas in reprisal for his brutal ravaging of the ports and towns of England. The realisation that the Admirals were dead panicked the Dieppe and Picardy soldiers and sailors in the second line. Once more they succumbed to the English archers and the ships were boarded. Meanwhile, Barbavera with his fleet of Genovese galleys had raised anchor and escaped to sea. As night fell the Flemings organised by Jacque Van Artevelde attacked the French in the third line from the rear. Admiral Hélie escaped with the royal galleys and a few ships. Survivors came ashore and were to be seen naked and wounded, struggling across Flanders away from the disaster. The French lost all but a few ships – 190, and 16,000 were killed. The English loss was 4,000 men and four knights. At the French court subsequently no one dared to speak to King Philip VI about the outcome of the battle.

King Edward III remained that night at Sluys, celebrating his victory. The next day he went to a mass at the convent of Our Lady of Ardenborg to give thanksgiving for the outcome and rode on to Ghent to meet the Queen, Philippa of Hainault, and reunite her with her court ladies, come from England. The victory opened France to invasion, but Edward III did not act to do so until 1346. French sea power was not entirely destroyed: in August they landed on the Isle of Wight and on another occasion burnt Teignmouth. The French land forces withdrew into Artois.

28th June 1743

The Battle of Dettingen

The Battle of Dettingen was one of the incidents in the war of the Austrian succession, which commenced when King Frederick II of Prussia made an unjustified attack on the Empress Maria Theresa of Austria, with a view to taking Silesia from Austria. When the Emperor Charles VI died he had no son. During his life he had sought by treaty to obtain the consent for the Empress Marie Theresa to succeed to the Hapsburg land of Austria and to have her husband elected as Holy Roman Emperor, the purely nominal ruler of all Germany. Since 1713 all the greater European powers had adhered to the treaty (known as 'the Pragmatic Sanction') supporting Maria Theresa – Britain, France, Spain, Prussia, Bavaria and Hanover and the smaller principalities such as Saxony. On Frederick II's attack on Austria, the Elector of Bavaria and Saxony repudiated the treaty and France, Spain and Saxony, seeing advantages from the dismemberment of Austria, transferred their support from the Emperor to the Elector Charles Albert of Bavaria, who was crowned as the Emperor in 1742. The French, for example, thought that the humiliation of Austria would deliver to them the Austrian Netherlands (modern Belgium) and some borderlands, and in the tradition of the French state welcomed the opportunity to seize them. The course of the war, its shifting alliances, sharp successes and reversals is a tangled story, almost interminable to study. Britain sometimes feebly and sometimes strongly continued to support the Emperor and its treaty obligation of 1731.

The British position was however compromised by King George II's interest in protecting the Electorate of Hanover, which occupied largely the eastern part of the region of North-Rhine – Westphalia in Germany. The Hanoverian dynasty had secured the throne of England in 1715, on the death of Queen Anne without surviving issue, under the Act of Settlement of 1701, which had transferred the right to the Crown from the main Stuart line to the descendants of the Electress Sophia Dorothea, if Protestant, who was herself the grand-daughter of King James I. George II was devoted to Hannover; had German as his first language; in character was touchy and, although of small stature, obsessed with the idea of being a successful soldier-king. He kept mistresses, whom he was said to have paid with sweepstake tickets, but kept the Queen informed of them.

The years 1740 – 1742 saw shifting alliances and varying outcomes in the war. Marshal Belle-Isle was sent to Germany as a roving Ambassador to unite the Electors behind Charles Albert of Bavaria. Frederick II took Silesia, an act recognised by France, and France used its extensive military resources to capture Prague,

271

although in the winter of 1742 the French were forced to retreat. The Austrians in their turn ravaged Bavaria, driving Charles Albert from his Electorate.

In 1740 Louis XV could field some 130,000 regular soldiers, apart from the militia, and had a navy of 80 ships of the line, with 60,000 sailors. The low tax policy of Sir Robert Walpole, the first Prime Minister, over twenty years had left the Navy decayed and resulted in Britain being able to field only some 16,000 troops in 1742. These were sent to the Netherlands under the Earl of Stair to join the Dutch in the creation of the Pragmatic Army. The Dutch however refused to stir themselves and it was not until 1743 that a Pragmatic Army was able to move into Germany to campaign. The total army amounted to 30,000, of which the British were about half. The British were not themselves at war (indeed war was not declared by France until 1744), but acted as the ally of the Empress as Queen of Hungary. France fought as the ally of Charles Albert of Bavaria. The war was however very popular in England, and Walpole was forced to agree to a £300,000 subsidy and to pay contingents of Danish and Hessian troops to support her. Once Walpole retired, the Pelham Government with Lord Carteret as Secretary of State for Foreign Affairs, increased the subsidy to £500,000 and abandoned Hannoverian neutrality. George II therefore, against the advice of his ministers, went to take command in the field. In order to provide for his needs he took a baggage train of 662 horses, 13 Berlin carriages, 35 wagons and 54 carts. The luggage included 900 dozen napkins.

The Pragmatic Army had a destructive march south to the River Main because the commissariat failed to supply the troops and in mid-June they arrived in a poor state to camp at Aschaffenburg on the north bank of the River Main, west of modern Frankfurt, from which they went out to seize the peasant's cattle for food. Their plight was great and the French were so positioned that they were able to block new supplies from the east. The Earl of Stair was held responsible for the state of the army by George II and virtually ignored. In the context the issue arose of what course the army was to take. It was decided to retreat along the River Main west to Hanau where 12,000 further Hessian and Hannoverian troops were stationed.

Marshal Noailles with a force of 50,000 was on the south bank. He was of the view that the Pragmatic Army would retreat and thus had anticipated the decision made by George II and his generals. At midnight on 27th June the Pragmatic Army began its retreat. Soon after, Marshal Noailles made his dispositions. A French force under the Duke of Grammont, Marshal Noaille's nephew, of some 26,000 were sent across the river to the west of the retreating force to block its way, and the Marshal proposed to cross at Aschaffenburg and thus box the Pragmatic Army in. The route along the north of the river was narrow, hemmed in to the north by the wooded Spressart Hills, and was within the range of the guns on the south bank. Near Klein Ostheim heavy gunfire fell on the cavalry, which they endured as the infantry was shielded. Guns were fired at George II but the balls flew over his head. Just before Dettingen the route came to a swampy ravine crossed by a narrow bridge restricting further movement west. The Duke of Grammont on his own initiative placed his army on the east side of the marshy ravine in order to intercept the oncoming army. On coming to the waiting enemy George II halted his troops.

Some three hours passed before the Duke of Grammont, losing patience, launched his cavalry, breaking through a regiment of dragoons. The charge was dissipated by the fire of the British infantry, who stood firm. Three times the French charged, almost overwhelming the left wing. As the battle progressed George II's horse took the bit and bolted to the rear: the King sawed with the reins at the horse and brought it to a standstill. He dismounted, remarking that he could trust his legs better. The King on foot in front of the British infantry drew his sword and shouted in broken English, 'Now, boys, for the honour of England: fire and behave bravely, and the French will soon run.' Putting himself at their head, he marched the British infantry towards the French, to within sixty yards, putting into the latter's troops volley after volley as they advanced. The French infantry broke and were pushed towards the swamp and the River Main, where many drowned. There followed a cavalry fight near the river, the 3rd Dragoons, who had been subject to the gunfire as they came towards Dettingen, charging again and again. The Blues and the 1st and 7th Dragoons were pushed back by the French, but their success was nullified by volley after volley from the 21st and 23rd of Foot who shot them down. The trap had been opened. The Earl of Stair urged King George II to pursue the defeated French, but he decided, abandoning the wounded, to march on to Hanau. The French had lost 4,000 men. Marshal Noailles re-crossed the Rhine in order to defend France and the Duke de Broglie with the retreating French Army, pursued by the Austrians, abandoned on the orders of Louis XV the town of Donauworth to return home. The war was to be renewed in 1744 when Marshal de Saxe was sent to seize the fortresses in the Austrian Netherlands. George II was elated at his martial prowess and he rewarded the Earl of Stair immediately with a knighthood. One was also conferred on Trooper Thomas Brown of the 3rd Dragoons.

The victory was at first popular in England, but polite enthusiasm diminished when it was heard that George II wore a Hannoverian uniform in battle, a logical choice for him, however, as Britian was not at war with France. Nonetheless, Handel comprised a Te Deum in honour of the Battle, which was first performed before the King and Royal family at the Chapel Royal on 27th November 1743.

July

2nd	The Storming of the Schellenberg	1704
3rd	The Seizure and Destruction of the French Fleet	1940
4th	The Battle of Maida	1806
11th	The Battle of Oudenarde	1708
14th	The Surrender of Lebanon and Syria	1941
22nd	The Battle of Salamanca	1812
23rd	The Battle of Garcia Hernandez	1812
24th	The Taking of Gibraltar	1704
25th	The Battle of the North Foreland	1666
28th	The Battle of Talavera	1809
	The Battle of Sorauren	1813
29th	The Defeat of the Spanish Armada	1588
31st	The Battle of the Texel	1653

2nd July 1704

The Storming of the Schellenborg

The war of the Spanish succession commenced in 1701 but Britain did not declare war on France until May 1702. After the death of King William III, the Duke of Marlborough was appointed Captain-General of the allied English and Dutch forces in the Netherlands. Britain was part of an alliance headed by the Emperor of Austria, including the Markgraf of Baden, the King of Prussia, the Elector of Hanover and other German princes. Maximilian Emmanuel, the Prince and Elector of Bavaria, was in alliance with the French, as he hoped to gain the Imperial throne for himself. The summers of 1702 and 1703 were spent by the Duke of Marlborough, hampered by his Dutch allies, in Flanders. The French in Southern Germany in 1703 advanced and threatened Vienna, while the Emperor of Austria had also to deal with an insurrection in Hungary. The failure of the Elector of Bavaria to support his French allies by indulging in an attack on the Tyrol saved Vienna. The Emperor called back Prince Eugene of Savoy, his successful commander in Italy, and appointed him to command the Imperial Armies. Because of the chain of fortresses, seized by Louis XIV and the others, which he had built, Marlborough appreciated that a successful war against France would best be served in 1704 by a joint attack by the alliance forces on the Elector in the heart of Bavaria. He was also well aware of the difficulty which he would face from the Dutch, were he to tell them of his strategy. He therefore prepared in secret to achieve his ends.

In order to campaign in Bavaria a massive logistic problem arose. Some 40,000 men and horses would have to march some two hundred and fifty miles across difficult country, across rivers and on poor roads; Marlborough regarded it as crucial to ensure that his troops were provided with the necessary supplies. The Quartermaster General, Cadogan, was instructed to provide depots along the route where food, baking ovens, supplies (even replacement shoes) and forage could be collected to provision the march, which involved 1,700 wagons, 4,000 draught beasts as well as the cavalry and artillery horses. All was to be done in the utmost secrecy – indeed, apart from Marlborough and Cadogan only five people were privy to the secret, including Queen Anne and the Emperor. Publicly talk was of an invasion of France along the Moselle, thus outflanking the line of fortresses in the Low Countries.

The French had started the war with a massive army, amounting in May 1702 to some 400,000 men to whom would be added 45,000 Bavarians. In the Spring of 1704 Louis XIV had significant armies in the field: Marshal Villeroi in Flanders,

Marshal Tallard in Lorraine facing the Rhine and Marshal Marsin in Southern Germany, acting in concert with the Elector of Bavaria.

At the beginning of May the Duke left Liege leaving General Overkirk and a Dutch army to guard Holland. On 18th May he arrived at Bedburg, just north-west of Cologne. Louis XIV, aware of the openly expressed purpose of invading France up the Moselle valley, ordered Marshal Villeroi to shadow the Alliance army to the west and he therefore left a reduced force in Flanders and began to go south. On 20th May the Duke struck camp with a force of sixty battalions of infantry and forty-six squadrons of cavalry, of which 14,000 men were British and Irish. The long red train of men, wagons, horses, beasts and guns trailed south. Each day the march began at dawn and ended at 9.00 am, so that the ten to twelve miles a day march was accomplished before the sun was too high in the sky. Along the way the troops found the commissariat established and food and supplies ready. The cavalry in general preceded the infantry and the artillery and paused periodically to permit their catching up. As the train moved south, the pretence of an attack along the Moselle Valley was maintained. The army marched along the Rhine and on 25th May arrived at Coblenz, where the Moselle and the Rhine joined. Marlborough crossed the Moselle and marched through the town where he prepared to cross to the east bank. He crossed on two bridges of boats which had been especially constructed for that purpose, and then struck south-eastwards towards Mainz. The change of direction left the French uncertain as to the destination of the allied army and the commanders of the armies consulted Louis XIV, who after some time spent in deliberation gave orders based on the notion that Alsace would be the object of attack. Villeroi was to proceed to Landau where he would join Marshal Tallard on the west bank of the Rhine. Marlborough continued his deceit on the enemy by having a bridge of boats built at Philippsburg.

At Braubach on 30th May the Duke had heard that the Dutch were sending reinforcements. On 6th June the army moved east from Wiesloch and crossed the River Neckar at Lauffen. On 10th June at Mundelsheim the Duke of Marlborough and Prince Eugene met for the first time and instantly establish a mutual trust, sympathy and respect which made their co-operation in the war formidable. They agreed a strategy in which Marlborough was to press on to join the Markgraf of Baden and Prince Eugene was to go to the Rhine to block attempts by Villeroi and Tallard to strike at Marlborough's flank. When Marshal Marsin and the Elector of Bavaria realised, as Marlborough moved towards them, that they were isolated, they appealed to Louis XIV to send Tallard to reinforce them. In late May 10,000 ill-trained militia had been sent to Marsin, but Louis XIV was not prepared to send Tallard forward because of the danger which he perceived on the Rhine. After two weeks, he ordered Tallard to go on a long southern detour through the Black Forest with a view to supporting Bavaria.

On 14th June at the Lamb Inn at Gross Heppach Prince Eugene, the Markgraf of Baden and Marlborough met. Neither Prince Eugene nor Marlborough trusted the Markgraf completely since they suspected him of negotiating with Maximilian Emmanuel and of standing by while Tallard had reinforced Marsin. After discussion it was agreed that Eugene should go as planned to the Rhine and that Marlborough and the Markgraf should share command of the combined army, alternating day by day as Generalissimo.

On 27th June at Geislingen near Ulm, the whole army was united. The army which had come from Holland, had marched through difficult country for the last thirty-two days in downpours of rain, but had arrived in good heart and condition. The Markgraf's army, the Dutch and the Danish under the Duke of Wurtemberg all had joined. To strike into Bavaria a base was needed and the choice fell on Donauworth. The town also had the advantage of enabling a supply link to the north-east to the established.

The march from Holland was for the age a shining example of moving an army: as Winston Churchill remarked in his *Life of Marlborough*, there was no more heroic episode than this march in army annals. The challenge now was to take Donauworth. The city was situated on the River Danube on the north bank protected by the small River Wernitz on its east and a high mountain plateau known as the Schellenburg beyond the river. The town was approached from the north through a village called Berg and the city was protected on this side by the Schellenberg, whose steepest banks were to the west. To the north of the plateau was dense woodland, but the half-mile square flat summit had on it a fort constructed by the Swedish King Gustavus Adolphus during the Thirty Years War in 1632. The fort had long been neglected and was in ruins. There were scarcely any remains of this defensive ring in the south-west where the fort came down to the River Wernitz and the city.

The Elector of Bavaria and the French, having formed a view that Donauworth would be the object of the allied army, hurried a force there under Count D'Arco of some 13,000 men, including 2,500 French under Colonel La Colonie. Feverish attempts began to restore the fortifications, which Marshal Villeroi had warned in 1703 should be repaired. The eastern side was the first part attempted, where the slope was shallower to the summit. The west was left until last. A trench outside the fort was prepared and slowly the walls were repaired as the allied army approached. Count D'Arco, the commander, thought that he would be able to complete the work by 3rd July. There was a division of view as to the proper approach between the Markgraf of Baden and Marlborough. The former was traditionally a soldier used to the besieging of towns as the preferred method of warfare, while Marlborough favoured open crushing battles. News came that the main French-Bavarian Army was a days march to the south. On 1st July the Markgraf commanded the force and thought in terms of a long siege. Marlborough was determined that on 2nd July, his day of command, the Schellenberg should be attacked. He rose early and at 3.00 am, with thirty-two squadrons of cavalry and engineers to pave the way for the artillery, he set out for the city of Donauworth.

He arrived at 9.00 am and reconnoitred the situation. Count D'Arco had the majority of his force on the Schellenberg and had posted La Colonie and the French on the flat summit as a reserve. Marlborough decided to concentrate his initial attack on the north-west point of the hill on the steepest slope and await the result before committing reserves and the forces of the Markgraf at the weaker end of the western line between the hill and the town. Drenching heavy rain slowed the main body of the troops, who only arrived at midday: 6,000 infantry adding to the cavalry already present. The Markgraf was still following on. It took three hours to bridge the River Wernitz in order to permit troops and guns to form up on the lower slopes of the Schellenberg. During the day troops under Lord Cadogan, the Quarter Master General, had spent time measuring out a camp as if for a long siege. This deception on Marlborough's part led Count D'Arco to ignore the threat to the fort and to neglect to hurry on with the fortification works.

By 5.00pm, following a cannonade from both sides, the infantry were ready for the attack. La Colonie's French troops, drawn up on the plateau, had suffered particularly from the British cannon because there was no shelter for them. Five regiments of British troops and the Dutch led by General Van Goor were to attack the fort. The five regiments - the 1st Royal Regiment of Foot, the Queen's Royal Regiment of Foot, the Cameronians, Colonel Meredith's Regiment of Foot and Colonel Dearing's Regiment of Foot – represented the elite of the army and contained English, Scottish and Welsh. The troops had been provided with fascines to throw into the trench before the walls to ease its crossing. The cannonade fell off and at 6.00 pm the infantry, with Van Goor to the front started to mount the slope. Into their ranks the Bavarians poured volley after volley of musquetry fire, but they went on. Mistaking a long hole made by the rain for the trench the fascines were thrown in, so that they were not available at the wall. Nonetheless, they marched on; at eighty paces General Van Goor was killed. The troops began to shout to encourage their attack, so loudly that Count D'Arco ordered his drummers to drown out the noise. Savage hand-to-hand fighting took place over and around the fortifications but gradually the Bavarians forced the Anglo-Dutch infantry to draw back. Lord Marchant, Marlborough's tear-away son-in-law, later 3rd Earl of Peterborough and victor in 1705 at Barcelona, led a forlorn hope of fifty men as the spearhead of the attack. Out of fifty men, only he and ten others survived.

A second attack was ordered after the infantry had reformed and once more they mounted the hill, their generals and colonels at their head. Again the murderous fire halted their progress. The Bavarians and French moved to the counter-attack and swept back the assault, only being halted by the cavalry on the lower slopes. The stalwart endeavours made had been met by Count D'Arco in part by removing the defenders from the south-west wall in order to strengthen the resistance to the assault. Marlborough probed that end of the defensive fortification with a platoon of infantry. The defence was found weak behind the uncompleted fortifications, which had not been repaired. By this time the Markgraf of Baden had arrived and his troops, passing by the town walls from which the French did not fire, assaulted the gap and streamed into the fort.

A third attack was made on the north-west wall, un-mounted dragoons from the 2nd Regiment (Scots Greys) joining in. The defenders began to give way and La Colonie and his French on the plateau found the Imperial infantry attacking them to the flank and rear. One French regiment broke and fled back into the town. Gradually the attackers gained the upper hand and the defending troops hurried away in flight from the savage fighting which was overwhelming them. In less than two hours the Schellenberg had been taken. The Bavarian French army in its tempestuous flight lost all but 3,000 men. 7,000 were killed and 2,000 wounded. The pontoon bridge over the Danube collapsed under the weight of fleeing wagons and many drowned in the fast-flowing waters of the river. Donauworth was set on fire and abandoned, but the inhabitants put out the fires. 12 colours, 16 guns and Count D'Arco's silver plate were taken. The cost of the storming of the fort for the allies was significant: the British lost one in four of their force, as did the other allied forces. 1,200 were killed and 2,000 wounded. Heavy rain fell in the night, aggravating the condition of the wounded. Marlborough's improved medical services applied such palliatives as they could.

Maximilian Emmanuel with the French-Bavarian army removed to Augsburg. Marlborough, although he had cleared the route to Vienna, had an intense problem of supply and the dual command did not press on towards Munich. They marched to take Rain and then wandered around Bavaria destroying 372 towns and villages in the hope that the Elector, out of pity for his subjects, would negotiate. Marlborough had real misgivings about this policy, which as he wrote to his wife was against his nature, but he agreed to it out of necessity. After initial vacillation, the Elector of Bavaria decided to continue to adhere to the French.

3rd July 1940
The Seizure and Destruction
of the French Fleet

 In June 1940 the French fleet was the fourth-largest navy in the world. It was a major concern for the British Government, as the French Government moved toward the desertion of its allies, that this fleet should not fall under the control of either the Germans or the Italians, and thus jeopardise naval supremacy around our shores or in the Mediterranean. Winston Churchill, in the closing days before France sought an Armistice, hastened to France three times to endeavour to stiffen French morale and strengthen the Prime Minister, Paul Reynaud in his attempts to keep France in the war opposed, as he was by the commander of the army, General Weygand, and a soldier-hero of the Great War, Marshal Pétain, who had been brought into the Government. France had every opportunity, and the strength, to continue the war with the troops, aeroplanes and naval fleet in its extensive colonies throughout the world, and in particular in Algeria and Tunisia. As the cry for an Armistice became more insistent, led by General Weygand, the French Government sought the release by Britain of its treaty commitment to continue the war to ultimate victory over Germany. The British agreed to that release, but subject to the proviso that the French fleet should sail to British ports where it would be out of control of the Germans.

There was diplomatic confusion over the delivery of this message because of the sudden offer by Britain of indissoluble union with France. Marshal Pétain described the offer as 'fusion with a corpse'. Both he and General Weygand believed Britain would collapse too: Weygand indeed had told Petain that in three weeks England would have her neck wrung like a chicken. However, before the negotiations with the Germans, the request was put to Marshal Petain, who became Prime Minister in Paul Reynaud's place. A delegation was also sent to Bordeaux, where the French Government came to rest, to discuss the issue with Admiral Darlan. To be fair, the latter had told Churchill on one of his visits to France that the French navy would not be handed over to the Germans. However, the Armistice signed by France on 21st June 1940 contained a provision (Article 8) that the French fleet 'shall be collected in ports to be specified and there demobilised and disarmed under German or Italian control.'

Hitler gave a further assurance that the Germans would not take the vessels for their own use. The Armistice terms therefore in no way met the condition which Britain had stipulated as necessary for the release of France from the treaty obligation to continue the war. Given the scant reliance which could be placed on Hitler's promises, and the potential accessibility to the Germans of the French fleet under this arrangement, the French fleet proved a potential threat to the survival of Britain and the interests of the United States, who had also urged the French to secure their fleet outside potential German control. The French Government remained in France, with Admiral Darlan as Minister of Marine, when it could have continued the war in Africa. It was the only government of the states invaded by Germany not to continue the fight. Even the Belgian Government went to London, although King Leopold had surrendered his army to the Germans and stayed in Belgium.

The outlook for Britain in late June 1940 was bleak, although the islands had still the guard of its navy and the Royal Air Force, which were to fend off invasion. Nonetheless, the collapse of France did not fill the general population with undue dismay. The popular view was summarised by Vice Admiral Tovey on his visit to Admiral Cunningham on 24th June, as set out in the latter's memoirs. Arriving on the flagship in Alexandria he smilingly told Cunningham 'Now I know we shall win the war, Sir. We have no more allies.' Churchill, however, knew and appreciated the problem he faced politically and militarily, given the failure by France to put the fleet out of German reach. The American defence establishment, and President Roosevelt, were not sanguine about Britain's chances, and hesitated to send military aid, which was likely to fall ultimately into German hands. Roosevelt indeed told his associate James Farley on 13th June that British chances of survival were only one in three. There was a need therefore to demonstrate that Britain would fight on ruthlessly to the end. Churchill also appreciated in this context two essential premises on which war policy should be based: first, the maxim of Lord Palmerston that Britain should have no permanent friends, no permanent enemies but only permanent interests, and second, Lord Nelson's doctrine that in dealing with enemy forces the overall object should be annihilation. The logic of the situation led him and the Cabinet to regard it as necessary that the French fleet should be removed effectively from the war so far as possible. The decision was made to launch Operation Catapult on 3rd July. Many Naval officers, locked in sentiments of friendship for their former allies, lacked the clarity of vision to realise the necessity, and argued against the operation, but they were quite properly over ridden.

At the time of the operation, much of the French navy was dispersed from Toulon. In Portsmouth and Plymouth there were two battleships, four light cruisers, submarines, including the large submarine Surcouf, and two hundred other vessels. At Alexandria there were one battleship (the Lorraine), four cruisers, of which three were modern with 8' guns, and smaller ships under Admiral Godfroy. Cunningham in his memoirs said their presence presented a dilemma for the navy since, if they left, the ships could sail to Beirut or France. At Oran, at Mers El Kebir, there were the modern battle-cruisers Dunkerque and Strasbourg, each of 26,500 tons with eight 13' and sixteen 5.1' guns and a speed of 29.5 knots, both therefore superior to the German Gneisenau and Scharnhorst; two battleships (the Bretagne and the Provence), several light cruisers, destroyers, submarines and other vessels. At Algiers there were seven cruisers, four of them with 8' guns. At Casablanca lay the incomplete Jean Bart, not fully engined, but which had left France on 18th June from St. Nazare, before the Germans took the port, and at Dakar the Richelieu, an almost completed battleship with 15' guns. Away in the Caribbean was an aircraft carrier and two light cruisers.

On 2nd July the Admiralty alerted the naval units involved that Operation Catapult was to be executed on the following day. Seizures were to be made of the ships in Portsmouth and Plymouth. At Mers El Kebir and Alexandria, Admirals Somerville and Cunningham were ordered to present to the French alternative choices for them. At Mers El Kebir: first, the French vessels could join our forces to continue the war, effectively becoming part of the free French organisation forming under General de Gaulle; second, they could sail with reduced crews to British ports or third, if they were not to be used during the Armistice, they could sail with reduced crews to the West Indies - such as Martinique - where they could be demobilised or entrusted to the United States. At Alexandria the choices were: first, to reduce crews and immobilise the vessels so that they were not in sea-going condition, only coming into use if the Armistice was broken, while the British paid skeleton crews of personnel left to maintain the ships and second, to sink the ships at sea. As before, the opportunity was given to the officers and crews to continue to use their vessels in the war. In the event of no adequate reply before dusk, the British commanders were ordered by every means at their disposal to destroy the French ships.

At Plymouth and Portsmouth on 3rd July, although Admiral Cayol suspected that some action might occur, a strong force of armed patrols went onto the French vessels at 3.45 am. The watches on board were overpowered and the crews sent on shore. An hour later all the ships were in British control. Resistance was met on the Surcouf, and two deaths took place. When the crews were offered the opportunity to join the free French or go home, 19,000 chose to return to France, including most of the officers. Only 900 stayed to fight the war.

On 1st July Admiral Somerville had been ordered to proceed to Mers El Kebir to carry out the operation. Force H left Gibraltar comprising the battle cruiser Hood, (the 4th of that name) the battleships Valiant (4th of that name) and Resolution (13th of that name), the aircraft carrier Ark Royal (3rd of that name), two cruisers and eleven destroyers. Somerville was ordered that if none of the alternatives was accepted within six hours the French ships were to be destroyed. Captain Holland, who had been Naval Attaché in Paris, had protested against the action, allowing friendship for France to stand before political necessity. Churchill remained adamant. Somerville arrived off Oran at 9.30 am and Captain Holland was sent to see the French Admiral Gensoul, who, on orders from Admiral Darlan to have no contact with the British, would not see him. A message was therefore sent. Admiral Gensoul replied that the ships would not be allowed to fall into German hands and that he would meet force with force. Gensoul had telegraphed the French Ministry of Marine at Vichy, but did not present all the alternatives in asking for instructions. He merely sent the message that the British intended to sink the ships and that he was indicating that he would retaliate. Negotiations continued all day, and Gensoul played for time. Late in the afternoon the Ministry of Marine informed him that it had ordered all French forces in the Mediterranean to his support, including aeroplanes and submarines. In London Winston Churchill grew restless. Holland was received by Gensoul at 3 pm on the Dunkerque, the flag ship, and the men argued, Gensoul relying on a secret order from Darlan to scuttle the ships. Finally, Somerville radioed Gensoul setting 5.30 pm as the deadline for acceptance of the alternatives.

At 5.45 pm Summerville opened fire. The French warships were tied up along the mole, their fore guns pointing away from the sea. The stern guns' range of fire was impeded by raised land. Under the smoke screen created by destroyers, the British warships pounded the French fleet. Ark Royal sent its aircraft to torpedo and bomb. In fifteen minutes the Bretagne blew up and sank. The Dunkerque and Provence were beached, having been badly damaged. Only the Strasbung escaped, although it was crippled on its way to Toulon. Ironically, after the engagement Somerville received a telegraph from the Admiralty, inspired by Churchill, that 'French ships must comply with our terms or sink themselves or be sunk by you before dark.' The order had in fact already been carried out.

At Alexandria the position for Admiral Cunningham was more difficult, since the French ships were in the naval harbour where the Eastern Mediterranean fleet had its base. He was on friendly terms with Admiral Godfroy, the French commander as were the officers of both navies. In his memoirs he says that he therefore found the order 'utterly repugnant'. Cunningham received Admiral Godfroy with full naval ceremonial on the flagship Warspite at 7 am. He put the alternatives before him. Godfroy said that he had to consult his government, but indicated that the alternative of demobilisation in harbour might be acceptable. He then returned to the Duquesne at 8.30 am. At noon Cunningham received a reply by letter. The alternative of sinking the ships at sea was accepted, although immobilisation was preferable, but he indicated that that would require the consent of the Vichy Government. He sought forty-eight hours to make arrangements for the crews. Cunningham accepted the proposal to sink the ships with forty-eight hours grace to 5th July. The arrangement did not meet the requirement in the orders of the British Government. Cunningham therefore in the afternoon tried again, on the basis of immobilising the French ships by discharging the oil and taking the warheads of the torpedoes. That was agreed and by 5.30 pm was in process. At 8.15 pm the Admiralty in London telegraphed Cunningham insisting that crew reduction should begin before dark and that he was not to fail. Soon after, Admiral Godfroy sent a further note that he had been ordered to sail and that he had stopped discharging oil. Cunningham sent Rear–Admiral Willis to Godfroy for further discussion, but the latter remained adamant that if faced by force he would scuttle the ships in harbour, should he be unable to leave. Cunningham rejected seizing the ships by boarding as impracticable, realised the difficulties of striking them by gunfire in the naval harbour, and thought that the only alternative was to intern the ships or seek their surrender. The British warships were prepared to bombard or torpedo the French, but on the morning of 4th July Cunningham decided to appeal over Admiral Godfroy's head to the officers and crews of the French ships. Signals were sent explaining the situation and stressing the British Government's generous terms of surrender. Notices were taken round on boats; ships meetings of crews, men and officers, were seen to take place on the French warships. The captains of the ships went jointly to visit Godfroy. About an hour after lunch Godfroy came on board the Warspite and an agreement was concluded. All fuel oil was to be discharged from the French ships forthwith; the ships were to be immobilised so that they could not fight, and discharge and reduction of the crews was to be agreed. The standoff between the British and French in the harbour was over. The British Government's policy had been implemented. Cunningham had achieved a success in carrying out his orders, although he persisted in his inability to appreciate the necessities that drove the policy which he had to apply. Even in 1951, he still recorded that he believed the decision to take the French fleet inept in its unwisdom.

On 4th July Winston Churchill announced to the House of Commons the results of Operation Catapult. Previously the Conservative benches had greeted him as Prime Minister indifferently, and his principal support had come from the Labour and Liberal parties. But on this occasion all sides of the House rose waving their order papers to cheer loudly at the news which he brought. President Roosevelt in Washington noted the determination of the British to fight on at all costs, and the enthusiastic response of the House of Commons. The American political establishment at last appreciated that Britain was not France, and the flow of military support which helped to save the country began.

On 8th July aircraft from the Hermes severely damaged the Richelieu in the Harbour at Dakar and after negotiations involving the United States, the ships in Martinique were immobilised. Admiral Godfroy remained on board in Alexandria harbour until 1943, when he accepted the legitimacy of the French authorities set up in North Africa. The Surcouf went down on 19th February 1942 with all its crew fighting for the free French. The Strasburg and the six light cruisers from Algiers which escaped to Toulon remained there. On 19th November 1942 Hitler ordered the occupation of Vichy France. At Toulon there were eight warships, about one-third of the 1939 fleet. On 27th November the Germans attacked the dockyard. They were fired on by the French, who scuttled their fleet, apart from five submarines. It has been argued that Churchill should have believed Admiral Darlan's pledge to him, but given the deceits and manoeuvrings of the French politicians in June 1940, the need to ensure British survival and to persuade the world of the nation's determination to fight, the removal from the war of the French fleet under Vichy control was crucial.

4th July 1806

The Battle of Maida

The southern part of Italy at the time of the Napoleonic Wars formed a separate kingdom ruled by Ferdinand IV and his wife Queen Maria Carolina, the daughter of the Emperor of Austria and the sister of Queen Marie Antoinette of France, whom the revolutionaries beheaded. The kingdom, called the Kingdom of the Two Sicilies, comprised the mainland areas, with a capital at Naples, and the Island of Sicily, with a capital at Palermo. It was at Naples that Lord Nelson after his victory at the Nile met Lady Hamilton, the wife of the Ambassador Sir William Hamilton, who became his mistress and mother of his daughter. The ambition of the French to control all Italy resulted in the flight of Ferdinand IV and Queen Maria Carolina to Sicily in February 1806; only the peninsular town and fort of Gaeta held out against French armies amounting to 35,000. On 31st March 1806 the Emperor Napoleon conferred on his brother Joseph Buonaparte the crown of Naples, which he had until 1808 when he was made King of Spain. The British, by use of the navy, and by sending an expeditionary force of troops, supported the beleaguered royal family in Sicily.

A squadron under Admiral Sir Sidney Smith was sent by Admiral Collingwood, Nelson's successor, to succour Sicily and prevent its invasion. The Admiral was kind-hearted and agreeable but vain: he was daring and quick and thus considered unreliable by some. Sir Sidney Smith arrived at Palermo on 20th April with four ships of the line – Pompée (74 guns), Excellent (74 guns) (1st of the name) Intrepid (2nd of the name with 64 guns) and Athenian (64 guns) – two British frigates and one Neapolitan. Sir John Stuart, who had been born in Georgia in the United States, fought for the British in the Rebellion of the Colonies and was captured at Yorktown in 1781, was the acting Commander of some 7,500 British troops on the island, including Sicilian and Corsican Battalions. Like Nelson before him, Sir Sidney Smith became a devotee of Queen Maria Carolina, who not surprisingly had a visceral hatred of the French and a desire to regain the Kingdom of Naples. Encouraged by her and without orders, he collected munitions and supplies and sailed for Gaeta, where the garrison of 600 was resisting 12,000 French, on 12th May. Ordnance and supplies were landed and he was joined by the Eagle (12th of the name with 74 guns). On his return he passed Naples; seeing the town and Palazzo Reale fully illuminated for the coronation of King Joseph he was tempted to bombard the palace, but refrained and went on to seize Capri, where a small garrison was left. On returning to Sicily he was pressed by the Queen to take an expedition to the mainland to harry the French in Calabria. The Marques Circeller and the French émigrés argued for such an attack, but it was opposed by the Sicilian Prime Minister, Sir John Acton, who was British, and the military commanders. Nonetheless Sir Sidney Smith, swayed by the Queen, prepared an expedition on the basis that the Calabrese would rise and harass the French, after which troops would be put ashore.

At the end of June he sailed with Sir John Stuart and 5,000 troops and anchored in the Golfo di Santa Eufemia. Two days were spent disembarking the troops and the guns: there was but one squadron of cavalry and some mules which could be ridden. The small force moved inland along the coast among the olive trees and pines, and they emerged on a low ridge above a shallow river valley. Meanwhile, General Reynier, who was Minister of War and Marine to King Joseph of Naples, moved south with 5,000 French, including 1,000 cavalry. They took up position at the bottom of the hill, on which perched the village of San Pietro di Maida.

On the morning of 4th July Calabrese sharpshooters in the woods behind Reynier started to pick off soldiers in Reynier's rear and he decided, although in an impregnable position deterring a British attack, to advance across the river plain towards the strung-out companies which he saw. The French cavalry made several passes in the plain and then went, to reveal three columns of French infantry advancing under General Compere towards the red lines of troops, two men deep, stationed along the small ridge. Crashing deadly fire from the muskets felled the advancing columns and the light infantry led the charge into the disordered columns. The left wing dissolved, and gradually the other columns followed. The French cavalry charged again, but was caught by fire in the flank. By midday the French were in retreat but because of the absence of cavalry, effective pursuit was impossible. The French had 700 dead and 1,000 wounded, the British 300. Not since the Revolution had the columns of oncoming French not prevailed, and the Battle of Maida pointed the way to the future, the superiority of ranked lines of proficient soldiers capable of quick musketry fire into the massed marching columns.

On the beach the British force stripped off and bathed in the sea. A thunderous drumming like the galloping of horses was heard and the cry rose that the French had returned. The troops, stark naked, hastily stood to with their arms, only to see a passing mass of cattle.

There was little that Sidney Smith and Stuart could achieve with their victory, for Marshal Massena was moving south with a large army. The naval squadron under Sir Sidney Smith continued to fall on the mainland coast, supplying and encouraging the guerrillas. On 17th July Gaeta fell to the French, but during the year the guerrilla operations, encouraged by Smith, cost the French 12,000 soldiers. The French continued to wish to take Sicily and indeed, Sir John Stuart reported an attempted invasion in 1810. King Ferdinand IV and Queen Maria Carolina were not restored to the Kingdom of Naples until 1815.

The Battle of Oudenarde

After the Battle of Ramillies (23 May 1706), the War of the Spanish Succession continued, but 1707 was mainly spent by both sides merely manoeuvring in Flanders. The French however won a significant victory in Spain at Almanza in the April of that year. At the beginning of 1708 the Duke of Marlborough was depressed at the state of politics in England, the constant complaints of the Dutch about the war, and the ineffectiveness of Austria. The prospects for the year appeared poor and the spring was to come late. In March in the Hague the Duke met Prince Eugene of Savoy, the Imperial Commander, and discussed the strategy for the year, which was finally settled in April at a meeting between the Duke, Heinsius the Grand Pensionary of Holland and Prince Eugene. The Elector of Hanover (later King George I) was to be responsible for the campaign in Alsace and South Germany. Prince Eugene was to proceed to the Moselle to threaten invasion of France, and Marlborough was to remain in the Low Countries, endeavouring to bring the French to battle, where on his request Prince Eugene would return from the Moselle to his support.

To prepare for the spring campaign Louis XIV sent an army of 100,000 French to assemble at Lille. The command he gave to his grandson, the young Duc de Bourgogne. The latter had no experience of war and was a man of deep religious piety. He was to be accompanied by his brother the Due de Berry and the son of James II, the Chevalier de St.George. The effective commander of the army was the Duc de Vendome, descended from a bastard of King Henri IV of France. The Duc at the age of fifty-four had his nose eaten away by syphilis, and the appearance of a diseased old woman. According to the Duc de Saint-Simon he was filthy of habit, slept in his bed with his dogs and bitches, who pupped while with him, and relieved the needs of nature in any place in which he found himself. He had a penchant for most of the deadly sins, but was liked by the soldiers. He also was usually to be found in battle immersed in the fiercest fighting on the battlefield. The Duc was a grand-nephew, as was Prince Eugene, of Cardinal Mazarin, the ruler of France under King Louis XIII and during most of the minority of Louis XIV. Prince Eugene had only become an Imperial General, although his mother Olympic Mancini was childhood playmate and late mistress to Louis XIV, because the latter wished to make him a priest, and objecting to that he had fled in 1681 to Vienna. In all Bourgogne and Vendome had on the Netherlands border one hundred and twenty-four battalions of infantry and one hundred and ninety-eight squadrons of cavalry. Marlborough and the Dutch General Overkirk could muster one hundred and twelve battalions of infantry, one hundred and eighty-one squadrons of cavalry and one hundred and thirteen guns.

The French moved just up to Soignies south of Brussels and then to Nivelle and Braine L'Alland. Marlborough faced Vendome near Louvain on 3rd June, where he was joined by the Elector of Hannover. Both sides paused, and Marlborough sent off a message to Prince Eugene to return from the Moselle. Prince Eugene hurried back in his coach, escorted by Hungarian Hussars. On 3rd July the French suddenly turned and marched westwards, capturing Alost fifteen miles north-west of Brussels. Bruges and Ghent were handed over to the French by the inhabitants, restless over Dutch rule. At Ghent three hundred British soldiers held out in the citadel for five days, but the loss of these two towns, and the general disaffection of the local population, depressed the Duke of Marlborough. He had lost access to the Scheldt and was in danger of being cut off from Ostend. Prince Eugene arrived to join his army at Assche and gave him encouragement to join issue again with the French. They formed the view that the next French target would be Oudenarde, and planned to meet the threat.

On 8th July the French started from Alost to go south towards Lessines, thus covering the fortress of Oudenarde. At 2 am on the 9th, in order to forestall them, Marlborough started for Herfelingen, arriving there at 11 am, where the army had a five-hour rest. At 4pm Cadogan, with eight battalions of infantry and eight squadrons of infantry was sent the thirteen miles remaining to Lessines. He arrived at midnight to find the town still free of French. The French, finding that the Allied army was to their front, turned west at Voorde to cross the Scheldt at Gavere, north of Oudenarde. Marlborough slept out with the troops at Lessines on the night of 10th July and at daybreak sent Cadogan with 16 battalions of infantry, 15 squadrons of cavalry, 32 guns and the pontoon train on to Oudenarde. He arrived at the Scheldt at 9 am and set to work as soon as the pontoon train arrived to bridge the River Scheldt north of Oudenarde, since the town had but two stone bridges. Seeing the French in the distance deploying after having crossed the River at Gravere, Cadogan sent a messenger to Marlborough, who was on the march with the main army, to give him that information. Immediately Marlborough ordered the army to step out, and together with Prince Eugene and 20 squadrons of Prussian cavalry he galloped forward to the river.

The River Scheldt at Oudenarde runs almost north to south. Beyond the river leaving the town was the village of Bevere, and the road there turns north towards Ghent. Due west of Bevere, an outcrop in the form of a ridge runs to the west. On the north of the town, across the river were a number of small villages – Eyne the nearest and beyond that Heurne. Both stand in the river plain, which is itself to the west, edged by a long ridge running from Wannegen in the south to Huise in the north. In front of the ridge were the villages of Lede and Mullem.

The former possessed a windmill to east of the village. The country between the river and this western ridge was very broken, with hedges, coppices and a stream running through – the River Diefenbeck, which joined the River Scheldt to the east beyond Eyne.

Both armies as they deployed became aware of the other's presence – meeting during cavalry foraging near Eyne. Vendome, seeing Cadogan's force, was of the view that the French should attack, but the Duc de Bourgogne insisted that the French should form up on the ridge to the west of the river. The initial position taken up put the French right between the villages of Wannegem and Huise and the left to the east of the latter village, stretching towards the river.

By mid-day the pontoons were complete and Cadogan at 3 pm crossed the river with 16 battalions of infantry and eight squadrons of cavalry. Four battalions of Swiss troops had been sent by the Conte de Biron to Eyne and that was the first point of attack. Marlborough had waited for the whole army to arrive and, as Vendome at luncheon saw them debouch to cross the river, could only express his surprise by commenting that the Devil must have carried the troops from Assche. Cadogan's infantry soon overwhelmed the Swiss – three battalions were captured, including their commander, Pfeiffer; one was destroyed and a further three, seeing the Hannoverian cavalry take Eyne, retired. In an ecstasy of success, the cavalry then saw 12 squadrons of de Biron's cavalry and threw themselves upon them, scattering them.

Beyond stood the whole cavalry for the French left wing; the Hannoverians charged them as well. An intensive meleé began in which George Augustus, son of the Elector of Hannover and the future King George II, was heavily involved. His horse was shot beneath him, and as he was being assisted to mount another, a cannonball took off the head of the colonel helping him. De Biron responded to the attack by bringing up guns and more cavalry so that Rantzow, the commander of the Hannoverian cavalry, thought it prudent to retire, which they carried out in good order, being held in reserve for the rest of the day.

The destruction of the Swiss led the Duc de Burgogne to change his mind and, contrary once again to the advice of the Duc de Vendome, he ordered the right wing of the French army, as the allied army continued to come across the pontoon bridge, to move onto the field towards them. He, the Duc de Berry and the Chevalier de St. George took up their position in the vantage point offered by the windmill at Royegem. The French struggled through the difficult country west of Eyne to come to terms with the left wing of the army under Cadogan. The hedges, small streams and broken country reduced the two sides to vigorous hand-to-hand fighting. The advantage went this way and that. On the right wing, commanded by Prince Eugene, where were stationed the British infantry, devastating attacks were made and the British pushed north twelve hundred yards beyond Eyne. The village of Groenewald was taken. At one time two battalions of infantry were being attacked by 30 French. Reinforcements were sent – some 20 infantry battalions and 17 squadrons of cavalry to help Prince Eugene's forces. In the middle of the French second line, the Duc de Vendome was seen vigorously fighting with a pike. Between 4 and 5 pm he asked the Duc de Bourgogne to throw the left wing into the battle, but the latter refused to do so, saying that there was a morass between the troops and the fighting.

Meanwhile Marlborough, who had been controlling the action, sent General Overkirk with the Dutch infantry and cavalry through Oudenarde to the ridge west of Bevere. This treeless ridge was the ideal route for cavalry action, and the force begin to filter west and north round the plain where the fighting was in progress. By 7 pm, with the sun behind them in the west, Overkirk ordered the attack, and the Dutch threw themselves on the flank and to the rear of the French left wing, which had gradually been drawn into a noose by this outflanking movement. As dusk came and darkness fell the fighting died away, a position having been reached where the Dutch and Prince Eugene's troops were firing on one another. There were 6,000 Frenchmen lost and 9,000 prisoners. The Duc de Bourgogne, his brother and the Chevalier St.George proceeded with the remnant of the army, the left wing, which had stood immobile all day, to Ghent. There the Duc de Vendome went to bed for three days. Louis XIV, on the day when he received the news of Oudenarde, is said to have spent dinner complaining about the quality of every course. At the Court of Versailles the pious had the satisfaction of the Duc de Vendome's defeat, as it had confirmed their belief that he was too wicked for God to give him a victory, a belief soon rendered unsustainable by a series of victories won by him in Spain.

On the field of Oudenarde the wounded lay dying as a gentle rain fell in the night. Marlborough rested the army for two days and then moved towards Lille. He conceived the project of marching past the fortress in Flanders to Abbeville, from which he could threaten Paris, but his allies, including Prince Eugene, would not agree to it. They resolved to besiege and take Lille. On 13th August Prince Eugene invested the town. Marlborough and his army were to be the shielding force preventing the French from falling on the besiegers. Vendome and the Marshal Duke of Berwick (the illegitimate son of King James II by Arabella Churchill, Marlborough's older sister) united their forces at Tournai, but Marlborough could not bring them to battle. Louis XIV in fact ordered the Duc de Bourgogne and Berwick to attack the besiegers at Lille, but they refused and the Duc de Vendome resigned. Prince Eugene was wounded in an attempt to storm Lille on 20th September. At that stage the besiegers were in urgent need of supplies and had none arrived, would have needed to end the siege within four days. Marlborough ordered supplies to be brought from Ostend and he sent an escort of 12 battalions of infantry and 15 squadrons of cavalry under General Webb to protect them. Cadogan, with 18 squadrons of cavalry, went to Roulers, on the route, to cover the convoy.

At noon on the day after leaving Ostend, the supply train came upon 22,000 French commanded by General De La Motte, two miles from Vryriendael. Webb ordered the troops forward with such artillery as he had. The French fired on the lines, which were lying down, and about 5 pm attacked as a mass. The men stood up and pounded the French, volley after volley, and with cannon at close range. Cadogan with his cavalry attacked at 7 pm and the French retreated. The firmness, high morale and professional skill of the hugely outnumbered British army had saved the convoy. On 3rd October the siege was pressed again and on 22nd October, being short of food and ammunition, General Boufflers surrendered, retaining only the citadel, which fell on 11th December. Marlborough then forced the Scheldt to take his army to Brussels and on 29th December took Ghent from General De La Motte. The campaign of 1708 was over. On 12th January 1709 the great freeze began, gripping Western Europe in ice for two months: even the Tagus froze at Lisbon. Famine and cold stalked France. The public finances were disastrous. Louis XIV began to realise that he should make peace.

14th July 1941
The Surrender of Lebanon and Syria

In 1919 the League of Nations, under the provisions of the Treaty of Versailles, confirmed a mandate to France to act as the occupying and protecting power in the Lebanon and Syria. Prior to June 1940 General Weygand built up a substantial army in the two countries and, when France abandoned the war, control remained with the Government in Vichy. The agreement between Marshal Petain and the Fuehrer Adolf Hitler in October 1940, to the effect that France and Germany had a shared interest in defeating Britain, meant that the French position in the Lebanon and Syria was a potential danger to the British Empire in relation to Egypt, the Suez Canal and to the sources of oil supply, from Iraq to Haifa in Palestine and at Abadan in Iran. The High Commissioner of France in the two countries in 1941 was General Dentz, an enthusiastic supporter of Marshal Petain. There were also Italian and German Armistice Commissioners in Syria, who had the task of supervising the implementation of the armistice terms of 1940, but in fact exercised high levels of influence over the French administration.

In the spring of 1941 General Sir Archibald Wavell, the Commander in Chief of the British forces in the Near East, was entangled in a military situation which required troops to be deployed in North Africa, East Africa, Greece and Palestine, and the forces were over-extended. Although Adolf Hitler was focussed on a war with Russia, his involvement in the Balkans and Greece had led his strategists to ponder the advantages of securing a position in the Middle East, which might turn the flank of Turkey, penetrate into Iraq and threaten the Suez Canal from the north-east. Before a coherent policy could however be formulated and put into operation, events in Iraq were to take a hand and force the pace.

Under the Anglo-Iraq Treaty of 1930, Britain being the protecting state under the mandate of the League of Nations, the British were granted the right to maintain military bases at Basra and the airfield of Habbaniya, the right of transit for its armed forces and in war the right to use the transport, docks and other facilities of the country. In the spring of 1941 there were some 2,200 military and air force personnel at Habbaniya, with their civilian dependants. Anti-British elements, prompted by the Germans and encouraged by the Mufti of Jerusalem, who pre-war had fermented violence in Palestine and who had fled to Baghdad, were causing civil unrest in the country and in March a sympathiser, Rashid Ali, became Prime Minister. The pro-British Regent, the Emir Adbel-Ileh, fled. The threat posed to British interests led to the diversion to Iraq of forces from the Indian command,

and on 18th April, under cover of an airborne battalion, an infantry brigade and regiment of field artillery arrived at Shaiba near Basra, of whose arrival Rashid Ali was told. The 10th Indian Division, commanded by General Slim, was to become famous in the Burma campaign against the Japanese. On 30th April however, on the plateau overlooking Habbaniya air field, there arrived a force of 9,000 Iraqi troops with 50 guns. Air Vice Marshal Smart, in command, organised four squadrons from the 82 aircraft scraped together. There was an attempt to parley between the British and Iraqi troops, but on 2nd May the Iraqis began to bombard the airfield. Fighting was to continue for three days. General Wavell, pressed on all sides, was reluctant to divert troops to Iraq, but was ordered to do so. A brigade was improvised from motorised cavalry in Palestine (1st Cavalry Division), containing units of the Blues, Life Guards and Essex Yeomanry, but it was not to arrive at Habbaniya until 18th May. In the three days of fighting, the Iraqis dared not assault the airfield, and were subject to raids from it, while Blenheim bombers from Shaiba bombed the troops on the plateau, and other aircraft policed the skies to such devastating effect that when the Royal Air force was overhead the Iraqi gunners would not stand to their guns. On the 5th the enemy forces on the plateau began to retire, and on the 7th the siege was over, but the airfield still remained isolated in a country in revolt.

Rashid Ali had moved too early and the Germans and Italians were not in a position to give him effective support. However, the French General Dentz, with the support of the Armistice Commission, began to send supplies to the Iraqis and Syrian airfields were made available to the Luftwaffe and the Italian air force. Adolf Hitler issued a Fuehrer directive ordering every support for Iraq. On 13th May the first German planes landed at Mosul airfield and on the 14th began to arrive on the French aerodromes in Syria. The arrival of these aircraft led the Prime Minister, Winston Churchill, to consider the pressing need to invade and counter German intervention in Syria. General Wavell, conscious of his shortage of troops and weapons, and their deployment over the several areas of fighting, opposed that notion, stressing also that the Free French formations were unreliable; he had in any event already resisted the request of General De Gaulle to support the Free French forces to invade Syria. The Prime Minister and Chiefs of Staff however ordered the attack, and work was begun on 'Operation Explorer,' Meanwhile, the position in Iraq needed to be stabilised. The Royal Air Force had further been reinforced with aircraft from the East. On 19th May the land forces, supplemented by men from the garrison, attacked the bridge over the Euphrates River at Falluja and on the 27th the advance on Baghdad began. It took three days, as the armoured force faced the river inundations and the broken bridges and negotiated the irrigation waterways. On 30th May Baghdad fell and Rashid Ali and the Mufti of Jerusalem hurriedly left the city and Iraq. The insurrection was at an end. Determination and the fighting qualities of the army and the air force had prevailed, when the force available was scant. A serious threat had been averted.

By the beginning of June Wavell had assembled a small force in order to invade Syria and the Lebanon. It comprised two brigades of the 7th Australian Division, part of the 1st Cavalry (Motorised) Division and the Free French force of 6 battalions under General LeGentilhomme with their 8 guns and 10 light aircraft. From Iraq, the other part of the cavalry Motorised Division was to be sent in (Habforce), and the 5th Indian Infantry Brigade was added. This small force was to take on the French forces comprising some 18 battalions of French troops, bolstered with colonial troops, including four battalions of the French Foreign Legion, the whole amounting to 35,000, armed with 120 guns, 90 tanks and 90 aircraft.

Operation Explorer envisaged an advance in three columns, with the Australians on the right moving up the coast, the British in the centre and the Free French on the right, pushing via Deraa and Kiswe to Damascus. As the loyalty of the Vichy French and General Dentz to Petain was wrongly thought to be suspect, the forces were told to advance, distributing propaganda and leaflets and only to use the utmost force if their approach was not accepted. Thus on 8th June the Australians advanced in their slouch hats and were promptly machine-gunned. The Free French marched forward with a white flag and the Tricolore, behind a band playing the Marseillaise. They were initially to meet little resistance, but that was to mount, when General Dertz discovered how small the attacking force was. Orders were nonetheless given by him to shoot any troops who endeavoured to parley under the white flag. The civil war element of the conflict between the Vichy French and the Free French did give rise to difficulty: one battalion of the Free French Foreign Legion refused to fire on a Vichy French battalion. Progress, as resistance mounted, became slow. The Free French were stopped ten miles from Damascus; the Australians, having gone through Tyre, came to a standstill stopped on the Litani River, a green flowing barrier among the banana groves. In the centre fighting wavered back and forth around Merj Ayoon, Jessine and Kunaitra, where a British battalion was overwhelmed by two battalions with tanks. The Germans, using bases in the Dodecanese belonging to the Italians, bombed Haifa and targets along the coast, while the Royal Navy supported the army on shore. Initially two cruisers were assigned – Phoebe (5th of the name, launched 1939) and Ajax (7th of the name, launched 1934) with the destroyers Kandahar, Kimberley, Jackal and Janus. These bombarded the coast from 4,000 to 5,000 yards out, aiming at supply trains and dumps. On the 9th Phoebe was almost hit by a torpedo but Janus, attacked by the two French flotilla leaders from Beirut, had her bridge and boiler room wrecked. On 15th June Sidon was bombarded and two destroyers, Isis and Ilex, were damaged by German Junkers bombers. The following day however, the French Chevalier Paul was bombed and sunk.

After ten days or more of stalemate the campaign began to move again. The 5th Indian Brigade, with contingents of the Arab Legion, came up to Damascus near the Free French. On the 21st, the 21st Australian Brigade managed to cross the

Litani River. The prelude to their success was a landing behind the French lines by 11th Commando under Colonel Pedder. Unfortunately, information about this attack reached the French, and the beach was covered by a 75-mm gun. When the men landed, they waded in up to their shoulders led by Colonel Pedder with his walking stick and revolver. Despite the intense fire he, together with a sergeant, who was wounded, was able to take a battery and direct fire on the French. Despite heavy casualties the raid was successful, and gave the opportunity for the Australians to take a bridgehead and place a pontoon bridge across the river.

On the 21st, the 25th Australian Brigade and the 5th Indian Infantry Brigade fought their way into Damascus. The city was the subject of a three-way threat, from the east by General Collet and his French Circassians, from the south by the Free French force, and from the west through Messe by the Australians and Indians, who effectively took the city. The campaign from the east from Iraq gathered momentum. 'Habforce' of the 1st Cavalry Motorised Brigade moved along the pipeline neared Palmyra at the end of June, where the Foreign Legion held out for nine days until 3rd July. Further north the 21st Indian Brigade and the 17th were moving towards Aleppo. By the first week of July, General Dentz was being pressed north and although he still had a force of 24,000 men, his air force had been reduced by four fifths. Although he had sent an officer to North Africa to ask support from Rommel, no help was forthcoming. He also had German consent to move a French Division from Salamanca to Syria, but Turkey refused to consent to its passage and the Royal Navy harried his supplies. On 11th July therefore he asked for an Armistice, and General Verdillac and the British Commander, General Sir Henry Maitland–Wilson, met at Acre to discuss it. The Free French were excluded.

The Armistice talks were to be prolonged for three days. Their basis was that the French should have the honours of war, all British and other prisoners were to be returned, weapons to be handed over and an opportunity given for the Free French to recruit among the French prisoners before they returned to France. Even while talks on these lines proceeded, General Dentz hurried to break its terms. British officers were shipped out of Syria and in some cases handed over to the Germans. Aircraft were flown away to other French possessions; the British merchantmen Pegasus was sunk in the entrance to Beirut harbour and recruiting by the Free French obstructed. Spies were recruited to work to keep the Germans and Italians informed after the occupation. The terms were finally agreed on 14th July. In view of the acts in breach of the Armistice, the British subsequently interned General Dentz and 35 of his officers as hostages for the return of the British officers.

Syria was to remain, even while under British control in the war, a source of irritation. At the time of the proposed invasion, in order to secure support from the people of the two countries, Winston Churchill had guaranteed them independence after the war. General de Gaulle, of the Free French, grudgingly agreed. He tried however constantly to take control of the countries for France.

Despite a request not to do so by Winston Churchill, he placed General Catroux in Damascus on 23rd July as his Delegate General and Plenipotentiary, and subsequently refused to accept the terms of the Armistice. Both General Auchinleck and General Maitland-Wilson were concerned to maintain military control and were hostile to Free French involvement. De Gaulle threatened to remove his troops from the occupying army and join with General Dentz to overturn the Armistice arrangements. The British Cabinet Minister, the Rt Hon Oliver Lyttelton, in Cairo, arranged a compromise which was to leave the position in Syria and Lebanon as a constant irritant, while De Gaulle manoeuvred to reassert French colonial power despite the pledge of independence. The final clash came in May 1945.

It was recognised that new treaty arrangements would be required to endorse the lawful existence of Syria and the Lebanon as independent states, and the British Prime Minister encouraged negotiations with De Gaulle, who had taken over the Government in France. He however was still determined to reassert French control in the countries. The French therefore decided to reinforce their troops and on 17th May landed new units at Beirut. The population of the two countries immediately rose. Strikes and riots took place and people demonstrating on the streets of Aleppo were killed by the French. The British Government protested at the landing of the troops, but was told by the French that the protest had no justification, as the British had many times landed troops in the two countries without their consent. On 28th May the Syrian Government said that it was no longer able to maintain order. The French were shelling towns and had an armoured force in the streets of Damascus. French aircraft were buzzing the mosques. On the 29th the French began to suppress the people of Damascus; artillery fire killed many people and damaged the city. The Parliament building was occupied.

The whole French operation to retake Syria and the Lebanon was a clear breach of the independence promise given in 1941. In view of our guarantee, General Sir Bernard Paget, the Commander-in-Chief Middle East, was instructed to use British forces to restore order and that decision was communicated to Paris. De Gaulle, backing down, replied by saying that the French had been 'attacked' but had regained control and that he would order a 'Ceasefire'. Conciliatory notes were sent to Paris and to the President of Syria and on 3rd June the French left Damascus for a camp outside. The same day a British force entered the city to preserve the peace and the guarantee of independence.

In this short war to take Syria and the Lebanon there were, because of the savage fighting, significant casualties. The British forces had 4,600 killed and wounded (mainly Australians) and the French 6,500. Of the 24,000 French troops remaining at the end of hostilities, as at Plymouth, Portsmouth and Alexandria in July 1940, only a fraction were prepared to adhere to the Free French and continue the war. Four-fifths went back to France.

22nd July 1812

The Battle of Salamanca

The campaign of 1812 commenced with the taking by the Duke of Wellington of the frontier fortresses of Ciudad Rodrigo (19 January 1812) and Badajoz (6 April 1812), which guarded the entry into Portugal. With these in his hands he was able to contemplate a campaign in Spain to dislodge French control over broad areas of the north of the country. The strategic situation was helpful in that the French armies, although amounting to 250,000 troops in all, were divided and needed to cover different areas of the peninsula, where Spanish military and guerilla activity troubled them. Marshal Soult had problems in Andalucia and could not - or would not - support Marshal Marmont and the Army of Portugal. Marshal Suchet was in Catalonia and King Joseph had the Army of the Centre in Madrid. It was arranged that General Ballesteros and Sir Rowland Hill would keep Soult engaged in the south, that a force of 19,000 should come from Sicily to land at Valencia and that Sir Home Popham with the Navy should operate on the Basque Coast to keep General Caferelli occupied. In this context Wellington decided to move into Spain north-east to Salamanca and Valladolid. If he could reach Burgos, the French in Madrid and Seville would be cut off from France in the west.

On 13th June Wellington crossed the River Agueda with an army of 51,000, including 18,000 Portuguese and 3,000 Spanish. On 17th June the army entered Salamanca, where it was received joyfully by much of the population, Wellington being mobbed by women in the town plaza. The French still held three forts, the largest of which was the fortified convent of San Cayetano. An attack on the fort began on 19th June, but it was not be to be concluded until 27th June when the French commander surrendered, together with the commanders of the other town forts. A Te Deum was sung in the Cathedral, which Wellington and his senior officers attended. Meanwhile, the two armies – British and French – manoeuvred around one another in the vicinity of the city. Limited engagements took place but neither side came to battle: by mid-July Wellington was withdrawing towards the Tormes River and Salamanca shadowed by Marshal Marmont, who had conceived the notion of outflanking the British and thus cutting their retreat back to the Portuguese frontier. On 7th July General Bonnet had arrived from the north to reinforce Marmont. The latter's force now amounted to 43,000, 2,200 of which were cavalry but of poor quality, and 78 guns. On 18th July Marmont attacked

the rearguard and Wellington only just avoided capture. The armies marched on in sight of one another. On 20th July the French cannonaded the allied army, but to little effect, although their position was such that a general action could have been possible within half an hour. On the march this day Tomkinson in his *Diary of a Cavalry Officer* noted the eagles and vultures hovering over the dead of a previous engagement and wondered about the horror of their presence if he were wounded and could not move from the battlefield. On 21st July the French crossed the River Tormes at the ford at Huerta and the British at San Marta. Both armies were on the west of the river. As dark fell a fierce storm occurred with crashing thunder. The horses of the 4th Dragoon Guards panicked and galloped off, running over the soldiers sleeping at their head and almost trampling to death the Colonel of the Regiment and his wife, Mrs D'Albiac whom he saved by covering her under a gun. Eighteen dragoons were injured and thirty-one horses lost.

On the morning of 22nd July the Duke of Wellington formed up the army in the configuration of a large letter L. The country to the South-east of Salamanca was broken with small grassed hills, through which the route being used by the French ran. On either side of the road stood distinctive hills, near the village of Los Arapiles. They stood out, steep, rising to up to four hundred feet and flat-topped. The lower hills were to the north of the road on the west of the village and the higher, the Greater Arapiles, stood to the south in the form of a long ridge. Wellington stationed the 1st and 2nd Divisions facing east towards the French route, which at that point came from the north-east. The main position on the lesser heights faced the route after it turned east around the village of Los Arapiles. Packenham, a relation with the 3rd Division, was ordered to quit Salamanca and proceed to Aldea Tejada, to the west of the low hills and at a short distance from the route the French would take to the west. Wellington had at last determined to make a stand as he had news that King Joseph and Marshal Jourdan, with 15,000 troops, were marching to the assistance of the Army of Portugal.

Marmont, in pursuit of the retreating British, saw the dust from the baggage train on the distant Salamanca to Ciudad Rodrigo road, and mistook the movement of these wagons as signs of hurrying retreat. He therefore ordered his army on. The low undulations of the country chosen by Wellington for his stand hid his troops, and the French quickly marched on past his position. In doing so the army became strung out, with gaps appearing between the van, centre and rear. The French moved to the south of the road and had taken the Great Arapiles hill before the British could reach it, although about noon the 1st Dragoon Guards were ordered to attempt to take it, but called back before the order could be implemented. By the time that the French leading Corps under Thomières had reached the west of the British position, a gap of a mile had opened up between him and the centre comprising Mancune, Clausel and Brennier, and further a mile between them and the four remaining Corps under Ferey and Foy. As the French had passed, Wellington had moved Packenham and his 3rd Division (about 6,000 men) supported by D'Urban's Portuguese cavalry, forward among the low hills, and between 3 and 4pm moved the 5th, 6th and 7th Divisions right at the double. The French cannonaded the 11th and 16th Brigades of cavalry as they went but to no effect. Packenham and the 3rd were given the order to attack and about 5 pm they fell upon the flank of Thomières' column, supported by D'Urbans' cavalry. The 45th (Nottinghamshire Regiment of Foot), the 74th (Highland Regiment of Foot) and the 88th (Connaught Rangers Regiment) and the Portuguese went in cheering. The column broke; Thomières was killed, two-thirds of the leading regiments were dead and half of the rear. His guns were captured. The French cavalry retired and the British swept on to Mancune's corps, which was also being attacked by General Leith's 5th Division.

About the same time as the 3rd Division was attacking, Marshal Marmont was struck down by a cannonball while standing on the Greater Arapiles, injuring his arm and two ribs. Command of the French army devolved first on Bonnet, who was then also immediately himself seriously injured, so that Clausel took over the command. Following bombardment, the 4th and 5th Divisions were ordered forward to attack the French centre. The 5th charged Mancune and his corps on the ridge, and the French formed squares. Leith and his division flung themselves on the squares and Le Marchant's Brigade of 1,000 cavalry, in the smoke and dust, came crashing into the squares, sabreing and cutting their way through these formations. Both Generals Leith and Le Marchant were killed, but the force not only devastated Mancune's corps, but harried Brennier's, who were marching in column. The French fired suddenly and a quarter of the cavalry fell, but they pressed on. In the outcome about a third of the French army in the van and centre had been overcome.

The 4th Division, which contained a Portuguese Brigade and a battalion of the Lusitanian Legion and was supported by Pack's Portuguese infantry, had launched itself at the Great Arapiles but already decimated as it advanced through the rye fields, they were stopped by the final steep escarpment from making the summit. The French counter-attacked; Cole was injured and the Portuguese broke under the impact of Boyer's French cavalry. Cole's Division was outflanked on both sides. Wellington immediately sent the 6th Division under General Clinton to their support and it moved forward to where the French under Clausel, who had been joined by Ferey, were endeavouring to press on. The 6th came on in two lines, the Portuguese in the front line, the British in the second line. The heavy fire took a great toll of the Portuguese but the second line came on firing volley after volley;

the French left went back under the impact and finally returned to the Palagarcia woods to their south-east, the fields and woods breaking into fire under the impact of the battle cannonade. Clinton's 6th Division had taken a heavy toll.

The survivors of the battle moved to join Foy's corps, which had been in the rear in the east and which had not been engaged in the fighting. Together the defeated army retreated towards Alba de Tormes, where a castle overlooked the river bridge. Dark was falling and Wellington did not hasten the retreat. He believed the castle to be in the hands of the Spanish under General Carlos de Espana, but the latter had deserted his post, unknown to Wellington, and the French crossed the river unimpeded. 30,000 French escaped, but they lost 6,000 killed and wounded, and 7,000 were taken prisoner. 20 guns, 2 Eagles, 20 standards and much equipment was taken. Wellington lost 5,220 men, of which 694 were killed, 4,970 were wounded and 256 were missing.

The French fell back towards Valladolid and Burgos. Wellington took the opportunity to take Segovia and on 12th August entered Madrid, from which King Joseph and Marshal Jourdan had fled to join Marshal Suchet in Catalonia. He did not remain there long but left with half the army for Valladolid, with the intent of stopping at Burgos. Hill was left to cover central Spain in case Marshal Soult moved from the south. On 16th September Burgos was besieged, but after losing 2,000 men Wellington returned from there on 21st October. The French had started to unite their remaining forces and he was being threatened by the French army in the north and by Soult and Suchet with 60,000 men. Wellington gradually fell back to Salamanca where on 9th November the army was concentrated on the Tormes River. The French decided not to face Wellington, but managed to cross the river and again moved to outflank him. On 15th November the retreat was ordered. Torrential rain fell over the retreat in biting cold. The roads became flowing torrents and deep in mud. The men were foodless, because the Commissariat had mistakenly taken the wrong route. The only foods were acorns and raw onion. They could not bivouac for five days. 3,000 fell on the way from exhaustion. At last the River Agueda was reached and the army halted. 1812 had ended with many of the campaign gains lost, but the frontier towns remained in British hands – Ciudad Rodrigo, Badajoz, Almarez and Alcantera.

At Salamanca the higher command suffered significant casualties. General Le Marchant was killed at the head of his Brigade. Marshal Beresford was wounded heading the Portuguese in the 6th Division. General Leith was killed and Generals Cole and Alten wounded. The Commander of the cavalry, Sir Stapleton Cotton, was shot in the arm by one of his own sentries after dark when the battle was over. Tomkinson records that Mrs D'Albiac, accompanied by a Dragoon of the 4th, set out to search the battlefield for her husband. The Dragoon lost her and she spent the night among the dragoons on the field in her search on the ridge where the action had taken place.

23rd July 1812

The Battle of Garcia Hernandez

Not all the limited actions of the Peninsular War fought by Wellington's armies have been noted, but the Battle of Garcia Hernandez deserves its place among the victories of Britain because, as the French General Foy remarked, it was the most audacious charge by cavalry in the whole campaign. The victory was gained by the King's German Legion, raised in 1803-1804 from Hannoverians who had fled northern Germany following the seizure by the Emperor Napoleon of the Electorate of Hannover, of which King George III of Britain was the Elector. Initially comprising the 1st, 2nd and 3rd Hussars and the 1st and 2nd Dragoons, it was built up with infantry, engineers and a staff. By 1812 the Legion was a seasoned force of troops, having been for four years in the peninsula under the command of Major-General Baron von Alten. Major –General Von Bock commanded six squadrons of heavy cavalry and the 1st and 2nd Dragoons of the Legion.

On 22nd July the cavalry of the Legion had been held on the left flank in reserve behind the Light and 1st Division opposite Foy. In the course of the previous day General von Alten had been wounded in the thigh and taken to Salamanca, but he left instructions that in the event of army action he was to be informed by a galloper, as he had no intention of falling into the hands of the French. Warned of the action he dressed despite his wound, had his horse saddled, and started off to the army. On the way a message came that the Allied army were beating the French and, his overall trousers drenched in blood, he returned to Salamanca to his sickbed.

At night-fall the regiments went to bivouac, but at midnight Wellington sent a message to General von Bock to pursue the retreating French army the following day. The Legion saddled up before dawn on the 23rd and were joined by General Anson's Light cavalry and the First Light Division of Sir Thomas Graham. The Legion formed the van of the troops deployed to go after the French. The latter were retreating along a valley formed by a deep tributary stream of the River Tormes, called the Garcia Cabellero, which flowed through a long defile and then came out into a stone-strewn plain, which the road to Garcia Hernandez crossed. The plain was flanked by stony small hills. Foy had retreated in order and deployed two regiments to guard the rear of the retiring army.

Wellington, scanning the plain from a distance, saw squadrons of cavalry passing on the plain, but was unable to see the infantry regiments drawn up in three squares on the shallow rises of the hills because they were masked by the edge of the defile and were effectively in part in a shallow dip. He, seeing the cavalry, ordered General von Bock with his Dragoons to charge it. Because of the narrowness of the valley, Von Bock could not lead the squadrons into line to charge, and emerged on the plain in echelon, the 1st Dragoons to the fore. In any event his shortsightedness made it difficult for him to see the enemy. The French cavalry turned and, as the 1st Dragoons, whose motto was 'Tapfer und Trau' (Brave and True) and whose uniform King George III sometimes wore, advanced towards it, they were enfiladed by the French infantry on their left. Captain von Decken, about two to three hundred yards to the rear, was not prepared to follow the 1st Dragoons and, even though there was no artillery support, he launched his squadron on the nearest French square. Such a course, as Waterloo would show, was not a sound cavalry tactic. The infantry in the square, in six lines, two kneeling and four standing, fired volley after volley into the advancing horsemen. Von Becken fell killed but his men rode on. One Dragoon shot near the first file fell with his horse onto the ranks of the square, opening a hole in the screen. The Dragoons poured through, slashing with their sabres and raising piercing yells; the square disintegrated and the survivors fled.

The charge of Von Decken's squadron was followed up by Captain Von Reitzeuslen, who attacked a second square. The soldiers, having seen the slaughter and carnage of the charge on the first square, had their morale shaken and began to break ranks, creating gaps through which again the cavalry entered, sabreing their way to the other side. The dispersed French infantry tried to come together in a third square, but that in its turn was charged by two squadrons of the 2nd Dragoons. The rearguard of the French army was shattered, Anson and his Light Cavalry throwing themselves on the French cavalry. The French infantry in disorder mounted the shallow hills, where the spent horses could not follow, even throwing rocks at the horses. The Legion cavalry were ordered by Wellington to retire and as they made their way back through the ranks of the British infantry they were acclaimed with loud cheers. They had lost, according to Tomkinson (Diary of a Cavalry Officer) 39 dragoons killed and 40 to 50 wounded, out of their total of 800 horsemen. 2,000 prisoners were taken; Wellington said that he had never seen a more gallant charge.

Tomkinson described the heavy cavalry of the Kings German Legion as fine regiments, although the men were full-sized for their horses; perhaps the reason that the unhorsed dragoon broke the line of the French square. Save when charging, they never apparently went beyond a trot. The infantry distinguished themselves at La Haye Sainte at the Battle of Waterloo.

After the Napoleonic Wars the Legion returned to Hannover and formed the army of the new Kingdom of Hannover, carrying the battle honours of these wars on their guerdons and flags. Even after the seizure and annexation of Hannover, which had become in 1837 a separate kingdom from Britain, by Prussia in 1866, the 1st and 2nd Dragoons became the 13th and 14th Uhlans, still carrying the honours on their colours. After 1918, the 13th battalion became the first Battalion of the 13th (Prussian) Cavalry Regiment. In the mould of all populist governments impatient with history and tradition, Adolf Hitler ended the line of descent, and the honours won so gallantly were no longer carried. The faded colours are still in the museum at Celle, and a statue of a mounted Lancer of the 14th Uhlans stands outside the Cathedral at Verden.

24th July 1704

The Taking of Gibralter

It was the Duke of Marlborough in the War of the Spanish succession, who recognised the need to fight against the French in the Mediterranean as well as in Flanders. The use of the fleet to attack the French Mediterranean bases such as Toulon, in order to help sustain Britain's Austrian allies and to carry armies to convey the allied claimant to the Spanish throne, Charles III, back to Spain, had the strategic value of precluding the French from mobilising their resources on one front. In 1703 a demonstration was made with a fleet of 47 ships sailing to Leghorn and back. No battle was fought, but disease killed a tenth of the seamen on the voyage. Because of the position of Lisbon, put at British disposal by our Portuguese allies, the fleet under Sir George Rooke, with 20 ships of the line, left early for the Mediterranean, where he was joined by 6 Dutch warships.

Sir George Rooke was born in 1650. He fought in the Second Dutch war and took part in the battle of Barfleur-La Hogue (19th May 1692) where he entered the harbour of La Hogue with a flotilla of boats to burn the French fleet lying there. After the battle he was knighted. In 1702 he was the Victor of the Battle of Vigo (12th October).

By April, Rooke has been joined by further ships and his fleet had risen to 40. King Charles III was landed with troops at Lisbon. Rooke had been told that he should capture Toulon and co-operate with the Duke of Savoy. On 9th May orders arrived suggesting that Cadiz should be taken or a landing made in Catalonia. Queen Anne pressed on her part for the destruction of the French fleet. The Comte de Toulouse meantime had left Brest with 26 ships of the line and met Admiral Du Quesne-Mosnier from Toulon, with six, at Cadiz. Having met up they entered the Mediterranean. There then followed a period during which the fleets moved about, neither meeting nor coming to battle. An attempt was made on Barcelona, which failed. On 16th June Rooke was off Lagos, where Sir Clowdisley Shovell met him with 23 ships of the line. The latter had previously been appointed to guard the Channel, but the French fleet having gone south, he followed. A council took place, in which an attack on Cadiz was contemplated, provided more soldiers were available. None such came. The Admirals reconsidered the position on 18th July while off Tetuan, and decided however to attack Gibraltar. The significance of Gibraltar, in order to control the Mediterranean, had led Oliver Cromwell in 1656 to consider its taking and use as a base. He was told that he would need four or five thousand well-trained soldiers for that ambitious operation and the project was abandoned. Rooke and Shovell had a large fleet, but not such a force of soldiers.

On 21st July the fleet arrived in the Bay of Gibraltar. Their strength amounted to 63 ships. In the afternoon about 2,000 soldiers, predecessors of the marines, were landed on the isthmus in the vicinity of La Linea, under the command of Prince George of Hesse-Darmstadt. The garrison thus was deprived of the land link. The Governor was called upon to surrender in the name of King Charles III, but refused saying that he would bury himself under the ruins rather than surrender. His defence force, however, consisted of only 50 regular soldiers, 150 from the militia and volunteer townspeople. There were 100 guns. A few bombs from ketches were slung into the town. 22nd July, a day of light wind, was spent with the fleet manoeuvring 16 ships of the line into position under Rear-Admiral Byng, and 6 Dutch under Admiral Van der Dussen, in order to bombard the fortifications. The morning of 23rd July opened at daybreak to the bombardment of the fort and town. A consistent cannonade was kept up until mid-day. 15,000 balls of shot hammered the bastions and the walls.

The troops landed on the isthmus advanced to take the landward defences. From the sea the British fleet launched small boats of seamen to take the mole and seaward defences. Captain Whittaker of the Dorsetshire (1st of the name with 80 guns), Captain Hicks of the Yarmouth, and Captain Jumper of the Lenox moved in with their crews and seized the batteries. The fortifications were mined, and as they were taken, the train was fired, killing 2 lieutenants and 40 seamen, and wounding 60. Captain Whittaker and his band stormed on up to the redoubt between the mole and the town. The standard of Queen Anne was raised on the defences. The Governor and garrison were now hemmed in and he accepted an offer for an honourable surrender. On 24th July the garrison capitulated and the troops marched into the town. Most of the inhabitants had fled; the town, but for one church, was sacked. The next few days were spent in re-fortifying the defences, landing fresh supplies (including 60 great guns) and in providing 1,900 troops under the Prince of Hesse to defend the Rock. The fleet sailed to rewater on the African coast. On the way the French fleet out of Toulon was encountered and the Battle of Malaga (14th August 1704) was fought, ending the first assault made by the French and the Spanish to recover Gibraltar.

After the Battle of Malaga, Rooke returned to England leaving Admiral Leake with a flotilla on station to protect Gibraltar. Louis XIV and the French tried again to retake Gibraltar, and invested the Rock with an army of 3,000 Spaniards supported by 13 ships of the line. The Prince of Hesse held out with his body of marines and in October was succoured by Leake. The French fleet escaped but extra troops were landed, supported by four further regiments, in December. In early 1705 the siege was renewed. Sir John Leake again came from Lisbon and defeated the French at the Battle of Marbella (10th March 1705) after which the siege was lifted.

The War of the Spanish Succession was finally terminated by a series of treaties in 1713 and 1714. On 13th July 1713 King Philip V of Spain signed a treaty ceding Gibraltar to Great Britain, who since then have retained the Rock. It was besieged by the Spanish unsuccessfully in 1727 and again in 1780, when it was relieved by Admiral Rodney and the fleet. British politicians, whenever anxious to curry favour with Spain, have offered to return the territory. Even such a patriot as Pitt the Elder contemplated such an offer in 1727, admittedly before the full value of the colony was realised. The most intensive attempts to use Gibraltar to gain Spanish favour have been in recent years, since the European Union came into existence. British public opinion has always fortunately stood in the way of such endeavours and today the people of Gibraltar have shown their resolution to remain British. Visitors to Gibraltar will see more Union flags flying than in any other town. Many of the residents descend from Muslims and Jews who fled the oppression and tyranny of Spain.

25th July 1666

The Battle of the North Foreland

In 1665 the English had won a substantial naval victory over the Dutch at the Battle of Lowestoft (3rd June). The second Dutch War had not ended and both nations prepared in 1666 to join battle again with their fleets. In January of that year France had declared war on England and joined the Dutch in alliance. Pepys, the Clerk of the Acts in the Navy office, in the same month recorded that there was only £1.5milion available to meet obligations amounting to £2.3 million. While this want of money affected but little the campaign of 1666, it was to create the circumstances that led in the next year to the taking by the Dutch of Sheerness and the Medway. The fleet was only prepared for the summer campaign; the Earl of Sandwich having retired, the command was given to Monk, the Duke of Albermarle, and to Prince Rupert, but the burden of preparation and administration fell on the shoulders of Sir William Coventry, who was himself against the war. In all the fleet contained 89 men-of-war, the smallest of which was a 40-gun frigate, and 18 fireships. The Dutch had also been rebuilding and refurbishing their fleet, strengthening it with bigger ships like De Zeven Provincien (80 guns). In all the Dutch had 71 sail of the line, 12 frigates and 13 fireships.

The problem which the English faced was that the Dutch and French could attack by sea both from the east and from the west. The fleet was therefore divided, 20 ships of the line accompanying Prince Rupert, who was given the task of guarding the Channel mouth and watching out for the French. Albermarle with the remainder of the fleet was to deal with the Dutch. On 31st May he sailed from the Downs and on 1st June, near the Goodwins, sighted the Dutch heading north. A four-day battle was to begin. Albermarle had a significantly inferior force to the Dutch, but nonetheless he bore down on them and went on to the attack. De Ruyter was sailing northerly on a port tack, the wind being fresh and from the south-west, so that the English had the weather gauge. That had the disadvantage that the lower-deck ports on the lee had to be closed, while the Dutch with theirs open could maintain their gunfire. The Dutch line was not properly formed and Albermarle was able to break through and round to attack again. He attacked the rear squadron under Tromp, whose flagship was damaged. The Dutch ship blew up. Sir William Berkeley's flagship, the Swiftsure was however, taken with three other ships after fighting valiantly. Sir John Harman, Vice–Admiral of the White, although strongly attacked, sank three fireships. The struggle went on until evening, when each side retired to effectuate repairs.

On the second day the wind was negligible until a light afternoon breeze came up from the south. Albermarle now had only 50 vessels to the Dutch 77 and the day was spent by the fleets passing and re-passing for ten hours on opposite tacks. On the third day (3rd June) the wind had turned easterly and Albermarle began to retire from the Dutch, bearing up towards Prince Rupert and his Channel fleet, who were sighted in the afternoon. The Galloper shoal lay between the two squadrons of the English fleet, which were striving to unite, and a number of ships including the Royal Prince (78 guns), one of the best ships in the fleet, beached upon it. After firm resistance, Sir George Ayscough, who was attacked, surrendered and became a prisoner, the most senior officer ever to be taken. The Royal Prince was burned. Others managed to save themselves. The evening saw Albermarle and Prince Rupert and their fleets united. On the last day of the fight, the Dutch still having superiority of numbers, the English renewed the fight and were counter-attacked by De Ruyter. Shot was short in both fleets, but the battle continued to rage. Prince Rupert's flagship was dismasted. Sir Christopher Myngs, who had started the battle, was shot twice by musket balls in the throat and was killed. Both sides, severely mauled and damaged, withdrew to sail home. The English had suffered a severe blow - two admirals and ten captains killed, ten ships lost and 3,700 men killed, wounded or captured.

Pepys the diarist discussed this battle with Sir William Penn, an admiral present at the Battle of Lowestoft (3rd June 1665). The latter was of the view that the conduct of the battle was ill, and was contrary to the views of the fleet's commanding officers, who were against fighting that day with the disproportion of force and the detrimental effect of the wind precluding the opening of the lower ports. Penn had added that it was 'pure dismaying and fear' that made so many men beach on the Galloper, 'not having their wits with them' and that it was a miracle that all were not lost.

Within seven weeks near the North Foreland battle was to be joined again, but on this occasion the fleets were evenly matched and the Dutch had no advantage such as that in the earlier four-day battle. The command was once more in the hands of Albermarle and Prince Rupert, Sir Thomas Allen commanding the White in Revenge (3rd of that name with 52 guns) and Sir Jeremy Smith the Blue in the Loyal London (second of the name London with 96 guns). The roll of battleships in this fleet was to survive down the centuries, for example Warspite, Royal Sovereign and Lion. The English met the Dutch fleet, again under De Ruyter and Tromp, east of the Galloper shoal and a three-hour meleé resulted, as the English attacked the snaking Dutch line. Resistance by the Dutch was determined but ultimately De Ruyter, hard pressed, bore to leeward to join his fleet together, pursued by ships of the White and Red squadrons of the fleet. Sir Jeremy Smith with the Blue squadron took on Tromp with his squadron in what was virtually a separate battle, reducing Tromp's flagship to a wreck. By evening there was nothing for the Dutch but to retire to Holland. The English had lost the Resolution (2nd of that name with 60 guns) which was destroyed by a fireship. The Dutch had suffered great damage, different assessments of which are made, and went to shelter in their ports. The English pursued under Sir Richard Holmes and were able to destroy off the Dutch coast, Pepys says by chance, 160 merchantmen and 2 men-of-war, landing on the island of Terschelling to burn the town and naval stores. Tromp was dismissed on his arrival home for leaving De Ruyter and fighting a lone naval battle of his own. In September 1666 the fleets were out again but never came to battle.

The diarist Samuel Pepys notes without much enthusiasm that a victory had been won at the North Foreland. He was told that only two great ships had been taken which he thought ' a poor result after the fighting of two so great fleets' but consoled himself by the thought that, 'This is all; only we keep the sea, which denoted a victory, or at least that we are not beaten.' A Thanksgiving Day was held on 14th August and he attended a party, throwing Serpents and Rockets, burning themselves and the people over the way. His friends then retired to his house to wine and dance, Pepys and a Mr Banister dressing themselves as women after smutting one another with candle grease and soot.

The campaign of 1666 exhausted the money supply for the navy; ships were decommissioned in port, seamen discharged. The way was open for De Ruyter in 1667 to attack Sheerness and the Medway and devastate the battle fleet.

28th July 1809
The Battle of Talavera

The first British intervention in the Iberian Peninsula ended in January 1809 with the evacuation of the army and the death of its commander Sir John Moore at Coruna. In April 1809 Sir Arthur Wellesley (the future Duke of Wellington) arrived with an army to reinforce the troops who remained. After striking at Oporto and taking it, thus driving the French from Northern Portugal, the question arose as to the nature of the campaign to be waged in the summer of that year. The French forces were divided, under pressure from Spanish armies and insurgents, as they endeavoured to resist the uprising of the people in Galicia and the Asturias, the forces of the Junta (the government of Spain) in the south, and hold Madrid. Wellesley was given authority by the Government to extend his campaigning into Spain in order to support the Spanish. By June 1809 he commanded 25,000 British and Germans, but the state of the army left much to be desired. There was a need for boots and uniforms after five weeks marching, but Wellesley was limited in securing supplies for want of funds. Discipline was undermined and the army was disorderly. Food was a problem.

Marshal Victor, the commander of the nearest French army to Wellesley, had withdrawn up the Tagus River towards Talavera. On 27th June the latter was ready to move with the objective of joining to wage a co-ordinated campaign with the nearest Spanish army. On 8th July Wellesley reached Plasencia, which was to be established as a base. He was sixty miles from the Spanish at the bridge of Almaraz. On 10th July he rode over to meet their commander and inspected their army by torchlight. Don Gregorio de la Cuesta, the Captain-General of Estramadura, was over seventy, unfit, none too fastidious of dress, and unrecovered from having his own cavalry ride over him three months before. He travelled in a ponderous carriage drawn by nine mules and had to be lifted and supported on his horse by two pages. He never inspected the country, when engaging in battle, but relied on instinct. His army shocked Wellesley, being a rabble of 35,000 infantry and cavalry, undisciplined, and arrayed in ragged tatterdemalion uniforms. Cuesta avoided discussions with Wellesley, leaving his second-in-command, O'Donoju, to evolve any joint plan. Wellesley envisaged a co-ordinated strike against the French, involving the Spanish General Venegas, who would advance to threaten Madrid with the Army of La Mancha; the northern passes of Banos and Pavales were to be held against Marshal Soult by a Spanish force in order to protect the flank, and he and Cuesta would unite to pursue Marshal Victor along the Tagus towards Madrid. Wellesley made his condition for entering Spain the provision of his army with food, supplies and transport, promises the Spanish accepted with no hope of their fulfilment. On 16th July the British Army moved forward and on the 20th arrived after hot, dusty marching at Oropesa. Cuesta in his coach inspected the army massed on parade. He was surprised by their solid red lines and rigid, disciplined character. They for their part, seeing him and his army, saw little that made them think that they could depend on their allies.

The united army started to march and on 22nd July reached Talavera. Spanish dragoons trotted through the city and advanced towards the River Albreche, where Victor was waiting. Artillery checked the advance guard. Wellesley, having surprised Marshal Victor, was keen to attack but Cuesta refused. On the 23rd, the French left. Cuesta was now anxious to move forward but Wellesley, who needed rations for the troops, refused to budge. The Spanish army then left, a motley of undisciplined soldiery, cattle, sheep, hangers-on and tattered cavalry. A rearguard was left on the west side of the River Albreche from Dakin's brigade of two brigades of infantry and some cavalry. The main army retired to a position at Talavera already identified by Wellesley to the north of the town.

The River Tagus runs to the south of the town in an east to west direction. The city was walled and to the north of it there stretched cultivated ground and woods of pines and olive trees ending at a small knoll. There was then a dusty scrubby plain for a mile or two which rose to a ridge, the Cerro de Medellin, rising with a gentle slope out of the plain. The ridge stretched from east to west, being bounded on the east by a steepish valley in which ran a stream, the Portina Brook. Beyond the steep valley the ridge continued towards the east, the latter height being the Cerro de Casagel. The northern slope of the Cerro de Medellin was formed by steep cliffs bordering the 800 yard-wide Medellin valley, through which the Portina ran. North of the valley rose the hills and mountains of the Sierra de Segurilla. The Portina Brook joined the Tagus through the city of Talavera.

On 26th July the Spanish returned in confusion, little more than a mob. They had near Toledo come up against the now combined army, in all amounting to 46,000 men, of Marshal Victor, General Sebastian and King Joseph of Spain, the brother of Emperor Napoleon, who had placed him on the throne. Cuesta came to a standstill about three or four miles east of Wellesley and refused to move further. Wellesley went to persuade him, even kneeling to implore him to move back. Finally Cuesta decided to rejoin him and his army and the forward British brigade returned toward the position chosen.

Wellesley hurried to make his arrangements. Cuesta and the 35,000 Spanish were posted in the walled city and on the line to the north, shielded by the cultivated lands and woods, with hastily formed earth defensive works. North of the small knoll in the plain, the Pajar de Vergera, linking with the Spanish were stationed Lieutenant-

General Campbell's Division, and further north Lieutenant-General Sherbrooke's. To his north on the Cerro de Medellin was Sir Rowland Hill's Division. Lieutenant General Mackenzie's was placed in the centre of the plain as a reserve. North of the Cerro de Medellin were cavalry under Anson and Fane, Spanish cavalry under the Duca de Albuquerque and infantry under General Bassecourt.

The French gradually came up and Wellesley went forward to the position of his forward troops, in order to inspect what was happening. He arrived in the middle of the day, when Dorkin's brigades were taking 'a siesta'. He mounted the tower of the Casa de Salinas to view the country and while there French forces under General Lapisse came up through the woods and surprised the British troops, some of whom were routed, although the 45th (Nottinghamshire) Regiment of Foot stood firm. The 31st (Huntingdonshire) Regiment of Foot rallied. Wellesley himself was almost taken with his staff as the French skirmishers came up to the Casa de Salinas. The force, shielded by cavalry, successfully retired, however, to the position on the west side of the Portina Brook.

Later in the day French cavalry came into distant sight of the Spanish north of the city and the Spanish troops started to blaze away in a heavy fusillade of musketry fire, with no hope of hitting the cavalry as it passed. Four regiments, amounting to 2,000 men, fled to the rear, looting the British baggage train, and never returned. Cuesta ordered that one in forty of the deserters should be shot.

The French started to form position on the east side of the Portina Brook, taking the height of the Cerro da Casagel. Marshal Victor was anxious to attack and decided without conferring with King Joseph or Marshal Jourdan on a night-time attempt on the British left on the Cerro de Medellin. General Ruffin's Division was assigned this task. Two of his regiments were stopped by a chasm in the valley, but one mounted the steep eastern hillside and came up on troops of the Kings German Legion taking their leisure in their bivouacs. Disorder and rout took hold, but the firing was heard by Sir Rowland Hill who galloped up the hill, almost being taken by a French soldier, who caught his bridle, and he brought up the seasoned troops of the 29th (Worcestershire) Regiment of Foot. Led forward, the troops pushed the French off the summit and down the hill to the brook and their own lines.

Dawn came with a thin drifting mist and a light easterly wind. The whole French army of 34,000 men were drawn up opposite the British lines of 21,000. No French were stationed opposite Cuesta and his army, reliance being placed on containing them with cavalry. General Ruffin remained on the right. General Villatte held the Cerro de Casagel and the Divisions of Generals Lapisse, Sebastiani and Leval occupied the plain opposite the left centre, centre and right of the British force. At 5 am a single gun was fired, signalling the opening of the bombardment which was to precede the attack. 50 guns hammered the British on the summit of the Medellin which once again was to be the initial focus of attack. Hill ordered his Division towards the eastern reverse slope and told them to lie down. Ruffin's Division laboured up the steep eastern slope to the summit in three close columns, a formation which precluded the bringing to bear of total musket fire. Up they laboured and on through the mist and smoke blown onto the summit by the wind. As they crossed it, Hill gave the command: the British troops rose and doubled forward to stand in line at forty yards, pouring volleys of musket shot into the French. Men of Sherbrooke's Division attacked the French flank. Three times the French endeavoured to take the summit but finally the British charged; the experienced troops of the 29th and 45th pushed the French back and down the hill. At 8 am the attack was over and a truce was called. French and British soldiers mingled at the Portina Brook. The British on the Medellin collected their dead.

The French during the truce had held a council of their commanders. King Joseph had received two messages; first, that Marshal Soult with his army from the north-west could not arrive to cut Wellesley's link to Portugal until at least 5th August and second that General Venegas, who despite the agreement to act together with the British had been dilatory, was at last beginning to threaten Madrid. He vacillated therefore whether to continue the battle or move back to Madrid to protect the capital. Marshal Victor vigorously argued for fighting on to crush the British and Spanish in the field. In the end the King gave way and the French in the late morning sounded the retreat for their troops to return to the lines.

At 2 pm the bombardment of the British lines again began. At last, the guns falling silent, the French advanced on the British right and centre, where the army stood in the plain in two long lines (three ranks of men per line). The Divisions of Generals Lappise and Sebastiani came on: General Leval attacked the left. Campbell's pickets were driven from the shelter of the olive trees, while 10 Spanish guns from the top of the Pajar de Vergera pounded Leval's left flank. The French hesitated and Campbell's men charged, assisted by Spanish cavalry, repelling Leval's Dutch and German contingents and taking seventeen guns. Meanwhile the columns of Lapisse and Sebastiani came stolidly on to be met by a withering volley of close fire from the steadfast British lines. More than one attempt was made, but each was met by the shattering musketry fire, even as close as fifty yards. Sherbrooke's men finally broke into a cheer and charged, the Guards regiments and Kings German Legion rushing the French back across the Portina Brook in their enthusiasm. Into the French lines they went, pushing forward to be all but overwhelmed. The Hannoverian General was killed and 600 men lost.

The charge had opened a large hole in the British lines, which the French reserves could use to advantage to outflank and gain the British rear. Wellesley from the Cerro de Medellin perceived the danger. General Mackenzie with three regiments of the reserve, the 21st (Royal North British) Fusiliers Regiment of Foot, the 31st (Huntingdonshire) Regiment of Foot and the 45th (Nottinghamshire)

Regiment of Foot, was ordered forward to plug the gap. Sir Rowland Hill from the Medellin with the 48th (Northamptonshire) Regiment of Foot was ordered to support. The break in the centre was stopped: the survivors of the returning Guards and Hannoverians went through the new lines to reform to loud cheering. Lapisse and his column came on once more to meet hard volleys of musket fire. The French were seven times as numerous as the men in the British lines. For twenty minutes the enemy was subjected to the murderous fire, which was returned. At last the columns began to break and retreat when they were assailed by Sir Stapleton Cotton's cavalry, brought up from the rear, and were thrown back to the Portina Brook. General Lapisse was killed and Mackenzie mortally wounded. But the thin red lines had held.

No new direct attack was made on the Cerro de Medellin, but Marshal Victor thought that it could be outflanked through the valley to the north. The infantry divisions of Ruffin and Villatte were therefore set in motion to work their way round the hill and up the valley. Wellesley, seeing the movement from the Medellin, reinforced Anson and Fane, who were stationed in the valley. The French moved up and as they reached the farm of Valdafuentes the order to charge was given. Away went Anson's cavalry to the cheers of the men on the Medellin, with all the excitement and elation of the British foxhunter at the gallop down the valley, the 23rd Light Dragoons and the 1st Hussars of the King's German Legion in the lead. Across and through the long grass, in which in front of them there lay hidden a deep chasm some ten-foot wide, they charged. The close packed men came up to it unseen: were stopped, tumbled in a struggling mass of men and horses down the slopes and were shattered. The survivors and latecomers worked their way across and rode on towards the French infantry, which had formed squares. Subject to intense firing and coming up against the Polish Lancers, the broken regiments were forced to retire, losing one in two troopers fallen. On the Medellin the guns had been turned to pound the French squares below. Brigadier Fane's cavalry and that of the Duca de Albuquerque pressed on towards the dissolving squares, pounded by guns from the heights and in the valley, and the French infantry broke and began to flow back.

At this point, with only a reserve left of 5,000, King Joseph decided to end the attack, despite vehement protests by Marshal Victor. He knew that he had to reform the broken army and hold on to the reserve in order to be in a position to protect Madrid. Although the French artillery continued to fire until dusk, the preparations to retire began and the French, partially reformed, began to withdraw. Wellesley and the British army were left in possession of the field, although one quarter of their force was dead. The French had lost 7,000 dead and wounded and 17 guns.

At dawn the Light Brigade, fresh from England, with a troop of the Royal Horse Artillery, entered the camp to cheers, having hurried the last forty-three miles as they heard distantly the sound of the guns. On the Medellin that night the scrub and grass had caught fire, burning and torching the dead and wounded. The army was down to one-third of its daily rations, lacked water and had no transport. The Spanish had still not met their obligations of supply, which had been made to Wellesley before he entered Spain. The problem in the circumstances was what use was to be made of the victory. There was still a desire by the Spanish to press on to Madrid, but the strategic position was rapidly changing. Wellesley learned that the pass of Banos had been taken by Marshal Soult, the Spanish having left only a few thousand troops there and not the numbers which he had been given to believe. This French army now numbered 50,000 and was well towards cutting off his retreat to Portugal. He therefore on 3rd August started to retire on Orepesa, leaving 1,500 wounded to the Spanish, with 2,500 accompanying the army.

On the way Wellesley heard that Marshal Soult had taken his base at Plasencia and so at Puente del Arzobispo he crossed to the south of the Tagus. General Cuesta subsequently followed him, abandoning the British wounded in Talavera. Wellesley pushed on to Almaraz. The retreat was rapid, the army was without water and with little food in countryside devastated and plundered by war. General Cuesta paused at Arzobispo and was defeated by the French, losing the seventeen guns captured at Talavera. The next day he suffered a paralytic stroke. On 21st August the British Army left, having no other choice, for Portugal through Trujillo and Merida. They arrived at Badajoz on the River Guadiana on 3rd September, starving and fever-ridden. One-third of the army had been lost. Spain however remained in turmoil, as the battered armies and the guerrillas continued to harry the French. In November, Wellesley retired further to the River Mondego and Beira, leaving General Crawford and the Light Brigade to contain and watch the French beyond the River Agueda. The objective of the Emperor Napoleon of ejecting the British from Spain and Portugal had not been achieved.

In England, when the news of Talavera arrived, the signal victory over the French brought encouragement, but the retreat led to criticism and political attacks by the Whigs on the Tory Government and Wellesley. Nonetheless, Wellesley was created Viscount Wellington of Talavera, and Baron Douro of Wellesley in the County of Somerset.

Sir Stapleton Cotton, the commander of the cavalry, who remained so throughout the Peninsular War, became Baron Combermere in 1814 and Viscount in 1826. Sir Rowland Hill became Baron Hill of Almaraz and Hardwick in 1814 and Viscount in 1842. The 5th Lord Combermere and the 8th Viscount Hill were ejected from the House of Lords in 1999.

28th July 1813

The Battle of Sorauren
(also known as the Battle of Pyrenees)

The advance after the Battle of Vitoria (21st June 1813) had taken the Duke of Wellington and the Allied army to the borders of France, along the line of the River Bidassoa. Wellington was not prepared to go further, since negotiations under a truce were taking place at Dresden between the Emperor Napoleon and Prussia and Russia. He therefore paused. He still had to deal with the threat across his line of communications implicit in the French occupation of San Sebastian and Pamplona, which he believed would be the subject of an attempt at their relief. Sir Thomas Graham was sent to besiege San Sebastian, and the Spaniards left to blockade Pamplona. His other task was to guard the left flank on the lower Bidassoa near Irun. On his right the 7th and Light Brigades held the pass of Echalor and the heights above Vera. Sir Rowland Hill was posted in the Bastan with the 2nd Division, less one Brigade, in the Maya Pass. On the right flank the Pass of Roncesvalles was held by Sir Lowry Cole with the 4th Division, Byng's brigade from the 2nd Division and four thousand Spaniards. The 6th and 3rd Divisions were posted beyond the passes in reserve. The country away from the coast comprised the rocky foothills and mountains of the Pyrenees, with the army positions separated from one another by the ranges of these hills, such as the Sierra de Aralar. Cavalry was of little use in this countryside, and apart from two brigades was left at Vitoria. It was Wellington's view that the French would seek to relieve San Sebastian prior to Pamplona, and his headquarters were therefore at Lesaca in the left of centre.

The news of Vitoria had enraged the Emperor Napoleon. Marshal Jourdan and King Joseph were removed from command and Marshal Soult, the Duke of Dalmatia, known to the British soldier as the Duke of Damnation, was sent to reorganise the defeated army. He was ordered to recover Spain, first relieving the cities of San Sebastian and Pamplona, and was given a warrant secretly to arrest the Emperor's brother, King Joseph, if necessary. He arrived on 12th July and within a fortnight had re-established order in the army and seen to its supply. There was now to be a single army under his command – the Army of Spain – of 72,000 infantry and 7,000 cavalry, from which had to be deducted the garrisons and the sick and wounded, amounting to 14,000. He divided the army into three corps of three-divisions. The artillery was divided discretely among the various corps, the cavalry and the reserve.

Because Soult knew that General Rey was holding out at San Sebastian, and that the topography of the country hindered communication and contact between the contingents of the army on their right wing, he decided first to move towards Pamplona. His tactics were therefore the reverse of those conceived as likely by Wellington. Troops and boat-bridges were placed on the lower Bidassoa, but only as a feint. The problem of supply was such that the French troops had only supplies of food for four days, and the country was too bare and mountainous to live on the land. There was therefore a heavy pressure upon the French to reach Pamplona in four days of campaigning. The mountain passes were potentially strong obstacles to assault.

On 25th July news was brought to Wellington of the failure to storm San Sebastian at Lesaca. He rode over to visit Sir Thomas Graham and, while he was away, fighting was heard on the right in Lesaca. A French force had attacked Lord Dalhousie on the Pass of Echalor but had been repulsed. General Murray, the Quartermaster-General, warned the 7th and Light divisions that they might have to move and despatched a troop of artillery south. Wellington returned at 8 pm, when he was told that Byng had been attacked at Roncesvalles, although he was holding his own.

Marshal Soult had in fact launched his campaign based on St Jean Pied de Port. General D'Erlon with 20,000 troops was to attack the Maya Pass and Generals Clausel and Reille the Pass de Roncesvalles, the latter with 31,000 troops to the 6,000 there with Sir Lowry Cole and Byng. General Stewart on the Maya pass, hearing firing, left his troops to investigate the forces under the inexperienced Brigadier Pringle, new out from England. D'Erlon had managed to take him by surprise, since the French were only spotted when half a mile away. His troops managed to reach the Maya plateau and Pringle, having sent for help from the 7th Division, resorted to sending forward the infantry in a series of charges. In these charges the 34th (Cumberland) Regiment of Foot and the 39th (Dorsetshire) Regiment of Foot were mowed down by the French volleys. On the French right wing the 50th (West Kent) Regiment of Foot was repulsed and sixty per cent of the 92nd (Highland) regiment of Foot and of the 28th (North and South Gloucestershire) Regiments of Foot fell. After Stewart returned, further ground was lost, but recovered by the 82nd (2nd Somersetshire) Regiment of Foot, the 6th (1st Warwickshire) Regiment of Foot and the Brunswick Regiment. In the end General D'Erlon discontinued the fight, as he formed the view that two divisions were now present on the pass.

At Roncesvalles the position held by General Byng was so strong that frontal assault was effectively impossible. General Clausel thought that he needed to outflank the position and the French prepared to do that. General Reille began to filter troops across the Lindez Plateau to the west. General Clausel tried to filter across the mountains, outflanking Byng's forward troops, who had to retire.

As the French pressed forward, an impenetrable fog descended, clothing the battlefield in darkness, which left both sides unsure of their positions.

At 3 am on July 26th news was brought to Wellington that Sir Lowry Cole, fearful of being outflanked in the fog, had retired from the Roncesvalles pass and joined with Picton. Sir Rowland Hill, worried that his right flank was turned, also ordered a retreat from the Maya pass. The passes were therefore open for the French to press on to Pamplona. Leaving the 3rd Division to act as a shield to Graham at San Sebastian, Wellington began to move his forces southwards toward Pamplona. The 26th July saw no movement by General D'Erlon, who remained on the Maya, but Clausel and Reille marched forward, where Sir Lowry Cole had retreated. The move by the latter had left Sir Rowland Hill's division exposed on the right flank, and although his 9,000 troops were entrenched on the Elizonda Road, only the Sierra de Aralar lay between him and General D'Erlon's 18,000 troops. He too therefore was forced to retire. On 27th July D'Erlon began to probe again after Hill. In their retreat Cole and Picton finally came to a standstill on a ridge at Sorauren, some eight miles north of Pamplona. The village of Sorauren stood at the foot of a central ridge in a valley at the northwest end of the ridge. The ridge, rising to about one thousand feet, itself overlooked a valley, and at the east end, where the valley turned south, was the village of Zabaldica. Opposite the main ridge there was to the north of this valley a south-facing ridge, on either side of which there were the road to Ostiz in the west valley and the River Arga in the east. South of the main ridge a valley separated it from a further broken ridge, to the east of the river Arga valley in which lay the village of Huarte. The road to Pamplona ran though the villages of Zabaldica and Huarte in the valley of the River Arga.

The Anglo-Portuguese forces straddled the valley on the ridges. In the heights to the west of the western valley were stationed Brigadier-General Pack's Brigades of Portuguese. On the central height between Sorauren and Zabaidica in the Arga Valley were Cole's three brigades of the 4th Division, Byng's British brigade, a Portuguese brigade and two battalions of Spanish. On the second ridge beyond the southern valley the Spanish were on the left, west of Huarte and the 3rd under Sir Thomas Picton on the eastern ridge threatening the Arga valley and covering the road to Pamplona.

On 27th July about noon the army of General Clausel began to debouch from the River Arga valley on the north-east. General Reille's division was in the rear, having lost itself in the mountains. It took all day for the French Divisions to deploy across a front occupying the ridge to the north of the east-west valley opposite the British and also moving south along the River Arga valley to Zabaldica, and taking the height opposite Picton to the west. Meanwhile the British 6th division was marching south down the Ostiz road.

As the French arrived and moved west from the Arga valley, their forward cavalry patrols of dragoons reached the outskirts of the village of Sorauren just as the Duke of Wellington, having outpaced his staff and accompanied only by his aide-de-camp Lord Fitzroy Somerset, then only twenty-three, galloped into the village. Realising that the village could not be held and the deployment of troops to it was now impracticable, he scribbled orders for the Quartermaster General while leaning on the bridge. Lord Fitroy Somerset galloped north out of the village, evading the French patrols up the Ostiz road. Wellington turned south and vigorously mounted the rise to cries from the Portuguese as they recognised him of 'Douro, Douro', their name for him, changing gradually to the throaty loud cheer of the British. The French heard the roar of salute, but not having fully taken position and thinking new troops may have arrived, Marshal Soult decided to wait, calmly having dinner. In the later afternoon a torrential thunderstorm covered the battlefield and lashed the country with rain, precluding army action.

It was at noon on 28th July that the action began. The French right near Sorauren launched assaults on Pack's Portuguese, who withstood the attack and tried unsuccessfully to take the village, while their left under General Foy assaulted Picton's Division, but the main assault was to be on the central ridge across the northern valley. As the attack began, the 6th Division began to approach and come on to the field from the north-west, and Marshal Soult detached part of his force to stem their approach. On the ridge there stood in the front line the 27th (Inniskillen) Regiment of Foot, the 40th (2nd Somersetshire) Regiment of Foot, and the 50th (West Kent) Regiment of Foot. Byng's brigade formed a reserve, comprising a battalion of the 50th (West Kent's), two battalions of Highland Light Infantry (the 71st and the 74th) and the 92nd Highland Regiment of Foot. The French columns in their blue masses, with drums and flags flying, began to struggle up the ridge. They were preceded by a heavy screen of skirmishers especially sent in advance by Marshal Soult, and inexorably they came up the rise in their deep masses. The volleys of British fire mowed down the advancing masses, but they pressed hard on the British left and on the right centre the assault caused the British line to disintegrate, leaving the Brigades of Campbell and Ross liable to be outflanked. On the right Anson's Brigade repulsed the French, but the Spanish battalions fled leaving the 40th Regiment to bear the brunt of the attack. The 40th stand was undaunted – after the foot charge, they went forward downhill to bayonet the retiring French; two more attempts were made and again the 40th stemmed the French columns by their volleys and disordered them by their bayonet charge. They lost 130 killed. Along the line the troops held and the French assault was beaten back. In late afternoon the French paused and abandoned the assault. The 40th in particular had performed outstandingly and Wellington in his despatches referred to their 'enthusiastic conduct', which led to the 4th Division being nicknamed the Enthusiastics.

Not having carried the day, and having suffered large losses Marshal Soult faced a dilemma. His lack of food and supplies, which had been planned to last until Pamplona was reached, was such that another attack and advance against the background of his losses was impracticable. Retreat to his base appeared to be the only alternative. The 29th of July was spent by the two armies re-organising themselves and waiting. On the 29th Soult decided that he would not retire directly to France, but would move north-west to join up with General D'Erlon for an attempt to relieve San Sebastian. Such a manoeuvre meant that the bulk of his army would cross the front of the British to the Ostiz road in order to move on the city. Needing cover, the redeployment began on the night of the 29th. The terrain however was so difficult and ill-adapted to the movement of armies that by dawn on 30th July little progress had been made, and the greater part of the French force was still crossing the British front. Only General Clausel's Division had passed by during the night. On the previous day Sir Lowry Cole had fortified the ridge with additional guns. A cannonade and intermittent attacks on the straggling army reduced the French to disorder. The assault brought back the Divisions of General Mancune and Corroux to Sorauren and the 2nd Division, backed by Packenham's Brigade, attacked them there. After an artillery bombardment the French retired. General Foy's troops, who had opposed Picton's Brigade, lost their way north and ended up returning directly to France.

D'Erlon meanwhile had come up with Hill at Lizasco, where he was solidly entrenched. An all-out assault was made on the ridge on which he was placed, and by superior numbers he was forced off the ridge and had to retire. The way to France was now unobstructed. Soult gave up the attempt to relieve San Sebastian, returning directly to France. Wellington and the British army pursued the retreating French, but were unsuccessful in preventing their retreat across the Bidassoa River. The two sides then stood in the same positions as before the campaign started on 25th July. Wellington still had regard to the existence of the Armistice in Central Europe, which did not end until 12th August, the news of which reached him on 2nd September. He began then to plan to invade France. On 31st October Pamplona surrendered.

30th July 1588

The Defeat of the Spanish Armada

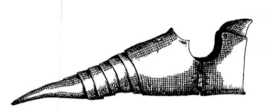

The creator of the self-governing British state was King Henry VIII (1509 – 1547), who threw off the hegemony of Catholic Europe, of the Pope and the sovereigns who supported him (like the Emperor Charles V of Germany and Spain, who stood between Henry VIII and his ability to divorce Catherine of Aragon, the aunt of the Emperor) and with the help of the people in Parliament established a national church and sovereign independence, which was to remain until thrown away by twentieth-century politicians after 1970. The Church which he established was both Catholic and Protestant, as the Church of England still remains. The purpose of his divorce was to secure a male heir, which ultimately he did by his third wife Jane Seymour. His son Edward VI (1547-1533) succeeded him, ruling because of his youth through a regency, which pursued a vigorous policy of shifting England towards Protestantism. His successor, Queen Mary, King Henry VIII's eldest daughter by Catherine of Aragon, was a convinced Roman Catholic and she reversed the policy of her predecessor, seeking to restore Roman Catholicism and the subjection of the church to the Pope in Rome. In July 1554 Queen Mary married King Philip II of Spain, the son of the Emperor Charles V. Philip, who became King of England, remained in England only a year, but returned again in 1557. During the course of his stay he met Elizabeth, the youngest daughter of Henry VIII, who was to become Queen on the death of Mary in 1558. The severe prosecution of persecution under Mary, burning bishops and clergy, as well as lay people, in the fires of Smithfield and Oxford and elsewhere, so well related in Foxe's Book of Martyrs, led the English people to welcome Elizabeth as Queen with delight. She inaugurated her reign by reinstating the national church, the Church of England, on the basis of her father's compromise. Her Roman Catholic subjects and the more extreme Protestants, despite laws to enforce conformity, were treated with a light hand, unless driven by fanaticism they conspired to attack her or the state. Her Church settlement, renewed in 1660, remains substantially today, apart from the liturgy and the use of the King James Bible, uprooted by populist bishops and clergy since 1960. In foreign affairs, while sympathetic to Protestants in northern Europe, especially the Dutch, her policy was one essentially of peace, particularly with Spain. Both Philip II and Elizabeth for many years co-existed without difficulty, not involving themselves in conflicts which might lead to war. As time went on, particularly after 1580, when Philip II annexed

Portugal, English sailors began to harass the Spanish in the Caribbean and South America, attacking and taking the treasure ships carrying gold and silver from the colonies. While Elizabeth sought openly to condemn their actions, she connived at them, often taking a share of the treasure captured. As Philip lost the hope of marrying Elizabeth and he became progressively a more fanatical Catholic, building the great Escorial Church and Palace near Madrid, he came more to dwell on the need to recover England for Catholicism. The idea arose in a context where Pope Paul V in 1570 had relieved all subjects of Queen Elizabeth of their oath of fealty, implicitly sanctioning the legality in Catholic eyes of her assassination, while his successor Pope Gregory favoured and urged an invasion. In the 1580s Philip II was also involved in a war in the Low Countries against Holland, to which Elizabeth sent money, supplies and soldiers. These considerations drove him towards war, a view that hardened with the execution of Mary, Queen of Scots, on 8th February 1587. Mary was a Catholic and legal successor to Elizabeth, should she die childless. Despite her constant plotting with the more fanatical Catholics, who contemplated killing the Queen, and which culminated in Babington's Conspiracy in 1586, Elizabeth had protected her from the wishes of the Council and Parliament who sought her death. Philip II, relying on a will made in 1577 and his descent from the House of Lancaster, stated his claim to the throne and finally, after seeking a subsidy from Pope Sixtus V, who only agreed to a payment of a million crowns after Philip's army landed in England, he began preparation of a huge force to invade. Work went on to assemble a fleet and to gather the men and supplies, but the assembling fleet was attacked, burnt and destroyed by Drake in the harbour at Cadiz in April 1587. Work had to begin again and the project was delayed until 1588. The Marques de Santa Cruz, Spain's most successful sailor, was in charge.

Philip II had been offered three strategies for the invasion of England. The Marques de Santa Cruz had commended a plan to sail to England with an army and take a West Country port for a base. He said that he would need 556 ships, of which 180 would be frontline galleons, 3,000 seamen and 65,000 troops. The cost would be 4 million ducats. The huge cost made this strategy impracticable. Mendoza, a soldier of great experience, suggested a small force to encourage the rising of the Catholic Scots, and, if that succeeded, the invasion of England with a rising by English Catholics. The third scheme was that of the Duke of Parma, who commanded the Spanish army in the Netherlands. A leading soldier with an experienced army, he suggested the secret building of flotillas of barges to land a force on the Kent coast before the English were prepared. Philip II adopted none of these strategies, but combined two of them. He envisaged a smaller fleet and force than that wanted by Santa Cruz, which would sail from Spain and move to join the Duke of Parma's fleet of barges, then crossing to England with 15,000 troops from the Flanders army. His adoption of this strategy also depended on the notion, of which he had been persuaded by emigré Catholics, that much of the English population would rise against the government in order to restore Catholicism. Detailed instructions were to be issued by Philip II to implement the adopted strategy.

The English received reports of a proposed invasion as early as December 1585 and in 1586 orders went out to lay down preparations for such an invasion – warning beacons on the coasts and hills, the mustering of foot bands of soldiers in counties, the provision of watches and a defensive strategy. Sir John Hawkins had worked to improve naval administration and the quality of the fleet. New warships were built to a radical design – the hull length became three times as long as the beam with a deeper keel. The stern and forecastles were lowered and the waist decked. The mainmast was stepped further forward. The lengthening of the boat and the change in position of the mainmast increased the speed and power of the boat to sail. By the time the Armada arrived there were 40 of the new warships. English guns had a longer range and the sailors were used to firing broadsides, a practice inaugurated by Henry VIII; moreover the new galleons rolled less than the Spanish, so that they were less affected by the tendency to fire directed down into the sea or up to the air.

The Marques de Santa Cruz twice expressed his reservations about the proposed invasion and the Duke of Parma informed Philip II of his opposition. Philip, however, was determined to go ahead. Since the commander of the Spanish army in the Low Countries, the Duke was a prince in his own right, possibly pursuing to some degree his own interest, he continued well into the spring of 1588 to negotiate with Elizabeth with a view to preserving the peace. After urging forward the restoration of the fleet following Drake's raid on Cadiz, the Marques de Santa Cruz fell ill and died in February 1588. Philip needed someone to complete the administrative task and so, over his protests of ill health, unsuitability and inability, he appointed the Duke de Medina Sidonia, a well-tried administrator, to command the expedition.

By the time the expedition sailed in May 1588, Medina Sidonia had a fleet of 137 ships, of which 109 were fighting ships. The fleet was a mixture of galleons of up to 1,000 tons, carrying 50 guns and 5,000 men, merchantmen rebuilt with forecastles of 60-100 tons, heavy built and slow moving fighting hulks, and light and fast sloops. There were 5 galleasses, of which one was lost en route; a highly manoeuvrable ship which both sailed and could be rowed by the 300 galley slaves. In total manpower there were about 32,000 men of which 19,000 were soldiers. There were included on board servants of the noblemen and 180 monks. The fleet contained galleons sailed by the ablest sailors of Spain. The Duke of Medina Sidonia was advised on board the San Martin by Don Diego Flores de Valdes, an expert in seas, tides and currents. Admiral Juan Martinez de Recalde was on the San Juan de Portugal, Don Pedro de Valdes on the Nuestra Senora del Rosario, Don Miguel Oquendo on the Santa Ana, Lieutenant General Almas de Leyva on the Rata Encoronada, Don Martin de Bertendoma on La Regazona and the galleasses were under Don Hugo de Moncada, with his flag on the San Lorenzo. All these were to play a distinguished and active part in the fighting. The fleet was divided into nine squadrons. In terms of the supplies of the fleet and its health matters were not ideal: there was a shortage of shot and gunpowder; the biscuit supply would last but four months and typhus was already on board. Even as it left, gamblers in Paris were offering 6 to 1 against that the fleet would not reach its objectives in the Channel.

In England the spring found the nation calm; Elizabeth continued to negotiate with the Duke of Parma. Drake persuaded Lord Howard of Effingham to press the Queen to allow the navy to attack the Armada before it left Spain, as had happened in 1587. The queen would not be moved, holding to the hope of peace. At last, after information was brought about the departure of the Spanish fleet, the fleet was mobilised and dispositions made. Lord Howard of Effingham was given command of the fleet, with 16 warships at Queenborough. He was a cousin of the Queen, Member of Parliament for Surrey 1563 – 1573, Lord Chamberlain and a staunch Protestant. Sir Francis Drake was to be based at Plymouth. He had been born in 1545 in a Lutheran family and brought up in Chatham, living on the river in a hulk. By 1588 he was regarded as the greatest English sailor, having circumnavigated the world, taken rich Spanish treasure galleons and in 1587 sacked the Spanish fleet in Cadiz. Sir John Hawkins and Sir Martin Frobisher were also prominent commanders in the fleet. The former was Treasurer of the Navy and had been responsible for forcing the evolution of the new type warship, and the latter had tried piracy and made three trips to the Artic, giving his name to Frobisher's Bay. A tough, unruly man, he carried his flag in the Triumph, the largest ship – a vessel of 1,100 tons with a crew of 500. Howard was aboard his flagship, the Ark of 800 tons with a crew of 400, and Drake on Revenge, of 500 tons with a crew of 250. Drake continued to urge Howard to persuade the Queen to permit the fleet to strike again at the Spanish in harbour but she did not release the fleet until 17ᵗʰ June, after Cardinal Allen had issued a manifesto calling on all Catholics to rise against her. Cardinal Allen's pamphlet, *an Admonition to the Nobility and People of England Concerning the Present War*, cited Elizabeth as a heretic, sacrilegious and a person living an abandoned life, so that it was the duty of the faithful 'to help towards the restoring of the Catholic faith and deposing the usurper.' The fleet released, an attempt was made in early July by Lord Howard of Effingham's fleet and that of Sir Francis Drake, to strike at the Armada in harbour, but lack of provisions and strong southerly winds forced the fleet to return to Plymouth.

On 18ᵗʰ May the Duke of Medina Sidonia sailed, but off Finisterre the fleet was scattered by storm and had to enter Coruna and the Biscay ports for repair and revictualling. The Duke pleaded again with Philip II to give up the project, but he replied that the storm could not have been a signal by God since the war was righteous. On 11th July the fleet was again under way and reached the Channel off the Lizard at 4 pm on 19th July. The fleet hove to in order to wait for the slowest vessels and the great banner, blessed by the Pope and embroidered with the Crucifixion, the Virgin Mary and Mary of Magdalene and carrying the motto - 'Essurge, Domnie, et judica causam tuam', was raised on the flagship, the San Martin. Slowly, at three knots, and mustered closely in the form of a crescent two to three miles long , the great war galleons on the wings, the Spanish fleet started on its journey up the Channel, aided by a south-westerly wind. On the same afternoon news reached Plymouth from a Captain Fleming on the barque the Golden Hind that the Armada had arrived. It is recounted that Sir Francis Drake was playing bowls in the presence of Lord Howard of Effingham when he received the news and calmly went on, remarking that there was time to finish the game. In the harbour, intense preparations of the fleet took place as it was readied to sail. The Queen in London on hearing of the arrival of the Armada issued a special prayer:

'We do instantly beseech thee of they special goodness to be merciful to the Church Militant here upon earth and at this time, compassed about with the most strong and subtle adversaries. O let thine enemies know that thou hast received England into thine own protection. Set a wall about it, O Lord, and evermore mightily defend it.'

The prayer was given effect as subsequently and in the centuries to come.

While he was hove to, the Duke of Medina Sidonia held a council. He was urged to attack the English fleet in harbour in Plymouth before it could put to sea. He rejected this plan, relying on his instructions from Philip II that his main object was to achieve a juncture with the Duke of Parma in order to ferry the army in the Low Countries to England, that he should not initiate sea battles on the way and only take the Isle of Wight or land after a meeting with the Duke of Parma had failed. Like any modern bureaucrat he remained inflexible, tied by his instructions.

In England the warning beacons were being lit, and by dark the fleet was on the ebb tide, being slowly warped out of the Catwater and the Sound by the ship's boats in the damp south-westerly. Once out the fleet crossed the front of the Spanish crescent and then began a tack up on to a beat as the wind veered north north-west in order to get behind the Spanish fleet and take the weather gauge.

Saturday 20th July dawned with thick drizzly weather. The English fleet had not at this stage any defined structure of squadrons, but it was agreed that Drake with Frobisher should attack the landward end of the crescent and Howard the seaward end. The form of the dense crescent was akin to a castle on the sea; it precluded safe assault on the inward vessels and made the English tactic the only one feasible. Moreover the English, with their longer range guns, had no intention of going in to grapple with the Spaniards and attempt to board them, as the latter expected. When the Duke of Medina Sidonia found the English to the windward he did not change course or formation; indeed under his instructions he had no choice. At 9 am Howard began a cannonade and the two fleets exchanged fire until 1 pm, with a succession of passes in line by the English, as they fired broadsides into the Spanish fleet. Little damage was done by either. Drake in the Revenge, Frobisher in Triumph and Hawkins attacked Recalde's San Juan and the Gran Grin, which had become separated, but only damaged the superstructure. Medina Sidonia in the San Martin with three other vessels beat up to the rescue and fought for almost two hours, but neither side closed. For all the fighting the only disaster suffered by the Armada was of its own making. Carelessness in dealing with gunpowder in the San Salvador resulted in the galleon blowing up, tearing out the forecastle and damaging the masts. 250 men were killed out of a crew of 396. Howard in the confusion attacked, but withdrew when the Spanish sought to rescue the ship and transfer the bullion it was carrying to other vessels. Elsewhere the San Catalina and the Nuestra Senora del Rosario collided. The latter lost its bowsprit and the mainstay of the foremast broke. Initially the ship was taken in tow by the San Martin but Don Diego de Valdes advised the Duke of Medina Sidonia that he should not falter in his mission by succouring damaged vessels. The Duke therefore left six small vessels as a guard and rejoined the fleet.

As darkness fell Howard decided that in no circumstances should the English lose the Spanish fleet, and he instructed Drake to lead the fleet with his stern lantern lit. During the six hours of darkness Drake extinguished his poop light, the fleet became dispersed and Howard in the Ark, the White Bear and Mary Rose came up close to the Spaniards, thinking that the light they had followed was Drake's.

At dawn on Sunday 21st July Drake, who had veered south, had come up to the damaged galleon, the Rosario. He went in to two or three cables length, bombarding the ship, but De Valdes parleyed and on the generous terms given by Drake surrendered. Only part of the gold and silver bullion on board is thought to have ended up in the Treasury after the ship was taken to Torbay. Howard in the Ark, the Mary Rose and Bear hurriedly went about and were not pressed by the fast galleasses, which might have taken them. The Spanish slowly sailed on and the day was spent reassembling the dispersed English fleet.

On Monday 22nd July the wind dropped and the Armada, followed by the English, crawled across Lyme Bay towards Portland Bill. All day long and into Tuesday the calm continued, until at 5 am on 23rd July the wind came again from the north-east quarter. The Spanish now had the weather gauge. Howard, anxious once more to outflank the Spanish, began to beat up to the north-west. The Spanish rearguard, with De Leyra in the Rata Encoronada, turned to intercept the English and fierce exchanges of gunfire took place. The morning had also found Frobisher in the Triumph with five converted merchantmen too close to Portland Bill to weather it in the changed wind. They were forced to drop anchor. Seizing their opportunity, the four galleasses led by De Moncada in the San Lorenzo attacked. With their 40 brass guns mounted fore and aft and up among the rowers, who gave them manoeuvrability in any wind, they were a potent danger. Frobisher and his companions put up a strong resistance to the attack, aiming at the oarsmen. As the fight went on, the easterly began to fall and the wind veered into south south-west. Lord Howard of Effingham decided to go to Frobisher's assistance. Medina Sidonia, seeing this movement, took the San Martin with five other galleons towards Frobisher. Before he arrived, Drake's attack on the fleet led him to detach the five accompanying galleons and alone he proceeded on towards Howard and his ships – the Ark, Elizabeth Jonas, Leicester, Golden Lion, Victory, Mary Rose, Dreadnought and Swallow. As he came up he backed his foretop sail, inviting the English to grapple and board with all the courage and honour that befitted a great hidalgo of Spain. The English replied by standing off and in line pouring broadsides into the San Martin. It was an hour before the flagship was rescued, but the great banner blessed by the Pope had been shredded. Meanwhile, on the change of wind Drake had sailed in to attack, coming out of the smoke to harry the seaward wing. The English warships bombarded the Spanish, pouring shot into Recalde's San Juan de Portugal, thus drawing off the Spanish from the attack on Frobisher. Medina Sidonia once more reformed his fleet, drew off and sailed on, now bunched into a ball.

On 24th July, Wednesday, a passing engagement took place just after dawn when Drake attacked the Gran Grifon, which had become separated from the fleet. Recalde on the San Juan, Oquendo on the Santa Anna and Bartendona on La Regazone all joined the fray. Drake lost his main yard in the fight and the Gran Grifon was badly damaged. The English withdrew when Medina Sidonia and his great galleons came near, and after two hours all was over. A galleass took the damaged Gran Grifon in tow. The rest of the day was quiet, with light airs and fitful breezes. The Armada was sailing on to the Isle of Wight. The Duke of Medina Sidonia had now twice sent messages to the Duke of Parma to alert him to co-ordinate his arrival with the army, but the latter seemed to lack the will to forward matters, an approach partly induced by the blockade of his harbours by the Dutch in their small boats. The Spanish captains again urged that the fleet should pause, enter the Solent and take the Isle of Wight, but Medina Sidonia, acting on his instructions, pressed on. Howard also took the opportunity to put some order into the formless English fleet, breaking it into four groups commanded by himself, Drake, Hawkins and Frobisher. So far the Armada, despite the attacks made, had lost only two vessels, although both fleets were becoming short of powder and shot. Howard sought to alleviate this problem by sending small ships to shore to obtain supplies, but not with great success.

Following the gentle breezes of Wednesday night, on 25th July in the morning calm the fleets were only about one to two miles apart. There were two Spanish laggards, the San Luis (830 tons and 38 guns) and the Duquesa (900 tons and 23 guns). They were too tempting to Hawkins in the Victory, and relying on being towed by longboats and on the slight gusts of wind he went to do battle with them. Howard in the Ark and Lord Thomas Howard on the Golden Lion had themselves towed into range but three galleasses sent by Medina Sidonia and supported by De Leyva's great coracle La Rata Encoronada were sent to the rescue. A confused battle took place which developed later into a more general engagement throughout the Spanish fleet. The galleasses however were able to take the San Luis and Duquesa under tow, although the Gerona was holed in the bows and the San Lorenzo had numerous casualties. A low wind developed and the Spanish attacked the English centre, doing damage to the Ark and driving the English back. Drake utilised the wind to get out to sea and then fell on the seaward end of the Spanish fleet, creating havoc and disarray. Medina Sidonia again regrouped and turned his great galleons to succour the south wing of the fleet and once more Drake and the English fleet broke off. Even if he had decided to disobey his instructions, Medina Sidonia had now lost his opportunity to enter the Solent.

The next two days, Friday 26th July and Saturday the 27th, were cloudless and hot. Howard on the Friday had a council and knighted Hawkins and Frobisher. Medina Sidonia continued to press the Duke of Parma to action and the fleets just sailed on, not firing a shot. The latter stressed in reply his problems with the blockade and indicated that the Armada might have to clear the way for him. On Saturday evening the Armada reached and anchored at Calais. The English, still astern, anchored half a mile away and were joined by Lord Henry Seymour, with 24 large ships and 18 others. The two Dukes of Medina Sidonia and Parma were now only twenty-five miles apart, but both faced the problem of coming together. Parma was under blockade and said that in any event he needed at least six days to prepare to cross. Medina Sidonia had no vessels capable of fighting in the shoals off Flanders to break that constraint. The Sunday passed in re-provisioning the galleons with the help of the French Governor of Calais, who was pro-Spanish. Sightseers came to see the fleets and the French vendors happily exploited the Spanish seamen, charging them twenty-five times the price in London for an egg. Meanwhile, although the English had intended having fireships ready in the Thames, none came. They therefore took eight small vessels, for example the Thames of 200 tons, and spent the day preparing them – corking them with tar, putting in them powder and inflammables and mounting guns on them to fire when ignited. The Duke of Medina Sidonia was well aware of the danger to an anchored fleet of fireships, and ordered his crews to launch their longboats and take grapnels ready to head off any fireships sent. He also ordered that the fleet should be prepared to slip their anchors and mark them with buoys, go out to sea and return to pick them up after the danger was past.

Soon after midnight eight points of light could be seen setting off from the English fleet. The fireships had been launched, and helped by wind and the tide they came on abreast towards the Spanish fleet, winking and glowing, growing ever in size as their crews, who would leave them only at the last moment, brought them on. The nearer they came, the larger they loomed. The Spaniards' ships boats were not adequate to deal with these large two hundred-ton vessels, and panic set in. The fireships were impossible to stop; only the two outside ships were deflected and, as the fire mounted, the guns on board started to boom. Ignoring Medina Sidonia's instructions, the bulk of the Spanish fleet severed their anchor chains and scattered out to sea and along the coast. In the confusion ships collided and were damaged. The fireships were driven on by sea and wind and came to rest on the beaches to burn themselves out. When dawn came, only six ships were still anchored at Calais and the others were strung out along the coast towards Dunkirk. The San Lorenzo galleass had collided with the San Juan de Sicilia and was near the shore.

The Duke ordered the six galleons to weigh anchor so that he could reform nearer Dunkirk. At that the English, with the favourable south-west wind, attacked once again in squadrons abreast. As they moved forward, Lord Howard of Effingham and his squadron diverged to go towards the now-beached San Lorenzo, which had gone aground and was heeled over with its oars in the sky. The Ark put out its longboats for the attack, which De Moncada bravely resisted, until he was killed by a musket ball, at which point the crew surrendered. The English looted the ship, but the French Governor of Calais fired upon them, claiming the ship as his prize. Howard turned away to join the battle of Gravelines.

The Spanish had to some extent been able to reform near Gravelines. In the first hour the San Martin and the other galleons had come about to resist the English squadrons, but thereafter the battle became a confused series of melées on a sea covered with clouds of smoke. Drake on the Revenge went in close and ceaselessly pounded the San Martin, to be immediately followed by the Nonpareil and White Bear. The Revenge suffered great damage, but sailed on into the galleon fleet. Frobisher and Hawkins joined and the battle raged in confusion, while the ships of both fleets were intermingled. All the time the action edged the Spanish towards the Flemish shore, its shoals and shallows. Howard in the Ark, with the Victory and the Rainbow and with his other fresh ships, hammered Oquendo's Santa Ana and De Leyva's Rata Encoronada and Bartendona's La Regazana. All were pounded, the San Felipe and San Mateo so severely that the scuppers ran blood. Sorely crippled, the two of them drifted towards the shore, where the Dutch fly-boats destroyed them.

By four o'clock the fight had almost fallen off; the Spanish had fought with great courage, but were (as were the English) running out of shot. Many of their ships were semi-wrecks; the English had not closed to board but stood off, relying on the range of their guns. By six o'clock sudden violent squalls were developing near the coast. The Duke of Medina Sidonia and his captains gathered the battered fleet and slipped away into the mists and darkness of the North Sea. For a time the fleet drifted and went parallel with the coast but on Tuesday 31st July Medina Sidonia, the wind blowing north-west, decided to return to Spain, sailing round the British Isles and out into the Atlantic. He did not regard his captains' plan of a return to Dunkirk in order to take it as practicable. The wind veered south-west and the long dangerous voyage could begin. For a time the English shadowed the Spanish, but running out of supplies, they turned for home.

At the end of July, when invasion was expected, the Queen and Council collected an army, mainly of trained militia bands from the counties, at Tilbury, in order to defend London. Elizabeth made the Earl of Leicester Commander in Chief. Although the Armada was seriously damaged on 30th July, its destination remained uncertain and the force of ninety ships could still prove a danger. Parma with his army and flat boats stood mustered on the coast of Flanders. The emergency did not seem over and the threat was perceived as not yet lifted. Elizabeth insisted that she wanted to visit the army, but Leicester and the Council sought to dissuade her. Many people were, it was thought, secret Catholics, among which were a fanatical minority, stirred up by their leaders, the Pope and Cardinal Allen, to wage war against and kill the Queen. The Government was worried by the potential religious fifth-column, and the action of its fundamentalist leaders. This was the context in which she set out to visit the troops. Elizabeth overrode her Council's doubts and on 9th August inspected the troops, who knelt as she proceeded, mounted and wearing a cuirass, through their ranks. She then addressed them in the famous speech which expressed so eloquently the English patriotic ideal, central to which is the tight bond between Crown and people. This army did not of course have to resist invasion and slowly the English people came to realise that they had achieved a sensational defeat of Spanish power. All over Europe people began to sense that a new force had come into international affairs. The English nation, born by Henry VIII, had come to lively adolescence. The triumphs in the future, the consistent record of resistance to European tyrants and their oppression, were yet to come.

The voyage of return by the Spanish fleet to Spain was beset by storms. Ships were smashed; some wrecked on the west coasts of the British Isles had their crews robbed and massacred. Some sank. The fleet was dispersed by Atlantic gales. Of the seventy or so ships which returned many were beyond repair: fifty-five never came home, the fate of over thirty not being known. The English lost not one barque or pinnace. The Duke of Medina Sidonia was grief-stricken. Only one-third of the men who embarked returned and Spain was smitten with mourning. Philip II ordered the sick and wounded to be relieved, but had no resentment for the Duke, whom he told, 'I sent you to fight against men, not against God'. He then began to build a new fleet. Twice more Armadas were to be launched against England. In November 1596 the Second Armada was broken by gales on its way, and the third was the subject of violent storms off the Lizard, which lasted for three days in 1597. Recalde arrived in Coruna on 7th October, but died four days after his arrival. Miguel Oquendo died of typhus shortly after he arrived home; Diego de Valdes was imprisoned for poor advice and De Leyra only arrived back after a series of adventures in which three ships were lost, the last being the galleass Gerona, wrecked on the Giants' Causeway.

In November 1588 Elizabeth progressed to a magnificent scene of Thanksgiving in St. Paul's Cathedral, where she knelt for a time on her knees on the steps of the Cathedral. The war with Spain went on but England was not again to be the subject of so threatening an attack. Sir John Hawkins and Sir Francis Drake died at sea in 1596. Drake's ship the Revenge was destroyed in an heroic attack at Flores in the Azores in August 1591. The Revenge fought fifteen ships all day and sunk two: in the end the Revenge, with six feet of water in the hold and many of the crew dead or wounded, surrendered. Sir Richard Grenville, the commander on the flagship and who came from Bideford, was taken wounded onto the Spanish flagship and there was treated with great courtesy until he died. Lord Howard of Effingham continued to command the fleet and became Earl of Nottingham, dying in 1619. The bulk of the old Catholic population remained loyal, as they were for the main part at the time of the Armada. The threat of religious fanaticism remained; one incident being the Gunpowder plot of 1605.

The Queen's Gracious Speech at Tilbury

'My loving people, we have been persuaded by some that are careful for our safety, to take heed how we commit ourselves to armed multitudes for fear of treachery: but I assure you, I do not desire to live in distrust of my faithful and loving people. Let tyrants fear. I have always so behaved myself that under God, I have placed my chiefest strength and goodwill in the loyal hearts and the goodwill of my subjects; and therefore I am come amongst you, as you see, at this time, not for my recreation and disport, but being resolved, in the midst and heat of the battle, to live or die amongst you all; to lay down for God, my kingdom, and for my people, my honour and my blood, even in the dust. I know I have but the body of a weak and feeble woman; but I have the heart and stomach of a King, and a King of England too, and think it foul scorn that Parma or Spain or any Prince of Europe, should dare to invade the borders of my realm; to which, rather than any dishonour should grow by me, I myself will take up arms, I myself will be General, Judge and Rewarder of every one of your virtues in the field.

'I know already for your forwardness you have deserved rewards and crowns; and we do assure you, on the word of a Prince, they shall be duly paid you. In the meantime, my Lieutenant-General shall be in my stead, than whom never Prince commanded a more noble or worthy subject: not doubting that by your obedience to my General, by your concord in the camp and your valour in the field, we shall shortly have a famous victory over these enemies of my God, of my kingdom and of my people.'

31st July 1653

The Battle of the Texel

After the Battle of the Gabbard Bank (3rd June 1653) the Dutch fleet had regained Holland, sheltering in the estuary of the Maas and at the Texel. The English under Monk followed and established a coastal blockade, interfering with Dutch trade and striking at their economy. Gradually the blockading fleet grew low in victuals, and on 16th July returned to Sole Bay on the Suffolk coast to take on supplies. Monk then returned to the Dutch coast with 120 ships carrying 4,000 guns, and lay between Tromp in the Maas and De Witt at Texel. The Dutch with great energy had repaired and refitted their fleet. Tromp had 83 ships and De Witt 31 and it was clearly necessary for the Dutch to unite their fleet before action: Tromp took the initiative on 30th July and came out, drawing Monk and the English fleet southwards. The wind was rising and the English for fear of coastal shoals stood out to sea. The Dutch, knowledgeable about their coast, took their opportunity and in the night re-united.

Clarendon in his *History of the Rebellion* described the battle fought the next day as 'the most bloody that had yet been fought'. Off Schveningen the two fleets met, the English with a little more sea, having tacked about. The Dutch fleet, which was more poorly organised, awaited their attack with courage. The Dutch had 116 ships to the 120 English. They had the weather-gauge. At six in the morning the English tacked down in the fair weather into the Dutch, and the thunderous battle commenced. Monk had ordered that no quarter should be given and no ships captured but destroyed. The English in line tacked through the Dutch, changed tack and returned. During the first pass Tromp was hit by a musket ball to the heart and fell dead. The Oak and the Worcester were set afire by the Dutch fireships. The Triumph (2nd of the name with 70 guns) was sorely pressed, being set on fire and only saved with difficulty. Smoke covered the battle scene; the skies thundered with guns and the seas surged with shot. Sails were rent and ships dismasted. The loss of Tromp affected Dutch morale, and as the weather-gauge was lost and the English tacked again to go through the Dutch fleet, ship by ship its cohesion disintegrated, and the Dutch captains and De Witt made sail to reach the Texel. Clarendon records that the Dutch left 20 to 30 ships behind, and 100 prisoners were taken. 1,200 Dutch seamen had been slain and 1,500 drowned; the wounded were 2,500. On the English side, Clarendon records 8 captains and 400 seamen killed, 5 captains and 700 men wounded. Only one ship was lost, although two or three were disabled from service. The extensive damage done precluded pursuit of the enemy to the Texel, and Monk and his badly mauled ships returned home.

With Monk gone, De Witt was able to run a convoy north and escort one back. A lull settled in the war, while the English and the Dutch quietly negotiated a settlement of their disputes. The Treaty of Westminster was signed in April 1654. Among it terms the Dutch accepted the right of English warships to have the flag saluted, the basis of the incident which had inaugurated the war in 1652.

August

1st	The Battle of Minden	1759
	The Battle of the Nile	1798
11th	The Capture of Havana	1762
	The Battle of Passaro	1718
13th	The Battle of Blenheim	1704
14th	The Battle of Malaga	1704
15th	V J Day	1945
16th	The Conquest of Sicily	1943
17th	The Battle of Verneuil	1424
	The Battle of Rolica	1808
18th	The Battle of Lagos	1759
20th	The Battle of Normandy	1944
21st	The Battle of Vimiero	1808
26th	The Battle of Crecy	1346

1st August 1759

The Battle of Minden

The Treaty of Aix-la-Chapelle at the end of the War of the Austrian Succession (1748) did not result in the resolution of the underlying issues between the powers of Europe. No settlement was made of the English and French differences in North America, as to the boundary between the American Colonies and the French settlements in Canada and at New Orleans. The area west of the Allegheny and up to the Ohio River and beyond was left as a no-man's land in the possession of Indian tribes such as the Iroquois. The other issue which the treaty did resolve, but which remained important, was that of the possession of Silesia. The Treaty gave the province to King Frederick II of Prussia, but Queen Maria Theresa of Austria and Hungary was determined to recover it.

The North American problem was the first to arise. In 1753 the French Government instructed the Marquis Duquesne to clear the English traders out of the area of western Pennsylvania and Ohio up to Lake Erie and establish a series of forts, which would link Quebec with New Orleans along the line of the Ohio and Mississippi Rivers. The Virginian colonists, who were anxious to keep their trade into the Ohio area, responded and, entering the territory in order to protect their rights, built Fort Pitt on the site of modern Pittsburgh. In 1754 George Washington (the first President of the United States) led a small force into the area after the French took Fort Pitt, and replaced it with a stronger work, Fort Dusquesne. His small band was defeated after he had fought and killed the Sieur de Jumonville and his party, who were on a mission to the Indians to make good their claim to the land. The Prime Minister in London, the Duke of Newcastle, was most reluctant to go to war despite the provocation and outright aggression of the French. He temporised, merely sending General Braddock and two regiments to America supported by the navy under Commodore Keppel. In conjunction with the colonists Braddock devised a campaign against French positions in Canada, upper New York State and Ohio. In 1755, on 9th July, Braddock was surprised by Indians allied to the French and defeated within twelve miles of Fort Duquesne. Washington, with great heroism, managed to escape and return, and was to play an active part with the Virginia militia in the border war, which continued. Britain sent more troops. The Duke of Newcastle still avoided outright war.

Queen Maria Theresa's determination to recover Silesia from Frederick II led to an upheaval in the pattern of alliances in Europe in the early 1750s. Traditional alliances were abandoned and she linked Austria with the France of Louis XV.

Prussia, the previous ally of France, hurried to make a treaty with the British. On 16th January 1756 the two powers signed the Convention of Westminster, to act together against any foreign power attacking and entering Germany. Austria abandoned the Dutch removing support for their occupation of the Barrier fortresses in the Netherlands. The British interest in these matters arose from the fact that King George II was Elector of the German State of Hannover, and he feared for his state. The Prussian treaty gave him protection and Frederick II a shield from the French in the west. Events moved on and Russia joined the alliance of France and Austria. The latter began to build up troops and strengthen the fortifications in Bohemia. Frederick II, surrounded to south and east by enemies and threatened by France in the west in relation to the Rhineland provinces, decided that a pre-emptive strike was needed and, after seeking a passage across Saxony in order to attack Austria, which was refused by its ruler, he struck and seized Dresden. In January 1757 the Imperial Diet declared war on him, and in the spring of 1757 the War became general.

George II's son, the Duke of Cumberland, was sent to Germany to command the British and Hannoverian troops. William Pitt the Elder, later Earl of Chatham, became Prime Minister. He was one of the greatest war prime ministers that Britain has ever had and he understood the need to weigh British efforts to oppose the French worldwide against persisting in a presence in the European War to divert French effort to that sphere. He had the incomparable advantage in conducting the war that he thought France to be evil, ruled by tyrants who were devoted to enslaving their neighbours. Cumberland, however, was defeated at Hastenbach on 26th July 1757 and in September 1757 yielded Hannover to the French. George II dismissed his son as commander-in-chief and on the advice of King Frederick II appointed a talented Prussian General, Prince Ferdinand of Brunswick, to command the troops in Germany. Pitt persuaded Parliament to raise sufficient monies to give £670,000 to Prussia and £1,800,000 to finance the army of Prince Ferdinand. In June 1758 he won the Battle of Krefeld and drove the French from Hannover. On 31st December the French seized Frankfurt, which they were to use as their base in 1759. The winter was spent in restoring the French armies, which were short of supplies. By spring 1759 the French had under the Marquis de Contades 50 battalions of infantry and 50 squadrons of cavalry, amounting to 31,000 men in the Army of the Lower Rhine, and 100 battalions of infantry and 91 squadrons of cavalry in the Army of the Main under the Duc de Broglie, amounting to 100,000 men. The first agreed object of their campaign was to drive Prince Ferdinand of Brunswick and his army beyond the River Weser.

Prince Ferdinand decided to strike first and marched the army out of Münster, planning to set siege to Frankfurt on 22nd March. In order to protect Frankfurt, the French had fortified Bergen to the north-east and had garrisoned Frankfurt with 30,000 men. The British and Hannoverian army had 27,000 men. A day-long fight took place on his arrival and he then decided to withdraw. The Duc de Broglie did not pursue him. In June 1759 the French finally advanced; both Münster and Minden were taken, the latter being looted. As Prince Ferdinand of Brunswick retired, ceaseless criticism came from George II and Frederick II of Prussia. He and the French skirmished without doing battle along the River Weser. Finally he decided to try to bring the French to battle. Stationing his troops on both sides of the river, he detached 10,000 men to attack the French at Lübbecke, to the west of Minden. The Erbprinz of Brunswick successfully pressed the French, clashed with them at Bunde on 31st July, and moved on towards Quernheim. The Marquis de Contades at Minden became concerned about his communications and Prince Ferdinand, trying to force a battle, drew his army up on the plain to the north-west of Minden with the River Weser on the left flank. In his army of 41,000 men he had six regiments of British infantry: they were the 12th Regiment of Foot (later the Suffolk Regiment), the 20th Regiment of Foot (later the Lancashire Fusiliers), the 23rd (Royal Welsh Fusiliers) Regiment of Foot, the 25th (Edinburgh) Regiment of Foot (later the King's Own Scottish Borderers), the 37th Regiment of Foot (later the Hampshire Regiment), and the 51st Regiment of Foot (later the King's Own (Yorkshire) Light Infantry). All these, after the Battle, carried Minden on their colours. A contingent of cavalry was also present, commanded by Lord George Sackville, whose conduct was such that they played no effective role in the battle. On the march the men picked wild roses for their hats.

Prince Ferdinand stationed his troops in a semi-circle from the village of Hahlen, due west of Minden, to Stermer in the north-west, then on to Kutenhausen and the river in the north-east. The cavalry were to the rear of the right flank. To the north of the village of Hahlen the plain broke into a scattered pattern of smallholdings, orchards and pine coverts. Contades was under pressure to win a victory from the Royal Court at Versailles and he therefore resolved on a plan for a surprise attack at night.

At 6 pm on 31st July the French commanders agreed their plan of attack. By night the army was to form up on the plain opposite the army of Prince Ferdinand with the left flank in the village of Hahlen, the infantry stretching north behind the guns, the cavalry under the Duke of Fitzjames in the centre, further infantry on the centre right joining with artillery and infantry, under the Duc de Broglie on the far right.

At 5 am Lieutenant-General Von Wangenheim, with the Hannoverians, was taken by surprise when the French under the Duc de Broglie commenced firing with their artillery at the left flank of the Allied army. The noise of the gunfire echoed against the thunder of a storm. The artillery replied and Von Wangenheim and his troops stood firm. Contades ordered the Duc de Broglie to advance to outflank his opponents by looping round to the village of Kutenhausen. Delays occurred and the French were so irresolute that the attack petered out, influenced by the fear of a cavalry charge.

While the Allied left was being drawn into battle, the French left under the Comte de Lusace moved to occupy the village of Hahlen, reinforcing a force of 16 battalions already there. Prince Ferdinand ordered Karl, Prince of Anhalt-Bernberg to occupy the village and fierce fighting broke out. Gradually the French were pushed back, forced in part by fire and flames from the buildings, which a strong wind drove before them. At the same time the Prince instructed General Freiherr von Störken in the centre right to move on the French centre. The British regiments were under his command and hurried forward at the double through the broken landscape of woods and small farms. Their pace was so great that they were soon forward of the Allied army and started to veer to the left towards the French cavalry in the centre. Alone in a forward position the British regiments became subject to a sustained and fierce attack from guns on their flank, to the rear and from the cavalry ahead. The regiments stood solid, firing off volley after volley from their muskets. Prince Ferdinand aided them with artillery fire helping to silence the French guns. The French cavalry under the Duke of Fitzjames, grandson of King James II, charged, to be torn by the musket fire and, when in close contact, bayoneted. The rearmost lines of the British turned to form a rudimentary square and battered once more with their musketry fire at the charging elite French cavalry, the Gens d'Armes, which had now been sent forward. The close, accurate fire, systematically delivered, broke the cavalry, which lost half of its strength. The infantry sent to their succour were driven back as Prince Ferdinand brought up more artillery and reinforcements from the centre. By 9 am the French centre and left had been soundly beaten. General Von Wangenheim on the Allied left had launched his cavalry against that of the Duc de Broglie, smashing though the force on the latter's left. In Hahlen a recovery by the French was beaten off by the artillery.

The Marquis de Contades decided to order a general retreat. The moment had come when the French defeat could have been turned into annihilation. Prince Ferdinand of Brunswick ordered Lord George Sackville with the cavalry to advance. The latter enjoyed a bitter relationship with the Prince and queried the order, riding to see him. In his absence the second-in-command, the Marquis of Granby, gave the order, but Sackville returned to countermand it. He then devoted his time to forming up and reforming the cavalry squadrons, going nowhere. The cavalry never charged, and the French flowing from the field went unimpeded. They retreated through Minden and by 12 pm the battle was done and the field belonged to the Allied army. The French retired to Kassel, and Hannover was saved. Prince Ferdinand moved the army to Münster to besiege the town, which fell on 22nd November.

The Prince had lost 2,762 casualties, of which 1,392 were in the British Regiments, who lost thirty per cent of their strength. Their role in the battle, through their unmoving, solid courage, had been decisive. The Prince wrote an astringent letter to George II relating to the conduct of Lord George Sackville. The latter was brought before a general court-martial for disobeying the order of a superior officer in the face of the enemy, found guilty and discharged. The report of his disgrace and sentence was read to every regiment of the army on the orders of William Pitt, the Prime Minister, a friend and political ally, so that 'officers may be convinced that neither high birth nor great employments can shelter offences of such a nature.'

1st August 1798

The Battle of the Nile

Since the opening of the Revolutionary War in 1793, the French had continued to press forward their ambitions to become the masters of Europe. By 1798 they had achieved significant success although Britain, protected by the navy, still stood defiant against them. In February 1798 the French marched into Rome in breach of treaties made, and seized the Papal Treasury and the silver and gold of the churches, in order to melt it into bullion. In March, on a trumped up charge, they invaded Switzerland to obtain the bullion held by the Swiss bankers and traders, ransacking churches and looting. The Directory, the Government of France, debated how to strike against Britain and persuaded by General Napoleon Buonaparte, the victor of the campaign in Italy, resolved on striking across the Mediterranean to Egypt and threatening India, thus affecting commerce and trading with the East. By 1798 the British had for all purposes abandoned the Mediterranean, but just as later, its control had a crucial role in enabling contact to be made and kept with prospective allies such as Austria, the Kingdom of the Two Sicilies and Russia. William Pitt the younger, the British Prime Minister, and the Cabinet, realising the strategic advantages of holding the Mediterranean Sea, despite the threat of invasion to Britain and Ireland, decided to order the navy back. A strong motivation was the intelligence they had received that the French along the coast of Provence and at Toulon were collecting a huge fleet of merchantmen and supplies, with eighteen ships of the line. The British Government worried over the possible destination of this assembly and so decided to reinforce Earl St. Vincent, who was blockading Cadiz, and send a fleet to cover the operations at Toulon. Lord Spencer, the first Lord of the Admiralty, sent a private letter to the latter, recommending that this detached fleet should be commanded by Sir Horatio Nelson, then aged 41. When the appointment became public, senior Admirals made a protest, but by that time Nelson had gone to win the fame which awaited him.

Earl St. Vincent had in fact already decided on a reconnaissance and on 8th May Nelson left Gibraltar with Vanguard, Orion (1st of the name with 74 guns), Alexander and five frigates to carry out this duty. On 17th May he learnt from the captain of a captured frigate that General Buonaparte was at Toulon and was preparing to sail with 300 transport ships and 50 warships, including 15 ships of the line. 40,000 troops were to be carried. On 19th May Buonaparte left Toulon, sailing along the coast and then east of Corsica and Sardinia. Nelson had no idea whether the objective of the French was to the east or the west through the Straits. A great storm blew up on 20th May of ferocious proportions. Nelson's squadron was shattered and the Vanguard lost the main topmast, foremast and mizen topmast. A tow given by the Alexander saved the Vanguard, but four days were spent refurbishing the ship with a jury rig before he could sail on. The frigates had not found him at the appointed rendezvous and returned to Gibraltar. The French had just avoided the storm. Meanwhile Earl St. Vincent had received his orders and had detached ten ships of the line, largely 74-gunners, to join Nelson. On 10th June they found Nelson and his fleet was joined by Culloden, Theseus, Swiftsure, Minotaur, Defence, Audacious, Zealous, Goliath, Majestic and Bellerophon. On 14th June news reached Nelson that a fleet had been seen west of Sicily ten days before. On 17th June he arrived at Naples to be told that Buonaparte and the fleet had gone south towards Malta; the Kingdom of the Two Scillies was not therefore the object of the convoy and Nelson concluded that the likely destination was Egypt. Nelson therefore pressed on south, and on 21st June set off for Alexandria, taking advantage of the westerly winds which had been blowing, carrying the French eastwards. Meanwhile, Buonaparte had taken Malta from the Knights of Malta and left a small garrison there.

On 22nd June the night was, as summer nights in the Mediterranean can be, misty and hazy over the warm sea. The two fleets came close to one another. The French could hear the British signal guns in the mist. Rear Admiral Brueys ordered the French northwards and the fleets crossed, Nelson sailing on hard along the African coast. At dawn the French were below the horizon. The French moved slowly with their lumbering transports, but the British on full sail steamed on. On 29th June Nelson and the British fleet reached Alexandria to find the harbour empty. Nelson, depressed by the absence of the French and doubting his own judgement, turned east and north to search the coast of Turkey and Southern Greece. On the evening of the same day the French arrived. Buonaparte landed and spent July conquering Egypt and taking Cairo after the Battle of the Pyramids, when the French army crushed the Mamelukes. Nelson beat back along the Mediterranean from Greece and made Syracuse on 19th July, short of water. The fleet was refurbished and re-supplied and on 25th July he again left for the east. South of Greece near Koroni news was confirmed that the French had passed and gone on south-east.

These sweeps from west to east were not without value, although the French had evaded the navy's surveillance. Every opportunity was taken to train the men and improve the working of the ships and the efficacy of the gunnery. Nelson had constant conferences with his captains to work out tactics and secure unity of action. Strategies were developed so that wherever the French fleet were met, the captains knew automatically, without orders, the nature of the action each should take. Nelson was a natural leader of men, inspiring all those under him with his vision and example. For sense of duty, intelligence and courage he embodied all that was best in the English. His background as the son of a country person imbued him with a simple piety and a real consideration for his men. The Battle of the Nile, remarkably, shows all these virtues and exemplifies them. By the time the fleet reached Egypt it was wielded into one efficient cutting force.

On the morning of 1st August the lighthouse at Alexandria came into sight and the harbour was viewed for the masts of the French warships. While there were a crowd of vessels there, none was a warship. Rear-Admiral Brueys had rejected the harbour as his base, since the largest warships could not enter, and he sailed along the coast to Aboukir Bay, about fifteen miles to the east at the mouth of the Nile. Aboukir Bay was sheltered by a point, on which stood Aboukir Castle and a small island, which Brueys had fortified, some mile away from the point to the east. The point and island formed part of a promontory which became a long shoal guarding the entrance to the harbour at the east. The bay shelved on all sides and much of the water depth was less than four fathoms. A ship of the line needed at least five fathoms in which to sail: much of the Bay therefore was inaccessible to the larger ships. Brueys had drawn up his thirteen warships in a line stretching from west to east, the bows facing west. Each ship was anchored only by the bows so that it was free to swing with wind and tide. The van and centre was sheltered by the promontory, island and the long easterly shoal.

The breeze on 1st August was a light north north-westerly and the British edged east along the coast. At 2 pm Midshipman Elliott on the royal yard of the Goliath first spotted the masts of the French fleet, slid down the backstay and on deck the signal was prepared. The Zealous, interpreting the activity on deck, hastened and was in fact the first to raise the signal that told the fleet that the French were seen. Nelson was delighted and, knowing that there would be a delay, sat down to enjoy dinner. At 3 pm the signal was given to prepare for battle and anchor by the stern. Later he signalled that the attack was to be made on the van and centre and that the line of battle should be formed as convenient. Based on the councils preparing for the battle the captains knew the action expected of them.

Rear-Admiral Brueys watched the approach of the British and expected the loose formation merely to sail past with a view to battle the next day. Many of his seamen were on shore, the ships were unprepared and on the larboard side the gun-lids were closed. Nelson, as the Vanguard approached, realised, having no proper navigation charts of the bay, that the gap between the ships at anchor and the fact that they were free to swing from the bows indicated that within the limits of swing there was sufficient depth to permit his ships to pass and come up the inner side of the French fleet, having rounded the front ship of the van. The Vanguard fell back and the Goliath took the lead, as the only vessel with a primitive chart of the bay.

At 6 pm, having passed seaward of Aboukir and the castle, the island and the shoal, the fleet bore down into the bay, rounding the east end of the shoal and turning towards the van of the French fleet. Goliath led under fire, sounding the lead as the ships moved forward. The first in line, Le Guérrier, was bombarded on the starboard side, and at 6.15 pm raked on the bows as Goliath turned, brushing aside the frigate, La Sérieuse, which tried to intercept it, and again on the larboard side. Then Goliath came to a standstill anchored opposite the next ship, Le Conquérant. The Zealous, which at one point seemed to be overtaking the Goliath, anchored beside the first ship in the line, Le Guérrier. The Orion sailed on and round to the fifth in line, Le Peuple Souverain. The Theseus rounded so close that there was but six feet between its rigging and the jib-boom of the Guérrier. It went down the line to the Spartiate, the third ship. Audacious stopped between Le Guerrier and Le Conquérant to come to anchor near to the fourth and fifth in line, L'Aquilon and Le Peuple Souverain. The advance squadron was therefore on the larboard side of the French. As each rounded and went down the line to anchor, the French ships were pounded by constant broadsides, replied to by the French in kind, firing often so high that there was little risk to the oncoming British. The French ships all carried 74 guns, save in their centre and rear, where the flagships L'Orient carried 120 guns, Le Franklin and Le Tonnant 80 guns. The bay thundered with noise and smoke lay across it.

Within seven minutes of the action starting Le Guérrier had lost her foremast and, pounded by Theseus as she turned, the mainmast and mizzen mast were also lost. The sunset was sinking in a flaming orb and darkness quickly fell, illuminated by the flashes of the guns as the fleets bombarded each other. At 6.40 pm on the starboard side, Nelson on Vanguard had led the centre of the line, his ship coming up to the Spartiate, which then lay between Theseus to larboard and himself. The Spartiate resisted hotly, only striking its colours at 9 pm. In the heart of the battle, under raking fire from L'Aquilon and Le Spartiate, Nelson on the quarterdeck was struck by a flying metal remnant above the forehead of his good eye. Falling blinded by the hanging flesh, he was carried below to the surgeons in the cockpit. They left the wounded to attend him, but he told them, 'No, I will take my turn with my brave fellows'. The wound fortunately was not deep but superficial and his head was bound up; slightly concussed, he returned to his post. In all the Vanguard was to have 30 killed, including the captain of marines and two midshipmen, and 76 wounded. The Minotaur behind Vanguard came up to anchor by L'Aquilon; Bellerophon turned to come down to the L'Orient, her 74 guns challenging the three-decker, 120-gun flagship. Defence sailed up towards Le Franklin, Majestic up to anchor by Le Tonnant with its 80 guns, Alexander passing between L'Orient and Le Tonnant, anchored to the starboard of the latter.

The constant fire of Goliath on the Le Conquérant, coupled with the passing fire of the Audacious, reduced the French warship to a wreck and she was the first to strike her colours after twelve minutes, having lost her fore and mizzenmasts and with the mainmast tottering. Le Guérrier was to surrender at 9 pm. L'Aquilon, battered by Theseus to port and Minotaur to starboard, surrendered to the former. Le Peuple Sovereign was engaged by Orion and Audacious on the larboard and Defence on the seaward. The fore and main masts came crashing down; the cable cut, the warship drifted out of line with fires on board and anchored 400 yards from the L'Orient, ultimately to strike its colours.

Bellerophon had stationed itself near the L'Orient at about 7 pm. It was subjected to withering fire from the larger, better-gunned ship. By 8 pm Bellerophon was dismasted, Captain Darby wounded, and the ship seriously damaged; 143 of her seamen were killed. She slipped her anchor and drifted away down the line. She had given a good account of herself and Rear-Admiral Brueys had himself been mortally wounded, dying from a round shot wound. As Bellerophon slipped away, the 50-gun Leander took her place, and Swiftsure came up on the starboard side while Alexander crossed the line behind the L'Orient to anchor on the larboard quarter. The pounding went on. Shortly before 9 pm the L'Orient was seen to be on fire. The wadding from the British guns appears to have ignited oilcans and paint left on the poop by the seamen painting the ship. The ship's rigging began to burn and the fire spread. Nelson was still below having his wound tended when Captain Berry told him of the fire. As it took hold the British ships nearby began to take precautions to avoid danger and damage to themselves from the growing fire. The advancing fire clearly would get to the magazine and at 10 pm L'Orient blew up with a devastating explosion, audible in Alexandria. The whole sky was illuminated, as the burning fragments were sent skyward to fall on the sea and the ships around.

One of the Alexander's sails caught fire, but it was extinguished. The sea was littered with the broken bodies of those killed and with the fractured pieces of the great ship. Nelson ordered the Vanguard's longboat out to pick up survivors and the nearest British ships followed his lead. The explosion so affected all the combatants in the battle that a total silence fell over the bay, which lasted for three minutes. The silence was broken by Le Franklin cannonading the Defence and Swiftsure. Together with the Orion, the latter reduced the vessel to a wrecked and ineffective state until at 2 am, having lost half the crew and main mizzenmast, Le Franklin surrendered. Le Tonnant, to the stern of L'Orient, battered on with the Majestic until 3 am, when the latter lost her main and mizzenmasts. These had hardly gone before Le Tonnant lost her masts over the side, disabling her guns. The captain had before his death left orders to fight to the last, and she changed position to lie ahead of Le Guillaume Tell, one of the French ships of the line that had no part in the engagement. Le Heureuse and Le Mercure in advance of the Guillaume Tell had cut their cables before the explosion of the L'Oreint and drifted out of range. Both were taken and burnt.

As the sun rose, Le Tonnant and the three undamaged ships, Le Guillaume Tell, Le Timoleon and Le Généreux, opened fire on the Alexander and Minotaur as they bore down on them. Zealous, Goliath and Theseus came up to assist: as they bore down the three French warships commanded by Admiral Villeneuve got under way towards the sea, accompanied by his two frigates. Hood in Zealous went to the chase, but as Nelson had no undamaged ships to follow and exhausted crews, the pursuit was abandoned. Le Tonnant remained flying her colours and only surrendered on 3rd August. Culloden had never joined the fight, since it had grounded on the shoal entering the bay. Despite desperate attempts to free it with the assistance of the Mutine, fired on the while by batteries from the Island and fort, it was not refloated until 2nd August.

On the morning of 2nd August, Nelson mustered his crew for a service of thanksgiving for the victory which had been given, and commended his captains to do likewise. He realised the extent of his success and considered the Battle of the Nile to be more than a victory – it amounted to a conquest. In terms of the ships of the line taken as a proportion of the fleet attacked, the Battle of the Nile was his greatest battle and not exceeded in the long history of the navy. Of 13 ships of the line, the French lost 9 captured and 2 burnt. Only 2 escaped with 2 out of 4 frigates. 900 men were lost, including Captain Westcott on the Majestic. The outcome of the battle was however of the utmost importance. Napoleon Buonaparte and his army were isolated in Egypt, with no hope of supplies and reinforcement from France across a Mediterranean sea which Britain again dominated. Austria and Naples were heartened and began to contemplate resistance to the French. The threat to India and Indian trade was gone. On 19th August Nelson in Vanguard, with Alexander and Culloden, left for Naples. Hood was left to blockade Alexandria with Zealous, Goliath and Swiftsure. Sir James Saumarez left for England with the prizes taken to enable their repair for addition to the navy – the Franklin, renamed the Canopus, Le Tonnant, L'Aquilon, Conquérant, Le Peuple Sovereign and Spartiate. Le Heureux, Le Guérrier and Le Mercure were too damaged and were burnt.

Messages had been sent in advance to Earl St. Vincent and to London, the latter going by way of Naples. On 22nd September Vanguard was off Capri. Shortly a large flotilla of boats came out for the entry into Naples. Bands on board played *Rule Britannia* and *See the Conquering Hero Comes* as Vanguard approached. King Ferdinand and Queen Maria Carolina were in the Royal Barge to welcome Nelson. Sir William Hamilton, the British Ambassador, and his wide Emma were in the party. Nelson, half-blinded by his injury, went ashore to stay with the British Ambassador, where Emma began to care for him and arrange glittering festivities to welcome him and his officers. Naples was illuminated and receptions, balls and parties filled the Palace. Lady Hamilton, then thirty-three, devoted herself to Nelson. She had been born Emily Lynn, daughter of a blacksmith on the Wirral, and risen because of her charm and beauty as a courtesan in London society, becoming the mistress and live-in lover of Charles Greville, cousin of Sir William Hamilton. He had lost his wife and was in later middle age. On a visit to London from Naples Charles Greville offered him Emily, now called Emma, as a wife, in return for a share in his inheritance. The deal was done and Emma accompanied Sir William as his second wife to Naples to live in his palace. There she captivated society and the Queen, showing off her beauty in classical tableaux at parties. Nelson in his turn was charmed and Sir William, Emma and he began to have a shared life-style. In time she was to have a daughter by Nelson, Horatia.

On 2nd October the news reached London. The church bells rang, houses and shops were decorated and illuminated that night. Salutes were fired at the Tower and in Hyde Park. King George III, who was at Weymouth, read the despatch three times to those around him. Norfolk rejoiced in its local hero. Nelson was made a Baron, with a pension of £2,000 per year. The Sultan of Turkey and Emperor of Russia honoured him; subsequently King Ferdinand of the Two Sicilies made him Duke of Bronte. Nelson did not return to London until November 1800, where he received a mixed reception from the court, which disapproved of his liaison with Lady Hamilton. King George III was particularly displeased, during Nelson's reception at court, by the Neapolitan orders worn by Nelson, and the diamond-studded aigrette (given by the Sultan) on his hat. The Mayor and Corporation of London, however, gave him a grand and enthusiastic luncheon at the Guildhall. The cheering crowds, as he went, took the horses out of his carriage and dragged it up Ludgate Hill to Cheapside.

11th August 1762

The Capture of Havana

In August 1758 King Ferdinand VI of Spain died and was succeeded by his half-brother, the King of Naples, as Charles III. The latter was an ardent believer in the unity of the Bourbon royal family, which ruled both France and Spain. He was fiercely anti-British, and had a developed sense of the importance of sea power. In March 1761 France, being in the grip of acute financial crisis, put out feelers for peace, and discussions began between Britain and France. Before those discussions had advanced far and the powers involved – Prussia, Austria and Russia – joined in, the chief Minister of France, the Duc de Choiseul, opened a negotiation with Spain and on 15 August 1761 concluded the *Pacte de Famille*, or Third Family Compact. The treaty bound Spain and France to make war and peace together, and Spain was to declare war by May 1762. The secret treaty became known to William Pitt the Elder, the Prime Minister and later Earl of Chatham. The peace negotiations lapsed and Pitt tried to press the Cabinet to take pre-emptive action against Spain. He could not carry his colleagues and resigned in October 1761. Newcastle, who had opposed war, continued in office, but on 4th January 1762 reluctantly declared war on Spain. The latter, in April 1762, attacked Britain's long-term ally Portugal.

The Navy under Lord Anson, the First Lord of the Admiralty, began work to plan strikes at Spain's overseas possessions within two days of the declaration of war. One scheme which was planned and undertaken was that of the capture of Havana. Sir George Pocock was to command the fleet, and the Earl of Albermarle the army, and the operation was conceived as a combined operation. The strategy was Lord Anson's, but he was not to live to see the scheme come to fruition. The principal element was an attack on the city, to come from the east. The usual route for approaching large ships was to the south of Cuba and having rounded Cap Antonis and the west of the island, to beat two hundred miles back to Havana. Anson's plan was to use the Old Bahamas Channel to the North of the island, and come down to Havana with a following wind. The Spanish were of the view that this route was impracticable for large ships. Sir George Pocock was an experienced fighting admiral, a talented navigator and seaman, and had commanded in the West Indies in the Leeward Isles. The Earl of Albemarle had never previously held a major command, having been at sieges in the Low Countries and served for most of his career as Lord of the Bedchamber to the Duke of Cumberland.

351

The success of the operation was dependent on achieving a result before the rainy season, which gave a window of only six months for the campaign to be successful. The fleet and army were organised to leave quickly, with reinforcement to come from British forces in Martinique, which had been taken from the French, and from America. Pocock sailed from Ireland on 22nd March, carrying his flag in the Namur, and accompanied by among others the Temeraire (1st of the name, taken from the French in 1759, with 74 guns), Dragon (7th of the name with 74 guns), Defiance (4th of the name with 64 guns), Valiant (1st of the name with 74 guns) and Merlin (7th of the name, a sloop of 16 guns). Albemarle sailed with 4,000 men, the intention being to make this number up to 14,000. On 20th April Pocock reached Barbados, took up six months' stores and departed to rendezvous at Cas Navires Bay on Martinique, which Rodney had taken. He found no fleet, but further transports with soldiers on board. Aware of the likely naval strength of the Spanish at Havana, he was disconcerted, but added to his fleet Rodney's flagship, the Marlborough, and three other ships of the line. He had been left to carry on the operation and face the danger of two fleets, the Spanish and the French under Blénac. Albemarle wasted two weeks re-organising the troops and their transports. At last on 6th May Pocock set sail for St Kitts, having asked Douglas with the Jamaican squadron to join him there. Having passed through the Mona channel he reached Cape St Nicholas on 17th May. On 18th May Harvey's squadron arrived, and Douglas's on 23rd May. All told 200 sail had collected, and the convoy included 12,000 men, with over 2,000 more to come. On 27th May, after detaching Douglas for Port Royal, he sailed on, leaving the American reinforcements to make their own way with little protection from the French. The difficult part of the voyage had arrived.

The charts of the Old Bahamas Channel made by the Spanish were inadequate and the pilots recruited without skill. Pocock had therefore sent Captain Elphinstone forward in the frigate Richmond to survey the channel. On the southern side the channel was bounded by the Cuban coast, and on the approach to Havana in the west the shoals and rocks of the outlying islands. In the north the shallow shoals and seas off the west of the Bahamas stretched up to the channel, the nearest to Cuba within fifteen miles at Cay Lobos, with another to the west, Cay Sol. Elphinstone returned with excellent charts as far as Cay Sol. Pocock divided his fleet into seven divisions of transport, each accompanied by ships of the line, and began the passage of the channel. The narrowest point, between Cay Lobos and Cay Comfite, was passed at night, and the rocks were lit by beacon fires. On 5th June the fleet was off Cay Sol, one hundred miles from its objective, having accomplished an outstandingly skilful feat of navigation.

Havana was the most significant city of the Spanish colonies, with a population of 50,000 people. The fortress and the defences were provided with 350 guns and the garrison amounted to 3,000 regulars, including soldiers and seamen. In the harbour were 12 sail of the line, with two under construction, and three frigates. The Governor, Don Juan del Prado, was relaxed and confident of the inability of an enemy to mount an attack on the city, and his overall attitude was complacent. The Admiral, the Marques de Reale Transporte, was more effective, but both were under strict instructions from Madrid to defend Havana and thus did not attempt to join the French Admiral Blénac at Cap Francois. The fleet was therefore kept in harbour to meet emergencies. The city itself lay to the west and south of the harbour, whose half-mile entrance was guarded by the Punta fort on the west side and the Castle of El Morro on the east, sited at the north end of the north-south ridge, the Cabana ridge, which dominated the city. The Castle of El Morro was defended by Captain Don Luis Vincente de Velasco, who was for his defence to become a national hero of Spain. In the castle he had 300 infantry, 50 seamen, 50 gunners and 70 guns. The gate was blocked up so access was by ladders in and out.

On 6th June at the El Morro Castle a look-out discerned the sails in the east of the on-coming fleet, now amounting to 22 sail of the line, 10 frigates, sloops and transports carrying 11,000 men. A message was sent to the Governor but he refused to believe the news, accusing the messenger of raising a false alarm. Once the news was accepted as true, some precautions were taken: three ships were sunk in the entrance of the harbour to prevent entry, but this also had the disadvantage that the Spanish fleet was itself imprisoned. On 6th June the Hon Augustus Keppel disembarked the troops on the bay, at the entrance the Coximar River, some fifteen miles east of the city. Albemarle proceeded thereafter to inaugurate and pursue a static siege of the kind he had witnessed in the Low Countries. His second-in-command, General Sir George Elliott, afterwards Lord Heathfield, and a soldier of ability, highly regarded by Prince Ferdinand of Brunswick (see the Battle of Minden 1st August 1759), was sent to clear the woods below the ridge towards Guanabacoa, which he successfully achieved. He thereafter took no part in the action.

The defences of Havana were not in an effective state; there were no works at the landward end of the Cabana ridge, initial works having been abandoned because of yellow fever. The city walls were old in places, broken down and in ruins. Spirited and effective attack would likely have resulted in a quick and relatively costless victory. The army, having landed, slowly assembled and ponderously cut its way to the ridge. In fact Keppel's seamen on the night of landing had discovered the way open by the shore to Castle Morro. Albemarle, however, adhered to his plan. On 11th June Colonel Carlton took the landward end of the ridge, reconnoitred the hill, put a Spanish force to flight and spiked twelve guns. Nothing however was done to follow this up. Albemarle was determined not to attempt action but only to besiege Castle Morro until it surrendered, then consider the position in the city. Sir George Pocock in the meanwhile and the navy discovered that a landing could be made west of the city at the Chorera River, and urged Albermarle to attack the city from the west. Nothing happened. The grinding siege of Castle

Morro continued: the siege works had to proceed in rocky soil, requiring stones to be removed. The heat was unbearable as the hot summer with its rains came on, and the soldiers and seamen dropped at work, worn out by heat and thirst.

Albemarle authorised Colonel Howe to land at Chorera, but only to cut the road to the interior. At last on 1st July the siege batteries were ready. As they opened, a combined operation requested by Albermarle was launched by Pocock: Hervey with three ships of the line went in to bombard the fort. Sir George had not wished to make the attack because of the inability of the ships to fire high enough to hit the fort, but nonetheless agreed. Of the three ships, one could not withstand the fire and turned away (the captain later being cashiered); one, the Dragon, ran aground, continuing the attack until two o'clock in the afternoon and the other, the Cambridgeshire, had its captain killed. The landward batteries had not been properly placed and, while damage was done to the guns of the fort, in Albermarle's view the position remained such that no assault should be made. A new cannonade followed from the navy and its guns, which had been brought up – the sailors firing at the quick rate of 149 times in 16 hours. So furious was the attack that the fascines went on fire and the battery works were damaged.

Albermarle still did not attack, although Don Vincente de Velasco was temporarily reduced to two guns. Food was becoming scarce, the weather hotter and wetter – up to 5,000 soldiers and 3,000 seamen fell sick and numbers died daily. On 12th July Douglas arrived with the home-going Jamaica convoy, with labour and cotton bales to use for constructing new batteries. Within days there were 20 guns to the Castle Morro's five or six, and the sap along the seashore had reached the castle. Don Luis Vincente had been wounded, but remained to inspire two sorties from the castle, which Colonel Carleton repulsed on 24th July. On 28th July Burton and another part of the American contingent arrived. Vincente de Velasco sought orders as to the course he should take – fight or surrender, but was told to make up his own mind. The next day there was a sudden thunderous explosion followed by the storming of the castle in the gap made by the British Grenadiers. The castle was soon overwhelmed. Don Vincente de Velasco was treated chivalrously and at his request taken back to the city, where he died two days later.

Attention was then turned to the city: a route was found in, poorly defended and shielded from the guns of Fort Punta. Nonetheless, Albermarle refused to attack, settling down to another siege. More Americans arrived and at Fort Punta and around the city the batteries were positioned. Albermarle called on the city to surrender on 10th August but the offer was refused. Early on 11th August bombardment of the fort and city began: by 10 am Fort Punta was silenced. White flags appeared everywhere after noon. Negotiations between the two sides began, but it was not until the 14th that these were finally concluded. The city of Havana, thought impregnable, had surrendered and been taken. The lost opportunities to take the city earlier and the obstinacy of Albermarle's plan for a long-drawn out conventional siege had led to a situation where on the day of victory, out of 11,000 troops landed, only 3,000 remained fit for action. 4,700 were to die from disease by October, as against 560 killed or dead from wounds. The booty taken was enormous – the prize money to be divided amounting to three-quarter of a million pounds. One-fifth of the Spanish navy was captured – 9 ships of the line, 2 under construction, 6 frigates and 100 merchantmen.

Later in 1762 a Treaty of Peace was signed between Great Britain, France and Spain, care being taken to protect the interests of Austria, Prussia and Portugal, the latter becoming also a signatory. As part of the terms, Havana and its dependencies (Cuba) were returned to Spain. Britain retained Minorca and obtained Florida by way of exchange. William Pitt, Earl of Chatham, the successful war Prime Minister, urged the House of Lords to reject the Treaty when it came for parliamentary approval, on the grounds that it restored too many French losses to them, allowing their recovery on the seas, and involved the desertion of our ally, King Frederick the Great of Prussia. The latter never again trusted Britain, and his abandonment left a legacy of mistrust to affect German history.

The 10th Earl of Albermarle was ejected from the House of Lords in 1999.

11th August 1718

The Battle of Passaro

The treaty of Utrecht in 1715 ended the fourteen year-old War of the Spanish Succession. The participants were weary of war and its economic consequences, particularly in France, and were determined to preserve the peace, even though their vital interests still continued to conflict. Philip V of Spain, recognised as king by the treaties, was however restless and urged by his wife Queen Elizabeth, of the princely Italian family of Farnese, resented the replacement of Spanish rule in parts of Italy by that of the Austrians. Thus in 1718 Spanish expeditions were fitted out to sieze Sardinia and Sicily. The latter had been awarded by the treaties to King Amadeo II of Savoy. After taking Sardinia, a Spanish army of 30,000 troops under the Marquis de Lede, landing on Sicily, captured Palermo and besieged Messina.

The Governments of Britain, France, Austria and Holland resolved to act on hearing of preparations for the expeditions, in order to maintain the peace settlement of the treaties. Despite there being no declaration of war Britain, as its contribution to the alliance, despatched a fleet of twenty-one men-of-war supported by frigates to the Mediterranean under Sir George Byng. His instructions were to avoid hostilities if the object of securing a Spanish withdrawal could be achieved by negotiation. Pausing at Naples to pick up an Austrian army, he arrived off Messina and suggested a two-month truce for negotiations, which was rejected by the Spanish commander, Admiral Casteneda. The fleets were fairly evenly matched. Byng's twenty-one men-of-war carryied 1,380 guns and Castenada's twenty-six, although some were small, mounted 1,284 guns.

The Spanish fleet was anchored in the Paradise Roads in deep water, where there are strong currents of velocities up to four and a quarter knots through the straits. In light and fickle summer winds, giving battle in such conditions was difficult and uncertain. Despite the relative safety given, Castenada decided to flee south and weighed anchor, giving Byng his opportunity to attack. Byng held a Council of War and on 10th August the decision was made to go into battle. There then began a strung-out pursuit of the Spanish, who had formed into line. Superior seamanship was required to catch up and overtake the fleeing fleet, ground being gained in the night. Early on 11th August the British were in a position to attack, and onwards from 10 am there commenced a running fight. The Santa Rosa (64 guns) was taken early by the Orford and the San Carlos (60 guns) by the Kent (2nd of the name, a third rate of 70 guns built in 1679). Captain Haddock of the Grafton had raked them with broadsides, while passing up to the flagship of Vice-Admiral Chacon, whom he engaged. The Breda and the Captain came to join him; the Principe de Asturias was shattered by the heavy broadsides and struck her colours to the Captain. By 1 pm the fleet was drawing up to the flagship of Admiral Castenada, the St. Philip, and Kent and Superb engaged with her for two hours. Kent was able to cross her stern, pouring a raking shot into her and coming up on the lee quarter. Superb on the weather quarter pounded in broadside after broadside. Admiral Castenada, badly wounded, with two hundred crewmen killed, finally surrendered. Byng's flagship the Barfleur was engaged with two 60-gunners in the midst of this battle, which both ran for land. Early on, a squadron of the Spanish had made off, to be pursued by a small squadron under Captain Walton, and destroyed.

In all Byng and his fleet sank or captured 16 ships, including the three flagships. Admiral Castanada was put ashore in Sicily but died of his wounds. The St. Philip was taken to Port Mahon, where it caught fire and was destroyed. The Spanish citadel garrison held out in Messina and the Spanish remained in Sicily. Despite that, the battle had struck a strong pre-emptive blow at the Spanish campaign to restore their power in Italy. Byng spent the next two years in the Mediterranean, patrolling the waters of Naples and Sicily. War was not declared until 18th December 1718 and peace did not come until 1721. By the Treaties of Madrid, finally signed by the Austrians and Spanish in 1725, Philip V abandoned his Italian claims. Sicily was handed to Austria and linked into the Kingdom of the Two Sicilies. Amadeo II was given Sardinia and the son of Philip V the Principalities of Parma and Piacenza. There was an understanding that the latter might became Grand Duke of Tuscany on the likely ending of the Medici dynasty. When however the last Medici Grand Duke died in 1737, Tuscany was taken over by the Austrians. The Kingdom of the Two Sicilies survived into the mid-nineteenth century, until Italy became united. Sir George Byng returned to London to be acclaimed and was made 1st Viscount Torrington.

The 11th Viscount Torrington was ejected from the House of Lords in 1999.

13th August 1704

The Battle of Blenheim

After the taking of the Schellenberg (2nd July 1704) the Duke of Marlborough advanced into western Bavaria and, in an endeavour to bring the Elector Maximilian Emmanuel to the conference table, reluctantly pursued a policy of laying waste the country. Prince Eugene of Savoy, the commander of the Imperial armies, following his agreement with Marlborough at Mundelsheim in June, had remained marking Marshal Villeroi in the Rhineland, to protect the Allied army's communications. Having heard that on the orders of Louis XIV Marshal Tallard had marched through the Black Forest to join Marshal Marsin and the Elector of Bavaria, he left part of his army to continue to watch that of Marshal Villeroi and set out with 20 battalions of infantry and 70 squadrons of cavalry to join Marlborough in Bavaria. On 6th August Prince Eugene and the Duke met at Schrobenhausen, north-east of Augsburg, in order to confer. The strategic position was discussed the next day with the Markgraf of Baden, who was anxious to besiege Ingolstadt to the east, lower down the Danube. Both Prince Eugene and Marlborough were anxious to rid themselves of the Markgraf, who did not understand their strategy of movement. They therefore encouraged him and his 15,000 troops to undertake the siege, and he left on 9th August. They, however, for their part examined how they should bring the Franco-Bavarians to battle and resist them. The latter had met up on 5th August, and were encamped at Biberach, south of them.

The enemies were now some twenty miles apart. Prince Eugene's force from the Rhineland reached Höchstadt, north of the Danube, on 7th August. Marshals Tallard and Marsin and the Elector of Bavaria decided to move on Eugene's Imperial army. By 10th August Prince Eugene was threatened, having moved east along the Danube, abandoning Höchstadt. The French, having crossed at Laningen, followed him. An urgent message was sent to the Duke, now at Rain, that Eugene needed assistance and confronted the united Franco-Bavarian army. Three hours after the message was received General Churchill, the brother of the Duke, left with 20 battalions of infantry to reinforce Prince Eugene. By 3 am on 11th August the whole army was on the move, gaining the north bank of the Danube at Donauwörth. The French, following Prince Eugene, had taken Höchstadt and come to rest north-east of the town, between Lutzingen and Blenheim. On 12th August Prince Eugene and the Duke of Marlborough, their forces now united some four miles east of the French position, went forward to reconnoitre, climbing the church tower at Tapfheim to view the enemy. The battleground was not of course of their choosing but both, as skilful, highly intelligent field commanders, were able flexibly to respond to situations which arose and adapt their tactics. Having viewed the plain before the French camp and the disposition of the army, they decided to attack, despite the inherent strength of the enemy position.

The French camp lay on a low ridge shelving gently down to a plain and the shallow valley of a large stream, the Nebel, which flowed into the Danube just north-east of Blenheim. Blenheim, a large village of farms and walled enclosures, lay on the French right flank. There was then a two-mile gap to the village of Oberglau, potentially another fortifiable strongpoint. The camp then stretched west towards Lutzingen. In front of the villages ran the Nebel stream, about twelve feet wide with swampy ground on both sides. The plain and valley were screened on the north and west by dense impenetrable woodland and three villages lay to the north of the Nebel – Schwennanbach in the west, Unterglau facing the centre of the French camp with Wolperstetten to the north.

In all, the French and Bavarians had some 60,000 troops and 100 guns, and the Allied forces 52,000 with some 60 guns, but a preponderance of cavalry. The British element in this army amounted to some 9,000, including five regiments of Dragoon Guards (the 1st, 3rd, 5th, 6th and 7th), two regiments of Dragoons (the 2nd (Scots Greys) and the 5th) and twelve regiments of foot (the 1st (two battalions), 3rd, 8th, 10th, 15th, 16th, 18th, 21st, 23rd, 24th, 26th and 37th) bearing subsequently famous names (Royal Scots, for example, Royal Scots Fusiliers, The Buffs (East Kent Regiment), Lincolnshire, Royal Irish, Royal Scots Fusiliers, Royal Welsh Fusiliers, South Wales Borderers and the Hampshire Regiment).

The Duke of Marlborough as commander was at Blenheim to face the greatest test: whether his military career would be sustained with honour by victory, or whether by defeat his military and political career and influence would be eclipsed. John Churchill, the future Duke, had come from the poverty-stricken country gentry, his father a Cavalier ruined by the Puritan regime after the Civil war, his property subject to fine and confiscation. His career started as a page at court, a position given as part recompense for the family's suffering, where his sister Arabella was the mistress of the King's brother, the Duke of York, later James II. He won the interest, because of his fine looks, of the Duchess of Cleveland, mistress of King Charles II, and more than her interest. He was once, at the age of twenty, discovered by the King in her bedroom, having on his arrival hidden in a cupboard. King Charles II, sophisticated and generously spirited, dismissed him telling him 'you are a rascal, but I forgive you because you do it to get your bread.' His career did not suffer: he rose to be Lieutenant-General in the army of King James II. On the arrival of King William III in 1688 he deftly changed sides, and throughout the wars of his reign played an active part, becoming Earl of Marlborough in 1689 and Duke in 1702 after a successful campaign in the Low countries, including the surrender of Liege.

On the morning of 13th August the army was roused at 2 am in order for preparations to begin for the march to the battlefield at Blenheim. 66 battalions, pioneers to lead the way, artillery and 160 squadrons of cavalry were to be organised. The army was to march in eight columns and by dawn all was ready. Morning came and the ground was covered by a heavy summer mist. Marlborough had passed the later hours of the night in prayer and taken communion from his chaplain. The pioneers led the way, bridging the River Kessel and lighting the way for the army. After passing a defile next to the Danube the army, having bunched up, split into nine columns, that on the left being led by Lord Cutts and containing 20 battalions of infantry and 15 squadrons of cavalry, mainly British. His role was to attack the village of Blenheim, a daunting task for with its farmhouses, walls and fences it could be easily changed into a virtual fort or redoubt. Marlborough brought up to the north-east bank of the Nebel River between Oberglau and Blenheim some 28 battalions of infantry and 71 squadrons of Cavalry. At Oberglau the Prince of Holstein–Beck was posted with 10 battalions of infantry. Beyond Oberglau towards Lutzingen Prince Eugene on the Allied right flank was to deploy with 18 battalions and 74 squadrons of cavalry comprising Danes, Prussians and the Imperial Cuirassiers on his left near Oberglau. Prince Eugene had by far the most testing manoeuvre to perform, since he had the furthest to go and the last section of his route north of the Nebel was hemmed in by the woods and across a broken country of ditches, thickets, brambles and scrub. All the troops had to cross the Nebel in order to attack the French and it was therefore necessary for pioneers to build 'paths' to cross it before the troops could finally deploy.

Between 6 and 7 am, as the mist was thinning and dispersing, the Allied army came in view of the French. They were wholly unprepared, asleep in their bivouacs, not expecting an allied attack. On first viewing the troops coming up in the distance, Marshal Tallard and his French officers were of the view that the allies were crossing the front to retreat to the north-east, and he sent a messenger so commenting in despatches to King Louis XIV of France. The allied armies came on and the French and Bavarians finally realised that they were under attack. The Duke of Marlborough and Prince Eugene had taken them by surprise. The emergency meant that far from the troop dispositions reflecting an informed response to the approaching enemy, the French more or less disposed their force in an order reflecting their encampment. Marshal Marsin and the Elector of Bavaria provided the left flank between Lutzingen and Oberglau. At Oberglau 8 battalions of infantry were in the village, with 30 nearby on reserve, including the Royal French Irish. Marshal Tallard with the French cavalry formations made up the line from Oberglau to Blenheim with only limited infantry, 9 battalions. At Blenheim a strong infantry defence was mounted. 16 battalions were posted in the village under the Marquis de Clérambault, being constituted from the crack troops of the French army. 11 Battalions were held outside in reserve and 12 dismounted squadrons of cavalry. The French cavalry were stationed for the most part half a mile away from the Nebel on the top of the ridge.

At 8 am the French fired a signal gun recalling their outlying troops, who set fire to the villages of Schwennanbach, Unterglau and Wolberstetten. They then began their deployment, including the stationing or four 10-pounder guns near Blenheim, and the rest along their front. The Allied pioneers began working on creating new causeways and a repaired bridge on which the troops could cross the Nebel and were not for the most part harried by the French. The Allied army in the centre began to deploy across the Nebel using the unsophisticated infantry marching movements of the age, which slowed the process down. Under Marlborough's direction counter-batteries were sited, particularly to deal with the gun position at Blenheim. At 10 am the French began a cannonade of the Allied lines, which was duly answered. The troops were to have to sit or lie down facing the bombardment for over two hours. The Duke of Marlborough, conspicuous on his white horse with the blue order of the Garter across his breast, rode up and down the lines encouraging his men and steadying them. On one occasion he was splattered with earth by a cannonball hitting the ground behind him.

Marshal Tallard had the meanwhile done nothing; he mounted no attack, it is thought, because his tactics were to await the arrival of the Allied troops on the south side of the Nebel, where his cavalry could drive them back onto the river. Marlborough arranged his lines in four ranks of interspersed infantry and cavalry – the cavalry shielded by the front line of infantry with a similar arrangement for the third and fourth lines. Unhappy as he was at the damage to his army being done by the cannonade, which caused many casualties, although the pace of the cannonballs at the time was so slow that they could often be seen coming and avoided, unless they ricocheted on landing, he was forced to wait before commencing action until Prince Eugene on the right wing was able to get into place. The Quartermaster General, Lord Cadogan, was sent to the Prince to ascertain how matters were progressing. His army was under constant French bombardment struggling through the difficult broken country, and was delayed in its endeavours to bring up the artillery. Cadogan returned to tell Marlborough there was no help but to wait. As the bombardment crashed on, the soldiers sat on the stubble waiting with complete stoicism and raw courage. At last at 12.30 am a messenger arrived for Marlborough from Prince Eugene that he was ready and in place. In the cannonade over 1,000 men had already been lost.

Marlborough too was ready; an aide-de-camp was sent to Lord Cutts on the left flank opposite Blenheim to attack the village. The Duke galloped over to observe the action. The brigades of Rowe and Ferguson waded the Nebel to dry ground without opposition. Brigadier Rowe had told his men not to open fire until he struck the palisades defending the village with his sword. Five battalions of British troops and one Hessian advanced. At 30 yards out from the palisade the French fired, Rowe went up, struck the palisade and from the shattered ranks, one third of which had fallen at the first volley, the crashing British musket fire came. Rowe himself was mortally wounded in the thigh and fell. His brigade began to recoil, but other regiments came on with ear-splitting cries and yells. The French cavalry launched a flank attack, to be met with the crash of musketry from the Hessians. A small force of English cavalry drove them back, retaking a captured colour.

Tallard then ordered forward eight squadrons of the Gens d'Armes, the elite cavalry of France. The Duke riposted with five squadrons under Colonel Palmes. At a slow trot the British cavalry crashed into the French, broke them and threw them back. Although larger in numbers, the primary French cavalry weapon was the flintlock; after a volley was fired, the troops needed to regroup before firing again. Marlborough had changed British cavalry practice, making the sword the principal weapon and limiting troops to three bullets for their pistols per campaign. The slashing horsemen were therefore difficult to resist, particularly as the Duke had also increased the pace of the charge to a canter or gallop. The infantry persisted, taking point by point in the village and pressing back the French defenders. In a welter of murderous hand-to-hand fighting the houses fell one by one. The commander at Blenheim, the Marquis de Clérambault, began to lose his nerve and ordered eight battalions from the reserve into the village. The village was now stuffed full with infantry, hardly able to move and presenting a solid target for the British muskets. The centre of the French line was now denuded of its infantry reserve.

Meanwhile Prince Eugene had crossed the Nebel and attacked Marshal Marsin and the Bavarians. The bulk of his infantry were Prussian, the rest from Denmark. At first his army had some success, seizing guns and pushing back the Bavarians. Then, over-excited, the Imperial Cavalry went too far forward and were in their turn repulsed and the guns retaken. The Prussian infantry with Prince Leopold of Anhalt-Dessau (the Old Dessauer) stood firm. From the age of seventeen to seventy the Prince served in the army and was the creator of the modern Prussian army. He married the daughter of a chemist, although he was a cousin of the King. He was both unrefined and coarse, but a devout Protestant, loved by his men. His philosophy of war was clear: 'Fire well, reload quickly: intrepidity and spirited attack are the surest road to victory.' They were precepts that the Allied armies at Blenheim put into action. The steadiness of the infantry, although the Danish wavered, enabled Prince Eugene to regroup and once more the Imperial forces attacked. The Elector of Bavaria's cavalry fell on them and they were forced back, saved only by fire of the Dutch infantry who were stationed near Oberglau.

By early afternoon the Allied forces were in place over the Nebel. News was brought to Marlborough that Tallard had reinforced Blenheim village. The Duke immediately ordered Lord Cutts to withdraw his troops and to close the village on three sides, shooting any French that tried to leave. The fortified village of Oberglau still needed to be taken or isolated to prevent a flanking attack on the Allied centre as it moved forward. The Duke of Würtemburg and his troops made an attempt, but were pushed back from the village and Marlborough, who had now ridden over to be near, ordered forward The Prince of Holstein Beck. Only two battalions were over the Nebel when nine battalions of French fell on his advance. He was wounded and taken prisoner, subsequently dying, and his troops driven back. A dangerous hole had been torn in the Allied line, which could have enabled the French to turn the flank of the centre force. Marlborough with his usual resolution quickly organised infantry and artillery to plug the gap. The flying troops were rallied and the Duke led them back. A messenger had been sent to Prince Eugene requesting that the Imperial Cuirassiers on his left should be sent to assist the fighting troops at Oberglau, now also threatened by French cavalry and the Irish regiments of foot serving the French which had wildly advanced. Although sorely pressed, the Prince instantly complied, trusting Marlborough's judgement. The flank of the French cavalry was engaged and the crisis at Oberglau was over. Prince Eugene had reformed the cavalry to the west of the village and tried to attack for a third time. He advanced on the French, but both they and the Imperial Cavalry came to a standstill, neither moving, while Prince Eugene and the Elector of Bavaria harangued their exhausted troops. Finally Prince Eugene left the cavalry in anger to fight with his brave Prussians, leaving them in the hands of the Elector of Hannover.

By 4 pm, in the centre between Oberglau and Blenheim firing was continuous along the two-mile line. The troops were submerged in smoke, drenched in sweat in the hot sun, the fallen lying in the dusty stubble. The Duke now had 28 battalions of infantry and 71 squadrons of cavalry across the Nebel, compared with Marshall Tallard's 64 squadrons of cavalry in the centre and only 9 battalions of infantry, the others being concentrated at Oberglau and Blenhem. Tallard had launched his first line of cavalry downhill under the Marquis d'Humières, who led them wearing a gilt cuirass. The Allied cavalry retired through the gaps left in the infantry line and the lines of infantry and the artillery poured their fire into the French cavalry, who halted and began to give way, retreating back up the ridge where they came on to the second line. Tallard tried to rally the cavalry and sent to Marshal Marsin for help, but he was still heavily engaged with the forces of Prince Eugene, where the Prussians doggedly battled on. He refused therefore to send assistance.

By 5 pm the Duke of Marlborough saw that the French were beaten and gone back. The signal was given to advance and the 5,000 waiting cavalry, riding knee to knee, began to advance, thundering over the stubble plains and up the shallow ridge. The French, previously thrown back and partly disorganised, shot one round and then hurriedly retreated, the Allied cavalry crashing into them; the Maison du Roi, Louis XIV's royal horse guards fled with the rest. They galloped away, in the rush carrying away Marshal Tallard towards Höchstadt. The infantry and the guns battered the nine battalions of infantry who had been left unsupported in the plain, raw novice troops, who with heroism stood their ground. Most were found dead in their place when the battle was over. Marsin, learning of the disaster in the centre, organised his troops and started to retire in efficient order. Prince Eugene was freed to send his cavalry in pursuit of the fleeing French and Bavarians. At Höchstadt pursuing Hessians took Marshal Tallard prisoner. Many of the French in their rush were pushed into the Danube and drowned.

By 6 pm all was over save at Blenheim, where the French infantry crammed in the village continued to resist. They believed that surrender would disgrace them. The British troops there thus had to fight on, slowly closing the noose round the village, which was surrounded on all sides. The Marquis de Clérambault was no longer at his post, seemingly having left in the late stages of the afternoon battle when he realised that his bad decision to strengthen the village garrison had deprived Tallard of infantry reserve to support the cavalry in the centre. He could not swim, but nonetheless had plunged into the Danube and was drowned. Lord Orkney was entrusted with encircling Belenheim and more troops were sent. Howitzers began to pound the village, setting it on fire: two battalions tried to flee but were captured. 20 battalions of infantry and 12 squadrons of dismounted dragoons remained in the village. The surrounding troops were outnumbered and a break-out was feared. Negotiations took place with the Comte de Blanzac, and the Marquis Dénonville persuaded his fellow French to lay down their arms. At 9 pm Blenheim surrendered, giving rise to 10,000 prisoners. The battalion of Navarre, deploring the surrender, burnt their colours.

The battle won, the Duke scribbled news of the victory on the back of a tavern bill and sent it by a Virginian, Colonel Parke, to his wife, Sarah, in London and on to the Queen Anne at Windsor. The latter presented Parke with one thousand guineas and a miniature. On the news being received on 21st August the bells rang out and the guns boomed in victory. That victory however had been both costly and crushing. In the Allied Army 4,542 had been killed and 7,942 wounded; of the British contingent of just over 10,000 men one-fifth were killed or wounded, including 300 officers. The French had 30,000 killed, wounded or missing and counting prisoners their army was reduced to 20,000. The military equipment, supplies and stores taken included 34 carriages, 5,300 draught horses, 330 mules, 47 cannon, 3,000 tents, and 100 fat oxen ready skinned to eat, a welcome bounty for the men. The generals' silver was taken and 300 flags and standards. 20,000 lay dead or wounded on the field, whom plunderers stripped on the night of 13th August. Thousands of dead horses littered the field and soon in the heat of summer began to putrefy. The Duke of Marlborough did what he could for the wounded and ordered them assisted and taken to Nordlingen, eighteen miles to the north. On 17th August a day of thanksgiving was held, with a formal Te Deum at Steinheim. The Duke did not immediately return to London, but continued to campaign, moving towards the Rhine and Trier preparatory for future action in 1705.

The news was taken to Versailles by a paroled French Officer. The Court and aristocracy of France were stunned. As the diarist the Duc de St Simon noted, 'One was not accustomed to misfortune'. King Louis XIV took the news stonily, without reaction. There is no doubt that he appreciated the cataclysmic effect of the victory. He turned his attention however to a planned Grand Fête with fireworks to celebrate the birth of a son to the Duc and Duchesse de Bourgogne, who died a few months later. Europe was shaken by the catastrophe which had struck the French army. It was the greatest land victory by a British commander since Agincourt. France was no longer seen as invincible; Austria was succoured and the ambitions of the French to establish their hegemony up to and beyond the Rhine ruptured. Never again in the eighteenth century would the French army believe itself incapable of defeat.

The Duke of Marlborough did not return to England until 24th December, when he landed at Greenwich with his prisoners, Marshal Tallard and fifteen generals. He brought 34 captured colours and 128 standards. In January he was feted at the Guildhall by the Corporation of London. The Queen and Parliament marked his victory with the grant to him of the Royal Manor of Woodstock of 15,000 acres, and the grant of monies to build himself a palace. Queen Anne appointed Sir John Vanbrugh as architect, a playwright and designer of stage sets, who was the supreme genius of the Baroque style in England. He provided the great palace of Blenheim as a royal and patriotic monument to the Duke as general, and to his armies. On walls and tapestries, ceilings and carvings, his military genius is celebrated, but it is a celebration too of the people whom he led. 'Corporal John ', as his soldiers called him, was well aware that his success was due to the extraordinary bravery, discipline and courage of his soldiers and officers. He led always from the front, used his forces with wisdom and showed that he cared for his men.

Austria recognised the victory by making Marlborough Prince of Mündelheim, a small principality taken from him at the Treaty of Utrecht 1713. Prince Eugene went on to lead the Imperial armies with success in Italy and returned to co-operate with Marlborough in the Low Countries. He fought the Turks and finally, in the war of the Polish Succession, he died in April 1736 in Vienna. Marshal Tallard and the generals remained in England nine years at Nottingham. The Markgraf of Baden finally took Ingolstadt, but suspecting that he had been sidelined, remained angry that he had been excluded from the devastating victory won over the Franco–Bavarian forces at Blenheim.

The 11th Duke of Marlborough was ejected from House of Lords in 1999.

14th August 1704

The Battle of Malaga

After taking Gibraltar (24th July 1704), Sir George Rooke left the Rock with the fleet, to rewater on the coast of North Africa. In the course of their progress they came upon the French fleet out of Toulon moving on Gibraltar. The French were commanded by the Comte de Toulouse, an illegitimate son of King Louis XIV, whose mother was the Marquise de Montespan. He was a young man of twenty-six and had been Admiral of France since the age of four. His second-in-command was Admiral Victor Marie d'Estrées, an experienced sailor and seasoned fighter. Toulouse had sailed from Brest in May 1704, followed south by Sir Clowdisley Shovell and 23 ships of the line. Toulouse had gone on to Toulon and had returned with a united fleet of 50 ships of the line, 22 galleys and 17 frigates. Sir George Rooke and Sir Clowdisley Shovell had united their squadrons and had a combined force of 41 English ships of the line, and 12 Dutch, making 53 in all, with frigates and bomb-ships.

When they encountered the French fleet, the latter were off Malaga, where they had been taking on water. The fleets were evenly matched in guns, with a marginal preponderance on the part of the French in that some of their warships were larger (Le Foudroyant, for example, had 102 guns) and they were accompanied by the galleys, which in the event did not participate in the battle save to tow disabled ships away. The English fleet sailed with Sir John Leake and Sir Clowdisley Shovell in the van (the blue), Sir George Rooke in the centre (the red) and Admiral Callenburgh in the rear with the Dutch fleet. Among the ships present were Warspite (3rd of the name with 70 guns), Kent (2nd of the name with 70 guns), Eagle (6th of the name with 70 guns), Centurion (5th of the name with 48 guns), St.George (96 guns), Monmouth (70 guns), Shrewsbury (80 guns), Barfleur (96 guns), Prince, Namur (96 guns) and Yarmouth.

When the French fleet was sighted, the fleets were sailing each in line, the French to leeward. They were sailing south between the Anglo-Dutch fleet and Gibraltar. A light easterly was blowing and the tide running from the Atlantic into the Mediterranean. The Anglo-Dutch fleet, on the weather-gauge, came down on the French in line abreast. The Admiral of the French van, the Marquis de Villette-Mursay, tried to weather the leading English, a manoeuvre Leake saw and anticipated.

Battle was joined at about ten o'clock in the morning. The struggle in the van became almost separate from that in the centre and the rear. L'Éclatant and the Yarmouth fought fiercely until the latter was forced out of the line. The Prince was pounded, suffering ninety dead. The bombardment went on all day. In the centre

Le Sérieux (60 guns) tried to force through the line between Shovell in the rear of the van and Rear-Admiral Dilkes in the centre. The Monarch stopped the gap and Le Sérieux was so badly damaged that it had to be taken away by the galleys. The Anglo-Dutch fleet, because of their part in the taking of Gibraltar, were short of shot, and four ships of the line in Rooke's centre squadron were soon forced to retire from the battle. By 3 pm Sir George Rooke was left with only the Royal Katherine, Shrewsbury, St George and Monarch. They had to battle against Le Foudroyant (104 guns), Le Terrible (102 guns) and Le Vainqueur (86 guns). The St George bore much of the brunt of the attack. By 4 pm Byng, in the centre-rear with four more ships of the line, was forced to retire for want of shot. At about that time the French van bore off to leeward about one and a half miles. Sir John Leake invited Sir Clowdisley Shovell to pursue them with him, but the latter chose to go to the help of Rooke in the centre, with the Barfleur and the Namur. In the late afternoon two bomb-ships, the Star and the Terror, disabled Le Fier (90 guns) and Le Magnific (90 guns). The Dutch until that time had not been engaged, being becalmed, but as they came into action a fierce engagement ensued between the Albermarle and Le Soleil-Royale. As dusk fell and the light went, the contest ended and the fleets drew apart. Sir George Rooke reviewed his supply position and, after everything available was shared out, there were only 10 rounds of shot for each gun, as against the requirement of 50. He was in no position to re-engage effectively. The Comte de Toulouse called his captains to conference to discuss whether he should return to Toulon. Admiral D'Estrées was strongly of the view that the next day the attack should be renewed but he was over-ruled. The Comte de Toulouse had decided to return to France.

The next day the wind changed westerly, giving the French the weather gauge. Rooke had decided that he should return to Gibraltar for new supplies and repair. Both fleets stood off from one another – the French slipping away in the night and Rooke making for Gibraltar when the wind once more turned easterly.

King Louis XIV of France on the return of his son ordered a great Te Deum in Notre Dame in Paris for a victory won, despite the fact that the French had been severely mauled and retired from battle. In London the action at Malaga was also acclaimed as a victory. The Tories, who needed a hero as a foil to the Whig Duke of Marlborough and the success at Blenheim, particularly argued the importance of the victory. In terms of the battle itself the action was inconclusive, but its effects were real. The French had strained every resource to mount a sea-challenge and still had not despatched the Anglo-Dutch navy. Louis XIV, faced by the military challenge in the Low Countries and Germany and realising the equivocal nature of the outcome of the Malaga battle, disbanded the seamen, ordered the navy to port and thereafter never attempted a major sea challenge during the War of the Spanish Succession. French naval power was only used opportunistically afterwards to harry commerce and trade. After Malaga, command of the Mediterranean had been won, and Gibraltar was safe. Not unlike Jutland, the action left the Allied fleet in possession of the sea.

15th August 1945
Victory Over Japan Day

Strictly, Victory over Japan Day is outside the scope of the history of victories over Britain's European partners, but it embodies a moment when the means of making war as an instrument of policy by powerful states was changed for all time. It also marked the final end of the Second World War, signalling that the civilian armies, navy and air forces that fought that long war could go home. The United States in early July had tested the atomic bomb in the Nevada desert, and the weapon had proved successful. Given its overwhelming destructive force, a difficult ethical problem arose on whether it should be used against cities and their populations. Winston Churchill, the British Prime Minister and President Truman conferred about the issue at the Potsdam Conference, where the negotiations were in progress dealing with problems that had arisen as a result of the war. The need to end the war and the fact that any assault on Japan might entail a million American casualties and half as many from the British Empire and Commonwealth, given the likely all-out fierce defence which could be expected from the Japanese, weighted the argument heavily in favour of using the atomic weapon, despite its cruelty. The use of the bomb was agreed and President Truman decided to authorise it. In an attempt to secure peace without the necessity for the use of the atomic bomb, a declaration was sent to the Japanese Government from the Potsdam Conference calling upon Japan, in order to avoid the destruction of its forces and homeland, to agree to the unconditional surrender of its armed forces. On the 26th the ultimatum was rejected by the Japanese Prime Minister, Admiral Kantaro Suzuki.

The first atomic bomb was dropped on Hiroshima on 6th August. The slaughter of civilians and destruction was without parallel. 62,000 out of 90,000 buildings were destroyed and ultimately some 138,890 people died as a result of the attack. The United States Government decided to drop another bomb and on 9th August one was dropped on Nagasaki, where 48,857 people died. On that day the Japanese Supreme War Direction Council met in Tokyo to discuss whether Japan should accept unconditional surrender following the bombing of Hiroshima. There was no agreement, but the matter was referred to Emperor Hirohito. He ruled that the Potsdam ultimatum should be accepted and a message was sent to that effect. At midday on 15th August the Japanese people heard the voice of the Emperor on the wireless for the first time, informing them that Japan accepted unconditional surrender to the Allies.

The war ended; the sacrifice of those who took part calls for the day to be remembered, even at the price of the horror done at its end. A new era had in fact begun, in which the use of war as an instrument of policy in human affairs had radically changed from the past, carrying the potential for the destruction of mankind and its civilisation rather than its transient wounding.

16ᵗʰ August 1943
The Conquest of Sicily

After the carrying out of 'Operation Torch' in North Africa, when the Prime Minister, Winston Churchill, and President Roosevelt met in Casablanca in January 1943, the issue arose as to the next step to be taken in the Mediterranean theatre. The possibilities discussed covered Sardinia, Corsica and Sicily. There was still a pressing need to clear the sea route from Gibraltar to Suez of enemy threat, and Sicily had the advantage in that respect as the prime objective, and it was so decided. Planning began for an operation which, prior to the Normandy landing, was to be the largest amphibian landing ever carried out. One of the advantages of extensive sea power against an enemy is that he cannot be sure where the power is to be used and armies landed, and is forced to disperse his defence to cover the options. The Sicily operation was therefore backed by use of deception to persuade the German High Command that the target for invasion would be Greece. The core of the deception was to place plans for a strike at Greece into the hands of the Germans. A submarine released a dead body disguised and accoutred as a Royal Marine Major. Locked to his wrist was a briefcase with the secret plans. As intended the body, supposedly the victim of an air crash, was washed up on the beach at Huelva, where the Spanish police allowed the German Consul to copy the plans and send them to Berlin. Admiral Canaris's intelligence unit had their veracity checked and were persuaded that Major Martin had been real and the plans genuine. Army units were as a result strengthened in Greece. A few days before the invasion itself cruisers from Force H, based in Gibraltar, were sent to make a demonstration at sea off south-west Crete.

The overall command of all forces was in the hands of General Eisenhower, but the land armies were commanded by General Sir Harold Alexander. Air-vice Marshal Tedder had overall command of the air forces and Admiral Cunningham of the navy, which was eighty per cent British. The forces to be mustered comprised 160,000 men with their equipment of 14,000 vehicles, 600 tanks and 1,800 guns, all of which had to be transferred from their bases in Britain, North Africa, Gibraltar and Suez. 2,590 ships and landing craft were to be used to transport this force to the invasion beaches. 121 British squadrons and 146 American, amounting to 4,000 aircraft, were to be used. Organisation of this massive combined operation was a logistic triumph, much of the achievement being due to General Eisenhower and the close co-operation be encouraged with the British Commanders. General Alexander's 15ᵗʰ Army Group comprised two army groups under General Montgomery (8ᵗʰ Army) and General Patton (United States 7ᵗʰ Army). The 8ᵗʰ Army comprised the 13ᵗʰ and 30ᵗʰ Corps, the former containing the 5th and 50th Divisions, 4th Armoured Brigade and 1st Airborne Division, the latter, 51st Division, 231st Infantry Division, 23rd Armoured Brigade and 1st Canadian Armoured Brigade. The United States 7th Army was made up of the 2nd United States Corps under General Bradley, the 3rd United States Division, 2nd Armoured Division and included airborne troops and Rangers.

Planning for this campaign began in January 1943 and it was hoped to move straight from Tunisia to Italy, but shortage of landing craft, many of which required refit and repair, resulted in a six-week gap between the end of the northern African campaign and the landings in Sicily. One novelty of the landings was to be the first appearance of the D.U.K.W.S ('ducks') which were amphibious vehicles, able to go into the beaches as a craft on sea and become a transport vehicle on land. The period of delay was however used for the continuous strategic bombing of enemy airfields, transport facilities and supply dumps. The Italians were forced to move the long-range bombers to Italy, and four out of five train ferries across the Straits of Messina were sunk. On Sicily, in order to defend the island were eight regular Italian Divisions, eight Coastal Divisions and two German, the 15th Panzer Grenadier Division and a reconstructed Herman Goering Division. Both the latter were embedded in the Italian army and to be found in the west. Later in the campaign they were to be reinforced by the 1st Paratroop Division and parts of 29th Panzer Grenadier Division. The Axis Powers' air forces on the Western Mediterranean were substantially weaker than those of the Allies and were to play only an insignificant role in the campaign.

Between Tunisia and Sicily are the small islands of Pantelleria, Lampedusa and Limosa. The former had a garrison of 11,000 troops and an airfield with underground aircraft hangers. From 18th May until 17th June the island was subjected to intensive air bombing. Some 6,750 tons of bombs were dropped. The island surrendered on the approach of a sea armada on the 17th. Despite the savage air attack only 2 out of 54 gun batteries had been put out of action and most of the aircraft were intact in their hangers. The ineffectiveness of such heavy bombing was to be repeated throughout the Italian campaign. Lampedusa and Limosa also surrendered.

On 9th July the convoys bringing the invasion forces moved to join up near Malta. On the morning of that day the weather began to deteriorate, with a strong wind from the north-west whipping up the sea and bringing a storm. Despite this, no decision to cancel the attack was made. Throughout the afternoon the intensity of the wind grew and the seas mounted, but in the Mediterranean these heavy storms and squalls in summer are not long sustained. As the landing craft however set out from Malta, on leaving harbour they disappeared in the heavy seas, vanishing in the spray. By evening the wind was falling. The young inexperienced R.N.V.R. officers and ratings thrashed on however into the seas, most reaching the beaches on time.

There had initially been disagreement as to the position of the landings, General Montgomery arguing for them to be close together, and not on different ends of the island as the Americans suggested. In the end it was decided to land in the south-west of Sicily to gain access to the airfields in that area. The British were to land between Syracuse and Cape Passaro on the east side of the island and the US 7th Army on the south-western shore between Cape Scarama and Licata. The landings were still about fifty miles apart.

Prior to the landing a preliminary bombardment was made by air and sea. The airborne drop, which was to precede the beach landing, left Kairouan in Tunisia in 400 transport planes and 137 gliders. On the fresh gale, still blowing at Beaufort Force 8, the drop was to be difficult: it was compounded by the inexperienced glider crews who released the gliders too soon. Of the 134 British gliders, 50 came down in the sea and 232 men of 1st Airborne drowned, although the small ships of the Royal Navy attempted a rescue. The wind meant that the airborne troops were dispersed away from their objectives, the Americans being scattered over fifty square miles in small groups. Only 12 gliders landed near their target objectives. For one group of men whose objective was to take and hold an essential bridge, the work was done by only eight officers and 65 men, of whom twelve hours after the drop only 19 had survived the fighting, when the ground force came up. The bad weather had caused the Italian troops to relax and the landings themselves were not strenuously opposed. The Royal Engineers went in small groups on to the beach in order to clear mines and at 2.45 am, guided by submarines using their lights as markers, the troops landed and moved off the beaches.

By the end of the 10th the British 13th Corps had taken Syracuse. Although the United States 7th Army met stronger opposition and their landings were made more difficult by wind and sea, by the end of the day all three divisions were ashore. The Italian coastal troops just faded away and fled. On 11th July the Germans counter-attacked at Gela, and heavy fighting went on from eight-thirty in the morning to four thirty in the afternoon, the Germans tanks even reaching the beaches. HMS Abercrombie, a monitor built in 1913 with its 15" guns, was however able to give the Americans support from the sea. To keep the focus of the enemy forces in the west of the island the Howe, King George Vth, Sirius (16th of the name and a new cruiser) and Dido were sent on the 11th and 12th to bombard western towns and defences. The British advance north to Messina had been conceived on the basis that the 13th Corps would hug the coast and the 30th go inland to round Mount Etna on the west. The volcano, rising to 10,588 feet, and the foothills to it guarded the routes to Messina, of which there were but three, one along the west coast from Taormina, one along the north coast from Cefalu and the last to the west of the mountain from Centuripe, through Adrano and Randozzo to Castiglione.

On 13th July, 1st Airborne troops and commandos landed and took the bridge over the River Simieto, and established a bridgehead on the coast road to Catania, which was bombarded by Warspite (8th of the name and launched in 1913) with its 15" guns. The 30th Corps meanwhile had gone inland towards Leonforte, which was taken on the 22nd. The US 7th Army was held back to some extent to guard the British flank, which made General Patton increasingly restless and prevented a quick mobile thrust by General Omar Bradley to the north coast to cut the island in two. The Italian overall Commander, General Gazzoni, was superseded by the German General Hube, who moved to regroup the German forces ready to defend the north-east of the island. He was to establish a defensive line running south-east from between Stan Stefano and San Agato on the north coast, through Troina to just south of Catania on the east coast. As the 30th British corps went north to Leonforte, Patton's 2nd US Armoured Division was to race for Palermo, which was taken on 22nd July. By that time General Omar Bradley had reached the north coast and on the 25th the town of Termini surrendered. General Montgomery's advance had meanwhile come to a standstill against the German reinforcements now in the north-west of island. The nature of the country precluded quick movement forward, particularly to the west of Mount Etna.

In Rome, however, the desire of the Italians to continue the war had ebbed. The Fascist Party Grand Council met on 25th July and after an acerbic debate voted 19 to 7 to oust the Duce, Benito Mussolini. The next day he was called to the Quirinale Palace and dismissed by King Victor Emmanuel II as Prime Minister. As he left, he was arrested and smuggled away. A new government was formed by Marshal Bagdolio, whose objective, shared by the King, was to end the participation of Italy in the war. Their action was however hampered by the presence in Rome of 10,000 Germans armed with machine guns and an armoured division outside. They were to tread warily, a tentative negotiation only beginning in Lisbon on 3rd August. These negotiations were to be bedevilled by the idea of 'unconditional surrender' put forward by Roosevelt and accepted too lightly by Churchill at Casablanca. The notion was to undermine progress with the Italians and help Dr Goebbels in Germany to strengthen the people's resistance.

The end of progress up the coast led General Alexander to transfer the 78th Division to Sicily and order an advance on 3rd August up the road from Centuripe to Castiglione. Progress was slow. The road was a narrow mountain road which wound through the foothills, giving to the Germans a continuous series of defensive positions. In most cases they established their positions to the rear of the villages, which the RAF and USAAF would ruthlessly bomb and raid prior to the ground attack. The civil population suffered as the buildings were reduced to rubble, collapsing and blocking the streets, giving rise to the need to bull-doze the rubble out of way before the troops could progress. On 5th August Catania fell to Montgomery's 13th Corps and on the 6th, after a five-day battle, the Americans took Troina, the centre of General Hube's first line. On the 8th the 3rd US Division carried out the first of three seaborne assaults on the north coast, moving closer to

Messina, the last being on the 15th August. As the area held contracted, General Hube, following the capture of Randozzo, organised the retreat of the German and Italian armies to Italy across the Straits of Messina. The straits were but three miles wide and heavily defended by anti-aircraft fire and shore batteries. Action to interfere with the evacuation, which was done at night from 11th August onwards, would have been difficult and limited. In a movement executed with great skill General Hube removed to Italy 39,650 German and Italian troops, 9,185 vehicles, the heavy weapons and 11,885 tons of stores. On 16th August the 3rd United States Division entered Messina to be followed by the British a few hours later. Sicily had been taken. It had been a thirty-eight day campaign in all, in which the enemy losses, amounting to 167,000 men, included the captured, of whom 37,000 were German. The Allies had 31,158 killed, wounded and missing.

17th August 1424

The Battle of Verneuil

After the Battle of Agincourt (25th October 1415) King Henry V made several attempts to subdue the North of France, principally along the coast in Normandy. Gradually the area taken was extended and on 21st May 1420 King Charles VI of France made with King Henry the Treaty of Troyes, providing that after the death of Charles VI the crown of France would be united with that of England. His daughter Katherine married King Henry and a son was born in 1422, who on his father's death became King Henry VI. King Charles VI died in the same year and the English, who by that year held much of Northern France including Paris, proclaimed King Henry VI to be successor to his grandfather. John, Duke of Bedford, brother of King Henry V, acted as Regent for the baby king. The lands of France were in total disorder when he arrived there in 1423. Crime, atrocity and murder flourished and the land was abandoned, uncultivated and neglected, which resulted in a shortage of food. English rule was challenged by the French, who controlled the area south of the Loire, under the leadership of the Dauphin, later to be crowned as Charles VII by Joan of Arc. The Duke of Bedford struggled with the problems with which he was beset, but suffered the handicap that English resources of manpower were always less than that required to hold conquered France. His diplomatic skills renewed the alliance with the Duke of Burgundy and he pursued the policy of Henry V of protecting Paris, Normandy and the North of France.

In 1424 the Dauphin was able to raise some 15,000 troops in southern France to enable resistance to be made to the English occupation, and to gather support from the Milanese. His commanders decided to make an attack on Le Mans. He was to be joined by 6,500 Scottish troops led by the Earls of Douglas and Buchan. They came in breach of a promise made that, were the captive King James to be returned to Scotland by Henry V, the Scots would join the English. As the Dauphin prepared to attack Le Mans, Bedford decided to wage a campaign in the summer to conquer Anjou and Maine. 5,000 additional English soldiers had joined him under John, Lord Talbot, and he reduced the garrisons in the occupied lands by half, taking 2,000 troops. The French and Scots started their campaign and took Ivry, a town thirty miles west of Paris. The Duke of Bedford sent the Earl of Suffolk to retake it. The town fell in June but the castle garrison only agreed to surrender if they were not relieved by 14th August. The beleagued garrison became an objective drawing both armies. The Duke of Bedford left Rouen and was joined at Evreux by the Burgundians under L'Isle Adam and by the Earl of Salisbury with his force. On 13th August Bedford reached Ivry and joined the Earl of Suffolk, conducting the siege. The garrison marched out and surrendered. Leaving troops to hold the town and castle, the Duke with his forces returned to Evreux. The Dauphin had by this time reached Noancourt, fifteen miles from Ivry. French and English patrols and skirmishing parties met one another, but the armies did not engage.

The French leaders met to discuss their tactics and there was a sharp division of view. The French, the Duc d'Alencon, Comte Narbonne, Comte Aumâle, Comte Tonnerre and Marshal La Fayette, all wished to retire and not confront the English and Burgundian forces but the Scots, the Earls of Douglas and Buchan, were anxious and zealous for the fight. The outcome of the argument was that they resolved to fall back, but endeavour on the way to capture towns in Normandy. The small town of Verneuil was chosen. Message was sent by the Earl of Suffolk, who had shadowed the French, that they have arrived there and were besieging it. The Duke of Bedford, who had paused to celebrate the Feast of the Assumption at Evreux, sent off with great confidence 3,000 Burgundians to wage war in Picardy and moved himself to join the Earl. The English approach occasioned another argument in the French camp, but this the Scots won. The Franco-Scottish army took station about a mile north of Verneuil on the Damville road, where there was a flat plain, on rising land before the road dipped into forest of Piseux. The French were lined up to the west of the road and the Scots to the right. The lines were dismounted, the men-at-arms interspersed with cross-bowmen, the mounted horse guarding the left and right flanks of the army.

The English marched up through the forest, emerging on the plain; the combined strength of the army amounted to 8,000-9,000 men, and there were present an array of successful soldiers, the Duke of Bedford himself, the Earls of Salisbury and Suffolk, Lord Scales, Sir John Fastolf and Captain Gladstone. Out of the forest they came and up the small rise where they began to assemble in orderly fashion, unlike their opponents, whose muster had been all confusion, with intense arguments among the Scots over precedence. The force formed, dismounted into two divisions, one under Bedford (the right) and one under Suffolk (the left). Men-at-arms were in the centre of each division and longbowmen on the flanks. A baggage guard of 2,000 archers was left to the rear of the line on the right flank and the wagons of the baggage formed into a square, outside of which the horses were tied head to head as a safeguard against horsemen, leaving the men in charge of the baggage free to fight.

It is said that before the battle commenced Bedford sent a herald to the Earl of Douglas to inquire the extent of their resolve to battle 'à l'outrance'. Their reply was that they would not give or receive quarter.

At four o'clock both armies began to move forward to close the gap in between. The English uttered loud cries as they moved forward, shouting 'For Bedford and St George', the French responding with cries of 'St Denis' and 'Montjoie'. The Scots advance was disorderly, but the French came on until at two hundred and fifty yards the English paused to admit the archers to the front to drive in the stakes, which they carried to form a protective palisade. The hard ground made that task nigh to impossible and before it was finished the French horsemen swept through the archers on Bedford's right flank. The latter reformed in groups but the horsemen charged on towards the baggage guard. By this time the two front lines had clashed and were in a tumult of hand-to-hand fighting, pike, axe and sword wielded one against another. Bedford fought on foot with a two-handed axe in the centre.

Meanwhile in the rear the French horsemen became engaged with the baggage guard and the Milanese from the right galloped to attack and loot the baggage. A Captain Young, fearing the oncoming cavalry, fled with 500 men, but the archers stood their ground, devastating the French horse with their arrows. They then turned on to the Milanese looting the baggage and drove them off.

For forty minutes the clash of the men-at-arms went on until the French line was pressed back and scattered, the survivors making for Verneuil. Pursuit began, but the Scots with unwavering courage fought on. Bedford reassembled his troops and fell on the Scottish rear. The archers, having disposed of the Milanese horsemen, marched to attack their flank. Ineluctably the Scots were overcome and being unwilling to receive quarter were slaughtered almost to a man. The Comte d'Aumale, Comte de Narbonne and Comte Tonnerre were all killed; the Duc d'Alencon and Marshal La Fayette with thirty-five Lords and Knights were captured. The Earl of Douglas fell and the Earl of Buchan was captured. Fifty Scots gentlemen of rank died. The English put the French dead at over 7,000 and their own losses at 1,000. Captain Young, taken after his desertion, was hung, drawn and quartered.

Like most victories in the Middle Ages the outcome did not live up to the achievement. The Duke of Bedford clung to his plan to pursue the summer campaign in Anjou and Maine, which were largely taken, and a thrust began towards the Loire. The Dauphin was however to continue his policy of resistance from his Loire base and the question of who should rule France, he or King Henry VI, remained unresolved.

17th August 1808
The Battle of Rolica

The Battle of Rolica was the first engagement fought by the British in the Peninsular War (1808 - 1814). It came about in response to the determination of the French under the Emperor Napoleon to subject the whole continent of Europe to their rule. As his sometime secretary Monsieur de Bourienne tells us, there was no doubt that Napoleon had the intention of becoming master of the entire continent. At Tilsit on 9th July 1807 Napoleon had concluded a Treaty with Emperor Alexander of Russia to make peace, enabling the imposition throughout all Europe of Napoleon's blockade of British exports. Spain, which was in alliance with France, was ruled by the enfeebled King Charles IV, his Queen and Minister Godoy, Prince of Peace, who was the Queen's lover. Napoleon was anxious to impose his continental blockade on Portugal, the only power giving help to the British. On 23rd September 1807 at the Court in Paris the Emperor Napoleon took aside the Portuguese Ambassador and threatened his country with war if they received a British Ambassador. He then began to build up pressure on the Prince Regent of Portugal.

On 29th October 1807 the Emperor signed a secret treaty at Fontainebleau with Godoy, the 'Prince of Peace', by which Portugal was to be divided into three parts – one part for France, one for Spain and one for Godoy himself. It was agreed that France would provide 28,000 troops for the invasion and Spain 27,000. On 13th November the Emperor announced that the House of Bragança has ceased to reign in Portugal. Marshal Junot, who was described by Bourrienne as having a ridiculous compound of vanity and ignorance, was given the command of the army of invasion and he arrived in Portugal in the latter part of November, where the Spanish joined him. The Prince Regent tried to make concessions, advised the people against resistance and fled on 29th November with his Government to Brazil, then a Portuguese colony, at the instigation of the British, who with a fleet under Sir Sidney Smith lay off Lisbon in the Tagus. The fleet had been sent to ensure that the Portuguese fleet did not fall to France. All Portugal was occupied.

In November 1807 conflicts within the Spanish Court came to a head. The heir apparent, Ferdinand, Prince of the Asturias, hated Godoy and manoeuvred against him. Charles IV accused Ferdinand of seeking to depose him and on 29th November, so informed the Emperor Napoleon, inviting his help to revoke the right of the Prince to the throne. The latter also sought the support of the Emperor. Napoleon promised to help the King and the French troops held in reserve for the campaign in Portugal entered Spain. Various towns and fortresses in northern Spain were occupied and on 16th February 1808 some further 100,000 French troops poured into the country. The proud Spanish people, incensed by the invasion of their country, rose in March in Madrid, and Godoy only avoided death in the palace by the intervention of the supporters of Ferdinand. Charles IV then abdicated and the Prince became King Ferdinand VII, to acclamation. On 8th April, Marshal Murat, Grand Duke of Berg and married to a sister of Emperor Napoleon, entered Madrid with an army of 40,000. He refused to support Ferdinand as King, saying that it was a matter for Napoleon to decide. Ferdinand then appealed to the latter for his support and General Savary was sent to persuade him to meet the Emperor. Reluctantly he agreed: at Vitoria he received from Napoleon a letter, said by Bourrienne to be full of deceitful promises and assurances about the crown of Spain. He decided to go on, although the townspeople removed the mules from their traces to his coach. He arrived at Bayonne on 20th April and there was met by an ultimatum to the effect that the House of Bourbon had ceased to reign in Spain and that he must abdicate. He was threatened with death and finally complied. Meantime, Charles IV, the Queen and Godoy were summoned to Bayonne and arrived on 4th May. In return for a pension and exile in Italy, the King renounced his rights.

In Madrid on 2nd May the Regent left by Ferdinand VII, his uncle, tried to leave for France but was prevented by the people, who rose in insurrection against the French, killing some 700 troops. The French army then entered the city and a massacre took place of unspeakable cruelty. Patriotic resentment was fuelled: all Spain exploded – the supporters of the French and Godoy were slain and executed with cruelty – at Cadiz, Seville, Carthagena and Valencia. The insurgency fuelled revolution in Portugal and the people rose against the French, led by the Bishop of Oporto and a Junta who organised resistance. By 25th June Junot held only the Lisbon area and the principal fortresses – Almeida, Elvas and Peniche.

The invasion of Portugal and the events in Spain had necessitated that the Tory Government of the Duke of Portland should work out a strategy to counter the changing position in the Peninsula. An army of 10,000 had been prepared at Cork to go to South America, but the events in Portugal persuaded the Government, in response to appeals made from Portugal and Spain, that it should be sent there. Sir Arthur Wellesley, a member of the Government as Chief Secretary for Ireland, was appointed to command, although only forty, based on his reputation gained for victories in India causing him to be called by jealous rivals 'The Sepoy General.' In answer to the appeals Wellesley left Cork, his troops following, and arrived at Oporto on 24th June. He appealed to the Bishop to collect wagons, oxen, mules and other transport for his army, contacted the Spanish Junta of Coruna and arranged to meet the Portuguese General Freire with his 6,000 troops at Leira. On 25th July Wellesley sailed south to meet Admiral Colton in order to organise the landing of troops. They settled on Figueira de Foz at the mouth of the River Mondego, despite the heavy surf, which pounded on the beach.

When the troops arrived, the fleet bore a letter from Lord Castlereagh telling Wellesley that he was to be superseded as Commander-in-Chief by Sir Hew Dalrymple, with Sir Harry Burrard as second-in-command, since more troops were to be sent and a more senior commander was required. Sir Hew, nicknamed 'The Dowager', at sixty had no military experience apart from in Flanders in 1793, and had been Governor of Gibraltar. Sir Henry Burrard was amiable, gentlemanly and ineffective. Wellesley resolved that he would take action before the new command took over. On 1st August the troops began disembarkation in small boats, aided through the surf by seamen, some losing their lives as the boats were capsized. It was not until 8th August that disembarkation was complete. Wellesley now had an army of 13,000, made up of the troops from Ireland and 4,000 brought by General Spencer from the Mediterranean. However, his cavalry were negligible, amounting to only 400, his artillery limited to five batteries. His army however was tough. Made up from the poorest and uneducated classes, the men had endurance, courage, self-confident patriotism and spirit. Theirs were qualities innate in the people of Britain and they needed to show them immediately as Wellesley sent them to march the twelve miles to Leiria along the beach in deep sand, overwhelming heat and assailed by the squeal of the oxcarts.

Wellesley met Freire on 10th August at Leiria and the Allies argued as to whether a coastal route in the west or an eastern through the mountains should be taken to Lisbon. The British needed to be near the coast in order to maintain touch with the fleet and their supplies: the Portuguese thought the mountain route safer. In the outcome Wellesley took 1,700 light troops from Freire and started off on the coast route. His army was welcomed, since news had come of an atrocity committed by the French under General Loison on 29th July, when a town was sacked and the population, including women and children, massacred. Junot had sent General Henri Francois Comte De Laborde to mount a rearguard to delay Wellesley's approach to Lisbon. It was at Obidos that the British first encountered the retreating French on 15th August. In a long single street of houses and gardens forward skirmishers and troops of the 60th (Royal American) Regiment of Foot and the 95th (Rifles) met the rearguard unawares and a hot tussle took place, the riflemen losing 2 officers and 27 men. De Laborde continued his retirement and on the 16th from the church tower of Obidos Wellesley saw how small was his force. The French that day halted at Rolica hoping that General Loison would come up in time to reinforce them. The village stood in a plain forming a bowl surrounded by a ring of hills.

On 17th August, with a superiority of three to one in numbers, no effective cavalry and only three gun batteries, Wellesley decided to attack. The British emerged in the plain in three massed columns, bands playing and flags flying. At the same time Major General Ferguson, with 500 troops, was sent round the rim of the valley to the east, and the Portuguese to the west, in order to outflank the French lines. De Laborde saw this movement and in good order retired to his next position, a mile back on the top of a steep ridge, difficult to take by frontal assault. The British came on and reached the ridge. The skirmishers of the Rifles pushed up gullies under fire and Colonel Lake took the 29th (Worcestershire) Regiment of Foot up a defile to emerge behind the French. The force took the full impact of the larger French numbers: Lake was killed and there were many casualties. The 9th (East Norfolk) Regiment of Foot soon aided them and the assault held while the mass of the columns came up to take the western half of the ridge. For two hours the struggle proceeded, but then De Laborde moved to retreat, which he managed in good order. He had lost 700 men and 3 guns. Wellesley had no means of pursuit and the army paused. The following morning Wellesley awoke to hear that a fleet had arrived with 4,000 more troops from England at the mouth of the River Maceira. He set off to Vimiero to cover the disembarkation. Sir Harry Burrard had arrived with the troops.

Many women accompanied their husbands or lovers with the army in the Peninsula attached to their husband's companies. They too endured and showed a Christian stoicism. Riflemen Harris, who had been a shepherd in Dorset, recounts the story of Mrs Cochan, whose husband he saw fall, hit in the throat by a musket ball. She insisted upon being taken to her dead husband. There 'she embraced the stiffened corpse, after rising and contemplating his disfigured face for some minutes, with hands clasped and tears streaming down her checks, she took a prayer book from her pocket, and kneeling down repeated the service for the dead over the body. When she had finished she appeared a good deal comforted.' Harris organised a party and Riflemen Cochan was buried. His wife went with the company to Vimiero and later took boat back to England.

18th August 1759

The Battle of Lagos

1759 was a year of victories, none more significant than the Battle of Lagos, where Admiral Boscawen destroyed the Toulon fleet, preventing its juncture with the main French fleet at Brest. For much of the year the Duc de Choiseul, the chief minister of King Louis XV of France, had planned the invasion of England and a similar attempt in Scotland. Essential to the project was the ability to have at sea a fleet capable of defending the transport barges needed to carry the army across the Channel against the British Navy. The latter in part defended the Channel and blockaded Brest, and in part blockaded Toulon to ensure command of the Mediterranean, as well as patrolling further away in the world. Boscawen took command in May 1759 at Toulon. His force contained 13 men-of-war and 12 frigates – including Namur (90 guns), the flagship, Prince (90 guns), the flagship of Rear-Admiral Broderick, Newark (80 guns) and the 74-gunners – Warspite (4th of the name built in 1758), Culloden, Conqueror and Swiftsure. Boscawen was a fearless admiral, well liked by the fleet, who had for him two nicknames 'Wry – necked Dick', because he carried his head to one side, and 'Old Dreadnought', a reflection of his determination and courage in battle. While Commander of Dreadnaught he was awakened by the officer of the watch who informed him that two French men-of-war were bearing down. He was asked what should be done. 'Do!,' he shouted coming on deck in his nightshirt, 'Do! Damn'em, Fight em!'

The French Commander in Toulon, Admiral Jean Francis de Bertet de La Clue-Sabran, had 11 ships of the line, mainly larger than the British, with frigates and sloops. Boscawen moved to Tarragona to take on water, but no attempt was made by La Clue-Sabran to leave harbour. The British tarried there until the end of July when they left to refit and revictual at Gibraltar. Once there, Boscawen received orders that his main objective was to prevent the union of the French fleets, and he was to follow La Clue whenever he went. With that in view he posted two frigates to patrol the entry to the Straits of Gibraltar, one off Malaga and one off Ceuta.

On 5th August Admiral La Clue left Toulon with 12 ships of the line and three frigates, among which was L'Océan (80 guns), new in 1756, Redoubtable (74 guns), Téméraire (74 guns), Terrible (64 guns) and Modeste (64 guns). By 17th August they had reached the Straits of Gibraltar, through which they were proposing to sail, close to the north African coast and at night. La Clue had given orders that his fleet, which was strung out because of the varying way which the ships could make, should make for Cadiz and there meet up. As they passed in the night the fleet was spotted by Captain McCleverty of the frigate Gibraltar.

He immediately made for port and the message was sent to Boscawen, who with his captains was dining with the Spanish Governor of San Roque, that the French had been sighted. With alacrity he left the dinner and the fleet was put in preparation to leave harbour. The task required a feat of administration: the fleet was part unmanned, the sailors being ashore, the ships unprepared, the sails unbent and refitting in various stages of progress. Within three hours Boscawen had eight vessels under way and off Cabrita point by 11 pm. The others were left to follow on.

La Clue realised that he had been seen and decided to signal his fleet with the poop-lantern that the rendezvous should be Cape St Vincent and not Cadiz. Whether through inadequate signalling or for some other reason, part of the fleet failed to take note of his message to abandon Cadiz as the meeting place. In the night five men-of-war and three frigates had become separated from the rest of the fleet. They searched the sea for La Clue and the main fleet but not finding them, they proceeded to the harbour at Cadiz. La Clue with the other eight ships of the line had turned north-west towards the Portugal shore. The strong easterly wind (the Levante) and a south sea aided Boscawen's pursuit and by the next morning the French fleet under La Clue was seen. La Clue, seeing the ships astern at 6 am on 18th August, started by believing them to be his rear squadron, but as he saw the British fleet join up, he realised his mistake and put on full sail. Boscawen pressed on carrying all sail possible, and gradually coming up, but it was not until the early afternoon that the fleets were to close. In his orders his captains were told to come up without regard to line of battle, but bear down individually, ship by ship.

At 2 pm the attack was signalled. At 2.30 pm the Culloden, in the van, came up with the Centaure (74 guns). Other British ships as they came up joined the attack, there finally being, to Boscawen's irritation, some four to five concentrating on that ship. The Admiral with his flagship went past the French, holding his fire, until at 4 pm he reached the L'Océan, delivering shattering broadsides. L'Océan replied in kind with its superior guns. Both sides battled one another until the Namur, having lost its mizzenmast and its fore and main topsail yards, was so disabled that it slipped astern. It came up with the battle around the Centaure, which had fought with valour for three hours, just as it struck its colours and surrendered. L'Océan, which had 86 dead and 100 wounded, leading the French fleet, sailed on. Boscawen transferred his flag to the Newark and the British followed in pursuit of the French into the night.

Dawn on 19th August found the French off Lagos. Two ships of the line had split off and four remained - L'Océan, Redoubtable, Téméraire and Modeste. As the British came up, La Clue ran L'Océan in full sail with flags flying on to the rocks. The proud new ship crashed into the shore and its masts broke over the bows. The Redoubtable followed suit. The Téméraire and Moleste went to anchor under the Portuguese fort at Lagos, but the British came up under the guns and seized them, the Téméraire striking to the Warspite. Admiral La Clue was taken ashore wounded and the crews made prisoner. The French had lost five ships and had 500 men killed and wounded. The British losses were 252. Rear-Admiral Broderick followed on to blockade the eight ships from the fleet bottled up in Cadiz, and they remained there into 1760.

Boscawen had achieved the objective of preventing the union of the French fleets, and struck a direct blow at the scheme for the invasion of England. Boscawen left for England on 20th August and the news of his victory reached London on 6th September. The Téméraire (1st of the name) was taken into the fleet and served in the navy until sold out in 1783. The second Téméraire was laid down in an Essex yard in 1793 and launched in 1798. It was to become the legendary fighting Téméraire of Trafalgar fame.

20th August 1944

The Battle of Normandy

The overwhelming success of the German Army in 1940 at the same time laid the foundation of a fundamental strategic problem, the need to defend and hold a sea frontier of over three thousand miles, from Norway to Spain. That problem was made more acute by the failure in 1941 to eliminate the Soviet Union from the war by a rapid blitzkrieg-type campaign. The Germans became committed to a war on two fronts, the one in the east endlessly consuming the resources of war in terms of men and armaments. After the entry of the USA into the war in 1941, following the declaration of war by Adolf Hitler in support of the Japanese, the German General Staff had to contemplate the inexorable certainty of an invasion into Western Europe. With the fall of Stalingrad in January 1943, Feldmarschall von Witzleben became sure that the battle against the Anglo-Saxon powers was being lost on the Eastern Front. That consumed all resources of men and weapon production. The defence of the West could only be contemplated on a basis of a static linear defence on the coast. That approach was embodied in Fuehrer Directive 51. That prescribed that the Channel coast was to be the main defensive position. In terms of tactics the enemy had to be held on the coast and thrown back into the sea. There was to be no withdrawal by any army from the positions set.

In pursuance of the Channel coast approach, a programme of fortification building was undertaken, the nub of the activity being the Pas de Calais coast of France nearest to England. The choice of that focus reflected the Army Command's (and Hitler's) belief that that would be the likeliest focus for invasion. In response to the Fuehrer Directive, Feldmarschall von Rundstedt, the Commander in Chief West, emphasised to Hitler the low quality of the army contingents in France; one Division, for example, the 70th, being full of men with stomach complaints, the limitations on their mobility, the absence of heavy weapons such as tanks and the non-existence of any strategic reserve. He also emphasised the weakness of General Sperle's Third Air Force and the supremacy of the Royal Force and the United States Air forces. Coastal protection was limited, the navy effort being confined to a few submarines and coastal launches. Supplies were promised by OKW, the Army Command, but most were diverted to meet crises in Russia on the Eastern Front.

At the end of 1943 Feldmarschall Rommel was appointed to advise on the adequacy of the coastal defences. He found many defects and set about an energetic programme, building underwater obstacles on the beach and 'Rommel-Asparagus', a pattern of posts driven in to the coastal fields and beaches in order to hamper gliders. Thousands of mines were also laid on the beach approaches. Rommel was then given command of Army Group B, comprising the Army Divisions in Holland, the 15th Army, stationed between Antwerp and the Meuse and the lower Seine, and the 7th Army west of the Seine and North of the Loire, occupying all Brittany and Normandy. The latter army had to be spread thinly along the coast, with over-large sections to watch in Normandy.

In terms of the tactics to be employed in relation to the 'beach' strategy, there was a difference of view between von Rundstedt and Rommel. The former wished to hold the army reserve and tanks back from the coast to counter-attack once a footing had been gained by the invading force, and the latter to hold such forces close up to the coast for immediate attack. In the outcome the deployment of these troops was an unhappy compromise.

Normandy throughout these preparations was largely neglected, because there were no large ports on the coast suitable for supplying a landed army apart from Cherbourg, at the northern end of the Cotentin peninsula, which had a twenty-five mile ring defence around it. From the Seine to the Cotentin the front was held by three divisions, the 716th, the 352nd and the 709th Infantry. Two infantry regiments were sent to the base of the Cotentin peninsula by Hitler, the 91st Air Landing Regiment and the 6th Parachute Regiment. The 21st Panzer Division, which was Rommel's mobile reserve, was stationed south-east of Caen. There were also in the West of France the 12th Hitler Jugende Panzer Division and the Panzer Lehr Division southwest of Paris. Neither of these was under the control of the Commander-in-Chief West; instead they were under the personal control of Hitler and the army command, OKW, and their consent was needed to move them.

An inherent defect of the large fortifications built on the coast was that their guns were designed to be used seawards. They were not properly defended from land attack and could be by-passed, leaving the garrisons as virtual prisoners. Von Rundstedt thought that the value of the fortresses was insignificant strategically and was cynical about the value of the Atlantic wall.

From the moment that Britain welcomed the Soviet Union as an ally in June 1941, Stalin and the Communist party in Britain sought the opening of a second front in Western Europe. In 1942 President Roosevelt also initially had the view that there should be an invasion of France. Winston Churchill and the British army, navy and air force were more sceptical, realising the huge problems of frontal attack on a defended line on the beaches. Churchill thought in any event that the initial challenge to the Axis powers should be in North Africa and the Mediterranean, and that strategy was adopted. A joint Committee of British and Americans under General Sir F.E. Morgan was however set up to produce a plan for an invasion in the West, and they worked on it in 1943. The COSSAC plan

evolved was ready by December
1943. The formulation of the
plan had the advantage that its
concepts could have full regard to
the lessons of the disastrous raid
on Dieppe in August 1942, where
the 5,000 troops of the Canadian
2nd Division suffered 900 killed
and had 2,000 made prisoner. That
showed how hard it was to sieze an

existing port for supply and also demonstrated the risk of its being taken as a ruin
and thus unusable. The need for new types of landing craft and other apparatus,
the importance of preliminary naval and aerial bombardment and support, the
crucial requirement for tight combined operations and the importance of assault
training influenced the planning as a result of that raid.

The COSSAC plan reviewed the various sectors where an invasion might be
attempted, and decided on the Normandy beaches between the estuaries of the
River Vire and the River Orne. There was the disadvantage that there was no port
on this stretch of coast, and the even more significant disadvantage that behind
the beaches the country consisted of land not well adapted to mobile warfare.
Fields were small, separated by high and impenetrable hedges, with narrow roads
between sunken banks. 'The *bocage*' had none of the advantages of the open
plains behind the coast to be found in the Pas de Calais. The need to achieve an
early supply base for reinforcements of men, petrol and oil, ammunition, food
and other needs of a great army led to the invention of the 'Gooseberries' and the
'Mulberries.' Work began on this project in 1943. The 'Gooseberries' comprised
breakwaters created at each landing beach from sunken block-ships to protect
the loading and unloading of the small vessels on the shore. 'Bombardons' or
floating rafts could be used to unload larger ships. The 'Mulberries' were two
complete harbour installations of the size of Dover harbour built in parts, which
could be floated across Channel and then re-erected as a landing stage with jetties
extending to the shore. There were two of these large harbours, one for the British
and one for the Americans.

The project to invade France hardened during 1943, with extensive preparation
and the transfer to England of the American Armies. Invasion was to be a joint
operation and the overall commander would clearly need diplomatic skills if the
combined team, involving elements which were Canadian, Polish and French, as
well as Anglo-American and from different arms of operation, were to function
without friction. General Eisenhower was chosen as Supreme Commander, but
he had as his Deputy Air Chief Marshal Sir Arthur Tedder, General Bedell Smith
as Chief of Staff, and as commander of the navy involved, Admiral Sir Bertram

Ramsay, of the Air Force, Air Chief Marshal Sir Trafford Leigh-Mallory, and finally as commander of all ground forces, General Bernard Montgomery, returned from his successes in North Africa. There had been hesitations over the latter's appointment, but on his taking command in January 1944 he began to revise the plan energetically, in conjunction with General Eisenhower. They both regarded a proposed initial landing of three divisions as inadequate, resulting in too narrow a front and thus increased the number to five. The landing area was stretched to the base of the Contentin peninsula on the west side of the River Vire.

The decision, because of the need for increased numbers of landing craft, effectively meant that a proposed simultaneous landing in southern France had to be delayed and reduced to one division. Landings on five beaches were now planned – the most easterly being Sword at the estuary of the River Orne, moving west to Juno and Gold in the vicinity of Asniles and Arromanches, Omaha between the latter town and the River Vire, and Utah on the west of the River in the vicinity of Sainte Mère Église. The attack on Sword, Juno and Gold was to be made by the 2nd British Army under General Dempsey, comprising two corps made up of both British and Canadian infantry and armoured brigades, that on Omaha and Utah by the 1st United States Army under General Omar Bradley. To the east of the River Orne the British 6th Airborne Division was to be sent to guard the beachhead flank and secure the bridges over the river. On the west flank behind Utah beach the 82nd and 101st US Airborne Divisions were to be dropped in order to perform a similar function and back up the Utah beach landing.

The basic strategy was first to create a sufficient bridgehead between the River Orne and Cotentin Peninsula and the objective for the first twenty-four hours was to have occupied a line south of Caen and Bayeux to the Vire river mouth. Thrusts forward were to be made in order to widen the beachhead, to permit the landing of massive quantities of military equipment and men, allowing the 3rd United States Army and 2nd Canadian Corps, 8th and 12th British Corps to land. The build-up period needed was thought to be four to six weeks. The second objective was to reach Avranches and to take Cherbourg and, finally, to break out in the west spearheaded by General Patton's 3rd Army, which would go south and west in order to occupy Brittany and the needed ports on the Bay of Biscay. It was envisaged that the attack would then turn east and reach the line of the Seine on D-Day plus 90.

The build-up of equipment for the invasion was massive. The south of England became a huge extensive armed camp and depot. 138 warships were collected – battleships, cruisers and destroyers, of which eighty per cent were British. There were escorts and minesweepers; 3,817 landing craft and barges for the assault; 800 motor boats and landing ships, 1,260 merchant ships for supply, and a fleet of other ships for laying petrol pipelines across the Channel and for transporting the Mulberry Harbours. In all there were over 7,000 vessels and an air force of 10,000 aircraft to bomb bridges, railways and enemy installations in France, tow gliders, drop parachutists and give fighter cover throughout military operations. The armies involved were to be backed up by endless supplies of tanks, guns, shells, hand weapons and ammunition. The operation involved the largest assembly of men and equipment ever made. The manpower for the landings was almost evenly divided, 20 United States Divisions, and 19 British, Canadian, French and Polish. Subsequently there was to be a build up of American manpower with their greater reserves of men.

During the spring a sustained bombing attack was made on the French railways, the marshalling yards, tracks and equipment. In tandem with the French resistance, allied bombing immobilised or destroyed three-quarters of the railway engines available. The railway links round Paris were especially targeted. In all 62,100 tons of bombs were used on the railways. The number of military trains which could use the system each day fell from 100 to 20. As D-Day drew nearer the attack moved to the bridges over the Lower Seine, Lower Loire and Meuse, isolating to some extent the 7th and 15th German armies from the areas beyond, and making communication difficult. Persistent attacks were made on the defences of the Atlantic Wall, with particular action devoted to the section along the Pas de Calais. Attack along all the coast helped to ensure that the Germans could not be sure on which beaches the invasion would come. The bombing reached a crescendo on D-Day minus one, when 14,000 tons of bombs were dropped along the Atlantic Wall.

To strengthen the uncertainty, a massive deception was undertaken. While the armies were being concentrated along the south coast to Devon, a whole phantom army - FUSAG - i.e. First United States Army under General Patton, was called into existence in the South East near the Pas de Calais. Constant wireless signals from its headquarters and other wireless activity was sustained. A British 'phantom' army was also placed in Scotland, to deter the movement of troops from Norway to France. Inflatable dummy tanks, lorries, landing craft and aircraft were stationed to mislead aerial intelligence. That, together with the distribution of the waiting invasion fleet along the coast from east to west, the pattern of the bombing and the fake army wireless traffic, ensured that the German command in the West remained fixed on the idea that the sea-borne invasion would come north of the Seine where the crossing was shortest. Hitler was less convinced initially and intuitively looked to Normandy, but became ultimately so convinced that the main attack would be in the Calais Region that, even after the army command had realised that the Normandy invasion was the real attack, he would not release forces from the 15th Army area until early August.

The strictest secrecy was imposed before the attack and the civilian population of southern England had to function within a virtual security zone. Troops were kept in camp and the details of the plan, adopted in May after their outline in conference by General Montgomery, and called 'Overlord', was made known only to the highest commanders. Even General de Gaulle was not told of the invasion plans until they were disclosed to him by Churchill a day or so before the invasion at Portsmouth. His reaction was typical; having heard Churchill out, he declined an invitation to dinner and insisted on returning immediately to London by car with his own aides. In order to achieve a dawn landing on a low tide, the window of opportunity was limited to a few periods a month. A low tide landing had the disadvantage that the troops had further to go over the beaches, but was needed so that beach obstacles were visible and could be destroyed. The period 5th, 6th, 7th June was picked for the operation, when conditions would be correct. Training exercises for beach landing became more intense. Along the German-occupied coast throughout May the troops were on constant alerts, but as May ended the fine weather dissolved. The 5th June had been fixed by General Eisenhower as the day for the landings. On the 4th the troops were embarked along the coast, the fleet mobilised and brought together, but the Channel was whipped by gales and incoming swells. The meteorologists were not confident that the conditions would abate, and the invasion was postponed for twenty-four hours. The troops were kept on board, fully briefed as to the plans; but they would have to disembark if the weather did not change. On the morning of the 5th the meteorologists forecast a lull between the existing storms, and a further sequence out in the Atlantic to come. Eisenhower met his deputy commanders and the decision was made to go. The invasion was fixed for 6th June. The bad weather had led the Germans to relax their guard. Rommel had gone to Germany, the troops were taken of alert and the field officers of the 7th Army departed to Rennes for a Conference.

That evening the vast armada of warships, transports, landing craft and supporting vessels set out in a heavy channel. Many of the soldiers were seasick as the smaller craft struggled with the sea, troubled and heaving from the aftermath of the storms. At 9.15 pm on 5th June the BBC began to transmit strange un-coded messages to the French Resistance with a concentration beamed to France north of the Seine. It was this message activity which was the first hint of invasion received at German army headquarters. Von Rundstedt's command ordered the 15th Army alerted, but not the 7th in Normandy. Unlike the position in Normandy, the area of the 15th Army had a second layer of defence away from the sea. Six out of ten Panzer Divisions in France were north of the Loire. In the area between the Seine and the Loire Feldmarschall Rommel had direct control of the 21st Panzer Division near Caen but as has been noted, the 13th Panzer Division 'Hitler Jugende' and the Panzer Lehr were directly controlled by the army command in Berlin and could not be moved without permission from Adolf Hitler. The latter were stationed away from the invasion coast. In all these three divisions had 600 tanks and were experienced, fanatically trained troops.

The first to land in France was a party of the Oxfordshire and Buckinghamshire Light Infantry with a party of engineers, who were brought in by glider and given the task of seizing the bridges across the River Orne and Caen Canal, the purpose being to impede any German armour moving up to the invasion zone. The party of 180 men soon seized the Caen Canal bridge against a German machine gun guard, and that over the River Orne without a shot. The 6th Airborne Division followed up, spreading out to occupy the designated drop area targeted, and a party attacked the coastal fortress at Merville at the mouth of the River Orne, which commanded the Sword landing beach. The fortress was first bombed and then attacked by 150 men, who took the casements, losing half their number. The defenders in fact retook the position, but their old-fashioned 100-mm howitzers could only cover the eastern end of Sword Beach. The American air drop on the Cotentin Peninsula was less successful. The planes carrying the troops flew too high and too fast and the 82nd; 101st Airborne Divisions were scattered over an area of twenty-five by fifteen miles, and the gliders came down well outside their landing zones. Out of 6,100 troops, only 1,000 reached their rendezvous. They were without signal equipment and anti-tank guns and had landed in the vicinity of the 91st Air Landing Regiment. Fighting became determined and intense, the Americans commonly fighting in small dispersed groups. At 2 am the parachute landings were reported at German Headquarters, and it was at once appreciated that a sea-borne invasion could soon follow. A report at 2.45 am that engine noise had been heard off the Cotentin Peninsula was however dismissed.

The night of 5th June was lit by a full moon and the low tide on the beaches was between 5 and 6 am. From 3 am, the 1,600 bombers of the US 8th and 9th Air forces started to bomb the beaches and the defences behind. The vast mass of vessels coming out of the dark appeared to waiting Germans in the defences like a massive wall out at sea. At 5.30 am the warships opened a devastating fire on the beach installations, the great guns of the battleships being able to reach well inland. The landing craft began to come in as the destroyers inshore pounded every yard of the beaches where the troops were to land. They were preceded and accompanied by the special prepared equipment designed by General Hobart's team of engineers. There were tanks fitted in front with revolving flails to explode the mines laid, assault vehicles carrying materials for bridging or ditch-filling, Churchill tanks fitted with flame throwers to destroy machine-gun positions, amphibious tanks and landing craft adapted to use for artillery. Combat engineers and the amphibian tanks were part of the first wave in. It had been intended that all the landings should be made at once, but local conditions meant that they were in fact made at different times. The first message of landings by sea reached Von Rundstedt's Headquarters just after 6 am. The Commander of 21st Panzer Division, Lieutenant General Feuchtinger, gave orders to move against 6th Airborne Division east of the Orne.

The invasion force had overwhelming superiority in the air, and the landing troops were supported by a constant air cover, although the haziness of the day until mid-day impeded the full effectiveness of that cover. As the landing craft, amounting to 4,266, went in, the troops moved onto the beaches to be met by fire from the waiting German guns and infantry. The beach at Sword, where there were heavy casualties, was secured within the hour and the troops started to move inland. In the van of the forces that had gone in were the 41st Royal Marine Commandos, as were the 47th and 48th Marine Commandos in Juno and Gold. It is said that the 15th Lord Lovat led his Commandos inland to the sound of the battle airs of Scotland played by his personal piper. It took three hours to overwhelm the coastal fortress at La Breche, between Lion-sur-Mer and Ouistreham. It was not until the afternoon that the 3rd British Infantry Division linked up with 6th Airborne. The push inland took the landing area some 4-5 miles inland by midnight, while 5-6 miles of coast had been taken.

At Juno, the next beach west, where the 3rd Canadian Division, supported by the 2nd Canadian Armoured Brigade was to land, the assault was delayed. A reef off the beach impeded the landing and the amphibious tanks had to be held back. A fortress at the mouth of the Seuilles River blasted the beach with heavy gunfire and a destroyer had to come in close, almost beaching itself to silence it. The sea battered the landing craft, and out of 300 some 90 were lost. The beach was soon taken with great heroism, but the small town of Courseuilles sur Mer had to be fought for street by street. Despite the difficulties, by the end of the day the Canadians were seven miles inland, within three miles of Caen. At Gold, where the assault was made by the 50th British Infantry Division and the 8th Armoured Brigade, the troops landing waded and moved across the beach before at two hundred yards from the sea they were hit by heavy defensive fire. The beach was alive with guns and explosions, but these experienced troops, despite the strong defence, pressed on and the beach was cleared within half and hour. Heavy casualties were incurred. The build up of troops grew as the joint infantry and armoured force moved off into the country. By mid-day a coastal area of three miles had been taken and the attack had been carried two and half miles inland.

The American landing at Omaha was almost a disaster. It was perhaps the most difficult beach to take: the beach itself was bounded by a shingle bank or low wall, while 100-foot high cliffs overlooked the beach, penetrated by four valleys which gave access to cliff-tops. The Americans did not precede their attack by a two-hour bombardment, but relied on one of forty minutes only. A dangerous sea had got up, and the amphibious tanks were thrown about, twenty-seven out of thirty-two being lost. The Americans had also rejected the special landing equipment invented and used by the British. They relied on a traditional infantry attack, unsupported as it had become because of the loss of the first wave tanks. A further misfortune was that the 716th German Infantry Division had been reinforced by the experienced 352nd Infantry Division. The incoming landing craft, launched too far out, came in to a heavy German defensive fire, which had not been disrupted significantly by the preceding bombing and bombardment.

The initial regiments on the beach took heavy casualties, became disorganised and were pinned down below the cliffs. Four hours after landing, General Bradley was told that obstacles to be taken were mined and progress was slow. The beach was a furnace of smoke, furious gunfire, and the dead. Bradley contemplated momentarily withdrawing from Omaha, but determined and courageous conduct, particularly by the 2nd Rangers and General Cota, saved the attack. The Rangers climbed the cliffs while the navy bombarded the defending troops and swept the tops clear in order to allow the beach forces to penetrate through the Vierville ravine to the open land beyond the beach: Cota rallied the broken 116th Regiment by standing exposed to fire on the seawall urging them on. By 1.30 pm the Rangers and the 116th were on the cliffs, the tanks were coming off the beach and the Americans began to push inland. On Utah beach opposition was slight and the Americans were helped by being carried by the sea away from the designated landing place to a beach where the obstacles were fewer. Within three hours of landing, control over the causeways through the flooded land behind the beach had been taken.

By mid-day the landings were complete and the 7th German Army had been severely mauled. Its defensive line had disintegrated and its cohesion had broken down. The strong counter-attack contemplated to drive the Allies back to the sea had not occurred. The move by 21st Panzer, started at 6 am, had made little progress, and that slow, under the threat of air attack. At 10 am however, Feuchtinger was ordered by Von Rundstedt to divert west of Caen and leave the 6th Airborne east of the River Orne. About ten miles from the sea the 21st Panzer met three British Infantry divisions and three Canadian, whose anti-tank fire destroyed 11 tanks. Sections of the division pushed on and reached the sea near Lion-Sur-Mer in the gap between Sword and Juno beaches. However, new airborne troop landings and tanks pushing inland on the flanks of the attack forced Feuchtinger and his tanks to retire to a line north of Caen. He had lost twenty-five per cent of his tanks. This was the sole counter-attack on the day of landing. At 4 am Von Rundstedt's headquarters had sought to obtain the consent of OKW to move the 12th SS Panzer 'Hitler Jugende' and the Panzer Lehr Division to attack the beaches. Berlin refused to consent until the Fuehrer had given his permission. Hitler was asleep, having had a late night with his mistress Eva Braun, watching cinema films. The Fuehrer's consent was not given until 4 pm. By that time a co-ordinated armoured attack for that day could not be launched. By midnight on D-Day the beachheads had been created. Sword had penetrated four miles inland and had a width of five miles; Juno and Gold were united along eleven miles of coast covering Arromanches and had penetrated six miles inland; Omaha was established but had only gained a depth of two miles and Utah was in being, the troops moving inland beyond the flooded area to join up with the embattled pockets of the 82nd and 101st Airborne Divisions. The objectives of the first day and the planned invasion line had not been achieved but the Allies were ashore and entrenched. There was space to begin the build-up in the beachheads. The taking of Arromanches and the establishment of Omaha beach allowed orders to be given for the two 'Mulberries' to be brought across the Channel from England.

In Paris, Feldmarschall von Rundstedt continued to receive orders from OKW at the instance of the Fuehrer to throw the allied forces back into the sea. The British were to continue to press towards Caen, but on the morning of the 7th June the first sustained German counter-attack was to be launched. After the release of the two panzer divisions by OKW at 4 pm on the 6th, the 12th SS Panzer Division (Hitler Jugende) under Major General Meyer began to move forward. Meyer was a fanatical Nazi aged 25, and led indoctrinated young troops ready to die for the Fatherland. He ordered prisoners shot and after the war was convicted as a war criminal. Meyer met Lieutenant General Feuchtinger in Caen, who warned him of the difficulties of air attack and bombardment in any move forward, and who favoured waiting for the Panzer Lehr division to arrive for a co-ordinated attack.

Meyer decided to push on and passed through the city in the early morning in order to assemble for a push north-west of the city with 21st Panzer on his right flank. 260 tanks were to take part, but even before the 12th SS Panzer Division could go forward from the start line its was subjected to withering air onslaught and naval bombardment, including the 16-inch shells fired by H.M.S Rodney in the Channel. Only part of the division was able to move forward, in a spurt which succeeded, after a ferocious fight with the 27th Armoured Brigade, in pushing the British back about a mile and a half. By the end of the day the attack had failed and two Panzer Divisions were stranded, short of petrol as a defensive shield north of Caen. The Panzer Lehr division at Le Mans had a 100-mile journey to the front and had left on the afternoon of the 6th. General Bayerlein, its commander, relates how, out of its total strength of 150 tanks and 600 tracked vehicles, by nightfall air attack had destroyed 30 tanks. On the 7th from 5.30 am, reaching its apex at 12.00 pm, there was constant attack by a sky full of fighter bombers. The division had to shelter under trees and in woods so their progress was slow. On the night of the 7th the division motored on and finally arrived at Ellon, having lost 40 tanks and 90 other vehicles. It had taken seventy-two hours to cover the distance and it could only be ready for battle on the 10th.

On the 7th General Montgomery arrived to set up his headquarters as overall commander of the ground armies, an appointment which he would hold until September. He brought with him a new staff car to replace the Humber used previously. As he had learnt that the German Commanders used luxury Mercedes cars, he had acquired a 1939 Rolls-Royce Silver Wraith, which he was to use throughout the campaign until 1945, on the basis that he had to show the flag equally. Apart from keeping up pressure towards Caen, the troops moved along the coast and the beachheads of Sword, Juno and Gold were united to provide a 24-mile coastal strip under Allied control. The Americans also made progress, fighting to unite Omaha and Utah beaches and consolidating their position. While there was disappointment at the failure to capture Caen, the foundation of the Overlord Plan was being implemented. The British were attracting the weight of the German counter-attack, especially their mobile arm in the east, and by so doing opening the way to the delivery of the major campaign by the Americans in the west. Reliance had to be placed by the Germans on their armoured divisions as the second line of defence, because bringing up infantry involved huge difficulties and delays.

Movement by train and road was prevented by air attack and reserves were driven to walking or bicycling and night movement. On 8th June, following air attack and naval bombardment, Gold Beach and Omaha were joined as the Royal Marines of the 30th British Corps went west along the coast. On the 10th, Panzer Lehr were ordered by Rommel to move on Bayeux, which had been captured, but they became entangled with a British push south towards Tilly sur Seuilles and withdrew. Around Tilly the battle was intense and went on until the 11th. On the 9th Rommel wrote to Berlin stressing the technological resources being relied on by the Allies and the extent of their bottomless supply of aeroplanes and weapons. Both Rommel and von Rundstedt had reached the conclusion that the German army should withdraw to a new defensive line on the Seine and demanded a meeting with Hitler. By the 10th, the British – Canadian beachhead was beyond Bayeux, near Tilly, and the Americans had established the Utah beach with eight miles depth along ten miles of coast. On that day a tank counter-attack was renewed by 1st SS Panzer Corps, but lack of fuel inhibited the attempt and Panzer Lehr was forced to withdraw with the loss of 100 tanks. Once more Hitler and the OKW issued orders for the troops to fight and fall without withdrawal. On 11th June the Americans took Carentan and Utah beach was united effectively to the rest of the beachhead, now sixty miles long. By the 12th June that beachhead contained 326,547 men, 54,186 vehicles and 104,428 tons of stores. The build-up was well in progress. In the week since D-Day some 35,000 air sorties had been flown and the German retaliation effort was paralysed. There was however only one airfield within the beachhead.

On 12th June Winston Churchill, who had been prevented by King George VI from being present at the landings on a cruiser, arrived to confer with General Montgomery. The latter was able to stress that the general strategy had progressed well, but was perhaps less than frank about the difficulties around Caen, which he said he soon expected to take. There were three factors which made forward moves difficult. First Montgomery, in the long tradition of British generals and influenced by the First World War, was protective of his men and was not prepared to dash regiments of infantry into battle unsupported by the softening-up of air bombing and bombardment, and unprotected by armoured forces. Second, he was faced by the most experienced and motivated troops on the western front, embedded in their tanks, which had come to perform a semi-static role. From 15th June to 25th July the British faced three times the number of tanks which faced the Americans.

The Tiger tanks and 88-mm anti-tank guns moreover, outclassed in protection and firepower the Shermans, Crusaders and Churchills available to the British. Third, there was the nature of the country. Wide-ranging mobile warfare in great number was impossible and the infantry and armoured brigades had to attack through small fields with dense boundaries of hedge and tree coverage. The sunken roads were narrow and the country undulating. German and British troops could move beside one another separated only by hedges without realising the others' presence. Field gaps could be commanded easily and woods used for ambush. It was inevitable that the going would be slow.

In reply to the request made by von Rundstedt and Rommel, the Fuehrer came to his French headquarters at Margival near Soissons. Hitler was at first conciliatory but when the issue of withdrawal was raised he became angry and told Rommel, who wanted political decisions to follow from the position in the West, to concern himself only with military matters. Towards the end of the conference news came of the American break out north-west from Utah beach in order to encircle Cherbourg and cut it off. Hitler said he would visit the front. However, a V1 rocket fired at London that day went astray, travelled in a circle and exploded near the headquarters. He changed his mind and flew back to Berchtesgaden. The orders issued remained the same, Cherbourg and every inch of Normandy was to be held to the last man: there was to be no withdrawal. Von Rundstedt discreetly altered this order from 'man' to 'bullet'. One consequence of this conference was that there was afterwards a much stiffer resistance by the Germans. By 17th June the US 7th Corps had reached Carteret and Porbail and Cherbourg was cut off.

On the 12th Montgomery had explained to Churchill the current operation to encircle Caen. The 51st Highland Division had been ordered to move east of Caen and the 7th Armoured and 50th Division to press south to Villers-Bocage. The attack to the south led by the County of London Yeomanry proceeded well, being flanked by the American Vth Corps advancing to the west, and being some two miles from the Panzer Lehr position. On the 13th Villers-Bocage was reached, but the heavily-armoured 101st Heavy Panzer Division with their Tiger tanks came up to the attack, and the Panzer Lehr Division and the 2nd Panzer Corps began to squeeze the corridor. On the 14th the Germans Panzer divisions moved to counter-attack but were halted by the British air bombardment and artillery. At midnight the 7th Armoured Brigade withdrew. East of the Orne no significant progress was made. On the 14th the Americans took Caumont, nineteen miles inland from the coast. In accordance with the overall strategy the west of the beachhead was being successfully enlarged. Montgomery had never been popular with the traditional establishment of the armed forces and Air Chief Marshal Tedder began to influence Eisenhower, suggesting that the land battle was not going successfully on the basis that the needed airfields were not being taken. Montgomery played into their hands by being too sanguine about the lack of progress. He stressed however to Eisenhower's headquarters that the use by Von Rundstedt and Rommel of the mobile reserve to fill the gaps at Caen helped the final strategy of break-out in the west.

On the 19th the Channel weather changed dramatically. A violent gale blew and tumultuous seas arose and raged for three days. The storm was the worst for many years and the off-shore structure of the beachhead and the ships were torn apart, damaged and sunk. The American Mulberry at Omaha beach was completely destroyed, the British Mulberry so severely damaged that it was not in full use again until 30th June. A dozen ships were sunk, and three hundred smaller vessels were driven ashore. The storm and its damage clearly underlined the need to take Cherbourg. On 21st June the Americans were within three miles of the city. Montgomery had prepared for the 19th yet another attempt to take Caen, Operation Epsom, but the bad weather delayed it. General Sir Richard O' Connor was to mount the attack with troops from the 8th British and 2nd Canadian Corps on a five-mile front west of Caen with 600 tanks. By this time the three strong Panzer Divisions had been stationed in the bocage for up to three weeks. Tanks dug in, with trench shelters underneath, minefields laid and some 60-80 88-mm guns, lethal to the tanks, were in place. The bad weather delayed the start of the operation, but on 25th June a push was made east of Tilly sur Seuilles, to help protect the right flank on the planned move forward by the 49th Division and 8th Armoured Brigade; but the thrust met fierce resistance. It was to be renewed on the 26th in the direction of Evrecy, crossing the Odon River. The action began with a huge artillery barrage bolstered by the large naval guns afloat. The 15th Scottish Division moved forward, but just as in the First World War the defenders appeared from their foxholes and hiding places to mount the defences. Nonetheless villages were taken with hand-to-hand fighting, Cheux under shell-fire being totally destroyed.

At mid-day the 8th Armoured Brigade went through the infantry in order to take the Odon River crossings. The 12th SS Panzer division sustained a violent attack, losing 700 dead and wounded, but the attack had lost momentum and came to a standstill two miles north of the Odon River. In pouring rain the 43rd Wessex Division was brought up that night. Early on the 27th the 2nd Argyle and Sutherland Highlanders managed to seize two of the bridges and the armoured brigades began to move across the river, taking Hill 112, about a mile south of the river. German reinforcements had begun to arrive, the 9th and 10th SS Panzer Divisions from the Russian front and 1st Panzer Division – Leibstandarte Adolf Hitler. Fighting circled round Hill 112 and the salient over the Odon for a day or two. The corridor made by the British was narrow, so that on 29th June the villages on the east flank were the subject of attack by the 43rd Wessex Division. The Germans were ready and prepared to counter-attack on 30th June, and the tanks of the Panzer Corps began to move up to the line. The day was bright and the skies clear. As they came into place, a murderous five was raised on them from the warships' naval guns in the Channel, the waiting naval artillery and the constant flights of fighter-bombers. It was afternoon before any attack could be attempted and that was again held. By this time Operation Epsom had run its course and the armour was withdrawn from across the Odon, leaving a small infantry salient.

After the Americans reached the west coast of the Cotentin Peninsula on 17th June they turned north and came to within three miles of Cherbourg by 21st June. It took until 27th June to capture the city and its arsenal. Despite the order to defend the place to the last man, the commander surrendered when faced by the reality of heavy tank attack. The fall of Cherbourg and the defeat of the combined attack of the Panzer Divisions in the Evrecy sector on 30th June resulted in a change of German command in the West. In late June Von Rundstedt, Rommel and General Freiherr Geyr von Schweppenberg commanding the Armoured Divisions in Panzer Group West complained to Hitler about the static use of the tanks around Caen. They demanded to see him and went to Berchtesgaden to meet him. There they were kept waiting and treated to a monologue by Hitler on 'the miracle weapons' now coming into use, the V1 and V2. No new orders were issued. Back in Normandy von Rundstedt telephoned Feldmarschall Keitel at Hitler's headquarters suggesting that a younger man was needed. Keitel asked what should be done. Von Rundstedt replied with clarity, 'End the war, you fools.' On 3rd July Feldmarschall von Kluge arrived to supersede von Rundstedt while von Sweppenburg also was relieved of his command. The former, having had a record of sound defence on the Eastern Front, had been brainwashed on the way into a state of optimism at the possibility of holding the allies and had been ordered to throw them back to the sea. Inspection of the front soon brought to him the reality of the problems which the German army had in Normandy.

After the fall of Cherbourg and the continuing build-up by the Americans, Montgomery and General Omar Bradley turned to the next phase of the Overlord Plan, the break-out in the west. General Patton had landed in France on 6th July and began to organise his American Third Army. The relative lack of progress in the British sector of the beachhead, where Montgomery was in command, continued to result in mounting criticism. The public in the United States and England cavilled at the lack of action. Tedder told Eisenhower that he doubted Montgomery's fighting leadership. The Government in London became restless. Omar Bradley however appreciated Montgomery's control of the battle. He did not join the criticism, but recognised that the constant activity around Caen hoodwinked the Germans into keeping six Panzer Divisions there for most of the time, and that the British army was acting in a 'sacrificial' role. It was knowledge of that role that influenced Montgomery's natural instinct to avoid casualties, and made British army moves 'hesitant' to some extent in the eyes of their opponents in the SS Panzer Divisions.

The plan agreed was for a major break-out west of St Lo, and then west and south to Coutances and Avranches. Subsequently the Americans would turn west across the plains north of the Loire eastwards; the British would press south and south-east so that the armies could join, having surrounded the German positions. Montgomery kept up the pressure in the Caen area. On 7th July an attack on the town was mounted. 2,200 bombers were launched against the city and 7,000 tons of bombs dropped. By the 9th the north-west of the city had been taken and the Germans had evacuated to the east of the River Orne. The city had been reduced to rubble, with 2,000 of its inhabitants killed in the action. The co-ordinated joint action of the Allies to break out was timed for mid-July. Operation Goodwood was timed for 18th July and the break out from St Lo on the 19th. The British did not achieve the break-out planned but even though they were opposed by seven out of the ten Panzer divisions in Normandy, they forced the front line southwards, abandoning the operation in torrential rain on the 20th.

The American Operation Cobra, because of the bad weather, was delayed to the 25th. The move began with a devastating air attack on the German defensive positions west of St Lo. Some 3,000 United States Air Force planes dropped 4,000 tons of bombs. Lt General Bayerlein, who was there in command, described the action as turning the front into a moonscape, leaving his military force with the majority of soldiers killed, wounded and demented. In fierce fighting in the bocage, US 12th Army Group started to move first on Coutances. The Germans riposted at once by sending two Panzer Divisions west from Caen (although only 17 new tanks had been sent to replace the 225 lost) and seven infantry divisions. The infantry attack west of St Lo was on a four-mile front, with tight co-ordination of infantry, tanks and air attack. The fighter aircraft communicated directly with the tanks, and ground officers could call up aircraft to the attack. On 28th July Coutances was taken. On 3rd August General Patton's 3rd Army was officially constituted as a separate command, although its armour had already on 31st July entered and taken Avranches.

On 17th July Feldmarschall Rommel was injured when his car was attacked by a fighter on his way to his headquarters. He returned to Germany. On 20th July Adolf Hitler survived the bomb attack carried out by Graf von Stauffenberg and his associates in the army command, supported by other members of the old establishment such as Graf von Moltke, leader of the Kreisau circle, and the future Ambassador to London Von Herwath. There was no change therefore in the 'stand firm' policy imposed on the army command in the west. The taking of Avranches however stimulated Hitler to order von Kluge to attack to the west, with a view to cutting off Patton's troops as they moved south and west. Some 6 Panzer Divisions were now deployed near Mortain. The German logistic problems, without effective air cover, meant that it was not until 7th August that the counter-attack could be launched. By 3rd August Patton was already at Rennes and on the 8th the 15th US Corps was at Le Mans. The open country was beginning to allow the campaign to become mobile.

The thrust forward towards Avranches ordered by Adolf Hitler was an immense gamble, but if it had had some success it could have seriously impeded the American move to the south and east. The high command in the west was against the attempt because of the danger of the German armies becoming entrapped and encircled. Von Kluge had no choice however, since the Fuehrer had ordered it and to some extent accepted that its risk was reduced when the British drive by the 1st Canadians stalled south-west of Caen. The 1st Canadians had attacked on the night of 7th August following a fierce aerial bombardment. The remnants of the 12th SS Panzer Division, a battalion of the 101st Heavy Tank Corps, and the 272nd Infantry Division, strongly led by General Meyer, put up stout resistance. The deployment of some 88-mm anti-tank guns made available by the Luftwaffe wreaked havoc among the advancing tanks, and 150 Sherman tanks were destroyed. Only fifteen miles were gained before the attack came to a standstill.

The same day, having assembled five Panzer Divisions near Mortain under General Eberbach, who had superseded Geyr von Schweppenburg on 4th July, amounting to 400 tanks, infantry transferred from the 5th Army and a force of bomber aircraft, an attack was launched just after midnight to drive the thirty miles to Avranches. Mortain was taken and the drive forward went on for a further seven miles. With the early disappearance of the mist on the morning of the 8th the RAF Typhoons and Hurricanes were able to come in to strike the advancing armour in support of the US 7th Corps, who had put up a stalwart defence. The rocket fire of the Typhoons was particularly damaging, and by mid-day the armoured thrust had come to a standstill. Hitler ordered three more Panzer Divisions from Caen, and on the 9th pressure was kept up to forward the attack. That day General Omar Bradley suggested to Eisenhower and Montgomery that the concentration of the enemy force so far west would permit a quick encirclement of those armies by shifting the existing drive east in part northwards to Argentan and Falaise, where the British and Americans could unite and close in the opposing armies. General Montgomery gave the necessary orders and the Allies moved to effect the capture of the Germans in Normandy.

Meanwhile the Germans continued to try to sustain their position near Mortain, with diminishing success, for a few days. A planned renewal of their assault on 10th August became abortive as the Allies went over to the attack. Just to the north-east of Mortain, the 5th US corps and the 2nd British Army, consisting of the 8th, 30th and 12th Corps, began to push south-east, squeezing the pocket on

11th and 12th of August. On the 13th the German forces began to retire in ordered fashion. Their pocket was also squeezed in the south as General Patton and the 3rd US Army diverted north from Le Mans and, passing Alençon, reached Argentan on the 12th. The concentration of the German, Normandy army south of Caen and at Mortain had meant that Patton had been able to advance rapidly, against little resistance. He wished to press on to Falaise, but General Omar Bradley ordered him to stop, concerned that the US 3rd Army had lost its cohesion and would be unable to withstand a determined attempt of the 80,000 strong army to escape through a thin cordon line.

The British, using the 12th Corps and the Canadian Corps, renewed their attack at Caen on 11th August. The Canadians, who were on the left and in the lead under General Crerar, faced a defence of attrition by the committed and experienced troops embedded north of Falaise. The Canadian Armoured force was inexperienced and although there were only 50 tanks left of the Panzer Divisions to the Canadians' 700, progress was painfully slow. By the 13th they were still ten miles from Falaise. On their left the 1st Canadian Corps were moving towards the River Dives.

As the Germans retired, von Kluge went to inspect the pocket and was effectively missing for a day from his headquarters. Adolf Hitler suspected him of trying to arrange a truce with the Americans and promptly dismissed him. A third commander was appointed, Feldmarschall Model. On 15th August the Americans and Free French landed on the Riviera. According to General Zimmerman, that caused the Fuehrer to permit the retreat from the gap of the German armies, and as his last act von Kluge issued such orders on the 16th. The retreat disintegrated into a total rout, the army units breaking up and becoming disorganised. On the 17th Falaise fell to the Canadians. There was now only a fifteen-mile gap through which the disordered remains of the 5th Panzer Corps, Panzer Group Eberbach and the 7th Army could retreat to safety. Feldmarschall von Kluge, recalled to Berlin, made his farewells in Paris stopped his car near Metz for lunch and committed suicide by poison. He left a strange letter for the Fuehrer attesting to his loyalty, the real attempts made to follow orders and stating his devotion to Germany and the Fuehrer. The letter has been much discussed, but its purpose was probably to protect his family. After the 20th July plot, Hitler had treated the conspirators' wives and children as also responsible for the plot, imprisoning the women and dispersing the children to unknown Nazi families.

Within the shrinking pocket, the retreating troops were subject to constant air attack, some 3,000 sorties a day being flown. The result was a growing carnage of indescribable horror. Along the roads lay dead and dismembered men, fragments of bodies, overturned and burnt-out tanks and lorries; everywhere mutilated and dead horses choked the sides of the roads. The air was full of the noise of aircraft, bombs and machine guns, of the cries of the wounded and the screams and the frightened loud whinnying of the transport horses. Smoke and burning and the growing stench of dead horses filled the air. Roads were blocked, vehicles abandoned. Much of the movement had to be done at night, and as the men moved east the gap grew ever narrower. By 18th August it was down to around four miles. On that day the remnants of two Panzer Divisions attacked near the River Dives, unsuccessfully, in a vain attempt to keep the gap open. On the 19th Polish and American armoured units first met at Chambois. On the 20th the gap was effectively closed. There remained a narrow road link until 22nd August, under constant heavy artillery fire from the 240 guns of the US 90th infantry on one flank, and the Canadians and British on the other. Movement had to be by night and the River Dives had to be crossed. By 22nd August even that was unusable. Some 80,000 men had been surrounded, the remnants of 14 Divisions and 2 Panzer Divisions. Of these some 10,000 were killed and 50,000 prisoners taken. Those who escaped fled along the roads of France east, disorganised and harried on the ground and in the air.

While these events were taking place, the United States armoured forces continued their fast advance to the west against minimal resistance. On 16th August the 15th US Corps took Dreux and on the 19th was on the Seine at Mantes-Gassicourt. On the 15th the 12th US Corps had taken Chateaudun and on the 17th Orleans. The 20th and 5th Corps were advancing on Paris. The Fuehrer had ordered the destruction of the city and its bridges on the Seine. General von Boineburg–Lensfeld was Commander of Paris when those orders were given. He told his staff privately that he would not carry them out. On 14th August he was relieved of his command in the aftermath of the July 20th plot, to be succeeded by General von Choltitz. The latter pursued the same approach as his predecessor, on the ground that it was too late to arrange a defence of the city. The Resistance emerged from hiding and a strange half insurrection and half truce came into being in Paris. As the 5th US Corps approached Paris, the Americans, who had a down to earth common sense view of General de Gaulle, unlike the almost romantic view held by Churchill, which led to his toleration of his activities, drew back and allowed General Le Clerc and the 2nd Free French Armoured Division to enter the city first, so that the French had the illusion that they had liberated it. General von Choltitz and his 10,000 German troops offered no resistance and at once surrendered. Paris had been saved by the traditional aristocracy in the German General staff.

On the same day the American 19th Corps reached Elboeuf on the Lower Seine against fierce resistance, as the Germany army tried to save its crossing points, while the 1st British Corps and 2nd Canadian Corps were advancing at the same time towards the lower reaches of the river. The taking of Paris with its Seine crossings meant that a defensive line along the Seine was no longer viable for the Germans, even if their fleeing armies had been able to organise it. The Allied forces continued their pursuit of the shattered armies. The objective of Overlord, to reach the Seine by D-Day plus 90, had been more than achieved by D-Day plus 79. There was to be no standstill, as the original plan envisaged and the British and Canadians were to advance north on the left and the Americans swing north-east and north on the right. The 15th German Army, with a remnant of five Divisions of the 7th Army, still remained near the coast to protect the sites of the 'miracle weapons', and it was a particular interest of the British to take that area, while maintaining the forward push north, which began after the Seine crossing, Amiens being taken and the Somme crossed by 1st September. In the inland area away from the coast, the Allied armies made rapid progress. The American 2nd Corps reached Mons on the 2nd September and had taken Verdun by the 1st.

On that day General Montgomery was superseded as commander of the Allied Ground Forces in Europe by General Eisenhower, and made a Fieldmarshal. Within four days the 2nd British Army armour, comprised of the 30th Corps and 12th Corps, had moved two hundred and fifty miles north and captured Arras, Brussels, Louvain and Antwerp. The Guards Armoured Divisions led the way into Brussels and the 11th Armoured Division into Antwerp. Even the bombastic General Patton, who had attributed the stop ordered by Bradley at Falaise as due to the jealousy of the British, was impressed. By 17th September a front line had been established from north of Bruges and Ghent, across the Albert Canal and south to Luxemburg and Nancy. The 1st Canadian Army had however a stiffer task in dislodging the 15th Army under General Gustav von Zangen, who as a Nazi was trusted by Hitler.

The first of the Fuehrer's 'miracle weapons' eulogised by Hitler at the meeting with von Rundstedt, Rommel and von Schweppenburg at Berchtesgaden at the end of June had been launched from northern France a week after D-Day. By late 1943 the threat from bombing in England had all but disappeared. The opening of the V1 campaign therefore came to people as an unwanted surprise. The *Vergeltungswaffe Ein* was a diesel powered rocket carrying a 2,300lb bomb head. It was only twenty-five feet long and had a firing radius of one hundred and fifty miles. It flew low in the sky, looked like a cigar with wings and emitted a fierce fire trail from its rear. Its engine had a characteristic thudding tone, like several Honda lawnmowers in the sky. Its passage could easily be watched and when the engine cut, by counting in a measured way the distance to its explosion could be broadly assessed. If it was near, the displacement of air sent out a loud rushing noise prior to the explosion. Its capacity for damage in built-up areas was considerable. Its directional control was imprecise and it needed a target as large as London to make much impact and even then its impacts were very scattered. Between June and September some 7,400 were launched against Britain, but only 2,300 reached London. Some 5,649 civilians were however killed and 16,194 injured.

The V2 (*Vergeltungswaffe Zwei*) was a rocket with a range of two hundred miles in the air, and had a maximum speed of three thousand five hundred miles an hour. Its targeting was difficult and imprecise. Its speed meant that its approach could not be seen and heard until its presence was made known by a double loud explosion, one after another, sounding in the clear air as one lived one's life, perhaps walking home from evensong to tea. In total 1,100 of them landed in England between 8th September 1944 and 27th March 1945, centred on London. The causalities amounted to 2,754 killed and 6,254 injured. The destruction or damage of homes by the rockets was always extensive, given that the explosions produced craters fifty feet long and ten deep.

The weapons were fired from especially constructed concrete bunkers, most centred along the coast from Dieppe in the south to Calais, although others, mainly rockets (V2) were fired further north in Holland. There was no effective defence against the V2 rockets, but techniques were developed against the V1. They could be intercepted by anti-aircraft guns, by mounting chains of barrage balloons, such as was done along the Kent and Sussex coast, and by lines nearer to London, and by fighter aircraft which developed techniques to tip their wings and send them down. By these methods the numbers getting through were reduced from 67 percent to 30 percent over the period of the attack. In addition, from 1st August, constant bombing was kept up on the launching sites. Attempts had of course been made in the war to delay or prevent the making of these weapons by the bombing of the research centre at Peenemunde, where Dr von Braun was developing his programme. When he was captured at the end of the war he was hurried away to America to apply his expertise to the American rocket and space programme.

While the Canadian drive was in part to take the Channel ports in order to improve the petrol supply system, which was becoming more difficult as the German frontier was approached, the main priority was to end the V1 and V2 attacks. General von Zangen, who took up his command on 25th August, had to plan after the crossing of the Somme how to extricate the 100,000 troops along the coast. He considered two possibilities, a powerful break-out in the north, or an evacuation by sea across the Scheldt River to Holland. On 5th September however, he was ordered by a new Commander-in-Chief West, Model having been replaced, to abandon his break-out plan. Feldmarschall von Rundstedt, called from retirement for the third time, arrived back at Headquarters West on 5th September. With his usual wisdom and skill he devised a plan, which was to hamper further Allied advance and give an opportunity to re-establish a 'Siegfried' line to protect Germany. Von Zangen was to retreat north, endeavouring to delay the Canadians, leave strong garrisons in the ports of Le Havre, Dieppe, Bologne, Calais, Dunkirk and Ostend, and then to cross the Scheldt from Brescens to Flushing. Once over he was to hold south of the river at the mouth and deploy on Walcheren and South Beveland to prevent access to the deep water port of Antwerp. By this means the allies would still have to rely on long supply lines.

The Germans at the ports were strengthened by Von Zangen, a division being sent to Dunkirk. He slowly retreated, blowing up the launching sites as he went.

General Schwable organised the shipping for the crossing of the Scheldt and in sixteen days took across 65,000 men, 225 guns, 750 trucks and 1,000 horses. Step by step the Canadians took the ports – Dieppe on 1st September, Ostend on the 9th, Le Havre on the 12th, Boulogne on the 22nd, Dunkirk on 28th and Calais on the 30th. The last to become operational was Calais on 21st October.

Operation Overlord and the consequences of it were complete, and a new phase of the invasion was to begin in order to achieve the crossing of the Rhine and the defeat of Germany. The campaign in Normandy had resulted in the Germans losing 400,000 men, of which half were killed or wounded and half captured; some 1,300 tanks, 20,000 vehicles, 2,000 guns and 3,545 aircraft had also been lost. The allies had 209,672 casualties, of which 36,976 were killed. Compared with the First World War, victory had been won at an economical cost in lives. The strategy had been evolved by Fieldmarshal Montgomery with the approval of General Eisenhower, and Montgomery was responsible for its overall execution by the British and United States ground forces. It was in reality his victory, and achieved because he pursued ruthlessly his campaign objectives, despite being undermined at SHAEF, criticised by public opinion in both America and Britain and doubted by their Governments. The success had relied on the solid virtues of the British troops, the courage, endurance and firmness of mind and action which their forebears had shown in the past. Their 'sacrificial role' against the weight of the Panzer divisions and the most fanatical troops of the German army was the enabling action which allowed the American break-out and guaranteed its success.

Undoubtedly the Americans fought bravely and with determination on Omaha and Utah beaches, in the initial stages of the break-out at St Lo and to prevent the Mortain counter-attack, but the broad sweep made across France by the US armoured and infantry columns were through softened groups of fleeing defeated men and against little resistance, the major surviving German armies having been in the north-west. It was not surprising therefore that General Patton for example, appeared to be able to make glittering progress and unduly try to claim the credit for victory in France. The hard work was done in Normandy, the victory won by the men of Bradley and Montgomery's armies, who made the early beachhead and held it against determined assault. A main contributor to the victory was the Fuehrer, Adolf Hitler. His orders to throw the Allies back to the beaches, to hold every yard to the last man, the counter-attack at Mortain and the retention of the 15th Army north of the Seine until early August brought about the destruction of his armies. Feldmarschall von Rundstedt, had he had control of the mobile arm and been allowed to evolve his own strategy, would have cost the Allies far more dear in men and weapons. After General Eisenhower became both overall and ground forces Commander on 1st September, the strategy and tactics to move forward became less focussed, and were lacking to some extent the previous clarity.

21st August 1808

The Battle of Vimiero

After the Battle of Rolica (17th August) Sir Arthur Wellesley, the victorious commander, had been unable to pursue General Junot and the French for want of cavalry. Having been told of the arrival of more British troops at the mouth of the River Maceira, he marched therefore towards the landing place and took position at Vimiero inland. Despite the fact that, in a memorandum to the Government written by him in March, he was the author of the war strategy to fight the French in the Peninsula and particularly in Portugal, he had first been given the command and then, as more troops were sent, superseded by the Duke of York and the Horse Guards, the administration of the army, who disapproved of the appointment since Wellesley was the youngest Lieutenant General and the least senior in the army. His appointment had been solely due to George Canning, the Tory Secretary of State for Foreign Affairs, who admired and recognised his military ability. The new second-in-command of the army, Sir Harry Burrard, had arrived with the troops. The reinforcements landed on 18th, 19th and 20th of August, bringing the total British force to 17,000. Wellesley tried to persuade Sir Harry to advance immediately on Lisbon while the French were disorganised and off balance. Sir Harry, believing Junot to have 30,000 troops available, refused to act until Sir John Moore arrived with further forces. He neglected to take account of the fact that Junot had left part of his force to garrison the fortresses still held and a large body (7,000) in Lisbon to prevent insurrection. Having rejected Wellesley's request, Sir Harry retired to bed and Wellesley returned to the troops.

At midnight a German dragoon arrived to see Wellesley with the message that General Junot had left Lisbon and had met up with De Laborde and Loison at Montechnique, and resolved to go on the attack. The French general had given Wellesley his opportunity. The estuary of the River Maceira was protected by a horseshoe of hills, the river passing though the ring at the village of Vimiero. Initially Wellesley drew up the army on the hills to the west of Vimiero, expecting Junot to appear on the road from Torres Vedras. At dawn there was no sign of the French and the army was told to stand down until the Sunday morning service. Before much time had gone, the dust clouds which rose to the east indicated that the French army was approaching from a different direction. Wellesley, with great care and efficiency, began the deployment of his troops onto the ridges of the hills further east, so that far from Vimiero being on the right of his position, it became the left of centre. The exercise was accomplished with great skill. The English front now occupied the lines upon which the battle was to be fought.

The village of Vimiero in the valley of the Maceira was the pivot of the position chosen by Wellesley. To the south of the village was a hill on which were stationed the troops of Anstruther and Fane, amounting to seven battalions protected by a screen of riflemen. To the left of that position on the ridge from Vimiero to the sea was Hill's brigade (3 battalions). To the north of the village and the river was the cavalry, such as it was, and Acland's brigade (3 Battalions). From the position taken up by Acland the ridge of hills extended inland to the north-west. It was protected by a ravine on its southern side with steep slopes. The first significant defile enabling access to be obtained to the ridge was two miles along it near the village of Ventosa. To the west of Ventosa was a less accessible defile up the ridge. At Ventosa, Wellesley stationed the Brigades of Nightingale, Bowes and Ferguson, amounting to seven battalions. Beyond Ventosa the ridge turned back towards the sea, and there were stationed the Portuguese troops.

General Junot's plan was to attack on his left centre up the hill at Vimiero, and at the same time outflank the British position in the east, on the British right. The steepness of the ridge and the absence of large defiles from Vimiero to Ventosa through the ravine meant that his flanking force needed to move east until a way up the ridge was found. Wellesley's position was immensely strong, but Junot thought nonetheless that it could be carried. The French army was divided; 6 battalions under Brennier and Solignac were deputed to carry out the outflanking movement, and the rest of the army moved to the attack of Vimiero and the village. The 2,000 cavalry came up to the rear of the infantry destined to attack that position.

Junot launched the initial attack on the hill, the French advancing in massed columns in their customary formation with lines of 32 men 40 deep, preceded by a screen of skirmishers. On the lower slope the riflemen from behind bushes and walls picked off the advancing troops, aiming for selected officers. The twelve guns positioned there carved lanes through their ranks and the howitzers fired shrapnel over their heads. With a confidence born of their victories against Austrians, Prussians and Russians they came on undaunted. The 97th (West Kent) Regiment of Foot was forced back as Charlot's Division moved forward but the 52nd (Oxford Light Infantry) Regiment attacked their flank with devastating fire. The 50th (West Kent) on the left of the 97th took the other flank of the French column, which under the steady fire broke and retreated. It is likely that there was intense hand-to-hand fighting as the British used their bayonets on the French, the proud colours of England flying over the field. Thomières too was sent forward to meet the same intense flanking fire and again in a confused mass the French withdrew. At eleven o'clock Junot switched to attack Vimiero village and made progress, although Acland's troops to the north of the village harried them from positions which the French could not see. To follow his first two battalions, two more were sent forward: the Grenadier reserve with twelve guns. They found Anstruther with the 43rd (Monmouthshire Light Infantry) on their left and Acland on their right with his three battalions. In fierce hand-to-hand fighting the French were pushed back. At this time Sir Harry Burrard arrived on the field but took no action to supersede Wellesley. As the French broke, Colonel Taylor and the limited cavalry contingent of Light Dragoons swept to the attack to show the enthusiasm that resulted in disaster so often through the Peninsular War, riding fast through to the French cavalry, where Colonel Taylor was killed and many of his men lost.

General Junot had intended that the main attack on the centre and the flanking attack should occur reasonably at the same time. The divisions sent to outflank the British however, lost their way and had difficulty in finding a way up the ridge. At last just after 10.30 am Solignac made the first attempt to the west of Ventosa. The British troops under Ferguson, Bowes and Nightingale could not be seen lodged on the top of the reverse slope. Once again the marching French met a withering fire and, as they mounted, with intimidating cheers and the pipes skirling, the British rose and fell upon them. Solignac was wounded and the French broke, leaving three guns. Before the 71st (Highland) Regiment of Foot and the 82nd (2nd Somersetshire) Regiment of Foot could regroup fully, Brennier with his brigade fell on the British, emerging from a defile to the east of Ventosa. The regiments were pushed back and the three guns recaptured. A ruthless battle ensued, until Brennier being wounded, the French turned and retreated.

After the assault on the village had been repulsed Junot had used his infantry fully and, had no reserves; he therefore decided to abandon the attack and began to withdraw screened by his cavalry. Sir Arthur Wellesley went up to Sir Harry Burrard, as he saw the French retreating, raised his hat and invited Sir Harry to order the advance. His answer was a no. As Wellesley left in anger, he turned to his officers and told them acidly that they might as well go off to shoot red-legged quail. Sir Harry was not without some justification, since the expeditionary force had no cavalry. It gave however an opportunity for the French to re-organise and made it inevitable that Lisbon could only be taken by a siege. The French had 2,000 men killed, wounded and taken prisoner, and 15 out of 23 cannons were taken.

Junot for his part was in a difficult situation. The situation for the French in the Peninsula was dire. After the first, easy, occupation of Spain, insurrection had spread rapidly, and the Juntas had organised armies, which with guerrillas had taken over parts of country. On 16th July General Castanos had fallen on General Dupont at Baylen and had forced the surrender of the army. 20,000 French soldiers had laid down their arms. King Joseph fled from Madrid to Vitoria and the French were backed into the northwest and Barcelona with some 60,000 troops only. In Portugal the whole country was in insurrection and a British army was on the threshold of Lisbon. Junot decided his only option was to seek an armistice and treaty. Kellerman was sent to negotiate with Sir Hew Dalrympole, the Commander in Chief, who had now arrived and was of the same view as Burrard.

The French negotiators sought terms on the basis that the French would quit Portugal if they could be conveyed to France with their arms and property. Sir Hew thought this offer satisfactory and, although he was opposed to it, Wellesley was induced to add his signature to the treaty, although he had no part in the terms. On 31st August the Convention of Cintra was signed. On 13th September the French withdrawal began and was to take some seven weeks. The news of the victory of Vimiero and the Convention of Cintra reached London on 18th September. Public joy at the victory was only equalled by anger at the Convention which the three generals had signed.

Wellesley left Lisbon for London and arrived on 4th October. Dalrympole and Burrard were recalled. Samuel Whitbread, the Radical MP, reflecting a rancour stemming from his political interest, rejoiced in the public anger and the humbling of Wellesley. Others like Captain Paget urged a loud huzza for the old British bayonet. The Government was under pressure from the House of Commons and an inquiry was set up. Wellesley conceded that, once it had been decided not to pursue Junot and the French, there was a case for the Convention. On 22nd December 1808 the inquiry approved the Convention six to one, but only by four to three in relation to its details. The particular element of criticism was the fact that 'the property' removed included all the loot-carriages, pictures, bullion and silver taken from Portugal. Sir Hew Dalrympole and Sir Harry Burrard were never to be employed again. Sir John Moore became commander of the army in the Peninsula and, following his death in January 1809, Wellesley was to return to Portugal to lead the army in April 1809.

26th August 1346

The Battle of Crecy

After the Battle of Sluys (24th June 1340), the war between King Edward III and King Philip VI of France continued without decisive outcome. Troops were sent to Brittany in 1342 to support the Duke, John de Montfort and Henry, Earl of Derby on 30th September won a battle at Morlaix. Parts of north-west France were invaded and occupied. Finally a three-year truce was signed at Morbihan, each side retaining the land won. In 1345 the war was renewed in Brittany and Aquitaine.

In Brittany Sir Thomas Dagworth was sent to rescue the province on behalf of John de Montfort, who had done fealty to King Edward III. He fought a battle at Ploermel, but John de Montfort fell sick and died, leaving a six-year-old son and his countess, who became deranged by her sufferings. In Aquitaine Henry, Earl of Derby, who was a distant cousin of the King, who became Earl and Duke of Lancaster and whose daughter Blanche married John of Gaunt, the King's third son, the father of King Henry IV, landed at Bayonne, took Bordeaux supported by four hundred men-at-arms and two thousand archers. Henry was an archetypal medieval knight. He was simple in taste, pious and courteous and had crusaded in Prussia, Cyprus and Grenada. Later he wrote a book, being for a great nobleman and warrior highly literate, *Mercy Gramercy*, asking God for forgiveness for sins done and mercy for those still to be done. His campaign was carried on during the summer and early autumn throughout the south-west of France, finally taking the town and Castle of Aiguillon. King Edward went to Flanders, but was forced to return after his ally Jacques d'Artevelde was assassinated.

The campaign season of 1346 opened with a large French army at Toulouse under the Duke of Normandy preparing to assault Aiguillon and retake the conquered provinces. Edward III at first had it in mind to raise a new army to assist the war in Guienne. He needed however his debts met and new monies for the war. A great Council was called and the nobles and commons there voted him a one-tenth levy from the demesne lands and the boroughs and one-fifteenth from the rest of the country. The notion of the King taxing only with the consent of Parliament was thus impelled forward. On this basis, and with a loan from the City of London, he began to muster an effective paid army, attracting recruits by the payment of generous wages. The bulk of the army was to be made up of longbowmen. In origin a weapon from Wales, the longbow had twice the range of the crossbow, with a more rapid rate of fire. It was light and versatile. In battle the longbowmen protected their front by iron-tipped stakes and small holes about one foot by one foot, which protected them from horsemen. The bowmen, mainly of yeoman stock, were helmeted and wore metal or strong leather chest armour. There were also light horsemen with spears, often Welsh and Irish.

A corps of 'engineers' was recruited: miners, woodworkers, builders and waggoners. Great nobles with names echoing in English history led their supporters and henchmen – Mortimer, Arundel, Beauchamp, Despenser, Hastings, de Vere, Warrenne, Sir John Chandos and Sir Robert Knollys, both the latter yeoman who rose high on the basis of military achievement. All met and camped in May and June on Southsea common. All ships over thirty tons had been requisitioned. King Edward discussed a number of objectives for this force, but publicly gave out that he was going to Gascony. He sailed on 11th July 1346, but contrary winds blowing from the Atlantic penned the fleet near the Isle of Wight. Sir Godfrey de Harcourt, a fugitive from the French king, who had sworn fealty to the king and whose brother Count Harcourt remained in France, suggested to Edward III that the English would be welcomed in Normandy and that the country would not be defended. The King accepted that advice and the fleet crossed to land on the Cotentin Peninsula near La Hogue. On 18th July the march began to Rouen. The army took supplies, looted and burnt coastal towns and villages en route, partly as a riposte to the French coastal raids. The King tried to prohibit such attacks, but towns like Barfleur in the tradition of medieval war were sacked, the gold and silver bullion taken being sent back to England.

On 25th July the English army reached Caen. King Edward summoned the town to surrender but the Bishop of Bayeux tore up his summons. The town had at that time no walls and was poorly fortified. It was held for King Philip VI of France by the Count of Eu, Constable of France, and the Count of Tancarville. They both wished to defend the city within its boundaries, but the townspeople had other views. King Edward was encamped five miles away and the fleet was at Ouistreham at the mouth of the River Orne. The town forces came out to meet him in fields beyond the town. On the morning of the battle King Edward rose early, heard mass, and led by his marshals, the Earls of Warwick and Huntingdon, the army advanced in three 'battles' on the waiting force. On their approach the waiting French fled, the fugitives being cut down by the advancing troops, and crowded into the town. The Counts of Eu and Tancarville tried to defend the Island of St Stephen between two limbs of the River Orne. The defenders of the bridges fell rapidly as the longbowmen showered them with arrows. The Counts of Eu and Tancarville in the upper tower, seeing Sir Thomas Holland, with whom they had been in East Prussia and Grenada, called out to him and asked to be taken prisoner. They and twenty-five knights were taken. Sir Thomas rode into the town with several English knights and took steps to prevent the pillage and rape of the inhabitants, including the nuns who held one of the two great abbeys of St Stephen and of Trinity.

Caen was taken on the 26th and King Edward and the army remained there three days. The fleet, with the wounded Earl of Huntingdon, prisoners comprising sixty knights and three hundred wealthy citizens and the booty taken, left Ouistreham for England. Thereafter the King had no sea base of supplies and had to find them on the march. He resolved to march on to Rouen and the north with the object of linking up with his allies in Flanders. On 6th August he reached Lisieux. On that day King Philip VI with a feudal army hastily gathered, partly including nobles and knights who had been at Aiguillon in the south, entered Rouen. The bridges on the Seine were broken down, the object being to cut off the English from the north, where the Flemings their allies were setting out from Ypres. Edward reached the Seine at Elbeof, where its width prevented crossing. He turned south-east along the southern bank towards Paris, and reached a point twelve miles from the city, shadowed on the north bank by the army of King Philip. His approach to Paris alarmed its citizens and they sought to have Philip come to the capital. Uncertain as to which course to take, he began to divide his forces and moved to St Denis. The English however at Poisy had found the remains of a bridge, a single sixty-foot beam left on the supports across the river. It was but lightly guarded. The carpenters and builders were put to work and in order to distract attention the English army attacked and sacked the suburbs of the city at St Cloud and St Germain en Laye. On the night of 15th August the English army crossed the River Seine and marched north until the 20th, hoping to find a crossing of the River Somme between Amiens and Abbeville with a view to joining the Flemings, now fifty miles away in Bethune.

King Philip VI, having found that the English were across and to the north of the Seine, collected his forces and in three days pressed on to Amiens. The marshy River Somme was a further formidable barrier and the English were isolated from the allies, now unsupported by the fleet and, the bridges being broken, without a way over the river. Food was limited; after a 300-mile walk, boots were worn out, and forage for the horses almost non-existent. King Edward slowly moved west seeking a way over, and Philip began to follow along the south bank, reaching Airaines. The situation of the English was becoming desperate. They left Airaines in the morning, abandoning the provisions, and the French King arrived at noon. His whole army not having arrived he paused there.

King Edward had the prisoners questioned about crossings beyond Abbeville to the sea, promising a reward to anyone with knowledge. A groom, Gobin Agace, told him of a ford passable at low tide at Blanchetaque. His reward was to be allowed to go free with twenty companions and a gift of one hundred nobles once the English were led to the ford. At midnight the whole camp was roused by trumpeters and the army set out with a view to crossing on the morning of the 24th at low tide. Just before dawn the van of the army reached the river. The crossing allowed ten men abreast to cross with water to their knees and the firm white gravel in the shallows could carry carts. The French had however anticipated that the ford might be attempted and had positioned on the north bank a large force of five thousand Genoese crossbowmen, and a thousand men-at-arms under Sir Godemor de Fay.

The English archers ten abreast, led by Hugh Despenser, whose tomb is to be seen in Tewkesbury Abbey, their bows held out of the water, waded into the river and across the ford; as they advanced they commenced firing and showered the waiting troops with arrows at a range beyond that of the crossbows. Once nearly across they stood aside, and mounted horsemen galloped across to harry the French. Fights took place in the shallows of the river but the archers continued to pick off the French, who with their order broken, spread out over the fields to be pursued by the English pike men. The army was free to cross, hurrying to beat the rising tide: the horses, baggage wagons and mounted men were the last to go over in the rising tide, assailed by the French arriving on the south bank. It was too late for them to cross over in pursuit: the English had just barely escaped. King Philip turned away to cross at Abbeville. The English moved north, taking Crotoy and capturing there merchant ships, whose cargo of wine was supplied to the army.

The inevitable point had come when Edward III needed to stand and fight in order to have a secure march north. The King spent 25th August looking for a suitable defensive site on the road from Abbeville and that he found on the height of a shallow valley running south-west north-east near Crecy. The low ridge faced southwest and the valley had to its north-west the wood of Crecy-Grange and on its south-westerly flank and running along the south ridge the Forest of Crecy. The position chosen by Edward III lay between Crecy and the village of Wadicourt. The French coming from Abbeville were bound to enter from the south-east, since the forest road was but a track. The whole valley could be overseen from a windmill on the ridge towards the Crecy end. Here on the plateau above the village the army encamped for the night, checking and polishing their armour and weapons.

King Philip VI that night mustered his army at Abbeville. He had sent out for support throughout all Europe and his army included men from France itself, Genoa, Luxemburg and parts of the Holy Roman Empire across Germany. There was John, King of Bohemia, who had lost his sight at Samaiten in Lithuania fighting for the Teutonic knights, Charles of Luxemburg, his son and later Holy Roman Emperor, the Duke of Lorraine, the Counts of Salm, Saarbrück, Flanders and Namur together with Sir John of Hainault. All the flower of European chivalry was there, confident of victory.

After feasting, King Edward III went to his Oratory to pray and to bed about midnight. At dawn he rose to attend early mass together with much of the army. Under his orders the Marshals put the troops into their battle positions. The English army amounted to some 13,000 men, of which over half were archers and 3,000 knights and men-at-arms. The army was divided into three battles, one commanded by the King, one by the young Prince of Wales and the Earls of Oxford and Warwick with Sir Godofroy de Harcourt, Sir Thomas Holland, Lord Morton, Lord Delaware and Sir Thomas Clifford and one by the Earls of Arundel and Northampton supported by Lord De Ross, Lord Willoughby and Lord St Aubyn. That commanded by the Prince of Wales was placed on the ridge on the right, that under the Earls of Northampton and Arundel on the left. On each flank of the two battles were stationed a body of archers projecting from the line forward. The line itself was probably from three to four ranks in depth. Behind the line the King posted the third battle, commanded by himself, as a reserve. He was to take up his own position in a windmill situated on the left centre, from which the whole valley could be seen. The knights and men-at-arms had their horses taken, to be kept in the laager of wagons to the far rear. Great nobles, knights and the ordinary swordsmen and pike men stood together on foot to wage the struggle which was to come. The archers drove into the soft earth their iron-spiked piles, and dug holes in front of them on the hill to trip the horses as they came up.

At 10 am the King, accompanied by his marshals and some of the greater nobles, rode on a small white horse along the lines, the royal standard held high and also the dragon banner of Wessex, like that used by King Harold at Hastings. He paused, as he went, to talk, calm and encourage the men and urged them all as Englishmen to play their part for God and St. George. The troops were then stood down to have a meal in the rear encampment, followed by a flagon of wine. A sharp shower brought them back to their places to unstring the bows and shelter the strings below their helmets. Then the whole army sat down to wait or relaxed.

King Philip VI and the French at Abbeville set out in pursuit of the English at sunrise. They marched for five miles before moving into battle order. In the van marched King John of Bohemia, the king's brother, the Count of Alençon and the Count of Flanders. The centre was commanded by the Duke of Lorraine and the Count of Blois, while the rear was commanded by the King himself, with Charles of Luxembourg and the exiled King of Majorca. The total numbers were said to amount to 40,000, three times the number of the English, of which 12,000 were mounted knights and men-at-arms. The most ordered contingent was that of 6,000 Genoese bowmen who marched in the van. These were recruited mercenaries; the rest of the foot soldiers were serfs summoned and ordered to march by their Lords. Initially the French took an eastern route north, although King Edward had taken the western road. After eight miles King Philip sent out a party to reconnoitre. Four knights rode forward – Lord Moyre of Bastelburg, the Lord of Noyers, the Lords of Beaujeu and Anceris. They found the English in the valley, were seen by them and returned to the King. Lord Moyre, who was attached to the King of Bohemia, with diffidence advised the King that the English awaited them refreshed and united at Crecy and that he should wait until morning before going to the attack. King Philip accepted that advice and gave orders for the army to halt. Those in the van did so, but those in the rear pressed on, anxious to be in the field to show their prowess and out of cupidity in their desire to take prisoners and ransoms. The whole army fell into confusion and was swept on; the only ordered contingent remaining the Genoese in front.

About four o'clock in the afternoon the head of the French columns came into the valley in view of the English, just as one of the passing heavy showers broke and the black scudding clouds passed over in rolling thunder. The sun then shone out, glinting on the arms and the flying coloured pennants and banners of the French. In a phalanx in the fore marched the Genoese crossbowmen and behind them a wedge of knights, their horses and themselves a multi-coloured pattern of the emblems of chivalry. They came on freshly despite their tiredness from the fifteen-mile march.

The crossbowmen stepped up to a halt, led by Odone Doria and Carlo Grimaldi, families whose names would appear again in British history with the Armada. The Genoese gave a great threatening shout and then moved forward. The English army stood unmoved. Once and once again the shout went up as they went forward, but still the English remained unmoved. Not a step was taken or an arrow shot, until the Genoese came within range of the longbows, while their volleys fell short of the mark. Then in a deluge, like the rain just fallen, the arrows were loosed time after time on the advancing Genoese. Smitten, some dropped their bows, some unstringed them and under the hail of arrows they turned and began to retreat at the run. The Count of Alençon then cried – 'This is what happens for employing such rabble: they fail us in the hour of need.' In arrogance and with the contempt for the people innate in the French elite, the knights behind did not open to let the beaten crossbowmen through, but rode them down. The French front became a formless mêlée as the knights crashed forward and began to ride uphill. Aiming for the line of standing English, they came riding hard between the archers in their protected 'stands' forward of the line and the arrows flew again, aimed at the horses and bringing the heavily armoured riders to the ground in a struggling mass of broken horses, men too heavy to rise and men pinned by the wounded beasts.

In wave on wave the horsemen came on, the archers invulnerable behind their barriers of stakes. Perhaps fifteen times they came on, adding to the carnage on the slopes. The weight of numbers told and through the heaps of wounded, dying horses and men, the French knights and men-at-arms reached the English lines and cutting, slashing hand-to-hand fighting began and spread along the line. The noble King John of Bohemia, the epitome of the idea of chivalry, of piety, duty and courage, aware of the fighting by the noise of the battle, asked that, although blind, he be taken to play his part. 'Take me', he said 'far enough forward to strike a blow with my sword.' As the request went to his honour as a knight, Sir Le Moine de Bazeilles and several others linked their bridles with that of the king and went forward to the heart of the fray. There they were found after the battle still linked together, all dead. Doubtless out of respect and admiration for the chivalry of the dead king, the three white plumes of his helmet and the motto 'Ich Dien' were taken by the Prince of Wales as a badge of honour and have been kept ever since.

The English lines on left and right were all under pressure from contingents led by the Count of Alençon and the Count of Flanders, but that of the right under the Prince of Wales and the Earls of Oxford and Warwick was being forced back and wavering. The archers on the flank began to break under the force of the young German, Savoyard and some French squires. Sir Thomas Norwich was sent to the king asking for aid but he refused, saying that the commanders, the Earls of Warwick and Oxford, should not come again unless his son was killed, but should let his son win his spurs. No aid was sent. The murderous battle went on as darkness fell; the English lines held, Sir Reginald Cobham and Sir John Chandos, who were with the Prince, distinguishing themselves. The flower of Europe's knighthood fought to the death and many were slain – the Counts of Aumale, of Alençon, of Flanders, of St Pol, of Auxenne and of Blois, the Duke of Lorraine and Count Harcourt. The latter's brother, Sir Godefroy de Harcourt, had tried to save his brother but had failed. As conflict faded, a band of Welsh and Cornish foot soldiers flooded out in the dark over the battlefield and started to kill and plunder mercilessly the wounded knights and men-at-arms, conduct which was not endorsed when it came to the knowledge of King Edward.

Late in the evening King Philip, depressed and shaken by the destruction of the nobility and knighthood of France, was led away with five knights by Sir John of Hainault. The son of King John of Bohemia, Charles of Luxemburg, seems to have slipped away from the field. The English held the field and lit their camp with fires and great torches. The soldiers gave thanks to God many times in the night. Philip retreated first to the castle at Brage and them to Abbeville.

The next morning the English awoke to a dense fog, which lay heavy across the field and heavy over the countryside. King Edward decided to send out a force of 500 men-at-arms and 2,000 archers to scout for any detached French troops. This body fell upon a contingent of 7,000, which had come from Rouen and Saint Ricquier expecting King Philip to attack that day. A fierce fight ensued and the French retreated in disorder. Another fight took place when forces led by two clergymen, the Archbishop of Rouen and the Grand Prior of France, met the scouting English. The French men-at-arms fought well, but they were dispersed and their two commanders killed.

As the fog lifted, the King sent Sir Reginald Cobham and Sir Richard Stafford to identify the fallen knights and lords by their coats of arms. At the end of the day they returned to tell the King that they had found the bodies of eleven princes and twelve hundred knights. The number of other soldiers which the searchers found was huge and probably unreliable. The King lamented the losses, particularly the death of King John of Bohemia, and on the next day the King ordered the bodies of the chief nobles to be buried in consecrated ground at Maintenay. After three days the King moved north, taking and attacking towns on the way, until he came to rest with the army outside Calais, which he began to besiege. The destruction of the French nobility and knighthood broke the morale of the King of France, and the English marched unhampered.

In the south the campaign had brought about the withdrawal of the French from Aiguillon. This allowed Henry, Earl of Derby and Lancaster, to renew his campaign. He took St Jean d'Angelys, Poitou, Lusignan and on 4th October Poitiers. When he returned to Bordeaux at the end of October, he had recovered four provinces, half of Poitou and reached Toulouse.

September

7th	The Taking of Copenhagen	1807
8th	The Taking of St Sebastian	1813
11th	The Battle of Malplaquet	1709
15th	Battle of Britain Day	1940
	(Celebrated on the nearest Sunday)	
18th	The Surrender of Québec	1759
19th	The Battle of Poitiers	1356
22nd	The Surrender of Harfleur	1415
27th	The Battle of Bussaco	1810
28th	The Battle of the Kentish Knock	1652

7th September 1807

The Taking of Copenhagen

On 14th June 1807 the Emperor Napoleon inflicted a devastating defeat on the Russians at the Battle of Friedland. The Czar, Alexander I, found himself in a situation in which there was a strong motive to make peace. The Emperors met at Tilsit on 7th July and a treaty was made which reduced Prussia to a 'rump', gave a kingdom to Napoleon's brother Jerome in west Germany, resolved on a Europe-wide embargo on British exports, and endorsed a secret clause to the effect that the Czar would coerce, with the aid of France, the northern powers in the Baltic to merge their navies under Russian command and break British sea power in the Baltic. The news of this arrangement became quickly known in London by the new Government of the Duke of Portland, of which George Canning was Foreign Secretary and Viscount Castlereagh the Secretary of State for War, both deeply committed to the overwhelming defeat of the French. The two Secretaries of State regarded it as essential to prevent the Danish fleet (of eighteen ships of the line, and frigates) from falling into the hands of the French, and resolved to act with expedition. Lord Cathcart, with a force of British and Hannoverians, had already been sent (on 16th June) to the island of Rugen, to co-operate with their Swedish and Prussian allies at Stralsund. Canning and Castlereagh realised that this object, attacking the Emperor Napoleon's communications, was rendered hopeless by Tilsit, and they decided it was far more important to divert all resources to neutering the threat of the Danish fleet. The decision was quickly made to send a mixed force of troops and ships to secure the fleet at Copenhagen.

On 26th July Admiral Sir James Gambier sailed for the Baltic with seventeen ships of the line and twenty-one frigates. On the 29th, ten days after Lord Castlereagh had issued his orders, transports with 18,000 troops were ordered to follow. Prior to their departure, a diplomat, Mr Frank Jackson, was sent to the Crown Prince of Denmark to negotiate the giving over to the British of the Danish fleet and naval stores while the threat from the French lasted. The Danes were of course in an impossible position, because Marshal Bernadotte with an army of 70,000 Frenchmen was in north-west Germany near Hamburg. The Crown Prince refused and Jackson returned to London.

On 31st July the fleet anchored off the Skaw near Elsinore and four ships of the line and more frigates were sent under Commodore Keats through the Great Belt to control the Baltic sea access. On 8th August the transports from Yarmouth arrived to join the fleet, and on the 12th the army brought off from Rugen under Lord Cathcart. On the same day the French Ambassador to Denmark, Monsieur Didelot, arrived in Hamburg to report that he had seen the British fleet. The message was forwarded to Paris, evoking anger from the Emperor Napoleon that he had been forestalled. On 16th August the troops disembarked under Sir Arthur Wellesley at Vedbock. The Danish troops on the island of Zealand were poor levies, the Danish main army being in Holstein. They were soon routed at Koge on 29th August and Copenhagen was besieged. It took until 2nd September for the engineers to prepare battery positions for the siege. Lord Cathcart and his easy-going second-in-command Sir Harry Burrard hoped that the Danish Governor of the city would in that period surrender, as requested, the fleet and naval stores.

The city had since the success of Nelson (2nd April 1801) reinforced the defences. The Trekroner battery now comprised 68 guns and mortars, the Citadel 20 guns and mortars and at the Arsenal 50 guns and 12 mortars. The mode of attack used by Nelson would have been one of great risk. The city needed to be reduced. The Danes were invited to send women and children out of the city. On 2nd September the bombardment began, the army hurling red-hot shot and Congreve's rockets into the city from land and the navy cannonading from mortar vessels and ketches on the sea. For three days the city was bombarded, the night skies being lit up by the onslaught. For those three days the Danes heroically endured, but on the morning of 7th September the Governor General Peiman surrendered. The fleet fell to the British, the object of the expedition secured. Some fifteen Danish ships of the line were removed and thirty smaller frigates and sloops. The naval stores taken, it is said, filled ninety-two transports. Having achieved their object the British re-embarked and the army returned to England, the fleet bringing their prizes.

On their return Sir James Gambier was made a Baron and Lord Cathcart a peer of the United Kingdom. The preventive strike so successfully made by Canning and Castlereagh against a neutral nation was subject to loud criticism by the opposition in Parliament as flagrantly immoral and an abuse of power, but the character of the arguments for and against the action were sufficiently embodied in a comment from Cobden, that the ministry might be impeached for making war or equally impeached for not doing so. On the basis of Samuel Pepys' approach, that the main point is to keep the sea, the taking of the Danish fleet had ample justification.

The 6th Earl of Cathcart was ejected from the House of Lords in 2001.

8th September 1818

The Taking of San Sebastian

After the Battle of Vitoria (21st June 1813), the French retired from north-west Spain, apart from the fortresses of San Sebastian and Pamplona. The Duke of Wellington had only a limited amount of siege equipment, and he therefore decided that priority in its use should be the taking of San Sebastian, in order to acquire its harbour. The army stood on the frontier of France, with its left wing on the Bidassoa River at Irun under Sir Thomas Graham. It was his division (the 5th, comprising the 1st or the Royal Scots Regiment of Foot, the 9th (East Norfolk Regiment of Foot) and the 38th (1st Staffordshire Regiment of Foot)), with Bradford's Portuguese, who were given the task of taking the town.

The defensive position occupied by San Sebastian was formidable. The town lay on an isthmus between the shell-shaped harbour and the estuary of the River Vranca. The northern tip of the isthmus comprised Monta Urgell on which, above the town, was the Castle of La Mota. The bay was shielded by the Isla de Santa Clara to the west of Mont Urgell and linked to it by a reef. On the riverside to the east the waters of the estuary lapped the walls at all times save low tide. On the isthmus the southern side of the town was defended by a castellated wall – the hornwork, and the Cask Redoubt on the harbour side of the isthmus. On the east was the convent of Santa Catolina and at the landward end of the isthmus the convent of San Bartolemé, on the heights of Ayote. The town was garrisoned by 3,000 men under General Rey, with 60 guns. Rey was a seasoned campaigner, a soldier before the Revolution, and was made a Baron of the Empire by Napoleon in 1808. He was determined and intelligent.

Sir Thomas Graham arrived before the town on 9th July. The first need was to take the convent of San Bartolemé. That had been taken by the Spanish in June, but they had been driven out and the convent armed with guns and the walls loopholed. Placing batteries to bombard the town, whether on the isthmus or across the river, involved planting them on the sand hills, and the task of digging the standings and moving the guns was slow and tedious. As one engineer remarked, it was necessary to cry 'Viva' twenty times to move artillery an inch. On 14th July the bombardment of the convent began. An assault was made on 15th July, but driven off with some losses. The bombardment was intensified and on the 17th a new attack was made and entry to the convent was effected. The French retreated through the small village of San Martin back to the hornwork, and on the 19th abandoned the Cask Redoubt. From San Martin the engineers began to send out, despite the heavy rain, a mine towards the fortifications. They came upon a great sewer and were able to plant a large mine under the hornwork. The bombardment went on.

It had been decided by Wellington and Graham that an assault along the isthmus itself was impracticable, but the acquisition of the convent and San Martin gave them access to the west bank of the river and the ability at low tide to advance along the river to the east wall. Against the background of Marshal Soult reforming the French on the Bidassoa and the mountain passes of the western Pyrenees, Wellington urged Graham to launch an early attack.

By 24th July the barrage of shot, carried on continuously, had created a break in the eastern wall. The assault was timed for that day early in the morning but, fire breaking out in houses near the breach, the attack was postponed. It was to take place at dawn the next day. At 5 am the mine under the western end of the hornwork was exploded as the signal for the storming force to move.

Led by the 1st or Royal Regiment of Foot, later the Royal Scots, a 300-yard rush along the beach to the breach was made, the troops slipping and sliding on the seaweed and rocks, and the head of the force clambered up the breach. Under fire from the walls, undaunted they arrived at the top to find an impossible situation. The street was still twenty-two feet from the top of the breach and Rey had had the street and ramparts blocked by walls, from which French marksmen poured a withering fire, while on the flanks the troops were pulverised from the damaged bastions each side of breach. The Royal Scots, however, suffering huge casualties, hung on for half an hour before they were beaten back. 100 were killed and 300 wounded. So heavy was the loss, and with the troops falling back, Graham called off the assault. Wounded were left at the foot of the breach and as the river rose Rey and the French rescued as many as they could from the rising water.

Wellington, on hearing the news at his headquarters at Lesaca, rode over to consult Graham and urge a new attempt. On his return six hours later he was told that Marshal Soult was now attacking on his right wing in the passes. Other needs had arisen, and Graham was ordered to discontinue the siege, protect the siege equipment, and watch for any crossing of the Bidossoa by the French rear Irun. A battle was fought by Wellington against Soult at Sorauren and the French defeated. Graham had transferred his siege guns to the fleet, and they were not restored to him until 6th August. On the 18th troops, ammunition and artillery arrived from England. Between the 6th and 24th the artillery was repositioned. Graham now had twenty 24-pounders, four 8-inch howitzers, four 10-inch mortars and four 68-pound cannons. Each day each gun fired three hundred rounds from daybreak to sunset.

General Rey had used the time between 25th July and the end of August to repair damage done, fortify his walls and strong points, bring in supplies and ammunition by boat and send out the wounded. Although Graham had been ordered to blockade the town by Wellington, part of that task involved the navy. At no time was the naval blockade effective, however, and Wellington had a correspondence of some asperity with the Secretary to the Board about the navy's failure. He seemed however to take no account of the obvious difficulties in poor weather of a blockade by sailing vessels along the northern Spanish coast in the Bay of Biscay, where there could be sea mists, the winds were generally to some extent onshore, making the coast a leeward shore; and the high cliffs and hills, backed by mountains as at San Sebastian, gave rise to the reinforcement of the speed of winds, and to gales known as the 'Galern', if the winds arose from depressions and were north-westerly. The war effort being made by the Navy was also extended beyond Europe to the war with the United States of America from June 1812 to June 1815, in which Americans warships were active off the Biscay coast.

On 26th August the bombardment began again: it went on for five days until the guns in the city were silenced. At the end of the days of firing there was a 300-yard break in the eastern wall and a smaller one further north in it. The hornwork was subject to fire from the Isla de Santa Clara. Wellington and Graham planned the new assault for 31st August. Wellington's annoyance at the failure in July had resulted in a peevishness with the 5th Division, although Graham had written to the Horse guards of 'the distinguished gallantry of the troops employed' and of how perseverance would have resulted in a useless sacrifice of life. Wellington therefore sought volunteers 'to show the 5th how to assault the city' from other divisions and regiments. 150 came from the Light Division, the 52nd (Oxfordshire Light Infantry) Regiment, 200 from the Guards, 100 from the King's German Legion and 100 from the Light Division of the Legion. These volunteers did not however take the lead in the assault, which fell to General Leith and the 5th Division, backed up by the volunteers.

General Rey, again anticipating the assault at the breach, had reinforced his walls and built up his defences, mounting on them his soldiers so that they could subject the breach to intense fire. Small mines had been planted at the breach and a large one in the breach itself.

Wellington and Graham were again to duplicate the tactics of the earlier attempt, principally because there was no more effective option. On the morning of 31st August low tide was at 11 am. The men drank a glass of wine each, raised a toast to health and success, and at 10.55 am, in an almost tropical heat, set out from San Martin along the western shore. Colonel Tomkinson, the diarist and an officer in the 16th (the Queen's) Regiment of (Light) Dragoons, went with others to view the attack in the village. From the moment that the Royal Scots and the volunteers began to move along the beach, they and St Martin were peppered with musketry fire from the hornwork and the walls. Bullets flew into the huts where Tomkinson stood, smashing the mud walls and plaster. He could see men falling on the beach as they went. The dum-dum-dum of the French drums could be heard from the town. General Leith accompanied the regiment. Under fire they reached the breach, the two small mines laid on the way exploding to no effect. The 1st stormed up the breach to find once more a strongly fortified inner curtain beyond the breach from which a withering fire came. The men valiantly strove to hold on the rampart, the volunteers backing the men of the 5th Division, but casualties were great, General Leith being wounded. After half an hour on the top the Royal Scots retreated to reform below the breach. The great mine set in the breach failed to explode.

Sir Thomas Graham, seeing the Royal Scots repulsed as in July, took a courageous and unprecedented decision. He ordered his guns to fire above the sheltering troops at the French on the top of the fortifications. The defenders were subject to a massive cannonade, shot after shot reaching the positions where they were arrayed. Among the British crouched below there was at first incomprehension, and a cry arose to come away, as our batteries had opened on us. The troops were steadied, and once more the attempt on the breach was made. Under Colonel Greville new troops aided the storming from the 38th Staffordshire Regiment. The Portuguese on the far right could be seen wading across the river in three feet of water in a courageous attempt on the lesser breach. The second assault, after the cannonade, cleared the south rampart and the British fought towards the southern defences. As they went, a terrible explosion shook the city; red-hot shot had ignited combustibles left by the French. They began to leap from the curtain walls and abandoned the hornwork. The breach was taken and the troops began to fight their way into the town. As they went, a violent storm filled the air with rolls of thunder and lightening. The 5th fought its way along the rampart to the lesser breach and the men of Bradford's brigade, the 7th Royal Fusiliers, the 23rd Royal Welsh Fusiliers and the 48th Northamptonshire Regiment, joined the 5th in the town.

General Rey defended the town house by house and street by street, and ultimately was forced back until with 1,300 men he retreated up Monta Urgell to the Castle of La Mota. The captured city blazed as fire took hold from abandoned powder casks, and the victorious troops, out of hand, began to drink and loot the churches, houses and shops. Sir Thomas Graham had before the siege commended General Rey to evacuate the women and children, and few remained. For three days San Sebastian was given over to an orgy of drinking, plundering and atrocity. There were so many officers lost in the attack that the army was difficult to control, and the resistance made by the town with the consequent loss of life had inflamed the men, as had the collaboration of the city's inhabitants in helping with erecting the inner curtains and walls around the breaches. In the breaches the tally of loss could be seen – scarred and disfigured faces, torn stomachs, limbless men, torn severed arms, killed and wounded, all entangled in grotesque heaps. The cost of the taking of the town was great. Tomkinson records 500 were killed and 1,500 wounded in the breach, without casualties elsewhere. By 4th September fire had consumed the whole town.

The same day that the city was stormed, Marshal Soult made an attempt to relieve San Sebastian. Seven divisions (45,000 men) were sent across the Bidassoa

River in the early morning mist. In the night General Reille with three divisions attacked the Spanish positioned on the heights at San Marcial, but was successfully repulsed. General Friere had posted his men on the heights and at his second attack the French fled. On the left were three divisions under General Clausel, and they gained ground. The failure on the right led to their recall, but before a retirement could be put into effect a great storm caused the Bidassoa to rise. Four brigades were left and General Vandermaesen decided to force the bridge at Vera, guarded by only two companies of the 9th (Derbyshire Regiment of Foot). These were defeated after suffering 61 casualties out of 100 men, in a stiff resistance in which General Vandermaesen was killed. The isolated companies had sent to General Skerret for help but he refused to give it, being sent on 'sick leave' afterwards, not to return. The French lost 500 at the bridge.

On 2nd September, with the army once more under control, the attack on the Castle began. For five days the heavy siege guns, some 60 guns in all, fired at the Castle, day in day out. At last an attack was begun with a morning bombardment of 33 guns, but at noon General Rey raised a white flag to request a truce. His original force was reduced to 80 officers and 1,756 men, of whom about a third were wounded. Sir Thomas Graham arranged a surrender and General Rey marched out with the honours of war. San Sebastian had been taken.

Sir Thomas Graham had warned Wellington that he intended to retire because of eye trouble, and in October he returned home. He commanded one more campaign in the Low Countries, but then finally retired. He was made a peer as Lord Lynedoch and lived until the age of ninety-five in 1842. He occupied his time hunting, exhibiting an almost youthful vigour and courage, with the Midland packs from Cosgrove in Northamptonshire, and in travelling. He detested trains and preferred to travel by coach. In Russia, like the Baroness Staël, society hostess in Paris and novelist, he complained of the incessant bed bugs in the inns and at Kiev slept nights in his own carriage. When he could no longer hunt, he started to race on the flat, and his very last note before he died was to direct that his horses were to be sold at Tattershalls.

Colonel Tomkinson, the diarist, who had seen the taking of San Sebastian, returned to England in October 1813 and took with him his cavalry charger, 'Bob'. Bob had carried him for five campaigns and was out of England for four and half years, but on arriving home knew his way back to the stable at Dorfold unhesitatingly. Bob carried Colonel Tomkinson for many years with his own pack of harriers.

NOTE: Bed-bugs still infested the Hotel Astoria in St Petersburg in 1961.

11th September 1709

The Battle of Malplaquet

The winter of 1709 was one of devastating cold. In France in particular the population were reduced by famine; the economy, due to the cost of all the campaigns in the War of the Spanish Succession, had reached a dire condition. King Louis XIV, following the disastrous campaign of 1708 (see the Battle of Oudenarde 11th July 1708), came to the conclusion that he should seek a peace with his opponents. The Duke of Marlborough and Prince Eugene of Savoy acted initially as go-betweens, but the matter was taken out of their hands and the Whig Government in London and the Emperor demanded of France rigorous terms for peace, amounting to forty-one in all. Louis XIV was prepared to accept most of the terms, but baulked at that which required the French armies within two months of the treaty to escort his grandson, Philip V, out of Spain. He refused, he said, to make war on his family and on 2nd June at Versailles refused the terms offered. He had begun already to rebuild his army with the help of the French people, who were asked to give the king their bullion in order to finance the cost. Even the King disposed of his gold plate, replacing it with silver-gilt. Spanish bankers also came to his rescue, and by June a new army had been rebuilt. The troops were of course less seasoned and experienced than those lost in the great battles of preceding years. The new army was put into the hands of Marshal the Duc de Villars with Marshal the Duc de Bouffleurs as second-in-command.

The Duke of Marlborough and Prince Eugene of Savoy were both less than enthusiastic to renew the war, but stood in the Low Countries at the head of an army concentrated near Lille of 120,000. Of the 197 squadrons of cavalry and the 129 nine battalions of infantry, only 14 squadrons of cavalry and 20 battalions of infantry were British. Prince Eugene for his part had 123 squadrons of cavalry and 66 six battalions of infantry. The Imperial and Allied army represented, apart from the British, the whole coalition led by the Emperor, Hannoverians, Prussians, Danes, Dutch, troops from many smaller Germans states, together with the Imperial troops themselves.

Marshal Villars, who had fought successfully at Friedlingen (1702), Höchstadt (1703) and Stollhaufen (1707), spent the early summer building a line of barricades to prevent the Allied army from entering France. The northern border was protected by a belt of forests so that any attack needed to penetrate through them on established routes and required the taking of bridges over rivers on the way. Marlborough and Prince Eugene decided that the line should not be attacked and so moved, after a feint towards the frontier, to besiege Toumai on 23rd June. The town had been taken by the French in 1697 and had been fortified by the great French fortress-builder, Vauban. The besiegers faced great fortifications protected by ground and land so waterlogged that they had to wade up to their thighs in mud and water. Mines were dug to be met by countermines. No assault was made and Marshal Villars did not attack. On 30th July, after a bombardment begun on 11th July, the town surrendered and the French commander, the Marquis de Serville retired to the citadel with his garrison. Marshal Villars collected troops, even from the Rhine, in order to advance to relieve Tournai, but the citadel surrendered on 3rd September. The Duke of Marlborough found there a large bust of King Louis XIV, which was taken back to his new house, then being built at Blenheim, where it remains. The Duke and Prince Eugene now decided to march on Mons and besiege it. Marshal Villars, with 9,500 men, moved forward quickly and established himself on a site south of the town at Malplaquet, near to the besiegers. King Louis XIV had approved his fighting a battle and the Marshal was all too ready for a fight.

Marlborough and Eugene were slow to react. Not all the Allied troops had arrived; they were only half-convinced of the need to fight, and were accompanied by the Dutch representatives, who were always difficult. On 9th September, however, they rode over to Malplaquet to inspect the site where the French were encamped. There they found the French engaged in defensive works.

The position chosen by Marshal Villars was a strong one. It occupied a gap in the forest chain on the road leading south-west from Mons known as the Trou d'Aulrois. On the west lay the large wood of Taisnières and on the east the wood of Lanieres. In between the two woods lay the Bois de Tiry, which separated the gap into two branches. The French left occupied the eastern rim of the wood of Taisnières and from there to the wood of Lanières used the timber of the woods to close the gap with wood and earth palisades, through which the only openings were those left through which the cavalry stationed in the rear could charge out forward to the field. The village of Malplaquet lay in the gap to the south of the French lines near the wood of Lanières. Two villages lay to the west of the position: La Louverie and La Folie. Marshal Villars commanded from the left centre and Marshal Bouffleurs the French right.

For two days the works felling timber and the building of the barricades proceeded with desultory bombardments while the Duke of Marlborough and Prince Eugene waited for the army to assemble. General Withers, with 19 battalions of infantry, four of which were British, had not arrived when the battle began on the morning of 11th September. He was still moving west towards the battle site. Although the attack on the entrenched French was similar to an attempt to storm an escarpment, Marlborough and Eugene had nonetheless decided to attack. Prince Eugene commanded the right with the Imperial troops under Schulenburg, the Prussians under General Lottum, the Hannoverians and one British Brigade under the Duke of Argyle. Lord Orkney was in the right centre where the British were placed, and the Dutch with the Prince of Orange on the left. Like the French had done, the cavalry was held at the rear. The assembly of the Allied army began at 3 am after prayers were said. After a bombardment for two hours, the attack began at 9 am. The plan was to launch the right wing on the French left at Taisnières wood and feint on the left where the Prince of Orange stood with his Dutchmen. Once progress had been made the centre, where the British battalions were mainly stationed, was to move forward.

The initial attack came from the Allied right, where the Imperial troops under Prince Eugene and the Prussians attacked into the Taisnières wood and tried to force its entrenchments. The advancing Prussians were struck in the flank by withering fire and the troops became embroiled in a savage struggle in the wood, including the Scots brigade under the Duke of Argyle. The losses were appalling. Prince Eugene vigorously called up the second and third lines to attack.

Meanwhile, half an hour after Prince Eugene had begun his assault, the Prince of Orange launched the Dutch against the entrenchment by the Lanières wood on the Allied left flank. They were enfiladed by twenty guns, but persevered and reached the French lines, but were too weak to attack. They and the Scots with them fell back. The Prince of Orange made his dispositions for a second attack despite heavy losses.

Prince Eugene's second attack on the Allied right was assisted by Lord Orkney's command, sending in the 1st Royal Regiment of Foot (later the Royal Scots) and the Guards, the Grenadiers and the Coldstreams. Crossing boggy ground, they joined the fierce struggle in the trees of the Taisnières wood, where yard by yard the presence of the allied force began to take effect. General Withers with his battalions began to near the field on the French flank as the fight went on.

On the left, the Prince of Orange made a second attempt to storm the Lanières wood position, but again was swept back. He planned a third try, but the Duke and Prince Eugene, who had ridden over to the flank, forbade it.

The approach of General Withers led to Prince Eugene deciding to send the Imperial Cavalry round the wood to outflank the French and that, together with the slow advance of the Allied force through the wood, led Marshal Villars to take infantry from the centre to reinforce the right flank of his forces. The Royal French Irish regiment was sent in, and where it met the 18th, the Royal Regiment of Ireland, later the Royal Irish, fighting of great ferocity and savagery took place. The French continued to mass infantry on their left by the wood. By now it was mid-day. The standing masses were exposed to the fire of the Imperial artillery now coming up. Marshal Villars, moving with his staff from the centre, was wounded by a cannonade, smashing his leg, and had to leave the field. Marshal Boufflers took command.

The Duke of Marlborough had reached the point when the centre could be launched and Lord Orkney moved forward with 13 battalions, only to find the entrenchments in part emptied. As the infantry stormed on, Marshal Boufflers launched the French cavalry. British cavalry, including the 2nd Dragoons (Scots Greys), joined by some 20 Dutch squadrons under the Prince of Hesse-Kassel, went on through the gaps and clashed with the French. The battle swayed to and fro, the French driving the Allies back to the gaps, where infantry fired devastatingly into the French cavalry. Marshal Boufflers drew off to level ground and the full forces of cavalry met in the greatest cavalry action of the eighteen-century.

On the left the Allied forces made progress out of the Taisnières woods, and General Withers took the French on the flank, coming from La Folie. The intense cavalry struggle began to go against the French and a third attempt by the Prince of Orange to storm the French right succeeded with the aid of three regiments of Danish Cavalry. Marshal Boufflers decided to order the retreat, and the French army disentangled itself from the combat and retired in good order. At 3 pm the battle was won, but the victors had no strength to pursue their opponents.

The battle had been the most murderous fought by the Duke. The allied losses were 18,000 to a French loss of 11,000. The Dutch were the worst sufferers, losing 43% of their troops. The British loss was 500 dead and 1,200 wounded. The Duke rode over the field and finding so many French dead in the wood of Taisnières, he sent to Marshal Boufflers to send carts to carry them away. The degree of loss was such that all Europe was shaken by the intensity of this battle. Far from bringing peace as Marlborough hoped, the relative success of the French stand strengthened their morale, and Louis XIV was to fight on. There were some who thought the battle need not have been fought. The Duke of Argyle hurried back to London and, attended by his company of swordsmen, campaigned against Marlborough in the public coffee houses and assemblies. It was the last battle which the Duke and Prince Eugene were to fight together. Later in the year they were to take Mons, but in 1710 the Whigs fell from power and the Tories took a majority in Parliament. The Duke was called home, no longer to command the armies in the Low Countries. While the war went on, it became solely one of sieges of the frontier fortresses and towns in a devastated countryside.

The Regiments which fought and won the battles for the Duke were largely the same in all his battles. General MacMunn in his book on Prince Eugene gives a list.

Cavalry

The 1st (later the Blues)
3rd (4th Regiment of House, the Prince of Wales Dragoon Guards)
5th (later 6th or 7th Regiment of Horse)
6th (The Carabineers)
7th (The Princess Royal's Dragoon Guards)

2nd Dragoons (Royal Regiment of Scots Dragoons – Scots Greys)
5th Dragoons (Royal Irish Dragoons).

Infantry

The Grenadier Guards
The Coldstream Guards
1st Royal Regiment of Foot (Royal Scots)
3rd Prince George of Denmark's Regiment (the Buffs)
5th Regiment of Foot
10th (later Lincolnshire Regiment)
15th (later East Yorkshire Regiment)
16th (later Bedfordshire Regiment)
18th Royal Regiment of Ireland (Royal Irish)
19th Yorkshire Regiment of Foot (later the Prince of Wales Own)
21st Scots Fusiliers Regiment of Foot
23rd (later Royal Welsh Fusiliers)
24th (later South Wales Borderers)
26th The Cameronians (later Scottish Rifles)
47th (later The Hampshire Regiment)

(In all cases when no contemporary name is given the regiment carried the Colonel's own name.)

In the second part of the twentieth century these regiments have lost their identities in larger formations, and with it in some part the history, tradition and local associations which gave to the regiments their special character.

15th September 1940

The Battle of Britain

Writing in relation to Armistice Day in 1937, Winston Churchill made the telling point that that day had brought no peace in the real sense, but reflecting its name, was a mere armistice between the powers. Unlike the Treaty of Vienna in 1815, the Treaty of Versailles of 1919 was turned into one of revenge and vindictiveness. President Wilson had formulated 14 points for the making of peace in 1917, which rested on mutual respect between nations and a proper justice. The Armistice accepted by the German Government in November 1918 was on the basis of these points. It was the Prime Minister of France, Clemenceau, who led the peace conference down the road to revenge, consistent with his delight at the telegram seeking an armistice, 'Il est arrivé, le jour de la revanche.' Instead of a just settlement, which the British Prime Minister Lloyd George endeavoured to support, conditions were placed on Germany which a sovereign country could scarcely be expected to accept. Territory was taken, the navy removed, disarmament forced to a level scarcely able to protect the country, reparations sought by France of an excessive order, and occupation of German territory in the Rhineland to guarantee payment of the sums imposed.

This settlement, aimed at the deliberate weakening of Germany, was bolstered by a series of Treaties with East European states, returning to France the hegemony of Europe which its politicians persistently seek. On this occasion the British unhappily acquiesced. The German representatives at Versailles were not consulted, but were offered a diktat which they were ordered to sign. It is not surprising therefore that the peace of the 1920s and 30s was, as Churchill thought it, unreal, even though the British electorate indulged in the illusion that they were secure. It was not surprising also that with economic collapse in 1930, Germany, with her wounded pride, battered economy and mass unemployment turned to the seeming redeemer, Adolf Hitler, who began to rebuild the country on the basis of Keynesian programmes of public works, rearmament of the army and navy and creation of an air force. A major aim was the revision of the Treaty of Versailles settlement.

Winston Churchill, with a few supporters, saw early and with clarity the need to rearm and restore to proper levels the Royal Navy and the Royal Air Force. For the period from 1924 to 1937 two politicians, Ramsay Macdonald and Stanley Baldwin, alternated as Prime Minister and both had the ability to leave the country quiescent and undisturbed in the false sense of security and peace which had fallen on the British people. However in 1935, with the rising tide of German rearmament, even they were lulled from their apathy and a policy of rearmament began, albeit badly forced forward and belatedly. Churchill constantly urged the need for air parity with Germany, and criticised the slowness of the re-equipment of the Royal Air Force. To that there was a half-hearted response, and the programme to rearm the air force constantly lagged behind predictions. Baldwin had promised for example 124 squadrons for the home defence force by 31st March 1937, but by 10th November 1936, as Churchill pointed out in Parliament, only 81 had been provided.

The British Government, conscious of the injustice of the Treaty of Versailles, also pursued a policy parallel to slow rearmament, of trying to come to terms with the German Government in a peaceful revision of the treaty, and in this context stood by when Hitler occupied the Rhineland in breach of the treaty. The foundations had however been laid to secure the means of defence which preserved Britain in 1940. On 26th February 1935 the Radar system of detection of aircraft developed by Sir Robert Watson-Watt was tested at Weedon and was demonstrated as workable. The first station was built in May 1935 and a chain around the coast was rising in 1937. By March 1939 there were 39 stations with 24-hour surveillance. Aircraft could be identified as they crossed the coast and the information as to their course, height and numbers went in forty seconds to Fighter Command Headquarters at Stanmore. From there instructions could be given to Groups and Sector Stations at aerodromes serving the group as to the action to be taken. This formed the basis of getting the fighter squadrons airborne in order to intercept the enemy. It was aided on land by a large ground corps of Observers.

The Hawker Hurricane fighter was tested and first flew in November 1935, but out of 1,000 ordered the first only appeared for No 111 Squadron in January 1938. The Hurricane was a heavier wood and fabric monoplane, not so fast as the Spitfire and not effective over 23,000 feet, but its efficiency was to be proved in 1940, for eighty per cent of the 'kills' of German aircraft were due to this plane. The faster Spitfire had a test flight on 5 March 1936 and 450 were ordered. It had eight machine guns, climbed at 2,530 feet in a minute with a maximum speed at 19,000 feet of 355 miles per hour. It was, said the air ace Pilot Officer Tuck, 'thirty feet of wicked beauty.' It was August 1938 before No. 19 Squadron traded in their planes for the first ones delivered. The bulk of the increasing air force in 1938 remained aircraft of older types, while Germany's air force was of planes no more than three years old.

In the summer of 1938 came the Sudetenland crisis, when Adolf Hitler began to threaten Czechoslovakia, unless the German borderlands were returned to the Reich. France was bound by treaty obligation to go to the aid of the Czechs should they be attacked, but had no enthusiasm for their treaty commitment. Britain prepared for war, but Chamberlain, thinking that the matter could be dealt with by negotiation and that a general settlement could be made, for like William Pitt the younger in 1792, he was reluctant to launch a war before all attempts for peace were tried, flew to Germany and the Munich Treaty resulted, giving German the Sudetenland borders of Czechoslovakia, an area which contained all its defences. On 5th October 1938, heckled by Nancy, Viscountess Astor, the first woman Member of Parliament, Winston Churchill denounced the settlement as a defeat stemming from the neglect of our defence. Only the security of airpower, he thundered, could regain our island independence. In hindsight it was improbable that Neville Chamberlain, advised on the defence inadequacies, could take any other practical course than he did. Sir Hugh Dowding, Commander of Fighter Command in 1940, was on record as saying that it was a good thing Chamberlain acted as he did. The RAF were just not ready. In March 1939 the Germans entered Czechoslovakia and the Czech state ceased to exist. Chamberlain, now conscious that no settlement had been reached at Munich, gave a pledge to Poland to come to their assistance if their independence was clearly threatened. As Lord Halifax pointed out in the House of Lords on 19 April 1939, the guarantee was founded 'on the principle that the rights of smaller states shall not be set aside by the stronger, that force shall not be the deciding factor in the relation between peoples, and that negotiations should not be overshadowed or overborne by constraint.'

The 1939 war came about over the desire of the German Government to revise the Versailles Treaty over the status of Danzig, a wholly German city, placed in a Polish corridor to the Baltic and under international control. Adolf Hitler wanted its return to Germany and the British Government had not been adverse to that revision, but their guarantee and treaty with the Poles in August 1939 gave rise to irreconcilable difficulty. Neither Hitler nor Britain desired war with the other, but both moved forward to war, having discussions in which there was no meeting of the minds. Adolf Hitler's conduct over Czechoslovakia meant that Chamberlain no longer trusted his word and the events of *Krystallnacht* in November 1938 had for the whole world clearly revealed the inhumane nature of the German Government. The failure of discussion was occasioned too by the total resistance of the Poles over Danzig, which Chamberlain had not entirely expected. Hitler, assessing that Britain would not fight, based on Munich and advice from von Ribbentrop, his Foreign Secretary, and armed by a treaty with the Soviet Union, invaded Poland on 31st August 1939. On 3rd September 1939 Mr Chamberlain declared war in accordance with his guarantee and treaty with Poland, and France reluctantly followed.

At the end of the war in 1918 Britain had built up an air force of 184 squadrons, which was reduced to 18 by 1920. During the inter-war period there was no systematic attempt to rebuild the air force until the late thirties. By April 1940 the Royal Air Force had only 2,279 aircraft, of which 638 were fighters. Squadrons of Hurricanes were sent to France with the British Expeditionary Force and fought there during the advance of the Germans to the Channel in May 1940. As the German Panzers advanced, the squadrons were disrupted and disorganised and severe losses occurred; for example 607 Squadron lost 26 pilots, and 204 squadron, a Canadian force, lost every pilot in May and June. At Dunkirk, while the RAF flew 3,000 sorties, 106 planes were lost. On 1st June only 238 fighters were serviceable. Churchill, dissatisfied with the rate of aircraft production when he came to power, charged Lord Beaverbrook in May 1940 with the task of producing more planes quickly, particularly fighters. Beaverbrook's campaign was strikingly successful. From May to August 1,975 fighters were built and 1,872 were repaired. After Dunkirk, as France collapsed under the defeatism of General Weygand and Marshal Petain, the sending of ten squadrons of Hurricanes to France was only just prevented and they were therefore still available, when the French Government sought an Armistice on 18th June with Germany and, instead of fighting on like the Governments of smaller countries such as Holland and Norway overseas, they deserted the Allied cause. A small minority only fought on, joining the Free French in London under General De Gaulle.

At the beginning of July Britain had about 600 fighters. Britain had on paper up to 29 divisions of troops in England, but only about six were of fighting value, since the equipment, tanks, guns and howitzers had been abandoned in France. Out of 200 destroyers only 70 were out of repair in the docks. Morale however was sustained by the echoing oratory of Winston Churchill, who on 4th June had pronounced that 'we shall go on to the end, we shall fight in France, we shall fight on the seas and oceans, we shall fight with growing confidence and growing strength in the air, we shall defend out island, whatever the cost may be, we shall fight on the beaches, we shall fight on the landing grounds, we shall fight in the fields and in the street, we shall fight in the hills: we shall never surrender and even if, which I do not for a moment believe, this island or a large part of it were subjugated and starving, then our Empire beyond the seas, armed and guarded by the British Fleet, would carry on the struggle until, in God's good time, the new world with all its power and might, steps forth to the rescue and the liberation of the old.' Those alive thanked themselves that we were not as the French and had a certain joy in the idea we were now alone.

The end of June brought a pause. Both the British and the Germans needed to re-organise and review their position. Desultory air engagements took place in the Channel, progressively reducing the ability of ships to pass through the Straits of Dover. The Germans sited long-range guns capable of hitting Dover, and howitzers to bombard the Channel, from Cap Gris Nez. No thought had been given by the Germans in terms of hard detailed planning for an invasion of England before July 1940, although Grand Admiral Raedar and the German Navy staff had considered the matter in broad terms in November 1939. They had required as a pre-requisite the complete control of the coast from Holland through Belgium to France. In late June 1940 they now had it. General Jodl of the German Army Command on 30th June thought that the final victory over England was only a question of time, and prepared a three-stage plan in principle to that end: first, there was to be an intensification of the air war, the increase of attacks on shipping, fuel storage depots and aircraft factories and the elimination of the Royal Air Force; second, terror attacks on centres of population and third, the landing of occupation troops.

On 2nd July Adolf Hitler issued a Fuehrer Directive authorising the preparation of plans, but stressed that, before invasion, air superiority was to be achieved. From the start there was an ambivalence in his approach, and he without doubt believed that Britain would come to terms either in 1940, as a result of the air campaign or after he had defeated the Soviet Union in 1941. Grand Admiral Raedar and the Navy were ordered to prepare a plan which took account of the state of their navy, much battered during the Norway campaign, and which provided for the establishment of a potential 'channel' from France to the south coast of England. This channel needed to be shielded on either side by minefields, with an outer screen of submarines. Vast quantities of shipping, the Navy staff said, were needed, amounting to 168 transports, 1,900 barges, 419 tugs and trawlers and 1,600 motorboats. It was essential, the Navy thought, to have air superiority in order to lay the channel and maintain the passage. The army wished for a landing on a wide front from North Foreland to Lyme Bay, but the Navy resisted that on the ground that such a wide channel could not be protected. On 21st July Hitler directed that invasion should be prepared for 15th September, despite Grand Admiral Raedar's objections that the Navy could not be ready, but he reduced the area of attack. In early July tentative peace feelers were put out through Sweden and on 19th July in a speech in Berlin Hitler made a so-called peace offer, which Lord Halifax rejected. On 1st August Fuehrer Directive No 17 was issued ordering the Luftwaffe to intensify the air war after 5th August, denominated as the Day of the Eagle (Adlerangriff). The first stage of the three-fold plan was to be put in operation.

The Germans assembled two air fleets for the attack. The first, in France and the Low Countries under Feldmarschall Kesselring (no 2) and General Sperrle (no 3) comprised 929 fighters, 875 bombers and 316 dive-bombers. The second, in Norway and Denmark under General Stumpf (No 5), comprised 123 bombers and only 34 Messerschmidt 110s. On land there were 13 Divisions under Feldmarschall Von Rundstedt in three armies, the 16th stationed north of Calais and which was planned to land in the vicinity of Eastbourne and Hythe, the 9th based on Le Havre to land between Brighton and Bognor, and the 6th to follow up the first two waves of assault at Weymouth. The first wave across was to comprise 90,000 troops and equipment and the second wave by Day 3 of the invasion 260,000, including 6 Panzer Divisions. All the plans however, depended on air superiority.

The air activity in the Channel in July by the Luftwaffe gradually led to shipping ceasing to move, and by 7th August no ship had stirred for nine days. The RAF had been avoiding staged large fights and had been husbanding their fighters and pilots, there being a marked shortage of the latter. Indeed on 17th July fighter training time had been reduced from six months to four weeks and on 17th August, when pilots were being sought from Fairey Battle pilots and Army pilots, it was to be further reduced from four weeks to two weeks. At the beginning of August Fighter Command had only 708 serviceable aircraft and 1,434 'trained' pilots. By 9th August however, the Navy had decided that the Channel should be forced and at 9 am a convoy of 25 ships set out from Southend for coastal ports in Sussex. Attacks by E-Boats in the night hours scattered the convoy in groups and on the 10th the Luftwaffe 8th Fighter Group under Baron von Richthofen (a cousin of the 1st World War Air Ace) attacked the convoy with Stuka dive-bombers. In 300 sorties 22 ships were sunk, but 13 Stukas were lost. The Battle of Britain had started.

Along the south coast the Radar towers stood at intervals with their 350-foot transmission towers and 240-foot receiver towers. They were the eyes and ears of 11 Group Command, which was to be the RAF group bearing the heat of the attack. They stood at Dunkirk, Rye, Pevensey and Ventnor. The Germans were uncertain of their exact use, but had formed the view that they did comprise a warning system. On August 12th the Lufwaffe attempted to destroy this system. Test Group 210 of adapted ME 109 and 110 fighters was sent against the stations. At 9.25 am Rye identified the attack formation coming at it. Manned in part by the Women's Auxiliary Air Force Services, the operating staffs stoically met the attack: sheltering from the bombs and returning to work once the raids were over. Damage was done to the ancillary buildings and at Pevensey the transmission tower shifted, but the towers survived intact. By mid-afternoon all but Ventnor, which was out for eleven days, were operational again. One more attack was made on the towers, but Feldmarschall Goering, head of the German Air force, thought the attacks useless and they were discontinued.

13th August saw the switch by the Lufwaffe to the attack on airfields, installations and factories serving the air force. The attack had started on Manston and Hawkinge, causing severe damage and dislocations, the latter closing for the day.

On 15th August the Lufwaffe struck in both the north and south of England. General Stumpf's 5th Air force sent a raid of 100 bombers escorted by 40 Messerschmidt 110s to Teeside. Fortunately there were 7 squadrons of Hurricanes and Spitfires, resting from the air war in the south, in the north. They were instantly made operational and 30 German aircraft, mostly Heinkel 111s, were shot down. In the south 800 aircraft crossed the coast and five major actions took place, engaging all 22 squadrons of Fighter Command two or three times. The Germans lost 76 aircraft to 34 British. The pattern of heavy raids had started and on 16th August Flight Lieutenant Nicholson was to earn the one Victoria Cross of

Fighter Command. The twenty-three year-old inexperienced fighter pilot was hit by a ME 110 at 18,000 feet with four cannon shells. Splinters from his hood left him blinded by blood, his plane caught fire and his left heel was disabled. The Hurricane however flew on straight and true for a Messerschmidt at full speed with flame lapping the cockpit; he fired and pursued it until it fell to the sea. At 5,000 feet, with flames around him, he baled out to fight again.

On succeeding days Short Brothers Aircraft factory was attacked, Eastchurch Bomber Station, Coastal Command's aerodrome at Detling, and the assault progressively mounted – Kenley, Biggin Hill, Hornchurch, Tangmere, North Weald and Middle Wallop. At some stations aeroplanes were destroyed on the ground: at Eastchurch on 13th August for example, 12 Spitfires of No 266 Squadron and 5 Blenheim bombers were destroyed. At most, buildings were damaged or devastated: at Kenley on 18th August 10 hangars were shattered and the Operations Room put out of action: By August 24th Manston was almost immobilised, with few buildings usable. The oil tanks at refineries such as Shellhaven and Thameshaven on the estuary of the Thames were set on fire. The silver flotillas of Heinkels and Dorniers, with their distinctive engine noise, a heavy reverberating droning, came on to be met by the diving fighters, filling the blue skies of summer with vapour trails and twisting aircraft. Children of nine in the Thames Valley east of London could see the savage tournament above, and the black smoke of the refinery fires billowing high into the sky to the clouds. The RAF fought back and on the ground indomitable efforts were made to restore the damaged aerodromes to operation; at Hornchurch, for example, where on 30th August 100 craters were made on the runway, all, officers, aircraftmen, Waafs and civilians worked to fill the holes made, and within four hours the aerodrome was operational. The battle raged on. On 1st September, for example, the attack struck at Hawkinge, Detling, Lympne, Biggin Hill, Debden, Rochford and North Weald.

The losses of fighter aircraft and pilots by the RAF were sapping. In August some 360 aeroplanes were lost, the largest number being in the last week, of 140. In the same month the Lufwaffe lost 662 aircraft. On 30th August, despite the more rapid production of aircraft, there were only 19 Spitfire Squadrons (with 372 aircraft) and 33 Hurricane Squadrons (with 709 aircraft) serviceable. From 24th August to 6th September alone 104 fighter pilots were killed and 128 seriously wounded. To fill the ranks the training period had been lowered, but the British airmen at the end of August were joined in their Spitfire and Hurricane squadrons by Poles, Czechs, Canadians and others. In the six weeks after 31st August the Poles destroyed 126 German aircraft to eight Polish aircraft lost, diving within twenty yards of the planes being attacked. From all over the Empire a contribution was made, and 10 Americans served in the squadrons.

On 22nd August the Luftwaffe bombed London by mistake and as a reprisal Churchill ordered a force sent to Berlin. On 24th August 81 bombers set out, of which 10 found the target. The night bombing force was sent four times in the next ten days. On the night of 28th August the first civilians were killed in Berlin. On 30th August the German Naval staff warned that because of British bombing attacks on the ports and harbours the naval invasion force could not be ready until after 15th September. These attacks had been made while the fight over England was proceeding and were to continue into September. On 1st September the German High Command began to collect the invasion boats and barges into the Channel ports near the Pas de Calais. As the battle raged over the airfields and air installations in the first week of September, Adolf Hitler on 4th September in the Sports-palast in Berlin, to an audience largely of women and nurses and to ecstatic applause, threatened to raze the cities of Britain to the ground. Feldmarschall Goering, who believed that the RAF had lost 1,115 aircraft to the German loss of 467 in the battle, was convinced that Britain could be reduced to making peace by all out attack on the cities in order to break the morale of the population and, overconfident that the Royal Air Force had been brought to the edge of elimination, decided to switch the attack to London. This decision was to prove crucial. Sir Hugh Dowding had begun to worry that the Royal Air Force could not sustain many more weeks of the campaign against the aerodromes and the wastage of pilots, and Air Vice Marshal Park thought the airfields pretty groggy. The first week in September had continued to take its toll. 144 British Fighters had been lost to the Germans' 187 and from 21st August the number of operational aircraft in Fighter Command had been steadily but slowly falling, a trend which was to continue to the end of September.

In September 1938 Winston Churchill, in relation to the Spanish Civil War, had written that attacks upon the civil population of Madrid, Barcelona and Valencia had the opposite psychological effects upon the civil population than that which the German and Italian air bombers expected. 'So far from producing panic and a wish to surrender, they have aroused a spirit of furious and unyielding resistance among all classes.' Nevertheless the Government worried about the effects of civilian bombing. On 7th September the test came. The Lufwaffe launched that day the largest air attack ever made on a city to that date. The force used comprised 625 bombers and 648 fighters and the first wave came at 4.30 pm up the Thames to the Woolwich Arsenal, the London power stations and the East End docks. Intertwined with the targets were the working-class terraces of East London. Despite Radar the opposing squadrons made operational were mainly still too low in height to prevent the bombers getting through. The Germans came one and half miles high and the air attack covered 500 square miles. The successive waves droned on until 4.30 am. After the first, the city was on fire, a burning cauldron in the docklands, the warehouses aflame, demolished buildings, a pall of smoke, trains and buses no longer running.

Heroically the Fire Brigade by river and land tried to stem the raging fires among the stricken buildings, and save the dead and wounded from the small houses which bombs had split and crushed. From over twenty miles away from London that night, the sky was like a violent red and orange formless globe, leading on successive waves of enemy aircraft to the target. The anti-aircraft guns after dark filled the night with continuous crashing explosions and devastating bangs as each wave came. The 7th September was not a good day for the Royal Air Force: out of the oncoming legions only 41 bombers were destroyed for the loss of 28 fighters, with 19 pilots killed. The anti-aircraft bombardment did not bring down a single aeroplane. On this day too by error the code word for invasion 'Cromwell' was given out and the army and Home Guard stood to. The church bells, the signal locally for invasion, were in many places rung, but it was all a mistake. On 8th September, with Feldmarschall Goering now personally in charge, the assault was renewed. On 9th September King George VI visited the bombed areas and Churchill went, noting the Union Jacks put on the rubble, and was reduced to tears of wonder and admiration for the fortitude of those bombed. On 13th September Buckingham Palace was bombed, just after the King and Queen arrived there. Queen Elizabeth thought she could now look the East End in the face without shame.

From the beginning of the collection of the invasion barges and supporting boats in the Channel ports, the Royal Air Force attacked the ports. On 10th September the German Naval Staff warned that air superiority over the Channel had not been achieved and warned of naval difficulties for the invasion force at Ostend, Dunkirk Calais and Boulogne, and for transport sunk at Le Havre and Antwerp. On 13th September 80 barges were sunk at Boulogne. On the same day Adolf Hitler had a meeting, in which he accepted that there was as yet no clear air superiority and Grand Admiral Raedar stressed the problems of the weather. General Jesshonneck of the Air force and Raedar both advocated the need for more terror bombing. Hitler was less certain of its significance but left the matter to the discretion of the air force.

On Sunday 15th September the Luftwaffe staged its greatest attack, a thousand aircraft aiming for London, Southampton, Bristol, Cardiff, Liverpool and Manchester. On that fine Sunday they were first intercepted early over the Channel. All 25 squadrons from No 11 Group were in the air and engaged and 3 came from No 12 Group. The German air armada advanced in streams on to London. The air fight once more covered the skies and was fought with the same skill and efficiency as previously. The Luftwaffe was to lose 56 aircraft and the Royal Air Force 23. Bomber Command that night bombed the ports gathering the invasion fleet from Boulogne to Antwerp, and on the 16th the Poles again attacked Boulogne. On 17th September by night 14 barges were sunk at Dunkirk and the harbour at Cherbourg was damaged. On 19th of September, the air war unwon, Adolf Hitler postponed the invasion indefinitely, turning to prepare for the attack in 1941 on the Soviet Union. Lacking air superiority, the daring 'enterprise of invasion', as he described it, was impracticable. He envisaged probably a short campaign to defeat Russia and then thought Britain would have to make peace or he could revive the invasion plans. On 12th October the invasion plan was abandoned.

From 15th September the 'terror' bombing of England continued by night for fifty-seven consecutive days until 3rd November. Not only London suffered as 200 bombers a night were sent on their missions. Londoners and those on the route of the bomber forces took to their shelters, where these existed, and others to protected places like the stations of the underground and reinforced cellars and buildings. The anti-aircraft barrage, which ringed London, pounded away as each wave came, filling the night with the deafening crash of guns. The sound of the First World War trench bombardment was transferred to the air above. Each generation kept their self-possession and courage: my grandmother, finding a lizard in her bunk on the second night of her stay in our underground shelter, left; 'Adolf Hitler', she said 'was not going to make her sleep with lizards', and she remained upstairs in her own bedroom for the rest of the war. Each day, boys emerged to seek for the largest lump of shrapnel to be found from the broken shells. Life among the bombs and fires went on. Commuters went to their work and the nation survived. Counselling was not offered and was not apparently needed.

By the time the end of the battle came – and the 'terror' bombing of the autumn was the last phase of the attack, done more as a reprisal for the bombing of Germany and Berlin than to achieve an outcome, the Royal Air Force had lost 915 fighters to the Luftwaffe's 1,733. The young pilots of Fighter Command – all of them, as well as the 'aces', like Douglas Bader, 'Sailor' Malan from South Africa, and Flight Lieutenant Deere from New Zealand, had saved Britain and stemmed the tide of Nazism, with courage and resolution doing battle against its darkness on behalf of the world of Christian reason and tolerance. While it is a trite remembrance, Churchill, as so often, spoke for Britain and its Empire and the wider world when he said never had so much been owed by so many to so few. That view was shared by Feldmarschall von Rundstedt, who expressed the opinion after the war that the Battle of Britain was the turning point of the war, rather than the Battle of Stalingrad.

Bomber Command, with gathering strength, took the attack back to Germany. Even by November 1940 the raids on Berlin had become significant. The Soviet Union's Foreign Minister Molotov visited Hitler that month. During discussions with von Ribbentrop, his German counterpart, he was led to an air raid shelter, as a raid took place. There he was treated to a long discourse to the effect that Britain was finished. Bored and aroused, he turned to Ribbentrop and asked, 'If that is so, why are we in this shelter, and whose are those bombs which fall?'

The Surrender of Quebec

Seventeen fifty-nine was a glorious year for victories in the Seven Years War. By September there had already been two (the Battle of Minden the 1st August and the Battle of Lagos 18th August); the taking of Quebec was to provide a third. William Pitt, subsequently Earl of Chatham, had become in 1757 the controller of military and naval strategy, although the Duke of Newcastle remained Prime Minister. Pitt's strategic vision encompassed a global view and was underpinned by a tactical strategy designed to stretch French resources in every direction, preventing their concentration on any single point, where the war was being waged. In Germany an Anglo-Hannoverian army was maintained and subsidies paid to Frederick II King of Prussia. In India the East India Company was encouraged to attack Indian states supporting the French. In the West Indies blows were struck at the French colonial islands. A focus of attack was Canada, where the French had colonised the St Laurence River area reaching into modern Ohio, and also settled at New Orleans in Louisiana. The British colonies in North America looked to Britain to protect them from the French and their Indian allies and to prevent French control spreading down their western boundaries along the rivers to New Orleans. Deliberate French incursion into this area had brought Britain into the war. Pitt's strategy involved removing the French threat to the colonies based on Canada, and he had a three-pronged strategy to strike in the west towards the Lakes, in the centre from New York on the line of Lake Champlain to attack Montreal, and by sea from Halifax up the St Laurence River to take Quebec. In 1758, based in Halifax, a combined army and navy force took the heavily fortified French fortress of Louisburg on Cape Breton Island, which dominated the entrance to the St Laurence. It was too late in the year to proceed up river, and preparation was made for a campaign in 1759. The strike against the French in the west had not been so successful, and so it was decided that General Amherst should take command on the frontiers and General Wolfe for the Quebec campaign.

Wolfe was one of Pitt's young men, appointed for their known ability. He was thirty-two, but suffered from ill health deriving from kidney complaints. He had a subtle, almost devious mind, and resplendent courage. His tactical grasp included a flair for joint operations with the Royal Navy, a talent he was fully to use in the taking of Quebec. He was fortunate there in having a young naval commander of the fleet, Sir Charles Saunders, who had been with Anson on his trip round the world and was to become First Sea Lord, and who knew the necessity for close co-operation in combined operations.

The winter of 1758-1759 was very hard and ice blocked the St Laurence until late in spring. Pitt had sent Admiral Durell early in the year with the task of blockading the river; however he had not remained in the mouth patrolling the ice edge, but had gone to Halifax, leaving only a single frigate. The Governor General of Canada, the Marquis de Vaudreuil and the army commander, the Marquis de Montcalm, had sent Colonel Bougainville to plead for reinforcements and supplies in Paris after the fall of Louisburg. He failed to persuade the Government to send a significant contingent of soldiers and returned with only 300 troops, a score of store-ships carrying ammunition and supplies, and three frigates. He arrived on 18th May having been ice-bound in the river for eighteen days. On the way however he had captured a letter which warned the French of Pitt's strategy of attacking up the St Laurence. The Marquis of Montcalm, who had gone to the west, returned with a large part of the army to Quebec. The convoy, through Admiral Durell's failure to maintain the blockade, was to sustain the colony in the coming year.

Sir Charles Saunders, with General Wolfe flying his flag in the 60-gun Stirling Castle, arrived off Cape Breton on 30th April, but the unfrozen ice forced their diversion to Halifax. Admiral Holmes was ordered to sea immediately to patrol the ice-edge, but it was not until 13th May that the fleet left Halifax for Louisburg. A fortnight was spent readying the army and the fleet for the expedition. Wolfe had only 9,000 men out of the 12,000 promised, but ample artillery, ammunition and supplies. He had been allowed to appoint his own commanders, apart from Brigadier Townsend, a nephew of the Prime Minister, the Duke of Newcastle. Both Brigadier Monckton, son of Lord Galway, and Brigadier Murray, son of Lord Elibank, were under thirty. Sir Charles Saunders commanded 22 ships of the line supported by frigates and sloops. On 1st June half the fleet under Saunders left Louisburg, the other half being detailed to patrol the mouth of the river, but impenetrable fogs lay over the mouth and lower reaches of the St Laurence. It took twenty-one days to reach the Isle of Bic, 165 miles downriver from Quebec. Between there and Quebec, west of the Isle of Coudres, lay a difficult channel of the river enclosed by steep cliffs and divided by lines of rocks in the water, the 'Traverse', which was thought by the French to be impassable to ships of the line

At Louisburg the British had taken charts made by the French of the river, but they had been indifferent and lacked accuracy. Lieutenant Samuel Holland and James Cook were commissioned to revise these charts and did so prior to the voyage of the fleet up the river. Captain James Cook was to become the discoverer of, and voyager to, Australia and New Zealand. The fleet arrived at the Traverse on 8th June. Saunders captured some French pilots on the Ile de Coudres and, led by soundings taken as they went by Cook and Holland in the channel, the fleet sailed through, the last ship getting past by 27th June. The skilled exercise of navigation based on the work of hydrography done was the Royal Navy's first contribution to the success of the expedition. It was the first time that a battle fleet had sailed up the St Laurence. On 26th June Saunders and Wolfe arrived at the Ile d'Orleans, just down river from the Bay of Quebec on which the city stood. The island divided the river into two channels which debouched into a basin, through which the river passed. The town of Quebec was built on a cliff promontary on the south-west side of the basin.

North of the river the French had constructed entrenchments and redoubts from the city for over three miles, to the village of Beaufort, where the cliffs began on the north of the basin and ran along the north channel. Further entrenchments and emplacements ran a further three miles to the River Montmorenci, which fell over two hundred feet onto the river shore. The western end of the Ile d'Orleans formed the north-east corner of the basin, separated by the south channel from the eastern shore. The basin narrowed opposite Quebec into the single channel of the river. Opposite the city cliff banks rose and continued south to the Chaudière River. The height facing the town on the east bank was Pointe Lévis. South-west of the city the heights on which the city stood almost 200 feet above the river continued as an open area of cornfields and pasture, named (after a previous owner) the Heights of Abraham. About three miles south of the city at two places, Sillery and Samos, batteries were to be positioned. Nearly 30 miles west of the city was Point aux Trembles on the north shore and 10 miles further the Jacques Cartier River. On the east bank about 10 miles from the Pointe Lévis was the Echimin River and a further 15 miles away lay St Nicholas.

Saunders anchored the fleet on the west shore of the island and disembarkation on the island began. The army tents and positions were taken up on the west end of the island. The same night a devastating storm caused the anchored ships to pull their chains, and some smaller boats necessary to convoy the soldiers were smashed. The fleet, he said, had to be moved therefore to the south channel, but that exposed the ships to the French on Point Lévis. He sought Wolfe's help in their removal.

The Marquis de Vaudreuil regarded himself as overall commander of the French by virtue of being Governor–General, but the regular army was under the command of the Marquis de Montcalm. This lack of overall control by one man was to lead to difficulties in meeting the challenge from the British, since they constantly bickered and gave contradictory orders. In all the French had in Canada 7,000 regular soldiers, 1,500 colonial marines and 14,000 militia men. In order to meet the three-pronged attack devised by Pitt, however, 2,600 regulars had been sent to Lake Champlain and 1,500 to Ontario. Montcalm was therefore left with about 5,000 trained troops, the militia and supporting Indians. While his numbers were therefore greater than those of Wolfe, the quality of the troops was not so adequate. Most of the ships which had been sent from France had gone sixty or seventy miles up river to Batiscan, where the frigates were left unmanned, the seamen being removed to defend Quebec. The harbour was therefore almost empty of major ships.

The problem which confronted Wolfe was the need to carry the troops across river to an attack, or to outflank a heavily fortified position. His first conception was to assault the city from the north, down river, and he conceived a plan to that end. An assault up river at that stage was not practicable as there would have been no naval support.

On the night of 28th June, out of the darkness there loomed seven ships, coming down towards the fleet on the tide. The French had converted their remaining transports at Quebec into fireships. As they came down on the anchored fleet they ignited, blazing and exploding, and threatened disaster. The seamen in their picket boats however grappled with them, took them under control and towed them to the shore, where they illuminated the night with their flames but did no damage. Admiral Saunders, having weathered the storm and dealt with the fireships, stressed once more the fleet would be safer in the south channel, but could not move there until the French were removed from Point Lévis which overshadowed the sound. The next day Brigadier Monckton with three battalions of the line, the Louisburg Grenadiers and some Highlanders were taken over to the south shore, surprised a French garrison, who fled, and took the heights. Work was immediately commenced to fortify the heights of the Point and guns put in place. On 1st July the navy, having prevented a counter-attack from across the river, began the bombardment of Quebec, which was to continue for ten weeks.

On 9th July Wolfe began his attempt to take the city. A feint using the navy was made up river which drew Montcalm from the city to the west and, under cover of darkness and the bombardment by Saunders of the entrenchments between the St Charles River and Beauport, Townsend and Murray took their brigades across the northern channel and up to the heights downriver from the Montmorenci Falls, from where the French entrenchments were overlooked. The next day there was a skirmish with the French, but Townsend was able to begin the building of his entrenchments. The same day Montcalm tried to recover Point Lévis under darkness. The two battalions sent landed, but lost contact, and when they came together, thinking the other the enemy, fired on one another, and retired in disorder without ever seeing the British.

On 18th July a move up river began. Under cover of bombardment from Point Lévis the Sutherland, (50 guns), the Diana (32 guns) and the Squirrel (20 guns) crept up river, subject to fire from Québec, although only three shot struck. They carried Colonel Carleton with three companies of grenadiers and a battalion of Royal Americans. They went on and landed to reconnoitre at Pointe aux Trembles on the north shore, some thirty miles from the city. On the 19th and 20th the force remained on the ground. Vaudreuil and Montcalm began to worry about their link to their supplies and Montreal and began to put defences in place up river. Two battalions of guns were placed at Samos and Sillery. The paths up the cliffs were broken and obstructed with logs.

On 23rd July Saunders, Wolfe and his commanders met to discuss the tactics for continuing the siege. Further ships were sent up river and Wolfe began to search for a landing place. In the meantime an attack was decided on at the Montmorenci Falls. It had been discovered that at low tide below the falls a firm beach emerged, and that the river was fordable. A redoubt had been placed on shore to defend this passage, but it still provided a route for an attack on the emplacements between Beauport and the river. The other decision was to pursue a punitive policy against the Canadians unless by 10th August they took an oath of neutrality. By this policy Wolfe hoped to put pressure on Montcalm to come out from the city. In the outcome 14,000 farms were burnt and laid waste.

The day before the attempt at the Montmorenci falls was planned to take place the French made a second attempt on the fleet. From small craft they constructed a great floating 'raft' linked by chains and turned the whole into one great 100-vessel fireship. Once more with the ebb tide it was sent down on the fleet, and once more the seamen in their picket boats were able to grapple it and tow it away from the fleet. On 31st July craft filled with troops and protected by frigates, together with the Centurion, passed up and down the position between the St Charles River and Beauport, where Montcalm was situated with his regulars, as if preparing to attack. The far left of the French position was there manned by the militia. After dark at low tide the troops assembled for the attack moved along the shore to attack the redoubt. That was soon taken, but in their enthusiasm the Grenadiers rushed on the entrenchments above, where Montcalm had arrived with some regulars. Fearsome volleys tore into the Grenadiers as they struggled to hold, but before the fight could be completed a devastating thunderstorm broke and ended the engagement. The attack was then abandoned, the steep slopes becoming too slippery to climb. Four hundred and fifty men had been killed, wounded or were missing.

Wolfe began again to rethink his plan of attack. He kept his resolution to himself, because of the problem of deserters, who carried knowledge of his movements to the French. Nor were his Brigadiers privy to his thinking, which led to some discontent and criticism from these commanding officers. The steps which he took were closely organised, however, with Admiral Saunders. On 5th August Saunders sent up-river twenty flat-bottomed boats, which passed undetected. He ordered up more ships to join Admiral Holmes, but owing to a westerly wind they did not leave until 27th August. On that day Murray was also sent up river with one battalion and two hundred marines to the Echimin River.

These movements at last lured Montcalm out of Quebec and he sent Monsieur de Bougainville with mounted infantry to defend the north shore. Brigadier Murray with his force mounted expeditions across the river. On 8th August Pointe aux Trembles was attacked. There was difficulty landing at low tide because of the rocks, and by high tide Bougainville had arrived and met Murray's force with heavy fire, killing 80 men. Murray seized St Antoine opposite across the river and began to build entrenchments. Both Vaudrevil and Montcalm tried to persuade Bougainville to assault the village, but he refused. Meanwhile Murray attacked at Deschambault on 16th August, twenty miles further on, undeterred by the French frigates, which were crewless. To counter Murray, Bougainville's force was raised to 1,500 men and the Chevalier de Lévis with 800 regulars was sent to Montreal, since the western expeditions in Ohio and New York states were advancing, having taken Fort Niagara. Many of the militia had been sent home by Vaudreuil to bring in the harvest, so that the defending forces at Quebec were weakened. The lower town had been all but destroyed by fire on 6th August as a result of bombardment, and much of the upper town ruined. Supplies were low as a result of the blockade of the upper river.

During August Wolfe was disabled by his illnesses, but continued to consider the solution to his problem. The key lay in the strategy he was applying for forcing Montcalm to spread his forces, while encouraging him still to believe that the attack would come between the St Charles River and Beauport. He also knew that he must keep secret his plans to retain the element of surprise and induce the commanders, who criticised him, to back his strategy. He was aware that Townsend in particular had power to influence the Government. On 27th August he held a Council of War and put three strategies to his Generals, all involving a renewed attack down river. They conceded none was practicable and urged an attack up river of the town. Wolfe had manoeuvred them into support for his strategy. On the 27th also Admiral Saunders sent the Lowestoft and the Hunter, up river and on 31st the Seahorse. He and Wolfe then began to embark on sorties to and from the upper river bases, which forced Bougainville to move continuously up and down the north bank to shadow the fleet and boats of troops. On 3rd September troops were withdrawn from the Montmorenci position under cloak of a naval feint at Beauport. On the 5th the whole army started up river. The camp at Ile d'Orleans remained with a small garrison to create the appearance that the army remained. The first stop was at St Michael but on the 6th Wolfe moved up to a position opposite Cap Rouge River. Vaudreuil had instructed Bougainville to shadow the flotilla and so he moved even further away from the city. Montcalm again added to his troops.

On the 8th and 9th, from a height over Murray's position at the Echimin River, Wolfe closely inspected the north shore. He discovered below the Heights of Abraham two possible small bays, but one, L'Anse de Foulon had leading from it to the plain at the top of the cliffs a path, albeit blocked, up which small guns could be brought. The plain was empty of troops, apart from a detachment of about 100 men at the top of the cliff. Reaching the crest of the cliffs involved a climb of one hundred and seventy feet. The cove was marked on the bluff by a jutting rock visible at night.

The attempt was set for the night of 12th September. The flotilla of boats commanded by Captain Chad was to float down the river to the cove on the ebb tide. Admiral Holmes used three factors to ensure success, the distance from St Nicholas of 8.7 miles, the estimate of the tide speed of 3.4 knots and the darkness of the night. The troops' boats, which only had capacity for 1,700 troops, were loaded on the shore side of the ships of the line and transports and two lanterns of the maintop of the Sutherland gave the signal to cast off. The boats began to slip down river. Twice they were challenged by French sentries, reply being made in French by one of the Scottish officers, who had lived in France. A convoy of supplies had been expected by the French that night, but unbeknown generally, Bougainville had cancelled it. The flotilla was thought to be the convoy, a mistake almost made by the Hunter, which ran out its guns to fire, desisting only after being given a last minute warning. Two hours after departure the boats carrying the troops had arrived at the landing place, which they slightly overshot. Wolfe was in the leading boat. He had made his will and handed over a locket given him by Miss Lowther, to whom he had become engaged, to Lieutenant John Jervis of the navy, later to become Earl St Vincent. On the way, it is said, that he read Thomas Gray's poem, Elegy in a Country Churchyard, out loud, and remarked that it was better to have written that than to have taken Quebec. He clambered ashore with his Adjutant-General Major Barré, captain Delaune and twenty-four volunteers making up the 'forlorn hope'. The Light Infantry and troops of Monckton's and Murray's Brigades began to scale the cliffs. It was not yet dawn and they had to scramble up holding on to shrubs and hawthorns. In emerging on the bluff they easily took the camp, one hundred yards away, of Monsieur de Vergor, who had allowed fifty of his men to go to the harvest. They then set out and took the batteries at Sillery and Samos. Vergor, who was wounded in the heel, did manage to send a message before capture to Montcalm that the British had arrived on the heights above the river. The obstructions on the cliff path were removed, and the second wave of 1,900 troops landed. Barré then sent off to bring over the reserves from Point Lévis, and the seamen from the transports began to land and manhandle the guns on the cliff path.

Montcalm had spent his night at Beauport with the troops stood to arms. While the invasion flotilla floated down to L'Anse de Foulon, Admiral Saunders and the navy had carried out a skilful exercise of deception. Ships of the fleet accompanied by small craft packed with seamen had sailed up and down between the St Charles River and Beauport during the night as if seeking a landing ground. The ships bombarded the lines and Montcalm was convinced that the attack, which he expected there, was about to be made. The message from de Vergor came as a complete surprise and Montcalm was at first not disposed to believe it. At last he set out with Chevalier Johnstone to inspect the position for himself.

Wolfe on landing had gone to view the plain, with the object of finding the place at which to station the troops. He had a force of 4,828 troops and initially they fell to with their backs to the river. He looked at a ridge across the plain not far from the city, the Butte de Neuveu, but rejected that because the troops would be unshielded from artillery fire from the city. He chose instead a line stretching about a mile long between some farm buildings inland, beyond which were woods and a 50-foot high knoll near the river. The troops then deployed to this position. On the left was Brigadier Townsend with the Royal Americans and Light Infantry, forming a wing protecting the lines on the plain from incursion on the flank from the woods. The regiments were then spread in two lines across the plain running from the left to right flank – the 15th Regiment of Foot (East Yorkshire) the 58th Regiment of Foot (Northamptonshire), the 78th (Highland) Regiment of Foot (Seaforth Highlanders), the 47th Regiment of Foot (North Lancashire), the 43rd Regiment of Foot (Oxfordshire Light Infantry), the 28th Regiment of Foot (Gloucestershire Regiment), the Louisburg Grenadiers and on the right flank the 35th Regiment of Foot (Royal Sussex). The Louisburg Grenadiers was a joint body of Grenadiers collected from other regiments. The Royal Americans were also positioned on the right near the taken batteries. By 8 am the army was in place; Wolfe, in a totally red-coloured uniform with brown top boots, was on the left of centre.

Montcalm was appalled to see the British on the heights to the west of the city and knew that the moment of decision had come. Wolfe was across his communications to his supplies and the main part of the colony. He sent orders to transfer the regular troops and some militia to the west of the city. Vaudreúil ordered the militia however not to move and Montcalm was left with 3,500 regulars and 1,500 Canadians and the Indians in the wood on his right. Messages were sent to Monsieur de Bougainville, whose troops had spent the previous day marching back and forth to shadow the fleet, to return to Quebec at once.

The British watched the French assemble on the field with their white uniforms in serried ranks emerging across the St Charles River bridge out of the town gates. As they assembled they brought out three field pieces and opened fire: Wolfe ordered the men to lie down to avoid the shot. By 9 am the seamen had arrived at the cliff-top with two brass 24-pounders, and they began to return the fire. Montcalm, on a black horse, rallied his troops and in dense groups six deep they advanced one hundred yards down the Butte de Neuveu; Canadians and Indians on the flanks meanwhile were harassing the British, who retaliated with skirmishers and sharp shooters. The British in answer to the French movement sprang up and moved forty yards. The armies were now a quarter of a mile apart. Wolfe ordered every man to load his musket with two bullets and not to fire until the French were forty yards away. As the soldiers waited the strange skirl of the pipes from the Highlanders in the centre curled across the field. At 9.30 Wolfe was wounded in the wrist as he stood in front of the 28th. He bound the wound with a borrowed handkerchief. The clouds parted and the sun began to shine as the French moved forward in three columns: two obliquely to the British left, firing from too great a distance. It was now five past ten. As they approached, the columns became disordered.

Wolfe was hit again in the groin; the British stood immobile, the ranks reforming as men fell. At forty paces Wolfe gave the order to fire. The volley came in one united explosion and the heads of the French columns were swept away. The remainder stood stock-still. The British advanced a few paces and fired for a second time. Wolfe, leading the 28th, ordered the advance, but he had scarcely gone two yards before being hit mortally by a musket ball in the chest. He begged Lieutenant Brown and Private Henderson not to let the men see that he was shot and they retired, supporting him, to the rear of the line. The soldiers continued their advance, the French moving to the rear, with the Highlanders falling on them with their claymores. The severed arms and limbs, the headless trunks reduced the French to panic and it was over in ten minutes. Montcalm, himself severely wounded, tried to rally the rearguard, but the French flowed on across the St Charles River and into the town. The Canadians and Indians on the French right did hold up the pursuit, and 200 Highlanders were wounded.

Wolfe did not linger, but lived long enough to know the result of the battle and turned on his side to die saying 'Now God be praised: I die in peace'. Command now devolved on Brigadier Townsend, who called off the pursuit and began to reform the troops in expectation that Bougainville might march back to the field. In fact Bouganville, who was at Pointe aux Trembles, did not receive Montcalm's message until after 9 am, but then came double marching back to Quebec with his 2,000 men. Townsend met them with two battalions and guns and Bougainville decided to retire.

Montcalm was lifted into the City and died the next morning. The Marquis de Vaudreuil decided that the only course was to retreat to the Jacques Cartier River and the troops and militia abandoned the Beauport entrenchments with its ammunition, guns and supplies. The retreating French swept though Cap Rouge, arriving at Jacques Cartier River on 15th September, where the Chevalier de Lévis set about reorganising them. The city did not surrender until the 18th, its inhabitants refusing to fight on. The city was occupied and a garrison of 7,000 left for the winter, since the fleet needed to return to Halifax before winter ice closed the St Laurence once again. The Power of France in Canada had been broken, and 1760 was to see it completely removed. Wolfe and Saunders, by their talents and combined action, had won the day and launched a new page in the history of British Empire. The victory was wholly due to the clever strategy of Wolfe to make Montcalm stretch out his forces and to Saunder's cleverness and ability to use the fleet in full backing of the strategy. It is perhaps sad that Admiral Saunders has been forgotten despite his distinguished part in the winning of Canada. When Montreal was taken in September 1760, the French nobility and richer merchants left Canada, the farmers and poorer inhabitants remaining, their religion and language protected, and gaining the protection of British law. These were to remain loyal during the Rebellion of the Colonies and the Anglo-American War of 1812.

19th September 1356

The Battle of Poitiers

After the victory at the Battle of Crecy (27 August 1345) and the taking of Calais in 1346, the war between King Edward III and King Philip VI of France went on, but in the Summer of 1348, an exceptionally wet year, the Black Death, which had been stalking across Europe, devastating as it went, reached England. The plague, which brought death within three days, had been carried by the black rat from Asia Minor, its fleas bringing the infection. It moved on from Melcome Regis north throughout 1348 and 1349. In its wake it brought death to thousands, economic disruption and the breaking down of all social activity. It carried off a third of the population, leaving the farms and countryside untended. Prices rose and labour became scarce. Some land was to remain untilled until 1354. Weakened, both England and France agreed to a truce. King Edward III, deprived of his own revenues, had to turn to his Great Council to help. Taxation and representative Government took some more infant steps. The shortage of manpower made it difficult to hold Guienne and Brittany and in August 1350 Philip VI died, to be replaced by King John II, 'Le bon'.

The truce expired and in 1352 the French invaded Brittany, and in 1353 the English lands in the west of France. In 1354 the truce was again renewed, while King Edward III dealt with problems in Scotland. Finally he determined for 1355 a three-fold plan of attack on France from Calais, in Normandy and in the south from Bordeaux in Aquitaine. In September 1355 the Prince of Wales, 'the Black Prince', sailed for Bordeaux with 3,500 troops, including a strong contingent of archers from Cheshire and Derbyshire. He was twenty-three years old and an experienced soldier, schooled by the able Sir Thomas Dagworth. The Comte d'Armangac had won towns in southwest Guienne, and the Black Prince decided to invade Languedoc to draw him out to battle. On 5th October, with a force of 5,000 but no siege train, he began his march, the 'grande chevauchée', through southern France. As the army marched, towns, villages and castles, stores and crops were burnt, although the Prince gave orders that no damage should be done to churches and monasteries, and that civilians should be spared. There were two French armies in the field, but neither moved to the attack. He marched on to Toulouse, where the Comte D'Armangac held the city, and by-passed it, reaching Carcassonne and Narbonne. From there he returned to La Reole, having marched seven hundred miles in nine weeks. In the North King Edward led a force from Calais in the same year, but the French would not come out from Amiens, and for want of forage he was forced to turn back, and returned to England to deal again with Scotland.

In June 1356 Henry Duke of Lancaster sailed for Brittany with the young Duke and landed at La Hogue on 18th June, where he met Sir Robert Knollys. Together they had 800 men-at-arms and 1,300 archers. On 28th June they reached Lisieux, going on to take Pont Audemar and Verneuil. By this time King John had organised his forces and tried to block the return to the Cotentin peninsula. The Duke evaded him and arriving back was re-supplied and set off south to Maine, in an endeavour to unite with the Black Prince, while King John endeavoured to recover the towns and castles taken. The Black Prince had himself started from Bergerac with the object of moving north to join Lancaster on the Loire, thus seizing a wide area of western France.

The Prince's first task was to recover the castle and towns taken previously on the borders of Guienne, and he re-established English rule as far north as Perigueux. On 4th August he crossed the River Dordogne, advancing ten miles a day and ravaging the countryside and towns of Touraine. Having come three hundred and forty miles he reached Amboise on the River Loire in the first week of September. Duke Henry of Lancaster had reached Domfront, which he was besieging. The river bridges were down and the Prince moved west to Tours, where he encamped for a week while the river Loire rose and it rained continuously. Supplies were short: Henry of Lancaster did not arrive and so he decided to retreat.

On 28th August King John was at Orleans, and he set off west on the north bank of the river, crossing at Blois and joining the Comte de Poitiers on 10th September, the same day as the Black Prince had begun his retreat. The latter had moved south and on the 15th paused for two days at Chatellarault. The French King meanwhile was moving south-west and reached Poitiers on 17th December, between the Prince and his route of retreat. That day, outlying elements of the armies clashed, and the Black Prince decided to take up a position south-east of Poitiers. The position chosen, six miles from Poitiers, was a strong one. The land immediately to the east of Poitiers was undulating plain, but the English took their stand in hilly countryside, where two roads from Poitiers came out along a shallow river valley. Along the east side of the more westerly road a sizeable hedge ran, from which the ground rose to a ridge. The hedge had only small gaps in it, allowing four riders through it abreast. Across the valley to the west was another ridge, not so high. Behind, to the east and south of the ridge on the eastern roadside, was the dense Noaille wood. The small River Moisson ran east to west south of the wood and the valley at whose southern tip, where the stream met the valley, was a marsh.

The Black Prince established his army between the hedge on the road and the Noaille wood on the rising ground. His army from England and Gascony numbered no more than 7,000 troops, of which 3,000 or so were knights and men-at-arms, 3,000 were archers with 1,000 light troops. It was divided into three 'battles'. The left wing was commanded by the Earl of Warwick with the Earl of Oxford, the Captal de Buch and, Sir John de Grailly, who had 300 armed horsemen and 300 archers on horse. These were stationed behind the ridge with the purpose of being available to strike the French in the flank or rear at an appropriate moment. The centre battle was under the direct command of the Prince with Sir John Chandos, Sir James Audley, Cobham and Burghersh. The knights and men-at-arms were dismounted, but their horses were stationed nearby so that they could be rapidly mounted. The third battle on the right was under the Earls of Salisbury and Suffolk, with a preponderance of archers and a number of Germans. As at Crecy, the archers were posted forward on the flanks of the army and the battles, among the hawthorn hedges and vines of the broken countryside. The day before the battle, 18th September, was spent strengthening the positions occupied by the archers with trenches and palisades of stakes. A defensive 'laager' of wagons was placed on the left near the marsh.

King John II gathered his troops on the plain outside Poitiers. The exact numbers are problematical. Froissart said there were three battles of 16,000 men in each, but the true figure is likely to have been less. The majority were lightly armoured troops of poor quality, but there could have been as many knights and men-at-arms as 8,000, and 2,000 crossbowmen. Unlike the situation at Crecy, the French King had time to order his troops, and they were divided into four battles. The first, which was to act as the vanguard, comprised two elements; part mounted under the two Marshals Sir John de Clermont and Sir Arnoul d'Audreham, and part on foot led by the Constable of France. The second battle was under the command of the Dauphin, the young Duke of Normandy, advised by the Duc de Bourbon, a seasoned warrior; the third, under the Duc d' Orleans, the brother of the King and the last under the King himself, with his son Philip and the Counts of Ponthieu, Eu, Longueville and Sancerre. The Oriflamme banner of France was to be carried near the King by Sir Gilbert de Charny. While the French army was forming, King John sent four knights – Sir Eustace de Ribeaumont, Sir John de Landas, Sir Guiscard de Beaujeu and Sir Guiscard d 'Angle to reconnoitre the English position. They returned to tell the King that the position was one of great strength and difficult to attack.

The 18th September was occupied by negotiations between the King and the Black Prince with a view to a solution which did not involve the clash of arms. They were induced to consider this through an initiative made by Cardinal de Perigord. The latter spent the day riding between the two sides endeavouring to arrive at terms. No doubt conscious of his weakness in numbers (about 1 to 4), the Black Prince offered to surrender the gains of his campaign back to France, restore the property taken and release the prisoners, and then to pledge himself not to take the field for seven years. King John II, with his overwhelming force, wanted unconditional surrender by the Black Prince, including the taking of him and 100 knights prisoner. The Cardinal made no progress, but tried for one last time on the early morning of the next day. The French King told him 'begone' back to Poitiers, and the Black Prince said the English had resolved to fight. As he returned to the city, some of the knights and young men with him, including his nephew Robert de Duras, broke away to join the French King, even though the traditions of the time precluded persons carrying out mediation from joining either side.

Advised by Sir William Douglas, the Scot, the King decided that the French should for the main part fight unmounted; the horsemen had to remove their spurs and the lances were pared to five feet. The exhausting march in armour to the field of battle commenced, and the French arrived from the north-west onto the ridge to the west of the road in the early morning. The English had been watering their horses in the valley, and the French initially mistook this operation for the beginning of a retreat. Before the vanguard under the Marshals began to advance, a knightly contest held the field.

Sir Eustace d' Aubrecicourt from Hainault in the Low Countries spurred his horse out between the armies, his shield carrying a field of ermine and two helmets gules (red). There came to meet him Sir Louis de Recombes from the Count of Nassau's contingent, carrying a shield with a field of silver on which were five roses gules. Riding forward, their lances at the ready, they crashed and were both unhorsed. Sir Louis de Recombes was wounded in the shoulder and slow at getting up; Sir Eustace quicker, but as he rose, he was set upon by five Nassau men-at-arms and taken prisoner. The latter tied him to a baggage wagon, but later in the day he was retaken, remounted and fought again bravely. The French began to move across the English front, D'Audreham shifting towards Warwick and the left wing and Sir John de Clermont towards Salisbury on the right. As they came to the lane and hedge, the storm of arrows from the longbows of the archers met them. Capable of shooting up to three hundreds yards and rapidly, near-to armour could be pierced. The riders in the battle were reduced by the murderous fire to confusion, their horses maddened by their injuries and the riders thrown, unable to rise without assistance. A few forced their way through the hedge to be swept back by an English counter-attack led by Salisbury. On the left flank Warwick withstood the on-rush, but some of his archers moved off to the marsh at the south end of the valley and began to shoot the French from the other flank, volley after volley at the hindquarters of the horses. The struggle along the front persisted; the archers spreading fear among the French and the men-at-arms clashing. Sir Arnoul de Audreham was taken prisoner and Sir John de Clermont killed. At last the French turned and fell back, meeting the next battle commanded by the Dauphin. The discipline of the English was such that they stood still and did not pursue.

The second battle was advancing well massed and formidable when the retreating vanguard ran into them, bringing news of the failure of the first attack. The rear of the Dauphin's formation began to disintegrate, numbers taking themselves from the field, including some knights. The head however of the column struggled on, losing fewer as they came up to the English position, for the supply of arrows for the longbows was much diminished. There was a long and desperate encounter as the men-at-arms clashed, but once more the French were driven back. The Counts of Saarbrück, Nassau and Nidau and their supporters were put to flight. While this encounter went on the battle led by the Duc d'Orleans moved off to the north-east away from the field, whether under orders or under the misapprehension that total defeat had occurred. There resulted as a consequence a pause, allowing the English archers to be replenished with arrows.

The last battle and the largest, led by King John himself, now appeared on the western ridge, a glitter of armour, banners and pennants, the heraldry of the surcoats and shields a kaleidoscope of vivid colour. Before he moved King John sent his four sons from the field, escorted by 100 Lances. Then, led by the King carrying an axe, the French marched towards the English position. The force led by crossbowmen looked intimidating: as they mounted up hill they loosed a storm of quarrels and the longbow men replied taking their toll. The Black Prince decided that the moment had come to charge, and he ordered the mounted knights and men-at-arms to their horses. Crying 'Sir George and Guienne' they thundered down on the French. The longbowmen dropped their bows and took to sword and entered the clashing, desperate mêlée of sword and axe, horse and foot. As the fight began to climax, the Captal de Buch with his 600 horse rode from the right into the French rear and flank. King John fought in the fiercest part of the battle. He came face to face with the Black Prince, according to Froissart, and more fine feats of arms were done that day than at Crecy. At the end the battles of the Prince, the Earl of Warwick, the Earl of Suffolk and the Captal de Buch were all engaged. Sir Gilbert de Charny was killed carrying the Oriflamme of France. The bannerets and pennants fell, and the French wavered as the bloody fight came towards it end. King John fought to the end, until he was forced to surrender. His taker was a knight from Artois, who had been expelled from France, Sir Denis de Morbecque. Others anxious to share or obtain the ransom money challenged him, and the King became surrounded by a dangerous jostling crowd. Sir John Audley was found wounded. The Prince, hearing of it, ordered that he be given an income of 500 marks for life, but Sir John, grateful to the care of four squires, who had looked after him and sewed up some wounds, transferred it to them.

The Black Prince retired from the fight and had his banner raised on a bush as a meeting point for his commanders. On his way he had seen the body of Robert de Duras, and he ordered it carried on his shield to the Cardinal de Perigord, as a riposte to the irritation which he felt from the liege men of mediators engaging in battle. A crimson tent was raised and as his commanders appeared they were served with wine. He asked after the King of France and sent the Earl of Warwick and Sir Reginald Cobham to find him. They came upon the mêlée, where the King was in danger and riding through it, took charge and escorted him to the Black

Price. That evening at a banquet King John with Philip, his son, Lord Jacques de Bourbon, Lord John of Artois, the Comtes of Tancarville, Etampes, Dammartin, the Lords of Joinville and Ponthenay, were all seated at a high table and the Prince out of courtesy served them and praised the King for his bravery.

The success of the battle was marked by the prisoners captured. In addition to the King and his son, there was one Archbishop, thirteen counts, five viscounts, twenty-one barons and 2,000 knights. 2,500 knights and men-at-arms were dead. The prisoners were so numerous that they amounted to twice the victorious army, even archers having five or six. Given the problem, there was no alternative but to make the knights and other men-at-arms give their recognizances to pay the ransom or return to Bordeaux by Christmas, and they were let go. The plunder taken comprised bullion, gold and silver plate, jewels and furs, all in quantity. Armour was so plentiful that there was little interest in it.

On the news reaching England there was prodigious rejoicing. The ransom of the King of France alone was worth 300,000 crowns, and the ransom money represented great wealth. In 1357 King John and the prisoners of wealth were brought back to London, to be greeted by King Edward with ostentatious pageantry and tournaments. Nonetheless King John II was to remain a prisoner for three and a half years. In 1359 King Edward III decided that he should be crowned King of France at Rheims, and in October mounted a great force to do so. The army sailed from Sandwich and in addition to the troops he took thirty falconers and sixty couple of greyhounds to give the King sport. As he moved through Artois and marched on to Rheims in October the torrential rain of autumn fell, forage was difficult to obtain and on arrival the Archbishop of Rheims and the citizens shut the gates against him. After two months siege in the appalling weather he marched south to Burgundy to spend Lent. April was still cold and food and forage were short. His failure induced in him the idea that he should make peace.

In France the victory of Poitiers was followed by a period of disorder and destruction. Many of the chivalry of France had been killed. Bands of soldiers ranged the country burning, looting, raping and stealing. The peasants rose to attack their lords. Trade was at a standstill. France too needed peace. The plenipotentiaries met at Bretigny on 1st May 1360 and a provisional Treaty was signed on 8th May. Under the Treaty King Edward III was to renounce his claim to the French throne and the over- lordship of Normandy, Anjou, Maine, Touraine and Flanders. Castles and cities were to be restored. For their part the French gave to the English King the sovereignty of Calais, Ponthieu and Aquitaine, a quarter of France. A list of cities to be included was made, but La Rochelle was unwilling to be given to the English. A ransom of 300,000 crowns was to be paid for King John and 200,000 more for his three sons. In the outcome the renunciation of the French throne did not appear in the treaty, and that was to become an issue under King Henry V. King John returned to France in October 1360.

22nd September 1415

The Surrender of Harfleur

After the treaty of Bretigny in 1360, following the Battle of Poitiers (19th September 1346) and the Black Death, King John II of France returned home after three and half years of captivity. Until his death in 1364, peace was preserved between England and France, but he was succeeded by his son Charles V who, like the French Prime Minister in 1918, Clemenceau in relation to the Germans, was consumed by a desire for revenge for the defeats inflicted by the English, which had resulted in a third of France coming under the control of King Edward III. A dispute arose over taxation imposed in Aquitaine by the Black Prince, and an appeal was made to King Edward III and Charles V. In 1369 the latter took the opportunity, despite the agreement to surrender sovereignty over Aquitaine at the time of the treaty of Bretigny, to declare the Duchy confiscated by France on the pretext that the Treaty did not bind him, as the agreement on sovereignty was not executed. From that date the war was renewed until a truce in 1396. English troops on five occasions made incursions into France, one of the most famous being the march made by John of Gaunt, third son of Edward III, from Calais to Bordeaux in 1377, a distance of some six hundred miles. The French under Bertrand du Guesclin by diplomacy and sieges gradually reoccupied territory under English occupation and control. During this period command of the sea was lost and it made assistance to the holdings in south-west France difficult. The truce of 1396 was based on the preservation of the status quo, and Calais. For the whole time the French had avoided battle with the English.

Under King Henry IV England was too much concerned with its own problems to contemplate recovery of the lost land, although the French took the opportunity to sieze more territory in Aquitaine, reducing English control to a strip along the littoral from Bordeaux to Bayonne. France itself gradually descended into civil strife around the Crown, Charles VI being subject to periods of insanity, between the Armagnacs and the Burgundians.

Henry IV died in 1413 to be succeeded by his eldest son as King Henry V. During his father's later years much policy had been decided by him, and sensing the opportunity to recover the lost lands he negotiated with the opposing parties in France separately. In 1411 he came to a secret agreement with the Burgundians. Henry V had been raised as a prince and a soldier, taking part at a young age in the warfare with the Welsh on the borders. He was seriously wounded at the Battle of Shrewsbury by an arrow through his cheek. A painful operation was necessary to extract the arrowhead, which was deeply embedded. His courage and endurance was only equalled by his piety, having a deep religious faith, and his learning, being a scholar in an age when great nobles and princes regarded literacy of low value as compared with knightly courage. On coming to the throne he was determined to recover his ancestral lands, and in view of the breach by the French of the Treaty of Bretigny, he revived the claim made by his grandfather King Edward III to the Crown of France, which the latter as a condition of the treaty arrangement had agreed to abandon, a treaty the French had breached.

Abortive negotiations took place but by spring 1415 Henry V was ready to go to France in order to assert his rights. In April a Great Council took place, resolving on war to deal with French duplicity and John Duke of Bedford, his brother, was appointed Regent in the absence of the King. The fleet and army were assembled in the early summer in the bays and estuaries of the Solent. 1,500 ships were collected, most requisitioned merchantmen, and massive quantities of equipment and supplies. There were numerous head of cattle and horses, oxen, wagons, ovens, thousands of round shot, guns and powder. There were, probably for the first time, twenty surgeons; heavy guns were taken with a crew of 65 gunners. There were assembled 2,000 men-at-arms, 8,000 archers and tradesmen to support the army-miners, builders, and carpenters. The whole was in place at Southampton and Portsmouth on the last day of July 1415. Henry V had arrived at Portsmouth on the 2nd July. Several weeks were needed to complete the arrangements and on 6th August he joined the flagship, the Trinity Royal, of five hundred tons. Four days were taken to concentrate the fleet in the Solent and on 11th August the invasion expedition sailed. Henry V had not at that point specified the destination and several landing places had been the subject of speculation in Gascony, Brittany, Normandy or Calais. On sailing, the King announced that the fleet was bound for Normandy. After a smooth passage across the Channel the English fleet cast anchor at 5 pm on 14th August at the mouth of the Seine. King Henry had determined to take the ancestral land of Normandy from which had come his Norman and Plantagenet forebears.

The French were aware of the threat, but they were disorganised and lackadaisical, and thinking that Boulogne was the destination, little was done. The Duc d'Orleans, the king's brother, hardly stirred and the Burgundians refused to assist. The Dauphin, aged 19, was made commander of the army assisted by Charles D'Abret, a talented soldier and Constable of France. Steps were taken to collect an army in the area of Rouen and Marshal Boucicault with 1,500 men moved south of the Seine towards the estuary. Among a population afflicted by taxation there was little enthusiasm for resistance to the invasion.

Early on the morning of 15th August the English army began to disembark at the Chef de Caux, about three miles from Harfleur, where Le Havre now stands. Sir Gilbert Umfraville and the Earl of Huntingdon were sent towards Harfleur to reconnoitre. No opposing force was found and the land was deserted. It was to take three days to land the army and its supplies, the men, horses and cattle. The first object of the campaign was to be Harfleur. King Henry V was one of the first to land and on reaching shore fell to his knees and prayed God to look kindly on his endeavours.

The city of Harfleur on the north bank of the Seine, today incorporated in the city of La Havre, was strategically sited to control movement on the river to Rouen, the capital of Normandy, and inland to Paris. It was strongly fortified by walls and towers newly built in the middle of the fourteenth century. The walls were penetrated by three well-defended gates to the south-west, north-east and south-east. Each gate was protected by a strong bastion or barbican outside the walls, and the city wall was enclosed for most of its length by a moat with a marsh on the eastern side. The River Lezarde ran through the city to join the Seine beyond. The harbour was protected by moles, ending with strongly built towers. The city lay about three miles from the Chef de Caux. The defence of the city was further strengthened by dams erected across the River Lezarde just at the city walls, flooding the valley of the river with water waist deep, which required a ten-mile journey to move round from west to east. The garrison under John, Sire de Estouteville, had only 300 men-at-arms.

Henry V and his army moved towards the city, coming from the west. There were only two strategies open to him, one to take the city by assault and the other to blockade it until it surrendered. As the English arrived, across the flooded valley of the River Lezarde was seen the arrival of reinforcement for the garrison, 300 men-at-arms led by Raoul, Sire de Gaucourt. The King at once sent a force under his brother, the Duke of Clarence, to block the approaches to the city from the east. The column had a ten-mile journey round the flooded valley and on the way captured a train of guns and ammunition on its way to the city. The French tried to affect a rescue but were driven off.

The English settled down in an encampment about one mile from the city. The fleet came up and blocked the River Seine, preventing any crossing by Marshal Boucicault from the south bank. Small boats were placed on the water in the flooded valley to the north so that access to the city was prevented on all sides. The French completed their works of protection by blocking the harbour mouth with a great chain between the moles. The King, before commencing the siege of the city, sent out a call for its surrender, but the French refused.

The King had brought twelve siege guns, the largest being 'the London', 'the Messenger', and the 'King's Daughter.' The bombardment of the city, concentrating on the towers and walls, began immediately, being kept up every day. As the guns destroyed the walls and defences by day, the French tried to repair them by night. The weather was an unusually hot August, so much so that the knights were in acute discomfort in their armour. The houses of the town were not spared and St Martins Church was damaged, but the main concentration was on the defences, particularly the three gates and their barbicans. The main attack however was on the south–western gate, which gave access to the west where the English were encamped. On the east where there was no moat, Welsh miners were employed, endeavouring to undermine the foundations of the south-east gate and wall. They were often met by counter-mines and hand-to-hand combat could result in the tunnels underground. Meanwhile, day in, day out, the troops waited. Supplies were plentiful, augmented by local fruit and shellfish. But the marshes and flood areas hampered proper sanitation and the dysentery bacteria thrived. The army began to fall ill, while King Henry drove himself to constant endeavours to forward the siege.

By 13th September the south-west barbican was in ruins and the moat had been filled with fascines over which the troops could advance into the breaches made. The ravages of dysentery grew; on the 15th among the dead was Bishop Courtenay of Norwich, the King's advisor, and on the 16th Marshal de La Pole. The same day as the Bishop died the French sallied forth from the south-west gate in a surface attack. A protective palisade was set on fire despite the efforts of the local commanders Sir John Holland, Sir John Cornewaille and Sir William Parker. On the 16th the Earl of Huntingdon launched an all-out assault against the gate. Balls loaded with combustible material were sent against the outer bulwarks to burn the fortifications. The troops drove in over the moat and pushed the French back to the main gates through which they retreated, blocking them. The fire of the palisade, started on the 16th, burnt for two days.

On 17th September King Henry V invited the Sire de Gaucourt to a meeting to discuss surrender and so avoid the need for a full assault on 18th September, which he was ordering. De Gaucourt was not receptive to the idea, hoping that the King of France would soon arrive to succour the city. The Burgesses had however in their view suffered enough: disease was rampant in the city, food and supplies low, houses and buildings destroyed by the bombardment. On the morning of the 18th emissaries of the town emerged from the south-west gate to inform the Duke of Clarence that surrender was being considered. The Bishop of Bangor, as representative of the King, promised that the English had not come to waste the town. Without support from the townspeople, de Gaucourt could not fight on and so by negotiation with the Bishop it was agreed that a request would be sent to the Dauphin to see whether the French army would move to relieve the city and that, if he failed to come within three days, the city would be surrendered. Twenty-four hostages were demanded, including the Sire de Estouteville.

Throughout the siege Charles VI and the Dauphin had been dilatory in the extreme. It was not until 28th August that a general call to arms was made. The Sire de Gaucourt had tried to seek the King's help without success. A mission under the Sire de Harqueville was sent to the Dauphin at Vernon under the terms of a truce, but he refused to march to the city on the ground that the army had not been fully assembled. On 22nd September Harfleur surrendered.

As a ceremony of surrender, King Henry V played out a repetition of the surrender of Calais in 1347. Seated on a golden throne and clothed in cloth of gold, the King with his waiting nobles had arranged to receive the city formally from the French commanders and the leading Burgesses. At one o'clock the procession emerged from the south-west gate, led by the Sire de Gaucourt with attending knights and the leading burgesses of the town. They climbed the hill clad only in their shirts and leg hose, with halter nooses about their neck. On arrival the Sire de Gaucourt knelt and presented King Henry with the keys of the city. The public relations exercise over, the King entertained the surrendering officials as guests to a banquet. He then turned his attention to reorganising the city as a permanent conquest. Over two hundred of the wealthier burgesses were sent to London or Calais until a ransom was paid; those that were prepared to take an oath of fealty were allowed to stay. The poorer citizens – men, women and children – were expelled and escorted to Lillebonne, where they came under the control of the King of France. Of the knights and men-at-arms, some 260 were paroled to appear at Calais by St Martin's day (the 11th November) to pay the King their ransom. Henry entered the city on 23rd September – leaving his horse, removing his shoes and walking as a penitent to St Martin's Church. Rauol de Gaucourt was sent on a mission to the Dauphin to challenge him to trial by battle with the King for the Crown of France, thus avoiding the sin of prolonging the war and saving life. The Dauphin avoided giving an answer, leaving an impression in the minds of the knighthood of cowardice.

Dysentery was still consuming the army. The dead were rising in number and included some of the King's commanders and advisors – the Earls of Mowbray, March and Arundel. The ill were sent home with most of the ships. The King was left with no more than 900 men-at-arms and 5,000 archers apart from the garrison. On 5th October proclamations were made in England for settlers of all trades to come to Harfleur to replace the expelled population. The King turned his mind to the next step. There were three choices – to return home, to march south to Bordeaux or go to Calais. The siege trains had been sent home and the winter season made going south difficult. The King was not prepared to go home and thus the army had to go north, as had King Edward III previously. On 8th October the King left Harfleur and the journey to Calais began.

27th September 1810

The Battle of Bussaco

Having been given the necessary authority by the Government, Lord Wellington advanced into Spain to assist the Spanish, and moved towards Madrid. On 28th July 1809 Wellington defeated King Joseph Buonaparte of Spain and Marshal Victor at Talavera. Despite the victory the circumstances were such that it was expedient for the army to retire to Portugal, and the French withdrew to defend Madrid. The British army fell back from the frontier to bases where the army could be re-supplied, repositioned and retrained. Marshal Beresford was given the task of creating a disciplined modern Portuguese army and Wellington conceived a strategy for the future. He was well aware that the Emperor Napoleon would be determined to drive him and the British from the Peninsula. In order to prevent that he began, as the ultimate safeguard, to create a defended area between the Atlantic and the Tagus which could bar the way to Lisbon and keep the British protected without fear of evacuation. In October 1809 the works began with great secrecy to construct the forts and redoubts, which were to become known as the Lines of Torres Vedras. The Light Division, supported by the Hussars of the King's German Legion and Major Ross's troops of horse artillery, were left on the frontier west of the River Agueda as a guard. General Crauford, who commanded the Division and was known as 'Black Bob', was a ferocious disciplinarian, but his men were devoted to him as a result of his constant care for their welfare.

The French were pre-occupied in Spain with the insurgency of the people and the threat of Spanish armies. However, on 17th April 1810 by Imperial Decree Marshal Massena was appointed to command the 'Army of Portugal', a force nominally of 70,000 infantry and 8,000 Cavalry. Massena served in the Royal Army from 1775 to 1789, when he was discharged, and for a time was a smuggler based in Antibes. In 1791 he returned to the army and rose rapidly, being made a General of Division after the siege of Toulon in 1793. He distinguished himself in Napoleon's Campaign in Italy, became a Marshal of France in 1804 and commanded in Italy. In 1809 he fought in the campaign in Germany and Austria. He had lost one eye as a result of a shooting accident when out with Napoleon. He was given to plundering and was avaricious. In the Spanish campaign he was accompanied by his mistress, who was the wife of one of his aides-de-camp, dressed as a hussar officer. As a general he was shrewd, fearless, tenacious and determined. In mid-May 1810 he arrived to take up his appointment. The French began to move forward into Portugal. In June Marshal Ney with his VIIth Corps of 24,000 men besieged Cuidad Rodrigo and on 10th July the city surrendered. In the third week of July the French began to move forward again: the Light Division fell back and was almost destroyed while crossing the River Coa on a narrow bridge. Crauford waited too long on the east side and Ney's corps came up before all were across the bridge. The French in their turn tried to rush the bridge and lost 500 men.

Almeida was invested on 15th August. It was garrisoned by 5,000 Portuguese under a British Governor, Walter Cox, and was provisioned with a million rations of bread and plentiful ammunition. On 26th August, when gunpowder was being taken from the store in the cathedral, a barrel leaked, leaving a powder trail back into the church. By chance a French shell fell on the powder line, which ignited, ran back and blew up the stored munitions in an infernal explosion which destroyed the Cathedral, the fortress and the centre of the town. 700 people were killed. As a consequence, on 28th August Cox and the garrison surrendered.

The catastrophe at Almeida made it inevitable that Wellington and the British army should fall back. He did, withdrawing further down the River Mondego. As part of his overall strategy the Portuguese civil population had been ordered to burn their crops, destroy their food and evacuate the country, taking their animals towards Lisbon. Leaving the country almost destitute of supplies, the trek of sad people began, miserably moving away from the advancing French. A problem which Wellington faced was to ascertain which of three routes the French might take. There were three possibilities; first, the main Almeida, Coimbra-Lisbon road, second, a southerly route joining the latter near Santererm or third, a northern route through Viseu. The French as they had advanced had been beset by logistic problems. The hilly barren country through which they had come was bare and inhospitable, made the worse after their penetration into Portugal by Wellington's scorched-earth policy. It was well adapted to guerrilla operations and as the Army passed, Spanish and Portuguese guerrillas, the *Ordinanza* or militia, closed the roads behind them. Supply columns were blocked and destroyed and as the French moved on supplies from the country itself became ever less obtainable. Massena ordered the Portuguese militia, a barefoot peasant army in their own brown cloaks, suppressed, and refused to accord them military status. Savagery and killing became perpetual on both sides. He was short of supplies and of horses, so that already one-third of the cannons had been left behind in Salamanca. Hoping that the northern route might be less devastated than the main and southern routes, the latter of which he heard was blocked by redoubts, he chose the worst road, the Viseu route, which wound over the hills and had to be widened by men working with picks and shovels to allow the artillery to pass. He left Almeida on 15th September with rations for fourteen days taken from the captured city. On the 17th Wellington received news that he had taken this road, 'the worst road in the kingdom' as he described it. Wellington had already chosen a defensive position on the main road to make a stand, but had to switch to another position to block the route taken. The choice made was the ridge north of the River Mondego at Bussaco.

Controversy has been excited on why Wellington decided to make a stand and not retire direct to Torres Vedras. In all probability the decision stemmed from a complex of factors; the hope that, as after Talavera, victory might lead to a French withdrawal, the need to persuade the Portuguese that the British would defend the country, the desire to help a Government under pressure in London with a victory and as a morale booster to the British army, and the newly formed Portuguese contingents, which the French viewed with contempt.

The Bussaco position eight miles North West of Coimbra showed all of Wellington's flair for picking and using the country to protect and strengthen his army in a battle. It comprised a nine to ten-mile ridge stretching north from granite cliffs descending to the Mondego. The sides were steep and rock strewn, falling into ravines and gullies at the bottom. The top of the ridge comprised a plateau about four hundred yards wide, rock-strewn, with basalt and limestone boulders, and deep heather among which grew aloes. The southern edge was crowned by the Nostra Senhora de Monte Alto. The highest point, at 800 feet, was two miles south of the northern end of the ridge, near the Convent of Bussaco and its park. This was to be the chosen command post of Lord Wellington. The road from the east to Coimbra ran through the villages of Moura and Sula, which lay on the hill climbing to the pass across the ridge. A southerly road branched off east of Moura and crossed the ridge in its centre from the village of San Antonio de Cantaro to Palherios west of the ridge. Below the western rim of the plateau ran a red mud track from north to south, from the Convent and down to the River Mondego at Penacova.

From 21st September Wellington concentrated his forces on the ridge and all were in place by the 25th. Sir Rowland Hill's 2nd Division had been recalled from the south when Wellington learnt that Reynier's 2nd Corps had been called back north. The Allied army comprised 52,000 troops, of which only half were British, and some 60 guns. The numbers meant that the ridge over its whole length could not be guarded without gaps between the divisions on the plateau. Cole's 4th Division was deployed north of the Coimbra road, Crauford's Light and some Portuguese barring the road, with the King's German Legion beyond the ridge in reserve. Spencer's 1st was south of the road. Then came Picton's 3rd Division north of the road from San Antonio de Cantaro, with Leith's 5th to the south. Finally Hill's 2nd Division occupied the ridge north of Senhora de Monte Alto. Forward from the ridge on the Coimbra road four companies of Rifles occupied Sula as a point of concentration for the skirmishers, while the rear brigade of the Light Division waited forward in Moura. The troops were stationed back from the crest and could not be seen from the ground as the ridge was approached.

Marshal Ney with the advance guard appeared along the Coimbra road from the west on 25th September. Advanced patrols identified skirmishers and a few guns on the ridge and came up against the soldiers of the Light Division in Moura, who defended the village until nightfall before rejoining the rest of the division. Ney reconnoitred the position and realised he had come upon the Allied army. Returning to camp at Mortagorda he sought out Massena, but had to hammer on his bedroom door to raise him from the arms of his mistress, Madame Liberton. Ney wanted to attack on the 25th, but Massena insisted on and carried out his inspection of the ridge on the morning of the 26th. He ordered the attack for dawn on the 27th. By reason of the activities of the Portuguese Ordenanza and the sullen opposition of such peasants as remained, the French had no proper intelligence of the dispositions and location of the Allied armies. Massena thought that Hill was still in the south and that facing him were only 20,000 British. He discounted the Portuguese as he considered them unreliable and likely to turn tail and run.

To him therefore there was no reason why with three Corps (Ney, Reynier and Junot) amounting to 60,000 men, he could not defeat the Allied army crushingly by frontal attack up-hill. He disregarded the difficulty that his artillery could not bombard the position on the crest and did not bother, confident of success, with the need to try to outflank Wellington. On those assumptions he thought that he had a strong chance of success. Reynier and Junot, who had fought the British, were more sceptical. The tactics were to be for Reynier coming up the road from San Antonio de Cantaro to turn the British right, pushing the centre along the ridge. Once Ney saw Reynier's Corps on the crest he was to launch his corps up the Sula Road over the pass to Bussaco, crushing the Allied left centre and permitting a division of the VIth Corps and the VIIIth Corps to press through towards Coimbra. As dark fell, the plain before the ridge glittered and twinkled with the fires of the French bivouacs. On the crest all was dark. Wellington had ordered that the troops should be fed only cold food and that no fires or lights were to be lit, in order to preserve the illusion which the French had that his army was smaller than it was. The men slept under their blankets as a cold wind blew in from the Atlantic.

When dawn came the lower slopes of the ridge were clothed in fog and the French corps could not be seen, the only sign of their presence being the drumming, music, shouting and noise of the columns forming up. At 6 am Lieutenant-General Picton, Commander of the 3rd Division, heard firing on the slopes below in the fog where there was a screen of skirmishers and light companies of the 45th (Nottinghamshire) Regiment of Foot, the 74th (Highland) Regiment of Foot and the 88th (Connaught Rangers) Regiment of Foot. General Hendelet's Division of 15 Battalions of the 2nd Corps had been launched up a spur to the south of the southerly road from San Antonio de Cantaro, attacking on the line of the road crossing the ridge to Palheiros. They advanced in columns a company width wide, drums hammering, driving back the skirmishers and finally emerging breathless and disorganised, having had to climb over the rocks into the sunlight above the fog. The pass itself was defended by half a battalion of British troops, and two battalions of Portuguese supported by artillery, which pounded the leading column, the French 31st Regiment, in the van. Between the 3rd and 5th Divisions on the ridge there had been a two-mile gap, but Picton had posted the 88th nearer to the pass in order to support the defenders in a detached position. The 74th Highlanders and the Portuguese brigade racked the columns with intense fire. The French were brought to a halt, torn by the artillery and devastating rifle fire, and finally veered to the right, pinned down on the hill.

At the same time General Merle's 1st Division of the Second Corps (12 battalions) moved up the hill from a dip one mile north of the Palheiros road. The Light Companies were driven back and the French reached the summit in a hole between the 88th and the Portuguese Regiments of the 3rd Division, one of which had been posted near the pass. The summit was occupied and the French could be seen at the top of the ridge. On their right the Portuguese were somewhat uncertain at first, but they rallied and helped by the half battalion of the 45th, poured a steady fire from fifty yards into the French now on the summit. On the left of the French the 88th, half savage Connaught Rangers from western Ireland, were formed in column and led by their Scots commander, Colonel Wallace, fixed bayonets and charged either side of the French along the summit. The 88th and four companies of the 45th fell so crushingly on the French that they were swept downhill, toppling back in headlong flight. Charles Napier, struck in the fall by a musket ball remarked, 'I could not die at a better moment'. General Foy with seven battalions then pushed forward up the north side of the pass, falling again on the defenders on the road, the half-battalion of the 45th, the Portuguese and the artillery support. They began to yield. Lieutenant General Leith, commanding the 5th Division to the south, moved quickly to assist the troops under pressure. Using the track to the west along the ridge, he dispatched the 9th (East Norfolk) Regiment of Foot, the 38th (1st Staffordshire) Regiment of Foot and the 1st (Royal) Regiment of Foot at the double to the pass. These came up to Foy's column, the 9th enfilading the advance and the 38th attacking the head of the columns. Foy was wounded and after fierce resistance the French fell back, pushed by the charging bayonets, encouraged by General Leith on his charger waving his hat.

When Marshal Ney saw the French on the top of the ridge after Merle's attempt with an officer waving his hat, he launched the other limb of the attack by the VIth Corps. General Loison's 3rd Division of 12 Battalions was to advance on the northerly side of the Coimbra road from Moura to the Bussaco Convent in its dry ravine and General Marchant with the 1st Division of 11 Battalions on the South. Loison emerged from the woods to dislodge the British and the Portuguese Cacadores from Sula. These fell back, skirmishing the while as they moved uphill.

At this stage Wellington in his plain grey coat, simple low hat and light sword could be seen reconnoitring the position of the Light Division, indifferent to the shot around him. Loison's Division struggled uphill, bombarded by 12 guns. As they moved up they could see on the crest only Captain Ross's battery and Major-General Crauford standing above. They struggled up against the gunfire and began to move towards the guns which they could see. Ross galloped off leaving Crauford alone. Just before they were twenty yards away, Crauford turned and shouted to the hidden Light Brigade who were lying down in dead ground on the crest, 'Now 52nd, avenge the death of Sir John Moore!' With a great huzza the 52nd (Oxfordshire Light Infantry) Regiment and the 43rd (Monmouthshire Light Infantry) Regiment rose up, 1,800 troops, and fired concentrated volleys into the French. The fusillade of shot was dense enough to slice off the heads of the leading French, and 1,000 fell. The remainder, in a confused mêlée, and pushed by the Light Infantry at the bayonet, slithered downhill. In sequence General Marchant had pushed forward south of the road to encounter Brigadier-General Pack's Brigades of Portuguese infantry, screened by the Cacadores (riflemen) and supported by artillery. So effective had been their training that they fired with all the effectiveness of the British Infantry, and following the rout of Loison Marchand's attack was called off.

No further attempt was made on the ridge that day, although firing had continued. The French had sent in some 45 battalions amounting to 40,000 men. Some 24 Allied battalions had put them to flight, while the 1st, 2nd and 4th Divisions had not been engaged. The French lost 4,500 men, of which 250 were officers. The British and Portuguese each had 626 causalities. The retrained and newly established Portuguese army had proved themselves. As Lieutenant Colonel Tomkinson wrote, 'the day gave the Portuguese confidence in themselves and with the army in general'. Wellington put the matter more laconically, 'it has given them a taste for an amusement to which they are little accustomed'.

On 28th September Marshal Massena, still determined on the conquest of Portugal, sent out cavalry patrols to seek out a route around the British position. He began to move into the Serra de Caramula and found a track to the north of the ridge which Trant and the Spanish had failed to guard. Wellington, realising he would be outflanked, decided to withdraw, and the army started to slip away that night, leaving straw-filled sentries and Crauford, the Light Division and Anson's cavalry Brigade to form a rearguard. He wished to cross the River Mondego at Coimbra before the French reached there. The retreat of the army after the victory affected morale and discipline as the army trudged back in days of unending rain, accompanied by a bedraggled and miserable column of Portuguese, without food, and whose animals starved and died. The French, behind, without adequate rations, since their troops marched living on the country, seized food from the local population, savagely sacked villages, slaughtered the peasants and committed endless atrocity in an endeavour to find hidden food supplies in the stripped country. The Allied army swept through Coimbra, which with the retreat had to be evacuated, looting and undisciplined. The inhabitants rich and poor joined the endless line of refugees struggling through the mud. On 7th October, having left another seventy miles of devastated countryside without inhabitants and provisions, the lines of Torres Vedras were reached, which Wellington had already had constructed.

These were in no sense a continuous line. The 'lines', using the escarpment of the hills, comprised 152 groups of forts set on the hills from the Atlantic to the Tagus over a twenty-mile distance. All woods giving cover before the forts had been removed and their guns commanded every road and valley entering the line. Roads had been constructed up to the forts, such as that to Monte Agnaco, where there were four redoubts on the crest, one of which, for example, was provided with twenty-four guns and a howitzer. It was here that Wellington had his headquarters, in a chapel on the Pero Negro. Revetments and entanglements were constructed from the felled trees. The Torres Vedras lines were only the first of three rings protecting Lisbon. Six miles beyond the outer ring was a second, and a third had been created enclosing two miles of shore on the Tagus between Lisbon and the sea.

In October the army in pouring rain entered the lines and the troops were assigned to their posts. Rations had run out but the army was immediately re-provisioned and re-supplied. The 50,000 odd refugees had to shift for themselves in the open countryside between the lines and the city. In early October Massena and his officers were sure that within seven days they would reach Lisbon with all its supplies. The supply position was dire. Five thousand French sick and wounded had been left in Coimbra but after the French army had passed on, the Portuguese Ordinanza had entered the city and taken it, massacring the sick and wounded and closing behind Massena to block his communications to Spain. The latter had no knowledge of the lines until a captured British cavalry patrol explained that they were seeking to enter them.

Wellington posted the Portuguese in the forts and defendable places, and deployed the British army to secure flexibility and mobility in action. By 10th October the lines were all manned and ready and on the 12th the French attacked and drove in some outposts at Sobral. On 14th October Massena reconnoitred the lines, seeking a way through. With dwindling food rations and no supplies Massena and the French army encamped outside the lines, sickness and starvation wearing away at his men and horses. It rained constantly. On 15th November Massena and the army retired thirty miles away north of Santarem, in hope of finding unravaged country. The ration supply was no better and mounting violence and atrocities were needed to force their hidden food from the remaining peasants. In December General Drouet arrived with 900 conscripted troops, but their presence worsened the problem. Finally on 5th March 1811 Massena struck camp and went into full retreat. He had argued with Marshal Ney about a move south in Portugal and Ney had wholly opposed the plan. Ney resigned and returned to Paris. Massena however set off southwards on 23rd March, his troops sick and starving, his cavalry and baggage hindered by the horses lost. Savage atrocities marked the retreat – for example, 200 people were killed in a church by fire at Porto de Mos. On 15th March he had been ordered back to Spain. The invasion of Portugal was soon to be over. He had lost 25,000 men, almost all his baggage and many of his guns. Half the horses were dead. 8,000 Portuguese citizens had been killed or starved and whole swathes of the country devastated.

After his retreat from Bussaco Wellington had been under criticism from the Government in London and the Portuguese, who suspected that he was abandoning them. Despite public outcry both he and Government kept their nerve and he waited for the strategy of the line of Torres Vedras to work, confidently awaiting the destruction of the French army by famine and disease. He was surprised how long the French remained, perhaps underestimating their ability to live off the country in the devastated areas. The Allied Army started to move forward on 3rd April; it caught up with Reynier's corps at Sabugal and defeated it (see the Battle of Sabugal3rd April 1811).

28th September 1652

The Battle of the Kentish Knock

The Battle of the Kentish Knock was an early naval incident in the first Dutch War and goes wholly unnoticed in Clarendon's History of the Rebellion. In 1652 the Dutch were the leading commercial nation, trading with Russia, the Middle and Far East and the Caribbean. Great convoys of merchantmen were shepherded about the seas by the Dutch navy, whose main duty was to protect for the five republics of the Netherlands the coming and going of these fleets. The determination of the City of London to challenge this supremacy in trade, together with their influence in the Long Parliament, led to war breaking out in the late spring of 1652.

The English and Dutch fleets carried out various sweeps at sea to bring the navies to battle and skirmishes took place, the navies ranging from the Shetlands to the Bay of Biscay. On 28th August Sir George Ayscue met the Dutch off the coast of Brittany in the late afternoon under Admiral De Ruyter. A confused fight took place, lasting until it was dark. De Ruyter had brought out from Holland a large merchant convoy, which he had shepherded through the Channel moving at no more than an average speed of two knots. Sir George Ayscue broke off the fight at nightfall and returned to Plymouth. The month of September was spent by De Ruyter sailing back and forth in the Channel. In late September De Ruyter returned to Holland, and the Dutch fleet, now under the command of Admiral Witte de With, came out in search of the English. De With was a convinced republican and a savage fighter, but the morale of Dutch crews was low.

The English fleet had united and was anchored in the Downs. There the Dutch found them, but a gale delayed the attack and the fleet only met up by the shoal known as the Kentish Knock. There were 68 ships under Blake and 57 under De With. At 3 pm Blake in the Resolution (80 guns and 1st of the name) and Admiral Penn in the James shortened sail and waited for the fleet to come up. The fleet was in three squadrons with the benefit of a south-westerly wind. Admiral Bourne with his squadron had became somewhat detached, and De With was first to concentrate on them. By 4 pm the fleet was gathered and the frigates began the cannonade. The English attack was somewhat handicapped in starting by the fact that the Sovereign (2nd of the name, built by King Charles I as the Sovereign of the Seas, with 100 guns) and Admiral Penn's flagship the James ran aground on the Kentish Knock and had to be got off. The bombardment by the fleets of one another, as they sailed past each other close hauled, was to last two hours. It was a heavy duel at close range. De With's flagship was so damaged that he had to transfer his flag, but mutinous sailors would not let him aboard, until finally he was taken up by the Prince William, a merchantmen whose pilot and crew were drunk. Darkness brought an end to the incidents of battle and under its cover the Dutch escaped to the Texel. At least four Dutch ships were lost and nine had deserted.

October

3rd	The Capture of Barcelona	1705
6th	The Capture of Manila	1762
7th	The Crossing of the River Bidassoa	1813
11th	The Battle of Camperdown	1797
12th	The Battle of Vigo Bay	1702
14th	The Second Battle of Finisterre	1749
21st	The Battle of Trafalgar	1805
25th	The Battle of Agincourt	1415
28th	The Battle of Arroyo dos Molinos	1811

3rd October 1705

The Capture of Barcelona

The Duke of Marlborough was a firm supporter of the need, in the War of the Spanish Succession, to promote a strategy of attacking the French in the Mediterranean as part of the attempt to force the division of their forces. The Emperor of Austria and the Allied candidate for the Spanish crown, King Charles III, was equally enthusiastic. A number of objectives were constantly canvassed by the British and their allies. In 1705 a Mediterranean campaign was organised and on 4th May a fleet under Sir Clowdisley Shovell, of 37 English men-of-war, 20 Dutch, and 20 frigates and fire ships, with seven bomb vessels, left England. They were accompanied by a force of 5,000 solders under the command of the third Earl of Peterborough. As Lord Moredaunt and something of a tearaway, he had led the 'forlorn hope' of guardsmen at the storming of the Schellenburg (2nd July 1704).

Sir Clowdisley Shovell and his fellow admirals worried as they sailed about the position of the French fleet. There were 20 ships of the line at Brest under the Marquis de Coëtlogan and 40 at Toulon under the Comte de Toulouse. At Ushant, however, the fleet divided and two squadrons were left under Sir George Byng and Sir John Jennings, a force inadequate to meet the fleet at Brest. In fact due to the neglected condition of the French navy, neither part of their fleet was fit to go to sea. On 10th June the main fleet reached the Tagus where a delay occurred while Shovell and Peterborough awaited troops from Ireland, and collected transport and forage for the Dragoons. On the 22nd June Shovell sailed on. There had been and was disagreement as to the destination. The Government had given instructions to attack the French naval base of Toulon, if the Duke of Savoy attacked by land. The latter however was in no position to do so, since he had just lost at Villa Franca. The Earl of Peterborough was keen to attack Catalonia, since that province was believed to be full of supporters of King Charles III, where the invasion force was said to be able to find help from 6,000 men and 1,200 horsemen. The Prince of Hesse-Kassel on the other hand preferred Valencia, because it was nearer Madrid. In the outcome a landing in Catalonia was to be made.

The fleet and its convoy arrived on 11th August about four miles east of Barcelona. The enemy did not move and the next few days was spent landing the dragoons, a force of marines, the baggage and stores. The quarrel about the objectives of the expedition persisted, since the commanders were lacking information about the position on shore and felt that their force was too small for a siege. They had noted that the French had needed 26,000 troops previously to retake Barcelona on an earlier occasion. The city was difficult to attack;

to the north-east and at St Martin the ground was partly a bog, which made mining difficult, and any attack would have to be over open ground. The ground conditions were not conducive to establishing batteries. On the southüwest the city was overlooked and dominated by the steep hill on which stood the citadel, the Castle of Montjuich and that could enfilade attacks from any direction. Contrary to expectation the Catalonians refused to go within reach of the guns. The Governor, the Conde Francisco de Velasco, had improved the northern and eastern defences and had a garrison of 4,000 horse and foot.

On the 17th August King Charles III landed and on the 18th ten siege guns and a number of field pieces were put ashore. There was still a division of view on account of the difficulty of the siege as to the course to be taken. The Earl of Peterborough wished to go to Italy, but the admirals opposed that suggestion as the sailing season was nearing an end. He then proposed a march to Tarragona and Tontosa but that was opposed by King Charles III and the Prince of Hesse-Kassel. The possibility of going to Nice was discussed, but the King continued to press for a siege. That won the support of the admirals and Peterborough, but not of fellow Generals. On 26th August a Council of War accepted the proposal, subject to the provision of seamen and guns on land to assist. On 28th August the Council met again and the sense of the meeting once more was that the siege was impracticable. The campaign had therefore spent over three weeks being irresolute and incapable of formulating a strategy. Once more Italy was considered, and a march to Tarragona with a decision finally made in favour of the latter. After the Council, Sir Clowdisley Shovell wondered whether the Earl of Peterborough should not consider taking Montjuich and assaulting the city from that side. The Earl reconnoitred the ground and accepted the suggestion. Under the cover of the preparation to leave by ship for Tarragona, which was visible to the city, dispositions were made for the army to move round to the south-west of the town and storm the hill of Montjuich. The route around used rocky paths in the foothills and was a hard terrain over which to take an army. King Charles III was not told and the army was informed that it was moving to take a pass on the road to Tarragona. Secrecy was tight. The attacking forces were organised into two columns: the first under Brigadier Lord Claremont, with half the Grenadiers under Lieutenant Colonel Southwell and other battalions, amounting to 1,000 troops; the second was commanded by Major General James Stanhope, comprising 1,000 infantry and Royal Dragoons.

In order to protect the batteries and siegeworks Sir Clowdisley Shovell transferred 2,600 marines on shore as a support for the attacking force. The march in the dark on the night of 2nd September over the rugged route chosen was slow and the first column did not arrive at the foot of the steep hill of Montjuich until just before dawn. The assault was made on both sides of the citadel; the sentries were aroused and the Spanish began to fire the castle's batteries. Lt. Colonel

Southwell with the Guards stormed a covered way into the castle, where many of the defenders were encamped in tents. These were driven out and the enemy garrison was rounded up and placed in a small fort as a dungeon. The Prince of Hesse-Kassel and the Earl of Peterborough came up with the second column. They resolved to move on the city whose garrison was now roused. Led by the Prince the troops moved along the great moat of the citadel. There they were subjected to musket fire from the Spanish, invisible behind the bank of the moat. The Prince of Hesse-Kassel was wounded in the right thigh, cutting the great artery in the leg, and he was dead within half an hour. Lord Claremont, abandoning some guns, drew the troops off, but as they went, suffering from heat and want of water, Spaniards moved towards them, shouting 'Hurrah for Charles III'. The British paused, thinking the garrison had changed sides, but as the Spaniards came into sight they fired volley after volley into the waiting British soldiers: the latter began in disorder to retreat, some being taken prisoner. The Earl of Peterborough, with all the bravery that he had shown at the storming of the Schellenburg, angry at the turn of events, turned the troops back and led them back to the citadel's defences, which they had previously taken. The Spanish, seeing the Earl leading his men, thought that he could not be unaccompanied but by strong forces and retreated back to the town. The hill of Montjuich was taken save for the fort where the Spanish garrison were imprisoned.

On 4th September Sir Clowdisley Shovell began to arrange the movement of naval guns and ships to continue the siege. In dirty weather and a pounding surf on 4th and 5th September the guns were landed to take their place on the Montjuich hill with a view to the bombardment of the town. Vice-Admiral Sir Stafford Fairbome with his flag on the Wessex (70 guns) leading an Anglo-Dutch squadron of eight ships of the line, seven fire ships and seven bomb vessels moved in to cannonade the city from the sea. The bomb vessels went in close and fire was returned from the harbour mole. On 6th September the guns brought up to Montjuich landed a shell on a magazine, killing the commander of the fort on the hill and blowing up one of the four corner bastions. The white flag was raised and 300 soldiers surrendered.

Supervised by Sir Clowdisley Shovell himself, the bombardment of the city commenced and continued. The fleet hammered away daily; for example, on 17th September between 11 am and 1 pm twenty shells were shot from seven vessels, amounting to 140. The defenders replied with fifty shots, not obtaining one hit. On shore the navy had landed 72 guns, mostly 18-pounders but with thirty-four 24-pounders. Raising the guns up the slope to the height of Montjuich was heavy work on the slippery rock at night. The fort battery opened on 12th September and on the 17th the great battery of fifty-eight guns began firing. Soon a break was made in the city wall. On 22nd September the Earl of Peterborough summoned the Governor to surrender. On the 23rd Don Francisco de Velasco asked for the terms of capitulation. It took six days to agree the terms, a significant problem being where to send the garrison. Even after their signature the Spanish garrison took no action, but the citizens of Barcelona desired peace and angrily rose against the garrison. In order to protect them the Earl of Peterborough on October 3ʳᵈ ordered the gates broken down and the British troops entered to protect their late opponents.

It was too late to pursue the taking of Minorca and Port Mahon. The fleet was short of provisions and ammunition and on 12ᵗʰ October Sir Clowdisley Shovell sailed home, leaving Sir John Leake and Baron van Wassenaer with an Anglo-Dutch squadron of 25 ships of the line to hold the Mediterranean. The absence of a base nearby meant that Leake had to return to Lisbon to refurbish and reprovision his ships. A garrison was left at Barcelona. In early 1706 Marshal de Tessé appeared outside the city with 20,000 troops and laid siege to it. His communications were harried by Catalonians, but his army was supported by the Comte de Toulouse with 30 ships of the line from Toulon. The British and Allied troops were dispersed around Catalonia supporting Charles III, and there was only a small garrison under Lord Donegall. News of the siege was brought to Leake at Lisbon and he waited for Sir George Byng to join him. At last he reappeared on 27ᵗʰ April with 57 transports and 5,000 troops. On news of his approach the French fleet returned to Toulon, and Marshal de Tessé, without naval support, raised the siege and retired.

The search for a Mediterranean base and the desire to destroy Toulon and the French fleet remained, and in 1707 an attempt was made on Toulon. The Duke of Savoy and Prince Eugene supplied the troops, many in British pay, and Sir Clowdisley Shovell with a naval force supported the attack by sea. The campaign was not well conducted and the Imperial commanders and the Duke of Savoy decided to give up the attempt. The only gain of the campaign was the destruction of the French fleet in harbour, partly by Shovell's eighteen-hour naval bombardment and partly by the scuttling by the French of their fleet. The French navy did not return to the Mediterranean for the rest of the war.

Sir Clowdisley Shovell returned to England and on 21ˢᵗ October was two hundred miles south south-west of the Lizard in the Association, and the ship's noon observations of latitude were good. Before a method of establishing longitude scientifically, ships had to rely on soundings and their own dead reckoning to know the longitude of their position. Any sailor will appreciate the difficulty of plotting dead reckoning without the help of position finders. In winter entry into the Channel could be difficult because of the wind direction prevailing from the west and south-west and the tidal movement across the Channel mouth, which could develop on occasion a strong northerly set. On 22ⁿᵈ October a strong gale blew, with dense heavy rain and no finding of latitude could be made. The Association and its accompanying vessels were steering east north-east. The force of the wind and the set of the current carried the fleet north and it was soon fifteen miles north of its dead reckoning. At four o'clock the fleet was brought to and soundings taken and it was still within the sixty fathoms line. Sir Clowdisley Shovell decided to go on despite murky misty weather.

At six o'clock the squadron bore away to east by north but at eight o'clock the Association found itself between breakers and rocks. The flagship went aground on the Gilstone ledges by the Bishop's Rock and was pounded to pieces by the gale and tempestuous waves, foundering within minutes. All the complement, mainly Norfolk men, was lost. The Eagle (70 guns and 6th of the name) and the Romsey (50 guns) which were to the lee of the flagship were also lost. The Royal Anne and St George were just saved. In all four vessels were lost and over 2,000 men. Sir Clowdisley Shovell was thrown up still alive in Porthellick Cove. A woman found him and decided to plunder him for the emerald ring on his finger. She struck him on the head and left him to die, only confessing the deed thirty years later. The body was taken to London and Sir Clowdisley was buried in Westminster Abbey. Having started before the mast he had risen by his capacities and exertions to admiral, and was well regarded by the seamen of his fleet.

In 1714 Parliament passed the Longitude Act, offering a £20,000 prize to the discoverer of a method to calculate longitude. The problem was solved by a clockmaker James Harrison, who nonetheless was denied the price and full recognition. Only after the intervention of King George III did he receive any substantial sum, but not the award. In 1708 Sir John Leake took Minorca and Port Mahon, giving the navy a base which remained in British hands until 1756.

6th October 1762

The Capture of Manila

When Spain entered the Seven Years War, Admiral Lord Anson conceived a strategy to strike at Spain both in the West and East Indies. In pursuance of this strategy Havana was captured (see 11th August 1762); the other limb of the plan was an attack on the Philippines and Manila. The Prime Minister, the Duke of Newcastle, had only half agreed the project, which had been brought to the Government by Colonel Draper. Colonel Draper had been a fellow of a Cambridge College in holy orders, but had abandoned the life divine for the life military. The expedition was co-ordinated with the East India Company at Madras, and from there half a brigade, of 2,300 Europeans and Sepoys were embarked, of which Draper described only 1,700 men as 'useful'. The troops were transported in a fleet comprising seven ships of the line and four frigates and sloops, commanded by Admiral Samuel Cornish, who was said to have begun his career before the mast,. The ships were not in good condition, they were leaking and in need of repair. The departure from Madras in early August was late, as there was a need to arrive and land before the monsoon season. The fleet anchored in Manila Bay on 23rd September.

The Spanish were totally unprepared and the defences of Manila were weak. The harbour however was dominated at its entrance by a citadel called the Cavita. The fleet had arrived in rough weather with heavy seas, the Pacific surf thundering on the landing beach. It took three days for the troops to be disembarked on the beach through the surf, an exercise carried out by the navy under the control of Captain Kempenfeldt. To the military force were added a thousand sailors and marines. General Draper organised the bombardment of the city and its walls and that proceeded until 6th October, when it became practicable to storm the walls where breaches had been created. The Spaniards initially resisted the attacking forces but after an hour's fierce fighting the place was taken. The Governor surrendered the city, the island of Luzon and all other Spanish possessions in the Philippines. The Citidel of Cavite gave up without firing a shot. In the terms of surrender the British agreed not to pillage the inhabitants in return for an indemnity of four million dollars. Admiral Cornish took the fleet into harbour where it underwent repair.

While the attack was taking place negotiations for peace had begun with the French, and the preliminaries were settled by 3rd November, when the Duke of Bedford was sent by the new Prime Minister Lord Bute to sign the Provisional Articles. News of the taking of Manila and the Philippines came therefore after the terms were settled. While General Draper had been given a secret order to take the island of Mindaneo for a permanent colony, the Treaty of Paris nevertheless returned the Philippines to Spain. British occupation of the colony was therefore short. The Treaty retained the right to the four million dollar indemnities, but that was never paid. The concern of the public about the return to Spain of this conquest was one of the factors that subsequently led to the defeat of Lord Bute in Parliament.

Captain Kempenfeldt had a distinguished naval career but on 29th August 1782 he was lost when the Royal George foundered as she lay at anchor at Spithead. Previously she had been coppered, as part of the general policy of giving the ships of the fleet copper hulls under the sea in order to improve performance and reduce maintenance. However, her timbers had become entirely rotted, probably because the iron fastenings of the copper bottom had corroded and let in seawater. The bottom just fell out. A court martial revealed that the poor condition of the hull had been seen before the loss and that her timbers were rotten. Her serious state was thus known. The findings of the court martial were suppressed, however. The poet William Cowper composed a poem in commemoration of the incident, 'On the loss of the Royal George'.

The 13th Duke of Bedford and the 7th Marquis of Bute were ejected from the House of Lords in 2001.

7th October 1813

The Crossing of the River Bidassoa

After the Battle of Sorauren (28th July 1813) and the fall of San Sebastian (9th September 1813) Marshal Soult and the French army tried a counter-attack at San Marcial, where they were held by the Spanish army alone. Their retreat however was stabilised along the Bidassoa River, where a defensive line was established. The line stretched from the estuary west of Béhobie, the lowest crossing point, some twenty-three miles inland, into the hilly and mountainous land of the Pyrenees. Works were undertaken to build redoubts and fortifications on the hills along the river, the most significant of which was La Grand Rhune. The bridges were broken down downstream and Marshal Soult was confident that the Allied army could be held.

The Duke of Wellington had not pursued the French ruthlessly after his earlier victories, having to contend with supply difficulties and the political problem of whether an invasion of France would be prudent in a situation where the Emperor Napoleon was in negotiation with Austria, Russia and Prussia during the campaign in central Germany.

The army therefore bided its time as it moved north, and had leisure for amusement. Throughout the war in the Peninsula the army had maintained two packs of foxhounds, one personal to the Duke of Wellington. Well-attended meets were held from time to time. It is recorded that while the army waited to cross the River Bidassoa, the hounds on one such occasion went away after a fox, which swam the river. The field came to a halt on the British side but the Master, waving his white handkerchief, crossed to the French side, where he was permitted to retrieve the hounds. It would be pleasant to think that the hounds did in fact kill their fox.

The crossing of the Bidassoa presented a difficult problem in that the Spaniards, who had suffered so much from the French, would plunder the countryside of France ruthlessly and alienate the French population. Wellington did not wish to be involved in the consequent insurgency which he foresaw. The Portuguese, far from their country, were beginning to lose their enthusiasm for the campaign, and there was a danger of their army melting away. In early September he received news of Napoleon's victory in the battle of Dresden and he began to prepare for the invasion of France.

The French position was a strong one, ending at St Jean Pied-de-Port in the east, north of the Pass of Roncesvalles. Marshal Soult had only some 39,000 troops to man the line and he was therefore thinly spread. He thought it unlikely that Wellington would cross the lower Bidasoa and decided to concentrate his troops in the centre and left–centre near Vera, while guarding against an outflanking movement at St Jean Pied de Port. General Foy was posted to guard the latter. The six Divisions of Generals Clausel and D'Erlon were placed in the centre and centre left near Vera, ensconced in the defences which had been built. General Mancune, with a weak division, was placed to guard the lower Bidassoa estuary. From a military point of view given his limited forces, Soult would have been better to retreat to a less strung-out position, but his fear of the anger of the Emperor Napoleon precluded that.

Local shrimpers gave information to Wellington that at low tide the mud of the estuary dried out, reducing the breadth of the river, and that there were causeways through the marshy land. Wellington therefore decided to attack the French position at two points. First, to carry out an outflanking movement across the estuary and second, to make a concentrated assault, in numbers, on the fortified front line in the vicinity of Vera. By carrying out demonstrations of force against the line on the right, the preconception of Soult was strengthened. Meanwhile, units were transferred to the west ready for the assault.

Thunderstorms shattered the night of 7th October as the British and Allied troops prepared themselves for the assault. Before dawn the 5th Division set off across the mud and wading the river, which came up to their armpits, crossed the mud to the north side. The troops of General Mancune's Division heard the force coming, but were too late to deploy fully to meet it. After some skirmishing the 5th Division found the French some three miles upstream and the took their camp. Béhobie was relinquished. General Reille, with the 105th Regiment and the remnants of Mancune's forces tried to make a stand, but they were defeated and retired. The French front was being rolled up from the west. Meanwhile, the Light and 4th Divisions had set off to scale the heights around and near Vera. With determination and resolve they climbed the escarpments and hills to reach the redoubts on the hills. One by one the redoubts fell, as in some only a token resistance was put up. The troops of Generals Conroux and Tampin's Divisions had a low morale and did not fight with the customary French firmness. In others a fierce resistance was made, necessitating their storming at the point of the bayonet. By the end of 7th October the French defensive line had however been swept away: only the redoubts on the Grande Rhune continued to resist. These were abandoned early the next day. Marshal Soult ordered retirement to the line of the River Nivelle, where he was to create a new line of fortifications. The allied loss had been small, amounting to 1,500 casualties only.

11ᵗʰ October 1797

The Battle of Camperdown

The winter of 1794 to 1795 was extremely severe, one of intense cold, when even harbours were frozen. A British army was forced to retreat across Gelderland in Holland back to Germany, and the French invaded and seized all Belgium and Holland. The Prince of Orange had to flee and the pro-French inhabitants among the Dutch rose establishing the Batavian Republic, which was to last until 1806. French cavalry and artillery took the Texel, where the Dutch fleet was icebound, and a significant naval force thus came into the hands of the French Government. In May the Dutch agreed that the French would be able to use it and on the 16ᵗʰ declared war on Britain. From 1795 until 1797 it was necessary to maintain a blockade at the Texel to deter the fleet from coming to sea. The task was entrusted to Admiral Adam Duncan, who, while a stern disciplinarian was respected by his men whom he treated humanely and fairly. The ships of the line which he had for the blockade were however old and well-used, being obsolete 64-gunners or well-used 74-gunners, since the North Sea blockade was not seen as so crucial a sphere of naval activity as the Channel or the Mediterranean. For two years he maintained an increasing watch over the Dutch fleet. 1797 was however to witness events which put the navy severely to the test.

Inadequate pay, delay in payment, poor on-board conditions, failure to accord seamen shore leave and on occasion tyrannic discipline led the fleet to mutiny at Spithead in April of that year. The Admiralty Board, with characteristic obstinacy and institutional inflexibility, which the British civil service still exhibits, was loath to deal with the complaints. The crews however refused to go to sea, although in every other way they observed discipline, respected the officers and ran the ships as if no 'strike' had taken place. In the end, wiser heads in the Government and among the Admirals prevailed, and undertakings were given to redress the grievances and give pardons to the mutineers. Earl Howe, victor of the Glorious First of June and who was trusted by the men, visited the fleet and the mutiny came to an end. Just as the mutiny at Spithead was in its last stages, the fleet stationed at the Nore mutinied. Unlike the mutiny at Spithead, the mutineers were more extreme and the outcome less happy. On the same day, 24ᵗʰ May, as the mutineers from the Nore came up to Duncan's fleet at Yarmouth roads, he received news that the Dutch were preparing to leave the Texel. He visited each of the ships in the fleet and appealed to the men to keep to their duty. On the

Adamant (50 guns) he was successful and also on his own ship the Venerable (74 guns). It is said that on the Adamant only one seamen challenged his appeal and Duncan lifted him up by one arm over the side and said this is the man who dares to deprive me of my command. The crew laughed loudly. The rest of the fleet departed for the Nore.

On 1st June the Venerable and Adamant and two or three smaller ships were outside the entrance to the Texel, where there were ninety-five Dutch vessels. Fortunately the wind was westerly and on shore and Duncan was able to maintain the pattern of his blockade, which was to be in shore in westerly winds and stand out on easterly winds. The entrance to the Texel was narrow and Duncan told his crew that from his soundings he knew that the entrance could be obstructed by the Venerable if sunk and her colours would still float above the sea. He had determined to fight to the last. The westerly wind however penned the Dutch in harbour, and Duncan kept up the pretence, used by Admiral Cornwallis, see Cornwallis's Retreat (17th June 1795), that his main fleet was below the horizon by having the frigates signalling to that effect. After three days he was joined by vessels from the Channel fleet, and a small Russian squadron. Once the mutiny at the Nore was settled his fleet rejoined him.

The French and Dutch spent the summer collecting supplies and assembling an army to invade Ireland, to assist the Irish rebel Wolfe Tone. The latter had hoped to take advantage of the mutinies to cross to Ireland, but these were over before the waiting troops who had been assembled could be used. By mid-June Duncan was back on his station with the whole fleet. In July the army was embarked ready to leave, but the wind for several weeks blew strongly from the west and finally in August the army disembarked. Duncan remained on his station until the equinoctial gales and the scurvy on board drove him home after nineteen weeks to Yarmouth, to reprovison and repair the fleet.

Although the invasion of Ireland had been abandoned, the Dutch Commander Admiral Jan Willem de Winter was ordered by his government to sea and to engage the British fleet if there were a reasonable chance of victory. Duncan had left Captain Trollope in the Russell (74 guns), with frigate support to watch the Texel. The winds turned easterly and on 6th October De Winter came out with his fleet of sixteen along the coast. Captain Trollope drew off and shadowed the fleet, sending a lugger to warn Duncan that the Dutch were at sea. The message arrived at Yarmouth Roads on 9th October, and without delay Duncan started out for the Dutch coast with sixteen ships of the line.

De Winter had, despite his orders, no intention of doing battle for no result, and after sailing south he turned to return to the Texel. It was on 11th October that the British fleet came up with him, sailing on a larboard tack on a north-easterly wind. The day was leaden-skied, the wind moderate with some variability, the sea broken. De Winter's fleet had formed a line in which the flagship Vrijheid was fifth from the van. His ships were smaller than those of the British; there were only four 74-gunners compared with seven British, and four 68-gunners compared with seven 64-gunners. The ships were more shallow-bottomed than the British and thus more manoeuvrable in and around the shoals which lay off the Dutch and Belgium coast. The shallower draft of his boats meant that De Winter could take his fleet nearer inshore than could Duncan and attain a degree of safety. Duncan sighted the Dutch fleet at 7 am some twelve miles from shore, and as he closed his original intention was to attack in line but De Winter ordered his fleet to move in shore. Duncan realised that he needed to get up to the Dutch fleet before they could reach the shallower waters, and so he ordered a general chase with a view to his ships attacking individually, breaking through the Dutch line and striking on the leeward side between the Dutch fleet and the shore.

The British fleet was in two divisions, one to the leeward under Vice Admiral Onslow and one under Duncan to the windward. The former reached the Dutch fleet first at 12.30 pm at the rear, passing through the Dutch line between the Jupiter (74 guns) and the Haarlem (68 guns). He then luffed up and engaged the Jupiter, while the Powerful (74 guns) took on the Harlem. Both these ships were taken. Duncan himself came up in the van, passing through the line behind the States-General (74 guns), smashing into it with broadsides from his guns and carronades, causing its retirement from the battle. The force of the carronades, which were short pieces with large bores and were easy to handle, gave the British a significant edge over their adversaries. The Venerable them came up to attack the Vrijheid and Ardent joined in. Duncan's flagship was itself under assault with destructive fire from Brutus (74 guns), Leyden (68 guns) and Mars (44 guns). The Triumph (74 guns) attacked the Wassener (74 guns) and the Bedford (74 guns) cut the line astern of the De Vries (68 guns) and engaged it. So fierce was the attack on Duncan's flagship, the Venerable, that on more than one occasion the flag was shot away. James Crawford from Sunderland took the Admiral's colours and nailed them to the stump of the main topgallant mast where they stayed for the rest of the battle. At one point only Duncan and the pilot were left alone on the quarterdeck. The mêlée was joined by the Director (64 guns) commanded by Captain Bligh, of mutiny on the Bounty fame, which raked the Dutch flagship with broadsides. The Powerful (74 guns) also came up and the Montagu (74 guns). In the course of the battle the Dutch 64-gunner the Hercules caught fire and the crew threw their powder overboard and surrendered. For two and half hours the Dutch fought with obstinate courage and strength of resolve, suffering intense damage to their ships. They surrendered only when the masts of the flagship Vrijheid collapsed on the starboard side and De Winter lowered his flag. Part of the Dutch fleet escaped, since not all were engaged in the action but the wind making, the danger of the shoals and the damage to the British fleet inhibited pursuit. The British had taken seven ships of the line, two fourth rates and two frigates. De Winter offered Duncan his sword as a symbol of surrender, but Duncan said that he preferred to take his hand rather than his sword.

Duncan was victorious, but as dusk came on, the wind rose to gale force and the sea was lashed by rainy squalls. He was only in nine fathoms of water and five miles from the lee shore. The damaged fleet and the wrecked prizes had to weather this storm before returning home on 13th October. The Dutch fleet were all peppered through with shot and mainly dismasted. The British too had suffered similar damage, since the Dutch shot downwards unlike the French and Spanish; the Ardent for example, had ninety-eight holes in the hull. The fleet limped back and two of the prizes were lost. The Delft (56 guns) by 14th October had ten foot of water in its hold; Lieutenant Bullen in charge of the prize crew sent them off and wished the Dutch to evacuate the ship. Lieutenant Heilburg, the officer in charge, refused to leave the wounded. Out of regard for him, his courage and humanity, Lieutenant Bullen stayed. When the ship finally foundered, Lieutenant Bullen jumped into the sea and was saved, but Lieutenant Heilburg went down with his ship.

By 17th October the fleet and its prizes had arrived at the Nore. The news of the victory was carried to the King, George III. William Pitt the younger, the Prime Minister, was at Walmer Castle and was given the news by a smuggler. King George III came down to the Nore with the intention of visiting Duncan on his ship, but the heavy weather prevented his going shipboard. The British had had 203 killed and 622 wounded, the Dutch 500, including De Winter himself. The prizes were so damaged that they were hardly useable.

A thanksgiving service attended by King George III was held at St Paul's Cathedral in November, at which the Bishop of Lincoln preached on the text 'Except these abide in the ship, ye cannot be saved'. William Pitt thought the Bishop should explain that God only saved those who saved themselves by their own exertions. Admiral Duncan was made Viscount Duncan of Camperdown and Vice-Admiral Onslow was made a baronet. Gold medals were presented by the City of London to the captains of the fleet.

12th October 1702

The Battle of Vigo Bay

The War of the Spanish Succession involved Britain in May 1702. King Louis XIV of France desired to put his grandson on the Spanish throne, and he was proclaimed as King Philip V. The Holy Roman Emperor, in concert with other powers, was not prepared to accept this solution to the succession to the crown of Spain. The clash of interests led to a war which was to last until 1715.

In the summer of 1702 the Marquis de Château-Renault was sent with a fleet and troops to the West Indies to besiege Barbados. He met General de Coëtlogon there but the campaign was abandoned. In July 1702 he left Havana to return to Europe escorting 'the flota', the Spanish merchant fleet, bringing home silver mined in America, and left with 15 French ships of the line, 17 armed galleons with 40–50 guns, and 60 merchantmen. Sir Clowdisley Shovell was blockading Brest, awaiting the return of the French battle fleet, and Sir George Rooke was at Cadiz with an Anglo-Dutch expedition, trying to sieze the city. The French were therefore faced with the need to bring the convoy to another port, and it was decided to go into Vigo Bay, arriving there in mid-September, sailing up to Redondela.

Vigo Bay, the Ensenada de San Simon, is a large shallow open water basin entered through a long entrance bordered by high land on both sides. About ten miles in from the sea the entrance narrows to about 600 yards in the Estrecho de Rande, before entering the inland open water. At that point the narrows were guarded by forts; one on the north shore, the Punta de Bestia, and one on the south, the Punta de Rande. Most of the bay has a depth of less than five fathoms, but deeper water gives access up to Redondela. The forts and batteries had 70 guns and de Château-Renault placed a boom across the entrance to the bay, anchoring his ships of the line on the inner side of the boom.

The Admiralty did not receive news that the French fleet and silver convoy were at Vigo until 4th October, by which time much of the silver had been landed. Messages were sent at once to Sir Clowdisley Shovell, who was moving south towards Coruna, and to Sir George Rooke. He had already heard from Captain Hardy of the Pembroke on 6th October that the fleet had arrived at Vigo. He immediately sailed north, sending frigates in advance. On 11th October he anchored in the Ria Vigo below the boom. The forts and the narrowness of the approach all presented a problem for any attack. It was resolved that the Duke of

Ormonde, with a military force which was returning from the failed attempt at Cadiz, should attack and storm the southern fort on the Punta de Rande, and that the navy should break the boom taking the narrows close in to the southern shore. The warships of the fleet were organised by Rooke into seven groups of three or four vessels, with accompanying fireships. The Torbay (80 guns), with Vice-Admiral Hopson, was in the van and the Association (90 guns) and the Barfleur (90 guns) were deputed to bombard the forts.

On the morning of 12th October some 2,600 soldiers under the Duke of Ormonde were to land. At 9 am they began their attack, soon driving 3,000 Spanish from their entrenchments, while the Barfleur bombarded the fort. The navy groups began to come up to the boom, but the wind died and the Torbay in the van had to anchor. Hopson on the Torbay began to worry about the strength of the defences and he and Rooke met, deciding immediate attack was the best course. Fortunately at 1 pm a fresh breeze began to blow from the north-west and the moment had come for the fleet to force its way in.

Torbay led the way, creeping close to the south shore and not answering the fire from the fort, which Ormonde's troops were attacking, taking one of the batteries. Crashing with its stern into the boom, the Torbay severed it and smashed through, followed by three groups of ships. Once through the Torbay opened fire, and was engaged with the Bourbon and the Hope. The Hope soon cut its sails loose, dropping its moorings and beginning to drift, but Torbay was able to get alongside and bombard it. The Torbay itself was exposed to a fireship, which came down upon it with a fire astern of its mainmast. It reached the ship before it was seen, and was able to fasten itself alongside on the larboard bow. The quarterdeck caught fire and the deck became hot. Some men went overboard and were drowned. Admiral Hopson was to leave the ship, ultimately joining Monmouth. In a great clap the fireship blew up and the Torbay's crew was able to work to extinguish the fire. In all 115 men were lost. Resistance from the other French ships was sustained, ceasing when the Hope was taken. The battle, while it proceeded, was fierce; nothing but cannonading, burning, men and guns flying in the air and on all sides horror and confusion. The French admiral finally fired five of his ships; four ran ashore and six were taken as prizes. Of the galleons six were burnt, six taken by the English and five by the Dutch. The remaining treasure which had not been unloaded was taken, amounting, it is suggested, to four million sterling. On 16th October Sir Clowdisley Shovell arrived from the north. He was too late for the battle, but was able to take the prizes back to England. The French navy had been effectively savaged and the Spanish eliminated.

The battle was to have decisive consequences. King Pedro II had initially taken the view that Portugal would be best served by joining the French and Spanish, but the victory at Vigo Bay caused him to change his mind. A main concern was for the Portuguese overseas possessions, which he did not wish to see threatened by any dominant naval power, and which he desired to retain. In 1703 Pedro II acted therefore to enter into the Methuan Treaties. The first treaty pledged him to the Grand Alliance, subject to Britain and Holland committing troops to Spain in support of the Imperial candidate for the Spanish throne. The effect of this obligation was to widen the war aims of the Allies into land warfare in the Peninsula and naval struggle in the Mediterranean. The second treaty was of a commercial nature, giving access to English goods in Portugal in return for a reduction of the tariff on port wine. The use of Lisbon and Portugal for a base for the navy and the trade agreement led to port becoming a popular and patriotic wine for the upper classes, as opposed to claret from France, which had chosen to assist the Jacobite King across the water. The analogy today would be for Eurosceptics to drink new world wines from Australia, New Zealand and South Africa rather than European, particularly from France.

14th October 1749

The Second Battle of Finisterre

After the first Battle of Finisterre, Anson and the fleet returned to harbour. After refitting, part of the fleet under Rear-Admiral Hawke was ordered to sea to patrol the waters of the Bay of Biscay from Ushant to Finnisterre, on the watch for any French convoy. Hawke left from Plymouth on 9th August. While the entrance to the Bay in summer is not unduly rough and windy, gales do occur and the winds can be very variable, with strong swells on occasion. Hawke and his squadron were to endure these conditions, as the weather worsened into autumn, for two months as they patrolled the Atlantic north and south. Information came to the Admiralty that a large convoy was being prepared in the Basque Roads, and Hawke was sent to search for it. The convoy comprised 250 ships guarded by a squadron of nine men-of-war under Admiral Desherbiers de L'Étendière. Hawke had a squadron of 14 men-of-war. At daybreak on 14th October the French frigate Castor signalled the presence of ships to the north-west, some sixty miles off Finisterre. The weather was fair and the wind south-easterly. L'Étendière, thinking the vessels seen were part of his convoy which had become detached in the night, started to sail towards them. It was only as the ships came full over the horizon that they were identified as a British fleet. The French Admiral, recognising the importance of saving the convoy, ordered the Content (64 guns) with the armed East Indiamen to sail on. He stood to, in order to await the oncoming British, hoping to make his escape before they neared. The wind backed to south south-east as Hawke came down to the French, and he ordered his scattered ships to form into line when he was about four miles away. As he neared, L'Étendière tried to escape, heading away from the convoy, all sails set and as near to the wind as possible. In order to close the gap Hawke ordered a general chase, to permit the quicker ships to press on.

The Lion (60 guns and 4th of the name) was the earliest to reach the French fleet and ran the whole line of the French squadron at 11.30 am, bombarding them and being pounded in return. The Princess Louisa (60 guns) soon joined and after tacking and standing to windward fell on the Terrible (74 guns), the leading French ship. By this time the British had come up and a general action ensued. Eagle (60 guns and 8th of the name, under Captain Rodney engaged with the Intrépide (74 guns) and was severely battered as was the Edinburgh (70 guns). Hawke in the flagship, the Devonshire (70 guns and third of the name), fired broadsides in passing at the Severn (50 guns) leaving her partially disabled to the frigates. He sailed into the smoke, which had begun to obscure the action seeking out the Tonnant (80 guns), the French flagship. Colliding with Eagle, the two ships became entangled. As Devonshire struggled away to engage, the lower deck guns lost their breechings, and firepower was affected. Tonnant was near to overwhelming the British flagship, but it was saved by a fierce attack on the Frenchman by Tilbury (64 guns) and Terrible (74). Yarmouth (64 guns) under Captain Saunders, who as an admiral worked with General Wolfe at Quebec, (see the Taking of Quebec 18th September 1759,) battered Neptune (70 guns) until with the captain killed, its masts gone and 200 killed and wounded, the Frenchman struck its colours.

The battle persisted until almost five o'clock, by which time Trident, Terrible, Monarque (70 guns) and Fougueux (64 guns) had also all been taken. The French flagship and Intrépide (74 guns) started to draw away down wind. Tonnant lacked both a mizzen and mainmast but L'Étendière struggled away. Seeing their flight, Captain Saunders on Yarmouth signalled to Eagle and Nottingham to join him. Only the latter under Captain Saumarez closed, and fought gallantly in an attempt to stop the escape. Saumarez was killed and Nottingham severely damaged. In the night both the Tonnant and Intrépide made good their escape. In all the French had lost six ships, with over 800 casualties. The convoy had however gone on, and the British fleet was in no state to pursue it. Hawke however sent the sloop Weazle to warn the fleet in the Caribbean, and some were taken in the Leeward Isles.

Hawke returned home with his victory on 31st October. Hawke demanded and obtained a court martial of Captain Fox of Kent, who had not obeyed an order given and, despite his having taken the Fougueux, he was dismissed from the service. Hawke went on to be victorious in the Battle of Quiberon Bay (see 20th November 1759) and Rodney was to defeat the French and Spanish at the Battle of the Saints (12th April 1782). Rodney became a Member of Parliament for Saltash in 1751.

The 10th Baron Rodney and the 11th Baron Hawke were ejected from the House of Lords in 1999.

21ˢᵗ October 1805
The Battle of Trafalgar

In March 1802 Britain signed the Treaty of Amiens with France, bringing peace after the ten-year Revolutionary War. Among the provisions of the treaty was the resolution of the status of Malta, which the British had captured. Valletta with its harbour was a significant base, covering the passage from Gibraltar to the eastern Mediterranean. Napoleon Buonaparte, during his expedition to Egypt, had seized the island from the Knights of St. John of Jerusalem, before Britain took it from France. While Britain agreed to its return to the Knights, it had sought assurances that guaranteed to them revenues from Spain, France and Italy in order to maintain their independence, while that independence was to be guaranteed by the six major powers – Britain, France, Russia, Austria, Prussia and Spain. These conditions were not met and Britain continued to occupy the island. Peace did not bring the reopening of Europe to British trade, and gradually relations with Napoleon Bonaparte became frayed. Britain was not going to leave Malta without guarantees, particularly as France had made threats against Egypt. In March 1803 Parliament voted 10,000 more men for the Navy. Napoleon Buonaparte began to collect invasion barges in the Channel ports, and in breach of treaties, he ordered permanent military occupation of Switzerland and Holland. On 4ᵗʰ April the British Government suggested terms for dealing with the disputes arising from the treaty. Talleyrand, the French Foreign Minister, temporised and began to trifle with the British. The discussions finally failed and on 18ᵗʰ May 1803 Britain declared war on France.

By the time war was declared the North Sea Fleet had been strengthened, and Admiral Cornwallis had been alerted to blockade Brest. On the same day upon which war was declared, Lord Nelson hoisted his flag at Portsmouth on Victory (100 guns, 7ᵗʰ of the name launched 1765 and still in commission) ready to take up his station as Commander in the Mediterranean. He was to be away from England until August 1805, leaving again on 15ᵗʰ September for his final campaign, culminating in the Battle of Trafalgar. Horatio Nelson was born in 1759, one of five sons of the Rector of Burnham Thorpe in Norfolk. He entered the navy as a midshipman in 1771 at the age of twelve. A relation of his mother secured his entry on a ship with a Captain Suckling, who nonetheless asked his father 'What has poor Horatio done, who is so weak, that he, above all the rest, should be sent to rough it out at sea. But let him come and the first time we go into action a cannon-ball may knock of his head and provide for him at once.' The latter comment was underpinned by harsh reality as 17 midshipmen were killed at Trafalgar and 41 wounded, eight being on the Colossus. Nelson had a naval career marked by his initiative, raw courage, gallantry and intelligence. His conduct at the Battle of St. Vincent (14th February 1797), his victories (the Battle of the Nile, 1st August 1798 and the Battle of Copenhagen, 2nd April 1801) had won him international renown, taking him to the highest ranks in the Royal Navy, and won him a viscountcy. The qualities which marked him in war were complemented by his humanity, intense love and concern for his men and his liberal Christian piety, the legacy of his Anglican childhood in a country parsonage. An instance of the latter is his request to the Society for the Promotion of Christian Knowledge to provide him with 874 prayer books and King James Version Bibles for the crew of Victory prior to his departure to the Mediterranean in 1803. He obviously regarded his men as well able to understand the language of these two pillars of English culture and civilisation. His qualities were balanced by human weaknesses of showmanship, vanity and a predilection for a beautiful married woman, Lady Hamilton, to the scandal of all but her husband. On his shoulders history was to let fall the task of delivering Britain from invasion and conquest by France.

Soon after the Treaty of Amiens in 1802 Napoleon Buonaparte became First Consul for life of the French Republic. In 1803 he established the Army of England of some 160,000 men, who were encamped at Boulogne through 1804 into 1805. Buonaparte himself spent some time with this army and devoted his Government to collecting barges for the army's transport across the Channel. In May 1804 he declared himself Emperor and, after a plebiscite, was crowned in December. His main problem in this period was how to take his invasion fleet across the Channel in the face of the blockade and threat from the Royal Navy. He thought he needed six clear hours to cross to England. The French Navy was scattered, being blockaded in Brest and Toulon and other ports and the Spanish navy (Spain having joined the war) was at Cadiz. Retaining Holland in 1802, now the Batavian Republic, he also had control of the Dutch fleet. Despite therefore occupying the whole coast of Western Europe, he still had the need to unite these forces or part of them in order to cross the Channel. The strategy adopted was to endeavour to draw off the British by a feint to the West Indies, uniting all the fleets there to return and sweep the Channel clean in a huge force of all the ships combined.

In January 1805 the French fleet at Toulon, commanded by Admiral Charles Baptiste de Villeneuve, who had escaped from the destruction of the French fleet at the Battle of the Nile in the Guillaume Tell, slipped out of port in stormy weather and evaded Nelson. He, having heard that they had gone east, set off to scour the Mediterranean sailing as far as Alexandria. The January gales had however forced Villeneuve to return to Toulon. In March 1805 Villeneuve escaped again.

Nelson heard the news of his departure while near Palermo, and that the French had gone west through the Straits of Gibraltar. He immediately followed, fearing that the French would sail north towards Brest but after having had difficulty in getting through the Straits because of the strong Poniente, which blew for days, he learned at Cape St.Vincent that the French had gone across the Atlantic. The rendezvous was to be Martinique, where the French and Spanish were to meet. Admiral Gravina with the main Spanish fleet sailed to join Villeneuve. The French were a month ahead.

It took Nelson twenty-four days to arrive at the Windward Islands, and in Barbados he was given mistaken intelligence that Villeneuve had gone south to Trinidad and Tobago. Having found that to be erroneous, he went north to Grenada. By this time his instinct for strategy and the absence of the French fleet led him to worry that the West Indies trip was a feint, and he hurried back to the Azores and Gibraltar. Meanwhile Villeneuve and Gravina, impatient that Ganteaume from Brest had not arrived and hearing that Nelson was in the West Indies, sailed back, meeting Sir Robert Calder's blockading squadron, with whom on 22nd July an inconsequential action was fought. Sir Robert Calder's 15 ships of the line, some of which were to be at Trafalgar, engaged the combined fleet of 18 off Finistere, being hampered by fog and light shifting winds, nonetheless capturing two ships. On 28th July the combined fleet entered Vigo. Four days after, they were at Ferrol. Ganteaume at Brest and the Rochefort fleet remained blockaded. At Ferrol, Villeneuve and Gravina were joined by 14 ships of the line from Coruna. Victory returned to England and between 21st August and 2nd September Nelson discussed future strategy with William Pitt the Younger, the Prime Minister, and the Admiralty.

While entertaining Captain Keats of the Superb at Merton Abbey, he explained to him the battle strategy which he envisaged that he might employ. It was to break the enemy line about one-third back, isolating the van, which could not easily turn to reach the battle, and at a second point to separate the centre and rear so that crushing force could be brought to bear on the centre and rear. On 2nd September news had come that Villeneuve and Gravina had sailed south to Cadiz. By that time the Emperor Napoleon had begun to send troops from the Army of England eastwards and had realised that the union of all the French fleet was less easy than he supposed. Nelson left immediately for the fleet. He was to command 27 ships of the line, of which four had more than 80 guns, the rest mostly being of 74 guns. He withdrew all but the frigates below the horizon at Cadiz, leaving some of them to patrol the harbour entrance. He began to occupy the waiting time with conferences with his captains, explaining his strategy and tactics and ensuring that they could act of their own initiative to implement them.

In Cadiz, Admiral Villeneuve had 18 ships of the line, four of 80 guns and the rest of 74: Admiral Gravina had 15, of which four had 100 guns, being 33 in all. The Emperor Napoleon was angry that Villeneuve had not succeeded in the earlier tactics to draw off the British and ordered him to try once more to unite the fleet, unjustly suspecting him of reluctance to fight. At last, towards the end of October, when a replacement commander was on the way from Paris, Villeneuve decided to leave port. The frigates on 18th and 19th October signalled that the combined fleet had left port. On the 20th the French and Spanish were heading south-west, but early on the 21st turned to go back to Cadiz. The wind was light from the north-west with a heavy Atlantic swell presaging coming foul weather. At 4 am the British were nine miles to the windward of the combined fleet, about thirty miles south-west of Cape Trafalgar. Slowly in the wind the British began to come down on the enemy; by 11 am they were three miles away, the enemy fleet stretching in line for four miles. Nelson had signalled to the fleet to make two divisions: one to windward, commanded by himself in Victory, and one just to leeward, commanded by Admiral Collingwood on the Royal Sovereign (100 guns and 4th of the name). He had made a new will, leaving Emma Hamilton as a legacy to his King and Country, asking that they should give her ample provision to maintain her rank in life and her illegitimate but adopted daughter, Horatia Nelson Thompson, desiring her only to use the name of Nelson, as an object of their benevolence. The famous signal was sent – 'England expects that every man will do his duty'. Nelson then composed himself to prayer and wrote into his daybook his moving plea to God embodying his beliefs and his patriotism.

As the fleet moved towards the French, it was cleared for action. The partitions came down; the gun decks were prepared, the hammocks stowed to give protection on the ships' sides, the shot brought up and the powder, the men stripping for action, and the guns run out of the ports. On some, bands played; 'Hearts of Oak are Our Men' rang out constantly, 'Rule Britannia' and 'Britons Strike Home.' On the guns of the Bellerophon the men had chalked 'Billy Ruffin, victory or death'. By noon the British were near the French and Spanish and the Royal Sovereign, the leading ship of Collingswood's division, came under fire. Nelson was on the quarterdeck, wearing a coat covered with his decorations. The surgeon, Dr Beatty tried to persuade him to change it, but he replied that it was too late to be shifting a coat. The light wind meant that the approaching British were not able to form a line abreast to break the enemies' line in several places, but had to go in line, exposing the bows of the leading ship first, and then the whole ship, to intense fire, to which no broadsides could be fired in reply. Thus, for the last half-hour before engagement the British seamen had to remain patient and solid under the storm of shot. As Nelson's Division came up to the French both Neptune (5th of the name with 98 guns) and Temeraire (2nd of the name with 98 guns) jockeyed with Victory for first and second position in line, but Nelson was determined to be the first through. Temeraire was however so close that its jib boom was almost into Victory's stern. The ship had been built in Essex and launched in 1798; its commander, Captain Eliab Harvey of Chigwell, was Member of Parliament for Essex, although it was manned mainly by men from Liverpool.

Collingwood's division joined the enemy with Royal Sovereign in the lead, then Belle Isle, Mars, Tonnant, Bellerophon and Colossus. The first British shot was fired inadvertently by Bellerophon, when a midshipman caught his foot in the loose end of a gun-lock lanyard and tripped. The Royal Sovereign was the first in about noon, and was subject to three or four broadsides from five or six ships before she could fire. She disappeared into the smoke and broke the French and Spanish line to the stern of the Santa Anna, which was raked by her broadsides; then she turned to starboard, firing on the Fougueux. Royal Sovereign and the Santa Anna were to fight for over an hour. Belle Isle came in slowly, the wind having become negligible, and fired into the Fougueux, going on to the Monarca. Mars and Tonnant (80 guns) joined the confused fighting in the swirling grey smoke, which made it difficult for each side, despite Union Jacks at the British peaks, to identify one another. Bellerophon started to fire at 12.20 pm to create a smokescreen and cut the line between Bahama and Montanez, delivering her broadsides from both sides. They had hardly done that when the Aigle loomed out of the smoke, with its greater height and heavier guns. The carronades in the bows of Bellerophon cleared, however, the decks of the Aigle and the French captain was wounded. The ships came together and the musket men in the tops fired down on to Bellerophon's after decks. For half an hour the ships fought locked together, with fire from other ships hitting Bellerophon from a distance. The captain was killed and the French prepared to board. The main and mizzen topmasts crashed down on the starboard side. The crews and soldiers on board both ships began to fight one with another, so close were the two ships. The French almost crossed on the starboard sprit-sail yardarm but it was crashed into the sea by untying the brace. The meanwhile, Bellerophon fired constantly upwards into the Aigle, although her upper decks were near cleared and fires had been started, which had to be extinguished. The French again prepared to board but quite suddenly, for no apparent reason, the ships drifted apart. As Aigle went, the broadsides of Bellerophon again raked her. Of 47 on the quarterdeck of the ship when the action began, only 7 were unwounded.

Victory, at the head of Nelson's division, had commenced firing at 12.20 am She was followed in immediately by Temeraire, Neptune (98 guns and 5th of the name), Leviathan and Conqueror. Nelson stood on the quarterdeck, with Captain Hardy, his secretary Blackwood, the Reverend Scott, his chaplain, and Dr Beatty. He had aimed for the sixth or seventh ship of the French and Spanish line, but on approach had veered, leading his division more towards the centre, seeking out the flagships of the enemy's Admirals, Villeneuve and Cisneras, the Bucentaire (80 guns) and the Santa Trinidad (140 guns). As she ran towards them, Victory was subjected to withering fire, crashing over the ship from bows to stern. The ship's wheel was smashed and she had to be steered by a large tiller manned by forty seamen on the lower deck. The marines were decimated: eight killed in line. 'This is too warm too last long', Nelson said to Hardy. Behind the Bucentaure, there sailed the Redoutable, the most efficiently trained ship of the French navy, under the skilled Captain Lucas, which had come up. Hardy asked for which he should aim but was told to take his choice. The helm was swung over behind the Bucentaure and, as Victory passed, a 50-gun broadside with two roundshot in each gun slammed into her stern; 20 guns were dismounted and half the crew killed and wounded.

Victory in turn was bombarded by the French Neptune, crossing her bows before Captain Hardy put over the helm to take on the Redoubtable. The guns of the latter and the Victory became engaged muzzle to muzzle. Grapeshot was used to sweep the deck of Redoutable of its waiting boarders. Smoke covered the conflict of five or six ships and the firing of the skirmishers in the tops of Redoutable began to strike the decks of Victory. A marksmen in the mizzenmast fifty feet up, at 1.15 pm hit Nelson in the chest. The bullet cut his pulmonary artery and lodged in his spine. Captain Hardy found him on his knees with blood over his hands. He fell on his left side and told his Captain, 'They have done for me at last Hardy. My backbone is shot through.' He was lifted and carried by a Sergeant of Marines and two seamen down to the surgeon on the orlop deck. On the way on the middle deck he saw Midshipmen Rivers with his leg shot away and turned to Hardy, saying 'Mind, Hardy, that young man is not forgot'. His face and decorations were hidden by a handkerchief to limit those who knew that he was wounded. In response, the Marines under Second Lieutenant Rotelay, later joined by Midshipmen Pollard and Collingwood, shot every man in the mizzenmast top. Above, the battle continued to rage, and Hardy, now effectively in command, returned to it. By this time Bucentaure had drawn away, but was being battered by Neptune, Agamemnon and Conqueror.

On the far side of Redoubtable, Temeraire had come up. On the way Temeraire cannonaded the French Neptune, but the wind was so light that it had difficulty getting through and up the line. The French Neptune, in the bombardment which she returned, took off the main topmast and halyard, the mizzenmast top and crippled the fore topmast and halyard. In the smoke Captain Harvey could not tell where he was, and stopped firing. Slowly, however, the Victory, interlocked with the Redoubtable, drifted down towards the Temeraire. Captain Lucas on his ship had assembled a force to board the Victory, whose upper decks were being subjected to devastating musketry. From the bows the Temeraire fired a carronade of 68lbs of grapeshot into these boarders, seriously shattering the assembled boarding party. Lucas still continued his attempt on Victory, but the Temeraire fired a double-shotted broadside into the boarders and swept the decks of the Redoutable clear of men: 200 were killed or wounded, the guns dismounted.

Fireballs flung from the masts of Redoutable started fires on both ships, which had to be extinguished.

The Fougueux came up on the starboard side of Temeraire. She had been severely damaged by Belle Isle and Mars. Her captain, Captain Baudoin, decided to board Temeraire, which was by this time a wreck aloft, and he closed with the shrouds full of men crying 'A L'abordage.' Temeraire had not fired on its starboard side and had the guns primed and double-shotted. Lieutenant Kennedy called the men to mount the guns; the 32-pounders and 18-pounders were ready, and in tempestuous broadsides at eight yards swept clear the rigging, forecastle and deck of Fougueux. The heavier guns below crushed the side of that ship into a battered mass. The vessel became uncontrollable and crashed into the Temeraire, whose crew lashed her to. Lieutenant Kennedy with a midshipman and 26 men clambered on board. There was a fight on the quarterdeck and Captain Baudoin was wounded. His second in command was shot down; the French driven off the quarterdeck. In twelve minutes the party were masters of the ship. The French crew were put in the holds and the Union Jack raised. Temeraire now turned again to Redoutable, which lay in the group of four now together, between Victory and herself. There was still firing from the masts, although the guns were silent. Victory began slowly to pull away and as she did the mainmast of Redoutable came crashing down on the poop of Temeraire. It was to form a bridge for the boarding party led by Second Lieutenant John Wallace. With only 100 men left in action out of 500, Captain Lucas surrendered. Temeraire had taken two prizes, but remained under attack by the French Neptune. Captain Harvey tried to return some guns to action, for five-sixths of them were masked. At that moment Leviathan came up and the French Neptune turned away.

In Collingwood's Division the Tonnant's broadside reduced the decks of the Monarca, hit her rigging and brought down her fore and cross-jack yards. The Tonnant moved on and was attacked by Algesiras, who crashed into her. A furious cannonade was exchanged, the 32-pounder carronades ripped apart the rigging of Algesiras and Lieutenant Clement ordered the decks to be cleared by grapeshot. As a midshipman he had been wounded three times at the Battle of Camperdown (11th October 1797). On board Algesiras Admiral Magon had promised his crew before action the opportunity to board an enemy ship, and the boarding party assembled. Lieutenant Clement ordered another crashing volley from the carronades on the poop and quarterdeck, devastating the boarding party. Admiral Magon was injured. Algesiras was joined by Monarca and Pluton. Tonnant was holed below the waterline in the firing, which continued. Gradually the guns of Algesiras were silenced, Admiral Magon killed, and a boarding party took the ship. The Royal Sovereign had kept up its heavy attack on the Santa Anna. Admiral Ignatio de Alava was wounded and at 2.10 pm the Santa Anna crossed the Royal Sovereign and raked her. The starboard guns of Royal Sovereign however crashed into the ship and the fore and mainmasts fell. At 2.20 pm the Santa Anna surrendered. Royal Sovereign had suffered substantial damage and its mainmast fell. At 3.00 pm she was to signal Euryalus, a frigate, to be taken in tow.

By 2 pm the rear of Collingwood's division had at last come up in the light wind, being about one knot faster than the Spanish squadrons. The Achille, Revenge (6th of the name with 74 guns), Defiance (6th of the name with 74 guns), Dreadnaught, Thunderer and Swiftsure all entered the battle. To the leeward were the French Achille, the Principe de Asturias, Berwick and San Juan Nepomuceno. The Colossus, which had followed up Bellerophon, engaged first the French Swiftsure, whose mizzenmast she brought down, and second the more powerful Argonaute. She suffered heavy damage and the most British casualties of the day, 40 killed and 160 wounded. Orion however appeared and crashed a broadside through the stern of the French Swiftsure, carrying away the masts and the wheel. Bellerophon and Colossus then attacked Bahama, killed her captain, brought down the mizzen and mainmast and seriously holed her. She decided to surrender. Bellerophon next engaged Monarcha, which also surrendered. Orion went on towards the Principe de Asturias, which was engaged with Dreadnaught and Britannia, but the Spanish ship was not taken, as the French Neptune and then the San Justo came to its aid. The Mars (74 guns) commanded by Captain Duff, was the third ship in Collingwood's division. As one of the lead ships it was subjected to concentrated fire first, being raked by four French ships of the line and second, while penetrating through the French line near the San Juan and heading for the Santa Anna, it was engaged by Pluton and raked by Monarcha and Algesiras. It also fought with the Fougueux and in the contests Captain Duff was killed, having his head shot off by roundshot. Revenge (64 guns), true to the line of the ship, was in the fiercest mêlée. It became joined with Aigle, having tangled its jib booms in the mizzen topsail of the French ship. It raked the Aigle, contributing to the damage to that ship, but became engaged by the Principe de Asturias, Indomptable and San Justo. Fighting hard at three to one, it was only saved by the Thunderer (74 guns) coming up.

In the van and centre Victory was engaged with Redoutable, until she went away. The Santa Trinidad, then the largest ship in the world, had suffered from Victory's broadside, as Nelson sailed towards Bucentaure, but sailed on in front of the latter. As has been said, it came under attack from Neptune, Agamemnon (64 guns) and Conqueror (74 guns), Neptune (98 guns) raking the stern. Fire was concentrated on her rigging. At 2.40 pm her mainmast crashed and as she swung away she lost her mizzenmast. Her sails and rigging slumped and she was left a hulk when her foremast came down too. At 3.00 pm Admiral Cisneros struck her colours. She was made a prize of Neptune. Belle Isle was under attack by both the San Justo and San Leandro. Aigle, as she left Bellerophon, fired broadsides into her. At 2.10 pm the mainmast came down on the poop. The French Neptune joined in and by 2.45 pm Belle Isle had lost her foremast and bowspit. She was little more than a hulk. She was saved by the appearance of Dreadnaught and Swiftsure. Bucentaure had been so pounded by Victory, Neptune, Conqueror and Agamemnon that, reduced virtually to a wreck, Admiral Villeneuve surrendered at 2.15 pm to Captain Israel Pellew of the Conqueror.

After he was taken below, Nelson lay propped on pillows in agony as his lungs filled with blood. He remained conscious both of his coming death and of the progress of the battle. On the orlop he was also, seaman that he was, plainly aware of the mounting swell under the ship that foreshadowed gales to come. At 2.30 pm Captain Hardy reported to him that twelve or thirteen of the combined fleet were in British possession. He continued to fail, becoming more breathless. Dr Beatty, the surgeon, among his extensive duties to the wounded, from time to time sought him out. After examination on one visit, Beatty told him 'My Lord, unhappily for our country nothing can be done for you'. His voice and strength were failing; he barely whispered 'God be praised I have done my duty.' It was fifty minutes before Captain Hardy could come again and he returned to Nelson to report that fourteen or fifteen had been taken. 'That is well', replied Nelson, 'but I had bargained for twenty'. He then, gathering his strength, ordered Hardy firmly to anchor the fleet once the battle was done. He asked him to take care of Lady Hamilton and Horatia and then, urged no doubt by his intense sense of human feeling, which had driven him throughout his life, he sought, as he sensed life fading, the consolation of the human touch. He asked Hardy, his brother officer of years and closest to him of the band of brothers who were his captains to kiss him. Hardy kissed him once and then again on the forehead, and left. Beatty then turned Nelson at his request onto his right side and his breathing became more laboured and shallower.

Aigle moved off from Bellerophon, shattered by the broadsides pumped into her. Defiance (6th of the name and 74 guns) was now up with her and after heavy bombardment prepared to board Aigle. No undamaged boat could be found on Defiance and so an Irishman, James Spratt, offered to lead fifty or sixty seamen over to Aigle by swimming to her. Taking his cutlass and with a tomahawk at his waist be managed to enter the stern and fought his way up to the poop deck. At one time he was fighting three Grenadiers. He was not followed, but Defiance and Aigle had come together and the first attacking party had tried to go aboard, but were thrown back by musketry and grenades from the tops. The second party succeeded and Spratt, who had been wounded, was saved. At 3.30 pm Aigle surrendered.

When Bucentaure had been so fiercely attacked, Admiral Villeneuve had signalled Admiral Dumanoir in Formidable to return to assist the centre. The light west south-westerly wind made this manoeuvre one of difficulty. Some ships could only turn with the assistance of rowing boats swinging the bows. It took three hours for the French van to turn and begin to come down to the battle.

Dumanoir's squadron had divided into three groups: the nearest to the battle comprised by Formidable, Mont Blanc, Duguay – Trouin and Scipion. A second comprised Rayo, San Francisco de Asis and Heros and the third, Intrépide and Neptuno. As Dumanoir arrived, he realised that the flagships were beyond help and failed to close with the British Neptune. He chose to endeavour to cut off Minotaur and Spartiate at the rear of Nelson's division. These came up to the bows of Formidable and bombarded the French line as they sailed along it. Dumanoir sailed down towards Victory, Mars, Royal Soveriegn and Temeraire, which had all been heavily damaged.

At 4 pm Collingwood, seeing this movement, signalled to Dreadnaught, Thunderer and Revenge, who were engaged with Admiral Gravina's flagship the Principe de Asturias. Dumanoir, under fire from Victory and damaged, was unwilling to engage the undamaged line of ships advancing on him, and bore away to turn to Cadiz. Intrépide and Neptune continued south: Rayo, San Francisco de Asis and Héros went north-east away from the battle. Intrépide was weakly armed and an old ship, but nonetheless she went on towards Bucentaure and Redoutable, but she passed Bucentaure and attacked the disabled Leviathan, which had lost its rigging and tiller. The latter had engaged and taken the San Augustin in a fierce and heavy engagement. The Intrépide had also been engaged by the Africa (64 guns) which had been far to windward. Codrington in Orion came to the aid of Leviathan and Africa and fired into Intrépide on the starboard quarter and into the stern smashing the wheel and the tiller. The French Neptune tried to rescue Santa Trinidad and Bucentaure, but was overwhelmed by the bombardment of Minotaur and Spartiate, who brought down its mizzenmast. By five o'clock Intrépide had surrendered and Neptuno had been taken by Minotaur. Defence (74 guns) towards the rear of the division exchanged broadsides with Berwick, and then within one hour compelled San Ildefonso to surrender. The Berwick was taken by the Achille (74 guns) after engaging with Polyphemus (64 guns) and Swiftsure (74 guns).

After Captain Hardy's visit Nelson's obvious distress increased; his voice became weaker. He told his chaplain that he had been a great sinner. He asked him to remember that he commended Lady Hamilton and Horatia as a legacy to his country. In the heat and with the growing sense of suffocation as his lungs filled, he pleaded for water and to be fanned. He became speechless. Supported by his Chaplain and the purser he quietly died. At 4.30 pm he was pronounced dead by Dr. Beatty.

About the same time firing stopped. Admiral de Escano in the Principe de Asturias tried to rally the Franco-Spanish fleet, and they made for Cadiz with twelve ships. The Prince at the end of the battle had been attacking, firing broadsides into the Achille, which was drifting and racked by fire. The attack was stopped and boats sent out to rescue her sailors. The frigates, Pickle, Entrepenante and

Naiad assisted. At 5.30 pm Achille blew up. The ships' boats maintained their work, saving sailors from the sea.

The combined fleet had lost 18 ships, 17 taken and one blown up. There is no record of their dead and wounded and the figures given vary, but over 11,000 prisoners were taken. The British had 449 dead and 1,214 wounded. The pain and agony endured by the latter, as they suffered the surgeon's work without anaesthetics, can today scarcely be contemplated. Such accounts as there are seem to show that amputation was undergone by many almost with the same insouciance as these men showed as they went into battle. Thomas Main, captain of the forecastle on Leviathan, sang 'Rule Britannia' as his left arm was amputated below the elbow. On Victory Midshipman Rivers, whom Nelson had asked should be cared for, had his leg sawn off below the knee. That evening, as the severed limbs were being taken to be thrown in the sea, he joked, as he asked for his leg, that he understood that 'old putty nose', the purser, was to use them for fresh meat for the wounded.

Nelson's final commands to the fleet given to Captain Hardy, to anchor, were taken to Admiral Collingwood, now in command. The wind had now begun to make and the storm presaged by the heavy swell arrived to hit the damaged fleet and its prizes. The ships were on a rock-bound lee shore in water some nine miles off land, which became shoaly as the approach was made to the coast. The prizes had been damaged to the point of almost being wrecked. The British ships were themselves severely damaged; Belle Isle had lost all its masts, Royal Sovereign, Temeraire and Britannia their main and mizzenmasts, Victory and Colossus their mizzenmasts and most others topmasts or topsail and lower mast yards. Collingwood did not act on Nelson's command and, as night came, storm turned to gale and blew at Beaufort Force 9 and 10. It blew on all through 22nd October, only abating by dawn on the 23rd. At nine o'clock on the 21st Collingwood finally ordered the fleet to anchor for the night, but it was too late. The fleet and the prizes were battered by the wind: the sheer task of survival for the broken and damaged ships required tenacity, skill and constant courage. French frigates took their opportunity to retake the drifting damaged prizes. Bucentaure, Fougueux, Indomitable, Rayo, San Francisco de Asis, Monarca and Aigle were wrecked on shore. In the Algesiras the prize crew was overpowered and French frigates took and made away in tow with Santa Anna and Neptuno. The Santa Trinidad could not be saved and was scuttled, as was the Argonauta. The British burnt the Intrépide and the San Augustin, which were damaged beyond hope. Only four prizes reached England – the San Ildefenso, Bahama, Swiftsure and the San Juan Nepomuceno. None of them ever left port again and were kept for use as hulks.

Nelson had asked Captain Hardy not to throw him overboard, a request Hardy honoured. His body was put into a brandy cask, while the fleet limped back to Gibraltar, and there transferred to a cask of spirits and wine, which was lashed to the mast of Victory for return to England. A small cemetery in the main street of the Rock contains the bodies of some of those who died in the battle. It was not until 6th November that Lord Barham at the Admiralty received Collingwood's despatch relating to the battle and he immediately informed the Prime Minister, William Pitt, and King George III. Newspapers spread the news to the country and the Morning Chronicle spoke of 'A sensation at once of patriotism, of pride and of gratitude.' The public rejoicing for victory was dampened by the death of Lord Nelson. Covent Garden staged a special performance for the event at which Rule Britannia was sung with added words ending, 'Rule, brave Britons, rule the main, Avenge the god-like Hero slain'. A thanksgiving service was held for victory at St Paul's Cathedral on 5th December. The day before, the demasted Victory, which had been towed from Gibraltar, arrived at Spithead. The coffin was taken up the Channel to the Nore, where Nelson's naval career had begun.

On 24th December his body was borne to Greenwich, where it lay in the Painted Hall. His coffin was fashioned out of the mast of the L'Orient and on 5th January was taken up the river to the Admiralty in a procession of black draped barges, watched from the river bank by crowds of thousands. The 6th January 1806 was the day of the procession and burial in St Paul's. The body, in an outer coffin of black and gilt, was carried though crowded silent streets accompanied by his crew carrying the war-torn white ensign of Victory. Thirty-one admirals and a hundred captains accompanied the hearse. It was a sunlit winter's day. The burial service lasted four hours. His sunburnt, tough, hard courageous seamen from Victory wept, and, as the moment of burial came, took the flag and ripped it into tiny shreds to have each a memento of their Nelson. As Casper Weinberger, Secretary of State for Defence of the United States said at a Trafalgar day dinner ' In Admiral Lord Nelson – ardent, unruly, supremely self-confident – a nation and a principle found concrete form in a man'.

The Battle of Trafalgar gave Britain unchallenged dominance over the Oceans for over one hundred years. It facilitated the growth of the Empire and was the linchpin of the fight to rid Europe of one more attempt by the French to fasten on its states their hegemony. Without Trafalgar, the Peninsular War and the campaigns in the Mediterranean would not have been possible.

The Government made Lord Nelson's brother, William, an earl, with a grant of £99,000 and a pension of £5,000 per annum in perpetuity. The latter was removed by the Socialist Government of 1945 to 1950. Nelson's wife Fanny was given £2,000 for life. William Pitt was ill and the issue of Lady Hamilton and Horatia was put aside. Nelson's request committing them to the nation was ignored, testimony to the all too common institutional ingratitude of Governments for the endeavours of those whose bravery serves the nation. Nelson's sisters and friends did help them. Horatia married the Reverend Philip Ward, had a large family and died in 1881. Admiral Villeneuve was soon exchanged and returned to France, to be found shot in a hotel on his way home. There has always been a question whether he committed suicide or was murdered. Captain Harvey of Temeraire was made a Rear-Admiral and a Knight Commander of the Bath in 1815. Nelson's message to the fleet was inscribed on a brass plaque and set in the deck before the mainmast of the ship. She remained in commission until 1838, the latter years spent as a guard ship at Sheerness. There her last commander was Captain Kennedy, who had organised the resistance to the boarders from the Fougueux and taken that ship at Trafalgar. Its guns were fired for the coronation of Queen Victoria in 1837. After its sale, on decommissioning it was taken up river to be broken. Its final journey was immortalised by J.A. Turner in his famous painting of the Fighting Temeraire. In 2005, responding to a survey organised by the BBC, those who took part, avoiding political correctness, voted the picture as Britain's favourite national painting.

The 9th Earl Nelson was ejected from the House of Lords in 1999.

Nelson's Prayer : 21st October 1805

> May the Great God, whom I worship, grant to my Country and for the benefit of Europe in general a great and glorious victory, and may no misconduct in anyone tarnish it, and may humanity after victory be the predominant feature in the British fleet. For myself individually I commit my life to him who made me and may his blessing light upon my endeavours for serving my country faithfully. To him I resign myself and the just cause which is entrusted me to defend. Amen, Amen, Amen.

SAILING ORDER
BRITISH FLEET

Weather Division
Victory (F)
Temeraire
Neptune
Leviatha
Conqueror
Britannia
Agamemnon
Africa
Ajax
Orion
Minotaur
Spartiate
Lee Division -

FRENCH AND SPANISH FLEET
(from the van)

Neptuno (S) (T)
Scipion
Intrépide (T)
Rayo (S)
Formidable
Duguay-Trouin
Mont Blanc
San Francisco de Asis (S)
San Augustin (S) (T)
Héros
Santissima Trinidad (S) (F) (T)
Bucentaure (F) (T)
Neptune

Royal Sovereign (F)
Belle Isle
Mars
Tonnant
Bellerophon
Colossus
Achille
Dreadnought
Polyphemus
Revenge
Swiftsure
Defiance
Thunderer
Defence
Prince

San Leandro (S)
Redoutable (T)
San Justo (S)
Indomptable
Santa Anna (S) (T)
Fougueux
Monarcha (S) (T)
Pluton
Algesiras (T)
Bahama (S) (T)
Aigle (T)
Swiftsure (T)
Argonaute
Montanez (S)
Argonauta (S) (T)
Berwick (T)
San Juan Nepomuceno (S) (T)
San Iledefenso (S) (T)
Achille (T)
Principe de Astorias (F) (S)

Key:
Ships Taken T
Flagships   F
Spanish   S

25th October 1415

The Battle of Agincourt

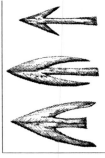

After the taking of Harfleur (22nd September 1415) King Henry V had to decide on the course of action to be taken next. His army had been afflicted by disease, and dysentery had reduced the active force available. He needed to garrison Harfleur, and effectively his army was reduced to 6,000 men. There were three courses open to him: first, to take a larger area around Harfleur; second, to carry out a chevauchée to Calais, similar to that of the Black Prince in the south of France before the battle of Poitiers; or third, to return home and reopen the campaign in 1416. His council with his leading nobles and commanders showed that they favoured a return to England. Henry V wished to go on and contrary to the advice given decided to march to Calais. It was a strategy involving risk, since the French forces had been reorganised by Marshal Boucicault and the Constable of France, Charles D'Albret, and by the beginning of October had risen to about 14,000.

The French stood along the line of the Seine from Mantes, near Paris, through Vernon to Rouen. Charles VI and the Dauphin with the sacred oriflamme of France, brought from St Denis, were at Mantes. The journey to Calais was one hundred and six miles and required the crossing of the Rivers Bethune, Bresle and Somme. The English had the advantage, however, that the French army had soldiers of poorer quality and was still poorly organised. With rations for eight days, and leaving behind his guns and heavy baggage, King Henry left Harfleur on about 8th October. The Rivers Bethune and Bresle were soon negotiated and King Henry marched north towards Abbeville. He had in mind crossing on the ford at Blanche Tacque below the town, used by Edward III in 1345, but he received intelligence that it had been protected by stakes and a large force under Marshal Boucicault. He therefore turned away and started to march up river, searching for a crossing.

The French advance guard was however already at Abbeville, on the Somme, and the bridges and the fords were guarded. He continued past Amiens, reaching the town a day before the main body of the French, who arrived from Rouen on 17th October. At Boves he turned north-east for Corbie. The bridge was intact and the army was subjected by the French to a sortie from the town, which was chased off. Henry V at this point decided on a clever tactic, which was to enable him to cross the river. The French marched at a slower pace than the English and the main guard was not at Corbie, which it did not reach until a day after the English had left. The King took advantage of the bend in the river to place his army upstream. Beyond Corbie the River Somme, which was extensively in flood due to the rain of the past weeks, executed a bend north-eastwards towards Peronne, before turning south-east again past Athies to Ham. The French on the north would have a greater distance to cover to keep up. To take advantage of the bend the English left the river, moving south-east to Nesle, where they turned north-east and reached the river east of Peronne. The rations were running out, the army had been on the march for nine days. The King had been told of the fords across the marshy river and these were found unguarded. The causeways across had been damaged but these he had repaired, and by eight o'clock in the evening of 19th October the last soldiers were across.

On the same day the French main army reached Peronne, seven miles away. Near Athies on Sunday 20th October King Henry rested the army, and three French Heralds attended upon him, challenging him to give battle with the Duc d'Orleans and the Duc de Bourbon to determine matters by trial by battle. The King, however, expressed his intention of going straight to Calais, and of going peaceably if the French allowed him to pass. The interchange led him to expect an attack on the morrow and he looked for a battle position. No attack was to come, for on the twentieth the French left the city to march north-east towards Bapaume, from where they could strike out towards all routes to Calais. Neither Charles VI or the Dauphin were with the army, since at a Great Council at Rouen the Duc de Berri had persuaded the king that he should not endanger himself, as had happened to John II at Poitiers. There was a major disagreement in the French command, however, which was to hamper its strategy even up to the field of battle. There were those who were content to let the English pass to Calais, and hotheads who were equally determined to fight.

On 21st October the English marched round Peronne and began to move north-east towards the coastal route to Calais. Buffeted by wind and rain they marched towards Albert and then to Frevent. The French marched on their flank, at first some ten miles distant, but from Frevent north the gap narrowed, as the French passed through St Pol, to one of three miles. On 24th October the English passed through Blagny in the valley of the River Fernoise, and breasting a ridge saw in the distance the whole array of the French strung out in advance of them. There is no precise record of the size of the French army, and various assessments have been given of its size. Shakespeare in his historical play suggests five to one as the ratio, but it was probably nearer three or four to one. The English marched forward towards Maisoncelles and as they did so the French moved across to straddle the road to Calais. The road ran north through a flat area of newly ploughed fields, sodden with rain and formed of heavy glutinous clay. To the west of the road was the dense wood of Agincourt, and to the east some nine hundred yards away at its narrowest was the wood of Framcourt, closing in the side of the open plain. The French were placed to the north of the woods and the English to the south. The

English had marched for sixteen days and had one day of rest. Food was in short supply, the army being reduced to corn, vegetables and nuts. Days of unremitting rain had left clothing soaked, armour rusted and shoes worn and sodden. The French, who were mostly mounted, had been on the march for only ten days. The 24th was the eve of the feast of St Crispin and St Crispianus. The legend that they were missionaries come to Soissons in the third century A.D. is probably inaccurate. Their relics however were enshrined there and they were the patron saints of leather workers, shoemakers and cobblers. At one time they had an altar in the church at Faversham in Kent.

The English were drawn up across the southern edge of the gap between the woods at the narrowest point. The form of line was similar to that at Crecy, with archers on the wings and embedded in the lines in formations in advance of the men-at-arms. Sir Thomas Erpingham was in command of the archers. He had begun his career as a soldier at eleven, and fought with John of Gaunt, son of King Edward III. He had ambushed the deposed King Richard II and kept him for a time as a prisoner. The English right was commanded by Edward, Duke of York, the second cousin of the King, and author of a book in celebration of hunting – The Master of Game; the centre was commanded by King Henry V himself, and the left by Lord Camoys. The limited forces of the English meant that all troops had to be placed in the battle line and there was no reserve. The baggage, with the priests, boy pages, young squires and the horses, were placed in the rear with only a limited guard.

The French under the Constable of France had evolved a battle plan with difficulty, because of the arguments between the chief nobles and knights as to the distribution of the commands. However, when the army took the field the plan did not survive and was modified. The size of the army enabled it to be divided into three 'battles' which could be each lined up behind one another. The first line comprised dismounted knights and men-at-arms under the Constable of France himself, Charles D'Albret, the Duc d'Orleans and Duc de Bourbon, Marshal Boucicault, and the Comtes of Eu and Richmont. The second, also of dismounted men-at-arms was led by the Duc d'Alencon and the Duc de Bar. The final line was led by Comtes Marle, Dammartin and Fauquemburg. In this line the knights remained mounted. In additional to the three battles, there were two companies of mounted horse of about 600 men, commanded by the Comte de Vendome, the Admiral of France, and Clignet de Brabant, on the flanks, which were to be directed against the archers. The crossbowmen were stationed behind the three battles.

Torrential rain fell through the night and the men had to keep their arms and bowstrings clean and dry. King Henry V released his prisoners on parole to give themselves up again should he win, and to go free if he lost. To guard against surprise night attack he ordered that the troops should maintain a strict silence, so that any enemy movement could be heard. The discipline of the English army for the fifteenth century was iron, surprising all who witnessed it. A monk of St Denis noted that in accordance with the King's order on the march the army 'paid regard for the welfare of the inhabitants, observed the full rules of military discipline and their King'. Indeed, a soldier who had stolen a brass pyx from the altar of a church at Caix, thinking it gold, was taken and hung, so firm was the discipline. The troops filled their time with being shriven, preparing for battle and eating such food as they could; then they slept on the rain sodden fields. The silence observed caused the French to fret that the English army was slipping away.

On the French side all was noise, bustle and confusion. They did not have the homogeneous nature of the English, from which came their strength, but were an ill-sorted mixture of people from all parts of France, hastily gathered and assembled in the army, little more than an undisciplined horde. Unlike the English, who fought in 'retinues' of men from the same estates and areas, they lacked identity one with another. Their overwhelming numbers induced a customary Gallic arrogance, which had them dicing for the capture of King Henry V and the great English nobles.

When the watery dawn came, the rain had stopped, but the field of battle between the armies was a sodden, deep clay mass, puddled and sticky. King Henry V attended 'lauds', the earliest service of the day and arrayed in his surcoat, quartered with the three leopards of England and the Lilies of France, and wearing on his bassinet a gold crown ornamented with crosses and lilies, he rode along the ranks on a grey palfrey encouraging the standing ranks of men. The French took position, a long glittering rank of metal and shining armour with the waving pennants of the knights, contrasting with the soil-worn appearance of the English, rusted armour, dirty leather jerkins and clothes battered by their long march. The French lines were about 1,000 yards away and extended over a wider front than the English, 1,250 yards as compared with 950. The English men-at-arms numbered 1,000 at most and were no more than four men deep. The bulk of the army were archers.

The armies stood motionless for four hours, during which time some parleys occurred to discuss terms on which the French would permit the English to go on to Calais. While Henry V might have considered the giving up of Harfleur, the terms sought by the Constable of France were wholly unacceptable. At eleven o'clock Henry V decided to advance. Dropping to the ground, each man made a cross on the ground, knelt down and kissed it, taking a small mouthful of soil. The archers had to remove the stakes in front quickly from the ground before they could move. The army advanced slowly into a new forward position within bowshot of the French. Despite the danger of attack the archers once more staked out their ground, pointing their stakes towards oncoming horses. While this proceeded, the French did not attack, many of their men-at-arms having wandered off, until the two wings of cavalry retained were launched on the new position of the archers. Of the total reserved, it seems that only a third of their numbers took part, the Bulgundians probably hanging back. These knights moved slowly in the heavy clay, mud up to the hocks, and the horses with labour sucking their hooves out of the gripping soil.

As they came up, Sir Thomas Erpingham gave the signal to the archers 'Strike' and the sky darkened as the flight of arrows struck into the approaching horses, bringing them down. In pain from the arrows the wounded horses became unmanageable: some fell on the stakes; their riders crashed to the ground often one upon another, crushing those below by the weight. The leading battle, which followed behind, became itself mired in mud as the men in armour struggled through the squelchy, clinging ground. The fleeing horses ran through it, breaking the line apart. As the French line advanced, the gap between the woods narrowed. The long line of French was pressed in, man upon man, congealing into clots of men hard together, scarcely able to raise their arms, as they struggled towards the English men-at-arms between the archers. Wearied from the long walk through the mud they, like the horsemen, arrived to volleys of arrows, thinning their ranks and felling them in piles. Their visors lowered against the arrows, air was lacking in the helmets as they hung their heads downwards. Finally the survivors clashed with the English men-at-arms in intensely strenuous fighting, in the centre of which was King Henry V. The archers for their part dropped their bows and nimbly passing over and among the piles of wounded and dying set themselves against the men-at-arms with swords, axes and mallets. The shock of the French line at first drove the English back but they soon recovered, fighting the oncoming men, who had to negotiate the heaps of fallen, pressed down into the mud with some suffocated. The *oriflamme* of France was trampled down and lost.

The King fought in the heart of the battle, standing over his brother Humphrey Duke of Gloucester, who was wounded in the groin, holding off attackers until he could be taken away. Eighteen French knights had pledged themselves to kill or take the King and they tried to fight towards him, all but one being slain on the way. The last reached him and cut off one *fleur-de-lys* from the crown on his head, before also falling. The second line was now engaged on the front. The second battle ended up in the same struggling mass as the first. Once more confusion reigned as the men fell, unable to rise, and kept down by neighbours who crashed onto them. The archers went on with their work, trying in the course of their fighting to take prisoners for ransom. Then a message came to the King that there had been an attack to the rear.

When the English moved up, the baggage had been brought up from Maisoncelles to behind the lines. The fear grew, given the size of the French forces, that they were about to attack both front and rear at once. In fact a band of peasants from Hesdin under Ysembart d' Agincourt, Robinet de Bourbonville and Rifflart de Plamasse had rushed the baggage, looting and seizing the supplies and stores and raising loud wails from the priests and putting to the sword the young boys and squires left there. They were able to make away with the crown of England and the King's seals of office.

Mistaking this affair for a real attack and worried that the fallen men-at-arms might join up with the third battle still unused, King Henry V ordered that no quarter should be given to prisoners. The third line of horsemen, equal to the whole English army, had indeed appeared ready to attack and to be assembling to move forward, as Antoine, Duc de Brabant came up. Some of its leaders however had moved forward to fight on foot and the battle was effectively uncertain and divided in view as to the course to take. The order given by King Henry V was contrary to the rules of chivalry, which exhorted the protection of prisoners, but the King had acted in emergency and possibly in anger at the slaughter of the young boys and squires. The archers went to their deadly work, stabbing the fallen through their visors. The third battle, seeing the massed piles of fallen, assaulted in their heaps by the English, realised that their way was blocked and began for the most part to fade away. The battle was effectively over. Only the Comte de Marle, the Comte de Fauquemburg and the Duc de Brabant with their men made a partial charge, checked as before by the arrows of archers.

The losses of the English were small, reputedly some 100, but they included the Duke of York and Earl of Suffolk. The French losses are uncertain but their numbers were significant including three Dukes, 1,500 Counts, Barons, Knights and nobles, 3,00 men-at-arms and 1,000 other troops. There were at least 1,000 prisoners including the Duc d' Orleans, the Duc de Bourbon and the Comtes of Eu, Vendome and Richmont and Marshal Boucicault. The English dead were cremated but the bodies of the Duke of York and the Earl of Suffolk were parboiled, so that their bones could be taken back to England. It took four days for the English, still lacking rations, to reach Calais, where they were met outside the town by its captain, the Earl of Warwick. On the news of the defeat reaching King Charles VI at Rouen, he wept and cried 'Now we are overthrown.'

In the next three years, with the aid of the Duke of Burgundy, Henry V was to occupy most of northern France. In 1420 the Treaty of Troyes was signed, promising that on the death of King Charles VI the crowns of France and England would be united in the person of King Henry V. The latter, it was agreed, was to marry the child loved best by the Queen of France, her daughter Katherine, and the marriage took place in June 1420. The child of the marriage was King Henry VI of England and France.

In the early part of the Second World War a film was made of the play King Henry V by Shakespeare, Laurence Olivier playing the part of the King. The manifest victory of the few English against the over mighty French stirred hearts and the words of Shakespeare, based on a recorded incident on the eve of the

Battle, in the speech of the King in Act IV Scene III, spoke to the time. According to Richard Holinshed, Sir Walter Hungerford had said to the King that he wished there were ten thousand more archers. The King disagreed: the numbers were courageous and enough.

> This day is call'd the feast of Crispian:
> He that outlives this day, and comes safe home,
> Will stand a tip-toe when this day is nam'd,
> And rouse him at the name of Crispian.
> He that shall see this day, and live old age,
> Will yearly on the vigil feast his neighbours,
> And say, To-morrow is saint Crispian:
> Then will he strip his sleeve, and show his scars:
> Old men forget; yet all shall be forgot,
> But he'll remember, with advantages,
> What feats he did that day: Then shall our names
> Familiar in his mouth as household words, -
> Harry the king, Bedford and Exeter,
> Warwick and Talbot, Salisbury and Gloster, -
> Be in their flowing cups fresh remember'd:
> This story shall the good man teach his son:
> And Crispin Crispian shall ne'er go by,
> From this day to the ending of the world,
> But we in it shall be remembered:
> We few, we happy few, we band of brothers;
> For he to-day that shed his blood with me
> Shall be my brother; be he ne'er so vile,
> This day shall gentle his condition:
> And gentlemen in England, now a-bed,
> Shall think themselves accurs'd they were not here;
>
> And hold their manhoods cheap, whiles any speaks
> That fought with us upon St.Crispin's day.

Few of the Baronial families of medieval England survive today. In some cases new families on ennoblement received old names. However, the 7th Baron Camoys, a title which was created in 1264 A.D. and revived in 1839 out of abeyance, was ejected from the house of Lords in 1999.

28th October 1811
The Battle of Arroyo Dos Molinos

The campaign of 1811 was dictated by the desire of the British to press on into Spain from Portugal, and of the French to bar their way. The northern routes required Wellington to subdue and take the Fortress of Cuidad Rodrigo, and to take and hold the Portuguese town of Almeida. The southern route required holding the fortress town of Elvas, and taking the Spanish fortress of Badajoz. Marshal Massena on the northern route endeavoured with the army of Portugal to relieve the French garrison in Almeida, but was defeated at the Battle of Fuentes de Onoro by Wellington on 5th May 1811. Meanwhile Marshal Beresford had gone south with a mixed British and Portuguese army to besiege Badajoz. He lacked a siege train and needed time to starve out the garrison. Threatening him from the south was Marshal Soult with a French army from Andaluiia. Beresford abandoned the siege and engaged the French at the Battle of Albuera on 16th May 1811. Soult then retired back towards Seville.

Joined by Wellington, Beresford returned to besiege the city, which was unsuccessfully assaulted on 6th and 9th June. Marshal Massena withdrew to Salamanca and was superseded by the young Marshal Marmont, who was thirty-six and highly ambitious. He without delay co-ordinated an attack on Wellington to be made by himself and Marshal Soult together, and on the 1st June 1811 took the road to Merida, where he met the French army from the south. Together the two Marshals commanded 60,000 men. Wellington had only 54,000 and on 17th June abandoned the siege of Badajoz and moved north-west across the River Guadiana, taking up a strong position on a line of hills over a ten mile distance. The two marshals entered Badajoz on the 20th June, revictualling the city. They reconnoitred Wellington's position but decided not to attack.

In Andaluiia, which Marshal Soult thought of almost as a private kingdom, the Spanish had risen and were supported by a Spanish army under Blake and an invasion from Murcia. Soult hurriedly abandoned Marmont and moved back south, leaving only the Vth Corps and part of Latour – Maubourg's cavalry. The forces to the west of Badajoz were left in deadlock. Marmont tried to hang on in the bleak lands of the Estramadera, but there were no local resources on which the French army, as was its custom, could live. Ultimately in mid-July he withdrew north-east to Placencia on the Salamanca-Merida road. Wellington moved north of the Tagus, leaving Sir Rowland Hill at Elvas.

In August, Wellington began to move on Ciudad Rodrigo and threaten the fortress, whose communications east had been cut by the fierce Spanish guerrillas under Julian Sanchez. All over Spain the French were hampered by such activities, and it made concentrating the armies more difficult. By the end of September, however, Marmont in conjunction with General Dorsenne had succeeded once more in concentrating an army of 60,000, including 4,500 cavalry, twenty miles east of Ciudad Rodrigo, consisting of elements from the army of the north, the army of Portugal and the Vth Corps detached from Marshal Soult in the south. They sent out a vanguard, and Wellington retreated to prepared positions at Sabugal, his army numbering only 46,000 of which 17,000 were Portuguese. The French pursued him to Sabugal, but coming on the prepared allied defensive positions decided not to attack. The move against Wellington of Marmont's army used up the supplies intended for the re-supply of Ciudad Rodrigo, which the army had carried, and the French were forced to disperse, Marmont going back to Salamanca and the Vth Corps south, where the IXth Corps was operating in an attempt to hold down the Estramadura and protect Badajoz. Drouet had had to disperse his troops for that purpose, and the First Division of the Vth Corps, commanded by General Girard, had become detached from any support at Cáceres.

Sir Rowland Hill, seizing his opportunity, having obtained Lord Wellington's consent, set off to attack the isolated Division with the 2nd Division of the army and Hamilton's Portuguese, amounting in all to 11,000 men. His base at Portalegre was sixty miles west of Cáceres, and he needed to intercept Girard before he could reach the safety of Merida. On 22nd October, observing the strictest secrecy, the army marched thirty miles through unbelievably desperate weather – strong rain, gales and freezing night temperatures. For three days they pushed on, determined, until they were within eight miles of Cáceres. Girard had however left for Merida. On 26th October the Allied army turned south, tramping along parallel to the French, but on the first day of this move, they covered twenty-eight miles while Girard's troops went twelve. That brought them to within five miles of the French, who had halted at the little town of Arroyo dos Molinos, six thousand feet above sea level. In the mountains Hill's troops paused for the night unsheltered from the freezing gale. Like his predecessor at Agincourt, Hill commanded that there be no campfires, no bugles and that silence be preserved.

At two o'clock in the morning the troops were roused and marched in icy rain and mountain fog towards the town. By dawn the Allied army was closing in on the French, who were not completely loaded up, and only just preparing themselves to move. General Girard and his officers were at breakfast. In three columns the 2nd Division pushed on around the town. Major-General Howarth's Brigade – comprising the 50th (West Kent) Regiment of Foot, the 71st (Glasgow Highland) Regiment of Foot and the 92nd (Highland Regiment) led by pipers playing 'Hey Johnny Cope, are ye waukin yet!', stormed the main street, which was littered with the baggage trains and baggage. There and in the fields around the town the French endeavoured to make a stand, but within thirty minutes it was all done. General Girard with others made their escape in isolated groups into the mountains around. Only one French brigade (it had already left the town) escaped. Hill's army captured General Bon, the second-in-command, took 1,500 prisoners, 3 guns and several hundred horses. The French dead amounted to 800. Sir Rowland Hill, having successfully caught his prey, returned to Portalegre. Wellington had a high regard for Hill, regarding him as one of the few of his generals on whom he could rely to act intelligently and reliably on their own initiative.

The 8th Viscount Hill was ejected from the House of Lords in 1999.

November

4th	The Battle of El Alamein	1942
10th	The Battle of Nivelle	1813
11th	Armistice Day	1918
	The Destruction of the Italian Fleet at Taranto	1940
20th	The Battle of Quiberon Bay	1759

The Battle of El Alamein

At the time of the 2nd World War Britain controlled the Kingdom of Egypt as a protectorate, put in place originally to secure the passage to India through the Mediterranean and Suez Canal. Cairo was the headquarters of British military power in the near East, from the Horn of Africa to the oil fields of Iraq. It was crucial for waging war worldwide that Egypt be held. Mussolini, the dictator of Italy, had ambitions to expand the Italian Empire, the principal elements of which were Libya, the conquered Ethiopia and Italian Somaliland. He had allied himself with Germany and Adolf Hitler and entered the war as part of the Axis on 10 June 1940, just before the collapse of France. The Italian navy constituted a threat to Britain in the Mediterranean, but their army based in Libya was equally a threat to Egypt. Stretched by the perils which encompassed them, the British had a Western Desert force of only two divisions to defend that country on the Libyan frontier.

It was not until September 1940 that the Italians attacked under General Berti, and they pushed the British back into Egypt to Sidi Barrani, where both sides established front lines and strong points, the Italians being well provisioned with the best of food. Courageously, Winston Churchill had despatched tanks and military supplies round the Cape to General Wavell, who was in command in the Near East, although in Britain these were few. With these reinforcements, on 9th December the Western Desert Army counter-attacked, driving on into Libya. On 22nd January 1941 Tobruk was taken, and the retreat of the Italian army was cut off by encirclement at Beda Fomm. 130,000 prisoners were taken, together with 400 tanks and 1,290 guns. The whole of Cyrenaica was taken, but the victory was to be short lived. Events in Greece required the removal of troops from North Africa to defend the latter country and to help in resisting its occupation. Only a weakened force was left.

The Germans, in order to assist the Italians, had despatched a German division to Tripoli, the 5th Light Division, and in the early spring Feldmarschall Rommel arrived to command the Afrika Corps of the Axis army. On 24th April 1941 he attacked at El Agheila and swept the British back to Sollum, almost on the Egyptian boundary. His army was strengthened by the 16th Panzer Division and he was advised to remain in the new position on the defensive. Tobruk remained invested and was fiercely held by two Australian Divisions for most of 1941, although at the end of the siege part of these had been replaced by British and Polish troops. In June an attempt to break through the Axis line was made unsuccessfully, but tanks, aircraft and ammunition were built up and on 20th November 1941 Operation Crusader was launched. Fierce and determined fighting took place, and, Rommel began to withdraw west. Tobruk was relieved on 26th November and the British pressed forward as Rommel and the Italians retired once more, through Cyrenaica to Mersa Brega. On 5th January 1942 Rommel received 55 new tanks and fuel. On 21st January he launched a new campaign spearheaded by the Panzer Army Afrika. The British hastily retreated and against orders Rommel pressed on to Benghazi, where he paused. In May he re-launched his attack and defeated the British at Gazzala, taking Tobruk on 25th June with 35,000 prisoners, and thrusting on to El Alamein inside Egypt, where the British had established a defensive line between the Quattara Depression and the sea, some sixty miles from Alexandria. Thus, for just over two years, the desert war had swung backwards and forwards across Libya with no final outcome.

The desert was peculiar in that the area covered comprised substantially a terrain of rock, sand and areas of camel scrub, was largely unpopulated and had few defensive positions and inadequate ports apart from Tripoli. Arising from the terrain and the distances to be covered (up to a thousand miles by means of the coastal road) was a need to transport supplies – water, food, ammunition and fuel, over vast distances. The burden which distance imposed can be judged from the fact that it took almost as much fuel as a vehicle could carry to go to El Alamein from Tripoli and back. The supply position of the Italians and the Germans was further worsened by the requirement to transport supplies to the ports across the Mediterranean Sea, which could be dominated by the Royal Navy and subject to Royal Air Force attack from Malta and elsewhere. During Rommel's spring campaign in 1942 the German and Italian air forces concentrated for some six weeks on reducing Malta and almost drove the base out of action, although it recovered when the German Air Corps was switched to assist Rommel at Gazzala. From the middle of 1942 the developing use of the ULTRA system of intelligence made interference with the supply chain of the Axis forces more effective.

The Germans sent out their signals in the clear, relying on the 'scrambling' of the message by use of a sophisticated machine called ENIGMA, and variable keys to the code, in order to preserve the security of the message. The British managed through the Poles to acquire a machine, and from various sources some of the codebooks. A team assembled at Bletchley Park in Bedfordshire worked out how to break the codes painstakingly and skilfully, with the use of mathematics. The information which they secured enabled them ultimately to pass on every message decoded by the Germans as to the movements of their troops - down to the postings of individual men - and their ships and aeroplanes. The recipients of the messages sent were as limited in number as possible and all sworn to secrecy, so that the fact that access had been obtained to German military and naval signals should not become known to the enemy. In the Mediterranean sphere messages were sent out to the Commander in Chief, General Alexander, for example, in late 1942 and to commanders of the various armies in action, to General Montgomery and to Naval and Air Force Commanders. Even at that stage the recipients had to be careful to use information received only in such a manner that, if action were taken, the Germans would treat that action as the result of some conventional means of intelligence. Thus where there was intelligence that supplies were being sent by sea to Libya, aerial or naval reconnaissance was sent out 'to find' the convoy or ships before an attack was made. Once ULTRA was in place and used, the percentage of total enemy supplies loaded for North Africa in the months from May to October 1942 which arrived never rose above forty per cent; mostly, however, the supplies totalled only one-fifth of monthly requirements. The fuel position was the worst. During the summer all tankers going to Libya were sunk, as during the Battle of El Alamein were both the Proserpina and Louisiana, which could have brought relief to Rommel, who had been effectively reduced to immobility. It was against this background that the first and second battles of El Alamein were fought.

The character of the fluctuating fortunes of the desert war had depended on the ability of the opposing sides to outflank the other in the desert, away from the coast. The El Alamein position to which the British retreated in 1942 was different in that the line established could not be turned. In the north it was bounded by the coast and in the south by the 6,000 square-mile Quattara Depression, an area of soft sand dunes, salt lakes and marshes impassable to tanks and other vehicles. The seventy-odd mile front between the two limits was mined along the front. Behind the minefields there were strong points established mainly with stonewalls, as digging trenches was often impossible. A number of ridges, mainly on an axis east to west, lay on either side of the line or dissecting it. In the north behind the German lines, there was the Kidney ridge, so called because of its shape and the Mitelriya Ridge on the north-west – south-east axis. Towards the centre of the line the Ruweisat ridge and south of that the Alam El Halfa Ridge lay on the British side of the line. The British had four positions in depth, the most easterly being located along a line of springs.

Throughout July 1942 the British under General Sir Claude Auchinleck made a number of attempts on the German lines, which were being gradually solidified by the laying of minefields. On 10th July the Australians captured Tel El Eisa on the main railway near the coast in the north, and on the 14th the New Zealand and Indian Divisions attacked along the Ruweisat Ridge in the centre. On the 16th the Australians launched an assault on the El Makh Ahad ridge in the south and held it. Counter-attacks by the Afrika Corps on 18th and 19th July on the Ruweisat Ridge failed. An attempt at a break-through by the Australians and New Zealanders did not succeed on 21st July; indeed on 22nd July 118 tanks were lost against 3 German. Nor did the Australians make further progress at Tel El Eisa on the 26th.

On 4th August Winston Churchill arrived in Cairo, dissatisfied with the progress made. As a result of his visit General Auchinleck was superseded as

Commander-in-Chief Near East by General Sir Harold Alexander, and General Sir Bernard Montgomery was put in command of the army in the desert. Montgomery was the son of a Church of England parson. He had fought in the First World War, served in India and had success in the Dunkirk campaign. He was determined that the British soldier would not suffer another Passchendaele (see Campaign of 191711th November 1918). He was single-minded, direct and determined to re-organise the army to make use of tanks and guns as a concentrated force, and to improve fighting morale. On arrival he shook up the command structure, removing officers whom he thought inadequate and visiting every unit. He established a particular public style, abandoning the General's hat for first an Australian bush hat and subsequently a beret. He was fearless under attack; at the battle at Alaim El Halfa, while talking during an air attack, he neither took cover nor ceased to talk to those with him. As part of morale building he deliberately improved the status and prestige of army chaplains, and on a so-called 'secret' visit to Cairo insisted on reading the lesson at a service in the Cathedral.

Almost immediately after taking up his command in mid-August he was faced by a final attempt by Rommel to break through the line to push on to Alexandria and ultimately Cairo. Helped by intelligence from Ultra, he was prepared to deal with this assault. Because of the limitation of supplies and the diversion in Germany of aircraft and armaments to Russia, Rommel was anxious to retreat to establish a new line at Sollum. Neither the Fuehrer nor Mussolini were prepared to accept this strategy and he was ordered to attack and break through the lines. He had made it clear that he needed fuel before he would proceed and on 27th August Feldmarschall Kesselring and Marshal Cavallero guaranteed 6,000 tons. On the night of he 31st August Rommel attacked. There were feints planned against the north of the British line, and a strong punch in the centre, but the main force was to be committed in the south along the edge of the Quattara depression, turning north towards the Alam El Halfa ridge and then to the sea, enveloping the main British forces. By dawn on the 31st the minefields had not been fully penetrated but the main attack went on, turning north-east early, taking the benefit of a dust storm blowing towards the ridge. There was trouble, the tanks getting stuck in the Ragil depression and the RAF constantly carpet-bombing the German formations. Artillery pounded the German tanks. Nonetheless on 1st September, despite the efforts of the 2nd Armoured Division, they almost broke through. On 3rd September Rommel ordered the retreat. He was out of fuel and the promised supplies had not come. The Germans and Italians went back to fortify their four mile-deep line more heavily, sowing more minefields, creating 'Devil's Gardens', the anti-personnel bomb 'entrenchments'. Rommel returned to Germany on sick leave, leaving General Stumme in command.

During the summer and early autumn a constant stream of supplies of all types arrived for the British, including Sherman and Grant tanks and heavier guns.

Thus by October the British armies had 1,079 tanks, of which 270 were Shermans and 210 Grants, 195,000 men, 849 6-pounder guns, and a Desert Air Force of 530 (without Air Marshal Tedder's Strategic Bombing Force). The Axis by contrast had only 507 tanks (of which 200 were German), 104,000 men, of which 54,000 were Italian, only 24 of the 88-mm guns comparable to the 6-pounders, and 350 aircraft. Even Rommel, on 3rd July had noted 'Our strength has faded away'. By October the British had thus an overwhelming superiority.

From north to south along the British line the troops were deployed for the final battle with the XXXth Corps on the north and the XIIIth in the south. Nearest the coast on a ten-mile front were the 9th Australian Division, then the 51st Highland Division, 2nd New Zealand Division and 1st South African Division. The Ruweisat Ridge area was held by the 4th Indian Division. South of the ridge to the Quattara Depression were respectively the 50th Division, the 44th and 7th Armoured Division and the Free French nearest the rim. The Xth Corps, comprising the 1st and 10th Armoured Divisions, was held behind the lines in the north near the coast. On the Axis side behind the minefields Rommel stationed his Italian troops embedded between German forces. The size of the army for the front meant that he could not hold the Panzer Armies Afrika in reserve. The only reserves held in the north were the 90th Light and Trieste Divisions. In the line nearest the coast was the 164th and Brescia Divisions, in the centre opposite the 4th Indian Division the Fallesch and Bologna Brigades and in the south three Italian Divisions, the Trento, Folgore and Pavia, backed by the 15th Panzer Division and the Littorio Divisions. In the far south were stationed the 21st Panzer and the Ariete Division. It should be noted in passing that the Italian tanks were obsolete and in their infantry divisions the ratio of guns and vehicles to men was only 1 to 33, compared with 1 to 8 in the British Divisions.

General Montgomery was faced by the tactical problem that the nature of the El Alamein position prevented any flanking attacks. The Axis line had to be assaulted head on, a situation not dissimilar from the western front in the First World War. The plan of attack involved punching lanes through the minefields by infantry and backing them up with concentrations of tanks, which would dig in to counter anti-tank gunfire if necessary. The front was to be 'crumbled away' by persistent pressure until the armoured divisions held in readiness could break through and out to roll up the enemy's line. The creation of the lanes through was to be secured by artillery barrage preceding attack and carpet-bombing in close co-ordination with the Royal Air Force. Montgomery developed a close relationship with Tedder and the success at El Alamein was due to the well co-ordinated co-operation of the navy and air force interfering with supplies and the air force acting on the battlefield as an arm of the ground forces. The air force in fact maintained in the attacks a rolling barrage of high explosive and napalm bombs, clearing paths for the advance known as 'Tedder's carpet.' The importance of that can be gauged by reference to Rommel's comment that 'to fight against an enemy who had air supremacy was to be in the position of a spear-armed savage against European maxim guns'.

In implementing his approach Montgomery decided that the weight of the attack should be in the north, punching two broad lanes through the minefields, with a feint in the south. To prepare the ground for this strategy an effective deception was evolved to persuade the Germans that the main attack would come on the southern part of the line, where XXIIIrd Corps under Lieutenant General Sir Brian Horrocks was to attempt to make a single lane through the minefields. Fake fuel dumps and fuel lines were placed in the desert behind the southern lines, while in the north guns and tanks were brought up by night, to be hidden under false frames that had the appearance of lorries from the air. In the outcome the launch of the campaign both in timing and position came as a surprise to the Germans. Indeed, German intelligence was of the view that the British would not attack in October.

The night of 23rd October was bright with moonlight. The attack opened with a barrage from 1,000 guns and aerial bombing of the German lines. The German lines were reduced to a hell of smoke, fire, explosion and destruction. At 10 pm the infantry advanced. The XXXth Corps in the north went in to create two lanes. The 9th Australian Division led the advance north of Mitelriya Ridge with the 50th Highland Division. The 2nd New Zealand Division with the 1st South African Division pushed south-west of the ridge clearing a second lane. The 4th Indian Division moved along the Ruweisat Ridge. The 1st and 10th Armoured Division followed into the cleared lanes with some 700 tanks. By dawn the lanes had not been fully established, but these seasoned and experienced divisions were through the minefield as far as the German front line. In the New Zealand lane the tanks became bogged down and had to be withdrawn. In the south the attack forced a corridor using the 44th Division and 7th Armoured Division through the eastern part of the minefield but not the west. The Australians did however manage to establish a salient either side of Kidney Ridge with 1st Armoured Division. On the 24th Adolf Hitler telephoned Rommel and asked him to return to North Africa. General Stumme was dead and the command of the Germans devolved to General Ritter Von Thoma.

24th and 25th October were taken up by persistent attacks and counter-attacks. The 15th Panzer and Ariete Divisions were committed to the attack. The infantry of the XXXth Corps and the 10th Armoured Brigade were jammed into the narrow lane. Heavy losses were inflicted on the Axis forces by artillery bombardment and raids by the RAF In the south the Italian Folgore Parachute Division re-established the position and the hole made was stopped up by the 15th Panzer and the Littorio Divisions, but the Axis lost 101 tanks out of 426. In the north General Lansden with the armour reached the far side of the Mitelriya Ridge, but wished to retire to the reverse side to protect the tanks from anti-tank gunfire. Montgomery refused this request as he wished to keep up constant pressure on the enemy. The focus of attack however turned north towards the Kidney Ridge. On 25th October Rommel returned to take command. He immediately planned a counterstroke. The 21st Panzer and Ariete Divisions were brought north. On the night of 25th October the British artillery began another heavy rolling barrage along the line, and night air bombing was persistent. By midnight Kidney Ridge was captured and the bridgehead beyond the line was being widened. The German 90th Light Division and the Trieste Division were committed and a desperate and bloody struggle took place around the ridge, in which the east and west flanks of the ridge were retaken. The German air cover of Stuka dive-bombers was swept away by the faster British planes and the counter-attack was brought to a halt by the Royal Air Force.

On 26th October Rommel was in the north directing the fighting around Kidney Ridge which was being continuously strengthened. An ammunition shortage was beginning to afflict the Axis armies. The Australians turned north towards the sea in the vicinity of Sidi Abd el Rahman, and the Trieste Division was moved up to El Daba in order to counter this. Fighting round Kidney Ridge was intense and although the objectives planned for Day 1 had been reached, there was still no break-through opened up behind the Axis lines. The dive-bombers once again attacked the British moving north-west, but they were set upon by 50 planes. The Italian air forces became confused in the mêlée of the battle and bombed their own troops. South of the ridge there were renewed attempts by the British armour to drive through. In the afternoon 150 tanks secured a deep penetration but were forced back, although 20 Royal Air Force bombers attacked the Germans every hour. News came to Rommel that the Proserpina, the fuel tanker being sent, was sunk outside Tobruk. The move of 21st Panzer north was now irreversible, since the fuel shortage was becoming acute. The British were tiring and the violence of the attack was diminishing, tank losses having been considerable. Montgomery was however able to regroup, still having 800 tanks and inexhaustible supplies. The 7th Armoured Division and infantry in the south were moved north.

27th October opened with heavy artillery fire on the Axis lines. Rommel, however, now tried to launch a counter-attack on Kidney Ridge and the Mitelriya Ridge, the former being attacked by the 90th Light Division and the latter by 15th and 21st Panzer Divisions. The tanks had to assemble in open desert and while doing so in the early afternoon they were attacked by the Royal Air Force as much as three times in fifteen minutes. German dive-bombers attacked in support of their tanks despite hot anti-aircraft fire, while the German armour came on with the sun behind them. Intense anti-tank and heavy anti-aircraft gunfire halted the attempt in its tracks. The 90th Light Division was devastated and there were heavy German casualties.

The next day Rommel reached a turning point in respect of his losses. There were three British attacks in the north, the Australians meeting with qualified success. The Royal Air Force unceasingly bombed the Axis. At 9 pm west of Kidney

Ridge a murderous artillery barrage was launched, followed by an assault leading to six hours' violent fighting; again the position was just held. The situation convinced Rommel that he should consider a retreat to Fuka, to save his army, where the escarpment would aid a defensive position.

On 29th October Rommel received news that the Louisiana, another fuel tanker, had been sunk and the Royal Air Force switched the bombing to supplies being sent forward on the road from Tobruk. General Alexander and Richard Casey, Minister of State for the Middle East, with Major McCreery, a tank warfare expert, visited Montgomery to discuss future tactics and progress, given that after six days of effort no complete break-though had been achieved. It was decided that there should be a new attack north of Kidney Ridge on the hinge between the German and Italian forces. The 2nd New Zealand Division was to be redeployed so that a westerly attack could be made creating a breach for the 10th Armoured Corps. General Freyberg indicated that the New Zealanders could not be ready until 1st November.

On the night of 30th October the 9th Australian Division renewed their northern push to the sea, assaulting frontally from the south after a one-hour artillery barrage. By dawn 30 tanks succeeded in getting through to the coast road, giving the potential to cut off the German infantry division in the north salient. 21st Panzer was not assembled ready to counter-attack, but Ritter Von Thoma, using units of it and the 90th Light Division was able to throw back the small force and get through to the encircled infantry. On 1st November Rommel once more reconnoitred the northern front in detail and ordered that British troops who were evacuating their wounded from a Red Cross post should not be fired on. That day the Axis northern front was raided 34 times and the supply columns pounded by fighter-bombers. Rommel was left with only 90 German tanks and 140 Italian. Once again his mind turned to retirement to the Fuka position.

On the night of to 2nd November Montgomery launched his campaign 'Supercharge' to achieve a final break-though. Having kept up the pressure on the Axis tenaciously for eight days, hammering their forces and attacking them to force their disintegration, the time had come to move forward. The offensive began with a three-hour shelling on the German front line. Wave after wave of RAF bombers bombed the defensive line. The 9th Australian Division was to move north and the 2nd New Zealand and 50th west of Kidney Ridge. The latter had developed by dawn a two and half-mile wedge, which the Afrika Corps tried to seal. Once more a violent tank battle ensued, while artillery and the RAF pounded the Axis line. The break-out was near but was not yet achieved. Rommel, knowing the precarious position, sent an aide-de-camp to Hitler in East Prussia to ask for the order to be given to retreat. While a reply was awaited the front held on 2nd November. The 21st and 15th Panzer, Littorio and Trieste Divisions were smashed by the powerful Sherman and Grant tanks, the Germans losing 70 and the Italians 50. The reply from Adolf Hitler ordered Rommel to stand firm to the last, assuring him that he would receive supplies. Rommel with difficulty accepted the order. He cancelled his order to retreat, although three divisions of Italians had already been put on the march to Fuka and were subject to attack by 200 bombers of the RAF. His contempt for the decision was shown in a comment which he made that 'What we needed was guns, fuel and planes; what we did not need were orders to hold fast.'

On 4th November the remnants of the Afrika Corps and the 90th Light Division still held a front without depth near the Tel Mampstra sand dune west of Kidney Ridge. General Ritter Von Thoma put on his dress uniform and medals that day and appeared with a small bag.

He told General Bayerlein that the Hitler order was a piece of madness. At 8.00 am. the British attacked with every arm employed so that the line became nothing but a place of death. All the tanks and anti-tank guns of the Afrika Corps were out of action by 11.00 am. Ritter von Thoma was observed standing by a burning tank surrounded by 20 Sherman tanks. A Bren-gun carrier and two tanks drove up to him and he was taken prisoner. A message was sent to Rommel that Ritter Von Thoma was a prisoner by the 10th Hussars. Rommel knew that despite the Hitler order the time had come to retire. He ordered disengagement after dark, setting out to save some part of his tanks, guns and transport. The break-through was complete and the battle of El Alamein won. The Indian 4th Division pushed a further mile south of Tel el Aggagir. On 5th November Hitler agreed to a retreat but by that time the Fuka position had been overrun. Rommel continued to retreat west towards Tunisia. On 8th November the Allied forces – largely American – invaded Morocco and Algeria and Rommel and the Axis faced war on two fronts.

In the battle 30,000 prisoners were taken and the Germans were left with 38 serviceable tanks. The British casualties were not light, amounting to 13,650. The New Zealanders, who bore with the Australians much of the brunt of the infantry fighting, lost one-third of their numbers. The victory had however opened the way to Tripoli, although the pursuit was in some respects cautious. However, after rearguard actions by Rommel at El Agheila and Buerat, Tripoli fell on 23rd January 1943. In February the army entered southern Tunisia, while the Americans moved in from the West. On 12th May all enemy resistance in North Africa ended. In early February Winston Churchill took the salute at a parade of the troops in Tripoli, led by the pipers of the 51st Highland Division. El Alamein was the greatest victory of the war achieved by the British Empire and its peoples. Henceforth the British and Americans were to form a joint force. The Africa Corps and the Italians had fought with a courage and determination to be admired.

The 2nd Earl Alexander of Tunis, the 2nd Viscount Montgomery of Alamein and the 3rd Lord Tedder were all ejected from the House of Lords in 1999.

10th November 1813

The Battle of The Nivelle

After the crossing of the River Bidassoa (7th October 1813) Marshal Soult had retired north to just beyond the River Nivelle, with a front twenty miles long, from St Jean de Luz to Ainhoue. Once more he built as he did on the River Bidassoa a line of fortifications. Wellington did not move the British Army up for an early attack. He had a number of concerns. General Casson still held out in Pamplona with his 80 guns and 3,000 men and did not surrender until 31st October. The supply situation from Santander was still in confusion and he still had the problem of the behaviour of the Spanish army in France, and of the Portuguese drifting home. Despite the German battles the political situation was still unclear, and the possibility of peace with the Emperor Napoleon was not yet dismissed.

The country chosen by Marshal Soult for his new line was yet again good defensive country, lending itself to the construction of redoubts on the hills. He still had 62,000 men, many of whom however were new conscripts. Although spread out along the line they were somewhat thin, they had ample guns for the redoubts. He believed that his position was strong enough to prevent its loss save in a fight in which the Allied armies were prepared to lose one-third of their force. His dispositions were not dissimilar from those at the Bidassoa. General Reille was on the French right on the lower Nivelle. General Clausel with three Divisions was in the centre. Generals D'Erlon and Foy were on the left. The movement of the latter to a position closer to D'Erlon enabled Sir Rowland Hill with his force of 22,000 men to emerge from the defiles of the Lower Pyrenees. The Duke of Wellington's strength was 82,000 men, with a large number of guns. Most of the troops were seasoned and experienced soldiers. Sir Rowland Hill was on the right, Marshal Beresford with 33,000 in the centre and General Sir John Hope with 25,000 on the left.

On 9th November Wellington met his Light Divisional Commanders, Alten, Colborne and Kempt, on the Grand Rhune, from where they observed the enemy position. After cold and storm, early November had become a time of sunshine. To them he expounded his tactics for the battle. He was to thrust strongly against Clausel in the centre and make feints on each wing. The troops moved up to their positions in the night and at dawn waded across the river. Sir John Hope drew General Reille into a sparring match, pinning down the French right wing, and Sir Rowland Hill attacked D'Erlon on the French left. In the centre Beresford's men climbed the hills under fire, pushing their lines forwards to the forts and defences. The Allied force was two to one in numbers against Clausel's divisions in the centre. Menaced by the shots of the British line and frightened by their firmness and determined climb forward, many of the new conscripts in the redoubts fled. One was even bluffed into surrender as General Colborne shouted to the defenders of the redoubt that the Spanish were on their left. Within two hours the Light Division took the outworks on the Petite Rhune. Cannon was brought up the tremendous steeps to bombard redoubts not taken. By noon the British were through deep into the French rear. Total victory was prevented by the shortness of the winter's day, but once more Marshal Soult retired north to Bayonne and the River Nive. The 1,200 defenders of St Jean de Luz and their 50 guns were abandoned. The French had 4,300 casualties, mainly in Clausel's divisions, and lost 59 guns apart from those in St Jean de Luz; Allied causalities were 3,000.

The Duke of Wellington moved forward after the battle and camped between St Jean de Luz and Espellette, where once more he paused. On 9th December Emperor Napoleon finally rejected the peace offers made and invasion of France became inevitable. The Allied army, hemmed in the south-west corner of France in a narrow salient, still had to cross another river. Soult had established a new defensive position based on Bayonne and the River Nive. The Duke of Wellington could not stay where he was and so decided to advance to the River Adour and Bayonne. On 9th December the Nive was crossed by means of pontoon bridges unopposed, the enemy troops returning to Bayonne. Sir John Hope advanced towards the city, only to be met on the 11th December by a counter-attack driving him back. On 13th December Soult attacked Sir Rowland Hill. Although separated by a River Nive in flood, Hill fought Soult to a standstill and reinforcement came from across a reconstructed pontoon bridge. The French retired on Bayonne. The British and Allied armies lost 1,100 men.

11th November 1914

Armistice Day 1918 brought to an end the First World War. The origins of that war, and how the powers in Europe came to stumble into it in the manner which they did, have been the subject of endless debate. Underlying the apparent slide to war were realities which had been growing in significance as the nineteenth century turned. In 1866 the Empire of Austria Hungary had been defeated by the Prussians at Sadowa and its influence in Germany destroyed, weakening its strength in central Europe. The Ottoman Empire in the Balkans had been progressively dissolving, attracting the attention of both Austria-Hungary and Russia in establishing influence and control over the area. In 1871, after the defeat of France, Prince von Bismarck had called into being a united Germany under the Prussian King, the Emperor Wilhelm I. His foreign policy rested on holding the balance of power evenly between the Empires of central Europe, and avoiding policies which involved suggestions of a threat to Britain. The Emperor Wilhelm II in 1890 dismissed Bismarck from office and German policy evolved in a direction which inevitably upset the careful balance which underlay the peace. Germany allied itself with Austria-Hungry to the exclusion of Russia, and the weakness of Austria made that Empire virtually dependent for its international influence on the German Government. France, concerned at the rise of a militant Germany and weakened by the Franco – Prussian War of 1870 – 1871, looked to find new allies, and turned to the Tsar of Russia.

The latter, meddling in the Balkans with the secret desire still to control access to the Black Sea at Constantinople, under Prime Minister Stolypin started to support the Slav state of Serbia. The latter, Austria-Hungary saw as part of the problem of the south Slavs within and without the Empire, which was under internal political pressures, threatening its continued existence. Slav populations existed within the Empire in southern Hungary, Croatia and Bosnia and Herzegovina, first occupied in 1878 and annexed in 1908. The emergence in Germany of an aggressive commercial interest backing a navy progressively persuaded British politicians that Imperial Germany could threaten its supremacy at sea. Actions by Kaiser Wilhelm II and the Anglophobe Admiral von Turpitz led the Liberal Government to re-arm the fleet under the leadership of Lord Fisher, who urged on the building of the new 'Dreadnought' battleships. In both the German and Austrian Army commands there existed too a body of opinion which saw war as desirable to increase the strength and influence of their countries worldwide.

On Sunday 28th June 1914 a nineteen-year old Serbian, Gavrilo Princip, assassinated the Archduke Francis Ferdinand, heir to the Emperor of Austria, and his wife at Sarajevo, where they were on an official visit. The Austrians suspected the involvement of a secret group of Serbian nationalists known as the Black Hand, and officers of the Serbian army. With the backing of Imperial Germany, Austria served an ultimatum on the Serbs on 24th July, requiring them to take steps to control the persons and bodies involved in nationalist plots, and to give Austria guarantees and rights to exercise control over acts done in Serbia. A reply was requested within 48 hours. Just in time the Serbians accepted most of the demands made, but also expressed some reservations on two items. The Germans and Austrians, intent on a war with Serbia, pressed on and on 28th July Austria declared war on Serbia.

From that moment war in Europe moved forward ineluctably and inevitably. The Russians on the same day announced 'partial' mobilisation, aiming to protect the Serbs (and their own influence in the Balkans) and the Germans warned them that their mobilisation would lead to war. The German Government on 31st July itself ordered mobilisation and a similar response on 1st August would emerge in France. In all cases the generals relied on their war plans and logistic requirements to justify putting the armies into deployment. Both Kaiser Wilhelm II and Tsar Nicholas II tried to restrain the march to war. On 31st July, however, the Tsar was persuaded to issue a *ukase* for mobilisation, and Austria likewise issued such orders. The same day the Germans sent ultimata to St. Petersburg and Paris demanding the suspension by Russia and France of war measures against Austro-Hungary and themselves. The Germans called on France to remain neutral in any war between Russia and Germany and permit the occupation of Verdun and Toul for the duration of the war as a guarantee. The Chief of the German General Staff, Helmut Graf von Moltke, told the Kaiser that the deployment of the army could not be stopped, and that in any event there was a favourable situation to strike against France.

In the evening of 2nd August Germany served an ultimatum on Belgium to permit the passage of the German army and the occupation of vital fortresses for the duration of the war against France. The ultimatum was to expire on the morning of 3rd August. On that day Germany declared war on France and the German army set out on their March through Belgium to France, crossing the frontier on 4th August.

The invasion was the result of a strategy devised by the German General Staff to combat both France and Russia together in the event of war, as the growing rapprochement of those powers was seen. It envisaged fighting on two fronts, the principal being in the west, while the Russians were held in the east. After the quick defeat of France, the attack was to take place on Russia. The plan evolved by Graf Von Schlieffen predicated in the west a swing by the German right wing through Belgium to encircle Paris on the west side, in order to outflank the French armies and attack them from the rear. The corollary was to feint with the left wing in Alsace-Lorraine and try to persuade the French to concentrate there. To achieve the success of the right wing it was heavily loaded, with 53 Divisions and contributions from the Landwehr. The plan contained an implicit risk that the French might achieve a break-through on the German left wing and move behind the Imperial army. The Schlieffen Plan was complemented by the plan of the French military to strike east into Germany through Alsace-Lorraine, on the theory of achieving victory by '*attaque*', a concept of which Lord Kitchener of Khartoum, who became Secretary of War in 1914, was deeply suspicious. Feldmarschall Graf Von Moltke, who succeeded Schlieffen, was of a more nervous disposition and between the formulation of the plan in 1905 and 1914 added eight of the nine new divisions raised to the left and only one to the right, but otherwise he adhered to the plan.

In Britain Sir Henry Wilson, a Francophile and arch-intriguer, had pushed the army down the route of staff discussions with the French in the event of Britain becoming entangled in a war, with France as an ally. The British army was to be used on the French left wing – six divisions were to be sent to France, the four infantry divisions four days after mobilisation. In 1912 General Sir Henry Wilson and Sir John French, who was to command the army to go to France, tried to persuade the Liberal Government to enter an alliance with France. Such an alliance had not been entered and was not to be prior to the war. In 1912 joint British and French naval planning was instituted.

The summer of 1914 was occupied by the crisis over Home Rule for Ireland, and July was passed full of rumours of civil war between the north and south, including the risk of army mutinies. On 21st July a conference at Buckingham Palace under the auspices of King George V tried to reconcile the difference between all the party interests involved, and that was uppermost in the mind of Mr Asquith, the Prime Minister, and of the Cabinet. On 24th July Sir Edward Grey, the Secretary of State for Foreign Affairs, told the Cabinet that the Austrian ultimatum to Serbia was likely to result in war between the four continental great powers, but as Asquith recorded in his diary, there was no reason why the British should be more than spectators. Sir Edward Grey tried unsuccessfully to arrange a conference to mediate between other parties. However, on 29th July warning signals to prepare were sent to military, naval and colonial stations. On the same day Britain considered the position, were Belgium to be invaded, and the Cabinet took the view that any action in the end was one of policy and not completely of law (involving the guarantee of Belgium independence and neutrality under Treaties of 1831 and 1839, which the powers including Prussia had signed).

On the same day Sir Edward Grey told the French and Germans that he could not pledge any action by the British if war came. At that stage the Cabinet was divided ten to ten as to the action to be taken, Lloyd-George being one of those against entering any war. On 30th July the City of London businessmen implored Lloyd-George to keep out of any war at all costs in order to protect Britain's economic and financial position. On 31st July the French pressed London to declare its support and on 1st August the Cabinet met to consider its position if the neutrality of Belgium were infringed. It was still divided. Sir John Simon and Lord Morley remained strong for non-intervention as did the bulk of the Liberal party in the House of Commons. Winston Churchill was all for mobilisation and Sir Edward Grey threatened to resign if Britain did not intervene, were Belgium to be invaded. On 2nd August there were two cabinet meetings and disagreement still continued. Lloyd-George led the opposition to intervention.

In the streets war fever was mounting. On 3rd August King Albert of Belgium and the Belgian Government rejected the German ultimatum. At the Cabinet meeting at 11 am Lloyd George had moved to favour intervention and the resignations from the Cabinet, which were mooted, were withheld until Sir Edward Grey had addressed the House of Commons in the afternoon. In a moving and coherent speech he swung the doubters and on 4th August Britain served an ultimatum on Germany to remove its armies from Belgium by midnight. That night Britain was at war with Germany. Once more, as in the past and future, Britain acted to protect a small nation from an European aggressor, aiming at domination of the continent, and to prevent the breach of solemn treaties. The majority of European rulers and generals thought that the war would be over in a short time. In Britain only Lord Kitchener of Khartoum predicted a long war over three years.

The Campaign of 1914

On 4th August the Germans crossed into Belgium and on 5th May succeeded in taken the heavily armed fortress of Liege, clearing the path of their advance. The Belgium army retired and took up a position east of Brussels on the River Gatte. In London that day and on the next Councils of War were held at which diverse views were voiced. General Haig wished to delay the movement to France and Lord Kitchener thought that the British Expeditionary Force should be centred at Amiens, and not Maubeuge on the French border as agreed. He distrusted the French tactics of 'L'Attaque' and wished to have the BEF where it could be extracted, if need be. It was finally agreed that only 4 divisions of Infantry, the 1st, 2nd, 3rd and 5th, would go to France, together with cavalry and artillery. From 6th August the Germans poured troops into Belgium, some 50 trains crossing on the Rhine bridges each day with troops and supplies. 1,500,000 men were assembled in seven armies. The BEF arrived in France from Southampton and Portsmouth between 12th and 21st of August landing 80,000 men, 125 machine guns, 30,000 horses and 315 field guns. Lord Kitchener gave way on the issue of concentration at Maubeuge and the BEF was moved up to Mons to act as an independent army in co-operation with the French on the left wing.

While the BEF were assembling in France, the French had attacked in the east in Alsace-Lorraine and, even reached the Rhine at one point on 19th August. In Belgium King Albert was forced to fall back from the Gatte, given the strong forces against him, and the Germans took Brussels on 20th August and reached Namur. The great relentless march was going on, but as it proceeded, German headquarters increasing lost touch with moving corps and with telephones and telegraphs destroyed, they gradually were without direct control in the field. On the 20th as well the French were defeated at the Battle of Mortange – Sarrebourg by a left wing under the Crown Prince which had been made too strong by Moltke. The Germans began to press the French back in eastern France. On the French left wing the BEF fought hard to hold the line of the Mons-Condeé canal, but on the 23rd General Lanrezac on their right with his fifth army retreated, leaving the British exposed.

Sir John French, the Commander-in-Chief of the BEF, ordered retirement south on the evening of the 23rd. He felt he had been abandoned by Lanrezac and he hurried to get as far south as possible to bring the small British army to safety nearer the Channel. A fierce stand was made by second Corps commanded by General Smith-Dorrien, contrary to orders, at Le Cateau on 26th August against General Von Kluck's first army. The British had 7,812 casualties and lost 38 guns. The retreat was resumed: the Germans did not pursue the British as Von Kluck's army marched on south-westwards. First Corps had retired under General Haig without significant attack upon it. General Joffre and Sir John French met and Joffre explained that the French left would have reinforcements transferred from the east and that a stand was envisaged on the Somme and the area of Laon and the Forest of St Gobain. Lanrezac in fact attacked General Von Bulow's second army on the 29th, but made no great progress, being fought to a standstill, while General D'Esperey, concentrating artillery on a three-mile front, launched an attack towards Guise.

While the march through Belgium and France had gone on, the Prussians had attacked in East Prussia, a province from which much of the officer corps of the German army came. Two Russian armies had moved forward: the first in the north, the First Army under Rennenkampf towards Gumbinnen; and the second, in the south, under General Samsonov. Rennenkampf was brought to a standstill at the Battle of Gumbinnen, but the German 8th army was threatened by Samsonov in the south and were forced back. General Von Prittwitz, who contemplated retirement to the Vistula, was replaced by General Hindenburg, with General Ludendorff as Chief of Staff. Von Moltke, worried by pressure put on him to defend East Prussia, withdrew two infantry corps and a cavalry division from the campaign in France to fortify the 8th Army. Before they arrived the Battle of Tannenburg was fought on 30th August, and the Russian 2nd Army destroyed. The campaign army in France was weakened: von Moltke in fact reduced the right wing during August from 17 to less than 12 corps and the 'strong' right wing conceived by Schlieffen no longer existed. The British and French retreat nonetheless went on, back by stages to the Marne.

The counter-attack by Lanrezac and D'Esperey in the St Quentin-Guise area had caused General Von Bulow to appeal to General Von Kluck to come to his assistance and the latter had moved his 1st Army south-eastwards. That, together with the weakening of the right wing meant that Kluck's First Army no longer would be able to wheel west of Paris. Moltke, influenced by the constant retirement of the Allied Armies and the victories in the engagements with them, endorsed this change of direction. The German Army was beginning to suffer foot problems after three weeks marching, with a shortage of food and fodder for the horses. Meanwhile, General Joffre, spurred on by General Gallieni, was trying to form a new army in Paris under General Manoury to defend the capital. Another was being formed under General Foch, the 9th Army, in the centre of his line. Sir John French had become increasingly gloomy at the prospects of the BEF and more suspicious of the French and their reliability. He proposed to continue his retreat and establish a new base position for evacuation at St. Nazaire. On 1st September Lord Kitchener hurried to Paris to meet Sir John French. In the outcome it was resolved that the BEF should not withdraw from the line, but continue to support the French, while making sure of their flanks in any action. Sir John further agreed with Joffre that the British should join the counter-attack in the gap that had opened between the 1st and 2nd German armies.

On 5th September von Moltke, worried by the threat of Manoury's 6th Army to the German right flank, ordered Kluck and Bulow to face west towards Paris. The former regarded the order as nonsense and continued to move on south of the Marne, leaving only one corps to shield Paris. On the same day Manoury's Army struck at the corps which had been left as a shield. The Battle of the Marne had commenced. It was to last for four days. Fighting took place along some twenty-four miles of line and involved over 2 million men. The gap between Kluck's and Bulow's armies widened. It was not until 9th September that the British turned north-east, entering the gap in five columns with one of French cavalry. Bulow, afraid of being outflanked, gave orders to retreat, as did Kluck, whose flank was equally likely to be threatened. Because of the British entry into the gap Kluck had to move north, making the gap longer. All along the line from Lorraine and Alsace, around Verdun and in the centre, the Germans were under pressure. General von Moltke accepted the situation and also ordered the retreats of the 3rd, 4th and 5th armies on the centre left and left wing. Sir John French did not however advance rapidly in pursuit into the gap; indeed, in the four days between

6th September and the 10th he marched but thirty-six miles. The 5th French Army was even slower.

The Germans were able therefore to gain the line of the Aisne and establish a defensive line. Primitive trenches were established. The 'Stellungskrieg' had begun. Further north the allied and German armies began the attempt to outflank each other. On 28th September Antwerp was bombarded and Winston Churchill sent marines to the support of the Belgians. The 7th British Division and the 3rd Cavalry under General Rawlinson was landed at Ostend and Zeebrugge. On 10th October Antwerp capitulated and the Belgium army retreated down the coast covered by General Rawlinson. Both sides planned campaigns in the north; General von Falkenhayn the War Minister also became Chief of Staff in von Moltke's place, and planned a renewed assault south along the coast towards the Channel ports to the rear of the French and British, with a second attack west south of Lille. Joffre and Foch however planned a move east towards Lille and Tournai. If the latter had occurred, it would have enabled a more effective achievement by the Germans of their goal. The BEF, in conjunction with these dispositions, moved back north, only after delay occasioned by Sir John French, worried in case he was left as had happened at Mons, having the fifth French army on his right and the Belgians, whose lines stretched to the North Sea, on his left.

By 18th October the move forward by the BEF had come to a halt long before Lille was reached. As it advanced the French left fell back. On the 19th the Germans launched their campaign on the Yser Line near the sea. The Belgians' line was attacked and a larger force moved towards Dixmude and Ypres. The forces clashed east of Ypres. French reinforcements were sent and the two campaigns came to a halt. On the Yser the Germans were successful in crossing the River, the Belgians giving way. On 25th October King Albert ordered the opening of the sluices and the sea began to pour in to cover the flat lands around the river. The Germans were forced back to avoid being cut off. In the area south of Neuve Chapelle on the 27th the Germans made a gap in the British line which was being established. The breach was filled by troops of the Indian Army who on 28th October took the village of Neuve Chapelle by hand-to-hand fighting. The sustained German counter-attack drove them out, only 68 out of 289 men escaping. In six days of fighting the Indian Corps lost 25 British officers and 500 Indian officers and men killed, with 1,465 wounded. On 31st October Khudadad Khan of the 129th Duke of Cannaught's Own Baluchis won the first Indian Army Victoria Cross of the war, many years later dying in Pakistan when eighty-three. In November the Germans vigorously renewed their attacks on the Ypres Salient, which Generals Haig and Dubois resisted, holding the line east of the town. On 11th November the last major attempt was made there by the Prussian Guards, who were in large measure repulsed by the 52nd Light Infantry. Thereafter the campaign withered away: the shallow defences around Ypres had held and the thin 'red' line was unbroken by reason of the courage and endurance of the fighting men who had withstood steadfastly the assault upon them.

The 1914 Campaign was now at an end. The war of movement was over and until 1918 the First World War on the Western front had the nature of a huge 'siege'. The opposing armies were embattled each in strong positions, which could only be taken by assault on heavily armed defences. As at Badajoz and San Sebastian, each attempt to pierce the 'wall' required deadly efforts to overcome the barrier created by the trenches, before the army could break in to take the enemy in a campaign of movement. All the assaults were to involve sacrifice, luminous courage and endurance and the men were time and time again to echo the role of 'the forlorn hope', which went forward in the van at the siege of towns and fortresses in the Peninsular War. The problem was that the war took place on the pivot of a time when firepower and technology had outpaced the development of the means of mobility. Until the tank was developed, men and cavalry horses were no effective opponents for the machine guns and intense artillery fire. The generals still hoped for mobility and believed that 'the siege lines' could be breached, but as was demonstrated, this was a futile hope, lacking substance much as their continuing belief in cavalry. Engaged as they were in a static siege, the Generals were to forget too the value of deception and surprise in warfare. The 'siege' of Germany on land was to be backed by blockade by the Royal Navy at sea, summoning the weapon of famine to the war.

The Campaign of 1915

The war in 1915 was dominated by events on the eastern front, where the Russians were under considerable pressure by the German and Austro-Hungarian armies. Politically, Britain and France were keen to help their allies, and the Gallipoli campaign was opened against Turkey in an endeavour to force the Dardanelles, enabling supplies to be sent to Russia through the Black Sea. Militarily on the western front a strategy was adopted to induce the Germans not to switch troops to the eastern front. To this end an attack was made on 10th March by General Haig, commanding the right wing of the BEF, using the 4th Corps and an Indian Army Corps, North of the La Bassée canal. The objectives were limited but only partially achieved. The village of Neuve Chappelle was taken after a short artillery bombardment, but not the Aubers Ridge. The Germans counter-attacked and Haig persisted but after three days the attack was called off. The casualties amounted to 12,982 and the gain was two miles wide and about half a mile deep.

On 22nd April the Germans attacked further north on the British left against the Ypres Salient, where the French were entrenched beyond the British, continuing the line to the sea. The attack was launched with the use of poison gas on a French Division and an Algerian Division holding the left of the salient next to Sir Henry Plumer's 5th Corps. Chlorine gas was discharged from large cylinders using the wind, after a bombardment. The yellowy-green cloud was blown down on the trench lines and reduced the defenders to a suffocating, dying, fleeing mass of men vomiting as they went. The ground turned yellow and the troops died in agony on the ground. A two-mile deep hole was punched in the Allied line over a four-mile front but the Germans halted, partly as a result of the lingering gas, deep into the salient: only stiff resistance by the Canadians, who were at first in isolated 'garrisons' behind the line, stopped them from going further, together with their lack of reserves.

On 23rd April the position of the Germans was dominating with 42 battalions against 21 ½.. On the morning of the 24th more gas was released and the salient further reduced, despite the desperate Canadian stand. On the 25th Sir John French ordered a counter-attack which was savaged, 2,400 men being lost. On the 26th another vain attack was made by the Indian Lahore Division and the Northumberland Territorial brigade. The losses were 4,000 . General Smith-Dorrien, successful in 1914 at Le Cateau, on 27th April suggested that the salient should be abandoned for a more logical line nearer Ypres in order to stop the slaughter, but Sir John French and General Foch refused, relieving him of his command. However, Sir Henry Plumer was ordered to shorten the line over the next few days and draw it nearer to Ypres, where it was to remain until the third Battle of Ypres in 1917. The French objected to the withdrawal but were in fact removing troops to the Arras sector, where Joffre planned his own attack. By the end of May fighting petered out as the Germans ran out of shells. On the Arras front the French attack was made and supported by General Haig on the British right wing. Haig's attack had no success, but cost on the day of action 458 officers and 1,161 men. By the end of May the Ypres Salient had been almost eliminated by the Germans, at a cost of 40,000 Germans and 60,000 British.

Meanwhile, General Joffre in June developed a new plan, as he said, to end the war. It was to comprise two thrusts, one, the most important, north between Verdun and Rheims to break out behind the Germans, and the other north of Arras on an eight-mile front towards Loos and Lens, with the object of taking Lille. President Poincaré of France was opposed to this plan but was over-ridden. Generals Haig and Rawlinson, who were to carry out the thrusts in the Arras sector, were also opposed to the plan, as was Sir John French's chief of staff Sir William Robertson. The latter's views were of course countered by the Francophile Sir Henry Wilson, who had total faith in the French military. Haig thought the supplies of artillery and ammunition for this offensive inadequate and that any attack should be delayed. Lord Kitchener, influenced by Joffre, the failure at Gallipoli and the need to help Russia, intervened to force the BEF to take part as envisaged, even though there might be heavy losses. Asquith, the Prime Minister, wrote to the King that Lord Kitchener was far from sanguine that any military advantage could be obtained by the proposed campaign, but that

Britain was forced to co-operate with General Joffre to avoid serious damage to the French alliance.

The proposed area of attack was flat countryside without cover, and during the summer the Germans constructed a second line of defence beyond the first. The Allies had overpowering force locally, 20 divisions to 6 1/3 German. Haig planned to use a bombardment and gas as part of his initial steps. French and Joffre limited his use of gas to only 2,500 cylinders (75 tons) for forty minutes. On 21st September the artillery bombardment commenced on the German trenches, and was to continue for four days. The heavy guns shot 90 rounds a day and the field guns 120. At 5.50 am on 25th September the release of gas was authorised by Haig. Its use was less than successful, drifting away on the left and in one place poisoning the British troops. Despite heavy losses the first day had some success, but the attack was ultimately stopped. Of the objectives only the mining village of Loos was taken. On the 26th the Xth Corps consisting of the Guards and the 21st and 24th Division, who were new in France and inexperienced, were sent in and mown down, losing 8,229 men. Sir John French had kept his cavalry sixteen miles in the rear and the troops were not in any event ready to exploit the gains. The French had some success south of Loos, taking Vimy Ridge. Further attempts were made after a slight pause on 2nd October and 13th October. In a period of heavy rain the thrust forward petered out, not having penetrated the German second lines. There had been 60,392 British casualties to 20,000 German. The attack in Champagne was no more successful in breaking the line. The winning of the war by the great break-through had proved to be a mirage. By the end of 1915 the BEF had had 285,107, casualties of which 44,158 were killed. The largely professional army of the BEF had been virtually destroyed. As Winston Churchill noted, out of 19,500 square miles of Belgium and France occupied by the Germans, eight had been retaken. Haig began to lobby in London and with King George V to remove Sir John French for 'his failures'. On 16th December Haig replaced French as Commander-in-Chief of the army in France.

The problem of mobility in war had much exercised the War Office, particularly the vulnerability of the cavalry to machineguns. In June 1915 the idea of 'the tank' was evolved; Lloyd-George, the Minister of Munitions, became enthusiastic and production was authorised. 150 were ordered but by September 1916 only 49 were available.

In the east on the Russian front the year ended with the Germans having occupied Poland, Lithuania, Kurland and part of old Russia. Lemburg had been retaken and Warsaw, Vilna and Brest Litovsk had fallen. The Germans had taken 300,000 prisoners. Despite their huge losses the Russians re-organised their armies and increased supplies of guns and ammunition ready for 1916.

In the Balkans the Germans and Austro-Hungarians were successfully driving through Serbia and pushing the Serbian army into the Albanian hills, opening a route to their ally Turkey. The latter had resisted the landing by the British at Gallipoli, much of the brunt of that campaign being borne by the Australians and New Zealanders. That attempt, despite the shining heroism of the troops, failed as a result of lack of resources, incompetence and the stern resistance of the Turks from a formidable position which they had been allowed to create. With the failure, those in Britain, like Winston Churchill, who wished to attack the Central powers from the east, knocking out Turkey and helping Russia, were discredited, and the focus of the war returned for Britain to the grim Western front.

The Campaigns of 1916

By 1916 the British naval blockade of Germany, coupled with the loss of imports from Russia in the east, was beginning to undermine the capacity of the Imperial Government to feed the German people and sustain the war. Kaiser Wilhelm II had almost withdrawn from decision-making and the Chancellor, the head of Government, was becoming marginalized by the generals and admirals conducting the war. Military domination had commenced over the Government of Germany. In 1914 neither side had begun the war with any long-term war aims, but following the successes of the army, always celebrated by Kaiser Wilhelm II with pink champagne, the generals and admirals in agreement with industrial and commercial interests envisaged peace only with gains for Germany in Western and Eastern Europe, indemnities for the cost of the war, and new colonies. After the losses in 1915 Chancellor Bethman-Hollweg sounded out General Eric von Falkenhayn as to the possible terms of a peace offer. The latter took the view that Germany should not negotiate until the will of its enemies was broken. It was Falkenhayn's view that the war had become one of attrition and he told the Kaiser that Britain should be shown that she could not win such a war. The need, he argued, was to eliminate Britain's allies, of which France was the strongest, and he argued for unrestrained submarine warfare to impede Britain's supply of food and armaments. These ideas underlay his approach to the war in 1916.

When on 7th August 1914 Lord Kitchener of Khartoum had predicted to the Cabinet a long war, he had also told them that armies of millions would need to be put in the field and maintained for several years to fight decisive battles on the European mainland. As Secretary of State for War he began a recruitment of volunteers, based on a poster portrait, in which he pointed a finger at the viewer with the slogan 'Your Country Needs You'. The campaign was marked by huge success, 175,000 men volunteering in the first week alone. In the first eighteen months of the war, in all 1,741,000 men were recruited for his new armies and 726,000 for the Territorial Army. By 1916 the Kitchener armies were ready to be tested. The old professional army of the BEF had been virtually destroyed in 1914 and 1915 and from then the civilian armies of volunteers and then conscripted citizens were to carry the burden of war. By his abounding energy and power of organisation Britain had been made ready for the long war which he had foreseen. The losses of 1915, against Kitchener's wishes, forced however, the country towards conscription, which was regarded as an alien continental practice. By May 1916 conscription was brought in for all males aged between 18 and 41.

A conference at Chantilly had met on 15th December 1915 to plan the campaign for 1916. General Joffre, the French commander-in-chief, described the battles of 1915 as 'brilliant tactical results' and ascribed failure to the weather and the lack of ammunition. His mindset was characteristic of a view shared with the British commanders, who had evolved no fully adequate method of curbing the power of the machine gun which was transforming the nature of infantry war. According to the French President Poincaré in his memoirs, Joffre like Falkenhayn had come to the view that the war was one of attrition to be largely fought by French allies, such as the British and Russians and even the Italians. He argued therefore for a large combined British and French attack over a forty-mile front on the Somme. General Sir John Haig, who superseded Sir John French as commander of the British armies in France in late December, favoured an attack further north. There was no strategic objective to be gained out of an attack on the Somme and the German position on the ridge overlooking the British was one of the strongest, if not the strongest point along the defensive line, and any preparations could not be kept secret. The choice made by Joffre for this location appeared to have stemmed solely from a desire to force the British to take part in a decisive action. The absence of a strategic objective was irrelevant, as he saw the campaign as part of the war of attrition to be waged by French Allies on their behalf. Haig resisted the proposal but he was finally forced in February 1916 to agree in order to avoid Joffre's demand for local attacks in April and May along the line, and to carry out the political objective of the Government of co-operating with and supporting the French. As before Loos, military commonsense was sacrificed to loyalty to the French, a loyalty not consistently reciprocated. The sound rule that a stronghold should only be assaulted at a point where it was weak or weakened, as events were to show, was to bring failure at an intolerable price.

In February 1915 the Germans attacked the French line at Verdun. General von Falkenhayn had decided that the 1915 campaign had brought France to the edge of collapse, and that a campaign of attrition should commence to bleed the French army by constant and persistent attacks at one location. The initial offensive by Crown Prince William's 5th Army began over a seven-mile front on the east side of the Meuse. Nine Divisions were employed and 1,000 guns, using millions of shells. Although Joffre heard of the proposed offensive in January, he dismissed its importance. The campaign began in snow and heavy rain and every hour 100,000 shells rained down on the obsolete forts. By the sixth day the Germans were six miles from Verdun. Joffre moved his 10th army from north of the British line, requiring its length to be extended to eighty miles. Marshal

Petain was sent to organise the defence. On 6th March the Germans followed on, attacking west of the Meuse. The French stood on the defensive but constant fighting went on, with appalling casualties to both sides. On 21st June west of the Meuse the Germans made their last large offensive strike, using phosgene gas, to be brought to a standstill by French artillery. The struggle however was to go on until the end of August.

The effect of the attack on Verdun was to compel the French to switch their armies to that area; indeed eighty-four percent of the French army became involved at Verdun. Joffre would not nonetheless abandon his plan for an attack on the Somme, but the original concept was scaled down to one where the greatest effort, and the brunt of the attack, was to be carried by the British. The French contribution shrunk to an eight-mile front with 16 Divisions. The British were to attack on a fifteen-mile front using 26 divisions for the offensive. From opposition Haig moved to enthusiasm for the plan, predicating four objectives: first, a break-through of the first line of defence; second, the taking of the ridge where the German second line was located; third, a wheel left from the Bapaume ridge towards Arras to 'roll up' the Germans; and fourth, an advance generally to Cambrai and Douai. The main attack was to be made by General Rawlinson's IVth Army of 18 divisions, five of which were in reserve, with cavalry held ready for the break-out. A subsidiary attack was to be made in the north at Gommecourt by General Allenby's IIIrd Corps. There were 1,537 guns strung along the front, one every twenty yards, a quarter of which were heavy guns.

The German position was strongly fortified, comprising a first and second line of elaborate defences of wire, trenches, dugouts and strongpoints. The second line ran along the ridge line, so all attacks had to be made uphill. It had until the Somme offensive been a quiet area and was only garrisoned by General Von Below's 2nd Army, who had five divisions north of the Somme and three in reserve. The sector was short of artillery and aeroplanes. Von Bulow, seeing the preparations of the British from the ridge, warned Falkenhayn of the coming offensive, but in the absence of any discernible strategic objective the latter did not believe that any offensive there would be a major one, but that it would come further north as Haig himself had wanted. The 2nd Army was not therefore reinforced and Falkenhayn remained unconvinced that it was the main battle until 5th July.

The tactics chosen contemplated a heavy bombardment preceding the attack. Rawlinson wished to attack just before dawn so that his men crossed no-man's land in the dark, thus shielding them from losses. Joffre and Foch however objected to this, since it impeded their artillery, whose bombardment should be in daylight before the French part of the attack. The advance was thus set for 29th June in the early morning. The men were told that the ruthless bombardment would silence the German machine guns and artillery and clear the way for the advance. On 24th June the bombardment of the German lines began. It was to last for seven days and seven nights during which 1.5 million shells hit the German position. A German soldier transferred from the eastern front said that the experience surpassed in horror all his previous experience of the war; every surface obstacle was flattened, while the defenders retreated below to their dugouts to sit out the storm. On the 29th the weather broke and torrential rain fell. The waiting troops stood and rested in trenches waterlogged with mud and standing pools.

1st July dawned with bright sunlight. The bombardment ceased. The Germans came out of their dugouts and repositioned their machine guns in the remains of their entrenchments and craters. The British clambered out of their trenches, shoulder to shoulder in waves one hundred yards apart. As they struggled across no-man's land to the front line the machine guns wreaked their slaughter. Some battalions were reduced to 100 men. Thousands fell. Despite the annihilating fire the front line was penetrated and small villages taken: the 30th and 18th Divisions took Montauban and the 7th Division Mametz. The French in the south under General Fayolle made more significant progress, but in the north little was gained. The 36th (Ulster) Division penetrated beyond Thiepval, but the latter village resisted strongly. Only 1,983 prisoners were taken that day. The British losses were the largest for any single day of any war, 20,000 killed and 37,000 wounded. At General Headquarters self-delusion led to an attitude that there had been a successful action with few casualties. The losses were so great that, although attacks took place in the south, leading to the French penetrating to the high ground overlooking Peronne and in the left and centre by Rawlinson's IVth Army, by 10th July the maximum British penetration amounted to a depth of about two and half miles over an eight-mile front. The second line was not pierced and the Germans were working on a new line to their rear.

On 14th July Rawlinson carried out a night attack using troops from Kitchener's new army. Guides put down markers in the night to lead the infantry forward and to set out the start line. At 3.20 am a barrage smashed the German lines and the troops moved forward. The second line was broken and, although the South Africans suffered heavy loses at Delville Wood, the 7th Division was able to move forward with cavalry battalions, their first use since 1914. Rawlinson was near as he could be to a 'break-through', but the Germans brought up reserves and the opportunity was lost. Haig thereafter through the rest of July and August engaged in petty attempts on the German line, making scant progress. The urge to break out, however, obsessed Haig and he resolved to have one more 'gamble' to break the line.

After three days of bombardment, on 15th September the attempt was made in the morning mist. The XVth corps, with a few tanks, was beyond Flers by 10 am; on the left the IIIrd corps cleared High Wood and on the extreme left the villages of Martinpuich and Courcelatte were taken. The right was held up, but on 25th September the Germans were forced to withdraw from Combles. On the 26th Thiepval fell finally to two divisions of the VIth Corps, aided by three tanks. In all only 32 tanks arrived at the starting point for the battle, of which nine broke down and five were ditched. They were used in small groups, instead of in a mass. As Winston Churchill wrote, 'This priceless conception was revealed to the Germans for the mere petty purpose of taking a few ruined villages.' The ridge and second line had been taken, but Haig fought on into October. Rain and shell craters reduced the ground to mud but the troops were pushed on over the ridge into the far valley, where during the winter they were to spend their time in water-sodden trenches. Haig was certain by 12th October that the campaign was effectively finished, but General Joffre urged him to continue. Limited attacks therefore continued, the most successful being by the 7th Division north of the River Ancre which captured Beaumont Hamel and took 7,000 prisoners.

When the Battle of the Somme ended, the British had suffered 419,564 casualties, the French 204,253 and the Germans 465,000. At Verdun the French lost 315,000 men and the Germans 281,000. On the Somme the horrifying cost of the battle had resulted in the taking of a salient twenty-five miles in length and of seven-mile depth. Only Haig's first two objectives had been gained and the Germans still stood on a third defensive line which they had constructed. The citizen army had however displayed a heroism and courage beyond imagination and an endurance strong as iron. Their service as volunteers to their King and country ennobled a patriotism of country that lived in them, rooted in the idea of a Christian monarchy governing in freedom and with humanity. Their sacrifice should still sober our hearts and re-awaken the desire to keep that idea alive, a nation in freedom sovereign and self-governed.

In the east 1916 saw a remarkable recovery by the Russians. By March the Russian 2nd Army, for example, comprised 360,000 men, with almost 1,000 guns. In March the Russians launched an assault at Lake Naroch and suffered 40,000 killed in the first three days. Mud slowed their advance and the Germans, reinforced, brought the thrust to a halt by the end of March, regaining the lost ground in April. In the south an offensive was planned in June and took place over a two hundred and fifty-mile front. Brusilov's armies (the 7th, 8th, 9th and 11th) with divergent attacks strained the ability of the Germans and Austro-Hungarians to resist these pushes. The offensive was a significant success - over 200,000 prisoners were taken and large numbers of guns. The offensive however came to a halt when Brusilov outran his supplies, and because of absence of a reserve. It drew however German divisions from the west and seriously damaged the Austro-Hungarian Army. By the end of August the series of offensives ended. The losses were beyond calculation on both sides, but Brusilov had taken 400,000 prisoners and nearly 500 guns. One million of the enemy were killed or wounded; his own casualties were possibly a million men.

These events led to political upheaval in all the countries involved. In Germany the Kaiser Wilhelm II had virtually abandoned any intervention in political or military action, but in August Feldmarschalls Hindenburg and Lundendorff induced him and the Chancellor, Bethman Hollweg, to dismiss General Von Falkenhayn, whose strategy in 1916 was seen as a failure. Hindenburg became commander in the west with Ludendorff Quartermaster General, but it was the latter who was in effective control. He was a believer in 'total' war on all fronts, including for the civil population. He was authoritarian in attitude and would only support a peace which gave Germany significant gains. The civilian Government became increasingly ineffective and in 1917 Imperial Germany would be moving to military dictatorship.

In England the conscription issue and Asquith's response to the 1916 Easter Rebellion in Ireland had divided the Liberal party and alienated Lloyd-George, while the Conservatives in the coalition were becoming restive over the conduct of the war by the Prime Minister, Asquith. The disaster on the Somme had increased public concern about the war. Kitchener had died on his way to Russia in June 1916, when HMS Hampshire hit a German mine and sank within fifteen minutes. It was felt that more decisive and stronger leadership was required. Lloyd-George thought himself to be the man to give it, and together with the Conservatives forced the resignation of Asquith in early December and became Prime Minister. Asquith would not serve in his Government and the Liberal Party was to begin its slide into irrelevance.

In Russia the strain of the campaigns of 1915 and 1916, the huge losses of men, the shortage of supplies and the gathering absence of food in the cities was feeding unrest and was to lead to the March Revolution in 1917. Imperial Russia, in loyalty to its Allies, had bled itself and destroyed the foundation of consent on which its government rested.

Germany was to gain another success in the year with the defeat and occupation of Romania, but in the autumn the Chancellor Bethman-Hollweg made one more attempt to promote a general peace. On 16th September, with the approval of Kaiser Wilhelm II, he proposed that President Woodrow Wilson should mediate and negotiate a peace between the warring parties. The United States was in the throes of an election and for a time nothing happened. Hindenburg and Ludendorff objected to the approach and the German Foreign Secretary was dismissed. On 20th December Wilson replied that he would not act as mediator but he invited each participant in the war to set out their terms for peace so that he could act as a negotiator in a context that no one should come out a winner. On 10th January the Allies replied that Germany was such an immoral aggressor that they were not interested in negotiations. Germany had already refused to supply her peace terms, as Bethman-Hollweg stated that she preferred to negotiate with her opponents directly.

The Campaign of 1917

At the beginning of 1917 all the participants of the war were to some measure exhausted by the constant struggle without outcome. In Germany the civil population was short of food, heating oil and coal. As Princess Blucher, married to the descendant of the Prussian leader at Waterloo, noted, everyone was gaunt and bony and thought only of where to find the next meal. The Allied blockade kept up by the Royal and French navies had cleared the German merchant marine from the seas. Food from Eastern Europe was no longer available. There were shortages of weapons and ammunition because of the comparative lack of raw materials. In this context Feldmarschall Ludendorff, who was the effective army commander, behind the largely 'ceremonial' figure of Feldmarschall Hindenburg, tried to coerce the civil government to militarise the whole German people. He decided that in the west there should be no offensive but that every attempt should be made to destroy Russia on the eastern front. To weaken the British war effort he became the advocate of unrestricted submarine warfare on the approaches to Britain on all ships, including neutrals. In this he was supported by Admiral von Turpitz and Admiral von Scheer, who had recommended it after the Battle of Jutland (31 May 1916).

Such open warfare had been tried for a short time in 1915, but discontinued after the sinking of the Cunard liner Lusitania by the U20 on 7th May with the loss of 1,198 lives, of which 124 were American, including A.G. Vanderbilt, and many women and children. Alfred Gwynne Vanderbilt had built the Vanderbilt Hotel on Park Avenue and was a son of Cornelius Vanderbilt II, one of America's super-rich. He is said to have been seen on deck handing his life jacket to a woman and helping to round up children for the ship's boats. He was last seen struggling in the water after the ship went down. The outcry in the United States led the German Government to back away from continuance of the policy. Kaiser Wilhelm II and the Chancellor Bethman – Hollweg still opposed it, but their influence weakened before the military and naval pressure in its favour. Admiral von Holzendorf told the Kaiser that England would want peace within six months and not one American soldier would get across the Atlantic, if war came. Ludendorff emphasised that the war would be over before the Americans could become engaged on the Western front. The Kaiser and Bethman-Hollweg gave way. On 31st January the submarine campaign started. Germany had 111 submarines, of which 46 were constantly at sea, rising to 75. Before the 1917 campaign started, the Allies in January lost 500,000 tons of merchant shipping.

In November 1916 the French and English military conferred on the campaign plans for the next year. No constructive ideas emerged other than to continue the strategies tried in that year, but Haig sensed that the French, with 1,675,000 casualties since 1914, would make no major effort, while the Prime Minister Lloyd-George did not wish to approve another Somme. In December General Joffre was replaced by General Nivelle as French Commander-in-Chief. He had had two limited successes pushing back the Germans at Verdun, and was the exponent of a major attack on a narrow front through which extensive reserves (28 Divisions) were to flow, opening out behind the enemy. In January 1917 he met Lloyd-George and persuaded him to approve a British attack as part of his overall battle plan. The British were to attack in the Arras – Bapaume area to pin the Germans down. Haig was less than pleased with this plan, as he envisaged an attack in Flanders ultimately to recover the Belgian ports of Ostend and Zeebrugge. The French were to strike on the Aisne. Preparations were made for the battle, but in mid-march the Germans suddenly shortened their front line. Crown Prince Rupprecht's 2nd Army retired fifteen to twenty-five miles over a seventy-mile sector from Arras to the Aisne, to a newly constructed front line, the Hindenburg line. The abandoned country was left ravaged, all buildings destroyed, booby-trapped and mined, the population removed. Haig wished to abandon his attack, but the French insisted, and the German withdrawal added to his difficulties, affecting the November plan and the place of attack. The British and French offensives were planned for April.

In mid-march revolution seized St Petersburg and the army and navy fell into disorder as all the bitterness at the war, its shortages and its sacrifices found expression. Tsar Nicholas II abdicated and a Provisional Government was formed, which pledged itself to continue the war even after a left-wing Socialist Kerensky had become Prime Minister. Russia nonetheless remained in disorder. The Bolsheviks, however, pledged that they would end the war. A Marxist millionaire, Alexander Helphand, persuaded Ludendorff that the revolution in Russia and its collapse would be furthered, if Lenin could go from Switzerland to Russia to campaign for the Bolsheviks. With the characteristic lack of long-term vision that Ludendorff showed in all his political decisions, he agreed. On April 8th Lenin in a sealed train, fit for the dangerous bacillus which he and his movement proved to be for Europe, left Switzerland for Russia.

From January onwards the campaign of unrestricted submarine warfare had began to achieve significant success. In February 800,000 tons of British shipping was sunk and the tally was rising. By April the total was a million tons, sixty percent of which was British, reducing the supply of raw materials and food. When the German Government had announced its campaign, the United States was told that only one passenger liner per week would be allowed to Britain. On 3rd February President Woodrow Wilson in response severed diplomatic relations with Germany. The German submarines persisted; on 28th February the S.S.Laconia was sunk and demands for war came to be voiced in the United States. In March the Germans tried to develop an alliance with Mexico, made public in the Zimmerman Telegram. The sinkings went on, including the American liner, SS Algonquin. On 1st April President Wilson invited Congress to declare war on Germany and on 6th April war was declared. The United States was wholly unprepared, but efforts began to raise a million-man army to go to France.

Meanwhile, the British and French were preparing for their April offensive. The German retreat to the Hindenburg Line meant that the British were to concentrate north of the line on either side of Arras. On the left the First Army, with 13 Divisions, was to attack north of Arras and take the Vimy Ridge. In the centre General Allenby with 18 Divisions, the 3rd Army, was to advance astride the Arras – Cambrai road to high ground beyond Arras; and on the right General Gough with 6 divisions was to mount a subsidiary attack at the pivot from which the front was to move forward. 60 tanks were divided between the three armies and the cavalry reserves were prepared to follow on the break-through. Allenby wished the attack to be made on the basis of a surprise with a short bombardment but General Headquarters envisaged a bombardment of eight days, including three days for wire cutting. The Germans were fully aware of the preparations and General Baron von Falkenhausen thought that the 6th Army could hold the attack. The bombardment began and continued over the front to be assaulted from 2,879 guns, of which 989 were heavy guns, equivalent to one gun every nine yards. The use of gas shells hampered the gun crews, who needed to keep on their masks, but on the morning of 9th April a creeping barrage was laid in front of the advancing troops. Within one hour of the 5.30 am start the first German line was captured: the Canadian Corps of the first Army took the Vimy ridge. South of the Scarpe River, which divided the front, the advance of 3rd, 12th and 15th Divisions was held up at Telegraph and Railway Triangle. North of the Scarpe 17th Corps, including the 51st Division, pressed forward.

The results of the first day were that many of the objectives set were met, but the narrowness of the front – some twelve miles – led to congestion in relation to the reserves intended to break out, and the guns could give only scant help, as they had been outdistanced. On the 10th the move forward wilted and German resistance increased. On the 11th Monchy Le Preux was taken with the assistance of four tanks. In the far south the 5th Army launched an assault led by the Australian Division on the Hindenburg line, with assistance from eleven tanks. The line involved a new complex of arrangements of outposts to give covering and interlocking machine gun fire, entangled entrenchments and deep shelters to give cover while any bombardment proceeded. The assault broke through the line but became the subject of counter-attack. The initial offensive ceased on 14th April. This did not prevent Haig from ordering, although the French offensive on the Aisne was over, attacks on 3rd and 5th May because he wanted a 'good defensive line'. When it was over, the British had gained four miles over a ten-mile front and suffered 84,000 casualties.

Nivelle's new-style attack on the Aisne, after several days of bombardment, started in an unseasonable snowstorm on 16th April and initially took 20,000 prisoners and 175 guns. Little ground however was gained, although a tank attack was successful in the night; Chemin de Dames was taken and the Moronvilliers heights east of Rheims. When the attack came to a standstill, the French had suffered 187,000 casualties. Nivelle wished to renew the offensive, but in May mutiny, no doubt nourished by the example of the revolution in Russia, broke out in 59 Divisions of the French army. The French army had reached the end, the men refusing to march against the machine-guns and the wire. The Government removed Nivelle and Marshal Petain was appointed Commander-in-Chief to re-establish order in the army. 55 mutineers were shot and others were deported to the penal colonies. Petain addressed the problems of pay and leave and settled down to re-order the army and await the coming of the Americans.

The continued losses of merchant ships, peaking in April, had became a serious concern of the British Government as food supplies, even with rationing, dropped to a six-week provision. Lloyd-George, despite arguments to the contrary made by the Admiralty, insisted on ships travelling to and from North America in convoy and that, together with new techniques for spotting and destroying U-boats, led to a falling of the tonnage of ships sunk, reducing to 200,000 a month by the end of the year. Lloyd-George was unwilling to allow Haig to go ahead with another offensive and withheld reinforcements from him. In June Haig went to London, reiterating the need to keep up pressure on the Germans and to take advantage of the Royal Navy's wish to close Belgium ports to U-boats. With great reluctance Lloyd-George gave way and sanctioned an offensive in Flanders. Meanwhile, and more effectively, the Americans laid a barrage of mines, amounting to 70,000, between Norway and the Orkneys, sealing the North Atlantic to the Germans. The attention of the British now focussed on the Ypres salient.

The salient was overlooked by high ground from Messines to Wynschaete and it was the object of Haig to secure it. Planning to that end had begun in 1916 and the engineers evolved a scheme to undermine the chalk ridge and, as in the model of historic sieges, to blow up the defensive line to permit the breaches to be stormed. Some 20 mines were commenced under the German trenches into the hill. The Germans sought to counter them and one on one occasion were within eighteen inches of the mine under Hill 60. Between January and June 8,000 yards of tunnelling was completed. Sir Henry Plumer, commanding the 2nd Army, was determined to carry out an attack based on surprise which would reduce the toll of casualties. The use of the mines, artillery, tanks and gas attacks were all to play their part. The 2nd Anzac Corps was on the right, the 9th Corps in the centre and the 10th on the left – amounting to nine divisions with three in reserve. 72 tanks were provided. There were 2,339 guns in the nine-mile front, amounting to one gun every seventy yards. A bombardment was mounted from the end of May for seven days to proceed the attack, which had only limited objectives, to take the ridge and end up on the Oosttaverne line at the base of the Salient. On the morning of 7th June the barrage fell and at 3.10 am, in one devastating explosion, 19 mines went up, each loaded with 600 tons of explosives. Within thirty-five minutes the ridge was taken, the German lines over-run. Within three hours the crest was secured. Behind a moving barrage the New Zealanders cleared the ruins of Messines: Wyschaete fell to a combined force of the 36th (Ulster) division and the 16th (Irish). At 10 am the White Chateau and the Ypres-Comines canal was reached and by 3.10 pm all objectives were achieved. 7,000 prisoners were taken with casualties of only 16,000. The Messines push based on surprise had been a success.

The Provisional Government in Russia had to some extent re-organised and re-supplied the army and authorised a new offensive under the command of General Brusilov from Riga to the Carpathians. The attempt began on 1st July and had success in Eastern Carpathia, where the Russian Army broke through the Austro-Hungarians and advanced thirty miles towards Lemberg. The other attacks failed and all was over by mid-July. On 19th July General Hoffman counter-attacked on a twelve-mile front southeast of Tarnapol. On the 24th Tarnapol fell and the Russian army began to retreat, dissolving as it went, as order collapsed and desertions intensified. The Brusilov offensive was to be the instrument for the destruction of the Provisional Government, as hatred for the war gripped the revolutionary population of Russia.

At last in July Lloyd-George gave the go-ahead for the third Battle of Ypres, even though fearing yet one more bloodbath. Haig had been preparing. He envisaged attacking to the north-east to take the ridge from Gheluvelt in the south to Passchendaele in the North, then to go on to take Roulers, the communication pivot for the Belgian ports, where the army would wheel west. On the far left was stationed General Anthoine's 1st French Army, then General Gough's 5th Army, which was to bear the main weight of attack together with one corps of the 2nd Army on the right. 3,091 guns, of which 999 were heavy guns, were provided at one gun for every six yards. As at Messines and in the Hindenburg line, the Germans had been evolving new front-line arrangements of disconnected strong points and concrete pill boxes with deep shelters commanding the arcs of machine gun fire, with reserves of troops further back and only light forces in the forward line. Twelve divisions were readied over the eleven-mile front. Before the offensive began Gough changed its axis to the north, slightly away from the ridge to be taken.

The country needing to be negotiated by the attack was below the ridges, low lying and depended on deep ditches and land drains to remain dry: its natural state was near to that of a swamp. The preliminary bombardment, which was to last over eight days, destroyed the drainage system of the land and for the four days prior to the assault torrential rain fell, changing the battered land into a plain of swamp and mud. General Gough thought that given the state of the ground the attack should be delayed, but Haig and G.H.Q. disregarded his advice. At 3.30 am on 31st July the attack began and the troops began to claw their way forward in the devastated landscape of mud. The tanks used, some 140, were stopped by the mud, taking hours to suck and press their way through and across the ground. On the left small gains were made including the Pilken Ridge and Steenbeck, and about two miles on the right.

In the centre little progress was made and the second objective was not reached. Each day it continued to rain heavily. Gough once more tried to persuade Haig to abandon the attack, but the latter persisted, sending reports to London on the progress made, exhausting, as he argued, German manpower. After four days there were 31,850 casualties. A new effort was made on 16th August and the Germans were forced back beyond Langenmark and Poelcapelle, while Sir Henry Plumer on the right had extended his front to the Menin Road. Four to five miles had been gained and by the end of August there were 68,180 casualties, of which 10,266 were dead. There came then a pause but on 20th September the offensive resumed with the 2nd Army, either side of the Menin Road, six Divisions going forward, of which two were Australian. This assault emphasised the use of artillery, some 1,295 guns, with the infantry held back and succeeded in gaining the Third German defence line and holding it to counter-attack. From 26th September to 4th October yet another staged attack went forward with eight divisions, of which four were from Australia and New Zealand.

The rain still went on, the mud was deeper and more grasping; each of three limited assaults, the infantry not outdistancing the effect of the guns, took ground and ended with the main ridge taken at Gheluvelt, Polygon Wood and Broodseinde and 10,000 prisoners. General Sixt Von Armin's 6th Army had initially held the offensive in check with success, but gradually had begun to bring in reinforcements. Haig yet again decided to press on to take the ridge up to Paschendaele, so that Gough's army would not be left in a defensively weak position. The army for so long having fought its way through mud was exhausted and the Germans had brought up fresh troops to defend their position. From 4th to 9th October it rained, on the 8th torrentially. The guns were up to their axles in mud, the men having to wade through wet crater holes and the deep ground. The cold and wet were so intense that sand bags had to be worn over their boots. On the 9th a new attack was made, but no ground was gained. Haig ordered the 2nd Army to attack once more on the 12th but that ended on the start line. The final attempt came at the end of October, spearheaded by the Canadians. The struggle fiercely contested three hundred yards of mud, but suddenly the German line broke and on November 4th the ruined site of Paschendaele was at last taken. Haig had used up all his reserves; the armies were exhausted. The salient had been turned into a quagmire and offensives after 20th September had added three miles in depth, at Paaschendaele. Casualties were 244,897.

The first use of the tank in 1915 had encouraged its advocates to press the army to exploit the potential successes that this weapon could give. It had been used at both Messines and the third Battle of Ypres, where the nature of the swampy muddy ground rendered its use difficult, many tanks becoming bogged down. General Elles and Colonel J.C. Fuller, who were keen supporters of the tank, wished to see it used en masse for a narrow attack, which would demonstrate the potential to breach the German defensive line. Colonel Fuller envisaged a raid south of Cambrai on firm ground for eight to twelve hours, taking no ground but penetrating the enemy position: General Sir Julian Byng, whose 3rd Army were deployed in the area, wanted to expand the action to take Cambrai. Haig only sanctioned the action when it was clear that the Ypres salient offensive was becoming impossible. Haig ordered the taking only of Bourlon Hill, but Byng kept to his wider objectives. His resources were however limited. He had the 3rd and 4th Corps, some 6 divisions of infantry, and the Cavalry Corps of three divisions. There were 381 tanks and 1000 guns. The offensive was to be on a narrow front between the Canal du Nord and the St Quentin – L'Escaut Canal, aiming at Bourlon Hill in the north and towards the east of Cambrai at Masnieres. The tanks were to lead the attack comprising an advanced guard, the main body concentrated and followed by infantry to mop up behind the tanks. Each tank carried 'fascines' in front to drop on reaching the twenty-four feet wide trenches of the Hindenburg Line in order to enable them to cross. The whole tank force was to be employed and no reserve held. General von der Marwitz was aware of the likelihood of the offensive in his sector, but was sceptical of the reports made. Like most German Generals of the time, he underestimated the tank.

On the misty November morning of the 20th at 6.20 am the roaring spluttering tanks mechanically clanked forward to the German lines on a six-mile front led by the commander, Brigadier Elles himself. There had been no bombardment, but the guns laid a moving barrage two hundred yards in front of the tanks. The tired German divisions sent to recuperate on this quiet front gave way. On the first day the advance penetrated across the German lines some six miles, the strongposts, wire and machine guns swept aside: only at Fesquiéres in the centre was the advance held up because the infantry were too far behind. Of the tank force, 65 had been hit by artillery, 71 suffered mechanical failure and 43 were ditched. A great hole had been punched in the German front, which was open to the west, but there were no reserves to move through it in mass. Some cavalry went forward, but did not carry the advance forward. The gap was open for many hours, but von der Marwitz brought up a reserve division to plug it. The tanks came to a stop on the reverse side of a ridge three miles from Cambrai. On 21st November Ludendorff and Crown Prince Rupprecht added three more divisions to the defence. No progress much was made save on the left centre where the advance went on to Bourlon Hill. Haig sent two extra divisions, but there were no more gains. On 30th November, using gas and smoke shells, the Germans counter-attacked using 'Stürmtruppen', experienced troops in small parties to penetrate through weak points in the line to the rear. By 7th December the offensive was over, the Germans having recovered much of the country taken and penetrated the British lines towards Gouzeaucourt in the south. Despite its failure by the want of any tank and infantry reserve, the example of the tank assault at Cambrai was to revolutionise land war and set an example which would echo down the twentieth century. The huge initial success was thrown away by a badly organised follow-up and the absence of an army reserve to exploit effectively the tanks' achievement in breaking the line. The cavalry once more were of no avail in a war of machine guns and artillery. Cambrai was the end of the British Campaign in 1917.

In both Germany and Austria-Hungary during the summer discussion of peace was mooted. The new Emperor Karl of Austria-Hungary tested whether peace could be made with Italy. Chancellor Bethman-Hollweg made suggestions for peace and there was an initiative by the Pope to the Central Powers. Ludendorff, backed by Hindenburg, opposed any discussion of peace without total victory. The Reichstag voted for peace negotiations. Under pressure the Chancellor was removed by the Kaiser and replaced by Ludendorff's creature, Michaelis. The Reichstag amended its resolution and the war went on. In September the Germans attacked in the east near Riga, pushing the Russians back towards St Petersburg, which might have been reached, had Ludendorff not switched divisions to the western front to meet the Ypres offensive. Then came the October Revolution in Russia; Lenin and the Bolsheviks took power by force, pledged to make peace. The disorder in the army, the threat of their opponents and the 'white' anti-Marxist armies which were forming made peace necessary to them. In mid-November General Krilenko, the Russian Commander-in-Chief, offered a one-month armistice. Talks were scheduled at Brest-Litovsk. The German attitude to making peace was divided: Kuhlman, the Foreign Minister, wanted no annexations but as ever Hindenburg and Ludendorff opposed that and were supported by the Kaiser, whom they had come to dominate.

The negotiations lingered on with Trotsky and representatives of the Ukraine. A new offensive against the Bolshevik army opened on 18th February 1918, but on 3rd March the Treaty of Brest-Litovsk was signed. Russia was out of the war, but the subject of an oppressive and ruthless peace, in which the Germans took control of Georgia, the Ukraine, Poland and the Baltic States. 6 million marks of reparations were demanded. Russia lost 1,250,000 square miles of territory and thirty-two per cent of her population. Germany was freed to send fighting divisions to the west, although it needed to maintain an army of a million men in these territories in order to hold them. As for Haig's belief that the offensives of 1917 were wearing out Germany's reserves of manpower; the manpower had been found to defeat and take Russia, to withstand attack in the west and to strengthen the Austrians at Caporeto, where the Italians were pushed back and 400,000 prisoners taken. In fact however the German state's ability to wage war was coming to an end, with intense starvation haunting the cities, discontented soldiers and sailors and limited access to food, forage and reserves of raw material.

Colonel J.C. Fuller rose to be a major-general in the army and continued during his career, mostly to the annoyance of the military establishment, to publish writings diagnosing the effects of technological change on war. Particularly he advocated, on the basis of Cambrai, the advantage of the concentrated tank attack. In Britain his advocacy was listened to but deafly. In 1932 there were only 9 tanks in service of less than four tons. Only in the late 1930s were the cavalry regiments changed over to tanks and armoured vehicles. He was heard in Germany and Russia. On April 20th 1939 he attended Adolf Hitler's Birthday Parade in Berlin and at a reception was asked by Hitler, having seen the three-hour parade of the mechanised army, whether he was pleased with his children. Fuller replied that he thought that they had grown up so quickly that he no longer recognised them. The attack on Poland in 1939 demonstrated their worth and in 1940 General Guderian's tank armies swept through France, bringing about defeat. The French had more tanks, but as at the Somme in 1916, split them into detached units with individual armies. Fuller's legacy was a twentieth-century theory of war to rival that of Karl von Clausewitz in the early nineteenth century.

The Campaign of 1918

In January 1918 the Allied blockade by sea had reduced Germany and Austria-Hungary to a pitiful state. Food shortages were universal; there was widespread malnutrition. Coal and oil for light and heating was almost unobtainable. Inflation had reduced many of the middle classes to pauperism. Medicines were hard to find. The cities were the worst hit: in Berlin the potato ration was one pound a person per week and, as Princess Blucher wrote, even that contained many which were bad. The army on the western front had falling morale: uniforms and boots were in tatters; medical services inadequate and the food ration poor. Army units had been reduced in numbers for want of available men. January was marked in Berlin by strikes in favour of peace and calls in the press and the Reichstag for the war to be ended. Feldmarschalls Hindenburg and Ludendorff, the army commanders who had obtained a dominance over the Kaiser Wilhelm II and the Chancellor, sought to control events internally in Germany by direction of labour and industry and measures of censorship. The civil population were accused by them of defeatism and they resisted all peace moves which did not give Germany control of Belgium and annexations in Belgium and France reflecting the western front victories since 1914. Haig was still obsessed with the offensive and only 2,700 men out of 100,000 available for labour were put on defensive works.

By the beginning of 1918 the United States had 225,000 troops in Europe and by the spring the monthly total of arrivals amounted to about 125,000.

The Americans insisted on their army being kept substantially as a single unit under General Pershing, and it was not to be battle ready before the late summer. They held only seventeen miles of a quiet sector of the front with four divisions, equivalent to eight British or French. In an address to Congress in January President Woodrow Wilson set out Fourteen Points which he believed should be applied to the peace settlement, spelling out his position further in subsequent declarations. The fourteen points and declarations provided, among other things, for the restoration of all occupied territory, the impartial adjustment of colonial claims, the righting of the annexation from France in 1871 of Alsace Lorraine, the restoration of a free Poland with access to the Baltic sea, equal and unrestrained trade between countries, and guarantees for the reduction to their lowest point of national arnaments consistent with safety. There were to be no annexations, no punitive expropriations or damages imposed; the self-determination of peoples was to be the imperative of the peace and the peace was to be just, without discrimination between those involved one to another. A League of Nations was to be established with a view to preserving and making peace secure.

The catastrophe of the third Battle of Ypres had so upset Lloyd-George, the Prime Minister, that he was determined to ensure that in 1918 the losses of 1917 should not be repeated. He tried to remove Haig, made a Fieldmarshal by King George V in January, or establish a command structure which would make him subordinate to others. He also withheld reserves of troops in Britain to prevent Haig from taking the offensive again. The latter opposed the Prime Minister, believing that the offensives were leading to the progressive attrition of the enemy. By 1918 the British had come to hold 126 miles of front line with 59 divisions, which in 1917 had been reduced each one from four to three battalions. In deploying the army, Haig was convinced that the northern Flanders end of the line was the most important; 14 Divisions were therefore held for a twenty-three mile front at Ypres, with the southernmost part of the line from Cambrai to the junction with the French held by only 14 Divisions and 3 cavalry brigades for its whole forty-two miles. Most of this part of the line had been recently taken over from the French and its trenches, outposts, wire and strongpoints were in a poor state, its telephone lines were unburied and French peasants constantly removed the barbed wire for their farms. Marshal Foch had become the French commander in the field in place of Petain, but neither he nor Haig could contemplate further large-scale offensive action until the Americans were ready.

Ludendorff had started in November 1917 to plan for the offensive on the western front, using the divisions from the east to reinforce the army, with a view to a decisive blow against the British, which would force them to make peace and drive them from the continent. His plan envisaged a blow struck in the area of St Quentin (Plan Michael) to be followed a fortnight later by a thrust in the Ypres sector towards Hazebrouck (Plan St George) rolling back the British and cutting them off from their bases. The plan lacked reality however, since the Germans were to have only a limited superiority of numbers, no replacements and a shortage of transport. Their lorries were unsuitable for the transport of troops and from lack of forage horses were in a weakened condition. The main objective was to punch holes in the front line, but their further exploitation was not so clearly conceived. In the east, after the threat of a renewed attack in February, the Treaty of Brest-Litovsk was signed, and although a million men were left in the east to control the land over which the Germans had gained control, combat divisions became transferable to France. The blow in the Ypres sector was, before its implementation, reduced in weight and thus effectiveness.

By March the German armies were ready for the launch of Plan Michael. 63 infantry divisions were assembled along a forty-mile front from Arras south to La Fere. General von Bulow commanded 19 on a front of nine miles on the right at Arras, General von der Marwitz the centre with 18 divisions on a nine and a half-mile front and General von Hutier on the left with 24 divisions on a twenty-mile front. The River Somme through St Quentin bisected the front so that the latter's army was largely south of the river. The massed forces had 6,608 guns. Opposing them in the north was the British 3rd Army under General Sir Julian Byng, with 14 divisions on a thirteen-mile front, and a reserve of six divisions, and in the centre and south Sir Hubert Gough's 5th Army of seven divisions north of the River Somme and seven divisions south, covering a twenty-six mile front, part of which comprised the ill-maintained trench system taken over from the French. Gough's reserve comprised only three divisions stationed too far back, which Haig refused to reinforce because he was fixated with the idea of an attack in the north, despite intelligence of the German preparations.

On the early morning of 21st March 1918 a five-hour bombardment from 4.40 am began the German offensive, pouring gas and high-explosive shells on to the supply dumps, trenches and dugouts of the front line, soaking the land with gas. The guns played up and down the British line. At 9.35 am in the morning mist, a creeping barrage moved forward, backed by the 'Stürmtruppen', who were to sweep through the line punching holes and leaving the oncoming main divisions to clear up behind them. These parties, with machine guns and other equipment, were designed to establish themselves in the rear, while the front was cleared. By mid-day all the forward zones had been taken. The push went on: von der Marwitz in the centre went though the second line with few casualties: von Hutier's force was half way to the Crozet Canal.

Only in the north did Byng's army hold the assault of von Bulow's army. By the evening of 23rd March the armies of Marwitz and Hutier had penetrated the British front line to a depth of fifteen miles and Gough's 5th Army was in full retreat. The overpowering force of the German offensive could not be held. That same day in the north the progress of the Germans had amounted to only four miles although the forward thrust of Marwitz's and Hutier's armies forced a retreat on Byng's 3rd Army on the flank. Despite Hutier's success, Ludendorff committed his reserves to von Bulow's army to press on in the Arras area. Kaiser Wilhelm II drank champagne for the 'victory' and awarded Hindenburg, as Commander-in-Chief, the Iron Cross with Golden Rays, not given since the 1815 award to Marshal Blucher, to which Hindenburg responded privately by asking what use were decorations, when a good and advantageous peace was to be preferred. Fieldmarshal Haig was relying on Petain to strengthen his right by sending General Fayolle's army to reinforce him, but Petain in fact ordered the general to fall back on Paris if need arose, in response to the shelling of Paris begun that day with an 8-inch gun firing shells of 264 pounds each. This shelling from the Laon salient, over seventy miles away, was to go on until 9th August. During these 139 days a shell was launched every twenty minutes. There was no military purpose for the bombardment other than to harry the civil population. The Pariskanone (wrongly referred to as 'Big Bertha' after Bertha Krupp, the proprietress of Krupps steel combine) had a range of eighty-one miles and the first shell burst in the Place de La Républque.

By 26th March the Germans were still advancing; von Hutier was about to reach Montdidier some forty miles from the front line, taking it on the next day, and von der Marwitz in the centre was up to the old Somme battlefield, within five miles of Albert. Bapaume had fallen in the northern area of attack and the River Ancre had been reached. The allied commanders met with Lord Milner and Clemenceau at Doullens that day. As Haig entered the conference, Petain whispered to the French President Poincaré. 'There is a man who will be forced to capitulate in open field within a fortnight, and very likely if we are not obliged to do the same'. As a result of the conference General Foch was appointed as overall commander, to co-ordinate the effort to beat back the offensive and save Amiens.

Ludendorff, despite the achievements south of the Somme, continued to field his reserve divisions in the north, where the weight of his attack had intended to be. On 28th March von Bulow's army launched an assault on the high ground near Arras defended by Byng's 3rd Army, only to be ferociously rebuffed, consuming some seven of his reserve divisions. The new front line established near Amiens was also assaulted and on the 29th the attack north of Arras was renewed. However by 30th March the German campaign was beginning to falter. The Germans were within seven miles of Amiens, but their momentum was gone. The German troops, as they advanced, had began to dissolve as disciplined forces. The under-nourished Germans were waylaid by the food and drink in the British stores captured. The transport to the front had broken down; the problems of crossing old devastated areas and the constant air attack of the Royal Flying Corps on the roads behind the advancing front slowed supplies. When the troops reached Albert, the tired divisions were mowed down by the machine-guns on the new line and the advance crumbled. British and French reserves sent by Foch had plugged the gap and all that Plan Michael had achieved was a huge new salient on the German line. The Germans had however taken 8,000 prisoners and 975 guns. They had suffered 250,000 casualties as compared with 177,739 British, of which 14,823 were killed. General Gough, perhaps unfairly, was relieved of his command.

The German High Command turned from the Plan Michael offensive to the northern limb of their dual thrust against the British on 9th April in the vicinity of Ypres to Béthune, but the strength of the blow had been weakened by the limitation of the reserves. The 6th Army of General von Quaast was to attack the 2nd British Army of Sir Henry Plumer and in the south near Béthune the 1st Army of General Sir Henry Horne. In the north the 4th German Army of General Sixt von Arnim also faced Plumer's 2nd Army. The latter had some six divisions, five of them transferred after the fight in the March offensive, and two Portuguese Divisions holding a twenty-four mile front. Although air observation had seen the Germans assemble for the offensive, Haig failed to reinforce the Portuguese because he was obsessed with the possible threat south of Béthune. At 4 am von Arnim's 4th Army began the bombardment on a narrow front between the La Bassée Canal and Armentieres, where the Portuguese were deployed. The trenches were hammered with high explosive and mustard gas on the flanks. At 8.45 am nine German Divisions marched on the Portuguese, who under the impact broke. By noon some three miles had been gained and by the evening of the 10th the Rivers Lavre and Lys had been crossed. A Salient five miles deep had been created, although the 55th Division had held the front in the far south. On 10th April Armentieres, Messines and Ploegstreet fell as the Germans expanded their front to twenty-four miles. Disorder reigned among the retreating divisions, although the 50th and 51st made a stand on the west bank of the Lavre and Lys. By the 12th the advancing Germans were within five miles of Hazebrouck, the railway junction critical to British military communications. There the 1st Guards Division and 1st Australian Division were to make a stand which brought von Quaast's 6th Army to a halt. So critical was the position that to the alarm of the British and French politicians, Fieldmarshal Haig issued his famous 'backs to the wall' call to the army to stand firm. Plumer in the north had decided to straighten the line and pulled back around Ypres to the original line just outside the city, giving up the Flanders mud won in 1917 at a cost of a quarter of a million lives.

Once more communication problems and the attacks on supplies by the Royal Flying Corps began to hamper the German advance. By 19th April it ground to a standstill as reinforcements including fresh French Divisions sent by Marshal Foch began to strengthen the new front. On 25th April, however, von Armin's 4th Army seized Mount Kemmel, but after a further unsuccessful attack the offensive was abandoned by Ludendorff. His success in the two offensives was measurable by the fact that he had taken the most territory occupied by any army in the war, but in the forty days of fighting his casualties have been estimated at 250,000. The British had suffered 236,000 casualties, the French 75,000.

Still pursuing his strategy of striking the Allied Front line by offensives at differing places, Ludendorff began to prepare for his Plan Blucher-Yorck, a thrust at the French between Soissons and Rheims. The offensive was envisaged as limited, striking a blow only to cross the River Aisne. Under the command of Crown Prince Wilhelm of Prussia, the 18th, 7th and 1st Armies, comprising 41 divisions, were to be launched on a front of twenty–two miles. Opposite them were seven French divisions along the west of the line with four British divisions, three of them being rested, in the east. Reserves were limited to three divisions. Despite American intelligence given to him of a proposed attack, General Duchesne ignored his orders to construct a defence in depth and concentrated his troops in the front line.

Before the offence could be launched the German Army needed a pause after the earlier attacks to train, recuperate and reorganise. It was not therefore until 27th May that the attack began. At 1 am bombardment started of the Chemin des Dames and at 4.30 am the torrents of infantry poured up the ridge, using the same pattern of attack as in the March and April offensives. By noon the ridge had been taken and the Germans were over un-destroyed bridges on the River Aisne by the end of the day. The 50th and 8th British Divisions stood firm against the onslaught protecting Rheims, and sacrificed themselves almost to a man. On 28th May Soissons was occupied and Fismes; 25,000 prisoners had been taken. By the evening of the 30th the Germans had reached Chateau-Thierry, which was taken on 1st June. The armies had advanced almost forty miles on a front of thirty miles to within thirty-nine miles of Paris. There they were held by reinforcements committed by Foch of fourteen infantry divisions and the 10th Army, with two divisions of Americans defending the Rheims-Paris Road. On 3rd June Ludendorff ordered the Crown Prince to abandon the attack. The number of prisoners was now 65,000. Once more the army had slipped out of control, with looting of Allied supplies and a growing number of desertions.

The Germans were to launch two more attacks. Plan Gneisenau was to be a thrust on the Noyon-Montdidier section of the front against General Fayolle's armies. The latter had however built up a defence in depth with seven divisions in the first line and five in the second, some of these Americans. There was a reserve of ten divisions. The 18th German army, of eleven divisions with seven in reserve commanded by General von Hutier, moved forward on 9th June. The army not only was under-nourished, but had begun to suffer from the flu epidemic which was to ravage Europe, and contained many inexperienced recruits. The usual pattern was followed of bombardment succeeded at 3.45 am by the 'Stürmtruppen' and then the massed divisions. Breaches were made, seven miles of front being taken to a depth of six and half miles, but most of the front held, and on the next day

General Mangin arrived with reserve defence divisions. On 11th June they counter-attacked, cleared the Aronde valley and halted the campaign. The Germans had 25,000 casualties and the French 40,000.

The final attack was on 15th July, both sides of Rheims, Plan Marneschutz and Rheims. Unintentionally it was to coincide with a planned offensive by the French and Americans against the Marne salient won by the Germans in June. The intent was to throw a two-pronged attack either side of Rheims to surround the city and move on Epernay and Chalons. Forty-nine divisions were committed. The German army as a whole however no longer had the strength which it enjoyed before the March attack began, some 207 Divisions with 82 in reserve. There were only now 66 in reserve, reduced in numbers and quality. The 7th Army had the problem of crossing the sixty-yard River Marne, but successfully achieved that under the cover of smoke, building bridges assembled for the purpose. A four-mile bridgehead was created. The attack of the 1st and 3rd Armies east of Rheims made only limited progress. On 16th July the offensive slowed down. Marshal Foch and General Pershing had as indicated, in fact planned for an assault on the Marne Salient and they had prepared their offensive. Petain after the German attack ordered the offensive cancelled but Foch ignored his order. On 18th, after a bombardment west of Chateau Thierry and spearheaded by tanks from the woods of Villiers Cotteret, the armies of Generals Mangin and Degoutte attacked. Spearheaded by 225 tanks, a mixed army of six French Infantry Divisions and two American with cavalry moved forward and by 22nd July had penetrated the salient for four miles, when they came to a standstill. In the centre the British 51st and 62nd Divisions penetrated up to nine miles. The chief of staff of the 4th German army wished to disengage, but that was prevented by Ludendorff. The fight raged on until 2nd August, by which time the Germans had withdrawn to the River Vesle and abandoned the Marne Salient. The German casualties amounted to 110,000 but the Allied 160,000.

By July the French and British had survived the great offensive campaign mounted by Hindenburg and Ludendorff. The build-up of American divisions and their gain in experience fortified the morale of the Allies and Haig, Foch, the over-all commander as from 14th April, and General Pershing began to evolve an offensive strategy for the remainder of the year. On 12th July Marshal Foch asked Haig to go over to the offensive north of the River Luce, but Haig preferred the Amiens front, which he felt he had to free from threat. Care was taken to ensure that all preparations for the offensive were disguised. All movements up were made at night and the extra artillery sprinkled among the batteries already there. The Royal Flying Corps hindered air reconnaissance by the Germans. The main thrust was to be in the centre by General Sir Henry Rawlinson's 4th Army, deploying 14 infantry divisions and 3 cavalry brigades. The Canadian and Australian Corps were to head the way south of the River Somme. The objective chosen by Haig was limited but Marshal Foch persuaded him to aim to go on twenty-eight miles to Roye. The German defence line from Albert to the River Avre was held by von der Marwitz's 2nd Army with six under-strength divisions amounting to 18,000 men. The French 3rd Army was to attack from north of Montdidier to Noyon, while the British 3rd Corps north of the Somme went forward to secure the left flank of the advance. Deception was pursued to the end, the Canadians and Australians coming up only at the last moment and spreading out in trenches, as if merely to strengthen defence. There was no bombardment.

At 4.20 am on 8th August, in a ground mist, led by the tank force, the Canadians on the right and the Australians on the left moved forward. Accompanied by the moving barrage of 2,000 guns on the ten-mile front, the waves of infantry went in. By the end of the first day the advance in the centre had been six to eight miles, but less north of the Somme where there were few tanks. 16,000 prisoners had been taken and 200 guns. Whole bodies of Germans surrendered, sometimes to one man; the officers lost control and the army was crumbling. As the reserve divisions came up, the defeated troops shouted to them 'Blackleg.' On the 9th Montdidier was taken, but the offensive slowed as Ludendorff sent up 18 reserve divisions and the advancing forces came up to the old battlefield. To avoid casualties Haig wished to stop, but Foch urged the advance on. On the 10th and 11th Ludendorff carried out a partial withdrawal. On 11th August the attack was abandoned. The Allies had 'only' lost 22,000 killed and wounded, while the Germans lost 75,000 men, 50,000 of them as prisoners, and 500 guns. The total gain did not exceed about twelve miles at its deepest, but Ludendorff described 8th August as the 'Black Day' of the German army. The dissolution of the troops as a disciplined determined fighting force led him and Hindenburg on 13th August at Spa to tell Kaiser Wilhelm II that the war could not be won, and that the army could only be held together while negotiations to end the war were carried on. The slow melting of the institutions and structures of the Imperial German Empire had begun and soon was to gather speed.

The assault at Amiens was but a precursor to a series of offensives upon which the Allied leaders had agreed all along the German line. In August Byng's 3rd Army struck towards Bapaume; the 10th French Army retook Soissons on the 17th; the 4th British Army resumed its advance and the Australians on the 26th took Peronne and Mont St Quentin. In September the Americans and French mounted a major attack on the St Mihiel Salient west of Verdun and by 13th September had retaken it and moved towards Metz. At the end of September co-ordinated attacks were mounted by Haig in the northern sector and by Pershing and the French in the southern sector of the line near Verdun, out of the Argonne Forest. The former in the Ypres salient had some success. The ground troops were supported by 500 aircraft. The New Zealand General Freyberg, nine times wounded and holder of the Victoria Cross, led the New Zealand Brigade mounted on an ugly white horse, until it was shot under him. The New Zealanders took Gheluvert and the offensive ended with 4,000 prisoners. On the Meuse-Argonne front the Americans attacked west of Verdun on 26th September with the object of breaking through to Mezieres. Only limited advances were made, so that by 4th October the offensive had come to a standstill some five miles beyond the start line. On 28th September Hindenburg and Ludendorff had a discussion in which they decided to insist on an immediate armistice and so advised Kaiser Wilhelm II.

October brought a continuing momentum to the constant offensive strikes. The British breached the Hindenburg line in early October. On 8th and 9th October on a twenty-mile front a British initiative pushed west and Canadians entered Cambrai, a cavalry division advancing eight miles beyond to near Le Cateau. On 13th and 14th October the British and French launched an assault between Dixmude and Courtrai, using in the initial bombardment gas shells. Adolf Hitler, the future Fuehrer, who in August had received the Iron Cross, 1st Class, an unusual honour for an ordinary soldier, suffered in that attack, being sent to the rear to hospital, and then to Munich to carry out political intelligence for the army. 12,000 prisoners were taken and 550 guns. On the 10th the Americans had renewed their assault and pushed forward, reaching a line just south of Buzancy by the end of the month. On the 13th the French took Laon and on the 17th the British took Lille.

The break-up of the resistance of the German armies in the field was matched at home by the disintegration of the Imperial Government and control over the civil population. After Hindenburg's and Ludendorff's request to Wilhelm II on 28th September, the Kaiser issued a decree pledging a new democratic constitution with proper powers given to a Reichstag for control of policy. A new Chancellor was appointed, Prince Max of Baden, and on 3rd October a Note was delivered to President Wilson that the Germans would accept an armistice based on the 14 points set out in January and the Declarations which he had made. The President replied on 9th October asking whether all the points were accepted and whether to show bona fides the occupied territories would be evacuated. This was unacceptable to the army command and on the 12th a non-committed reply was sent. In a second note, the President asked for an end to the U-boat campaign, the guarantee of democratic reform and the evacuation of the territories occupied. Despite protestation by the Kaiser, Prince Max of Baden, the new Chancellor, was under great pressure to accept the terms. Germany was near starvation; disorder was breaking out in the streets. The navy, ordered to sea for a last fight, was on the brink of mutiny and was in fact to do so. Bulgaria had collapsed and the Austro-Hungarian Armies were breaking up into their national groupings-Slav, Czech, Hungarian, Slovak and German. The Chancellor therefore accepted the terms, despite Hindenburg changing his mind and calling for resistance. Ludendorff resigned and General Groener took his place. On 23rd October Wilson had sent the German Government a new note implicitly requesting the abdication of the Kaiser. The latter resisted but on 8th November was persuaded by the army command to mount his silver train and flee for asylum in Holland. Prince Max had in part announced of his own accord the abdication in Berlin before the Kaiser had left and resigned. In Munich a Socialist Workers Republic was proclaimed.

On 28th October at Senlis the Allied military commanders had met to fix the armistice terms, a task left to them by President Wilson, who had been the most involved in the negotiations, and by the other political leaders. A delegation from Germany was received by Marshal Foch with representatives of the other powers in his Wagon-Lit carriage in the Forest of Compiegne. In the background the war continued; in the south the Americans were advancing on Sedan and on 4th November the New Zealanders took Le Quesnoy by storm with a five-mile advance, 10,000 prisoners and the capture of 200 guns. On 10th November the British entered Mons. The armistice terms were set out and agreed. There was to be immediate evacuation of the occupied territories. The army would surrender 5,000 heavy guns and artillery pieces, 2,500 machine guns, 3,000 trench mortars and 1,700 aeroplanes. The left bank of the Rhine was to be occupied by the Allies together with Cologne, Mainz and Coblenz. Germany would surrender 5,000 railway engines, 150,000 rail wagons and 5,000 lorries. The eastern lands occupied under the treaty of Brest-Litovsk were to be evacuated. All submarines were to be handed over and also the Imperial Navy to the total of 10 battleships, 6 battle cruisers, 8 light cruisers and 50 destroyers. The impact of these proposals can be measured by the fact that between 1st August and 8th November the Germany army lost half its guns to the Allies, totalling 6,400. The German army was to be left without the means therefore to renew the war. At 5 am on the morning of 11th November the German delegates signed and accepted the terms. The Armistice was to commence at 11 am on the 11th November. Action of a desultory character continued until then. General Freyberg, riding his command horse, once more at 9.30 am led his New Zealanders to capture an unblown river bridge on the Dendre. German outposts fired on him and a bullet hit his saddle. The bridge was however safely taken. At 11 am the guns fell silent: the war was over.

In retrospect the Allies had won an undoubted victory. No single land offensive on the western front had that characteristic. The destruction of Imperial Germany had been like a long siege of medieval times. Constant battering on the walls had progressively destroyed the defenders and the blockade of food and raw materials by sea had reduced the garrison and the inhabitants to starvation and poverty and robbed them of the means of war. Two elements were decisive, the blockade of Germany with the destruction of all sea trade, and the attrition of her forces by the constant attacks in the front line, including the feats in the east by Russia until the end of 1917. As at Badajoz, making a 'breach' was costly of life and each attempt sapped the attackers as well as the defenders. Given the obstacle to mobile war by cavalry that the new field guns and the machine gun presented before the coming of the tank, the war of attrition was the only practical course. Fieldmarshal Haig, Marshals Joffre and Foch were all forced to continue within that constraint, but the war of whole populations took a toll of death, which was unimaginable and barbarous. The savagery of the conflict can well argue that the Armistice was no victory, but celebration is for the heroic endurance and courage of those who took part and their achievement. Remembrance Sunday is the day to recall the sacrifice upon which the outcome of the war rested. The result ennobles man but leaves him sorrowing, and discomforted by the price of modern war.

The Peace

The leaders of the four victorious Allies were to react in different ways to the end of war. On 12th November the Prime Minister, David Lloyd George declared that 'No settlement which contravenes the principles of eternal justice will be a permanent one. Let us be warned by the example of 1871. We must not allow any spirit of greed, any grasping desire, to override the fundamental principle of righteousness'. Fieldmarshal Haig, writing to his wife on 1st November, had commented, 'I am afraid the Allied statesmen mean to exact humiliating terms from Germany. I think this is a mistake, because it is merely laying up trouble for the future and may encourage the wish for revenge.' Both attitudes reflected the concerns and desires of President Woodrow Wilson, who had formulated the basis of a fair peace in his fourteen points and declarations. The Armistice had been agreed by the Germans on the footing that these principles would be applied to the peace process. The reaction of the French, to whom Haig was close, and of the Italians, was less benevolent. The Italians had little interest in a liberal peace, as their concern was to sieze parts of the Austrian Empire in the south Tyrol and along the Adriatic. The French saw the peace as an opportunity to reassert their political hegemony over Europe, so often aimed at in the past. Clemenceau, the French Prime Minister, on receiving the telegram that the Armistice was signed, welled up with fervour, declaring that the day of revenge had arrived and that France would by reparations 'bust' the German Republic.

The initial driving force of the Peace Conference which opened in December 1914 was President Woodrow Wilson. He was a former President of Princeton University and a tormented intellectual of stern Presbyterian background, who had come to believe that he was a saviour appointed by God to save the nations and give a new order to the world on the basis of his policies in the fourteen points and the Declarations. He was welcomed almost with religious devotion by the people of Britain and France, as the harbinger of lasting peace. He insisted that before dealing with the practical problems of peace the nations at the conference should formulate and adopt a Covenant for a League of Nations to establish a worldwide regime of law, to outlaw the resort to war, to provide for diplomacy with justice and to guarantee the existence of all the member states. The Covenant was ready by January, before he returned to Washington for a short visit. Clemenceau was left to run the conference.

In Britain Lloyd-George had called a General Election before Christmas. His supporters and those of the Coalition were given approval, a 'coupon', as one party in the constituencies. 364 Conservatives received the Coupon, but only 108 Liberals. These were opposed by over 250 Liberals led by Mr Asquith and by the Labour Party. In the results 333 Conservatives were elected and 133 of the Coupon Liberals and others. In all supporters of the Government won 478 seats. Only 29 Asquith Liberals were elected. Lloyd-George became dependent on the Conservative Party for the sustaining of his premiership. The election was also notable for the enlargement of the franchise by 4 million men and 8 million women, diluting almost completely the selective electorate which had existed in the Victorian period. Britain had begun to move from the Aristotelian model of ideal government, the polity, to the 'degraded' form of outright popular democracy. Its first fruit was a campaign whipped up by the media and forced on the Coalition to make Germany pay, ruin its trade and force on 'the Huns' material guarantees of security. Lloyd-George, always feline in his understanding of his constituency, came to Paris with motivations different from those expressed on 12th November 1918. The tradition of magnanimity in peace by Britain in the past had come under assault by the new mass electorate.

Wilson returned from America to the Conference in February, but his nerves were shattered, his health reduced. The details of the settlement of Europe had little interest for him as long as he had his Treaty for the League of Nations. As the conference wound on and the French demands became even more incompatible with his fourteen points, which were the foundation of the Armistice, he only weakly fought for his beliefs, thinking that in any event the Treaties could be reviewed within the aegis of the League of Nations. French and Italian demands became even more insistent. On March 25th Lloyd-George tried again to urge reconciliation and moderation. 'Injustice, arrogance displayed in the hour of triumph will never be forgotten or forgiven,' he wrote in the memorandum, setting out his opposition to the transfer of Germans to other states. 'If we are wise' he added, 'we shall offer Germany a peace which, while just, will be preferable for all sensible men to the alternative of Bolshevism'. The settlement, he thought, needed to be drawn up as if we were impartial arbiters and contain within itself no provocation for future wars. Within a few days, his memorandum made public, Lloyd-George was sent a telegram urging him to maintain the policy to which he was pledged. It was signed by 370 Members of Parliament, most of whom to their discredit were Conservatives. Lloyd-George, with one eye on London, began to follow where the French led, to what they saw as the sweet rewards of revenge. The subjection of the making of British foreign policy, historically a matter of the

Royal Perogative, to the people in the new unsophisticated electorate and to the House of Commons which they had elected, was to bring its own long and bitter result, inimical to their own long-term interests.

By May the draft Treaty was drawn. If put beside the 14 points which both sides accepted as the basis of peace, the draft Treaty was a total betrayal of the principles. The French loaded Germany with every handicap. The breaches of promises made were formidable: of 20 points stated by Wilson only four were in the Treaty. The most obvious breaches were over the principle of no annexations, no punitive damages and the need for self-determination as the imperative principle of action. Two other important matters were open-minded and impartial adjustment of colonial claims, and the general reduction of armaments consistent with domestic safety. In the treaty, Eupen-Malmedy was annexed to Belgium; a swathe of East Prussia (the corridor) cutting off the East Prussian province from Prussia proper went to Poland and the Saar to France until 1935, then to be the subject of a plebiscite. In relation to punitive damages and reparations, the Germans lost three-quarters of their iron ore sources, half of their zinc, a quarter of their lead and a third of their coal. 20% of the Inland Water Tonnage was to be surrendered together with their merchant fleet. Fifty per cent of coal production was to go to France, together with 140,000 milch cows. The property of German nationals abroad and in the Saar was sequestered. No reparations figure was fixed, the final sums being left to a Commission, but the French claimed for property damaged the sum of £3,000 million, a sum in excess of the value of all the landed property and buildings of France. An initial payment of five billion dollars in gold marks was sought between 1919 and 1921. In relation to self-determination, Germany lost four million people to Poland and three and a half million Germans in the Sudeten borderlands of the Austro-Hungarian Empire were given to Czechoslovakia. The associated Treaty of St Germain precluded the union of Austria with Germany, and three million Hungarians were given to Czechoslovakia and Romania. No one sought the consent of those transferred. Danzig and Memel were made free cities under Polish control. The Austrian Adriatic was given to Italy and the new state of Yugoslavia. The colonies were not subject to 'impartial adjustment' but given by mandate of the League to Britain and France. General disarmament was limited to the disarmament of Germany, permitting an army of only 100,000 men with no air force and a navy limited to vessels of under 10,000 tons and no submarines, while France and its new allies, Poland and Czechoslovakia, stood fully armed on the German frontiers.

President Wilson in his fourteen points had pledged that all treaties should be openly discussed and openly arrived at. The Treaty of Versailles and the Treaty of St Germain were the antithesis of that pledge. No German was invited to the peace conference. In April the German Government was ordered to send a delegation to Paris. They were on arrival initially treated as prisoners and on

7th May were given the terms of the Treaty accompanied by a demand that they made their observations within fifteen days. In Germany the publication of the treaty led to widespread demonstrations. President Ebert described the terms as 'unrealisable and unbearable'. The Government was strongly against accepting the Treaty, backed by the German people as a whole. The army were consulted but Feldmarschall Hindenburg and General Groener advised that resistance was impossible. Graf Brockdorf-Rantzau, the head of the German delegation, presented modified proposals on 31st May, which the Allies did not allow to be published. A definite final answer was sought from the German Government, with an ultimatum for signature given expiring on 24th June. The Weimar Assembly, the new Parliament of Germany, voted to sign it on 24th June by 237 votes to 138 as a 'bitter necessity.' On 28th June 1919 the Treaty was signed in the Gallerie des Glaces at Versailles.

There were many in Britain who saw the folly of the Treaty, including the great South African leader General Smuts. Strangely it was the Independent Labour Party who distinctly expressed this view, saying that the terms expressly violated the conditions of the Armistice and did not give world peace but the certainty of other and more calamitous wars. In Germany the bitterness and hatred aroused by the treaty was fuelled too by the economic dislocation which resulted. In January 1923 the French aroused more embitterment by occupying the Ruhr, for failure by Germany to maintain its reparations. By November the exchange rate had fallen to four billion marks to one dollar. The nationalist forces of the right who had opposed the Treaty gathered support, and Adolf Hitler and Feldmarschall Ludendorff put themselves at the head of a putsch in Munich. The army fired on their procession, but Ludendorff, looking neither to left or right, marched erect in his uniform through the troops towards the Odeonsplatz. He swore never to wear his uniform again. Hitler was arrested, tried and sentenced to imprisonment, where he began work on his book, Mein Kampf. It was first published in 1925 and for the reader set out with clarity his policy and attitudes. Among the 25 points of the programme of the National Socialist German Workers' Party were the following –

i.   'We demand the union of all Germans to form a Great Germany on the basis of the right of self-determination enjoyed by nations.

ii. We demand equality of rights for the German people in its dealings with other nations, and abolition of the Peace Treaties of Versailles and St Germain'

After he came to power, with steadfastness and commitment unusual in politicians, he set out to implement his promises with an evil which grew into a flood. The treaty was unrevisable by agreement, since the French could by their single veto block any amendment under the League of Nations provisions.

Germany had only one feasible alternative of deceit and the threat and use of force, to face French opposition and intransigence.

The political leaders of Britain faced an impossible situation. The threat of communist rule hung over a Europe locked in economic collapse. Adolf Hitler, despite his perceived character as a ruthless dictator, seemed to promise a stability not otherwise achievable in the nineteen-thirties. The Governments of Macdonald, Baldwin and Chamberlain and many enlightened men in Britain had become ever more uneasy at the nature of the Versailles settlement, about which even at the time General Smuts had had such misgivings. Appeasement of Hitler as a policy seemed to serve two objectives, first, of revising the treaties and second, of hoping to bring Germany, its legitimate grievances redressed, into the peaceful comity of European nations. It was a policy wholly in tune with the tradition of Sir Robert Walpole and William Pitt the Younger, of preserving peace until events gave no alternative but war. The tragedy was the failure of the Anglo-Saxon powers in 1918 to press the policy of magnanimity in victory and to curb the revenge of France which was to embitter Germany, seed the political growth of Adolf Hitler and plunge Europe into yet another World War.

11th November 1940
The Destruction of the Italian Fleet

After France deserted Britain in 1940, British interests in the Mediterranean were in great danger. Italy had declared war in June 1940 and the Italian navy was potentially a considerable threat, particularly as its strength exceeded that of Admiral Sir Andrew Cunningham's Mediterranean Fleet. The principal base in southern Italy was at Taranto, which had a large, magnificent and well-defended harbour. The harbour was in two sections, the outer Harbour, Mar Grande, and the inner harbour, Mar Piccolo, to which a canal gave access through a promontory on which stood the town. The outer harbour had a single entrance, its sixteen square-mile area being blocked off on the north-west and south-west by submerged breakwaters. The south-eastern shore between the Cape San Vito and the town lay along the main enclosed area, which was shielded by a mole, the Diga di Tarantola. The shore here was lined with a dense screen of barrage balloons. In the centre of the bay torpedo nets had been laid to shield the anchorage for cruisers, and the northerly part of the harbour beyond the mole. The harbour was ringed with anti-aircraft batteries. In the inner harbour there were dockyards and anchorage for cruisers and destroyers, and an oil and seaplane depot. The naval installation was therefore well protected and guarded and difficult for torpedo attack.

Attack by torpedo needs the delivering aircraft to dive low to the sea to launch the 1,500-lb torpedo, judge carefully the moment of release and then to bear off from the warship regaining height. It requires skill, courage, experienced judgement and careful flying of the aircraft. The attack on Taranto, because of the defences, meant that the only paths open for the launch of torpedoes were from the north-west and across the town, evading the barrage balloon shield and the netting in the harbour. It had the further complication that the attack was to be made at night.

Careful planning was carried out by Cunningham and Vice-Admiral Sir Arthur Lyster, carrying his flag on the aircraft carrier, HMS Illustrious. The aircrews were intensively trained and close reconnaissance was mounted on a daily basis from Malta, 320 miles away, by Glen Martin aircraft and Sunderland flying boats. The original plan was fixed for 21st October (Trafalgar Day) but problems with HMS Eagle led to the delay of the operation and the withdrawal of Eagle, its Swordfish planes being transferred to Illustrious. On 6th November the fleet, including

Warspite, Valiant, Malaya, Ramillies and Illustrious, was led out of Alexandria and steamed to the west. On the 8th Italian bombers approached the fleet but were driven off by Fulmars from Illustrious. Two were shot down out of seven and no damage was done. On the 9th a further Italian reconnaissance flight was destroyed. On the morning of 11th November an RAF plane carried out a flight over the harbour. There were five major ships in the harbour, two of the new Littorio class and three of the older Cavour class of battleship. A sixth entered in the afternoon and was seen by the RAF.

As a feint at 1 pm Vice Admiral Sir Henry Pridham-Wippel with three cruisers – Orion (5th of the name) Sydney and Ajax (7th of the name) – left the fleet to enter the Adriatic between Brindesi and Valona in order to attack a supply convoy between those two ports. At 6 pm Illustrious escorted by destroyers left the fleet to take up station for the attack 170 miles east of Taranto. The attack was to be made in two waves. The first wave of twelve included two aircraft being sent in to drop flares to light up the harbour: the second wave was of nine. Eleven of the Swordfish carried torpedoes, the others bombs. At 8 pm the first wave led by Lieutenant Commander K. Wilkinson was ready on deck and, led by the two pathfinders, flew off to the attack. The planes dropping flares went in from the east, negotiating an intense anti-aircraft barrage and the screen of the barrage balloons. At half-mile intervals the flares were dropped along the shore, silhouetting the anchored battleships against the sky for aircraft flying in from the west. After the flares were dropped the two planes flew on to bomb the inner harbour. In came the first wave from the north-west and over the town, launching their torpedoes in the Grand harbour waters to the north of the netting. They dived in until the moment of launch through the fierce anti-aircraft fire from the land and the anchored fleet. The torpedoes launched streamed across the water at 42 knots. One of the Littorio class ship was hit and was soon on fire and hits were made on one of the Cavour class battleships. The leader of the formation was lost. At 11.40 pm the second wave, commanded by Lieutenant Commander Hale, came in and concentrated on the two Littorio class battleships. Those without torpedoes bombed the inner harbour and the docks. One more plane was lost. Two cruisers were damaged in the Inner Harbour.

On inspection on the morning of the 12th one of the Littorio battleships was so damaged that its bows were awash; an older Cavour class battleship was aground forward and its stern on starboard side was under water. Another had been beached. Half the Italian fleet, taken with the damage to the cruisers and destroyers, had been crippled. The dockyard too had been damaged.

A second attack was planned but bad weather on 12th November prevented it. In any event, reconnaissance showed that the undamaged fleet had left, going north. The Mediterranean fleet was no longer outnumbered and for at least six months untroubled in mastery of the sea. The success of Taranto signalled a new era in sea warfare. The battleship was to be rendered obsolete unless heavily protected in the air and aircraft carriers became the key element in the fleet. The Japanese were to study the attack on Taranto as a model for Pearl Harbour. The battleships Prince of Wales and Repulse were sunk off Singapore by aircraft, as they had no air cover, later in the war. Naval warfare had a new dimension. Half a fleet was destroyed by 21 aircraft courageously and skilfully flown, at a cost of two lost.

20th November 1759

The Battle of Quiberon Bay

The year 1759 was the climax of the Seven Years War, bringing a string of victories to Britain and its allies – the Taking of Fort Ticonderoga in America, the Battle of Minden (1st August) the Battle of Lagos (18th August), the Taking of Quebec (13th September) and the naval victory of Quiberon Bay. The latter was a feat of endurance, courage and unparalleled seamanship upon the part of the Royal Navy.

Throughout 1759 King Louis XV of France and his chief Minister, the Due de Choiseul, planned and plotted an invasion of Britain, hoping to co-operate with the Stuart pretender, Bonnie Prince Charlie of the 1745 revolt. The Prime Minister, the Duke of Newcastle, constantly worried about the threat and was fearful in relation to the policy of William Pitt, the Elder, the Secretary of State for War who pursued the war worldwide, believing that the navy 'keeping the sea' would prevent invasion. In the Autumn of 1759 the French collected an army to be commanded by the Duc d'Aiguillon in Brittany, where transports were collected. It became essential to prevent the sailing of this invasion fleet. The Marquis de Conflans was made responsible by Louis XV for ensuring that the transports were protected and arrived successfully at their destination. He had been made Admiral and Marshal of France in 1758 and he was to command the French navy, which was to assemble at Brest.

The state of the French navy made action with an enemy an undoubted risk: there was a shortage of victuals and naval provisions; the men-of war were not prepared, transports for horses were rotting and there was a lack of manpower. The captain of L'Orient for example, complained that he had only thirty well-experienced seamen on his ship. Conflans was faced therefore with a difficult task. To an inexperienced fleet was added the problem posed by the blockade of Brest. For most of 1759 Sir Edward Hawke had mounted a blockade of Brest. To continue that effort he had fought a constant battle with the Admiralty, dishonest victuallers and peculating civil servants to insure fresh food for his 14,000 men, decent beer, and vegetables to prevent scurvy. The ravages and remedies for that disease are well laid out in the First Edition of the Encyclopaedia Britannia. Among other remedies, every common sailor is recommended to lay in a stock of onions. Hawke's concern stemmed from his career. He entered the navy in 1720 at the age of 15 and was rated as able seamen. He was not commissioned third Lieutenant until 1729. He was a courageous officer and became a favourite of King George II, who had him made Rear-Admiral of the White in the Channel Fleet. He sat as Member of Parliament for Portsmouth for thirty years although, lacking the devious skills of politics, he remained unpopular with both William Pitt the Elder and Lord Anson, who opposed his appointment. Hawke was however with his developed skills of seamanship adapted perfectly to naval warfare in the storm-ridden seas of autumn in the western Channel and Bay of Biscay.

The invasion threat from France in October and November was at its apex, as was the likelihood of heavy weather in the northern Bay of Biscay. The passage of deep and moving depressions occasioned by the Iceland Low, and the anti-cylical effect of the Asian Anticyclone, leads to strong winds which can blow both westerly and easterly. The dominant winds come from the west, carrying swells of which over sixty percent are above seven feet and sixteen percent exceed thirteen feet. In November up to sixteen percent of winds can blow at gale force and above, twenty-nine knots or more. Because so often the winds are controlled by passing depressions, there is a high degree of variability in the winds, so that they are seldom stable even for a day in speed or direction. To fight in the worst of such conditions was not expected of the navies of the eighteenth century. Hawke and the Royal Navy was to prove that notion wrong.

The French collected their army at Vannes, where there were eight regiments, and at Auray where there were five regiments. Access to both towns is obtained from the Bay of Morbihan, an enclosed water full of shoals and narrow channels, with access to Quiberon Bay. The French collected their transports at Auray. Quiberon Bay is marked on the west by the peninsula protruding to Quiberon, the Teignouse Passage which separates the end of the Peninsula from Belle-Isle, an island lying north-west to south-east about fifteen miles long, with a coast of high steep cliffs. The eastern shore of the bay commences at the estuary of the River Vilaine and terminates at the headland, on which the village of Le Croisic stands. The southern boundary from Belle Isle in the west comprises outlying rocky shoals and outcrops until the rocks of the Cardinals are passed. East of that is a deep water entry some seven miles wide before the Four Shoal, a dangerous rock bank, is reached off Le Croisic. North of the shoal lies the Ile Dumet. Within the bay just off the west of its centre are the islands of Houart to the north-east of Belle Isle and of Hoedic to the east of Belle Isle, near each of which there are rocky outcrops and shoals.

Commodore Duff arrived off Morbihan in late September with a small flotilla, inspected the Bay and saw that the transports would not be able to leave. He therefore departed to the Ile de Croix himself in the Rochester with two frigates. In October the Duc d'Aiguillon arrived in Vannes. At Brest Conflans was not ready, although after three days of heavy westerly gales, in which Hawke had to go off shore and returned to Britain, there was a five-day period when the port was freed. Hawke after the 20th returned to lie off Brest. November opened with easterly winds turning south-west and from the 5th to the 8th a ferocious storm raged from the north north-west. Hawke was drawn westwards and on the 7th the French Admiral Bompart, with the fleet from the West Indies, entered the harbour. Conflans was able to take the experienced sailors from these ships and was at last ready to sail. From the 10th to the 12th a period of strong winds followed. Hawke's ships had suffered in the gales and although he tried to return to sea, when a south-westerly gale splitting sails arose on the 13th he returned to Plymouth for repairs. There he transferred his flag from Ramillies (2nd of the line with 90 guns) to the Royal George. In his absence on the 14th Conflans sailed out of Brest with 21 ships in three divisions, commanded by Budes de Guébriant, St André du Verger and the Chevalier de Bauffremont. He stood out for Quiberon and the Bay of Morbihan. At midday on the 16th he was half way, sixty miles south-west of Belle Isle. That afternoon the wind turned easterly and mounted to gale force. Conflans, having tried to beat up, was forced to turn and run before the wind, ending up 120 miles away.

Meanwhile Hawke had left Plymouth with the fleet and met up with Admiral Sir Charles Saunders who had reached the Lizard on the 15th and who informed the Admiralty of his resolve, made personally, to join in the pursuit of the French, whose sailing from Brest was made known to him. Hawke, with 22 ships of the line made a fast passage on the north north-easterly wind, and had arrived seventy miles west-of-north off Belle Isle. Because of the wind Conflans had to sail back south-eastwards. On the 19th the wind died, veered to give rise to south-easterly squalls and shifted about midnight to north north-west. He hove to about twenty miles from Belle-Isle. Hawke drove on with all sail and only hove to for four hours on the morning of the 20th with topsails backed.

Commodore Duff was warned on 19th November by Vengeance of the coming of the French fleet and collecting his flotilla had raised the blockade to sail west to seek out the British fleet running for the Teignouse Passage. At dawn on the 20th he was seen by Conflans who ordered a general chase, splitting his fleet into two squadrons north and south. The Rochester, which was slow, was gradually being overhauled, but about 8.30 am the Maidstone sighted the French fleet, which Duff and his flotilla were leading towards Hawke. She let go her topgallants, the signal for the sighting of a large fleet. Although the night was ending with strong westerlies rising to gale force, Hawke ordered up the top gallants and, the winds shifting northerly, he bore away towards the rocky lee waters of Belle Isle. The van of the British fleet having been seen, Conflans ordered that the chase of Duff's flotilla should be adandoned and that his ships should close up to the flagship. His mind was filled with indecision, whether he should stand and fight or run for the Bay of Quiberon and turn to fight there with the weather behind him, forcing the British towards the strong shoals and rocks at the east of the bay. Mindful of King Louis XV's injunction to use the fleet to protect the troop transports, he thought the latter course preferable. He therefore ordered his fleet to form line and make for the entrance of the Bay to round the Cardinal rocks, he being in the lead in his flagship the Soleil Royal. The winds freshened, blowing from the west north-west, reaching gale force at noon. Hawke, despite the lee shore, the violence of the wind and the mountainous swell, pressed on with all sail, flying before the wind. The topgallants were set despite the wind. At 11 am the Magnamine lost her main topgallant yard. The waves crashed round the ships and on to break ferociously on the reefs, rocks and cliffs; the wind howled through the rigging, shaking the shrouds and moaning round the sails. Hawke still pressed on. The British closed up on the French fleet. As Conflans in the Soleil Royal rounded the Cardinals into the bay about 2.30 pm, the opening guns of the battle could be heard.

Lord Howe in the Magnamine had led the van comprising his own and eight ships of the line, Torbay, Dorsetshire (2nd of the name with 70 guns) Resolution (6th of the name newly built in 1758), Warspite (4th of the name and new in 1758), Swiftsure, Revenge (5th of the name built in 1715 with 70 guns), Montague and Defiance. The French van coming up to the Cardinals rocks were drawn out in a long line, the rear comprising the Formidable, the flagship of Admiral du Verger, the Héros, Superbe and Thésée. In the distance the crashing swell with its plumes of spray and angry white caps could be seen on the Cardinal rocks. By 2.30 pm the British van was up with the French rear, although Hawke was six miles behind. Warspite fired early and the Revenge moved to attack the Formidable, firing its broadsides and going on towards the Magnifique. Dorsetshire and Defiance held their fire initially as they went up the line. As they came up an angry squall hit the fleet, and Temple had to double reef its topsails, but both it and Dorsetshire had to luff up suddenly to avoid the lee gun ports, which were open, going under water and filling the ship. Torbay almost broached. Magnamine, Montague and Warspite fouled one another, breaking jib booms and spritsail yards. Once free Magnamine attacked the Formidable, aided by Warspite.

The French had continued to round into the bay where Conflans had hoped to form a line but in the narrowed sea, the swell still ran long and the fierce wind went north-west, throwing the French fleet into confusion, as they knew that they had to stand off from the rocky shoals to their south and south-west. The British fleet followed them into the Bay, attacking as they went. Magnamine, having freed herself from the collision, went with Warspite up to the Formidable and subjected her to a half-hour of heavy bombardment, reducing the ship. Dorsetshire engaged at different times some five ships. Torbay attacked the Thésée, a new 74-gunner, when a further heavy squall struck, laying the latter on her beam ends with the lee ports open. She sank instantly, with the loss of all but 22 of her 600 crew, who were rescued by the British despite the wind and heavy seas. Magnamine and Chatham sought out Héros. The fore and mizzenmasts had gone and the helm was damaged. Having lost all her officers and midshipmen, she struck, but the seas were so tumultuous that a party could not be sent to board her.

Conflans had decided, following the confusion into which the French fleet had fallen, and the mounting presence of the British in the Bay, that his best recourse was to put out for sea. Not all his captains were of the same mind. Villars de La Brosse in the Glorieux with six others tacked among the shoals and made for the estuary of the River Vilaine. It is a feature of the north Bay of Biscay that the low pressure generated by a depression together with the effect of continued westerly gales can raise the sea level in the Bay. Conditions were therefore such together with the spring tide that de La Brosse's flotilla tried to seek entry up river over the bar. Whether they were forced over by the high gale or chose to make the attempt, three only remained usable and four broke their backs. As the French organised themselves to leave the Bay, Swiftsure fell among the French, suffering extensive damage and fell out of action near the Ile Dumet. The Royal George rounded the Cardinals about 4 pm, within distance of the Soleil Royal heading towards the entrance of the Bay. Seeing her, Hawke ordered the Master to lay the Royal George alongside. The Master pointed out the risks of this manoeuvre, but Hawke insisted: 'You have done your duty in this remonstrance: now obey my orders and lay me alongside the French Admiral'. The Royal George was duly turned and broadsides were promptly exchanged. After two or three broadsides, fighting around the flagships became confused, but as they drew apart the Intrépide (74 guns) interposed itself between them. Union, Mars and Hero joined the Royal George, which then bombarded the Superbe (70 guns) which after two broadsides suddenly foundered. The Soleil Royal was pushed by the wind and sea to leeward and she tried to tack but fell foul of two ships. She could no longer weather the Four Shoal and so ran east towards Croisic. About the same time, 4.30 pm, the Formidable lost its fore topmast and was battered ferociously; De Verger being killed, it finally struck to Resolution.

The light was fading while the storm became ever more ferocious, the sea continuing to rage. Hawke gave the signal for disengagement and the fleet anchored in fifteen fathoms in the Bay, virtually in its centre. Odd guns boomed in the night above the sound of the storm as both fleets lay at anchor. The Chevalier de Bauffremont, warned of the risks of the shoals in the Bay, decided to slip away and he in the Tonnant with others stood out to sea. These eight ships anchored in Aix roads late on the 21st November. The Juste also ran for St Nazaire, but went aground in the mouth of the Loire and the ship was destroyed by the sea. In the Bay about 10 pm the Resolution went aground on the Four Shoal and the Héros also was driven down on to it.

At dawn on 21st November the Soleil Royal found itself anchored in the vicinity of the British fleet and Conflans decided to sail away from the dangerous situation in which he found himself. If anything the gale was more ferocious and he was driven aground on the shoal, 'Rovelle', in the east of the Bay. Resolution was seen dismasted firing off distress guns: Essex sent to rescue her went aground on the Four Shoal. Hawke moved to attempt an attack on the men of war in the River Vilaine, but decided that the river estuary could not be safely penetrated. The wind did not moderate until 22nd November. The crew of Resolution and the Essex were taken off and rescued. An attempt to seize and destroy the Soleil Royal and the Héros was prevented by the French setting fire to the vessels before they abandoned them. The wounded from the Formidable were sent ashore and there was an exchange of fire with the French troops at Le Croisic, when the sailors trying to take off the guns of the Soleil Royal were fired on. Hawke tried to secure the ships lying in the Aix roads, but they entered the River Charente. The Ile d' Yeu was taken and its cattle seized to feed the fleet. Hawke himself remained on station, returning to England only in January.

Effectively the action at Quiberon Bay severely savaged the French fleet and the invasion plan became impracticable. In all the French lost some ten ships: the Soleil Royal and Héros destroyed, the Formidable taken, the Thésée, Superbe and Juste sunk, while four were with broken backs in the River Vilaine. Despite the risks arising from the heavy weather Hawke had lost only the Resolution and the Essex.

The news came to London and in early December a thanksgiving service was appointed to be said in the churches. David Garrick adapted his Christmas theatrical at the Theatre Royal, Drury Lane, by introducing into the middle of the Harlequin's Invasion a new song, 'Hearts of Oak', which was to become a constant anthem for the Royal Navy. The young Lord Robert Manners, who was to be seriously injured in Resolution at the Battle of the Saints, wrote to Hawke asking him to take him to sea.

Hawke returned in January 1760. His fellow members of Parliament greeted him with a solemn declaration thanking him for his victory. £2,000 a year was granted to him and his next two heirs, but Pitt and Anson failed to grant him a peerage. It was not until 1777 that he was made Baron Hawke.

A courtier at Versailles soon after the battle was in discussion with King Louis XV, who remained optimistic about the prospects of the war. In answer to his cheerfulness, the courtier said, 'But Sire, we no longer have a navy'. With the sophisticated detachment fit for a Bourbon King of the eighteenth century, Louis XV replied, 'Yes, Monseigneur, but we have that of Monsieur Vernet'. Vernet was the leading marine painter in France of the period.

The 11th Baron Hawke was ejected from the House of Lords in 1999.

Hearts of Oak

> Come cheer up, my lads, 'tis to glory we steer,
> To add something more to this wonderful year:
> To honour we call you, not press you like slaves,
> For who are so free as we sons of the waves?

Heart of Oak are our ships, heart of oak are our men;
We always are ready, steady boys, steady,
We'll fight, and we'll conquer again and again.

We ne'er see our foes, but we wish them to stay;
They never see us, but they wish us away;
If they run, why we follow, and run them ashore;
For, if they won't fight us, we cannot do more.
  Heart of Oak, & chorus

They swear they'll invade us, these terrible foes;
They frighten our women, our children, and beaus;
But should their flat-bottoms in darkness get o'er,
Still Britons they'll find, to receive them on shore.
  Heart of Oak, & chorus

We'll still make 'em run, and we'll still make 'em sweat,
In spite of the devil, and Brussels's gazette;
Then chear up, my lads, with one heart let us sing,
Our soldiers, our sailors, our statesmen and King.
  Heart of Oak, & chorus

December

8th December 1914
The Battle of the Falkland Islands

On the 2nd September ten cadets from Britannia, the naval training school, aged fifteen years old, joined HMS Monmouth, ready to sail for duty in the South Atlantic. It is said that a marine, echoing perhaps Captain Suckling's letter to Lord Nelson's father on his entry in the navy, remarked that here were some more poor little chaps being sent to be killed. HMS Monmouth was an armoured cruiser built in 1903 of 9800 tons whose effective broadside was only nine 6-inch guns. She was one of four ships destined for the coasts of South America, charged with the task of intercepting and destroying any German warships within that area.

At the outbreak of war in August 1914 the Imperial German Navy had stationed in the west pacific at its colony of Tsing-Tao a squadron of cruisers charged with protecting Germany's colonial interests in that ocean. Their intended function in the event of war was to prey on and destroy Britain's mercantile trade. In Tsing-Tao were the Scharnhorst and the Gneisenau, two heavy cruisers completed in 1907, displacing 11,600 tons and carrying eight 8.2-inch guns and six 5.9-inch guns. In addition there were three light cruisers – the Leipzig, Nurnburg and Emden. They had a displacement of about 3,500 tons, and were built between 1905 and 1909, carrying ten 4.1-inch guns. Elsewhere in the Pacific off the coast of North America was the Dresden, a cruiser of the same class. This squadron was commanded by Admiral Maximilian, Graf von Spee. He was a naval officer of strong character, a convinced Catholic, serene in battle, chivalrous but determined. He faced the problem at the outbreak of war that Japan was allied to Britain and was likely to enter the war. He feared being blockaded in the port of Tsing-Tao and of being destroyed there. Von Spee therefore set out on his mission to hamper Allied trade, at the same time endeavouring to return to Germany. The Emden went south to the Indian Ocean, sinking merchant ships on the way, but was sunk by the HMS Sydney, a light cruiser of the Royal Australian Navy. Von Spee himself decided with the remainder of the squadron to make for South America and return by way of Cape Horn. Tsing-Tao was abandoned and during September he threaded his way through the Pacific Islands, taking up supplies and coaling. By mid-October he was at Easter Island, where Leipzig joined him.

The Admiralty was conscious of the need to dispose of the Eastern Squadron of the Imperial Navy and detached elements of the fleet to cover the two possible routes of return – from the east up the west coast of Africa, or from the west moving north up the coast of South America. The wide stretches of ocean meant that the scouting groups formed had to cover vast expanses of the seas, while the threat of the High Seas Fleet in Kiel forced the retention of the bulk of the Grand Fleet to police the North Sea. A group was formed to go to South American waters. It comprised the HMS Good Hope, an armoured cruiser of 14,100 tons built in 1902 and carrying two 9.2-inch guns and sixteen 6-inch guns. Ninety per cent of the crew were drawn from the naval reserve, and the crew by 1st November had only fired their guns once. The Good Hope was accompanied by HMS Monmouth, and HMS Glasgow, a light cruiser built in 1911 of 4,800 tons displacement, with two 6-inch and ten 4-inch guns, Otranto, a converted liner with eight 4.7-inch guns and HMS Canopus, a pre-dreadnought battleship of 12,950 tons built in 1899 with four 12-inch guns and twelve 6-inch guns. Canopus, too, was manned by reservists with little gunnery practice and had defective engines, which reduced her speed to a maximum of seventeen knots. Glasgow could make twenty-five, the Good Hope twenty-two knots. The scouting group was commanded by Admiral Sir Christopher Cradock. Cradock was an officer moulded in the naval tradition of Lord Nelson, who would have thought it discreditable not to face the enemy with honour. He is reputed to have said that he always hoped that he would be killed in battle or break his neck in the hunting field. In theory his command was stronger than the combined German cruiser squadron, but that depended on the presence of the battleship Canopus. In fact the Admiralty had advised him of the need not to engage without the battleship's assistance, to which he was told to keep close.

The British and German forces steadily moved towards one another. During mid-September Cradock's group patrolled the Atlantic Ocean between the Abrolhos Rocks and the River Plate, only arriving at the Magellan Straits by the end of September. At the time von Spee's squadron was still in mid-Pacific at the Marquisa Islands. Cradock's group steamed on into the South Pacific searching for Dresden on 28th September, with Canopus still far behind at the River Plate. After a fruitless attempt to find her in Nassau Bay they returned to Port Stanley. On 3rd October Glasgow and Monmouth left to join attacks on German trade on the west coast of South America. The Canopus at last arrived on 18th October and the state of the engines was such that five days of repair were needed. Von Spee's squadron had maintained wireless silence as it approached South America, transmitting only from the Leipzig after it left the Easter Islands. It left there on 18th October. Cradock sailed from the Falklands on the 22nd to search, as he thought, for the Leipzig. Canopus followed on 23rd October. By 26th October von Spee had reached the Juan Fernandez Isles and left there on the 28th. Cradock was off the Vallenor Roads in Good Hope and he began to move north. The gap was inexorably closing as von Spee moved south-west and Craddock north. Canopus was far to the south having only reached Puntas Arenas on 27th October. By 1st November Cradock had collected up his squadron and was at Coronel. It was heavy weather and it was at 4.20 pm that Glasgow saw smoke on the horizon on the starboard bow and thought that she had met up with the Leipzig, which incidentally was the nearest German ship and had by 4.30 pm identified Glasgow. Cradock was told by signal of the presence of the Scharnhorst and Gneisenau and had the choice of pressing on or, knowing Canopus was three hundred miles distant, turning to draw off the Germans towards his protecting battleship. In the naval canon of history from Tudor times flight was not honourable, and there were cases of superior forces being defeated by inferior ones. Craddock decided to fight. At 5 pm he ordered the ships into line and at 6.40 pm the line turned to face the enemy between them and the sun. At 6.18 pm Cradock signalled action; the van of the two forces were only two miles apart and as the sun sank, at 12,300 yards the 8.2-inch guns of Scharnhorst and Gneisenau opened fire with deadly accuracy. At that range only the Good Hope with its 9.2-inch guns could reach the target.

By the time of the third salvo, Good Hope had these guns out of action. Monmouth was hit by the Gneisenau, going on fire. As the other ships closed, the British returned the fire, which in the smoke was questionably accurate. The heavy seas made firing the guns a struggle, and Good Hope and Monmouth were continually hit. By 7.35 pm Cradock had closed to 5,500 yards; Good Hope had suffered multiple hits and was burning along its length, while the fore turret of Monmouth was gone. At 7.50 pm there was an ear-rending explosion between the mainmast and the funnel, flames rising to two hundred feet, and the Good Hope quickly foundered with all on board. Monmouth was disabled, down by the bows and listing. The damaged Glasgow, her port guns out of action, turned away to use her speed to outrun the Germans and to warn Canopus. As she went north-west, Monmouth continued to fire on Dresden until her unprotected deck was torn open.

Continuous firing was seen from Glasgow until 9.20 pm. The Monmouth finally capsized and sank, her flags still flying. All the crew were lost. Only the ten midshipmen survived, as they had been transferred to another ship at St. Vincent on the way south. Cradock had ordered Otranto away and she fled through the night. At 10.30 pm von Spee abandoned the chase: he had won a naval victory for Germany and momentarily commanded the South Pacific. In Valparaiso he was welcomed by the German ambassador and the German community. At a dinner a German resident proposed a toast, 'Damnation to the Royal Navy.' Von Spee stood, raised his glass and firmly stated, 'I drink to the memory of a gallant and honourable foe.'

It was not until 4th November that news of this disaster began to electrify the Government, the Admiralty and then the nation. Winston Churchill, the First Lord of the Admiralty, and Lord Fisher, the First Sea Lord, acted with speed. HMS Carnarvon, an armoured cruiser built in 1904 of 10,850 tons with four 7.5-inch guns and six 6-inch guns, and HMS Cornwall, an armoured cruiser of similar displacement built in 1903 with fourteen 6-inch guns, were ordered to the Falkland Islands. In addition two battle cruisers were detached to go south to strengthen the group based at the islands. They were Inflexible and Invincible, both built in 1908, of 17,250 tons displacement with eight 12-inch guns and sixteen 4-inch guns. Admiral Sir Doveton Sturdee was appointed to command the squadron. They sailed on 11th November under orders of the First Lord, with the workmen doing repairs on board. The Kent, similar to the Cornwall, and the Bristol, a light cruiser similar to Glasgow, were also added. By the 24th the German Navy were aware that the battle cruisers were off the Abrolhos Rocks, but thereafter Inflexible and Invincible shut down their signals. On 7th December they with their associated armoured and light cruisers reached Port Stanley, where they intended to coal.

After his visit to Valparaiso on 3rd November von Spee sailed to join Leipzig and Dresden at Mas a Fuera, where he anchored for ten days. Berlin instructed him to break for home and he decided that he should return rounding the Horn. On the 21st the German flotilla arrived at St Quentin Bay, having moved south with the supply ships Baden and Santa Isabel. He stayed five days coaling, loading even the decks with coal. Once more von Spee lingered only to meet on leaving weather of great violence, with gales and mountainous waves. The deck coal had to be jettisoned and it was not until 28th November that the storms abated. On 1st December Cape Horn was on the beam and he made for Picton Island, where he anchored. There on the 6th he conferred with his captains and told them that he proposed to attack the Falkland Islands. He said that he had intelligence that there were no battleships at the islands. The captains of the Gneisenau, Dresden and Leipzig opposed the project, arguing that the flotilla should take a mid-ocean route away from the islands. Von Spee rejected their advice.

After the defeat at Coronel Glasgow, Canopus and the Otranto had returned to the Falklands. The Governor and Captain Heathcote Grant of the Canopus resolved that they had to prepare for an attack on Port Stanley. The Governor raised from the islanders a militia; Canopus was beached to protect the harbour and some of her guns landed on shore. On the day of von Spee's decision to attack, Port Stanley and Port William were not protected by any overpowering force, which as has been seen arrived the next day.

At 2.30 am on 8th December von Spee sighted the islands and Gneisenau and Nurnberg were sent forward. By 8.30 am the latter were some five miles east of Cape Pembroke with the rest of the squadron fifteen miles behind. Gneisenau observed the signal masts on shore and a column of smoke from the Macedonia. Beyond the headland smoke was seen, but it was assumed that the supplies of coal were being fired, as had occurred at Tahiti on the journey across the Pacific. Only at 9.00 am were the masts of the assembled warships seen. Gneisenau signalled to von Spee that they had identified the presence of three county-class cruisers, one light cruiser and Canopus with a smaller ship. The presence of the battle cruisers was not identified. Von Spee steamed on to the attack.

When the German flotilla was seen, Sturdee's ships were coaling. Orders were given to raise steam. By 8 am only Carnarvon and Glasgow were coaled; the colliers were with Inflexible and Invincible, Kent, Cornwall and Bristol were un-coaled. Sturdee ordered the ships to move when twelve knots could be raised. There was nothing to be done but wait and Sturdee went to breakfast. Kent was able to leave at 8.45 am At 9.20 am Gneisenau and Nurnburg trained their guns on the signal stations and Canopus responded at 11,500 yards, obtaining a hit at the base of a funnel on Gneisenau. By this time the presence of the masts of the battle cruisers had been seen and von Spee ordered Gneisenau to turn away from the harbour. He then set course for east by north at full speed, sending Baden and Isabel south-east.

It was not until between 9.45 and 10.00 am that Invincible, Inflexible, Carnarvon and Glasgow left. Cornwall and Bristol were to leave later yet. There then began a race to catch the German cruisers as they turned south-east. The British battle cruisers were five knots faster than Gneisenau and Scharnhorst and they pushed on following a parallel course. The Germans were twenty miles away and were steaming south in the hope that they could lose themselves in bad weather and mist. For a time the battle cruisers and Glasgow slowed so that Cornwall and Carnarvon could catch up, but Sturdee decided to revert to attack by Invincible, Inflexible and Glasgow. There was a clear sky and a heaving low sea. At 12.47 the battle cruisers opened fire on Leipzig, the rear ship, but the Germans were on the starboard bow and firing was confined to the two bow turrets. Two salvos were fired every half-minute but finding the range was difficult and visibility obscured by smoke. At 1.20 pm von Spee ordered Leipzig, Dresden and Nurnberg to leave the line and try to escape south. Von Spee turned north-east pursued by the battle cruisers: Inflexible and Invincible engaged in an exchange with Gneisenau and Scharnhorst and at 1.44 pm Invincible was hit. Sturdee decided that the accuracy of his fire was not aided by von Spee having the lee position. He decided to cross the line of the Germans, if he could. Von Spee frustrated that attempt by turning south, but remained in range, while the British were beyond the range of the Germans. At 2.45 pm von Spee turned to bring the British within the range of his 9.2-inch guns at 10,000 yards.

It was at that moment that a fully rigged French brigantine came between the fighting warships, her captain, ignorant of the war, blithely sailing the blue sea as the guns thundered, but rapidly went about as he came upon the fight. The German fire was accurate, but both Gneisenqu and Scharnhorst had suffered. Von Spee resumed his southward path, but Sturdee hung on with the battle cruisers. By 3.00 pm Gneisenau had lost some of its boiler rooms and was on fire, while Scharnhorst was holed fore and aft and on fire in places. By 3.30 pm Scharnhorst had lost her third funnel, and her port guns were out of action. She stopped firing and turning towards Inflexible was seen to be listing heavily to port, with her funnels at varied angles. At 4.04 pm she healed over and at 4.17 pm slid with her ensigns flying under the sea. Von Spee had signalled to Gneisenau to escape, but the damage to her boiler rooms had reduced her speed to sixteen knots. She continued to fire her salvoes vigorously as she went south-west. The smoke over the seas made it difficult for the battle cruisers and Carnarvon, which had joined up, to keep the line. At 5.15 pm Invincible was struck, as Gneiseanu fought on, but at 5.30 pm she stopped. She was listing heavily to starboard. Sturdee stopped firing, but then Gneisenau fired one of her guns. The bombardment re-commenced until 5.50 pm. By then, thoroughly wrecked, she began slowly to settle and at 6.00 pm disappeared, her propellers turning. Sturdee ordered the boats out to pick up survivors, but many had been damaged in the fighting, and Sturdee was particularly angry with Carnarvon whose rescue effort was non-existent. Unhappily few out of the 600 crew were saved.

When von Spee at 1.20 pm had ordered Dresden, Nurnberg and Leipzig to diverge south, Glasgow, Cornwall and Kent were detailed to follow them. Of the three German cruisers Dresden was in the van and the Leipzig in the rear. Although it had been intended that Glasgow should engage Dresden, Cornwall Leipzig and Kent, Nurnberg, early in the chase Glasgow and the slower Cornwall joined in. At 2.50 pm the Glasgow with its 6-inch guns engaged Leipzig at 12,000 yards. Captain Haun, his ship slowed by worn engines and boilers, and knowing that there was only a slight chance of escape, turned to bring to bear his 4-inch guns. In an hour-long fight Glasgow was hit twice. Cornwall gradually drew up and Leipzig concentrated her fire on her. At 4.17 pm Cornwall was to open fire on Leipzig, firing broadsides at 8,275 yards.

The engaged ships pressed south and the weather began to deteriorate, with drizzle and mist. By 6.00 pm at 800 yards Leipzig still bombarded Cornwall, although she was burning near the mainmast and forward. By 7.00 pm she was beginning to slow and her firing began to weaken. At 7.50 Captain Haun ordered the last torpedoes to be fired. They missed their mark and Leipzig fell silent. Both Cornwall and Glasgow approached, ceasing fire. The colours were still flying, so they fired again at short range. Haun had ordered the crew to abandon ship and they were mustering on the foredeck, since aft the ship was consumed by flames. Many were hit and wounded, but the British almost immediately ceased firing and the lowering of boats was ordered to affect a rescue. Leipzig began to roll as darkness fell and the crew were tipped into the icy South Atlantic. At 8.30 pm the cruiser healed to port and went down by the bows, carrying her captain and with flags flying. Only seven officers and eleven men were rescued.

Kent went after Nurnberg. To raise the speed to twenty-five knots, the wood fitments of the cruiser were ripped out to fuel the boilers. By 5.00 pm Nurnberg was close enough to open fire on Kent with its rear guns. Firing was accurate at 12,000 yards, but the two cruisers started to move on convergent courses, the range reducing. At 7,000 yards Nurnberg brought its port guns to bear and at

6,000 yards Kent fired off its starboard broadsides. Nurnberg began to go on fire forward and her pace slowed. By 6.35 pm she had stopped and ceased firing. Kent went towards her, ceased firing but saw her flags flying. She opened fire again and five minutes later Nurnberg lowered her colours. She was stern down and listing to starboard. Kent put out her undamaged boats but at 7.26 pm Nurnberg healed over and sank. Only twelve of the crew were recovered from the sea, of which only seven survived. Among the lost was Otto von Spee, the son of the Admiral. Kent stayed until 9 pm attempting a rescue, but then left to return to the Falklands. She had in the fight narrowly escaped destruction, when a flash from a shell, hitting the turret casement, went down the hoist. A Royal Marine Sergeant, Charles Mayes, removed a charge from the hoist and flooded the compartment, preventing the fire spreading to the mezzanine. His action was recognised by the award of the Conspicuous Gallantry Medal.

Glasgow being diverted from the chase for Dresden meant that Dresden was able to slip away in the raining, misty weather to return to the Pacific well south of Cape Horn. From time to time she anchored at various locations along the coast of Chile but was without the support of the supply ships, Baden and St Isabel, which had been sunk by Bristol and Macedonia on 8th December. Invincible returned to England, but the rest of the flotilla searched for Dresden until 29th December. On 14th February the Deutschland and the supply ship, Sierra Cordoba, were sailing north two hundred miles off the Chilean coast. In early March the Admiralty picked up a signal arranging for a rendezvous between Dresden and a collier. On 8th March she was found by Kent and as the sea fog dispersed was seen twelve miles to the west. Deutschland fled and was lost in the darkness in the evening. Kent was short of coal, but a further signal was intercepted that Deutschland had anchored at Mas a Tierra in Cumberland Bay on 9th March. She had 100 tons of coal left and the Imperial Naval Headquarters advised that she should accept internment. On 14th March Glasgow, Kent and Orama arrived and in breach of Chilean neutrality opened fire at 8.50 am The fire was returned at first, but Captain Ludecke raised the white flag. Firing ceased and the German crew began to abandon ship. Lieutenant Canaris was sent to the Glasgow to protest the attack because the ship was interned. A prolonged discussion took place, while Captain Ludecke prepared to scuttle Dresden. He followed his officers to shore and at 10.45 am the magazine blew up, the warship listed and sank, flying the white flag and the Imperial Naval colours. The Germans on shore and the British shipboard cheered as she vanished.

Sir Doveton Sturdee was made a Baronet, the first for a naval action since 1811, and given a grant of £10,000. Lt. Canaris was to rise high in the German Navy, and by the Second World War was an Admiral and head of the Intelligence section in the High Command. Despite that position he was a sympathiser with the resistance against Hitler from 1938 onwards. In April 1945, after having been arrested, he was shot by the Gestapo.

10th December 1941
The Relief of Tobruk

The Fuehrer, Adolf Hitler, and the German High Command (OKW) were slow to grasp the importance of the Mediterranean area to the survival of Britain and the Empire. As early as 26th September 1940 Grand Admiral Raedar, the Commander in Chief of the German Navy, met Hitler in Berlin and tried to impress on him that the Mediterranean was the 'pivot of the Empire' and that together with Vichy France early steps should be taken to secure Gibraltar and the Suez Canal before the United States entered the war. He also argued that from Egypt it would be possible to strike north to Iraq and Turkey. The Fuehrer in general agreed, but his mind was already concentrated on a campaign in Russia. In late October he set out to discuss these matters with General Franco, Marshal Petain and the Duce, Benito Mussolini. He met Franco at Hendaye on the Spanish frontier. Hitler expected gratitude from him for the help given to the nationalists in the Spanish Civil War, but the Caudillo, perhaps influenced by the failure of the plan to invade Britain, was cautious. He agreed to co-operate, but only on terms that demanded of Germany large commitments of weapons, supplies, tanks and guns and considerable areas of the French Empire as a reward. He signed no agreement to give access to Gibraltar and Hitler left Hendaye in his train to meet Marshal Petain the next day without any commitment on the part of Franco. He was to say later that he would prefer to have his teeth extracted rather than to have another meeting with the Caudillo.

Petain and Vichy France, however, ran true to French form. Hitler was able to leave with a secret agreement to the effect that the Axis Powers and France had an identical interest in seeing the defeat of England accomplished as soon as possible, and that the French Government would support to the best of their ability measures by the Axis powers to that end. On 28h October Hitler alighted from his train at Florence to be surprised by a jubilant Duce announcing that that day his armies in Albania had attacked Greece. The Fuehrer was furious, as he worried about his future position in the Balkans when he attacked Russia. Within a week the Italian armies were retreating and the Greeks were to manage to keep 27 Italian Divisions at bay with only six divisions of troops.

The plan for a campaign in the Western Mediterranean remained however a matter of discussion. Plan Felix was debated, to take Gibraltar and the Canary and Cape Verde islands. The French fleet in Toulon would be freed under the Armistice terms to fight in North Africa. The German Navy continued to press for a strategy to deal with Britain in the Mediterranean first, before an attack on Russia. They urged the sending of troops, aeroplanes and weapons for a campaign in this theatre, having a low opinion of the Italians. Indeed, General von Thoma had been sent on an inspection to Marshal Graziani to assess the situation. He had reported that four Panzer Divisions would be needed in Libya and cover by the Lufwaffe. He was not persuaded that the Italian armies were effective fighting forces. Hitler told the Navy that he might consider a campaign after the Italians reached Mersa Matruh in September 1940 seventy miles east from the position reached by their invasion. He promised once more to approach General Franco about Gibraltar, but before his request could be made the North African situation was transformed by the Battle of Sidi Barrani (15th December 1940) and The Victory at Beda Fomm (7th February 1941). His request reached General Franco on the day of the Italian surrender at Beda Fomm. The General replied that circumstances had changed since the meeting at Hendaye. The project for the attack in the West Mediterranean dissolved, because the Fuehrer had a new concern, the need to support the Italians in order to keep Italy in the war, given their failure in Greece and the surrender at Sidi Barrani.

At a meeting on 8th to 9th January at the Berghof, near Berchtesgaden, he resolved to support Italy in North Africa with anti-tank formations and Lufwaffe squadrons, and to send reinforcements to Tripoli. The Fuehrer also expressed his intent to invade Greece through Bulgaria and Yugoslavia. 26th March 1940 was to be the date to cross the frontier. The further surrender of Marshal Graziani's army at Beda Fomm led him to commit formations including heavy tanks, anti-tank guns, and heavy artillery. On 15th February 1941 Feldmarschall Rommel was appointed to command the German Afrika Korps to be sent to Libya, and the supporting Italian divisions. A dedicated soldier of talent for armoured warfare, as he had shown in France in 1940, Winston Churchill was to say of him in Parliament in January 1942, 'we have a very daring and skilful opponent against us, and, may I say across the havoc of war, a great general.' While he remained nominally under the supreme command of the Italians, Rommel with his army, which started to arrive in mid-February, was to shape the war in Libya for the next two years.

Fieldmarshal Wavell and Admiral Cunningham, who commanded the ground forces and the navy in the Mediterranean and near East, were despite the army's success in January 1941 beset with difficulties arising from their shortage of resources, the absence of significant air support and the extent of their potential obligations. Although the British stood on a line one hundred and fifty miles south of Benghazi (at Agheila) holding Cyrenaica, Malta needed to be protected, Axis supplies by sea to Libya had to be disrupted, the Suez Canal and Egypt held, the Italians in East Africa, who threatened the Red Sea route to Egypt, dislodged, Greece strengthened and any threat from the Vichy French in Syria to be kept under surveillance. In terms of naval power the Italian Navy remained a substantial threat. Apart from the four battleships – Warspite, Malaya, Royal Sovereign and Ramillies – and the aircraft carrier, Eagle, about to be replaced by Illustrious, the Italians had a preponderance of three to one. They could put to sea seven cruisers with 8-inch guns, twelve with 6-inch guns, 36 modern and 19 old destroyers The posting of Luftwaffe bombers, dive bombers and fighters to Sicily and Libya however, made the central Mediterranean impossible to use. The last convoy for two years came through in January 1941, protected in the west Mediterranean by Force H from Gibraltar, and was met by the main body of the east Mediterranean fleet just east of Sicily. It was there subjected to heavy bomber attack by Junker 87s and 88s and Illustrious, the protecting aircraft carrier was seriously damaged. Some cruisers were also damaged and the Southampton sunk. Illustrious went temporarily to Malta, where it was the target of bombing raids, and then back to Alexandria for a long period of repair. It was replaced by Formidable. The closing of the western route to Egypt made it imperative to protect the country through the Red Sea and the destruction of the Italian position in East Africa became urgent.

Britain had given a guarantee to Greece in 1939, as with Poland, to accord her assistance if attacked, should aid be requested. No such request was made until the spring of 1941. In accordance with Adolf Hitler's decisions in January to aid Mussolini and the Italians, the Fuehrer sought the agreement of Bulgaria and Yugoslavia to the passage of his armies for an assault on Greece. The former agreed, but the latter having accepted such an agreement, the people rose against the Prince Regent, installed the young King Peter on the throne and repudiated the consent. The Fuehrer, in a fury at action which he considered an insult to him and the German Reich, ordered the invasion of Yugoslavia, diverting armed forces bound for Russia and delaying his strike against the Soviet Union by three weeks, a main consequence of which, it is said, was the failure to take Moscow in December 1941 before the fighting armies became engulfed by bitter snow and ice.

Fieldmarshal Wavell, in order to honour the request by Greece, ordered over half the army in North Africa to Greece, comprising an armoured brigade, the New Zealand Division and part of an Australian division, amounting to 53,000 men. The North Africa force was left seriously weakened. The Agheila line was manned by a brigade of the 2nd Armoured Division and part of its Support Group and the 9th Australian Division, save one brigade held at Tobruk. The tank and transport position had been paired down for Greece and the troops were not experienced in desert warfare. That warfare was carried on in the area between the coast and the great sand sea to the south, in country which was open, mainly uninhabited, uncultivated, and comprising rock and scrub. Tank movement through it was more akin to the manoeuvre of ships on the open oceans than of vehicles on land. Static positions could be readily turned or evaded and the key to success was swiftness and mobility. The role of Rommel had been conceived by OKW in Berlin as defensive, but after forward reconnaissance and before approval of his plans by the High Command, on 31st March he struck.

On arrival he had persuaded the Italians to move their forces from the defence of Tripoli to the south-east of the Gulf of Sirte. Berlin had ordered him to await the arrival of the 15th Panzer Division with its heavy tanks before seeking to take Benghazi, and he submitted a plan for future action to OKW envisaging a two-pronged attack, the first along the coast north towards to Benghazi and a second north-east through the desert to Msus, Mekili and Derna on the coast. The need of the British to avoid encirclement, if the plan was successful, would compel the evacuation of Benghazi and the coast west of Derna. An essential role for the Luftwaffe was to deprive the British armoured troops and transport of fuel, to inhibit their movement by bombing their carriers and depots. Using his judgement of the situation, Rommel did not wait for the approval of this plan before it was implemented. The inexperienced troops of the 9th Australian Division (less one brigade in Greece), which had now come under the command of Lieutenant General Neame, who had been awarded the Victoria Cross for single-handedly holding up a German counter-attack on a section of trench at Neuve – Chapelle in 1914 for an hour, standing up in machine-gun fire to throw bombs at the attackers, were pushed in and for the next two days were to make a fighting withdrawal from El Agheila.

On 2nd April Rommel took Agedabia, driving out the Support Groups of the 2nd Armoured Division, who retreated to Antelat, thirty-five miles further north. The armoured forces had become disorganised and were suffering heavy losses. On 4th April 21st Panzer Division (5th Light) were reported at Msus and General Morshead and the Australians began the retreat along the coast from Benghazi towards Derna. Wavell had gone to the front and had asked O'Connor to return to command the armoured Division with Neame. The presence of the German armoured force at Msus made retreat along the coast imperative. 3rd Armoured Brigade were ordered with the 2nd Regiment of Indian Motorised Infantry to Meliki, but their effectiveness was slight, having been improvised from diverse sources. The 2nd Armoured Division dissolved by reason of breakdown and bombing: only parts of it and its headquarters arrived at Meliki and on the 6th the 21st Panzer and the Italian Ariete Armoured Division surrounded the place.

On that night coming upon the slow long columns retreating down the main coast road Generals O'Connor and Neame in their staff car turned off on to a track to bypass the main column and became stuck in yet another slowing-moving line of transport. A German desert patrol with motorcyclists ran along the column, only stopping at their car, and both were captured. Because of petrol shortage the remnant of the 3rd Armoured Brigade had gone on to Derna; it comprised just twelve tanks. The rest of the 2nd Division was attacked at Meliki on the 7th and received orders to withdraw. A breakout from Meliki was tried on 8th April but only the 1st Royal Horse Artillery and some Indian troops escaped the cordon. General Wavell was faced with a dissolving and retreating army. He decided that it was essential to defend Tobruk and on the 8th he flew there to discuss the position with General Laverack, an Australian General placed temporarily in command. At the same time a brigade of the 7th Australian Division were sent there, together with some tanks.

On the way back to Cairo after nightfall his plane was forced to crash land in the desert after the failure of an engine. Neither the Commander-in-Chief nor his staff knew where they were. Secret papers were burnt and the party waited long hours in the dark, not knowing whether the area in which they were was in British or German hands. At last the lights of a lorry were seen approaching; it was seen with relief to be a British patrol and Wavell returned to Cairo. The 9th Australian Division reached Tobruk in its retreat on 9th April and by the 11th Tobruk was totally invested outside the defensive lines which the Italians had constructed. On 12th April Bardia fell and Rommel and his armoured divisions reached Sollum on the frontier, where they stopped. Their resources of water and fuel were at an end. In twelve days however, they had reversed the triumphs of December and January, and Cyrenaica, apart from Tobruk, was again in Axis hands. The armies of each side needed reformation, re-equipment and reinforcement.

Immediately after Tobruk was invested, Rommel directed a strong assault on the lines, but with stoic resolution and firmness the Australians and British held the attack and repulsed it. That was the beginning of a siege which lasted 242 days to December 1941. The Germans and Italians had to commit four Italian Divisions and four German Battalions to the task of containing and trying to take the fortress which Tobruk became. Thus, they amassed there twice the strength of the garrison for the assault and deployed around the perimeters heavy guns and tanks and armoured heavy vehicles. For the first month, in addition to ground attacks and bombardment, the Luftwaffe struck hard with their Stuka dive bombers, Heinkels and Messerschmidts, but with the withdrawal of the air force for use elsewhere the air attack lessened in extent to be replaced by constant artillery bombardment and intermittent attacks on the perimeter. A major attack was made on 1st May after the arrival of 15th Panzer Division, but without success. The buildings, port installations and even the ground itself were demolished and cracked apart. The garrison under General Morshead, with all the endurance, fighting spirit and courage of its largely Australian force, hung on.

Much of life had to be carried on in underground cellars and bunkers or mere desert holes, leading to the sneer of Lord Haw-Haw (William Joyce) about the Rats of Tobruk. There was a shortage of water and fuel. Intense heat, burning sands and the always present mass of desert flies added to the horror and burden of the constant bombardment. Sleep could only be snatched. There were no facilities for leisure – no amusements, pictures or shows. Beer and spirits were unavailable. Entertainment was reduced to a swim in the ocean or a game of cricket on the beach. Successive strong assaults continued on the lines and some penetrated, but were thrown back. In response the garrison made regular probes behind the enemy lines to harass them and, as the German High Command thought, in order to test points for a breakout. Initially there was little anti-aircraft gun protection, and the defenders were driven to use Lewis-guns to fire on aircraft. By September anti-aircraft guns had been supplied in number, almost as many as on Malta. The continuance of supply of weapons, ammunition, food, water and fuel oil and petrol to the garrison was the key to its survival. As so often in British history the Royal Navy was to secure the existence of the nation's armies.

The 300 sea-mile route from Alexandria to Tobruk along the coast had to be maintained against constant air attack. After the middle of April there was no effective air cover in this theatre of operations, as the air force was called to deal with the difficulties in Greece, Crete and the campaign in Syria. Only thirteen fighter planes were left in the desert. All supply ships were substantially unprotected and it meant that supply could only be made by units of the Inshore Squadron, - destroyers, river boats and even schooners. Convoys were out of the question. Even when the long voyage was ending vessels had to enter Tobruk through a channel between minefields, and the Luftwaffe constantly dropped mines into it and awaited the arrival of ships at the channel's mouth. Minesweepers based in Tobruk had to work to clear the passage in. At the end of April two small merchant ships, Fiona and Chabla, maintaining the supply, were sunk. Thereafter, apart from the schooners, destroyers had to be used for reaching the garrison to meet its needs and evacuate the wounded. Only on moonless nights could water and petrol carriers be sent in.

The destroyers left by day for Tobruk, ending their journey as dusk fell and leaving before dawn, in order to protect themselves from air attack while loading and unloading. The aim was to maintain a rate of 70 tons of supplies a day. The valiant small destroyer Ladybird on 12th May was sunk by dive bombers in the shallows approaching Tobruk. The commander of the South Staffordshire Regiment cabled naval headquarters, having met the officers and men, the regiment's sympathy at the loss of this gallant ship. Sir Andrew Cunningham, the Admiral commanding in the Mediterranean, records how he was deeply moved by the pride and fine spirit of two young men wounded aboard, who lay in bed side by side in hospital with only one leg unamputated between them. The seamen of the Royal Navy were to have to continue to bear such sacrifices as night by night they ran their voyages of supply to the staunch fighting men in Tobruk. By August the rate of supply had risen to an average of 150 tons per day. The German heavy batteries fired daily on the harbour and four or five U-Boats lay in wait along the route in Bardia. In September, to strengthen the stream of supplies, ten landing craft were pressed into service. Despite their character a surface battle was fought with a U-Boat and they carried during their use 2,100 tons of stores to Tobruck, and 55 tanks and guns; of the 10 employed 6 were ultimately lost.

Rommel, despite interruptions in supply as a result of naval and air action from Malta, constantly pressed Feldmarschall Keitel at OKW to send weapons, men and aircraft to enable him to eliminate Tobruk and to continue his campaign into Egypt. Keitel was in constant attendance on the Fuehrer, earning him the nickname of Lakaital (lakai being in German a lackey). Prince von Bismarck, commenting on his attitude to North Africa, thought him an 'imbecile', and even Adolf Hitler dismissed him as 'a man with the mind of a movie doorman.' The High Command had two factors to weigh, first the Balkans involvement occasioned by the attack in Greece in April and May and second the strike against Russia in June, which meant that German resources were the subject of claims other than North Africa, which Keitel saw as a sphere of little to negligible importance. OKW admired Rommel's audacity but were sanguine, given his long and difficult communications from Sicily, about his chances of success. Keitel and General Cavallero, the Italian Army Commander-in-Chief, conferred twice in the course of the summer and agreed that until strong reinforcements of armour and heavy guns could be provided for Rommel, a move forward could not be made, certainly not until Tobruk was taken. Rommel was urged to gain Tobruk, but a major campaign had to wait.

The British made two efforts in the summer to relieve Tobruk. The first on 15th and 16th May near the coast was carried out with such weak forces that, although the Halfaya pass was taken on to the escarpment near Sollom, the attack could not be sustained and the pass was retaken on 27th May by Rommel with 160 tanks. The second attempt, Operation Battleaxe, was to take place on 15th June. A convoy in May carrying 295 tanks and 53 Hurricane aircraft was escorted through the Mediterranean first by Force H from Gibraltar and subsequently by the eastern Mediterranean force with the Illustrious. It was subjected near Sicily to fierce bombing attack and one ship was lost with 50 tanks, but the remainder arrived n Alexandria on 12th May. It took two weeks to unload them and they then had to be fitted with sand filters and the crews acclimatised to the new 'I' class tanks. The plan envisaged a three-pronged attack, one by the 4th Indian Division to recapture the Halfaya Pass, another by 22nd Guards Brigade and 4th Armoured to recapture Capuzzo, and in the south a move to the west of Sidi Omar of 7th Armoured, which had been reconstituted. Rommel held for the defence of the frontier the 15th Panzer Division with heavy 50-mm and 88-mm guns. The 21st Panzer (5th Light) was held back to watch Tobruk. The battle started on 15th June. There was fierce fighting. The 11th Indian Brigade failed however to capture the Halfaya pass and 7th Armoured was reduced to 22 tanks. On the 16th the latter was raided in the rear by 21st Panzer which had come up. 15th Panzer Division counter-attacked and forced 4th Armoured back to Capuzzo. Rommel planned for the 17th a Cannae-like pincer attack and the threat was such that the British armoured forces were forced to retreat to avoid being cut off. 64 out of 100 of the heavy 'I' tanks were lost and 27 cruiser tanks. Winston Churchill, who had from London pressed for this operation and was disappointed with the outcome, had Fieldmarshal Wavell replaced, and on 1st July Sir Claud Auchinleck became Commander-in-Chief for the Near East.

While these events were in progress, on 8th March the British force arrived in Greece, consisting of the 2nd New Zealand Division under General Freyberg, VC, part of the 6th Australian Division and an armoured brigade from 2nd Armoured Division. Events moved quickly; the Germans swept through Yugoslavia, where its army of 28 divisions surrendered at Sarajevo, and invaded Greece on 6th April. The Greek and British armies were forced to fall back and on 24th and 25th the British troops were evacuated by the navy from the beaches of Attica, abandoning their equipment. Out of some 57,000 landed, 43,000 were taken off over three nights, although 12 Hurricane fighters having been lost, there was little air cover. Part of the force was taken to Egypt and part landed in Crete, amounting to 27,000. The King of Greece and his Government, unlike the French Government, went into exile to finish the fight. On 28th May the Germans attacked Crete by air with paratroops, taking the airport and landing gliders. Freyberg and his New Zealanders were the core of the defence, although Freyberg complained that without air and naval support the defence could not be sustained. He was to be proved to be correct. Because of the loss of equipment, there were only 38 heavy anti-aircraft guns, the artillery were largely without guns and the tanks amounted to 9. The divided British forces in three centres with only limited inter-communication along the main east-west route on the island, were forced to retire to the south through the mountain passes. On 27th May Wavell agreed to the evacuation of the island, the final effort being made on 1st June.

18,000 men were evacuated. Some 11,835 were made prisoners, of which over 5,200 were Australians and New Zealanders. The Royal Navy under heavy air attack in these operations sustained substantial damage; one aircraft carrier, three battleships, six cruisers and seven destroyers were in fact damaged and three cruisers and six destroyers sunk. Elsewhere in East Africa, after a campaign begun in November 1940, the Duke of Aosta and the Italian armies surrendered in May 1941, although some limited resistance remained. In June a successful campaign in Syria defeated the Vichy French, but had required six squadrons of fighter aircraft, four of bombers and 200 tanks. While the Aegean was now in German and Italian hands, the Commander-in-Chief of the army could now concentrate on the problem of once more achieving success in the Libyan desert. Auchlinleck was clear about the need to build up his armoured forces and infantry again, re-equip them and to have proper air cover for the ground forces, but he remained under pressure from London to act. Rommel and the Italians were equally clear about the need to re-supply themselves before a further campaign, and both sides devoted themselves to that task. Throughout the summer and autumn the Germans maintained supplies (on average) to North Africa of over 100,000 tons a month; from July 1941, however, the percentage which arrived safely fell from 80% to 20% in November, due to the attacks made largely from Malta on German and Italian shipping. The British were to rebuild their weapons and manpower by using the route round the Cape of Good Hope and with the successful outcomes in Syria and East Africa were able to concentrate the army in Egypt. 600 tanks and 800 guns were brought in. As the autumn drew on both sides were to prepare to renew the attack, centring on the siege at Tobruk. Before that occurred however, political upheavals were to affect the garrison there.

Mr Robert Menzies, the Australian Prime Minister, had visited London in the summer, been fully informed of the war situation and signified his acceptance of the deployment of the Australian divisions which were involved in the defence of Tobruk. His Government had however a majority of only one in the Commonwealth Parliament and on 28th August he was defeated and resigned. The new Australian Government of Mr Fadden, who led the Labour party, immediately demanded the withdrawal of the Australian troops from the garrison and their return to Australia. Such an action, quite apart from its effect on the resources of the North African army, and given the desperate supply and transport difficulties from Alexandria to Tobruk, involved serious logistic problems and danger to those likely to be involved. Winston Churchill tried to dissuade Fadden from this course without success, and with heavy heart in mid-September he reluctantly agreed. On 29th September Mr Fadden was defeated in Parliament and a new Labour Government under Mr Curtin took power. Churchill tried again but the new government was equally opposed to the Australians remaining. Despite the dangers, the evacuation and replacement of troops was mounted in September and October. Two fast minesweepers, the Abdiel and Latona, which had arrived in July, were put to use with the other vessels employed and in the two-month period of this exchange, while heavy fighting still proceeded, the Navy in September replaced 6,000 Australian troops with men from Syria, taking in 6,300 troops and 2,100 tons of stores, and in October in a fortnight brought back 7,900 troops to Egypt and landed 1,400 tons of stores and 7,100 troops in Tobruk. The garrison now comprised the 70th Infantry Division, a Polish Brigade and a further regiment of tanks.

Sir Archibald Wavell appointed General Cunningham, who had commanded the campaign in East Africa so successfully and was the brother of Admiral Cunningham, the naval C-in-C, as commander of the operation to relieve Tobruk. He was however not experienced in armoured warfare in the desert. The operation (Operation Crusader) planned had a twin objective; first to destroy the armoured force commanded by Rommel and second to raise the siege at Tobruk. The main coastal road of Cyrenaica ran from Tobruk, where the garrison held the old Italian twenty-one mile perimeter, to Bardia and then turned south to Capuzzo and Sollum, beyond which was the Halfaya pass, one of the few routes which penetrated the escarpment which ran from south of Tobruk to Sollum, and which was an obstacle to tanks and armoured vehicles. Beyond the pass stood the British lines, which ran southwards to Sidi Omar and Sterferzan. Thirty miles further south along the line was Fort Madalena, the headquarters of the 8th Army, as the force had become. From the latter there ran a track crossing the British line through the desert villages of Gabr Salah and El Gubi west and then north to El Adem to the south of Tobruk. A branch went on west to Bir Hacheim. From Capuzzo in the north a middle track (Trigh Capuzzo) ran west through Sidi Aziz, Gasr El Amd to Sidi Razegh, south-east of Tobruk, where the focus of the battle was to be. Between Sidi Razegh and Tobruk was the small settlement of El Duda. This whole seventy-five mile front was to be the theatre in which a three-week battle was fought.

The British forces comprised two corps, the XIIIth Corps on the right north of Sherferzen to the sea, and the XXXth corps assembled in the area of Fort Madalena. The XIIIth corps comprised three brigades of the 2nd New Zealand Division under Major-General Freyberg VC, three brigades of Major-General Messervy's 4th Indian Division, each brigade comprising one British or Ghurkha battalion and two Indian, supported by the 1st Tank Army Brigade. The XXXth corps in the south on the left flank under Lieutenant General Willoughby Norrie consisted of the British 7th Armoured Division (comprising the 4th, 7th and 22nd Armoured Brigades), together with the infantry and artillery of 7th Support Group commanded by Brigadier 'Jock' Campbell, and finally the 1st South African Division, two brigades of which were South African and one the 22nd Guards Brigade. The 2nd South Africa Division was held in reserve together with 500 tanks. The two corps between them had 710 tanks, the substantial part of which constituted the XXXth Corps.

The Axis army under the overall Command of General Bassano comprised five Italian Divisions of XXIst Corps and a German Division (the 90th Light Division, and Feldmarschall Rommel's armoured formations, being the DAK (Deutsche Afrika Corps) and the Italian XXth Corps. The DAK (Afrika Corps) consisted of the 15th Panzer Division (8th Panzer Regiment and 155th Motorised Infantry Regiment), the 21st Panzer Division (5th Panzer Regiment and 104th Motorised Infantry Division) the Italian Ariete (armoured) Division and the Trieste (Mobilised) Division. The German Afrika Corps had 250 tanks, 105 of which were armed with machine guns or 75-mm guns, which could not pierce armour. The Italians had only 146 obsolete tanks. The kernel of Rommel's firepower rested, however, in ninety-six 50-mm anti-tank guns and thirty-five 88-mm anti-tank guns, which were capable of obliterating any tank, even the British heavy tanks. The Axis forces were deployed around Tobruk; part consisting of four Italian divisions and a German around Tobruk itself, one Italian Division to the west of the southern track at Bir Hackeim, the Ariete Division at El Gubi, the 15th and 21st Panzer Divisions on the coast between Tobruk and Bardia and on the frontier at Halfaya the 90th Light and an Italian Division.

The tactical plan evolved by the British contemplated first a strike north from the Fort Madalena area by XXXth Corps, towards Gabr Salah and Sidi Rezegh and towards the north between Tobruk and Bardia in order to draw south the German Afrika Korps and second an assault from the south to the rear of the German and Italian frontier defence by part of XIIIth corps from Sidi Omar, while holding the frontier. There was to be a break-out from Tobruk towards the advancing forces from the south-east. At the same time as the British were working up their plan, Rommel began to plan a new attack upon Tobruk and strike thereafter east. The Italians however, who had wind of the planned British offensive, told Rommel not to move. He challenged that decision and finally General Jodl at Fuehrer Headquarters gave him consent to make the attempt, which he envisaged for 23rd November. The British, in order to prepare for their new campaign, extended the fuel pipeline from Alexandria and brought up over 30,800 tons of supplies. In terms of air cover the Royal Air Force provided for the army six squadrons of medium bombers, nine of light and twelve squadrons of fighters. A further squadron of fighters and two of light bombers was held at headquarters. The Germans and Italians had 190 German aircraft, of which only 120 were serviceable, and 200 serviceable Italian aircraft. The RAF prior to the commencement of the campaign kept up a constant programme of bombing of the Axis forces and bases.

The extent has already been noted to which desert warfare by armoured columns is not dissimilar from sea operations. Variability on occasion of weather, dust storms and electric storms interfering with communication can affect the progress of operations, while as at sea drifting smoke from guns could obscure visibility. On 17th November, the day before Operation Crusader was due to be launched, furious thunderstorms struck and it was still raining on the 18th at dawn when XXXth Corps moved to the attack. On that day progress met with scant resistance and by nightfall the 22nd Armoured Brigade in the west was south-west of Gabr Salah and making for El Gubi. The 7th Armoured Brigade and the Support Group was within two miles of Gabr Salah and the 4th Armoured Brigade was across the southern track and moving north towards the escarpment. The weakness of the tactics was already in the making, as the armoured force went from concentration to fracturing into parts. It was the antithesis of the concentration of the Afrika Korps which Rommel used to effect and which almost tipped the campaign into another British defeat.

On the 19th, 7th Armoured Brigade reached Sidi Rezegh and the Support Groups took the escarpment there. The 22nd reached El Gubi, where the Italian Armoured Ariete Division was stationed, and a severe fight took place, in which the 22nd Brigade suffered significant losses. The 4th had continued its way north, engaging a German tank force to the north east of Gabr Salah, which withdrew. On the 20th Rommel's 15th and 21st Panzer Divisions struck at the isolated 4th Armoured Brigade to great effect. The severity of the blow led Cunningham to recall the 22nd Armoured Brigade from El Gubi to the support of the 4th. Rommel on that day followed up by going south and then turning north-west to Sidi Rezegh, to which the remnant of 4th and 2nd Armoured brigades were now ordered, in order to support 7th Armoured and its support group, part of the 1st South African Division being left to watch the Italians at El Gubi. By the 21st Rommel's columns had surrounded 7th Armoured and its support group before 4th and 22nd Armoured could arrive. That day, while the 4th Indian Division held the frontier, the 2nd New Zealand Division broke through south of Sheferzan and moved north towards Bardia, while the 70th Division started its break-out south-east at Tobruk.

For the next three days confused armoured fighting took place around Sidi Rezegh involving all three Brigades of 7th Armoured and its Support Group and 15th and 21st Panzer Divisions. The tank columns were entangled, in close contact and visibility affected by the smoke of the guns and the black columns of burning fuel from tanks which had been hit. With the poor visibility, moving across the battlefield was not easy. Brigadier 'Jock' Campbell was to lead his force in his open staff car, often standing up and visible as the gun fire struck about it. Even when wounded he continued at the front of his men, leading the van and inflicting with his batteries heavy losses on the German tanks, firing at point-blank range. For his leadership and heroism he was awarded the Victoria Cross, but sadly died in a car accident near Halfaya Pass on 26th November. The confusion of battle was so great that on 23rd November the Chief Medical Officer of a forward British military hospital led round to inspect it a person who he thought to be a Polish General. In fact it was Rommel, there by mistake, who carried off the visit calmly and then left.

7th Support Group was forced to retire towards Gabr Salah in the south and the escarpment was lost. Both sides had suffered heavily with tank losses: Rommel, because of the interference with supplies, had no reserves to call in, unlike the British. At this point General Cunningham suffered a failure of nerve; the tank battle had dissolved in confusion and significant losses had been sustained. He asked that he be given consent to retire.

Sir Claud Auchinleck flew at once to army headquarters and assessed the situation. In an act of decisive leadership and intelligence he ordered that there should be no retirement and that the battle should be continued. General Cunningham was replaced by General Ritchie, Auchinleck's chief of staff. Rommel now faced a dilemma; his garrisons still remained on the coast at Bardia and

Sollum, his mobile armed forces were however reduced and there was still a need to hold the British at Tobruk. He could retire to regroup in western Cyrenaica and abandon the coast and Tobruk, the cautious course which a more conventional general might have chosen, but instead he decided to strike at the rear of the XXXth Corps behind Sheferzen, and from there north to the rear of the Indian Brigade, drawing the British forces away from Sidi Rezegh and from the rear at Capuzzo, which the 2nd New Zealand Division had reached on the 22nd.

Thus, on the 23rd Rommel broke off the fight at Sidi Rezegh and hurried south to join with the Ariete Division at El Gubi. At the same time the 2nd New Zealand Division had turned away from Bardia and began to move up the Trigh Capuzzo towards Sidi Rezegh. On the 24th Rommel's armoured drive moved along the southern track far to the south of XXXth Corps forces to the frontier at Sheferzen. On the way he passed without pausing the six-mile square fuel dumps at FSD 63 east of El Gubi and at FSD 65 east of Gabr Salah, both of which were guarded by 22nd Guards Brigade and were distantly visible from the track. On the 25th the Germans broke through the frontier and travelled twenty miles into the rear, causing destruction in their path, taking prisoners and attacking the rear of the 4th Indian Brigade. An improvised armoured column was formed to attack Rommel in the rear, but he broke off his raid and on 26th November turned north towards Bardia. Throughout this manoeuvre he received little air support and his tank column suffered from attacks by the RAF. That day the 2nd New Zealand Division had finished its drive up the Trigh Capuzzo and retook Sidi Rezegh after two days heavy fighting. The 70th Infantry Division had in the interim taken El Duda and that night, pushing from their salient, they met up with the New Zealanders. The headquarters of XIIIth Corps and some New Zealander units entered Tobruk. The link was however broken on the 27th by a counter-attack and with the arrival of Rommel's armoured corps on the 29th the Germans retook Sidi Rezegh, despite a flank attack by the 120 tanks of 7th Armoured Division.

The 6th New Zealand Brigade was driven out with heavy losses. They and the 4th Armoured brigade were withdrawn to reform, but Tobruk, with the land taken, held on. On 4th December using the 88-mm anti-tank guns, an attempt was made yet again on Tobruk and, although there was at one point a significant penetration of the perimeter, the attack was repulsed. Rommel also made an attempt to release his garrisons in position on the coast, which was resisted, and being short of fuel, pinned between Tobruk and XXXth Corps flanking his line of retreat, and with his tanks savaged and depleted, he decided that his main need was to regroup and keep his army in being. To that end he withdrew south-west to El Gubi, where he concentrated his army. All available tanks were allocated to the 4th Armoured Brigade and 11th Indian Brigade and on the 5th December El Gubi was attacked. After an initial repulse and reinforcement by the Guards Brigade and the remainder of the 4th Indian Division, the position was taken and Rommel began his retreat, first to Gazzala, then via Meliki to Agedabia, which the rest of the army from the Tobruk area reached along the coast road. On 7th January he withdrew to Agheila.

Meanwhile on 10th December 7th Indian Brigade and the 70th Division from Tobruk joined up at El Edem to the south of the town. The siege had been lifted and Tobruk had been relieved. Bardia was to be taken on 2nd January 1942 and the garrison at the Halfaya pass surrendered on the 17th. The British pursuit was not however sufficiently decisive, and allowed the escape of the Axis armies. General Ritchie followed up along the coast but came to a halt at Agedabia because of the supply difficulties now besetting the 8th Army. At that point, as General Fuller points out, he could have either remained or retired. The former required the strength to resist attack, which the tired and worn army did not have. The proper choice to retire was not taken. Despite his losses Rommel was able to re-organise his armies and on 21st January struck at the British position at Agedabia. With his three armoured columns he pressed on to Antelat, then Msus and west to Benghazi, which he entered on the 28th. At last the British rallied east of Gazzala and there Rommel stopped. During the campaign Rommel's total loses were 33,000 men, of which 13,000 were German, 386 tanks and 850 aircraft. In the armies of the Empire, there were 2,908 officers and men killed, 7,339 wounded and 5,457 missing, together with 278 tanks.

The resistance of Tobruk would have been impossible without the Royal Navy. In all between 12th April and 10th December, some 32,667 men were taken in and 34,115 taken out, including 7,516 wounded and 7,097 prisoners. 92 guns and 72 tanks went in, 33,946 tons of stores and 108 sheep, undoubtedly for the Australians. The cost however was high: 27 naval vessels were sunk, including 2 destroyers, 7 anti-submarine vessels and minesweepers and one minelayer. 27 were damaged, including 7 destroyers and 11 anti-submarine vessels and minesweepers. 6 merchant men were sunk and 6 damaged.

1942 began with a serious situation for the Royal Navy in the Mediterranean. In October of 1941 the Germans switched to the Mediterranean a force of about 20 U-boats and strengthened the Luftwaffe cover in and around Sicily. In November Ark Royal was torpedoed and sank, while being towed damaged on the way to Gibraltar. The battleship Barham was sunk and the Queen Elizabeth and Valiant put out of action by an Italian miniature submarine torpedo attack in Alexandria harbour. The cruisers Neptune and Galatea were lost, the destroyer Kandahar and the submarines Perseus and Triumph. Control over the Mediterranean was jeopardised. Malta was to come once more under extreme attack and supplies could again flow to the Axis forces in Libya. Indeed, from February to May 1942 mounting supplies were sent to the latter, of which not more than 20% were stopped.

The spring period of 1942 saw the British ensconced on the Gazala line, which ran from that town on the coast forty miles south to Bir Hacheim. For the main part the line consisted of unmanned minefields, but there lay on and behind it four fortified positions, the first at Gazala held by the 1st South African Division, the second some fifteen miles south held by the 50th Division, a third twenty-five miles behind the minefield at 'Knightsbridge' on the Trigh Capuzzo where the 2nd Guards Brigade were stationed and finally a fourth at the end of the forty-mile line, Bir Hacheim, where there was a Free French brigade. Between these three were other 'boxes' and troops held in the rear. The British army still comprised the XIIIth and XXXth Corps, but the make up varied from that in the November battle in 1941. In the XIIIth there were three infantry divisions (1st and 2nd South African Divisions and 50th Infantry) and the XXXth comprised 1st Armoured Division (4th and 22nd Armoured Brigades) the 7th Armoured Division (4th Armoured Brigade), the 201st Guards Brigade Group, the 3rd Indian Motorised Brigade, 29th Tankers Brigade and a Free French brigade. Rommel's army still had the same basic structure of the German Afrika Corps (15th and 21st Panzer Divisions), the Ariete and Trieste Divisions, the German 90th Light Division and six Italian infantry divisions. With these forces Feldmarschall Rommel was to plan and execute a brilliant campaign, spectacular in its mobility and decisiveness, which the British failed to hold, despite their re-equipment with 260 heavy tanks and having a total armoured force of 631 to Rommel's 550. The concept involved a feint with a sea landing to the rear of the British and a massed armoured thrust from the Bir Hacheim area, striking north-east to the coast east of Tobruk, to draw out the British armoured forces.

The attack was launched at dawn on 27th May and was marked by sensational success. Rommel advanced with three columns, the Italian Ariete Division on the left, 21st Panzer Division in the centre and 15th Panzer on the right. The 3rd Indian Motorised Brigade was crushed, the 4th Armoured Brigade driven off, General Messervy of the 7th Armoured Division captured, 1st Armoured Division engaged at 'Knightsbridge', a point on the Trigh Capuzzo south-west of Tobruk, and at the day's end Rommel had reached El Duda and Sidi Rezegh, fifteen to twenty miles east of Knightsbridge and south-east of Tobruk. The feint and landing at Gazala failed and Bir Hacheim stood firm. The defensive boxes however were encircled and made subject to attack. From 28th to 31st May a violent armoured battle raged west of Knightsbridge during which the German sappers cleared two lanes ten miles apart through the minefields in the vicinity of the Trigh Capuzzo and on either side of the 50th Infantry 'Box'. On 1st June Rommel attacked the box of the British 150th Brigade and took 3,000 prisoners. From the 2nd to the 5th the British counter-attacked Rommel and his Afrika Korps west of 'Knightsbridge' without success, freeing him to take on the 10th Bir Hacheim, from which General Koenig and most of his Free French Brigade were able to escape. In this moving warfare of the mobile armies the engagement shifted north again to the 'Knightsbridge' area, where the 2nd and 4th Armoured Brigade made no progress against the German anti-tank guns. In the outcome the army had to withdraw leaving the 1st South African Division and the 50th Division utterly exposed. A retreat was therefore ordered by General Ritchie to the Egyptian frontier and these forces started to crowd back, protected on their flank by 1st Armoured and covered by the Royal Air Force.

The loss of naval superiority in the Mediterranean in early 1942 had meant that the Royal Navy could not sustain Tobruk throughout another siege and it had therefore been planned that in the event of a reverse the town should be abandoned. The perimeter defence ring was moreover in ruins, although abundant supplies were there. General Ritchie, however, decided on the retreat nonetheless to leave a garrison under Major-General Klopper of two brigades from 2nd South African Division, and 32nd Army Tank Brigade with heavy tanks. The 1st South African Division went through the town on 15th June. On the 20th Tobruk was bombed, to the extent that Klopper's headquarters was driven from place to place and all control over the troops there was lost. The German sappers cut through the minefields and the defence disintegrated into confusion as the Axis army came into the defended area. By dawn on 21st June Tobruk had fallen and Rommel had taken 30,000 prisoners and a mountain of supplies. Meanwhile the 50th, whose passage east had been blocked, turned west and then south towards Bir Hachiem, from which they made their way back towards the British lines. Having taken Tobruk, Rommel hurried on crossing into Egypt at Fort Maddalena and Sidi Omar, reaching Mersa Matruh on 27th June. From there the British once more retreated to the short thirty-five mile front at El Alamein. There was a three-day critical period of fighting but Rommel had once more come to the end of his supplies and had but 125 serviceable tanks left. The front held and the stage was set for the battles of El Alamein (see the Battle of El Alamein, 4th November 1942). Rommel's success was due to two factors, the concentration of his armoured forces and mobile artillery as compared with the British dispersal of the armoured divisions, and his realisation that in desert war, as Major-General Fuller points out, the commanding general, like the admiral with his fleet at sea, had to lead from within the force itself.

Fieldmarshal, command in India, become Viceroy from 1943 to 1947 and become an Earl. The Desert War was not only notable for the wide-sweeping character of the action fought but the conditions of war affecting those involved had a quality which crossed the embattled lines, a fact illustrated by the adaptation of the song Lili Marlene by both sides. The song was first broadcast by Karl-Heinz Reintgen from the German Belgrade army station in April 1941, and had been rescued from a series of banned songs held in Vienna. Its popularity arose from its being broadcast nightly before the ten o'clock news. General Bayerlein is on record as having said that in the desert it was heard by both sides daily with a pause in fighting. This First World War German poem was translated, and it was recorded most famously by Dame Vera Lynn and by Marlene Dietrich in the United States. The song was to continue throughout the 2nd World War to provide a universal pleasure and a kind of feeling for home to those engaged, although not equalled for the British by Dame Vera Lynn's 'The White Cliffs of Dover', which strangely was American in origin.

Lili Marlene, written by Hans Leip 1915, music by Norbert Schultze 1938. English lyric by John Connor.

1. Vor der Kaserne
Vor dem Grossen Tor
Stand eine Laterne
Und steht sie noch davor
So woll'n wir uns da wieder seh'n
Bei der Laterne wollen wir steh'n
　　Wie einst Lili Marleen:

Underneath the lantern
By the barrack gate
Darling I remember
The way you used to wait
T'was there that you whispered tenderly
That you loved me,
You'd always be,
My Lilli of the Lamplight
My own Lilli Marlene

2. Unsere beide Schatten
Sah'n wie einer aus
Dass wir so lieb uns hatten
Das sah man gleich daraus
Und alle Leute soll'n es seh'n
　　Wie einst Lili Marleen:

Time would come for roll – call,
Time for us to part,
Darling I'd caress you
And press you to my heart

3. Schon rief der Posten,
Sie blasen Zapfenstreich
Das kann drei Tage kosten
Kam'rad, ich komm sogleich
Da sagten wir auf Wiedersehen
Wie gerne wollt ich mit dirgeh'n
　　Mit dir Lili Marleen:

And here 'neath that far off Lantern
light
I'd hold you tight,
We'd kiss good night,
My Lilli of the Lamplight
My own Lilli Marlene

4. Dein Schritte kennt sie,
Deinen zieren Gang
Alle Abend brennt sie,
Doch mich vergass sie lang
Und sollte mir ein Leids gescgeh'n
Wer wird bei der Laterne stehen
　　Mit dir Lili Marleen?:

Orders came for sailing,
Somewhere over there
All confined to barracks
Was more than I could bear
I knew you were waiting in the street
I heard your feet,
But could not meet,
My Lilli of the Lamplight
My own Lilli Marlene

5. Aus dem stillen Raume,
Aus der Erde Grund
Hebt mich wie im Traume
Dein verliebter Mund
Wenn sich die späten Nebel drehn

Resting in our billets,
Just behind the lines

Werd'ich bei der Laterne steh'n
Wie einst Lili Marleen

Even tho' we're parted,
Your lips are close to mine
You wait where that lantern softly gleams
Your sweet face seems
To haunt my dreams
My Lilly of the Lamplight
My own Lilli Marlene

15th December 1940
The Battle of Sidi Barrani

The entry of Italy into the War in June 1940, just prior to the French desertion of the Allied cause in the Armistice made with Germany, presented grave problems to Britain in the Mediterranean area. The Mediterranean was the main axis of the Empire, passing through Egypt, and its availability was also essential to the maintenance of control over and access to the oil of the near East. The removal of the guard of the French fleet and its potential, if in German lands, to overwhelm the navy in the Mediterranean presented the Prime Minister, Winston Churchill, with a huge strategic problem; and the danger, if the area were lost, of a catastrophe for Britain second only to a successful invasion of the British Isles themselves. The problem however of the risk from the French navy was dealt with expeditiously (see the Destruction of the French fleet 3rd July 1940). The Italians nonetheless sat astride the Mediterranean in Italy itself, and in its colony of Libya, where some 215,000 troops were stationed under Marshal Balbo. They were also in a position in East Africa where from Abyssinia, Eritrea and Italian Somaliland they had forces which could threaten the eastern route to Egypt through the Red Sea. Between Gibraltar and Egypt the sole British staging point was Malta, which was to become the focus of battle and resistance, winning for its people an award of the George Cross. Syria and Lebanon were in the hands of Vichy France.

The Middle East command under General Sir Archibald Wavell had the responsibility of protecting this huge area, covering the Empire interests in Egypt, Palestine, the Sudan, Kenya and British Somaliland. His resources for this purpose were exiguous. There were some 36,000 troops in Egpt, 27,500 in Palestine, 5,500 in Kenya and limited forces in the Sudan and British Somaliland. Given the major Italian threat in Libya, the holding of Egypt was crucial. Winston Churchill understood clearly the essential nature of the need for a Mediterranean strategy and defence, an historic arm of British policy in European wars going back to the reign of Queen Anne. Adolf Hitler did not grasp its importance and was never to give it the full weight which it deserved.

Wavell had at his command in Egypt two partially equipped brigades which made up the 7th Armoured Division and some obsolete aircraft. Churchill was certain of the need to reinforce him. Commitment to do so in August 1940, when Britain's shattered armies had just returned from Dunkirk, had few weapons and invasion was feared, involved a decision which Churchill has described as 'awful

606

and right'. He proposed to the Cabinet the sending of part of Britain's small force of tanks to Egypt and they agreed. On 10th August 1940 he ordered out the convoy carrying a cruiser tank battalion of 52 heavy tanks, one light tank regiment of 50 tanks, infantry tank battalions with 50 vehicles, 48 anti-tank guns, 48 25-pounder guns, bren-guns, anti-tank rifles and ammunition. The risk of Italian naval attack on this precious shipment led the First Lord of the Admirately and the First Sea Lord to persuade Churchill to send the supplies round the Cape of Good Hope. Churchill worried that they would not arrive in time for the Italian attempt to invade Egypt. They reached there in the latter half of September. It was not until November that the attack on Taranto was to begin the task of wearing down the naval threat (see the Destruction of the Italian Fleet 11th November 1940).

The Italians did not invade Egypt at once on the declaration of war. General Wavell however sent raiding parties to harass the Italians on the front. To carry out these raids there was set up a Support Group of the 7th Armoured Division, comprising the 3rd Coldstream Guards, the 1st/60th Rifles, the 2nd Rifle Brigade, the 11th Hussars, a squadron of the 6th Royal Tank Battalion and two mechanised batteries of the Royal Horse Artillery. Over a sixty-mile front they struck at the Italians in surprise attacks, giving the Italian army the false idea that there was more than one armoured division in Egypt. In this period Fort Magdalena and Capuzzo were taken. Some bombing of the ports took place, and in August Marshal Balbo was killed in a raid on Tobruk. He was succeeded by Marshal Graziani, who told the Italian Foreign Minister, Ciano, that he could not be ready to invade for two or three months, and that there were problems over water supply. The Italian dictator Benito Mussolini was impatient for victories and ordered Graziani to attack in mid-September. He did so with six infantry divisions and eight battalions of tanks. A strong barrage preceded the assault across the frontier on Sollum, and the Italians advanced in three columns in review order, one along the coast road and two in the desert. That on the road was led by motor-cyclists and serried ranks of vehicles.

Despite taking a heavy toll of these columns, the troops on the frontier were forced back, the 3rd Coldstream Guards retreating slowly and in fighting order to the defensive line that General Wavell had established at Mersa Matruh, 180 miles from Alexandria at the head of the single line railway running to the city. On 17th September the Italians took Sidi Barrani and came to a halt. There then remained a seventy-mile no-man's land between them and the positions at Mersa Matruh. East of the town the Italians established some seven fortified camps: at Maktila and Point 90, further south at Tummar East and Tummar West, then at Nibeiwa, twenty miles south of which was Sofafi East and Sofafi west. It was this twenty-mile gap which O'Connor was to exploit in the attack which he mounted in December. Each of the camps was comfortably provisioned with civilian luxuries, food and wine, but the fortified perimeters were only on three sides, with the western boundaries left unprotected. None of these camps was mutually supporting.

The arrival of the precious shipment of tanks and men sent by Churchill enabled O'Connor to plan an assault on the Italians. His plan was to penetrate with armoured forces the gap between Nibeiwa and Sofafi East, swing north and take the northern forts one by one from the rear. Another force would go south to deal with Sofafi East and West. To prepare for this thrust the force had to cross the seventy miles of no man's land. On the night of 7th December the Western Desert Force, consisting of the 7th Armoured Division, 4th Indian Division, two infantry brigades and the 7th Battalion of the Royal Tank Regiment with the heavy new 'I' tanks, moved forward with its supplies some forty miles; on the 8th it spent the day in the desert waiting, failing to be observed by the Italian air force. On the night of the 9th it moved to the attack, piercing the gap and turning north to the rear of Nibeiwa. At 7am the artillery came up to the rear of the camp and opened fire. At 7.35 am the Royal Tank Regiment and the infantry struck. The Italian tanks were engulfed by heavy 'I' tanks and their 37-mm. anti-tank shells were wholly ineffective against the British tanks' armour. Within one hour the camp had fallen, yielding 3,000 prisoners. The next attack at 1.50 pm fell on Tummar West, which was carried by assault. By nightfall most of Tummar East had also fallen. The 7th Armoured Support Group had moved south to block the Italian retirement from Sofafi East and West. While the camps were under attack and being taken, the 4th Indian Division with 7th Armoured had hastened north and cut off the road from Sidi Barrani west to Buq Buq. 10th December was spent advancing on Sidi Barrani, where an attack was launched at 4.15pm. At Mersa Matruh that day the Coldstream Guards attacked the Italian front, covered by naval bombardment from the sea, and by evening had carried their assault. Their battalion headquarters signalled that there were as prisoners five acres of officers and two hundred acres of other ranks. Sidi Barrani was taken and the retreating Italian army was kept going by the 7th Armoured Division, the 16th British Infantry Brigade (motorised) and the 6th Australian Division to their rear. By the 12th the coast was cleared and the Italians had been forced back to the border. The British had captured 38,000 prisoners, 400 guns and 50 vehicles. Their casualties were 133 killed, 387 wounded and 8 missing.

17th December 1939
The Sinking of The Admiral Graf Spee

The 'Pocket' battleship Admiral Graf Spee, which had represented Germany at the 1937 Coronation Review at Spithead, was one of a number constructed to comply with the limitation of the Treaty of Versailles by Germany, having a displacement of 10,000 tons. It was however heavily armoured, carried six 11-inch guns and eight 6-inch guns, and was capable of a speed of 26 knots. It carried an Arado AV 196 aircraft for reconnaissance and had a primitive radar with a range of 18.5 miles. Designed for the purpose of raiding merchant shipping, it posed a substantial threat, moving outside heavily protected convoys. Prior to the outbreak of the Second World War it and its sister ship, Deutschland, later renamed Lützow, slipped out into the north Atlantic on 21st August 1939. When war broke out on 3rd September Deutschland was near the Denmark Straits by Iceland and the Admiral Graf Spee near the Azores moving south. The two raiders therefore threatened merchant shipping routes both north and south in the Atlantic. Both on 7th September were ordered by the German Naval command to remain within a 'waiting area' in the open ocean without taking action, while Adolf Hitler waited to see whether after the conquest of Poland Britain would continue the war. Their orders however were to pursue the destruction and dislocation of enemy shipping by all means possible and to avoid engagement with enemy naval forces. The Graf Spee travelled in touch with a supply ship for oil and stores, the Altmark, by which it could be refuelled and reprovisioned at sea. On 27th September Admiral Raeder ordered the two ships to leave the waiting areas and begin action.

To meet the threat in the broad spaces of the Atlantic, the Admiralty had to split the fleet into a number of groups, which could patrol the wide expanse of the ocean and seek out these raiders. Some seven groups were formed. In the south Atlantic below the line from Pernambuco in Brazil to Freetown in Sierra Leone, there were Force K comprising Renown, (a battle cruiser and 9th of the name), Ark Royal, (an aircraft carrier and 3rd of the name), accompanied by some French cruisers based at Dakar; Force H and K based around Cape town including Sussex, Shropshire, Dorsetshire (a cruiser and 3rd of the name) and Eagle (an Aircraft Carrier and 4th of the name); and on the South American section of the South Atlantic, Force G, comprising Ajax, the flagship (a 7,000-ton cruiser and 7th of the name), Exeter (a heavier cruiser and 4th of the name), Cumberland and Achilles (a cruiser and 7th of the name) which was part of the Royal New Zealand Navy. This force was commanded by Commodore Harwood. In terms of armament, the Exeter carried six 8-inch guns and Ajax and Achilles eight 6-inch guns each, so that they were inferior to the Graf Spee in the range and weight of firepower. The latter could fire a broadside of 4,700 tons while the three cruisers together combined could fire only 3,136 pounds.

The Graf Spee began its campaign on 30th September, sinking the SS Clement of 500 tons off Brazil. It then proceeded south, sinking more ships on the Freetown to Cape Town shipping route, and feinted into the Indian Ocean, sinking a ship, the Africa Shell, in the Mozambique Channel. The battleship retraced its steps and on 2nd December sunk the SS Doric Star in the middle of the South Atlantic. In all nine ships were sunk, amounting to 50,000 tons. Captain Langsdorff was however a man of honour and a careful observer of international naval law, so that on every occasion he evacuated the crews of the stricken boats before sinking them. The seamen taken were put aboard the Altmark for return to Germany or kept on the Graf Spee. His next course was towards the River Plate, prior to returning to Germany; whether to engage a convoy in that area or find time for repairs in the port of Buenos Aires, where the Government was pro-German, is unclear.

Commodore Harwood, made aware of the reappearance of the battleships in the Atlantic, had to assess the action which he needed to take to intercept it. He resolved without knowing Langsdorff's course that Graf Spee would go towards the River Plate and moved to position the force off the estuary. He lacked Cumberland, which had gone to the Falklands for repairs and supplies, and thus had to confront Graf Spee with an inferior force. He rehearsed tactics for meeting the pocket battleship and ordered that the force should divide, he in Ajax with Achilles to move on one side of the Graf Spee and Exeter on the other, forcing the Germans to divide their fire.

At 6.14 am on 13th December smoke was observed by the British force, who were steaming north-east, on the horizon to the north-west. A similar recognition occurred on Graf Spee, where it was thought at first that the smoke came from a convoy. Both sides began to close together, Force G splitting to proceed to the stations assigned. Exeter pressed on to investigate and came up on the quarter of Graf Spee. When Langsdorff began to realise that the group of ships were not a convoy, he could have turned and fired on the British out of range. Instead he came on, turning his 11-inch guns on Exeter. Exeter returned the fire with its 8-inch guns at nine and half miles, continuing to close up despite the intense and withering fire from the Graf Spee. She had torpedo tubes damaged, the B Turret gone, the guns out of action but for one, the bridge communications destroyed, and was on fire foreword of midships. Most of the crew on the bridge were killed. She was not fully under control and listing. In her turn Exeter had damaged the bows of Graf Spee and Ajax and Achilles struck at the battleship's superstructure. Exeter was left with only one gun, but Captain Bell and two or three officers kept the gun firing until about 7.40 am. Exeter then turned away under a smoke screen, having 62 dead and 29 wounded. Graf Spee was free to fire on Ajax and Achilles. Despite having only 6-inch guns they returned the fire, causing more damage to the Graf Spee. Achilles was damaged and the two aft turrets of Ajax were knocked out. Ajax had tried to sink the Graf Spee with its torpedoes, unsuccessfully, and came up with Achilles to a five-mile range. The fact that both suffered so little damage was due to the seamanship of the crews, which manoeuvred with continuous use of the helm under full power, kept up by the stokers in the boiler room, where the young crews stayed with their work unflinchingly.

The Admiral Graf Spee had suffered damage to its galleys, engines, food stores and gun hoists. The bows had been holed. In the last interchange with Ajax and Achilles two shells had landed, starting a fire. The reserves of shells were falling, only forty percent of the supply for the 11-inch guns remained and only fifty percent for the 6-inch guns. Langsdorff therefore decided to turn under a smoke screen and head for repairs and provisions to Montevideo in Uruguay. Ajax and Achilles shadowed the ship, with desultory fire being exchanged. In the evening the Admiral Graf Spee entered the port and dropped anchor in Montevideo Roads just after midnight.

Captain Langsdorff and the German Envoy sought the consent of the Uruguayan Government to remain in Montevideo for repairs. While Uruguay was formally neutral, its political stance was pro-British. Permission was only given to remain for seventy-two hours, an inadequate time to effect the required repairs. It was in the British interest, however, to keep Graf Spee in port for longer, since time was needed to bring to the estuary the ships to support Ajax and Achilles, both of which were damaged. Only Cumberland arrived in the evening of 14th December to replace Exeter from the Falkland Islands. The Renown and Ark Royal were at Rio de Janeiro, 2,000 miles away and it was 4,000 to Cape Town, where Force H and Dorsetshire were located.

In the naval tradition of Cornwallis's Retreat (17th June 1795), the British played out on the Germans an intelligence exercise designed to persuade Langsdorff that the arrival of the heavy ships was imminent. The impression was created that Revenge and Ark Royal had passed south from Rio de Janeiro and were nearing the River Plate at 30 knots. German Intelligence was persuaded that such were the facts. Langdorff was faced, in the situation which he believed existed, with only three choices: first, to allow Graf Spee to be interned in Uruguay for the duration of the war; second, to make a run for Buenos Aires; or, third, to scuttle the ship. Any attempt to return to Germany was in any event highly problematic, given the Royal Navy's knowledge of his position and the forces deployed, and incautious, because of the damage to the bows in the likely high Atlantic winter seas. He therefore contacted German Naval headquarters asking for instructions. Admiral Raedar discussed the position with the Fuehrer, who was angry beyond words, and with General Jodl, and they directed that he should seek more time, but if that were impossible, avoid internment and either fight to get to Buenos Aires or scuttle the ship. Uruguay refused to extend the time given. The British Ambassador however pointed out to the Uruguayan Government that under international maritime law a belligerent warship was not permitted to leave port until twenty-four hours after any large merchant ship had sailed. The application of this rule delayed the sailing an extra day and lessened the chances of success of any flight to Buenos Aires, as the British heavy fleet came up. Langsdorff therefore decided to scuttle Graf Spee in international waters in the estuary.

On 17th December, having unloaded stores and supplies, Langsdorff put the British prisoners on shore and left some 700 men, the bulk of her crew. Admiral Graf Spee weighed anchor at 6 pm and sailed out to sea for four miles, where she stopped. Captain Langsdorff and the skeleton crew left the ship. Six large explosions echoed in the calm and the Graf Spee burst into fire and smoke, settling to her grave. The German sailors and Captain Langsdorff left Montevideo on the Tacoma, a German tanker, for Buenos Aires, where on the 19th Captain Langsdorff shot himself. His body was found lying on the traditional German Navy Ensign brought from Graf Spee. Captain Pottinger, one of his prisoners from the SS Ashlea, attended his funeral.

The Altmark, the supply ship, had slipped away north carrying 299 British prisoners. She eluded the navy but was found finally on 14th February 1940 in Norway in the Jösing Fjord. The Germans had not disclosed to the Norwegian Government, which was neutral, that she carried any prisoners, but hid them in closed stores and an empty hold. HMS Cossack, a destroyer under Captain Vian was sent in, although Altmark was in Norwegian waters. He came alongside and a small party stormed and boarded the ship. A deck fight took place, but the prisoners were found and released. The Norwegian Government protested at the incursion into its territorial waters, but the incident strengthened the resolve of Adolf Hitler to invade Norway.

When the news of the gallant action of Exeter and Force G against the more powerful Graf Spee came to London, Commodore Harwood was raised to the rank of Admiral and King George VI made him a Knight Commander of the Bath. Captain Woodhouse of Ajax, Captain Parry of Achilles and Captain Bell of Exeter were all made Commanders of the Bath. In his despatch to the Admiralty, Admiral Harwood particularly noted the very high standard of efficiency, courage, and devotion to duty that had been displayed by all officers and men in the five-day action and he recognised the contribution of the men of New Zealand on Achilles for their conduct during their baptism of fire.

Exeter, which had been hit 100 times and was near to a wreck, limped back to Port Stanley, where the Admiralty wished to leave her un-repaired for the rest of the war. Winston Churchill, the First Lord of the Admiralty, insisted however on her return and she was patched and made seaworthy with metal taken from the beached Great Britain, built by Brunel. Despite determined attempts by the U-boats to find her and sink her, she arrived home in February 1940 in Plymouth Sound, where Winston Churchill went aboard to greet the crew. The crew were each presented with a medal by King George VI at the Guildhall on their enthusiastic reception in London. Between 1942 and 1943, Sir Henry Harwood went on to be Commander-in-Chief Mediterranean. Exeter returned to service but was sunk by the Japanese in 1942.

Bibliography and Sources

Arthur, Max, - Symbol of courage (Pan Books, 3rd Impression 2005)

Aspinall, C.-Oglander, Freshly Remembered (1956 Hogarth Press)

Asprey, Robert - The German High Command at War (Little, Brown & Co 1991)

Atkin, Ronald - Pillar of Fire (Sidgwick and Jackson 1990 Reprint)

Attwater, D - The Penguin Dictionary of Saints (1965)

Barnett, Correlli - Marlborough (Book Club Associates & Eyre Methuen 1974)

Bayerlein, Lt. Gen.F. - The Fatal Decisions: El Alamein (Michael Joesph Ltd 1956)

Bell, Douglas - Seamen of England (Thomas - Nelson & Sons Ltd 1943)

Bennett, R. - Ultra in the West (Hutchinson 1979)

Black, C. - Franklin Delano Rooseveldt (Weidenfeld and Nicholson 2003)

Black, J.B. - The Reign of Elizabeth (O.U.P. 1936)

De Bourrienne, F. - Memoirs of Napoleon Bonaparte (Hutchinson & Co. 1904)

Bryant, Arthur - The Age of Chivalry (Collins 1963)

Bryant, Arthur - The Turn of the Tide (Collins 1957)

Bryant, Arthur - Freedom's Own Island (Gould Publishing 1986)

Bryant, Arthur - Unfinished Victory (Macmillan 1940)

Bryant, Arthur - Years of Endurance (Collins 1942)

Bryant, Arthur - Years of Victory (Collins 1944)

Buchan, John - Oliver Cromwell (The Reprint Society 1941)

Burne, Alfred H. - The Agincourt War (Eyre & Spottiswoode 1956)

Butler, D and Jennie Freeman, British Political Facts (Papermac 1968)

Lord Byron's Works, Childe Harold's Pilgrimage (John Murray 1814)

Callender, Geoffrey - The Naval Side of British History (Christophers London)

Campbell, Thomas - Poetical works (George Routledge and Sons.c. 1878)

Carey, John - The Faber Book of Reportage (Faber & Faber Ltd 1987)

Fieldmarshal Lord Carver - Britain's Army in the 20th Century (Pan Books 1999)

Cawthorne, N. - Turning the Tide (Arcturus 2002)

Cecil, Henry, A Matter of Speculation (Hutchinson 1965)

Chalfont, A. - Montgomery of Alamein (Weidenfeld & Nicholson 1976)

Chandler, David - The Campaigns of Napoleon (The Folio Society 2002)

Chandler, David G. - Dictionary of the Napoleonic Wars (Greenhill Books 1993)

Chenevix Trench, C. - George II (The History Book Club 1973)

Churchill, Winston S. - Never Give In: Churchill's Best Speeches (Pimlico 2003)

Churchill, Winston S. - The Second World War (Folio Society Edition 2000)

Churchill, Winston S. - Step by Step (Odhams Press 1947)

Crawley, Aidan - de Gaulle (The Literary Guild)

Edward Earl of Clarendon - The History of the Rebellion (Oxford University Press 1840)

Connell, Brian - The Plains of Abraham (Hodder & Stoughton 1959)

Cochrane, Memoirs of a Fighting Captain (The Folio Society 2005)

Corbett, Julian S. – The Seven Years War (Folio Society 2001)

Cronin, Vincent. – Louis XIV (Collins Harvall 1990)

Cummins, John – Francis Drake (Weidenfeld & Nicholson 1995)

Cunningham of Hyndhope – A Sailor's Odyssey (Hutchinson and Co 1951)

Drabble, Oxford Companion to English Literature (O.U.P. 1995)

Debretts, People of Today 1998 (Debrett's Peerage Ltd)

Dupuy, R.E. and T.W. – The Encyclopaedia of Military History (Hero Books Partnership U.S.A 1986)

Edward, J. – El Alamein Revisited (American University in Cairo 2000)

Edwards. K. – Men of Action (Collins 1943)

Esdaile, Charles – The Peninsular War (Allen Lane 2002)

Flexner, J.T. – Washington, the Indispensable Man (W.Collins & Sons Ltd 1976)

Foxe.J: The Book of Martyrs (Revised by the Rev.W.Bramley – More) (Cassell. Potter and Galpin)

Fraser, Antonia, Cromwell – our Chief of Men (Weidenfeld and Nicholson 1973)

Fraser, Antonia, King Charles II (Book Club Associates 1979)

Fraser, Edward – Famous Fighters of the Fleet (Macmillan & Co. 1907)

Freud, Sigmund & Bullitt, W.C. – Thomas Woodrow Wilson (Weidenfeld & Nicholson 1967)

Froissart Chronicles (G.Brereton) (Penguin 1968)

Froissart Chronicles (Ed. Joliffe) (Harvill Press 1967)

Fuller, J.F.C. – The Second World War (Da Capo Press – 1993)

Gardiner, Juliet – Wartime Britain 1939 – 1945 (Headline Book Publishing 2004)

Gates, David – The Spanish Ulcer (Guild Publishing 1986)

Gilbert, Martin – First World War (Weidenfeld & Nicholson 1994)

Gilbert, Martin – Second World War (Weidenfeld & Nicholson 1989)

Glover, M. – Wellington, Peninsular Victories (Batsford 1963)

Graham, Winston – The Spanish Armadas (Collins 1972)

Green, David – The Battle of Poitiers 1356 (Tempus 2002)

Haines G and Cdr B.R. Coward, R.N. - Battleships, Cruisers, Destroyers (The Promotional Reprint Co 1994)

Hart, Liddell – History of the First World War (Book Club Associates 1973)

Harvey, Richard – Cochrane (Constable London 2000)

Hibbert, Christopher – Corunna (Batsford 1961)

Hitler, Adolf – My Struggle (Paternoster Books, 1938)

Hough, R. – Captain James Cook (Hodder & Stoughton 1994)

Hoyt, E.P.- The Vanderbilts and their fortunes (Frederick Muller 1963)

Huizinga, J. – The Waning of the Middle Ages (Penguin 1990)

Hutton, Ronald – Charles II (Oxford University Press 1991)

Jenkins, R. – Asquith (Fontana 1967)

Jones, Archer – The Art of War in the Western World (Barnes & Noble 1987)

Kaplan, Philip & Collier, Richard – The Few (Blandford 1989)

Lindsay Kerr, Sir David – The Constitutional History of Modern Britain (A and C Black 1961)

Kinglake A.W. – Eothen (Sampson Low, Marston And Co 1913)

King, Cecil – His Majesty's Ships and their Forbears (The Studio Publications 1940)

Kinross, The Ottoman Empire (The Folio Society 2003)

Latham & Matthews – Pepy's Diary (Vol.2) The Folio Society 1998)

Longford, Elizabeth – Wellington - Years of the Sword (Weidenfeld & Nicholson 1969)

Low, Charles R. – Great Battles of the British Navy (G.Routledge & Sons 1872)

Lunt, James – Charge to Glory (Heineman 1961)

Macdonald, G. – The Last Kaiser (Phoenix Press 2001)

MacGregor – Hastie – The Day of the Lion (Macdonald 1963)

Macmunn, G. – Prince Eugene (Sampson, Low, Marston & Co Ltd)

Magnus, P. – Kitchener (Grey Arrow 1961)

Manchester, J. – The Arms of Krupp (Bantam Books Inc. 1970)

Marcus, C.J. – A Naval History of England 1: The Formative Centuries (Longmans Green 1961)

Marcus C.J. – A Naval History of England II : The Age of Nelson (Longmans Green 1971)

Marcus, Geoffrey, Quiberon Bay (Hollis and Carter 1960)

McLynn, F. – 1759 (Pimlico Ed. 2005)

Mitford, N. – The Sun King (Book Club Associates 1969)

Monk, Commander W.B. – The Bay of Biscay Pilot (Hydrographic Department of Ministry of Defence 1970)

Monk, Commander W.B. – The West Coasts of Spain and Portugal Pilot (Hydrographic Dpt. Ministry of Defence 1970)

Moorman. J.R – A History of the Church of England (Adam and Charles Black 1976)

Mordal, J. 25 Siècles de Guerre sur Mer (1959 Collection Marabout Université)

Morehead, Alan – African Trilogy (Hamish Hamilton 1944)

Mowat, R.B. – A History of European Diplomacy 1451 – 1789 (Longham Green 1928)

Neill, Stephen – Anglicanism (Penguin Books 1965)

Nelson, W.H. – The Soldier Kings : The House of Hohenzollern (J.M. Dent & Sons Ltd 1971)

Norton, Lucy – Saint Simon at Versailles (Penguin Books 1985)

Norwich, John Julius – Shakespeare's Kings (Viking 1999)

Oman, Carola – Sir John Moore (Hodder and Stoughton 1953)

Oman, Sir Charles – The Art of War in the Middle Ages (Greenhill Books 1991)

Owen, J.H. – War at Sea Under Queen Anne (Cambridge University Press 1938)

Oxford Companion to English Literature – Oxford University Press Revised Edition 1955)

Parker, John . – Task Force (Bounty Books 2003)

Parker, Mathew – Monte Cassino (Headline Book Publishing 2004)

Parkinson, Roger – Clausewitz (Stein and Day 1971)

Pocock, Tom – Horatio Nelson (Cassell 1988)

Pocock, Tom – A Thirst for Glory (Aurum Press 1996)

Raynor, R.M. – European Histroy (Longmans 7th 1960)

R.C.C. Pilotage Foundation – Atlantic Spain and Portugal (Imray Laurie Norie & Wilson 1988)

Reddaway, W.F. – A History of Europe (Methuen & Co 1936)

Robertson, C. Grant – Select Statutes, Cases and Documents (Methuen & Co Ltd 9th Edition 1949)

Rodger, W.A.M. – The Command of the Ocean (Allen Lane 2004)

Rodger, W.A.M. – The Safeguard of the Sea (Harper Collins 1997)

Rogers, H.C.B. – The Mounted Troops of the British Army (Seeley Service and Co Ltd. (1967))

Seward, Desmond – The Monks of War (Folio Society Ed. 2000)

Shirer, William – The Collapse of the Third Republic (The Literary Guild 1970)

Shirer, William – The Rise & Fall of the Third Reich (The Reprint Society 1962)

Shulman, M. – The Defeat in the West (Masquerade 1995)

Sobel, D. – Longitude (Fourth Estate Ltd 1996)

Spears, Sir Edward – Assignment to Catastrophe (W.Heineman Ltd 1954)

Steinhoff, Pechel, Snowalter, Voices from the Third Reich (Grafton Books 1991)

Spencer, Charles – Blenheim (Phoenix 2005)

Stewart, Adrian – The Early Battles of the English Army (Lee Cooper 2002)

Strawson, John – Gentlemen in Khaki (Secker and Warburg 1989)

Taylor, A.J.P – The Origins of the Second World War (Book Club Associates 1978)

Thomson, G.M. – The First Churchill (Martin, Secker & Warburg Ltd 1979)

Trevelyan. G.M.- England Under the Stuarts (Penguin Books 1960)

Ullman, Walter – A History of Political Thought: The Middle Ages (Penguin Books 1965)

Urban, Mark – Generals (Faber & Faber 2005)

Vickers, Kenneth H. – England in the Later Middle Ages (Methuen & Co 6th Ed. 1937)

Wand. J.W.C. – St Augustine's City of God (Oxford University Press 1963)

Williams, A. – D-Day to Berlin (Hodder 2004)

Williams, Neville – Elizabeth I Queen of England (Weidenfeld & Nicholson 1967)

Wilson, Charles – Profit & Power (Longmans 1957)

Wilson, Trevor – The Downfall of the Liberal Party (Collins 1966)

Woodman, Richard – The Sea Warriors (Constable & Robinson 2001)

Young, Desmond – Rommel (Fontana – 10th Impression 1979)

B.Zimmerman, The Fatal Decisions: France 1944 (Michael Joseph 1956)

Index

The index employs the name by which the character, event or place is best known; so a commoner who becomes an earl and later a duke is indexed by their ultimate title. As regimental names have changed these have been grouped into their county or region. Few military divisions are indexed as they seldom indicate their components. All naval ships have been syled HMS for clarity. Ship names, like titles, were transferred so you will need to look at the context to separate these.

Printed in the United Kingdom
by Lightning Source UK Ltd.
125489UK00001B/1-21/A

9 781904 623533